ANNALS OF THE NEW YORK ACADEMY OF SCIENCES
Volume 774

DEHYDROEPIANDROSTERONE (DHEA) AND AGING

Edited by Francis L. Bellino, Raymond A. Daynes, Peter J. Hornsby, David H. Lavrin, and John E. Nestler

The New York Academy of Sciences
New York, New York
1995

DEHYDROEPIANDROSTERONE (DHEA) AND AGING

⊛ *The paper used in this publication meets the minimum requirements of American National Standard for Information Sciences—Permanence of Paper for Printed Library Materials, ANSI Z39.48-1984.*

Cover art: *"Age Confronting Youth," by Leonardo da Vinci.*

Library of Congress Cataloging-in-Publication Data

SP
Printed in the United States of America
ISBN 1-57331-004-2 (cloth)
ISBN 1-57331-005-0 (paper)
ISSN 0077-8923

ANNALS OF THE NEW YORK ACADEMY OF SCIENCES

Volume 774
December 29, 1995

DEHYDROEPIANDROSTERONE (DHEA) AND AGING[a]

Editors and Conference Organizers
FRANCIS L. BELLINO, RAYMOND A. DAYNES, PETER J. HORNSBY,
DAVID H. LAVRIN, and JOHN E. NESTLER

CONTENTS

[a]This volume is the result of a conference entitled **Dehydroepiandrosterone (DHEA) and
Aging** which was sponsored by the New York Academy of Sciences and held on June 17–19,
1995 in Washington, DC.

Poster Papers

Financial assistance was received from:
Major Funder
- National Institutes of Health
    - NIA
    - NIAMS
    - NCI

Contributors
- DIAGNOSTIC SYSTEMS LABORATORIES, INC.
- GLAXO WELLCOME INC.
- GLENN FOUNDATION FOR MEDICAL RESEARCH
- HENRY AND LUCY MOSES FUND, INC.
- MERCK RESEARCH LABORATORIES
- PARADIGM BIOSCIENCES, INC.
- PFIZER CENTRAL RESEARCH
- WYETH-AYERST RESEARCH

The New York Academy of Sciences believes it has a responsibility to provide an open forum for discussion of scientific questions. The positions taken by the participants in the reported conferences are their own and not necessarily those of the Academy. The Academy has no intent to influence legislation by providing such forums.

INTRODUCTION

DHEA: A Coming of Age

JOHN E. NESTLER

Division of Endocrinology and Metabolism
Medical College of Virginia/Virginia Commonwealth University
Richmond, Virginia 23298

One can almost hear the hucksters calling out: "Come get your DHEA, come get your Fountain of Youth. Cures all that ails you. Helps you live forever." For many years dehydroepiandrosterone (DHEA) has enjoyed a reputation akin to that of snake oil, in no small measure due to the perhaps understandable but nonetheless overzealous promotion by fellow scientists. DHEA was reputed to remedy almost any bodily ill, even though evidence for the beneficial effects of DHEA in humans was virtually nonexistent and its cellular or molecular mechanism(s) of action remained a mystery. Because of this nefarious reputation, DHEA research was regarded by many as a dubious or, at best, avant garde venture.

Fortunately for many of us, DHEA has come a long way in the past decade to divest itself of this status. As evidence for this, the New York Academy of Sciences (NYAS) sponsored an international conference on "Dehydroepiandrosterone (DHEA) and Aging" from June 17–19, 1995, and this volume of the Annals serves as a compendium for the conference's proceedings. To wit, DHEA has "come of age" and has regained legitimacy as an area for scientific inquiry.

Two seminal observations have sparked renewed interest among aging researchers in the adrenal steroids DHEA and its sulfate ester, DHEA sulfate (DHEAS). The first is that circulating levels of these steroids decline progressively and markedly with aging. This is in distinct contrast to other adrenal steroids, such as glucocorticoids or mineralocorticoids, whose serum levels are relatively preserved with aging. Moreover, human epidemiologic studies suggest that an elevated serum DHEAS level may confer beneficial effects in terms of increased longevity and prevention of heart disease. Hence, serum DHEA and/or DHEAS may represent biomarkers of healthy aging.

Secondly, numerous animal studies have convincingly demonstrated the beneficial effects of DHEA administration in preventing obesity, diabetes, cancer, and heart disease, in enhancing the immune system, and even in prolonging life span. Collectively, these observations have led investigators to speculate that some of the degenerative changes associated with human aging may be related to a progressive deficit in circulating DHEA or DHEAS.

However, it must be remembered that most of these animal experiments were conducted in rodents, which have little, if any, circulating DHEA. It is not immediately obvious that results obtained in these animal models can be extrapolated to humans. Hence, a major scientific question is whether any of the beneficial consequences of DHEA administration that have been demonstrated in animal models can be shown to be relevant in human beings.

It was therefore particularly exciting that several papers presented at the NYAS conference reported positive effects of DHEA on the human immune system. As reported in this volume of the Annals, a handful of respected investigators have administered DHEA to humans while monitoring immune status and observed results which suggest that DHEA boosts the immune system. A recent report[1] out of Stanford conducted in women, which suggests that DHEA administration might be useful clinically in the treatment of systemic lupus erythematosus, further supports the observations reported here and also demonstrates for the first time that DHEA might prove effective in the treatment of a human immunologic disease. Since aging is accompanied by progressive immune senescence, restoration of a competent immunologic response by DHEA can be considered an "anti-aging" or restorative action.

Another promising action of DHEA in humans is the prevention of atherosclerosis or acute myocardial infarction. Two epidemiologic reports in this volume of the Annals suggest that an elevated serum DHEAS level confers cardioprotection, although this protective action may be specific to men or of substantially lesser magnitude in women. One of the reports also raises the sobering possibility that the degree of cardioprotection in men may be less than previously reported. Nonetheless, these epidemiologic observations were bolstered by papers which demonstrated that DHEA can inhibit human platelet aggregation and beneficially influence circulating levels of plasminogen activator inhibitor type I and tissue plasminogen activator antigen.[2]

As alluded to earlier, I believe the challenge to clinical investigators in the coming decade will be to convincingly establish that DHEA exerts beneficial actions in men and women. Coincidentally, the clinical issues that will have to be addressed include optimal DHEA dosage form and amount, route of administration, and delineation of side effect profile. It is important that such studies be conducted before DHEA is casually administered to men and women, as some physicians in private practice are currently doing, because DHEA administration may be associated with some untoward effects. For example, DHEA can be converted to potent androgens, such as testosterone, which would masculinize women. Similarly, whether DHEA administration is associated with any change in prostatic volume or risk for prostatic cancer in men is currently unknown. Finally, there has been at least one report of transient hepatitis associated with oral DHEA administration in a woman.[3]

A second challenge to bench researchers and clinical investigators alike is to elucidate the mechanism or mechanisms underlying the selective and dramatic aged-related decline in serum DHEA and DHEAS levels. From a clinical viewpoint, this is an important issue because an understanding of DHEA regulation may allow us to raise circulating DHEA in humans in a physiologic fashion, avoiding any side effects that may prove to be associated with oral DHEA administration. As noted by Dr. Peter Hornsby in the accompanying introductory piece, several papers in the current volume of the Annals critically address the area of DHEA metabolism and regulation.

How DHEA exerts its biologic actions remains an enigma. As suggested by some papers in this volume of the Annals, DHEA may act by influencing several key metabolic enzymes, such as glucose-6-phosphate dehydrogenase or glycerol-3-phosphate dehydrogenase, by altering physicochemical parameters via interpolation into cellular membranes, or by conversion to androgens, estrogens, or other metabolites. Given the diverse nature of DHEA's putative biologic actions, it seems likely that several independent mechanisms for DHEA action may be operative.

An issue which unfortunately was not addressed in the NYAS conference was the molecular mechanism for DHEA's actions. A putative binding site for DHEA has been reported on hepatocytes and human leukocytes, but a specific DHEA receptor has not been characterized. Intriguingly, some actions of DHEA may not involve a classic steroid receptor or gene activation, as evidenced by the fact that DHEA can inhibit platelet aggregation. Platelets are anucleate, and hence some other mode of action must be invoked.

In closing, I would like to take off my hat as clinical investigator and don my hat as medical practitioner. As a physician, I believe a few words of caution are in order. It was evident from the NYAS conference that some physicians are dispensing DHEA in cavalier fashion for almost any indication. This is not justified. Although the results of human DHEA studies appear promising and tantalizing, as evidenced by the reports in this volume of the Annals, they still need to be confirmed in large-scale and properly controlled studies. A beneficial effect of DHEA administration in humans has not yet been firmly established, and we know virtually nothing about the side effect profile of chronic DHEA administration. Without confirmed beneficial actions in humans and a better understanding of associated risks, it does not seem reasonable to dispense DHEA. As always in medicine, we must first heed the maxim: *"Primum non nocere."*

Nonetheless, given the current groundswell in human DHEA-related research, I remain confident that these issues will be fully addressed within the next 5 to 10 years and predict that a therapeutic role for DHEA will be established. This could take the form of hormone replacement therapy (for example, starting DHEA administration around age 30 and keeping the serum level at its zenith) or pharmacologic therapy for specific disease indications. Again, however, this goal will be attained only through carefully designed and rigorously controlled scientific studies.

With this brief introduction in hand, I would now invite the reader to thoughtfully peruse the articles contained in this volume of the Annals. The reader will find them enjoyable, stimulating, exciting and, if nothing else, provocative. Certainly, they indicate that DHEA remains a promising and, perhaps more importantly, a legitimate and worthwhile field for future bench and clinical research. As the NYAS conference proved, DHEA has truly come of age.

REFERENCES

1. VAN VOLLENHOVEN, R.F., E.G. ENGLEMAN & J.L. MCGUIRE. 1994. An open study of dehydroepiandrosterone in systemic lupus erythematosus. Arthritis Rheum. **37:** 1305–1310.
2. BEER, N.A., D.J. JAKUBOWICZ, D.W. MATT, R.M. BEER & J.E. NESTLER. 1995. Oral dehydroepiandrosterone administration reduces plasma levels of plasminogen activator inhibitor type 1 and tissue plasminogen activator antigen in men. Am. J. Med. Sci. Submitted.
3. BUSTER, J.E., P.R. CASSON, A.B. STRAUGHN, D. DALE, E.S. UMSTOT, N. CHIAMORI & G.E. ABRAHAM. 1992. Postmenopausal steroid replacement with micronized dehydroepiandrosterone: Preliminary oral bioavailability and dose proportionality studies. Am. J. Obstet. Gynecol. **166:** 1163–1168.

Current Challenges for DHEA Research

PETER J. HORNSBY

Huffington Center on Aging
Baylor College of Medicine
Houston, Texas 77030

The steroid dehydroepiandosterone (DHEA) and its sulfated form, DHEAS, present many puzzles to biological and biomedical researchers. They are synthesized in high quantities by the adrenal cortex only in primates and a few other species, most laboratory and domestic species having very low plasma levels, these being often mainly or exclusively gonadal in origin. In contrast, the huge levels in humans are synthesized almost entirely by the adrenal. Even within primates, however, only humans and our close relatives among the apes show the following curious life history pattern—no secretion in childhood, then secretion in large amounts in young adulthood, and finally a continuous steep decline in secretion through old age. The pattern of absent secretion pre-puberty, rising at adrenarche to very high levels, is observed only in species closely related to humans such as the gorilla and chimpanzee. More distantly related primates such as the rhesus monkey have measurable DHEAS levels in plasma but no adrenarche. Because the restriction of DHEAS biosynthesis in humans to the period past adrenarche is a recent evolutionary development, we must conclude that there are important functions for DHEAS in adult life; yet what these may be has remained elusive.

An important idea, proposed by Dr. Fernand Labrie, is that DHEA provides a universal precursor of further androgenic and estrogenic products which are produced in peripheral tissues, supplying local requirements under the regulation of a series of DHEA-metabolizing enzymes which Dr. Labrie's group has cloned and characterized. The concept of *intracrinology* suggests that we should look for the function of DHEA based on what each individual tissue does with this abundant precursor hormone. This forms another unique aspect of primate endocrinology versus that in other mammalian species—a partial transfer of regulation of tissue sex steroid levels from the classical mode of gonadal biosynthesis and regulation of plasma levels to local synthesis by peripheral tissues from DHEAS precursor.

These factors, the unique life history pattern in higher primates and the local synthesis of androgens and estrogens from DHEA, present a considerable challenge to the researcher approaching the question of appropriate animal models to study the biosynthesis and functions of this hormone. Rodents and other common laboratory species produce extremely small amounts of this steroid, mostly not from the adrenal glands. Indeed, the normal circulating level of DHEAS in mice is probably about 5 orders of magnitude lower than the level in human plasma. An unanswered question is how such disparate levels are maintained. Apparently, DHEAS is rapidly excreted in rodents, as expected for a sulfate, yet in humans its metabolic clearance rate is extremely low, implying a specific mechanism for renal reabsorption, as yet unexplored.

Thus, although experiments in rodents on the effects of DHEA have been extremely valuable, we should always bear in mind the difficulty in applying rodent data to humans, where tissues have evolved DHEA-metabolizing systems in coordination with rising plasma levels of the precursor hormone. In rodents tissues may respond to DHEA quite differently since they do not normally have high levels of DHEA in their plasma.

The present conference yields many clues as to where future researchers should look for the function(s) of DHEA. For the biologist, however, the cycle of changes in DHEA biosynthesis over the life span in humans presents a different puzzle—how to account mechanistically for this curious pattern. Moreover, the age-related decline presents a challenge to the biologist interested in aging as a phenomenon requiring molecular and cellular explanations. Several of the chapters in this volume address these issues; as can be seen from these contributions, these questions need to be attacked at multiple levels: the regulation of DHEA biosynthesis by the key enzymes 3β-hydroxysteroid dehydrogenase and 17α-hydroxylase, their molecular biology, the cell biology of the adrenal cortex, and changes in tissue structure which occur in aging. By the integration of these different levels of analysis, we may obtain a complete picture of the changes in DHEA biosynthesis in early adult life and during aging.

The organizers hope that the exciting and broad range of research presented in this volume will provide a basis for future experimenters not currently within the DHEA field to find something of interest to which to apply their knowledge and skill.

An Abbreviated Account of Some Aspects of the Biochemistry of DHEA, 1934–1995

SEYMOUR LIEBERMAN

Department of Obstetrics and Gynecology
St. Luke's-Roosevelt Hospital Center
Institute for Health Sciences
1000 10 Avenue
New York, New York 10019

I propose to discuss some features of the biochemistry of dehydroepiandrosterone (DHEA) which I believe are incomplete. Attention needs to be given to these issues particularly in this volume because they may be relevant to some of the subjects that will be presented.

DHEA was first isolated in 1934 from urine by Butenandt and Dannenbaum.[1] Even at the very beginning the haze that envelops our understanding of the significance of this compound was evident. In this study DHEA itself was not isolated; the substance isolated was its 3-chloro derivative. The chlorine-containing substance was immediately recognized as an artifact produced from DHEA by boiling the urine with HCl. What was not known until 1944 was that the most probable precursor of the chloro compound was the conjugate, dehydroepiandrosterone-3-sulfate (DHEAS) which was isolated from urine by Munson, Gallagher, and Koch[2] in 1944. In 1954 Migeon and Plager[3] showed that complete extraction of DHEA from human plasma could be achieved only after acid solvolysis, and later in 1959 Baulieu[4] showed that DHEAS was also the form that was most abundant in plasma.

In the early years, confusion reigned even about the name of this compound. Butenandt and Dannenbaum[1] first named the compound dehydro-androsterone. Ruzicka *et al.*,[5] who synthesized the compound by degradation of cholesterol, called it trans-dehydroandrosterone. Fieser,[6] in the first edition of his famous 1936 book, "Chemistry of Natural Products Related to Phenanthracene," named it "dehydroisoandrosterone." Between the years 1936 and 1949, the biochemical and endocrine communities almost always used this designation. In 1949 Fieser, in the third edition of his book, declared that the compound should be dubbed dehydroepiandrosterone. Although both names, dehydroisoandrosterone and dehydroepiandrosterone, were trivial and the distinction between the two was minimal, the influence of Fieser at that time was dominant and the community generally accepted the new name. Ten years later, Fieser and Fieser[7] recommended still another name for this compound. In their classic book, "Steroids," published in 1959 they suggested the name "androstenolone." This time the new name did not prevail, and dehydroepiandrosterone retained acceptance.

To return to the conjugates of DHEA, its sulfate, DHEAS, is indicated in FIGURE 1 by the structure at the bottom left. R stands for the steroid moiety. At the top are shown the structures of the glucuronidate and the *N*-acetyl glucosaminidate. At the bottom right is the structure of the hypothetical and contentious sulfatide proposed by Oertel.[8] In the middle 1960s Oertel claimed that DHEA exists in tissue as a lipophilic derivative composed of the steroid sulfate esterified to a diacyl glycerol residue. The steroid moiety of one of Oertel's sulfatides was DHEA. During the

1

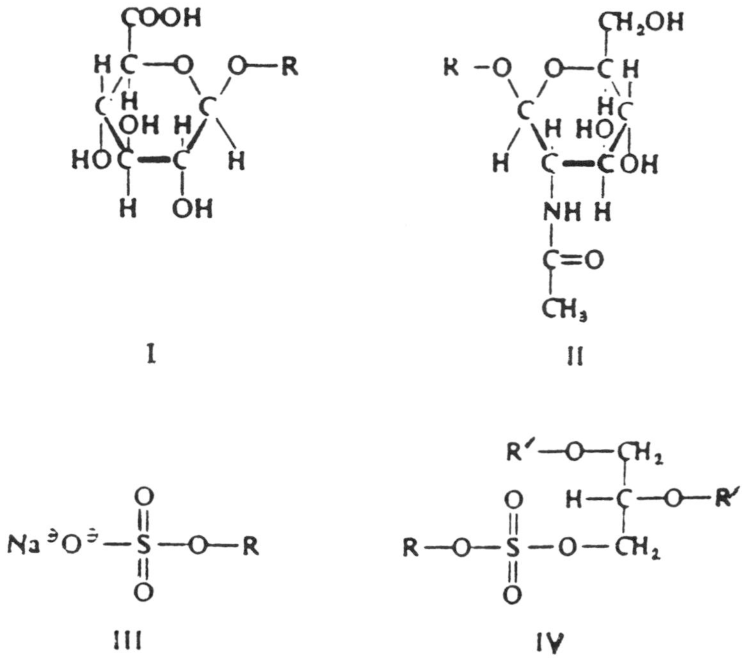

FIGURE 1. Structures of steroid conjugates.

1960s, Oertel[9,10] and coworkers described the properties of these conjugates, including their isolation, composition, and biochemical transformations. Several investigators have tried to confirm Oertel's observations, but they have been uniformly unsuccessful. Nevertheless, this subject deserves mention particularly because we have had results that may have relevance to this issue.[11] We have presented evidence that there exists in bovine brain lipophilic complexes of the sulfate esters of cholesterol and sitosterol. The complex is represented in FIGURE 2 as a diester of sulfuric acid which when treated with pyridine leads to the formation of a sterol sulfate, shown in the figure as cholesterol pyridinium sulfate. In this case, R is a lipophilic constituent of unknown structure. Proof that DHEAS occurs in tissues in an analogous form does not exist, but, like cholesterol, the steroids DHEA and pregnenolone both possess the 3β-hydroxy-5-ene grouping. What is true for cholesterol sulfate, that it exists in mammalian brain as a derivative that is soluble in nonpolar solvents and easily dissociable into cholesterol sulfate by nucleophilic reagents, perhaps even by methanol, may also be true for the sulfates of DHEA and pregnenolone. Dialkyl sulfates are very reactive, and this lability might make the isolation of such conjugates in intact form difficult. If DHEA does exist in tissue as such a conjugate, and if it per se has biologic properties, this molecule would have relevance to the theme of this volume.

Another kind of derivative of DHEA and pregnenolone should be mentioned. Several years ago we isolated from mammalian tissues, fatty acid esters of DHEA, pregnenolone, and other steroids.[12] The steroids have been shown to exist as esters of palmitic, stearic, oleic, linolenic, arachidonic, and eicosotrienoic acids. More recently Hochberg and his coworkers[13,14] found that both estradiol and testosterone

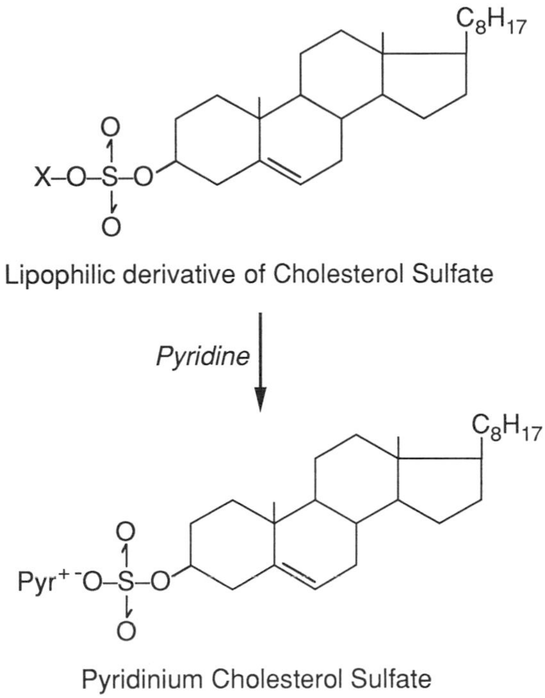

C$_8$H$_{17}$

Lipophilic derivative of Cholesterol Sulfate

Pyridine

C$_8$H$_{17}$

Pyridinium Cholesterol Sulfate

FIGURE 2. Proposed structure of a nonpolar derivative of cholesterol sulfate and the product formed upon treatment with pyridine.

are present in tissues, particularly fat, as long-lived lipoidal fatty acid esters. Esterification influences the biologic activity of these hormones possibly by increasing their half-lives. In any case the physiologic significance of these esters may also warrant further consideration.

The biosynthesis of DHEA may also be enveloped in some uncertainty. Despite the general acceptance by endocrinologists of the validity of the scheme shown in FIGURE 3, it is my contention that some uncertainty still exists about the proximal precursors of the C$_{19}$-steroids. In the scheme, cleavage of the C-17, C-20 bond of the C$_{21}$-steroid, such as pregnenolone or progesterone, is shown to involve the intermediacy of a metabolite that has oxygen functions on two vicinal carbon atoms, that is, 17-hydroxyprogesterone. 17-Hydroxylation and subsequent cleavage (lyase) of the

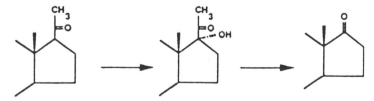

FIGURE 3. Traditional scheme for the conversion of C$_{21}$-steroids to C$_{19}$-steroids.

C-17, C-20 bond is catalyzed by a bifunctional cytochrome P450, 17-hydroxylase/17,20-lyase. This enzyme is present in adrenals, testes, and thecal cells of the ovary. It is apparently not present in granulosa cells of the ovary, trophoblasts of the human placenta, and mammalian brain, all sites of steroidogenesis.

Everything known about this enzyme by 1991 was admirably recorded in a scholarly review by Yanase et al.[15] Another review[16] published contemporaneously posed the question: Does this scheme, shown in FIGURE 3, satisfactorily explain all the facts known about the conversion of C_{21}-steroids to C_{19}-steroids? Our iconoclasm was specifically directed at the question: Was a 17-hydroxylated C_{21}-steroid an obligatory intermediate in the conversion as is required by this scheme?

By 1990 several reports had cast doubt on this formulation. The 1991 review by Yanase et al.[15] also recognized that not everything was known about cytochrome $P450_{17}$. They wrote: "the observation that $P450_{17}$ can catalyze two distinct reactions, namely the 17-hydroxylation and 17,20-lyase reactions required for the production of cortisol and androgens, raises the intriguing question: how can we explain the dissociation between secretion of androgens and cortisol observed at specific developmental stages in humans?" They go on to say: "little is known concerning the mechanism of reaction selectivity occurring in the . . . instances of variation in ratios of 17-hydroxylase and 17,20 lyase. This remains one of the interesting issues to be understood in the future."

These ideas contain the assumption that one enzyme, $P450_{17}$, is involved in two processes, cortisol formation and C_{19}-androgen production. No unequivocal evidence exists that establishes this assumption as fact. The enzymic properties of $P450_{17}$ are customarily established by demonstrating in vitro its capacity to convert progesterone to 17-hydroxyprogesterone and/or to cleave the latter compound to the C_{19}-17-ketosteroids. Its direct involvement in the biosynthesis of cortisol has not been established. The enzymic products from expression studies of cDNA clones of the human enzyme in COS-1 cells are also identified by their capacity to catalyze these same two reactions; cortisol formation was not determined.[17] What precursor of cortisol could be used as a substrate in these in vitro experiments? The coincidence of low levels of 17-ketosteroids and low levels of cortisol in 17-hydroxylase deficiency disease does not logically prove that the same P450 is involved in the two processes. In a parallel way, aldosterone secretion is also decreased in this disease. As this steroid does not have a 17-hydroxyl group, $P450_{17}$ is probably not directly involved in its decreased secretion. It has been suggested[15] that other factors are undoubtedly responsible for the decrease in aldosterone production. So too, factors other than $P450_{17}$ may be invoked to account for the coincidence of low levels of 17-ketosteroids and low levels of cortisol. It is possible to imagine explanations for the aforementioned coincidence other than that which assumes that the $P450_{17}$ involved in androgen production is the same as the enzyme that introduces a hydroxyl group on C-17 during cortisol formation.

The idea that a C-C bond could be split easily only if each C atom was substituted with an oxygen function, such as a glycol or α-ketol, came at a time when the chemical reactivities of reagents such as HIO_4 or $Pb(OAc)_4$ were readily known to every chemist. These properties were discovered in the early 1930s. Reichstein had elegantly used them to elucidate the structure of the glucocorticoids, again in the 1930s. A search to determine when the extrapolation of this idea was first applied to biochemical reactions involving naturally occurring steroids led to a paper in the August 1938 issue of the Journal of the American Chemical Society.[18] Its author was Russel E. Marker, who wrote: "products contain dihydroxy acetone residues which are readily susceptible to oxidation to yield carbonyl groups at C-17." He then mentioned the properties of HIO_4 and $Pb(OAc)_4$ and pointed to the C_{19}-steroids, adrenosterone and androstenedione, as products that may arise by analogous "biochemical" reactions. He also said that "this theory will predict the possible existence in urine or glandular extracts of related steroids."

On October 20, 1938, the Canadian, Guy Marrian, was the Harvey Lecturer in New York.[16] In his presentation he described how he established the structure of a C_{21}-triol that he had isolated from the urine of a patient with adrenal virilism. He had oxidized this triol with $Pb(OAc)_4$ and had identified the 17-ketosteroid produced as etiocholanolone. This 17-ketosteroid and also isoandrosterone were isolated from that same urine, and so Marrian concluded: "It seemed probable to us that an oxidation similar to that which can be effected in the lab with $Pb(OAc)_4$ must have occurred in the body."

By 1947 this idea that C-C bonds could only be cleaved when each was substituted with an oxygen function was generally accepted. The Hirschmanns[20] wrote, "in general it has been proposed that pregnane derivatives with oxygen substituents at C-17 and at C-20 are metabolized into 17-ketosteroids. This theory is not directly applicable to the formation of dehydroisoandrosterone." They believed this to be so because the compounds they had isolated from the examined urine did not contain a double bond in the 5-6 position.

The Hirschmanns then made two surprising speculations. They proposed to explain the fact "that adrenal hyperactivity is frequently associated with a subnormal output of urinary 17-ketosteroids" by assuming "that the reaction between C_{19}-17-ketosteroids and C_{21}-17-hydroxy-20-ketosteroids can proceed in both directions." Finally, they found it "conceivable that the dehydroisoandrosterone needed to initiate such a synthesis (of C_{21} compounds) may be formed from cholesterol without passing through an intermediate containing 21 carbon atoms." To the present, no proof for either of these two suggestions has been forthcoming.

In 1950 Hechter and his colleagues[21] demonstrated that enzymes in the adrenals could hydroxylate steroids at specific carbon atoms. It is of special interest that they isolated 17-hydroxyprogesterone after perfusing progesterone through an isolated bovine adrenal. These considerations led in 1953 to the proposal[22] that "hydroxylation at C-17 of a properly constituted precursor(s) possessing the Δ^5-3β-ol groups would yield . . . the 17-hydroxylated 20-oxygenated pregnane derivatives which would be the precursors of urinary 17-ketosteroids. One of these 17-ketosteroids is the Δ^5-3β-hydroxy-17-ketosteroid, DHEA. The suggestion was made then[22] that DHEA is "not the metabolite of a hormone but is the urinary product from an intermediate in the biosynthesis of the adrenal hormones." That intermediate obviously could be pregnenolone, which at that time (1953) had been isolated only from pig testes.[23]

The proposal that pregnenolone was a precursor of DHEA assumed that 17-hydroxylation was an essential feature of the steroidogenic processes leading to the C_{19}- and C_{18}-steroid hormones. At that time, most endocrine biochemists were fixated—and maybe they still are—on the absolute necessity of having oxygen functions on both carbon atoms of the side chain in order for cleavage of the C-17–C-20 bond to occur. If this were true, 17-hydroxypregnenolone and 17-hydroxyprogesterone would then be examples of obligatory intermediates not only for cortisol but also for the 17-ketosteroids such as DHEA and for the hormones testosterone and estradiol.

These considerations naturally led to the proposition that cytochrome $P450_{17}$ is an essential enzyme in the biosynthetic pathways by which testosterone and estradiol as well as cortisol and DHEA are produced. The two-dimensional representations of the pathways involved in steroid hormone biosynthesis published in every textbook that deals with this issue clearly propose this central feature, but these representations probably do not reflect the natural situation correctly. These schemes are

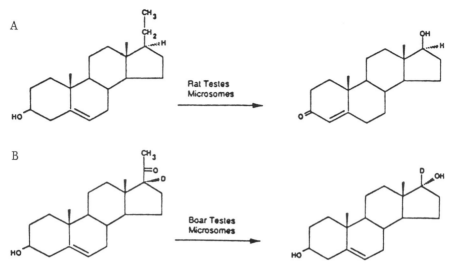

FIGURE 4. Summary of the results of Hochberg *et al.* (**A**) and Shimizu (**B**) which suggest that 17-hydroxylation is not essential for the conversion of a C_{21}-steroid to a C_{19}-steroid.

constructed (by biochemists) to systematize our biochemical knowledge and to present that knowledge in an easily assimilatable manner. The depicted chemical relationships, however, do not define the intercellular arrangements. These schemes may give the impression that the various hormone-producing processes are randomly distributed in the relevant endocrine cells. But a better view of the *in situ* situation may be had by considering that there exist intercellular structures (e.g., multienzyme complexes), each of which is dedicated to the production of one specific hormonal product. Within this view of reality, it may be possible to arrive at the proper evaluation of the role of $P450_{17}$.

From our current knowledge it is reasonable to hold that cytochrome $P450_{17}$ is involved in the formation of C_{19}-steroids. But it is not unreasonable to ask: Is the process shown in FIGURE 3 the only pathway by which DHEA can be formed?

A large part of the review Prasad and I wrote in 1990 was devoted to this question.[16] We pointed out that several papers suggested that there may be other pathways leading to C_{19}-steroids. FIGURE 4 presents the results of the two most compelling studies, those of Hochberg *et al.*[24] and Shimizu.[25]

Hochberg *et al.* incubated 20-deoxypregnenolone with rat testes microsomes and produced testosterone in about 3% yield.[24] The C-17–C-20 bond of the substrate was readily cleaved during the artificial *in vitro* incubation even though neither carbon atom of its side chain bears an oxygen function.

Shimizu[25] in 1978 incubated deuterated pregnenolone with boar testes microsomes and isolated deuterated androstenediol. The deuterium atom at C-17 present in the substrate was retained in the product. This result precluded the possibility of a 17-hydroxylated C_{21}-intermediate, because if it were involved in the process, it could only have been formed by displacement of the deuterium atom.

It is unclear why more attention has not been paid by the endocrine community to Shimizu's result. Hochberg's experiment may be criticized by pointing out that the substrate 20-deoxypregnenolone is unnatural and consequently the result is artificial.

Still, this unnatural substrate resembles cholesterol in that both it and the sterol have hydrocarbon substituents at C-17. On the other hand, the substrate in Shimizu's experiment is the naturally occurring substance pregnenolone, and the result obtained with it clearly indicates a second pathway from C_{21}-steroids to C_{19}-steroids, one that proceeds without the intermediacy of an isolatable 17-hydroxy-20-ketosteroid.

It may be logical to dub pregnenolone a "putative" precursor of C_{19}-steroids. Is scepticism about this point also warranted? The bulk of the evidence suggesting that a C-20 ketone, such as pregnenolone, is the necessary proximal precursor of C_{19}-steroids comes from *in vitro* experiments in which tissue preparations are

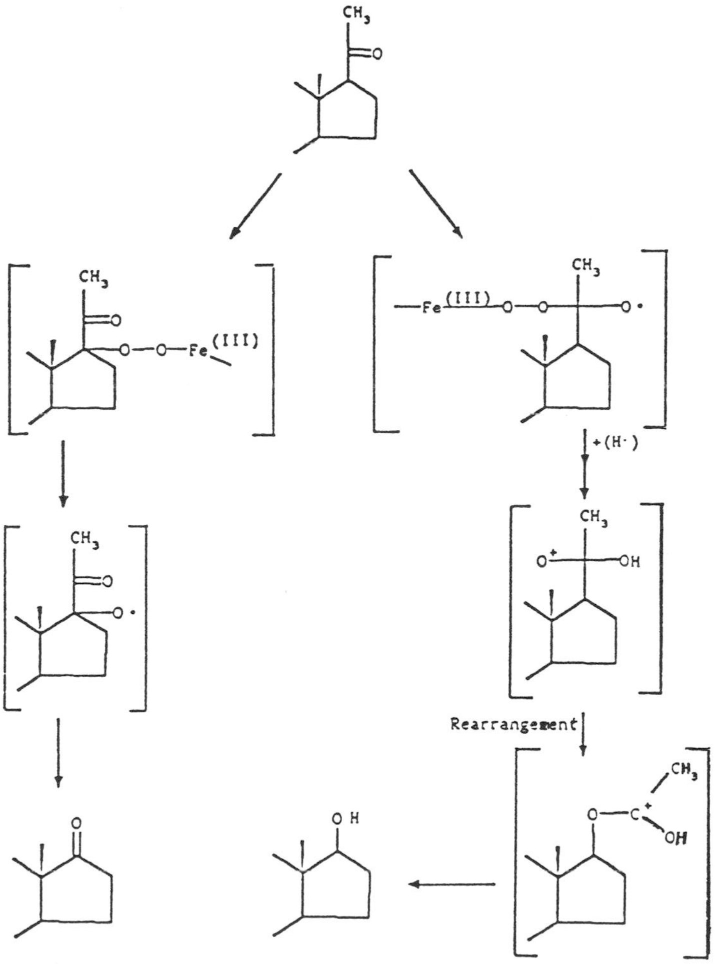

FIGURE 5. Proposed mechanism by which a C_{21}-20-ketosteroid is oxidized to (**a**) a C_{19}-17-ketosteroid by oxygenation at C_{17} or (**b**) a C_{19}-17-hydroxysteroid by oxygenation at the C-20 carbonyl group.

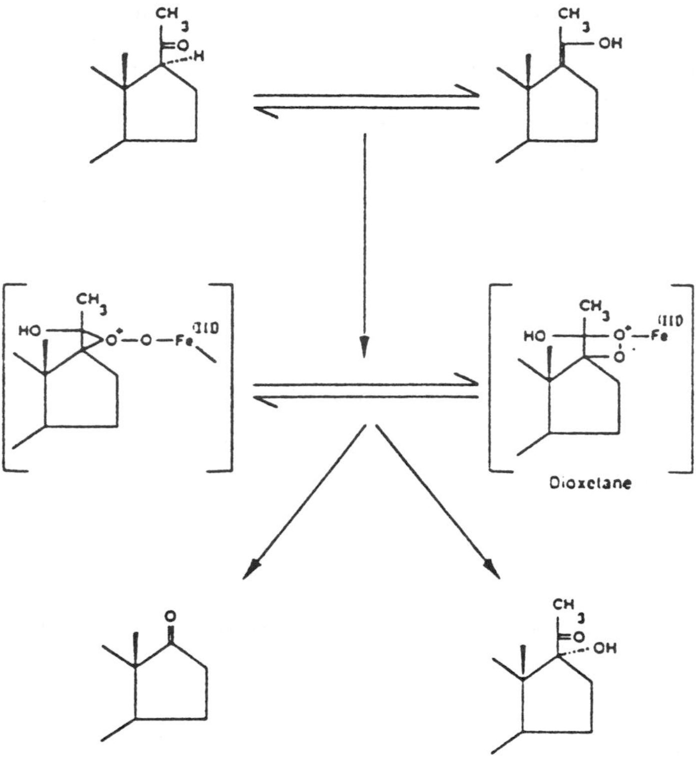

FIGURE 6. Proposed mechanism by which a C_{21}-20-ketosteroid is oxidized to a C_{19}-17-ketosteroid or a C_{21}-17-hydroxy-20-ketosteroid.

incubated with this C-20 ketone. Two possibilities are pertinent: the substrate is not a true reflection of the natural intermediate or it is. That it is not comes from the possibility that an unnatural substrate may yield, in such artificial *in vitro* experiments, a naturally occurring product, one the investigator expects. There are many examples of this phenomenon.[26] *In vitro* experiments, such as these, may suggest how various metabolic pathways proceed, but they do not reveal the true naturally occurring substrate. *In vitro* incubation experiments can suggest only what is possible. They do not reveal with certainty what actually prevails *in situ.* They certainly do not reveal the nature of true intermediates for these most likely are transient, nonisolatable (at present) species.

Even if pregnenolone is the true proximal precursor of C_{19}-steroids, it is possible to formulate oxidation patterns that do not involve the intermediacy of a 17-hydroxy-20-ketone. These are shown in FIGURE 5. On the left, oxygenation is shown to occur at C-17. Hydroxylation reactions catalyzed by specific cytochrome P450s are thought to occur by an H atom abstraction from a substrate followed by a free radical recombination mechanism. Currently, it is not uncommon to invoke the idea that some biochemical reactions are best formulated as free radical reactions. When the steroidogenic pathways were first being investigated 30–40 years ago, such ideas were not fashionable. Nowadays, it is acceptable to say that "free radicals play a significant role in metabolism."[27] The P450 reaction mechanism involves the reduction of molecular oxygen to reactive species, shown in FIGURE 5 in brackets. The alkoxy radical shown could fragment by β-scission, a well known property of such species, to give the 17-ketosteroid. Oxygenation at the C-20 carbonyl group (FIG. 5, right) could lead by a Baeyer-Villiger rearrangement reaction to yield the 17-hydroxy C_{19}-steroid. In neither case is an isolatable 17-hydroxy-20-ketosteroid an obligatory intermediate.

Even if pregnenolone is the natural precursor and even if oxygenation takes place at C_{17}, it is possible to formulate a process that accounts for the formation of both the C_{17}-ketone and 17-hydroxy-20-ketone without the latter being a precursor of the former. FIGURE 6 shows a scheme in which both products are formed from a common reactive nonisolatable species (shown in brackets).

The fact that the expected product is a 17-ketosteroid, such as DHEA, and is formed in *in vitro* experiments from pregnenolone is not logical proof that the experimental conditions mimic natural processes. Ketones, particularly those whose α-carbon atoms bear a hydrogen atom as a substituent, are readily susceptible to oxidation. A biologic system containing oxidases, peroxidases, and hydroxylases exposed in incubation experiments to dioxygen tension several times that prevailing *in situ* may generate many potent oxidants such as $.\overline{O}_2$, HO_2, HO., HOOH, and LOOH. How any one of these species may react with a methyl ketone such as pregnenolone must be taken into account before the result is assumed to mimic the *in situ* steroidogenic situation.

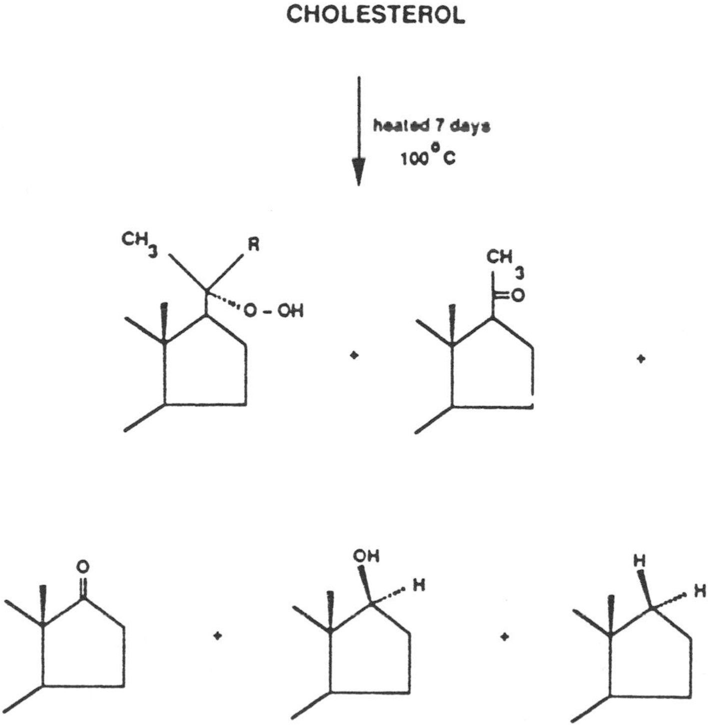

CHOLESTEROL

FIGURE 7. Products isolated from a sample of cholesterol heated at 100°C for 7 days. (A summary of the results of VanLier and Smith. 1970. J. Org. Chem. **25:** 2627.)

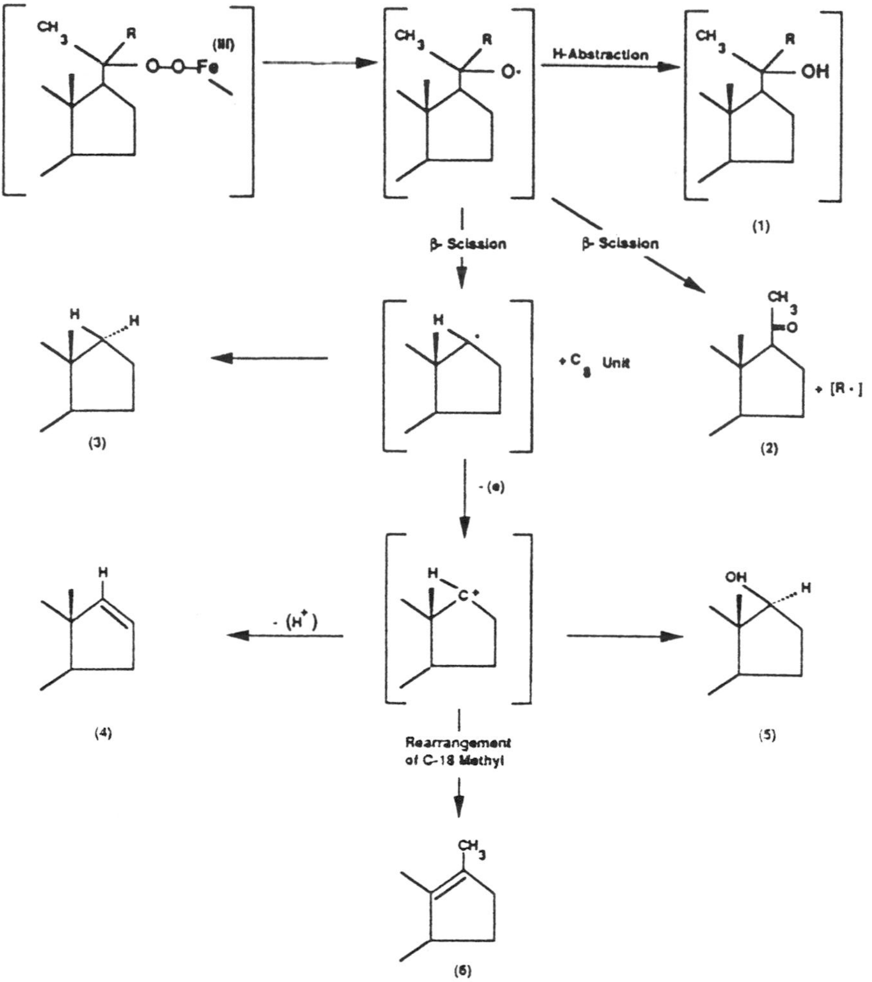

FIGURE 8. Some characteristic reactions of alkoxy radicals (RO).

Moreover, cytochrome P450s are known to act as peroxidases.[27,28] This leads to another proposal for the formation of C_{19} androgens. In this the proximal precursor of C_{19}-steroids is cholesterol. FIGURE 7 shows the oxidation products Smith and his colleague, VanLier,[29] isolated after heating cholesterol for 7 days at 100°C. One product is the 20-hydroperoxide of cholesterol. They also identified pregnenolone, DHEA, and androstenediol. Obviously no enzyme is involved in these reactions, but if in biochemical conversions the side-chain cleavage enzyme cytochrome P450scc reacts with cholesterol at C-20, as in FIGURE 8, to form an intermediate such as that shown in the top left corner, two cleavage routes can be imagined. Both follow the formation of the 20-alkoxy radical shown in the top center. Alkoxy radicals are known to cleave readily by β-scission. β-scission between C-20 and C-22 leads to the

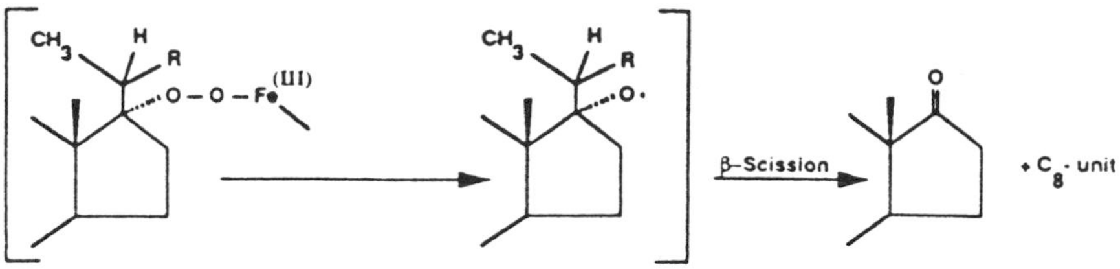

FIGURE 9. Proposed route by which a C_{19}-steroid could be formed from a sterolic precursor by oxygenation occurring at C-17.

20-ketosteroid pregnenolone and β-scission between C-17 and C-20 could lead to a C_{19}-steroid.

Another formulation is shown in FIGURE 9. In this the cytochrome is assumed to oxygenate at C-17. The resulting alkoxy radical could cleave between C-17 and C-20, forming the 17-ketosteroid. Some years ago we showed that cleavage between C-17 and C-20 could occur when an artificial, synthetic precursor, 20-phenyl-pregnene-diol (FIGURE 10), was used as a substrate with adrenal mitochondria.[30] Acetophenone was identified as one cleavage product, proving that cleavage between C-17 and C-20 had occurred.

More recent results support such a possibility. We recently reported that a nonketonic extract of rat brain from which all ketones had been removed (by a Girard Reagent) would generate pregnenolone and DHEA when treated with various chemicals, particularly $FeSO_4$.[31] FIGURE 11 shows our interpretation of this finding. If hydroperoxides or dioxetanes were present in this nonketonic extract, they would be expected to react with the reducing agent $FeSO_4$ to yield these ketosteroids. This extraordinary reaction, a reducing agent converting a nonketonic compound into a ketone, is a characteristic of hydroperoxides. Thus, in the brain, cytochrome P450$_{scc}$ catalyzes the conversion of cholesterol to pregnenolone (P). This 20-ketone as well as dehydroepiandrosterone (D) may be formed either enzymatically or by nonenzymatic autooxidation from the hydroperoxides or dioxetanes (cyclic peroxides) present in nonketonic fractions. Thus, the scheme in FIGURE 11 represents another pathway by which dehydroepiandrosterone may be formed *in vitro* by a process not involving a C_{21}-intermediate.

Finally, a few thoughts about the further metabolism of DHEA are relevant. FIGURE 12 shows some interconversions that DHEA may undergo. These interconversions have been known for decades, and they are shown here merely to demonstrate that DHEA can serve as a biosynthetic precursor of testosterone and therefore also of estradiol (not shown). Even here, however, with what appears to be straightforward, the natural history of DHEA is not simple; in addition to the

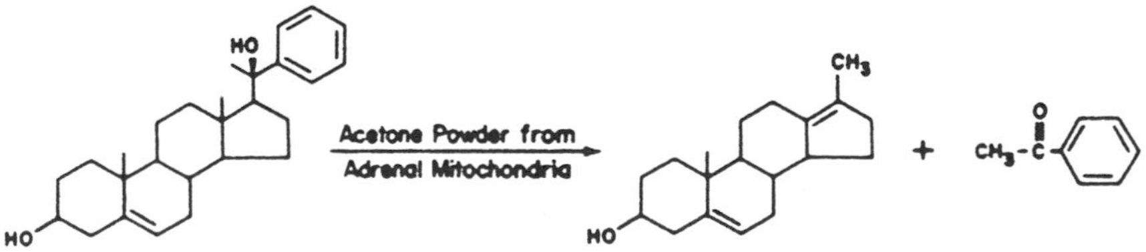

FIGURE 10. Example of cleavage between C-17 and C-20. One product is acetophenone and the other is a rearranged C_{19}-steroid.

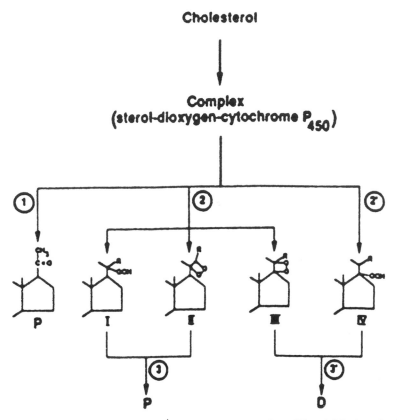

FIGURE 11. Reactions leading to the formation of pregnenolone (P) and dehydroepiandrosterone (D) from cholesterol. Reaction 1 represents the generally accepted side-chain cleavage catalyzed by $P450_{scc}$. Compounds I–IV are proposed as nonketonic peroxidic constituents of brain extracts which may lead to the formation of P and D. Reactions 2, 2', 3, and 3' may be enzymatic or nonenzymatic (autooxidation).

molecule itself, having its own biologic role (or perhaps more than one role), this C_{19}-steroid serves as a metabolic precursor for at least two other hormones, testosterone and estradiol.

There is nothing extraordinary about this finding. Other steroidal compounds, such as pregnenolone, serve as progenitors of hormones. For example, pregnenolone is considered to be a precursor of progesterone, cortisol, aldosterone, and also DHEA. But the circumstances in which DHEA and probably other C_{19}-steroids are used as precursors in estrogen biosynthesis are perceived to have a curious feature. Although the cellular factories that make progesterone, cortisol, or aldosterone are thought to contain all the components (enzymes, coenzymes, etc.) necessary to complete the process that transforms the sterol precursor, cholesterol, into the hormones, the cells that make the C_{18}-steroid estradiol are conceived to be "incompletely endowed." The cells that produce the estrogenic hormone are said to be unable by themselves to make the essential, proximal C_{19}-steroidal precursors, such as DHEA. The estradiol-producing cells in the ovary, the granulosa cells, and the syncotrophoblastic cells in the placenta are considered to be unable to synthesize from a C_{21}-precursor the C_{19}-intermediate necessary for the production of estradiol. For 25–30 years, this notion has generally been accepted: the granulosa cells[32] and the syncotrophoblastic cells[33,34] must obtain the essential C_{19}-steroidal precursors from other cells in order to feed the aromatization process. This thesis holds that the C_{19}-precursors of the estrogenic hormone must be made in one place; in the ovary it is the thecal cells and in the placenta it is the adrenal cells of the mother or fetus or both, following which the C_{19}-steroid is transported, in the ovary by diffusion and in the placenta by the blood, to the estrogen-producing cell where aromatization takes place. Support for this thesis comes from the finding that cytochrome $P450_{17}$ has not been found in either the granulosa cell or the placenta. Because this enzyme is considered essential for estradiol biosynthesis, its absence is considered to support this thesis.

So here, too, DHEA is a curiosity; it is involved in an extraordinary process, one in which the cells that require it as a building block for a process essential for the perpetuation of the species are supposedly unable to synthesize it. These cells are said to depend on help from other suppliers. This scenario has been repeated unquestioningly time and time again in textbooks and reviews written well into the 1990s. In my judgment evidence supporting this thesis is far from compelling and it is unwise to consider this thesis as an established fact. Further discussion of this facet of the biochemistry of DHEA here is inappropriate, but I mention it merely to reveal another unresolved problem at the center of which is DHEA. It is appropriate to mention here that in the brain where DHEA is found, the nature of its precursors is also unclear. In the brain, cholesterol can be converted into pregnenolone, but the biosynthesis of DHEA from pregnenolone in this organ has not been demonstrated.

This paper attempts to call attention to some gaps in our knowledge of the biochemistry of DHEA that may have relevance for some of the papers that follow.

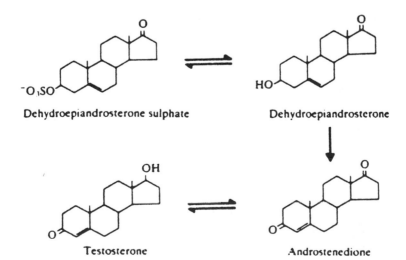

FIGURE 12. Some metabolic interconversions of dehydroepiandrosterone and its C_{19}-relatives.

REFERENCES

1. BUTENANDT, A. & H. DANNENBAUM. 1934. Isolierung eines neuen, physiologisch unwirksamen Sterinderivates aus Mannerharn, seine Verknupfung mit Dehydro-androsteron und Androsteron. Z. Physiol. Chem. **229:** 192–195.
2. MUNSON, P. L., T. F. GALLAGHER & F. C. KOCH. 1944. Isolation of dehydroisoandrosterone sulfate from normal male urine. J. Biol. Chem. **152:** 67–77.
3. MIGEON, C. J. & J. E. PLAGER. 1954. Identification and isolation of dehydroisoandrosterone from peripheral human blood. J. Biol. Chem. **209:** 767–772.
4. BAULIEU, E. E. 1960. Three sulfate esters of 17-ketosteroids in the plasma of human subjects and after the administration of ACTH. J. Clin. Endocrinol. **20:** 900–904.
5. RUZICKA, L., M. W. GOLDBERG & H. WIRZ. 1935. Sex hormones. III. Constitution of androsterone. Helv. Chim. Acta **18:** 61–68.
6. FIESER, L. F. 1936. The Chemistry of Natural Products Related to Phenanthrene. Reinhold Publ. Corp. New York.
7. FIESER, L. F. & M. FIESER. 1959. Steroids. Reinhold Publ. Corp. New York.
8. OERTEL, G. W. 1961. On steroid conjugates in plasma. I. Isolation of sulfate-, phosphate- and lipoid-containing 17-ketosteroid conjugates in human blood plasma. Biochem. Z. **33:** 431–440.
9. OERTEL, G. W. 1965. Uber Steroid-konjugate in plasma. XV11. Isolierung und Charakterislerung lipophiler steroid Conjugate aus Nebennierenrindengewebe, Plasma und Liquor. Hoppe Seyler Biochem Z. **343:** 276–281.
10. OERTEL, G. W., K. GROOT & D. WENZEL. 1965. On lipophile steroid conjugates. I. In vivo experiments with a biosynthetic lipophile dehydroepiandrosterone conjugate. Acta Endocrinol. (Kobenhavn) **49:** 533–540.
11. PRASAD, V. V. K., E. EL-MARAGHY, L. PONTICORVO & S. LIEBERMAN. 1985. Detection in bovine brain of lipophilic complexes of sulfate esters of cholesterol and sitosterol. Proc. Natl. Acad. Sci. USA **82:** 2657–2659.
12. ALBERT, D. H., L. PONTICORVO & S. LIEBERMAN. 1980. Identification of fatty acid esters of pregnenolone and allopregnanolone from bovine corpora lutea. J. Biol. Chem. **255:** 10618–10623.
13. LARNER, J. M., S. L. PAHUJA, C. H. SHACKLETON, W. J. MCMURRAY, G. GIORDANO & R. B. HOCHBERG. 1993. The isolation and characterization of estradiol-fatty acid esters in human ovarian follicular fluid. J. Biol. Chem. **288:** 13893–13899.
14. BORG, W., C. H. L. SHACKLETON, S. L. PAHUJA & R. B. HOCHBERG. 1995. Long-lived testosterone esters in the rat. Proc. Natl. Acad. Sci. USA **92:** 1545–1549.
15. YANASE, T., E. R. SIMPSON & M. R. WATERMAN. 1991. 17-Hydroxylase/17,20-lyase deficiency: From clinical investigation to molecular definition. Endocrine Rev. **12:** 91–107.
16. LIEBERMAN, S. & V. V. K. PRASAD. 1990 Heterodox notions on pathways of steroidogenesis. Endocrine Rev. **11:** 469–493.
17. ZUBER, M. K., E. R. SIMPSON & M. R. WATERMAN. 1986. Expression of bovine 17α-hydroxylase cytochrome P-450 cDNA in non-steroidogenic (COS-1) cells. Science **234:** 1258–1261.
18. MARKER, R. E. 1938. The origin and interrelationships of the steroidal hormones. J. Am. Chem. Soc. **60:** 1725–1734.
19. MARRIAN, G. F. 1938. Some aspects of the intermediary metabolism of the steroid hormones. Harvey Lect. **27:** 37–56.
20. HIRSCHMANN, H., & F. B. HIRSCHMANN. 1947. Steroid excretion in a case of adrenocortical carcinoma. J. Biol Chem. **167:** 7–24.
21. HECHTER, O. R., R. P. JACOBSON, R. JEANLOZ, H. LEVY, C. W. MARSHALL, G. PINCUS & V. SHENKER. 1949. The bio-oxygenation of 11-desoxycorticosterone at C-11. J. Am. Chem. Soc. **71:** 3261–3262.
22. LIEBERMAN, S. & S. TEICH. 1953. Metabolic precursors of urinary dehydroisoandrosterone. J. Clin. Endocrinol. Metab. **13:** 1140–1148.
23. RUZICKA, L. & V. PRELOG. 1943. Zur Kenutnis der Lipoide aus schweine Testes. Helv. Chim. Acta **26:** 975–995.

24. HOCHBERG, R. B., & LADANY & S. LIEBERMAN. 1976. Conversion of a C-20-deoxy-C_{21}-steroid, 5-pregnen-3β-ol to testosterone by rat testicular microsomes. J. Biol. Chem. **251:** 3320–3325.
25. SHIMIZU, K. 1978. Formation of 5-(17^3H)androstene-3, 17-diol from 3β-hydroxy-5-(17,21,21-^{3}H)pregnen-20-one by the microsomal fraction. J. Biol. Chem. **253:** 4237–4245.
26. HOCHBERG, R. B., P. D. MACDONALD, S. LADANY & S. LIEBERMAN. 1975. Transient intermediates in steroidogenesis. J. Steroid Biochem. **6:** 323–327.
27. ORTIZ DE MONTELLANO, P. R. 1986. Cytochrome P-450. Plenum Press. New York.
28. HRYCAY, E. G. & P. J. O'BRIEN. 1971. Cytochrome P-450 as a microsomal peroxidase in steroid hydroxylations. Biochem. J. **125:** 12.
29. VANLIER, J. E. & L. L. SMITH. 1970. Autoxidation of cholesterol via hydroperoxide intermediates. J. Org. Chem. **25:** 2627–2632.
30. HOCHBERG, R. B., P. D. MCDONALD, M. FELDMAN & S. LIEBERMAN. 1976. Fragments formed by the side-chain cleavage of 20-aryl analog of 20α-hydroxycholesterol by adrenal mitochondria. J. Biol. Chem. **251:** 2087–2093.
31. PRASAD, V. V. K., S. RAJU VEGESNA, M. WELCH & S. LIEBERMAN. 1994. Precursors of the neurosteroids. Proc. Natl. Acad. Sci. USA **91:** 3220–3223.
32. FORTUNE, J. E. & D. T. ARMSTRONG. 1977. Androgen production by theca and granulosa isolated from proestrous rat follicles. Endocrinology **100:** 1341–1347.
33. SIITERI, P. K. & P. C. MACDONALD. 1963. The utilization of circulating dehydroisoandrosterone sulfates for estrogen synthesis during human pregnancy. Steroids **2:** 713–730.
34. JAFFE, R., R. PION, G. ERIKSSON, N. WIQVIST & E. DISCFALUSY. 1965. Studies on the aromatisation of neutral steroids in pregnant women. Acta Endocrinol. **48:** 413–422.

DHEA and Peripheral Androgen and Estrogen Formation: Intracrinology

FERNAND LABRIE,[a] ALAIN BÉLANGER, JACQUES
SIMARD, VAN LUU-THE, AND CLAUDE LABRIE

Laboratory of Molecular Endocrinology
CHUL Research Center (Le Centre Hospitalier de l'Université Laval)
2705 Laurier Boulevard
Québec, G1V 4G2, Canada

Despite the fact that the concentration of dehydroepiandrosterone sulfate (DHEAS) in the circulation of adult men and women is higher than that of any other steroid, except cholesterol, the biologic function of this steroid as well as that of DHEA has received little attention. It is remarkable that man, in addition to possessing very sophisticated endocrine and paracrine systems, has largely vested sex steroid formation in peripheral tissues.[1–3] In fact, although the ovaries and testes are the exclusive sources of androgens and estrogens in lower mammals, the situation is very different in higher primates, where active sex steroids are in large part or entirely synthesized locally in peripheral tissues, thus providing control to target tissues which adjust the formation and metabolism of sex steroids to local requirements.

Man, with some other primates, is thus unique in having adrenals that secrete large amounts of the precursor steroids DHEAS and DHEA which are converted into androstenedione (4-dione) and then into potent androgens and/or estrogens in peripheral tissues.[1–3] Adrenal secretion of DHEA and DHEAS increases during adrenarche in children at the age of 6–8 years, and maximal values of circulating DHEAS are reached between the ages of 20 and 30 years. Thereafter, serum DHEA and DHEAS levels decrease markedly.[4–7] In fact, at 70 years of age, serum DHEAS levels are at approximately 20% of their peak values, whereas they decrease by up to 95% by the age of 85–90 years.[4] The 70–95% reduction in the formation of DHEAS by the adrenals during aging results in a dramatic reduction in the formation of androgens and estrogens in peripheral target tissues, which could well be involved in the pathogenesis of age-related diseases such as insulin resistance,[8,9] cardiovascular disease,[10] and obesity.[11,12] Low circulating levels of DHEAS and DHEA have been found in patients with breast[13] and prostate[14] cancer, and DHEA has been found to exert antioncogenic activity in a series of animal models.[15–17] DHEA has also been shown to have immunomodulatory effects *in vitro*[18] and *in vivo* in fungal and viral diseases[19] including HIV.[20] On the other hand, a stimulatory effect of DHEA on the immune system has been described in postmenopausal women.[21]

Transformation of the adrenal precursor steroids DHEAS and DHEA into androgens and/or estrogens in peripheral target tissues depends on the level of expression of the various steroidogenic and metabolizing enzymes in each of these tissues. This sector of endocrinology that focuses on intracellular hormone formation and action has been called intracrinology.[1,3] Knowledge in this area has recently made rapid progress with the elucidation of the structure of most of the tissue-specific genes that encode the steroidogenic enzymes responsible for the transforma-

[a] Address for correspondence: Professor Fernand Labrie, MRC Group in Molecular Endocrinology, CHUL Research Center, 2705 Laurier Boulevard, Québec, G1V 4G2, Canada.

tion of DHEAS and DHEA into androgens and/or estrogens in peripheral tissues.[22-25] The particular importance of DHEA and DHEAS is illustrated by the finding that approximately 50% of total androgens in adult men derive from these adrenal precursor steroids.[2,26-28] In women, our best estimate of the intracrine formation of estrogens in peripheral tissues is in the order of 75% before menopause and close to 100% after menopause.[1]

Because the molecular structure of the key non-P-450 dependent enzymes required for sex steroid formation has not been elucidated and knowing that local formation of sex steroids is most likely to play a major role in both normal and tumoral hormone-sensitive tissues, an important proportion of our research program has recently been devoted to this exciting and therapeutically promising area (for reviews, see refs. 23, 29, and 30).

HUMAN 3β-HSD ISOENZYMES AND THEIR GENES

Despite its essential role in the biosynthesis of all classes of hormonal steroids, structure of the 3β-hydroxysteroid dehydrogenase/Δ^5-Δ^4-isomerase gene family, hereafter called 3β-HSD, was only recently elucidated.[23,31-34]

The membrane-bound enzyme 3β-HSD catalyzes an essential step in the transformation of all 5-pregnen-3β-ol and 5-androsten-3β-ol steroids into the corresponding Δ^4-3-keto-steroids, namely, progesterone as well as the precursors of all androgens, estrogens, glucocorticoids, and mineralocorticoids. In addition, 3β-HSD is responsible for the interconversion of 3β-hydroxy- and 3-keto-5α-androstane steroids. 3β-HSD is found not only in classic steroidogenic tissues (placenta, adrenal cortex, ovary, and testis), but also in several peripheral tissues, including skin, adipose tissue, breast, lung, endometrium, prostate, liver, kidney, epididymis, and brain,[23,30,35,36] thus catalyzing the first step in the intracrine transformation of DHEA into androstenedione (4-dione), the precursor of both androgens and estrogens.

Following purification of 3β-HSD from human placenta and development of antibodies against the enzyme in rabbits, we isolated and characterized a first 3β-HSD cDNA type[31] and its corresponding gene.[32] The second 3β-HSD cDNA type, which corresponds to the almost exclusive mRNA species expressed in the adrenals and gonads, was chronologically designated human type 2 3β-HSD.[33] The structure of the corresponding human type 2 3β-HSD gene has also been elucidated[34] (FIG. 1). The human 3β-HSD genes corresponding to human cDNAs type 1 and 2 contain 4 exons and 3 introns within a total length of 7.7–7.8 kbp. These genes were assigned by *in situ* hybridization to the p13.1 region of chromosome 1 and are closely linked to D1S514 located at 1–2 cM of the centromeric marker D1Z5.[37]

We recently demonstrated that mutations in the type 2 3β-HSD gene are responsible for classic 3β-HSD deficiency, a form of congenital adrenal hyperplasia that impairs steroidogenesis in both the adrenals and gonads (refs. 38–40 and refs. therein). However, the absence of mutations in the type 1 gene provided the long-awaited molecular explanation for the persistence of peripheral steroidogenesis in these patients.

In addition to the characterization of the structure of the types of 3β-HSD expressed in the macaque and bovine ovary, the nucleotide sequence of four types of rat and four types of mouse 3β-HSD cDNAs and their corresponding deduced amino acid sequences have recently become available (FIG. 2, refs. 23, 29, 41, 42, and refs. therein). The existence of multiple members of the 3β-HSD gene family offers the unique possibility of gene regulation of tissue- and/or cell-specific expression of this enzymatic activity.

Human Type I 3β-Hydroxysteroid dehydrogenase / Δ5-Δ4 isomerase

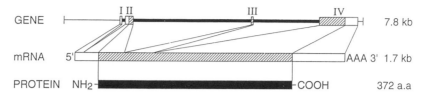

Human Type II 3β-Hydroxysteroid dehydrogenase / Δ5-Δ4 isomerase

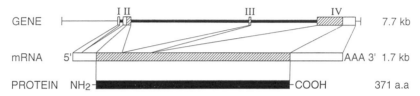

FIGURE 1. Structure of human type I and type II 3β-HSD genes, mRNA species, and the corresponding proteins. Exons are represented by boxes in which *hatched lines* demarcate the coding regions, whereas *open boxes* represent the noncoding regions. Introns are represented by *black bold lines.*

HUMAN 17β-HSD ENZYMES AND THEIR GENES

The enzymes of the 17β-HSD gene family are responsible for the interconversion of DHEA and 5-diol, 4-dione and testosterone, estrone, and E_2 as well as androstanedione and DHT, androsterone and androstane 3α,17β-diol, and epiandrosterone and androstane 3β-,17β-diol. This enzymatic activity is therefore required for the synthesis of all active androgens and all active estrogens as well as their inactivation. The molecular structure of a human type 1 17β-HSD cDNA and its corresponding gene, which encodes a predicted protein of 327 amino acids, was the first to be elucidated.[43-46] This enzyme is a member of the short-chain alcohol dehydrogenase superfamily. The type 1 17β-HSD gene consists of 6 exons and 5 introns within a genomic DNA fragment of 3.3 kbp. The type 1 17β-HSD gene was assigned by *in situ* hybridization to the 17q11-q21 region.[43] We have also taken advantage of our recent characterization of polymorphisms in the type 1 17β-HSD gene[47] to establish its precise localization by genetic linkage analysis as well as by physical mapping close to the BRCA 1 gene, which is responsible for the hereditary breast-ovarian cancer syndrome.[48,49]

The type 1 17β-HSD enzyme is a cytosolic protein that exists in a homodimeric form which catalyzes predominantly the interconversion of E_1 and E_2 using nicotinamide adenine dinucleotide (NAD[H]) or nicotinamide adenine dinucleotide phosphate (NADP[H]) as cofactor.[50,51] To pursue the structure function analysis of type 1 17β-HSD, the protein was overexpressed in baculovirus and has been crystallized by our group.[52,53] This work has led to the recent elucidation of its three-dimensional structure.[54]

The distribution of estrogenic 17β-HSD mRNA (type 1) and activity has been

```
                    10         20         30         40         50         60
HUMAN I       TGWSCLVTGA GGFLGQRIIR LLVKEKELKE IRVLDKAFGP ELREEFSKLQ NKTKLTVLEG
HUMAN II      .......... ..L...V.. ...E...... ..A.....R. .......... .R........
MACAQUE       .......... ......V... ...E...... ........R. .......... ..........
BOVINE        A.........G .......C ...E..D.Q. .....V.R. .V........ S.I...L...
MOUSE I       A.......... ....V.....K M..Q....Q. V.A...V.R. .TK....... T...V.....
MOUSE II      ---------- ---------- ---------- ---------- ---------- ----------
MOUSE III     ---------- ---------- ---------- ---------- ---------- ----------
MOUSE IV      P.......... .........Q ...Q..D.E. .....V.K. .T..Q.FN.G TSI.V.....
RAT I         P.......... .........V. M..Q.E..Q. ..A.FRT..R KQE..L.... T...V....K.
RAT II        P.......... .....V.... M..Q...Q. V.A...V.R. .TK....... T.A.V.M...
RAT III       P.......... .....V.... M..Q....Q. V.A...V.R. .TK....... T.A.V.M...
RAT IV        P.......... .......VQ M..Q....Q. V...YRT.S. KHK...L... T.A.V...R.
RAINBOW TROUT SLQ.DV.V.. C...E.LV. ..LE.DK.T. ..N..INVR. Q.IQCLEEIR GD.LVS.F..

                    70         80         90        100        110        120
HUMAN I       DILDEPFLKR ACQDVSVIIH TACIIDVFGV THRESIMHVN VKGTQLLLEA CVQASVPVFI
HUMAN II      .......... ......V... .......... .......... .......... ..........
MACAQUE       .......... ......V... .......... .......... .......... ..........
BOVINE        ....QC..Q .GT..V.. ..SV..RNA VP..T.... .......... ..........
MOUSE I       ...AQC.R.. ..GI..V.. ..AV...T.. IP.QT.LD.. L....N.... ......A...
MOUSE II      ---------- ---------- ---------- ---------- ....I....A...
MOUSE III     ...TQY.R.. ..GI..V.. ..A....T.. IP.QT.LD.. L....N.... ..I....A...
MOUSE IV      ...AQC.... ..GM.AV.. ..AA..PL.A AS.QT.LD.. L.......D. ..E.N..T..
RAT I         ...AQY.R.. ..GI..V.. ..AV...SH. LP.QT.LD.. L....NI... ..E.....A.
RAT II        ...AQY.R.. ..GI..V.. ..SVM.FSR. LP.QT.LD.. L....N.... GIH.....A.
RAT III       ..V.AQ..R. ..GM..... ..AAL.IA.F LP.QT.LD.. L....N.... ..E.....A.
RAT IV        ...TQC.R.. ..GI..V.. ..AL...T.. NP.QT.LD.. L....N.... ......A...
RAINBOW TROUT ..S.SEL.R. ..KGA.LVF. ..SL...T.K VLYSELHR.. .........T ..EN.VS..

                   130        140        150        160        170        180
HUMAN I       YTSSIEVAGP NSYKEIIQNG HEEEPLENTW PAPYPHSKKL AEKAVLAANG WNLKNGGTLY
HUMAN II      .......... .......... .......... ..T...Y... .......... ......D...
MACAQUE       ..TI...... .......... .........I .......... .........T ..........
BOVINE        H..T...... ......R...D. R...HH.SA. SS...Y.... ......G... .A........
MOUSE I       FC..VD.... ...K.VL... ...QNH.S.. SD...Y...M .......... SM........N
MOUSE II      FS..VD.... ......VL.. ...CH.S... SD...Y...M .......... SM........Q
MOUSE III     FS..VD.... ...D.VL... ...D.HR.S. SD...Y...M .......... SM........Q
MOUSE IV      .S..VL.... .....L.A ......HH.S. SN...Y...M .......... SI........H
RAT I         .C.TVD.... ...K.VL... ...HH.S... SDA..Y..RM .......... SI........H
RAT II        .C.TVD.... ...KT.L... R...HH.S.. SN...Y...M .......... SI........H
RAT III       .S..TG.... .....T.L.D R...HR.S.. SN...Y..RM .......... SI........FH
RAT IV        .C.TVD.... ....K.L... ....III.S. 3N...Y...M .......... SI........H
RAINBOW TROUT .......... .ANGDP.I.. D.NT.YTCSL KF..SKT..E .QVT.Q.Q. EV.Q...R.A

                   190        200        210        220        230        240
HUMAN I       TCALRPMYIY GEGSRFLSAS INEALNNNGI LSSVGKFSTV NPVYVGNVAW AHILALRALQ
HUMAN II      ......T... ...GP..... .......... .......... .......... ..........R
MACAQUE       .......... ...GP..... .......... .......... .......... ..........R
BOVINE        .......... ...P....Y MHG....... .TNHC...R. .......... ..........R
MOUSE I       .......... .R.P.IFNA .IR..K.K.. .CVT....IA ......E... ..A.G.R
MOUSE II      ......C... .R.PLI.NI .IM..KHK.. .R.F...N.A .......... ..A.G.R
MOUSE III     ......C... .R.Q...NT .IK..K.KF. .RGG....A .......... ..A.G.R
MOUSE IV      ......LSF. .ECQVT.TT VKT..K..S. IKKNAT..IA ......A... ..A.S..
RAT I         .......... .R.P...VM .LA..K.K.. .NVT....IA .......... ..A.G.R
RAT II        .......... .RGQ...RI .IM..K.K.V .NVT....I. .......... ..A.G.R
RAT III       ......LPF. .E.QII.TM V.R..K.NS. IKRHAT..IA ......A... ..A.G.R
RAT IV        .......... .R.P...VM .LA..K.K.. .NVT....IA .......... ..A.G.R
RAINBOW TROUT ......C..LGH MGDGIR.GDM .YRTSREAQ. .......... ..A.L .LQ.A..R

                   250        260        270        280        290        300
HUMAN I       DPKKAPSIRG QFYYISDDTP HQSYDNLNYT LSKEFGLRLD SRWSFPLSLM YWIGFLLEIV
HUMAN II      ......V... .......... .......I.. .......... ...L.T.... .........V.
MACAQUE       ...V.VQ. .......... .......I.. ....C.. ...L..A... .........V.
BOVINE        ...V.N.Q. .......... .......D... ...W.FC.. .M.L.I..Q .LA.......
MOUSE I       ....ST..Q. E......... ...D..... ....W....PN AS..L..P.L .LA....T.
MOUSE II      ...S.N.Q. E......... ...F.DIS.. ....W.FCP. .S..L.VP.L .LA....T.
MOUSE III     N...S.N.Q. E......... ...D..... ....W.FC.N ...YL.VPIL .LA....T.
MOUSE IV      ...S...Q. .......T... ...D.KC... ....W..... T3..L..P.L .LA....T.
RAT I         ....EQNVQ. .......... ...D..C... ....W..... .S..L..P.L .LA....T.
RAT II        ....SQN.Q. .......... ...D..C... ....W..... .S..L..P.L .LA....T.
RAT III       .E.SQ..Q. .......... ...D..C... ....W..... .S..L..P.L .LA....T.
RAT IV        ....SQNVQ. .......... ...D..... ....W.H.. .S..L.P.L .LA.....
RAINBOW TROUT ..QRRAA.G. N....... PV..SDF.HA VLSPL.FSIQ EKPIL.IPVL .LLC..M.ML

                   310        320        330        340        350        360
HUMAN I       SFLLRPIYTY RPPFNRHIVT LSNSVFTFSY KKAQRDLAYK PLYSWEEAKQ KTVEWVGSLV
HUMAN II      ....S...S. .......... .......... .......... .......... ..........
MACAQUE       ...S.V.S. Q.....T... .......... .......... .......... ..........
BOVINE        ....S...K. N.C...L.. .......... ......G.E ...T..... ...K..I....
MOUSE I       ....V.R... .....LI... .....T.... .......G.E .VN...... ..S..I.TI.
MOUSE II      ....S...R. I.....L.. ...G.T.... .......G.E .V....... ..S..I.T..
MOUSE III     ....S...R. I.....L.. ..TA.T.... .......G.E .V....... ..S..I.T..
MOUSE IV      ....V.N... ......LLI. VL....... .......G.E .V....... ../.I.T..
RAT I         ......F.N. ....C.L... .......K.. .......G.V .......... ..S..I.T..
RAT II        ......F.N. ....C.L... .......K.. .......G.E .V....... ..S..I.T..
RAT III       ......F.N. .....FM.. IL....I.. .......G.E .V....... ..S..I.T..
RAT IV        ..F.H.V.N. ..S...L.. .......K.. .......G.E .V....... ..S..I.T..
RAINBOW TROUT QI..C.FKRF T..I..QLL. ML.TP.S... RR....MG.A .R......RK R.MD...A.QL

                   370
HUMAN I       DRHKETLKSK TQ
HUMAN II      .......... ..
MACAQUE       .......... ..
BOVINE        KQ......T. IH
MOUSE I       EQ.R.I.DT. C.
MOUSE II      EQ.R...DT. S.
MOUSE III     EQ.R...DT. S.
MOUSE IV      MQ.R.IGNK. S.
RAT I         EQ.R...DT. S.
RAT II        EQ.R...DT. S.
RAT III       EQ.R...DT. S.
RAT IV        EQ.R...DT. S.
RAINBOW TROUT PKER.RI.V. --
```

FIGURE 2. Comparison of the deduced amino acid sequences of human types I and II, macaque ovary, bovine ovary, rainbow trout ovary, rat types I, II, III, and IV as well as mouse types I, II, III and IV members of the 3β-HSD enzyme family. Amino acid sequences are designated by the single-letter code. Residues common to human type I 3β-HSD are designated by a dot (.). The noncharacterized NH2-terminal sequence in mouse type II 3β-HSD is indicated by a dotted line (---). Note that the members of the mammalian 3β-HSD family have been chronologically designated as a function of their elucidation in each species.

studied in 15 human tissues (ref. 55 and refs. therein). Estrogenic 17β-HSD activity was detected in all tissues examined. The highest rates of estrogenic 17β-HSD activity were found in the placenta, liver, ovary, endometrium, testis, and adipose tissue. The differences observed between the reductive and the oxidative pathways are less important in human than in rat tissues.[55]

Androgenic 17β-HSD activity has also been demonstrated in the same 15 human tissues. The highest level of androgenic 17β-HSD activity was found in the placenta and liver followed by the testis, endometrium, prostate, adipose tissue, adrenal, and skin. In human tissues, contrary to the rat, the oxidative pathway of 4-dione formation is slightly favored only in the liver and placenta, while all other tissues favor testosterone formation (adipose tissue, adrenal, myometrium, ovary, prostate, skin, spleen, and ZR-75-1) or show no significant difference.[55] The presence of type 1 17β-HSD mRNA has been shown in the RNA from placenta, breast, ovary, endometrium, ZR-75-1 cells, LNCaP prostate cancer cells, adipose tissue, skin, and prostate.[44,55]

Recently, the structure of another type of 17β-HSD cDNA was reported[56] which encodes a predicted protein of 387 amino acids with a molecular weight of 42,782 and is most likely associated with the membranes of the endoplasmic reticulum. This enzyme catalyzes the interconversion of E_2 and estrone (E_1), testosterone (T) and 4-dione, DHT and A-dione, as well as 20α-dihydroprogesterone and progesterone. This enzyme, chronologically designated type 2 17β-HSD, is also a member of the short-chain alcohol dehydrogenase superfamily and shares only about 20% sequence identity with the cytoplasmic enzyme encoded by the type 1 17β-HSD gene.[43] This enzyme use NAD(H) as a cofactor.[56]

A novel type 2 17β-HSD cDNA, designated type 2B 17β-HSD, was isolated by screening a human placental cDNA library with the type 2 17β-HSD cDNA under stringent conditions.[25] In addition, both the type 2B 17β-HSD cDNAs and the longest type 2A cDNAs that we have isolated contain approximately 165 nucleotides upstream of the ATG initiation codon, 82 more nucleotides than were described in the 5′ untranslated region of the published type 2A cDNA.[56] The deduced amino acid sequence of the type 2B 17β-HSD cDNA open reading frame predicts a protein of 291 residues as opposed to the 387 amino acids found in the 2A protein. Both proteins are identical from the first methionine to glycine 222. However, the 109-base pair insertion present in the type 2B 17β-HSD cDNA causes a shift in the translational reading frame such that only two of the remaining 69 residues found in the unique COOH-terminal portion of the 2B protein, namely, glycine 263 and leucine 279, are also present in the IIA protein. The function of type 2B 17β-HSD remains to be determined.

The human type 2 17β-HSD gene is comprised of 7 exons and spans greater than 40 kbp of genomic DNA (FIG. 3.) Cloning of the human type 2 17β-HSD gene confirmed that the type 2A and 2B 17β-HSD transcripts originate from a single gene. We have also localized the type 2 17β-HSD gene to the q24.1-24.2 region of chromosome 16 by genetic linkage analysis.[57]

A third type of human 17β-HSD cDNA encoding a predicted protein of 310 amino acids with a molecular weight of 34,513 was also recently characterized.[58] Type 3 17β-HSD, a microsomal isozyme, uses NADP(H) as a cofactor and is expressed predominantly in the testes with an equilibrium of the reaction favoring testosterone production from 4-dione. This enzyme, which shares 23% sequence identity with the two other 17β-HSD enzymes, is the site of the mutations responsible for male pseudohermaphroditism from 17β-HSD deficiency.[58] The type 3 17β-HSD mRNA species was detected only in the testes in the 16 tissues tested by Northern blot analysis.[58]

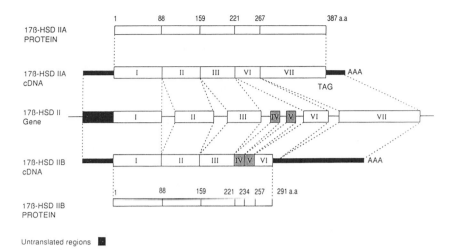

FIGURE 3. Structure of the human type II 17β-HSD gene, alternatively-spliced mRNA species, and the corresponding predicted proteins. *Open boxes* demarcate the coding region of exons, whereas *black boxes* represent the noncoding regions. Introns are represented by *solid lines*. a.a., amino acids.[25]

The human type 4 17β-HSD is a 736-amino acid protein of M_r 80 kD which shares 84% identity with the corresponding porcine enzyme and transforms E_2 into E_1 and 5-diol into DHEA.[59,60] The human type 4 17β-HSD mRNA is expressed in virtually all human tissues examined by Northern blot, including the liver, heart, prostate, testis, lung, skeletal muscle, kidney, pancreas, thymus, ovary, intestine, placenta, and several human breast cancer cell lines and is thus likely to play an important role in the inactivation of estrogens in peripheral tissues.

As multiple 17β-HSD genes are expressed selectively in various tissues, other types of intracrine dysfunction of 17β-HSD activity in peripheral tissues could also be expected.[1] 17β-HSD activity is indeed an obligatory step in the biosynthesis of all androgens and estrogens, namely, E_2, 5-diol, T, and DHT. These hormones bind much more strongly to their respective receptors in the 17β-hydroxy configuration than the corresponding 17-keto derivatives. It is then of particular interest to describe the characteristics of the oxidation/reduction activities of types 1, 2, and 3 17β-HSD as well as their inhibition by some selected inhibitors.

Comparative Activity of Transfected Human Types 1, 2, and 3 17β-HSD Activities in Intact Cells and in Cell Subfractions

As illustrated in FIGURE 4, type 1 17β-HSD measured in intact cells selectively catalyzed the reductive conversion of E_1 to E_2, while the reverse reaction was negligible. E_1 was thus the most favorable substrate, while DHEA was converted at a much smaller extent, and the transformation of 4-dione into T was negligible. By contrast, type 2 17β-HSD was selective for the oxidative reaction. It converts efficiently and almost equally T and E_2 into 4-dione and E_1, respectively. Type 3 17β-HSD specifically catalyzed the reductive transformation of 4-dione into T with a low level of transformation of E_1 into E_2.

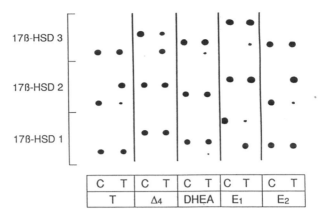

C	T	C	T	C	T	C	T	C	T
T		Δ_4		DHEA		E_1		E_2	

FIGURE 4. Enzymatic activities of expressed cDNAs encoding types 1, 2, and 3 17β-HSDs in intact transfected 293 cells. Autoradiograph of TLC of the transformation of 0.1 μM of [^{14}C]-labeled substrate by control mock-transfected cells (C) and cells transfected (T) with the pCMV-17β-HSDs 1, 2, and 3, respectively.[24]

FIGURE 5 shows that in contrast to the highly predominant unidirectional reaction observed in intact cells, the transfected 17β-HSD activities measured in cytosolic (type 1) or microsomal (types 2 and 3) subfractions catalyze both the oxidative and reductive reactions, the direction of the reaction depending on the added cofactor. However, the preferred reaction corresponds to that observed in intact cells.

The present data clearly show that in intact cells, which more closely reflect physiologic conditions, the activity catalyzed by each type of 17β-HSD is almost exclusively unidirectional: types 1 and 3 activities catalyze the reductive pathway,

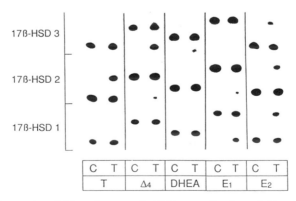

C	T	C	T	C	T	C	T	C	T
T		Δ_4		DHEA		E_1		E_2	

FIGURE 5. Enzymatic activities of expressed cDNAs encoding types 1, 2, and 3 17β-HSD in subfraction of transfected 293 cells. Autoradiograph of TLC of the transformation of 0.1 μM of [^{14}C]-labeled substrate by control mock-transfected cells (C) and cells transfected (T) with the pCMV-17β-HSDs 1, 2, and 3, respectively. In the reactions using types 1 and 3 17β-HSD, 0.4 mM of NADP$^+$ was added with T and E_2, while NADPH was added with 4-dione, DHEA, and E_1. In the reaction catalyzed by type 2 17β-HSD, 0.4 mM of NAD$^+$ was added with T and E_2 and NADH were used with 4-dione, DHEA, and E_1[24].

whereas type 2 17β-HSD activities catalyze the oxidative reaction. However, in cell homogenates, these 17β-HSDs can drive the interconversion of the product and substrate, but the direction corresponding to the physiologic direction is always favored.

In estrogen-target tissues, such as the placenta, ovary, and breast, the presence of type 1 17β-HSD ensures a high level of estradiol formation. Similarly, in the testis, type 3 17β-HSD drives the conversion of 4-dione to T needed for the development and growth of the internal male reproductive structures (epididymis, seminal vesicles, and vas deferens) as well as all secondary sex organs. In fact, impairment of type 3 17β-HSD leads to the well-characterized male pseudohermaphroditism.[58]

More recently, we cloned a human placental 20α-hydroxysteroid dehydrogenase that possesses reductive 17β-HSD activity designated type 5 17β-HSD (Luu-The et al., unpublished data). Thus, in peripheral tissues, it is likely that the expression of types 1, 2, or 5 17β-HSD activities plays an important role in regulating the formation (types 1 and 5) or inactivation (types 2 and 4) of active estrogens (E_2 and 5-diol) and/or androgens (T and DHT). Indeed, type 2 17β-HSD is highly expressed in the

TABLE 1. Relationship between Predominant Cofactor Specificity and Oxidative or Reductive Activity Catalyzed by 17β-HSDs and 11β-HSDs in Intact Cells

	Reaction			
	Reduction		Oxidation	
	NADPH	NADH	NADP$^+$	NAD$^+$
17β-HSD				
Type 1	+			
Type 2				+
Type 3	+			
Type 4				+
Type 5	+			
11β-HSD				
Type 1	+			
Type 2				+

NOTE: (+) indicates enzymatic activity.

liver, placenta, and endometrium. The contribution of types 1 and 3 17β-HSD activities in peripheral tissues could also be important, because using RT-PCR, we were able to detect type 3 17β-HSD in the prostate (Luu-the et al., unpublished data), while using RNase protection analysis, type 1 17β-HSD was detected in the prostate, adipose tissues, skin, prostate cancer cells (LNCaP), and endometrium.[55]

It is interesting to observe the correlation between the oxidation and reduction reactions with the presence of the NAD$^+$ or NADPH cofactor. Indeed, types 1 and 3 17β-HSDs, which preferentially catalyze the reductive reaction, use NADPH as cofactor, whereas types 2 and 4 17β-HSD, which preferentially catalyze the oxidative reaction, use NAD$^+$ as a cofactor. Similar results were observed with 11β-hydroxysteroid dehydrogenase enzymes (11β-HSD).[61,62] Type 1 11β-HSD, which catalyzes the reduction of cortisone to cortisol, uses NADPH as cofactor, while the type 2 enzyme, which catalyzes the oxidation of cortisol to cortisone, uses NAD$^+$. It is thus tempting to conclude that the enzymes that use NADPH as a cofactor preferentially catalyze the reductive reaction and that the enzymes that use the nicotinamide adenine dinucleotide cofactor (NAD$^+$) preferentially catalyze the oxidative reaction (TABLE 1). Such a conclusion has major physiologic implications, because it is well known that the intracellular concentration of NADPH versus $NADP^+$ is highly in favor of NADPH; in contrast, the intracellular concentration of NAD^+ versus NADH is highly in favor of NAD^+; the most abundant intracellular concentrations of nicotinamide adenine dinucleotide and nicotinamide adenine dinucleotide phosphate cofactors are thus NADPH and NAD^+.

HUMAN 5α-REDUCTASE

The enzyme 5α-reductase catalyzes the 5α-reduction of 4-dione, T, and other 4-ene-3-keto-steroids to the corresponding 5α-dihydro-3-keto-steroids. The best known role of this enzyme is the transformation of T into DHT, the most potent androgen, which is responsible for the differentiation of the male external genitalia and prostate as well as virilization at puberty. The major impact of 5α-reductase in men, however, is its role in prostate cancer and benign prostatic hyperplasia. Two types of human steroid 5α-reductases, chronologically identified as type 1 and type 2, were isolated from a human prostatic cDNA library.[63,64] The structure of the human type 1 5α-reductase gene has been elucidated.[65] This gene is not responsible for 5α-reductase deficiency, and it is relatively insensitive to the inhibitor finasteride.[64] Considering the crucial role of type 2 5α-reductase, we have elucidated the structure of its corresponding gene.[22] The type 2 5α-reductase gene contains 5 exons and 4 introns and shows splicing sites identical to those of the type 1 gene. Its coding region shares 57% homology with that of type 1 5α-reductase gene. Type I 5α-reductase is the predominant form expressed in human skin.[66] Type II 5α-reductase is the isozyme responsible for male pseudohermaphroditism from 5α-reductase deficiency.[64,67]

CONCLUSION

The adrenals of humans and some other primates secrete large amounts of adrenal steroids, especially DHEAS, which are metabolized into active androgens and estrogens in peripheral mammalian tissues.[1–3,68–70] It is estimated that 30–50% of total androgens in men are synthesized in peripheral intracrine tissues from inactive adrenal precursors, whereas in women, peripheral estrogen formation is even more important.[1,69]

As just mentioned, the formation of active sex steroids from the inactive adrenal precursors DHEA, DHEAS and/or 4-dione locally in the same cells where synthesis takes place without release in the extracellular space was recently described as intracrine activity.[1] Intracrinology represents an economical system which requires minimal amounts of hormone to exert maximal function. In classic endocrine systems, large amounts of hormones are needed with only a small fraction used for regulation while the rest is degraded. Because steroid receptors have high affinity, it is likely that the active androgens and estrogens synthesized intracellularly through intracrine activity bind to their specific receptors with minimal loss of concentration or time.

REFERENCES

1. LABRIE, F. 1991. Intracrinology. Mol. Cell. Endocrinol. **78:** C113–C118.
2. LABRIE, F., A. DUPONT & A. BÉLANGER. 1985. Complete androgen blockade for the treatment of prostate cancer. *In* Important Advances in Oncology. V. T. de Vita, S. Hellman & S. A. Rosenberg, Eds.:193–217. J. B. Lippincott. Philadelphia.

3. LABRIE, C., A. BÉLANGER & F. LABRIE. 1988. Androgenic activity of dehydroepiandrosterone and androstenedione in the rat ventral prostate. Endocrinology **123:** 1412–1417.
4. MIGEON, C. J., A. R. KELLER, B. LAWRENCE & T. H. SHEPART, II. 1957. Dehydroepiandrosterone and androsterone levels in human placenta. Effect of age and sex: day-to-day and diurnal variations. J. Clin. Endocrinol. Metab. **17:** 1051–1062.
5. ORENTREICH, N., J. L. BRIND, R. L. RIZER & J. H. VOGELMAN. 1984. Age changes and sex differences in serum dehydroepiandrosterone sulfate concentrations throughout adulthood. J. Clin. Endocrinol. Metab. **59:** 551–555.
6. VERMEULEN, A., J. P. DESLYPENE, W. SCHELTHOUT, L. VERDONCK & R. RUBENS. 1982. Adrenocortical function in old age: Response to acute adrenocorticotropin stimulation. J. Clin. Endocrinol. Metab. **54:** 187–191.
7. BÉLANGER, A., B. CANDAS, A. DUPONT, L. CUSAN, P. DIAMOND, J. L. GOMEZ & F. LABRIE. 1994. Changes in serum concentrations of conjugated and unconjugated steroids in 40- to 80-year-old men. J. Clin. Endocrinol. Metab. **79:** 1086–1090.
8. SCHRIOCK, E. D., C. K. BUFFINGTON, G. D. HUBERT, D. R. KURTZ, A. E. KITABCHI, J. E. BUSTER & J. R. GIVENS. 1988. Divergent correlations of circulating dehydroepiandrosterone sulfate and testosterone with insulin levels and insulin receptor binding. J. Clin. Endocrinol. Metab. **66:** 1329–1331.
9. COLEMAN, D. L., E. H. LEITER & R. W. SCHWIZER. 1982. Therapeutic effects of dehydroepiandrosterone (DHEA) in diabetic mice. Diabetes **31:** 380–383.
10. BARRETT-CONNER, E., K. T. KHAW & S. S. C. YEN. 1986. A prospective study of dehydroepiandrosterone sulfate, mortality and cardiovascular disease. N. Engl. J. Med. **315:** 1519–1524.
11. NESTLER, J. E., C. O. BARLASCINI, J. N. CLORE & W. G. BLACKARD. 1988. Dehydroepiandrosterone reduces serum low density lipoprotein levels and body fat but does not alter insulin sensitivity in normal men. J. Clin. Endocrinol. Metab. **66:** 57–61.
12. MACEWEN, E. G. & I. D. KURZMAN. 1991. Obesity in the dog: Role of the adrenal steroid dehydroepiandrosterone (DHEA). J. Nutr. **121:** S51–S55.
13. ZUMOFF, B., J. LEVIN, R. S. ROSENFELD, M. MARKHAM, G. W. STRAIN & D. K. FUKUSHIMA. 1981. Abnormal 24-hr mean plasma concentrations of dehydroepiandrosterone and dehydroisoandrosterone sulfate in women with primary operable breast cancer. Cancer Res. **41:** 3360–3363.
14. STAHL, F., D. SCHNORR, C. PILZ & G. DORNER. 1992. Dehydroepiandrosterone (DHEA) levels in patients with prostatic cancer, heart diseases and under surgery stress. Exp. Clin. Endocrinol. **99:** 68–70.
15. SCHWARTZ, A. G., L. PASHKO & J. M. WHITCOMB. 1986. Inhibition of tumor development by dehydroepiandrosterone and related steroids. Toxicol. Pathol. **14:** 357–362.
16. GORDON, G. B., L. M. SHANTZ & P. TALALAY. 1987. Modulation of growth, differentiation and carcinogenesis by dehydroepiandrosterone. Adv. Enzyme Regul. **26:** 355–382.
17. LI, S., X. YAN, A. BÉLANGER & F. LABRIE. 1993. Prevention by dehydroepiandrosterone of the development of mammary carcinoma induced by 7,12-dimethylbenz(a)anthracene (DMBA) in the rat. Breast Cancer Res. Treat. **29:** 203–217.
18. SUZUKI, T., N. SUZUKI, R. A. DAYNES & E. G. ENGLEMAN. 1991. Dehydroepiandrosterone enhances IL2 production and cytotoxic effector function of human T cells. Clin. Immunol. Immunopathol. **61:** 202–211.
19. RASMUSSON, K. R., M. J. ARROWOOD & M. C. HEALEY. 1992. Effectiveness of dehydroepiandrosterone in reduction of cryptosporidial activity in immunosuppressed rats. Antimicrob. Agents Chemother. **36:** 220–222.
20. HENDERSON, E., J. Y. YANG & A. SCHWARTZ. 1992. Dehydroepiandrosterone (DHEA) and synthetic DHEA analogs are modest inhibitors of HIV-1 IIIB replication. Aids Res. Hum. Retroviruses **8:** 625–631.
21. CASSON, R. P., R. N. ANDERSEN, H. G. HERROD, F. B. STENTZ, A. B. STRAUGHN, G. E. ABRAHAM & J. E. BUSTER. 1993. Oral dehydroepiandrosterone in physiologic doses modulates immune function in postmenopausal women. Am. J. Obstet. Gynecol. **169:** 1536–1539.
22. LABRIE, F., Y. SUGIMOTO, V. LUU-THE, J. SIMARD, Y. LACHANCE, D. BACHVAROV, G.

LEBLANC, F. DUROCHER & N. PAQUET. 1992. Structure of human type II 5α-reductase. Endocrinology 131: 1571–1573.

23. LABRIE, F., J. SIMARD, V. LUU-THE, A. BÉLANGER & G. PELLETIER. 1992. Structure, function and tissue-specific gene expression of 3β-hydroxysteroid dehydrogenase/5-ene-4-ene isomerase in classical and peripheral intracrine steroidogenic tissues. J. Steroid Biochem. Mol. Biol. 43: 805–826.

24. LUU-THE, V., Y. ZHANG, D. POIRIER & F. LABRIE. 1995. Characteristics of human types 1, 2 and 3 17β-hydroxysteroid dehydrogenase activities: Oxidation-reduction and inhibition. J. Steroid Biochem. Molec. Biol. In press.

25. LABRIE, Y., F. DUROCHER, Y. LACHANCE, C. TURGEON, J. SIMARD, C. LABRIE & F. LABRIE. 1995. The human type II 17β-hydroxysteroid dehydrogenase gene encodes two alternatively-spliced messenger RNA species. DNA Cell. Biol. In press.

26. BÉLANGER, A., M. BROCHU & J. CLICHE. 1986. Levels of plasma steroid glucuronides in intact and castrated men with prostatic cancer. J. Clin. Endocrinol. Metab. 62: 812–815.

27. LABRIE, F., A. BÉLANGER, A. DUPONT, V. LUU-THE, J. SIMARD & C. LABRIE. 1993. Science behind total androgen blockade: From gene to combination therapy. Clin. Invest. Med. 16: 487–504.

28. MOGHISSI, E., F. ABLAN & R. HORTON. 1984. Origin of plasma androstanediol glucuronide in men. J. Clin. Endocrinol. Metab. 59: 417–421.

29. LABRIE, F., J. SIMARD, V. LUU-THE, G. PELLETIER, K. BELGHMI & A. BÉLANGER. 1994. Structure, regulation and role of 3β-hydroxysteroid dehydrogenase, 17β-hydroxysteroid dehydrogenase and aromatase enzymes in formation of sex steroids in classical and peripheral intracrine tissues. In Hormone, Enzymes and Receptors. M. C. Sheppard & P. M. Stewart, Eds.: 451–474. Baillière's Clinical Endocrinology and Metabolism. Baillière Tindall Ltd. London.

30. PELLETIER, G., E. DUPONT, J. SIMARD, V. LUU-THE, A. BÉLANGER & F. LABRIE. 1992. Ontogeny and subcellular localization of 3β-hydroxysteroid dehydrogenase (3β-HSD) in the human and rat adrenal, ovary and testis. J. Steroid Biochem. Mol. Biol. 43: 451–467.

31. LUU-THE, V., Y. LACHANCE, C. LABRIE, G. LEBLANC, J. L. THOMAS, R. C. STRICKLER & F. LABRIE. 1989. Full length cDNA structure and deduced amino acid sequence of human 3β-hydroxy-5-ene steroid dehydrogenase. Mol. Endocrinol. 3: 1310–1312.

32. LACHANCE, Y., V. LUU-THE, C. LABRIE, J. SIMARD, M. DUMONT, Y. D. LAUNOIT, S. GUÉRIN, G. LEBLANC & F. LABRIE. 1990. Characterization of human 3β-hydroxysteroid dehydrogenase/Δ⁵−Δ⁴ isomerase gene and its expression in mammalian cells. J. Biol. Chem. 265: 20469–20475.

33. RHÉAUME, E., Y. LACHANCE, H. F. ZHAO, N. BRETON, Y. DE LAUNOIT, C. TRUDEL, V. LUU-THE, J. SIMARD & F. LABRIE. 1991. Structure and expression of a new cDNA encoding the almost exclusive 3β-hydroxysteroid dehydrogenase/Δ⁵−Δ⁴ isomerase in human adrenals and gonads. Mol. Endocrinol. 5: 1147–1157.

34. LACHANCE, Y., V. LUU-THE, H. VERREAULT, M. DUMONT, E. RHÉAUME, G. LEBLANC & F. LABRIE. 1991. Structure of the human type II 3β-hydroxysteroid dehydrogenase/Δ⁵−Δ⁴ isomerase (3β-HSD) gene: Adrenal and gonadal specificity. DNA Cell Biol. 10: 701-711.

35. MARTEL, C., M. H. MELNER, D. GAGNÉ, J. SIMARD & F. LABRIE. 1994. Widespread tissue distribution of steroid sulfatase, 3β-hydroxysteroid dehydrogenase/Δ⁵−Δ⁴ isomerase (3β-HSD), 17β-HSD 5α-reductase and aromatase activities in the rhesus monkey. Mol. Cell. Endocrinol. 104: 103–111.

36. MILEWICH, L., C. E. SHAW, J. I. MASON, B. R. CARR, C. H. BLOMQUIST & J. L. THOMAS. 1993. 3β-hydroxysteroid dehydrogenase activity in tissues of human fetus determined with 5α-androstane-3β,17β-diol and dehydroepiandrosterone as substrates. J. Steroid Biochem. Mol. Biol. 45: 525–537.

37. MORISSETTE, J., E. RHÉAUME, J. F. LEBLANC, V. LUU-THE, F. LABRIE & J. SIMARD. 1995. Genetic linkage mapping of the HSD3B1 and HSD3B2 genes encoding human types I and II 3β-hydroxysteroid dehydrogenase/Δ⁵−Δ⁴ isomerase close to D1S514 and the centromeric D1Z5 locus. Cytogenet. Cell Genet. 69: 59–62.

38. RHÉAUME, E., J. SIMARD, Y. MOREL, F. MEBARKI, M. ZACHMANN, M. FOREST, M. I. NEW

& F. LABRIE. 1992. Congenital adrenal hyperplasia due to point mutations in the type II 3β-hydroxysteroid dehydrogenase deficiency. Nature Genet. **1:** 239–245.

39. SIMARD, J., E. RHÉAUME, R. SANCHEZ, N. LAFLAMME, Y. DE LAUNOIT, A. P. VAN SETERS, R. D. GORDON, M. BETTENDORF, U. HEINRICH, T. MOSHANG, M. I. NEW & F. LABRIE. 1993. Molecular basis of congenital adrenal hyperplasia due to 3β-hydroxysteroid dehydrogenase deficiency. Mol. Endocrinol. **7:** 716–728.

40. SIMARD, J., E. RHÉAUME, F. MÉBARKI, R. SANCHEZ, M. I. NEW, Y. MOREL & F. LABRIE. 1995. Molecular basis of human 3β-hydroxysteroid dehydrogenase deficiency. J. Steroid Biochem. Mol. Biol. **53:** 127–138.

41. SIMARD, J., Y. DE LAUNOIT & F. LABRIE. 1991. Characterization of the structure-activity of rat type I and type II 3β-hydroxysteroid dehydrogenase/$\Delta^5-\Delta^4$ isomerase by site-directed mutagenesis and expression in HeLa cells. J. Biol. Chem. **266:** 14824–14845.

42. SIMARD, J., J. COUËT, F. DUROCHER, Y. LABRIE, R. SANCHEZ, N. BRETON, C. TURGEON & F. LABRIE. 1993. Structure and tissue-specific expression of a novel member of the rat 3β-hydroxysteroid dehydrogenase/$\Delta^5-\Delta^4$ isomerase (3β-HSD) family. J. Biol. Chem. **268:** 19569–19668.

43. LUU-THE V., C. LABRIE, H. F. ZHAO, J. COUËT, Y. LACHANCE, J. SIMARD, G. LEBLANC, J. CÔTÉ, D. BÉRUBÉ, R. GAGNÉ & F. LABRIE. 1989. Characterization of cDNAs for human estradiol 17β-dehydrogenase and assignment of the gene to chromosome 17: Evidence of two mRNA species with distinct 5′ termini in human placenta. Mol. Endocrinol. **3:** 1301–1309.

44. LUU-THE, V., C. LABRIE, J. SIMARD, Y. LACHANCE, H. F. ZHAO, J. COUËT, G. LEBLANC & F. LABRIE. 1990. Structure of two in tandem human 17β-hydroxysteroid dehydrogenase genes. Mol. Endocrinol. **4:** 268–275.

45. PELTOKETO, H., V. ISOMAA, O. MÄENTAUSTA & R. VIHKO. 1988. Complete amino acid sequence of human placental 17β-hydroxysteroid dehydrogenase deduced from cDNA. FEBS Lett. **239:** 73–77.

46. PELTOKETO, H., V. ISOMAA & R. VIHKO. 1992. Genomic organization and DNA sequences of human 17β-hydroxysteroid dehydrogenase genes and flanking regions: localization of multiple Alu sequences and putative cis-acting elements. Eur. J. Biochem. **209:** 459–466.

47. NORMAND, T., S. NAROD, F. LABRIE & J. SIMARD. 1993. Detection of polymorphisms in the estradiol 17β-hydroxysteroid dehydrogenase II gene at the EDH17B2 locus on 17q11-q21. Hum. Mol. Genet. **2:** 479–483.

48. SIMARD, J., J. FEUNTEUN, G. LENOIR, P. TONIN, T. NORMAND, V. LUU-THE, A. VIVIER, D. LASKO, K. MORGAN, G. A. ROULEAU, H. LINCH, F. LABRIE & S. NAROD. 1993. Genetic mapping of the breast-ovarian cancer syndrome to a small interval on chromosome 17q12-21: Exclusion of candidate genes EDH17B2 and RARA. Hum. Mol. Genet. **2:** 1193–1199.

49. ROMMENS, J. M., F. DUROCHER, J. MCARTHUR, P. TONIN, J. F. LEBLANC, T. ALLEN, C. SAMSON, L. FERRI, S. NAROD, K. MORGAN & J. SIMARD. 1995. Generation of a transcription map at the HSD17B locus centromeric to BRCA1 at 17q21. Genomics **28:** 530–542.

50. DUMONT, M., V. LUU-THE, Y. DE LAUNOIT & F. LABRIE. 1992. Expression of human 17β-hydroxysteroid dehydrogenase in mammalian cells. J. Steroid Biochem. Mol. Biol. **41:** 605–608.

51. LIN, S. X., F. YANG, J. Z. JIN, R. BRETON, D. W. ZHU, V. LUU-THE & F. LABRIE. 1992. Subunit identity of the dimeric 17β-hydroxysteroid dehydrogenase from human placenta. J. Biol. Chem. **267:** 16182–16187.

52. ZHU, D. W., X. LEE, R. BRETON, D. GHOSH, W. PANGBORN, W. DUAX & S. X. LIN. 1993. Crystallization and preliminary X-ray diffraction analysis of the complex of human placental 17β-hydroxysteroid dehydrogenase with NADP⁺. J. Mol. Biol. **234:** 242–244.

53. BRETON, R., F. YANG, J. Z. JIN, B. LI, F. LABRIE & S. X. LIN. 1994. Human 17β-hydroxysteroid hydrogenase: Overproduction using a baculovirus expression system and characterization. J. Steroid Biochem. Molec. Biol. **50:** 275–282.

54. GHOSH, D., V. PLETNEV, D. W. ZHU, Z. WAWRZAK, W. DUAX, W. PANGBORN, F. LABRIE &

S. X. LIN. 1995. Structure of human estrogenic 17β-hydroxysteroid dehydrogenase at 2.20Å resolution. Structure **3**: 503–513.

55. MARTEL, C., E. RHÉAUME, M. TAKAHASHI, C. TRUDEL, J. COUET, V. LUU-THE, J. SIMARD & F. LABRIE. 1992. Distribution of 17β-hydroxysteroid dehydrogenase gene expression and activity and human tissues. J. Steroid Biochem. Molec. Biol. **41**: 597–603.

56. WU, L., M. EINSTEIN, W. M. GEISSLER, K. H. CHAN, K. O. ELLISTON & S. ANDERSSON. 1993. Expression cloning and characterization of human 17β-hydroxysteroid dehydrogenase type 2, a microsomal enzyme possessing 20α-hydroxysteroid dehydrogenase activity. J. Biol. Chem. **268**: 12964–12969.

57. DUROCHER, F., J. MORISSETTE, Y. LABRIE, F. LABRIE & J. SIMARD. 1994. Mapping of the HSD17B2 gene encoding type II 17β-hydroxysteroid dehydrogenase close to D16S422 on chromosome 16q 24.1-q24.2. Genomics **25**: 724–726.

58. GEISSLER, W. M., D. L. DAVIS, L. WU, K. D. BRADSHAW, S. PATEL, B. B. MENDOÇA, K. O. ELLISTON, J. D. WILSON, D. W. RUSSEL & S. ANDERSSON. 1994. Male pseudohermaphroditism caused by mutations of testicular 17β-hydroxysteroid dehydrogenase 3. Nature Genet. **7**: 34–39.

59. LEENDERS, F., J. ADAMSKI, B. HUSEN, H. H. THOLE & P. W. JUNGBLUT. 1994. Molecular cloning and amino acid sequence of the porcine 17 beta-estradiol dehydrogenase. Eur. J. Biochem. **222**: 221–227.

60. ADAMSKI, J., T. NORMAND, F. IFFNDERS, D. MONTÉ, A. BEGUE, D. STEHELIN, P. W. JUNGSLUT & Y. DE LAUNOIT. 1995. Molecular cloning of a novel widely expressed human 80 kDa 17β-hydroxysteroid dehydrogenase IV. Biochem. J. **311**: in press.

61. AGARWAL, A. K., T. MUNE, C. MONDER & P. C. WHITE. 1994. NAD$^+$-dependent isoform of 11β-hydroxysteroid dehydrogenase: Cloning and characterization of cDNA from sheep kidney. J. Biol. Chem. **269**: 25959–25962.

62. AGARWAL, A. K., M. T. TUSIE-LUNA, C. MONDER & P. C. WHITE. 1990. Expression of 11β-hydroxysteroid dehydrogenase using recombinant vaccinia virus. Mol. Endocrinol. **4**: 1827–1832.

63. ANDERSSON, S. & D. W. RUSSEL. 1990. Structural and biochemical properties of cloned and expressed human and rat steroid 5α-reductases. Proc. Nat. Acad. Sci. USA **87**: 3640–3644.

64. ANDERSSON, S., D. M. BERGMAN, E. P. JENKINS & D. W. RUSSEL. 1991. Deletion of steroid 5α-reductase 2 gene in male pseudohermaphroditism. Nature **354**: 159–161.

65. JENKINS, E. P., C. L. HSIEH, A. MILATOVICH, K. NORMINGTON, D. M. BERMAN, U. FRANCKE & D. W. RUSSEL. 1991. Characterization and chromosomal mapping of human steroid 5α-reductase gene and pseudogene and mapping of the mouse homologue. Genomics **11**: 1102–1112.

66. LUU-THE V., Y. SUGIMOTO, L. PUY, Y. LABRIE, I. LOPEZ, M. SINGH & F. LABRIE. 1994. Characterization, expression and immunohistochemical localization of 5α-reductase in human skin. J. Invest. Dermatol. **102**: 221–226.

67. WILSON, J. D., J. E. GRIFFIN & D. W. RUSSEL. 1993. Steroid 5α-reductase 2 deficiency. Endocr. Rev. **14**: 577–593.

68. BÉLANGER, B., A. BÉLANGER, F. LABRIE, A. DUPONT, L. CUSAN & G. MONFETTE. 1989. Comparison of residual C-19 steroids in plasma and prostatic tissue of human, rat and guinea pig after castration: Unique importance of extratesticular androgens in men. J. Steroid Biochem. **32**: 695–698.

69. ADAMS, J. B. 1985. Control of secretion and the function of C19-Δ^5 steroids of the human adrenal gland. Molec. Cell. Endocrinol. **41**: 1–17.

70. MACDONALD, P., R.A. DOMBROSKI & M. L. CASEY. 1991. Recurrent secretion of progesterone in large amounts: An endocrine/metabolic disorder unique to young women? Endocrine Rev. **12**: 372–401.

Biosynthesis of DHEAS by the Human Adrenal Cortex and Its Age-Related Decline

PETER J. HORNSBY

Huffington Center on Aging
Baylor College of Medicine
1 Baylor Plaza M320
Houston, Texas 77030

Dehydroepiandrosterone sulfate (DHEAS) is the most abundant product of the young adult human adrenal cortex and fetal adrenal gland.[1-3] DHEAS secretion shows a dramatic cycle of high and low points over the life span in humans, as discussed in several other articles in this volume. Secretion from the adrenal cortex is very high in the fetus, drops sharply after birth to very low levels in childhood, rises again before puberty, a phenomenon termed adrenarche, and reaches high levels once again in young adulthood. Thereafter, DHEAS secretion progressively declines, often reaching very low or negligible levels after age 70. Plasma DHEAS levels reflect synthesis by the adrenal cortex, because the adrenal is normally the overwhelming source of DHEAS and the major contributor to unconjugated dehydroepiandrosterone (DHEA), which is present at much lower circulating levels and also is synthesized by the gonads.

Synthesis of the adrenal androgens DHEA and DHEAS in adult humans and other primates presents several puzzles to the researcher. First, why do the adrenal glands synthesize large amounts of these steroids in young adulthood, after a period from birth to pre-puberty during which little or none of these steroids is synthesized? Second, why does the high rate of secretion in young adulthood show such a strong age-related decline? Third, is the age-related decline in the adrenal androgens equivalent to deprivation of an essential hormone, and, therefore, is there a role for replacement therapy of DHEA(S) in later life as has successfully been achieved with estrogens? The question of the function of DHEA(S) in young adulthood and approaches to the concept of replacement therapy in older individuals are the subjects of several articles in this volume and will not be addressed here. Rather, the aim of this review is to account for the high rate of synthesis of DHEA(S) by the young adult adrenal gland at a cellular and molecular level, to examine the basis for the differences between humans and nonprimate species in DHEA(S) biosynthesis, and to offer some ideas for the mechanism of the age-related decline in secretion.

MORPHOLOGIC AND FUNCTIONAL ZONATION
OF THE ADRENAL CORTEX

The adult human adrenal cortex, like that of other mammals, has three morphologically defined zones. In most species, these zones are an outer zona glomerulosa, a middle zona fasciculata, and an inner zona reticularis. Although these traditional divisions have been recognized by histologists since the middle of the last century,[1,4] it has never been clear if the zona reticularis is really a homologous structure among all mammals and if it is functionally distinct from the zona fasciculata. Some species have other specialized sex-specific inner zones, such as the X-zone in the mouse and inner zones in some marsupials.[2,5] On the other hand, the zona glomerulosa is generally recognized as a homologous structure across different species. The glomerulosa is responsible for aldosterone synthesis, and so far as is known it has this function in all mammals.[1] Here evidence is reviewed that the zona reticularis is the zone responsible for the synthesis of DHEA(S) in humans and other higher primates. Some evidence indicates that the zona reticularis may secrete androgens and androgen precursors in other species.[2] However, it is not clear if the mechanisms for the formation and function of the reticularis in nonprimates are the same as those in primates, because of the vast difference in the rate of DHEA(S) biosynthesis and because the reticularis in nonprimates may have functions other than DHEA(S) biosynthesis. Thus, care must be exercised in applying conclusions derived from experiments on nonprimate adrenals to human steroidogenesis.

The model presented for the adult human adrenal cortex is therefore a three-cell model for steroidogenesis and its regulation, that is, the glomerulosa cell, producing mineralocorticoids, the fasciculata cell, producing glucocorticoids, and the reticularis cell, producing adrenal androgens. This three-cell model has an appealing simplicity and it underlies much of the discussion in the literature on adrenal androgen biosynthesis. However, most evidence that the morphologic boundary between the fasciculata and the reticularis forms a functional division between glucocorticoid and androgen secretion has been indirect. Here, direct and indirect evidence is reviewed together with recent cell culture experiments from this laboratory that strongly support this three-cell model. It is necessary to point out that the three cells, glomerulosa, fasciculata, and reticularis, are not separate cell types in the sense that adrenocortical cells, smooth muscle cells, and hepatocytes are separate cell types. Evidence from *in vivo* and *in vitro* observations suggests that the parenchymal cell of the adrenal cortex is a single cell type, the adrenocortical cell, whose phenotype, by mechanisms yet to be identified, can be modulated into a mineralocorticoid-, glucocorticoid- or androgen-secreting form.

Based on this three-cell model, regulation of each class of steroid synthesized by the adrenal cortex occurs at three levels:

1. Short-term regulation of steroidogenesis by hormones that increase the conversion of cholesterol to steroids by each zonal cell type, principally angiotensin II for the glomerulosa cell, adrenocorticotropic hormone (ACTH) for the fasciculata cell, and ACTH (with possibly other unknown factors) for the reticularis cell.
2. Long-term hormonal modulation of the enzyme levels within each cell type, causing the cells to have greater or lesser capacity for secreting zone-specific steroids and possibly changing the ratio of production of different steroid products; hormones that play this role are not necessarily the same as those that increase short-term steroidogenesis.
3. Longer-term shifting of boundaries between zones in the adrenal cortex by unknown mechanisms that modulate the zonal phenotype of adrenocortical cells, or by tissue remodeling by cell proliferation and/or apoptosis.

Controversy has long existed over whether the zona reticularis cell is regulated by factors other than ACTH. Acute stimulation with ACTH increases the adrenal production of cortisol, DHEA, and DHEAS in young adults.[3] Unconjugated DHEA and cortisol share a common circadian rhythm. The co-secretion of cortisol and DHEAS is not reflected in the circadian rhythm of plasma levels of these steroids, because of a much lower metabolic clearance rate for DHEAS,[6] resulting in uniformly high plasma DHEAS levels. However, in pregnancy the enhanced clearance of DHEAS resulting from placental metabolism results in lower plasma levels which then show a circadian rhythm concordant with that of cortisol/ACTH.[7]

Over long periods, the ratio of DHEA(S) and cortisol biosynthesis by the human adrenal cortex can vary. Following termination of glucocorticoid therapy[8,9] and after surgical remission of pituitary-dependent Cushing's syndrome,[10] cortisol synthesis normalizes rapidly but suppression of DHEAS synthesis is prolonged. In anorexia nervosa, DHEAS is selectively depressed and does not return to normal immediately after restoration of body weight.[11] In surgical stress, DHEAS shows a short-term rise, but levels are subsequently depressed for up to 30 days.[12] Burn trauma causes selective depression of DHEAS.[13] Plasma DHEAS levels correlate with many parameters of physical and mental well being.[14,15] One example is that DHEAS levels decrease as HIV-positive subjects progress to AIDS, the decrease occurring as symptoms develop.[16,17] These findings suggest that poor health generally may be associated with low DHEAS, consistent with a general dissociation of DHEAS and cortisol in chronic stress.

Because the rates of synthesis of DHEAS and cortisol are not always concordant, a separate DHEAS-stimulating hormone was postulated.[3] L. Parker isolated and partially characterized a proopiomelanocortin-derived peptide termed corticoadrenal androgen-stimulating hormone (CASH).[18] Other groups failed to find specific DHEA(S) stimulation by this peptide or other POMC-derived peptides.[19,20] However, according to the three-cell model for adrenal steroidogenesis, the critical experiment would be to test a putative CASH on isolated zona reticularis cells, and this to my knowledge has not been reported. In experiments on adult human adrenocortical cells, fasciculata cells were used,[20] and although it is not impossible that the addition of a factor to cultured fasciculata cells could cause them to convert to reticularis cells, this was not the proposed function of CASH. It was proposed to act as a short-term stimulus for DHEA(S) biosythesis, as angiotensin does on the zona glomerulosa cell or ACTH does on the zona fasciculata cell. On the other hand, experiments on both fetal human adrenocortical cells (definitive and fetal zone) and adult zona reticularis cells in culture show that ACTH is sufficient to maintain the biosynthesis of DHEA(S) and that a special hormone is not absolutely required (ref. 21 and experiments to be discussed in this article). In these DHEA(S)-producing cells, a high rate of DHEA(S) biosynthesis requires only increased intracellular cyclic AMP. However, as will be discussed, a high rate of DHEA(S) biosynthesis is dependent on the cell having the appropriate enzymatic pathway, and adult zona fasciculata cells produce very little of these steroids under the same conditions, that is, high intracellular cyclic AMP. Thus, the separate regulation of cortisol and DHEA(S) biosynthesis most likely results from changes in zonation, that is, modulation of the numbers of zona reticularis cells in the cortex, and possibly hormonal modulation of the ratio of cortisol/DHEA(S) biosynthesis within the reticularis and/or fasciculata, rather being the results of the short-term effects of a CASH-type factor.

DIRECT EVIDENCE THAT THE ZONA RETICULARIS IS THE DHEA(S)-SECRETING ZONE

The preceding overview assumes that the zona reticularis is predominantly or exclusively the source for DHEA(S) in the adrenal cortex. Curiously, direct measurements of steroidogenesis by separated human zona fasciculata and zona reticularis tissue or cells have been reported very infrequently. Notably, however, Tait and colleagues[22] separated dispersed human adrenocortical cells by unit gravity sedimentation, relying on the difference in size between the fasciculata and reticularis cells (FIG. 1). In their most purified fasciculata and reticularis fractions, they found significant differences in androgen/glucocorticoid ratios. By extrapolation, this experiment indicates that fractions with 100% fasciculata cells and 100% reticularis cells would secrete essentially only cortisol and only DHEA(S), respectively. In other work, inner zones of the human adrenal cortex were separated and placed in organ culture[23] or dispersed cell culture.[24] None of these experiments convincingly shows the clear separation of steroidogenic properties observed in Tait's experiment;

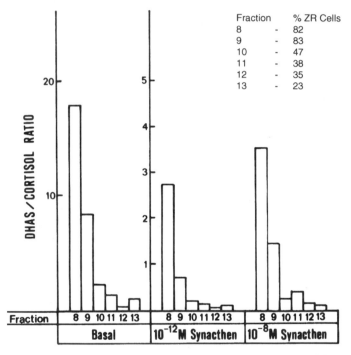

FIGURE 1. Production of DHEAS and cortisol by unit-gravity separated adult human zona fasciculata and zona reticularis cells. Reproduced with permission from Hyatt *et al.*[22]

however, the differences observed were consistent with a higher DHEA(S)/cortisol (DHEA(S)/F) ratio and higher sulfotransferase activity for the zona reticularis.

Recently, we tested the properties of separated adult human zona fasciculata and zona reticularis cells using the techniques of cell culture, Northern blotting, and radioimmunoassay.[25] We used microdissection to separate the zona reticularis and zona fasciculata on the basis of color (brown for zona reticularis and bright yellow for zona fasciculata). The DHEA(S)/F ratios from steroid precursor were vastly different between the zones. Expressed as a molar ratio of synthesis rates, DHEA(S)/F was ~0.5 in the zona reticularis cultures and ~0.02 in the zona fasciculata cultures, thus confirming Tait's earlier experiment. The ratio for the zona reticularis was still much lower than that for cultured fetal adrenocortical cells, as shown in these experiments and in previous studies.[26-30] Although these experiments are consistent with the concept that the zona fasciculata does not secrete DHEA(S), they leave open the question of whether the zona reticularis normally secretes cortisol. The question remains because, first, it is difficult to ensure that the zona reticularis is cleanly dissected away from the zona fasciculata. (Conversely, in the usual method of dissection of the adult human adrenal cortex used to prepare isolated adrenocortical cells, the zona reticularis, often a very narrow zone, is often destroyed when the gland is opened along the midline or it may be discarded with the medulla; therefore, unpurified adult adrenocortical cells are essentially fasciculata.) Second, the zona reticularis phenotype may have a tendency to change towards the zona fasciculata phenotype under culture conditions. We have no evidence for this, but the precedent is that the zona glomerulosa phenotype is difficult to maintain in culture, and zona glomerulosa cells stimulated with ACTH behave like zona fasciculata cells and secrete cortisol.[31,32] Such zonal changes are assumed to occur in the regulation of the boundaries between the zones *in vivo*.[33] However, maintenance of a 25-fold difference in the DHEA(S)/F ratio indicates that most likely DHEA(S) is the product solely of the zona reticularis and that regulation of DHEA(S) secretion in the adult human must be investigated in these cells, not in fasciculata cells or mixed zone preparations.

We compared the regulation of the mRNAs for the steroidogenic enzyme genes (cholesterol side-chain cleavage enzyme [SCC], type II 3β-hydroxysteroid dehydrogenase/$\Delta^{5,4}$-isomerase [3β-HSD], 17α-hydroxylase, 21-hydroxylase, and 11β-hydroxylase) in these zonal cultures. The principal reagents used were cyclic AMP analogs, because we previously showed that they potently induce cyclic AMP-dependent mRNAs in cultured fetal adrenocortical cells,[34] and insulin, because in other experiments with adult human adrenocortical cells we showed that insulin can modulate the DHEA(S)/F ratio.[35] When these inducers were added to the cells, the reticularis cells responded similarly to the fasciculata cells with respect to SCC, 17α-hydroxylase, 21-hydroxylase, and 11β-hydroxylase, but 3β-HSD mRNA did not increase in the reticularis cells as in the fasciculata cells.[25] Differences in DHEA(S)/F and 3β-HSD mRNA show that the cells "remember" their zonal cell type, at least over the 5 days of culture before they are exposed to the inducers. This occurs despite the fall of steroidogenic enzyme mRNAs to basal levels over this period, showing that the cells are no longer under the influence of the hormones that maintain transcription of the steroidogenic enzyme genes *in vivo*. Therefore, we conclude that transcription factors or other cellular machinery that differs between reticularis and fasciculata cells is stable under cell culture conditions, at least for these relatively short periods. These experiments do not rule out the possibility that longer-term culture and/or manipulation of the culture environment may modulate the properties of the cells between reticularis and fasciculata, as just discussed.

Thus, direct separation of the zona reticularis and zona fasciculata in the adult human adrenal cortex yields data that support a model in which the reticularis secretes most of the DHEA(S) made by the human adrenal cortex and that the fasciculata secretes essentially only glucocorticoids. A much larger literature supports this model indirectly. Most significant is the evidence derived from differences in adrenal androgen biosynthesis across the life span. In childhood, past the period of involution of the fetal zone after about 1 month of age,[1] there is no innermost zone in the cortex, and the adrenal secretes very low amounts of androgens. By adrenarche, when synthesis of the adrenal androgens begins again, a morphologically distinct zona reticularis has formed.[1] It reaches full development in young adulthood after age 20, the same point in the life span at which synthesis of adrenal androgens reaches its maximum level. From this we may conclude that the zona fasciculata in children produces essentially no androgens. It is not a large extension of this

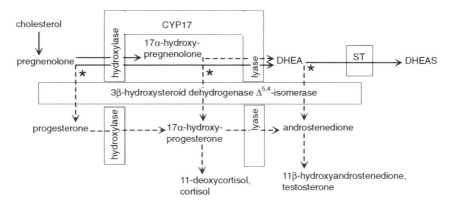

FIGURE 2. Pathway of DHEA(S) biosynthesis in the adrenal zona reticularis. For details, please see text. For clarity, the 17α-hydroxylase and $C_{17,20}$-lyase activities of CYP17 are shown as two "arms" of the protein, but in actuality these are activities at a single substrate binding site on the enzyme. ST = DHEA sulfotransferase. *Dashed arrows* indicate blocked or limited conversion pathways.

conclusion to suggest that the fasciculata in the young adult is likely the same, that is, essentially a glucocorticoid-producing and not an androgen-secreting zone. Other indirect evidence supports the concept of the reticularis as a DHEA(S)-secreting zone. This zone has the appropriate enzymatic machinery required for DHEA(S) biosynthesis (FIG. 2) in that it has low 3β-HSD expression and high DHEA sulfotransferase activity.[36–39] Histochemically, expression of DHEA sulfotransferase is restricted to the zona reticularis, the boundary of the zone of activity closely matching the extent of the morphologic zona reticularis.[39]

BIOCHEMICAL BASIS FOR DHEA(S) BIOSYNTHESIS BY THE ZONA RETICULARIS

Data from separated zonal cultures and other data reviewed here suggest that the level of expression of 3β-HSD is the sole or most important determinant of DHEA(S) biosynthesis and that without changing the activity of any enzymes other than 3β-HSD the DHEA(S)/F ratio can vary across a wide spectrum. Production of all steroids by the adrenal cortex is regulated in the short term by changes in the delivery of cholesterol to cholesterol side-chain cleavage enzyme (FIG. 2). Synthesis of different kinds of steroids is accomplished by differences in the levels of the enzymes beyond the cholesterol → pregnenolone step. The pathway of steroidogenesis in those adrenocortical cells that synthesize DHEA(S) is shown in FIGURE 2. The three asterisks indicate the three points of competition between 3β-HSD and another enzyme for substrate, points where the limitation of 3β-HSD activity keeps the steroid in the Δ^5 pathway.

The first two points of competition are between 3β-HSD and the two different enzyme activities, 17α-hydroxylase and $C_{17,20}$-lyase, of a single protein, CYP17.[40,41] The major pathway of DHEA biosynthesis from pregnenolone is thought to consist of two consecutive cycles of cytochrome P450 action on bound pregnenolone substrate, as 17α-hydroxypregnenolone does not compete well with pregnenolone for DHEA biosynthesis, although it is a substrate for the lyase activity of CYP17 when the concentration of pregnenolone is low.[42] FIGURE 2 indicates both a direct production of DHEA from pregnenolone and a pathway involving 17α-hydroxypregnenolone as a free intermediate. The high lyase activity of CYP17 applies only to Δ^5 substrates. With progesterone as substrate, hydroxylase activity is much more pronounced and lyase activity is hardly apparent; this is observed in both human and bovine CYP17 expressed in a heterologous cell system.[40,41] Evidently, however, 17α-hydroxyprogesterone at high concentrations can be converted by CYP17 to androstenedione, particularly in 21-hydroxylase deficiency.[43]

From studies of labeled precursors, it was concluded that the major pathway of cortisol biosynthesis in the adult human zona fasciculata is pregnenolone → 17α-hydroxypregnenolone → 17α-hydroxyprogesterone → 11-deoxycortisol → cortisol, based on the observation that progesterone was not efficiently converted to cortisol and did not accumulate when pregnenolone was used as steroidogenic precursor.[44,45] In our previous experiments on cortisol synthesis in cultured fetal human definitive zone adrenocortical cells it was also clear that 17α-hydroxypregnenolone and 17α-

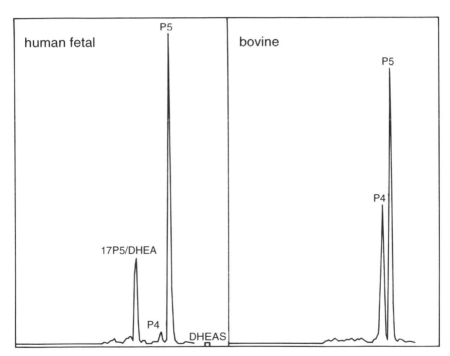

FIGURE 3. HPLC profiles of steroids synthesized from [³H]pregnenolone by cultured human and bovine adrenocortical cells without prior ACTH treatment. Human fetal definitive zone and bovine adrenocortical cells were grown for 12 days in the absence of ACTH. [³H]Pregnenolone (10 μM) was then added in serum-free medium. After 24 hours, the medium was taken for assay of radioactive products. **(Left)** Human cell culture; **(right)** bovine cell culture. P5 = pregnenolone; 17P5 = 17α-hydroxypregnenolone; P4 = progesterone. DHEAS was separately quantitated from the aqueous phase after solvent extraction. Reproduced with permission from Hornsby and Aldern.[21]

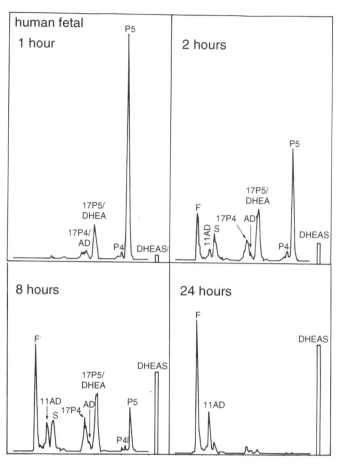

FIGURE 4. HPLC profiles of steroids synthesized from [³H]pregnenolone by cultured human adrenocortical cells after treatment with ACTH. Human fetal definitive zone cells were grown for 12 days in the absence of ACTH and then treated for 48 hours with 1 μM ACTH in serum-free medium. [³H]Pregnenolone (10 μM) was then added, and the medium was taken for assay of radioactive products after 1, 2, 8, and 24 hours of incubation. Abbreviations are defined in Figure 3. 17P4 = 17α-hydroxyprogesterone; AD = androstenedione; S = 11-deoxycortisol; F = cortisol; 11AD = 11β-hydroxyandrostenedione. Reproduced with permission from Hornsby and Aldern.[21]

hydroxyprogesterone, but not progesterone, are intermediates (FIGS. 3 and 4).[21] However, these cells also synthesize large amounts of DHEA(S), because low 3β-HSD activity traps the steroid in the Δ⁵ pathway and because CYP17 exhibits high lyase activity on pregnenolone substrate. The enzyme synthesizes a mixture of 17α-hydroxypregnenolone and DHEA from pregnenolone, and 17α-hydroxypregnenolone is then converted by the (very low) 3β-HSD activity to 17α-hydroxyprogesterone. The pathway in the zona reticularis is likely the same, again because of the limiting level of 3β-HSD activity.

   In these experiments we used bovine adrenocortical cells for comparison with human fetal definitive zone cells, as an example of most nonprimate adrenocortical cells, which synthesize very little DHEA(S) (FIGS. 3 and 5). 3β-HSD activity is about 10-fold higher in bovine adrenocortical cells than in fetal human adrenocortical cells under the same conditions in primary culture.[21] In bovine adrenocortical cells progesterone is clearly an intermediate in the biosynthesis of cortisol, because the higher 3β-HSD activity immediately diverts most Δ^5 steroid into the Δ^4 pathway at the pregnenolone to progesterone step and thereby also blocks the synthesis of adrenal androgens.

   It is not clear if the postnatal human zona fasciculata uses the Δ^4 or the Δ^5 pathway for the synthesis of cortisol. A related question is whether adrenarche is purely the development of a zona reticularis or whether there are also changes in the zona fasciculata. Studies of the changing patterns of adrenocortical steroid secretion in children at the time of adrenarche show changes indicating both a decrease in 3β-HSD activity in the cortex as a whole, consistent with the development of a zone with lower 3β-HSD activity (zona reticularis), and an apparent rise in $C_{17,20}$-lyase activity.[46,47] The latter could indicate a change in the enzymatic properties of the CYP17 protein in the adrenal cortex, but could also result indirectly from the development of the zona reticularis and greater use of the Δ^5 pathway by that zone, because of the higher lyase activity of CYP17 on Δ^5 substrates.

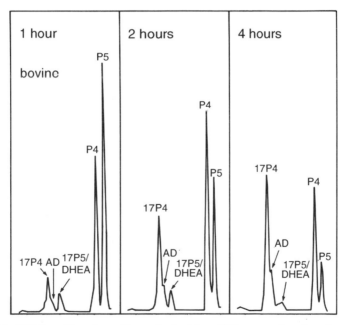

FIGURE 5. HPLC profiles of steroids synthesized from [³H]pregnenolone by cultured bovine adrenocortical cells after treatment with ACTH. Bovine cells were grown for 12 days in the absence of ACTH and then treated for 48 hours with 1 μM ACTH in serum-free medium. [³H]Pregnenolone (10 μM) was then added, and the medium was taken for assay of radioactive products after 1, 2, and 4 hours of incubation. Abbreviations are defined in Figures 3 and 4. Reproduced with permission from Hornsby and Aldern.[21]

This hypothesis requires that cortisol in the pre-adrenarchal (and presumably postadrenarchal) zona fasciculata be synthesized by the Δ^4 route with progesterone as intermediate, contrary to the conclusions of studies with labeled precursors; otherwise, if the Δ^5 route were used, the pre-adrenarchal zona fasciculata would be expected to synthesize substantial amounts of DHEA or other C19 steroids, because of the preference of the CYP17 protein for lyase activity on Δ^5 substrates. In favor of this notion, I refer to experiments on adult human zona fasciculata cells in which 3β-HSD activity is pharmacologically blocked. When fasciculata cells are incubated with trilostane, a potent inhibitor of 3β-HSD, they achieve a DHEA/F ratio higher than that of zona reticularis cells or even of fetal adrenocortical cells.[25] This is not unique to human cells; bovine adrenocortical cells treated with a 3β-HSD inhibitor also produce DHEA.[21] Thus, it is clear that the post-adrenarchal (and presumably pre-adrenarchal) zona fasciculata can synthesize DHEA (i.e., the cells have the necessary lyase activity) but that this capacity is blocked by the high 3β-HSD activity.

Additionally, when progesterone is added to cultured fetal human adrenocortical cells, they efficiently convert it to cortisol,[48] in contrast to the findings of older studies on noncultured adrenocortical preparations. Thus, more studies are needed to resolve the question of the predominant pathway of cortisol biosynthesis in the human adrenal cortex at different stages in the life span.

The third point of competition in the pathway shown in FIGURE 2 is for DHEA between sulfotransferase and 3β-HSD. Normally, about half the DHEA synthesized *in vivo* is converted to DHEAS, and much of the unconjugated steroid is converted extraadrenally to the sulfate, which accumulates at much higher levels in plasma than does the unconjugated steroid because of its low clearance rate.[1] Sulfation renders the steroid unavailable for transformation by other enzymes. If 3β-HSD activity is higher and sulfotransferase lower, as in the bovine gland, the small amounts of DHEA that are formed are converted to androstenedione which can serve as a precursor for 11β-hydroxyandrostenedione or testosterone.

These data are compatible with the hypothesis that the essential (but not the only) difference between DHEA(S)-secreting and non-DHEA(S)-secreting adrenocortical cells is the level of 3β-HSD. This accounts both for the difference between different kinds of human adrenal cells, the zona reticularis and the zones of the fetal cortex versus the zona fasciculata, and for the difference between cells of human origin which secrete adrenal androgens and those of the cow and other species which do not. The difference is reflected in the levels of mRNA,[34,49] protein,[50] and activity[21,30] of 3β-HSD. Thus, the dissociation between DHEAS and cortisol synthesis observed at different phases of the human life span and under different pathophysiologic conditions results from the relative levels of activity of 3β-HSD in the adrenal cortex as a whole, due principally to changes in the numbers of cells in zones with very low 3β-HSD activity (zona reticularis or fetal zone). There is the secondary question of whether the 3β-HSD level in the reticularis cell is to some extent modulated *in vivo* by circulating hormones, causing the cells to produce less or more androgens. Several hormones including angiotensin, acetylcholine, and insulin inhibit the production of DHEAS by fetal adrenocortical cells and reticularis cells, and this is associated with enhanced cortisol production and induction of 3β-HSD.[35,48] This effect of insulin is consistent with reported effects of insulin *in vivo* discussed in another chapter in this volume (Nestler). However, over long periods the most important determinant of the amount of DHEA(S) synthesized by the adrenal cortex is likely the number of reticularis cells.

MODELS FOR THE SEPARATE REGULATION
OF ZONA RETICULARIS FUNCTION

Is the function of the zona reticularis regulated separately from the function of the zona fasciculata? In generally accepted models for the regulation of mineralocorticoid and glucocorticoid biosynthesis, the level of steroidogenesis is under precise feedback regulation.[33] Long-term regulation of aldosterone biosynthesis is the result of a combination of the regulation of the width of the zona glomerulosa, the regulation of enzymes synthesizing aldosterone (particularly the CYP11B2 enzyme, aldosterone synthase/corticosterone methyl oxidase), and short-term activation of the conversion of cholesterol to pregnenolone. Both short- and long-term regulation of aldosterone synthesis, including regulation of the width of the zone, are mediated through a feedback loop by which aldosterone levels are maintained at a level appropriate for the function of this steroid, principally by regulation of the level of angiotensin II. The fact that angiotensin can also act on the fasciculata does not diminish the validity of this model, because the fasciculata does not synthesize aldosterone and, therefore, does not contribute to the feedback regulation of aldosterone biosynthesis.

Can this model be applied to the zona reticularis and adrenal androgen biosynthesis? Several gaps in our knowledge preclude the setting up of a feedback model. First, no hormone specifically stimulating adrenal androgen synthesis has yet been identified. As reviewed herein, ACTH is apparently sufficient to maintain adrenal androgen biosynthesis. Other hormones can change the balance of glucocorticoid and androgen biosynthesis towards glucocorticoids and away from androgens,[35,48] and so might be said to act as androgen-inhibiting hormones, but whether they have this function in vivo is yet unknown. Second, we have no evidence for a feedback mechanism in adrenal androgen biosynthesis. We do not know if there is a signaling mechanism in target cells for DHEA that is independent of its conversion to androgens and estrogens. If DHEA acts solely as a precursor for androgens and estrogens and does not have a unique signaling mechanism, we currently know of no mechanism by which androgens and estrogens can feed back on adrenal androgen synthesis. Obviously, if there were such a feedback mechanism, it is unlikely to be via ACTH, which is physiologically linked to monitoring glucocorticoid levels and not androgen and estrogen levels.

The idea of a separate adrenal androgen-stimulating hormone was appealing, because the adrenal androgen/glucocorticoid ratio can change over long periods of time. However, if these changes are linked principally to the number of zona reticularis cells, there may in fact be no feedback regulation of DHEAS biosynthesis. At adrenarche, unknown mechanisms cause the development of the zona reticularis and thereby set a certain level of adrenal androgen biosynthesis. The surge of adrenal androgen biosynthesis at adrenarche could be viewed as fulfilling an undetermined biologic requirement for DHEAS at this phase of the life span, where crossing a threshold of plasma levels of this steroid is needed but precise regulation is not required. The high variability of peak adrenal androgen levels in young adulthood is compatible with this concept and with a lack of feedback regulation of DHEAS biosynthesis. After adrenarche, the zona reticularis and adrenal androgen biosynthesis persist, but changes in adrenal androgens, for example, in surgical stress, anorexia nervosa, and other conditions, are mostly due to internal changes in the inner adrenal cortex resulting from the growth and death of adrenocortical cells. This model suggests the simplest explanation for the age-related change in DHEAS, namely, a slow loss of functional zona reticularis cells as a function of age, as will be discussed.

REGULATION OF ADRENOCORTICAL ZONATION

Little is known about how the adrenal cortex becomes zoned and how the zona reticularis develops. It is analogous to the question of setting up zonation between the glomerulosa and fasciculata. We previously proposed a model in which zonation is determined by the position of adrenocortical cells within the capillary bed across

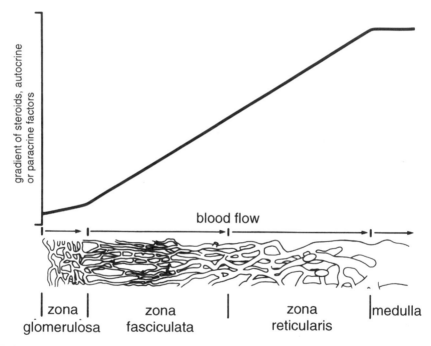

FIGURE 6. Hypothesis for the origination of zonation in the adrenal cortex by the action of a gradient of a factor across the capillary bed (see text).

the cortex, zona glomerulosa characteristics being a response to conditions on the arterial end of the bed, zona reticularis characteristics being a response to conditions on the venous end, with fasciculata in the middle (FIG. 6).[33,51] We hypothesized that the blood supply creates a gradient of an autocrine or paracrine factor across the capillary bed which signals the cells to adopt particular zonal characteristics.[33,52] The nature of such a factor is unknown. We previously speculated that steroids might fill such a role. Steroids do have direct actions on steroidogenic enzymes which mimic, to some extent, effects expected in zonation.[51] However, direct actions of steroids are unlikely to be responsible for normal zonation as opposed to pathologic states, because it has been established that differences among the zones principally reflect transcriptional differences for the steroidogenic enzyme genes and not posttranslational or posttranscriptional modifications. Although it is conceivable that steroids could regulate the transcription of genes in adrenocortical cells and thus cause zonation, we have no evidence of this. There are many other candidates for paracrine or autocrine factors that might be involved in zonation, but we have as yet no evidence on which to base a guess as to their identity.

According to this model of zonation, the important event at adrenarche is the achievement of a critical width of the cortex. The intraglandular environment within the inner cortex then dictates suppression of 3β-HSD expression and induces other aspects of the zona reticularis phenotype. The adrenocortical changes in adrenarche may arise first from a small reduction in the ability of the cortex to synthesize cortisol, because of lowered 3β-HSD activity, requiring a marginal increase in the secretion of ACTH to maintain cortisol production rates, thereby indirectly stimulating growth of the cortex and widening of the zona reticularis. Adrenarche thus can be viewed primarily as an adrenal event.[47] The dependence on adrenal growth for the occurrence of adrenarche can be inferred from data on patients treated with glucocorticoids for congenital adrenal hyperplasia resulting from 21-hydroxylase deficiency.[8,53] This treatment was associated in adult life with extremely low synthesis of DHEAS, even when the patients received no steroids for 6 weeks.[54] The authors suggested that steroid treatment interferes with adrenarche by suppressing growth of the cortex so that it does not achieve a width appropriate for the development of the zona reticularis.

Adrenarche is the prototype for the many other examples of changes in DHEAS/cortisol secretion ratios. These events may generally involve tissue remodeling, altering the total width of the cortex, thereby increasing or decreasing the appropriate intraglandular environment for the maintenance of the zona reticularis.

AGE-RELATED DECLINE IN ADRENAL ANDROGEN BIOSYNTHESIS

The long-term aim of research on the age-related decline in adrenal androgen biosynthesis is to account for the steep decline in adrenal biosynthesis of DHEAS and to clarify the effects of aging per se versus the effects of ill health. The decline in plasma DHEAS levels results from changes in adrenocortical production rates rather than gonadal changes, because it is also observed in ovariectomized women.[55] It shows a high interindividual variability.[55-57] The decline in DHEAS contrasts with the maintenance of plasma cortisol levels in aging. The rate of production of cortisol declines slightly, but this in response to an age-related decrease in metabolic clearance.[58] Plasma cortisol levels rise to the same extent in young and old subjects after administration of ACTH or CRH, whereas the increase in DHEAS is much smaller in old subjects.[59,60] The increment in plasma cortisol concentration is significantly higher in elderly patients undergoing operative procedures than in the younger group,[61] perhaps indicating a greater stress level in older patients. Aging may therefore be analogous in its effects on the adrenal cortex to chronic stress, with the interindividual variability caused by the heterogeneity of life histories in aging individuals.

The simplest hypothesis is that the decrease in DHEAS synthesis in aging results from a decrease in the number of functional zona reticularis cells, which may or may not precisely parallel changes in the morphologic zona reticularis.[62] The rate of loss of DHEAS biosynthesis with age is extremely variable. Unfortunately it has not been possible to correlate the decline in individual DHEAS levels in aging with the morphologic loss of the zona reticularis. In cross-sectional studies, there is a large, but variable loss of adrenal androgen biosynthesis with aging and variable changes in the zona reticularis, which are characterized as increasing irregularity rather than simple involution.[62] Thus, it is likely that there is a loss of zona reticularis cells with aging, causing a decline in adrenal androgen biosynthesis, but this hypothesis is difficult to prove directly. This model for loss of zona reticularis cells presumes that there is no feedback of adrenal androgen biosynthesis on the width of the reticularis. Without a feedback mechanism, a loss of cells occurs without triggering a compensatory increase in the stimulus to DHEAS synthesis.

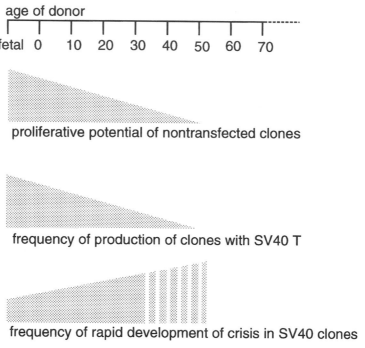

FIGURE 7. Diagrammatic representation of the effects of donor age on proliferative potential, rate of production of clones after transfection with SV40, and rate of entry of such clones into "crisis." This diagram is based on data derived from cultured human fetal definitive zone adrenocortical cells, from zona fasciculata-reticularis cells from postnatal donors 2, 11, and 18 years of age, and cells from one to three donors in each decade from age 20 to age 70. Reproduced with permission from Hornsby *et al.*[63]

What is the mechanism for the putative age-related loss of zona reticularis cells? One possibility is that loss of the zona reticularis is secondary to a decline in total width of the cortex caused by decreased growth ability of adrenocortical cells. This may result from an intrinsic change in the cells as evidenced by the failure of cells from older donors to proliferate in culture (FIG. 7)[63] or it could be secondary to vascular or other extracellular changes that deprive the cells of an appropriate supply of factors needed for proliferation. Elsewhere, I discuss the relationship of changes in adrenal androgen biosynthesis and changes in the adrenal gland to potential aging mechanisms generally and discuss the difficulty of understanding the basis for age-related changes in endocrine systems.[64]

REFERENCES

1. NEVILLE, A. M. & M. J. O'HARE. 1982. The Human Adrenal Cortex. Pathology and Biology—An Integrated Approach. Springer-Verlag. Berlin.
2. KIME, D. E., G. P. VINSON, P. W. MAJOR & R. KILPATRICK. 1980. Adrenal-gonad relationships. In General, Comparative and Clinical Endocrinology, Vol. 3. I. C. Jones & I. W. Henderson, Eds.: 183–200. Academic Press. London.
3. PARKER, L. N. & W. D. ODELL. 1980. Control of adrenal androgen secretion. Endocrinol. Rev. **1:** 392–410.
4. BACHMANN, R. 1954. Die Nebenniere. In Handbuch der mikroskopischen Anatomie des Menschen, Vol. 6. Blutgefass- und Lymphgefassapparat. Innersekretorische Drusen, Part 5. W. Bargmann, Ed.: 1–952. Springer-Verlag. Berlin.
5. SHIRE, J. G. M. 1979. Corticosteroids and adrenocortical function in animals. In Genetic Variation in Hormone Systems, Vol. 1. J. G. M. Shire, Ed.: 43–70. CRC Press. Boca Raton.
6. HANING, R. V., JR., M. CHABOT, C. A. FLOOD, R. HACKETT & C. LONGCOPE. 1989. Metabolic clearance rate (MCR) of dehydroepiandrosterone sulfate (DS), its metabolism to dehydroepiandrosterone, androstenedione, testosterone, and dihydrotestosterone, and the effect of increased plasma DS concentration on DS MCR in normal women. J. Clin. Endocrinol. Metab. **69:** 1047–1052.
7. PARRINI, D. C. GUIDONI, C. MASSAFRA & A. R. GENAZZANI. 1980. Spontaneous fluctuations, circadian variations, and pattern of DHAS during the last 20 weeks of pregnancy. In Adrenal Androgens. A. R. Genazzani, J. H. H. Thijssen & P. K. Siiteri, Eds. :199–206. Raven Press, New York.
8. DEWIS, P. & D. C. ANDERSON. 1985. The adrenarche and adrenal hirsutism. In Adrenal Cortex. D. C. Anderson & J. S. D. Winter, Eds.: 96–116. Butterworth. London.
9. BRIGELL, D. F., V. S. FANG & R. L. ROSENFIELD. 1992. Recovery of responses to ovine corticotropin-releasing hormone after withdrawal of a short course of glucocorticoid. J. Clin. Endocrinol. Metab. **74:** 1036–1039.
10. KLEIBER, H., F. REY, E. TEMLER & F. GOMEZ. 1991. Dissociated recovery of cortisol and dehydroepiandrosterone sulphate after treatment for Cushing's syndrome. J. Endocrinol. Invest. **14:** 489–492.
11. WINTERER, J., H. E. GWIRTSMAN, T. GEORGE, W. H. KAYE, D. L. LORIAUX & G. B. CUTLER, JR. 1985. Adrenocorticotropin-stimulated adrenal androgen secretion in anorexia nervosa: Impaired secretion at low weight with normalization after long term weight recovery. J. Clin. Endocrinol. **61:** 693–697.
12. LINDH, A., K. CARLSTROM, J. EKLUND & N. WILKING. 1992. Serum steroids and prolactin during and after major surgical trauma. Acta Anaesthesiol. Scand. **36:** 119–124.
13. PARKER, C. R., JR. & C. R. BAXTER. 1985. Divergence in adrenal steroid secretory pattern after thermal injury in adult patients. J. Trauma **25:** 508–510.
14. SEMPLE, C. G., C. E. GRAY & G. H. BEASTALL. 1987. Adrenal androgens and illness. Acta Endocrinol. (Copenh.) **116:** 155–160.
15. RUDMAN, D., K. R. SHETTY & D. E. MATTSON. 1990. Plasma dehydroepiandrosterone sulfate in nursing home men. J. Am. Geriatr. Soc. **38:** 421–427.
16. CHRISTEFF, N., S. GHARAKHANIAN, N. THOBIE, W. ROZENBAUM & E. A. NUNEZ. 1992. Evidence for changes in adrenal and testicular steroids during HIV infection. J. Acquired Immune Defic. Syndr. **5:** 841–846.
17. MULDER, J. W., P. H. FRISSEN, P. KRIJNEN, E. ENDERT, F. DE WOLF, J. GOUDSMIT, J. G. MASTERSON & J. M. LANGE. 1992. Dehydroepiandrosterone as predictor for progression to AIDS in asymptomatic human immunodeficiency virus-infected men. J. Infect. Dis. **165:** 413–418.
18. PARKER, L. N., E. T. LIFRAK & W. D. ODELL. 1983. A 60,000 molecular weight human

pituitary glycopeptide stimulates adrenal androgen secretion. Endocrinology **113:** 2092–2100.

19. MELLON, S. H., J. E. SHIVELY & W. L. MILLER. 1991. Human proopiomelanocortin-(79–96), a proposed androgen stimulatory hormone, does not affect steroidogenesis in cultured human fetal adrenal cells. J. Clin. Endocrinol. Metab. **72:** 19–22.

20. PENHOAT, A., P. SANCHEZ, C. JAILLARD, D. LANGLOIS, M. BEGEOT & J. M. SAEZ. 1991. Human proopiomelanocortin-(79–96), a proposed cortical androgen-stimulating hormone, does not affect steroidogenesis in cultured human adult adrenal cells. J. Clin. Endocrinol. Metab. **72:** 23–26.

21. HORNSBY, P. J. & K. A. ALDERN. 1984. Steroidogenic enzyme activities in cultured human definitive zone adrenocortical cells: Comparison with bovine adrenocortical cells and resultant differences in adrenal androgen synthesis. J. Clin. Endocrinol. Metab. **58:** 121–130.

22. HYATT, P. J., K. BHATT & J. F. TAIT. 1983. Steroid biosynthesis by zona fasciculata and zona reticularis cells purified from the mammalian adrenal cortex. J. Steroid Biochem. **19:** 953–960.

23. JONES, T., M. GROOM & K. GRIFFITHS. 1970. Steroid biosynthesis by cultures of normal human adrenal tissue. Biochem. Biophys. Res. Commun. **38:** 355–361.

24. O'HARE, M. J., E. C. NICE & A. M. NEVILLE. 1980. Regulation of androgen secretion and sulfoconjugation in the adult human adrenal cortex: Studies with primary monolayer cell cultures. *In* Adrenal Androgens. A. R. Genazzani, J. H. H. Thijssen & P. K. Siiteri, Eds.: 7–25. Raven Press. New York.

25. ENDOH, A., S. KRISTIANSEN, P. CASSON, J. E. BUSTER & P. J. HORNSBY. 1995. Submitted for publication.

26. BAIRD, A. C., G. BRISSON, K. W. KAN, W. C. DUGUID & S. SOLOMON. 1978. Control of steroid synthesis in human fetal adrenals in monolayer culture. Can. J. Biochem. **56:** 577–584.

27. VOUTILAINEN, R. & A. I. KAHRI. 1980. Placental origin of the suppression of 3β-hydroxysteroid dehydrogenase in the fetal zone cells of human fetal adrenals. J. Steroid Biochem. **13:** 39–43.

28. WINTER, J. S. D., K. FUJIEDA, C. FAIMAN, F. I. REYES & J. THLIVERIS. 1980. Control of steroidogenesis by human fetal adrenal cells in tissue culture. *In* Adrenal Androgens. A. R. Genazzani, J. H. H. Thijssen & P. K. Siiteri, Eds.: 55–62. Raven Press. New York.

29. CRICKARD, K., C. R. ILL & R. B. JAFFE. 1981. Control of proliferation of human fetal adrenal cells in vitro. J. Clin. Endocrinol. Metab. **53:** 790–796.

30. SIMONIAN, M. H. & M. W. CAPP. 1984. Characterization of steroidogenesis in cell cultures of the human fetal adrenal cortex: Comparison of definitive zone and fetal zone cells. J. Clin. Endocrinol. Metab. **59:** 643–651.

31. HORNSBY, P. J., M. J. O'HARE & A. M. NEVILLE. 1974. Functional and morphological observations on rat adrenal zona glomerulosa cells in monolayer culture. Endocrinology **95:** 1240–1251.

32. CRIVELLO, J. F. & G. N. GILL. 1983. Induction of cultured bovine adrenocortical zona glomerulosa cell 17-hydroxylase activity by ACTH. Mol. Cell. Endocrinol. **30:** 97–107.

33. HORNSBY, P. J. 1985. The regulation of adrenocortical function by control of growth and structure. *In* Adrenal Cortex. D. C. Anderson & J. S. D. Winter, Eds.: 1–31. Butterworth. London.

34. CHENG, C. Y., M. V. FLASCH & P. J. HORNSBY. 1992. Expression of 17α-hydroxylase and 3β-hydroxysteroid dehydrogenase in fetal human adrenocortical cells transfected with SV40 T antigen. J. Mol. Endocrinol. **9:** 7–17.

35. KRISTIANSEN, S., A. ENDOH, P. CASSON, J. E. BUSTER & P. J. HORNSBY. 1995. Submitted for publication.

36. CAMERON, E. H. D., T. JONES, D. JONES, A. B. M. ANDERSON & K. GRIFFITHS. 1969. Further studies on the relationship between C19- and C21-steroid synthesis in the human adrenal gland. J. Endocrinol. **45:** 215–230.

37. DAWSON, I. M. P., J. PRYSE-DAVIES & I. M. SNAPE. 1961. The distribution of six enzyme systems and of lipid in the human and rat adrenal cortex before and after administra-

tion of steroid and ACTH, with comments on the distribution in human foetuses and in some natural disease conditions. J. Pathol. Bacteriol. **81:** 181–190.

38. CAVALLERO, C. & G. CHIAPPINO. 1962. Histochemistry of steroid-3β-ol dehydrogenase in the human adrenal cortex. Experientia **18:** 119–120.

39. KENNERSON, A. R., D. A. McDONALD & J. B. ADAMS. 1983. Dehydroepiandrosterone sulfotransferase localization in human adrenal glands: A light and electron microscopic study. J. Clin. Endocrinol. Metab. **56:** 786–790.

40. ZUBER, M. X., E. R. SIMPSON & M. R. WATERMAN. 1986. Expression of bovine 17α-hydroxylase cytochrome P-450 cDNA in nonsteroidogenic (COS 1) cells. Science **234:** 1258–1261.

41. SWART, P., R. W. ESTABROOK, J. I. MASON & M. R. WATERMAN. 1989. Catalytic activity of human and bovine adrenal cytochromes P-450 17α,lyase expressed in Cos 1 cells. Biochem. Soc. Trans. **17:** 1025–1026.

42. YAMAZAKI, T., K. NAWA, S. KOMINAMI & S. TAKEMORI. 1992. Cytochrome P-450 (17α,lyase)-mediating pathway of androgen synthesis in bovine adrenocortical cultured cells. Biochim. Biophys. Acta **1134:** 143–148.

43. WHITE, P. C. & M. I. NEW. 1992. Genetic basis of endocrine disease 2: Congenital adrenal hyperplasia due to 21-hydroxylase deficiency. J. Clin. Endocrinol. Metab. **74:** 6–11.

44. WELIKY, I. & L. L. ENGEL. 1963. Metabolism of progesterone-4-C^{14} and pregnenolone-7α-H^3 by human adrenal tissue. Formation of 16α-hydroxyprogesterone-C^{14}, corticosterone-C^{14}, and cortisol-C^{14}-H^3. J. Biol. Chem. **238:** 1302–1307.

45. WHITEHOUSE, B. J. & G. P. VINSON. 1968. Corticosteroid biosynthesis from pregnenolone and progesterone by human adrenal tissue in vitro. A kinetic study. Steroids. **11:** 245–264.

46. RICH, B. H., R. L. ROSENFIELD, A. W. LUCKY, J. C. HELKE & P. OTTO. 1981. Adrenarche: Changing adrenal response to adrenocorticotropin. J. Clin. Endocrinol. Metab. **52:** 1129–1136.

47. KELNAR, C. J. H. & C. G. D. BROOK. 1983. A mixed longitudinal study of adrenal steroid excretion in childhood and the mechanism of adrenarche. Clin. Endocrinol. **19:** 117–129.

48. McALLISTER, J. M. & P. J. HORNSBY. 1988. Dual regulation of 3β-hydroxysteroid dehydrogenase, 17α-hydroxylase, and dehydroepiandrosterone sulfotransferase by adenosine 3′,5′-monophosphate and activators of protein kinase C in cultured human adrenocortical cells. Endocrinology **122:** 2012–2018.

49. VOUTILAINEN, R., V. ILVESMAKI & P. J. MIETTINEN. 1991. Low expression of 3β-hydroxy-5-ene steroid dehydrogenase gene in human fetal adrenals in vivo; adrenocorticotropin and protein kinase C-dependent regulation in adrenocortical cultures. J. Clin. Endocrinol. Metab. **72:** 761–767.

50. DOODY, K. M., B. R. CARR, W. E. RAINEY, W. BYRD, B. A. MURRY, R. C. STRICKLER, J. L. THOMAS & J. I. MASON. 1990. 3β-Hydroxysteroid dehydrogenase/isomerase in the fetal zone and neocortex of the human fetal adrenal gland. Endocrinology **126:** 2487–2492.

51. HORNSBY, P. J. 1987. Cytochrome P-450/pseudosubstrate interactions in the adrenal cortex and their possible role in adrenocortical pathology. *In* Corticosteroids and Peptide Hormones in Hypertension. F. Mantero & P. Vecsei, Eds.: 11–25. Raven Press. New York.

52. ANDERSON, D. C. 1980. Hypothesis: The adrenal androgen-stimulating hormone does not exist. Lancet **2:** 454–456.

53. REZVANI, I., L. R. GARIBALDI, A. M. DIGEORGE & H. G. ARTMAN. 1983. Disproportionate suppression of dehydroepiandrosterone sulfate (DHEAS) in treated patients with congenital adrenal hyperplasia due to 21-hydroxylase deficiency. Pediatr. Res. **17:** 131–134.

54. CONWAY, D. I., D. C. ANDERSON & D. E. BU'LOCK. 1982. The steroid response to controlled adrenal stimulation in congenital adrenal hyperplasia. Clin. Endocrinol. (Oxf.) **16:** 215–226.

55. VERMEULEN, A. 1980. Adrenal androgens and aging. *In* Adrenal Androgens. A. R. Genazzani, J. H. H. Thijssen & P. K. Siiteri, Eds.: 207–215. Raven Press. New York.

56. ADAMS, J. B. 1985. Control of secretion and the function of C19-Δ5-steroids of the human adrenal gland. Mol. Cell. Endocrinol. **41:** 1–17.
57. ORENTREICH, N., J. L. BRIND, J. H. VOGELMAN, R. ANDRES & H. BALDWIN. 1992. Long-term longitudinal measurements of plasma dehydroepiandrosterone sulfate in normal men. J. Clin. Endocrinol. Metab. **75:** 1002–1004.
58. WOLFSEN, A. R. 1982. Aging and the adrenals. *In* Endocrine Aspects of Aging. S. G. Korenman, Ed.: 55–74. Elsevier. New York.
59. VERMEULEN, A., J. P. DESLYPERE, W. SCHELFHOUT, L. VERDONCK & R. RUBENS. 1982. Adrenocortical function in old age: Response to acute adrenocorticotropin stimulation. J. Clin. Endocrinol. Metab. **54:** 187–195.
60. LIU, C. H., G. A. LAUGHLIN, U. G. FISCHER & S. S. YEN. 1990. Marked attenuation of ultradian and circadian rhythms of dehydroepiandrosterone in postmenopausal women: Evidence for a reduced 17,20-desmolase enzymatic activity. J. Clin. Endocrinol. Metab. **71:** 900–910.
61. BLICHERT-TOFT, M. 1978. The adrenal glands in old age. *In* Geriatric Endocrinology. R. B. Greenblatt, Ed.: 81–102. Raven Press. New York.
62. KREINER, E. & G. DHOM. 1979. Altersveranderungen der menschlichen Nebenniere. Zbl. Allg. Pathol. Pathol. Anat. **123:** 351–356.
63. HORNSBY, P. J., C. Y. CHENG, D. S. LALA, S. S. MAGHSOUDLOU, S. G. RAJU & L. YANG. 1992. Changes in gene expression during senescence of adrenocortical cells in culture. J. Steroid Biochem. Mol. Biol. **43:** 385–395.
64. HORNSBY, P. J. 1995. Genes, hormones, and aging. *In* Advances in Cell Aging and Senescence. P.S. Timiras, Ed. JAI Press. CT.

Adrenal Androgen Biosynthesis
with Special Attention to P450c17[a]

J. IAN MASON,[b,d] IAN M. BIRD,[c,d]
AND WILLIAM E. RAINEY[d]

[b]Department of Clinical Biochemistry
University of Edinburgh
Edinburgh Royal Infirmary NHS Trust
Edinburgh EH3 9YW, Scotland

[c]Department of Obstetrics & Gynecology
University of Wisconsin-Madison
Meriter/Park Hospital
Madison, Wisconsin 53715

[d]Cecil H. & Ida Green Center for Reproductive Biology Sciences and
Departments of Obstetrics & Gynecology and Biochemistry
University of Texas Southwestern Medical Center
Dallas, Texas 75235

The human adrenal gland is unique in its high secretion rate of dehydrocpiandros-terone (DHEA) and its sulfoconjugate, dehydroepiandrosterone sulfate (DHEAS).[1,2] Extremely high production rates of these C_{19}-steroids occur in the fetal adrenal, whereas minimal secretion occurs from the adrenal cortex of the child until adrenar-chy. The synthesis of adrenal C_{19}-steroids then increases, attaining a maximum in the young adult. Thereafter, a slow decline in adrenal C_{19}-steroid secretion continues through the remainder of adult life, while C_{21}-steroid secretion is little affected.

The last decade has seen considerable progress in the understanding of the molecular mechanisms controlling the expression of adrenocortical steroidogenic enzymes.[3,4] Nonetheless, the nature of mechanisms specifically controlling DHEA and DHEAS synthesis by human adrenocortical cells remains largely unresolved. Primary cultures of both fetal and adult human adrenocortical cells have acted as models for evaluating human adrenal DHEA production.[5–8] These cells, however, have certain limitations because of the availability and age of tissue and the difficulty in obtaining sufficient cells for molecular studies. Notwithstanding potential differ-ences in the nature of tumor or immortalized cells and primary parenchymal cells, a human adrenocortical cell line would facilitate investigations into the molecular parameters that regulate DHEA synthesis. The human adrenocortical cell line NCI-H295 appears to have retained the capacity to express all adrenal steroidogenic enzymes. Gazdar and colleagues[9] established the NCI-H295 cell line from an invasive primary adrenocortical carcinoma. The patient from whom the cell line was established showed signs of mineralocorticoid, glucocorticoid, and androgen excess. The tumor (a $14 \times 13 \times 11$-cm right adrenal mass) was surgically removed in

[a]These studies were supported in part by the National Institutes of Health (AG08175 and DK43140), American Heart Association (Texas Affiliate 93R-082), and Merck Sharp and Dohme. I. M. B. was also supported by National Institute of Health training grant T32-HD-07190.
[b]Address for correspondence.

December 1980. A portion of the adrenal tumor was finely minced and placed in culture in microwells using a variety of growth media. Because of fibroblast growth, a population of tumor cells that grew as a suspension was used to establish the H295 cell line. The initial description of the steroidogenic properties of the H295 cell line was performed after the cells had been in culture for 7–10 years. More than 30 steroids were detected in the culture medium from H295 cells, of which about 20 were identified. Importantly, depending on the culture conditions, the major steroids produced by these cells were glucocorticoids and C_{19}-steroids. Thus, these cells represented the first report of a human adrenal cell line which maintained the ability to secrete both C_{19}- and C_{21}-adrenocortical steroids. The ability of H295 cells to secrete C_{19}-steroids in response to activators of the protein kinase A signaling pathway as well as to express transcripts for the range of adrenal steroid enzymes was later demonstrated.[10,11]

Herein, we demonstrate that these H295 cells also retain a range of hormonal responsiveness and secrete steroids similar to those seen in normal human adrenocortical cells. The ability of these cells to produce cortisol, androstenedione, DHEA, and DHEAS suggests that these cells may well act as a model system to determine the factors controlling the production of C_{19}-steroids, the so-called adrenal androgens, and glucocorticosteroids.

MATERIALS AND METHODS

Cell Culture and Experimental Treatment

Human NCI-H295 adrenal tumor cells were obtained from the American Type Culture Collection (Rockville, Maryland). Cells were maintained in an equal mixture (v/v) of Dulbecco's modified Eagle's and Ham's F12 media (DME-F12) containing insulin (1 μg/ml), transferrin (1 μg/ml), selenium (1 ng/ml), linoleic acid (1 μg/ml), BSA (1.25 mg/m) added in the form of 1% ITS plus (Collaborative Research, Bedford, Massachusetts), and 2% Ultroser SF (Sepracor, Inc., Marlborough, Massachusetts) and antibiotics. Stock cultures were grown at 37°C on 75-cm² tissue culture plates (Costar, Cambridge, Massachusetts) in a humidified atmosphere of air (5 l/min) supplemented with carbon dioxide (0.2 l/min). Selection of an H295 cell population which remained attached during culture has been described. For experiments, cells were subcultured and after 48 hours rinsed and placed in fresh serum-free medium containing 0.01% BSA (defined medium) and treated with ACTH (Cortrosyn), forskolin, or dibutyryl cyclic AMP (dbcAMP). Cortrosyn (ACTH 1-24) was obtained from Organon (West Orange, New Jersey). Forskolin, angiotensin II (AII), 12-O-tetradecanoylphorbol 13-acetate (TPA), and dbcAMP were obtained from Sigma Chemical Co. (St. Louis, Missouri).

Analysis of Steroidogenic Enzyme Activity

Cells were washed in DME-F12 and incubated for 6 hours with 0.5 ml of medium consisting of DME-F12 and antibiotics supplemented with 2.5 μM pregnenolone, 100,000 dpm/ml [³H]pregnenolone (New England Nuclear-DuPont), and a potent 3β-hydroxysteroid dehydrogenase inhibitor, 4MA (17β-N,N-diethylcarbamoyl-4-diethyl-4-aza-5α-androstane-3-one, 1 μM; Merck Research Laboratories, Rahway, New Jersey). At the end of the incubation, medium was recovered and extracted with methylene chloride (2×3 ml), and the combined extracts were dried under air, reconstituted in methylene chloride (0.5 ml), and dried before final reconstitution (0.05 ml). Samples were then applied to Silica Gel 60 F254 plastic-backed TLC plates (EM Science, Gibbstown, New Jersey) and developed twice in chloroform-ethyl acetate (90:10, vol/vol). 17α-Hydroxylase activity was computed from the fractional conversion of pregnenolone to 17α-hydroxypregnenolone and DHEA, as identified against authentic standards. Results were expressed as nanomoles per milligram of protein per 2 hours.

Stimulation of Steroid Secretion and Analysis of Steroids

To assess the effects of treatment on steroid secretion, experiments were performed in media containing 0.5% LPSR-1 (Sigma Chemical Co.) containing 1% antibiotics. Cells subcultured onto 24-well plates were maintained for 24 hours in DMEM/F12 containing 0.5% LPSR-1. Medium was then renewed (1 ml/well) and treatment begun with the agents shown for a 48-hour period. The DHEA content of media recovered from each well was determined using an assay kit from Diagnostic Products Corp, Los Angeles, California. The cortisol or aldosterone contents of media were determined against cortisol or aldosterone standards, respectively, prepared in defined medium, using coated tube immunoassays from Diagnostic System Laboratories, Webster, Texas. Results of steroid assays were normalized to cellular protein per well and expressed as nanomoles per milligram of cell protein.

Protein Determination

Cells were solubilized in Tris-HCl (50 mM, pH 7.4), containing NaCl (150 mM), SDS (1%), EGTA (5 mM), $MgCl_2$ (0.5 mM), $MnCl_2$ (0.5 mM), and phenylmethylsulfonylfluoride (PMSF, 0.2 mM) and stored frozen at $-20°C$. Protein content of samples was then determined by bicinchoninic acid protein assay, using the BCA assay kit (Pierce, Rockford, Illinois).

Protein Separation and Immunoblotting Analysis

Protein samples were separated by polyacrylamide (12%) SDS gel electrophoresis at constant voltage. Proteins were then transferred to Immobilon P membrane (Millipore, Milford, Massachusetts) using a Transblot apparatus (Hoefer, San Francisco, California) at 100 V for 1.5 hours, in a transfer buffer of 20 mM Tris, 150 mM glycine, and 20% methanol. The Immobilon membrane was preblocked using a blocking buffer (10 mM Tris pH 7.4, 150 mM NaCl, 0.2% Nonidet P-40, 0.5% dried skimmed milk), before incubating with primary antibody (10 μg/ml in 10 mM Tris pH 7.4, 150 mM NaCl) for 2 hours. The membrane was then washed twice more in blocking buffer and incubated for 1 hour with [125I]-protein A (ICN Biomedicals, Irvine, CA) before final repeated washing (for 1 hour). Specific binding to the membrane was quantified by direct imaging (AMBIS) before final exposure to Kodak X-Omat AR film at $-70°C$. Primary antisera were those raised against human P450c17 (kindly provided by Dr. M. Waterman, Vanderbilt University) and human placental 3β-HSD.

Northern Analysis

Cells on 100-mm culture dishes were treated as described and then lysed at 4°C into 1 ml RNAzol B solution (Cinna Biotecx, Houston, Texas) before transfer to a microfuge tube. Phase separation was achieved by mixing with 0.15 ml CHCl$_3$, incubation at 4°C for 5 minutes, and centrifugation (12,000 × g; 20 minutes; 4°C). The upper phase (0.7 ml) was transferred to a second microfuge tube, and RNA was then precipitated by the addition of 0.8 ml isopropanol and standing for 1 hour at −20°C. RNA was recovered by centrifugation (30 minutes; 12,000 × g ; 4°C) and the recovered pellet was washed once in 75% ethanol (1.0 ml) before drying under air and dissolving in 1 mM EDTA, pH 7.0 (0.1 ml). After determination of recovery and purity by measuring absorbance at 260 and 280 nm, samples were precipitated by the addition of 1 ml absolute ethanol and 0.01 ml sodium acetate (3 M; pH 5.2) and stored at −70°C before analysis.

Samples were separated by electrophoresis on gels containing 1.1% agarose in the presence of formaldehyde. The presence and integrity of the major RNA species were examined under ultraviolet light to ensure consistency between lanes. RNA was transferred to a Magna NT membrane (MSI) by pressure blotting (75 psi, 1 hour; PossiBlot Pressure Blotter, Stratagene, La Jolla, California) and cross-linked under UV light. Prehybridization was carried out at 42°C overnight in a final buffer composition of 50% formamide, 5 × SSC, 1 × PE, and 50 mg/ml transfer RNA (20 × SSC contains 3.0 M NaCl and 0.3 M trisodium citrate, pH 7.0; 5 × PE contains 250 mM Tris-HCl [pH 7.5], 0.5% sodium pyrophosphate, 5% sodium dodecyl sulfate [SDS], 1% polyvinylpyrrolidone, 1% Ficoll, 25 mM EDTA, and 1% BSA). Hybridizations were performed sequentially in the same buffer at 42°C for 16–24 hours using antisense probes to 3β-HSD, then P450c17 and finally P450scc. Each antisense probe was labeled with [^{32}P] by asymmetric PCR in the presence of [^{32}P]dCTP; Amersham, Arlington Heights, Illinois. The blots were then washed in 2 × SSC containing 0.1% SDS at room temperature for 15 minutes and in 0.1 × SSC containing 0.1% SDS at room temperature for 2 × 30 minutes before direct radioimaging quantification of bound probe (Quantprobe V3.02, Ambis Systems Inc, San Diego, California) and exposure to film (Hyperfilm, Amersham). Blots were subsequently stripped by repeated washing in 0.1 × SSC/0.5% SDS at 65°C and checked for lack of radioactivity before reprobing. Finally, all blots were probed for glyceraldehyde 3-phosphate dehydrogenase (G3PDH) mRNA using an antisense probe generated by asymmetric polymerase chain reactions against bases 39–900 of the human cDNA and bound probe quantified as just described. Binding of G3PDH probe per lane was then used to normalize data for P450c17, P450scc, and 3β-HSD mRNA against minor variations in the RNA loading of the lanes.

Probe Preparation

Antisense probes were prepared by polymerase chain reaction in a 50-μl volume under standard conditions, but with the following modifications: forward to reverse primers were added at a 1:100 ratio (0.3 and 30 pmol), the free dCTP concentration reduced to 5 μM, and the addition of 50 μCi [^{32}P]dCTP (3000 Ci/mmol, Amersham). Template was added at 10 ng per kilobase. Labeling was performed through 40 cycles. Incorporation of label was routinely 60–75% by this procedure. Templates and oligonucleotides were as follows: Human P450c17 probe template was pCD-17αH[26] and the forward and reverse oligonucleotides were 5′-GCACCAAGACTA-CAGTG-3′ and 5′-ACTGACGGTGAGATGAG-3′. Human 3β-hydroxysteroid dehydrogenase (3β-HSD) probe template was the BglII/BglII sequence of human Type II cDNA (in PCR1000), and the forward and reverse oligonucleotides were 5'-CTCTCCAGCATCTTCTG-3' and 5'-TCACTACTTCCAGCAGG-3'. Human cytochrome P450-side chain cleavage (P450scc) probe template was a complete cDNA in Bluescript, kindly provided by Dr. Michael Waterman (Vanderbilt University). Forward and reverse oligonucleotides were 5'-TCTCCTGGTGACAATGG-3' and 5'-CTTGCACCAGTGTCTTG-3', respectively.

RESULTS

We have previously shown that treatment of H295 cells with elevated K$^+$ or AII results in an increase in [Ca^{2+}]$_i$ and increased aldosterone secretion.[12,13] The data shown in FIGURE 1 extend these findings to show the effects of K$^+$ (14 mM) on secretion of aldosterone, DHEA, and cortisol. Elevation of medium K$^+$ to 14 mM resulted in a 3.7-fold increase in DHEA secretion, but also increased secretion of aldosterone (3.5-fold) and, to a lesser extent, cortisol (2.9-fold) over a 48-hour period. These findings differ from those for AII (10 nM), which gave a greater increase in aldosterone secretion (5.7-fold) but lesser increases in DHEA (2.2-fold) and cortisol (2.7-fold) secretions. The effects of K$^+$ also contrast with those of dbcAMP which had the greatest effect on DHEA (23.0-fold) and cortisol (7.9-fold) secretions but a similar effect (3.3-fold) on aldosterone secretion. In contrast, treatment with TPA, a potent activator of protein kinase C, had little or no effect on DHEA, cortisol, or aldosterone secretion.

In addition to the stimulatory action of AII on aldosterone secretion in H295 cells, AII can also attenuate the positive effects of dbcAMP on DHEA and cortisol secretion. The data shown in FIGURE 1 confirm that in combination with dbcAMP, AII further increased aldosterone secretion, but attenuated the secretion of DHEA and cortisol over a 48-hour period. Combined treatment with dbcAMP and potassium also resulted in increased aldosterone, but it had a lesser attenuative effect on DHEA secretion and no effect on cortisol secretion compared to that of dbcAMP alone. However, combined treatment with TPA and dbcAMP resulted in almost no change in aldosterone secretion, but a marked attenuation in both DHEA and cortisol secretion.

Treatment of H295 cells with AII and dbcAMP or forskolin was previously shown to alter the expression of key steroid-metabolizing enzymes such as P450scc, P450c17, and 3β-HSD[25,34] within 20 hours. The results of northern blot analysis of changes in the levels of P450scc, P450c17, and 3β-HSD mRNA in response to the various effectors are shown in FIGURE 2. Time-dependent increases in the levels of P450c17 mRNA were seen with as little as 3 hours of treatment with K$^+$ and continued to increase thereafter (data not shown). Although more modest increases in P450scc were also seen, there was no effect on 3β-HSD mRNA at any time. Treatment with forskolin or dbcAMP most potently increased the levels of mRNA for P450c17 and to a lesser extent P450scc and 3β-HSD. AII treatment also increased mRNA levels for 3β-HSD and had a lesser effect on mRNA for both P450c17 and P450scc. While increased K$^+$ had no effect on 3β-HSD, the effect on P450c17 mRNA was greater than that of AII, but the effect on P450scc was similar in each case. On the other hand, phorbol ester treatment markedly increased 3β-HSD mRNA levels while suppressing the basal level of P450c17 mRNA.

These changes in the level of P450c17 mRNA were paralleled by changes in 17α-hydroxylase activity. Increased K$^+$ increased this activity to a level comparable to that in response to AII, while treatment with TPA resulted in a decrease in activity

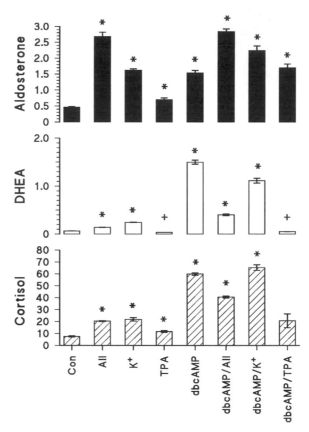

FIGURE 1. Effects of angiotensin II, potassium, TPA, and dbcAMP on the secretion of aldosterone, DHEA, and cortisol. Cells were treated for 48 hours in fresh media alone (control) or media containing AII (10 nM), K^+ (14 mM), TPA (10 nM), or dbcAMP (1 mM). At the end of this time, media were removed and assayed for aldosterone, DHEA, and cortisol as described. Cells were solubilized in protein lysis buffer and assayed for protein. Values represent the mean ± SE of data from one of two identical experiments, each performed with quadruplicate incubations, and are expressed as nanomoles of steroid per milligram of cellular protein per 48-hours.

(FIG. 3). Although AII and especially TPA attenuated the marked dbcAMP-promoted increase in 17α-hydroxylase activity, increased K^+ levels did not modulate the action of dbcAMP treatment on 17α-hydroxylase activity. It is noteworthy that all these changes in 17α-hydroxylase activity in response to 48 hours of treatment with AII, K^+, and TPA alone or in combination with dbcAMP correlated closely with changes in DHEA and cortisol secretion (FIG. 1), both of which depend on 17α-hydroxylase for their synthesis.

The results of western immunoblot analysis of levels of P450c17 and 3β-HSD proteins from H295 cells after various treatments are shown in FIGURE 4. Changes in P450c17 immunodetectable protein were consistent with those for P450c17 mRNA and the activity just described. Quantitatively, although each treatment increased the level of immunodetectable 3β-HSD protein twofold above basal, combined treatment with forskolin and TPA was not additive as was observed with mRNA, suggesting that posttranscriptional regulation of enzyme expression may also be occurring. Although the probe employed for northern analysis cannot distinguish between type I and type II isoforms of human 3β-HSD, western blot analysis indicates that the principal isoform expressed in H295 cells after various treatments remains the type II isoform as judged by its increased mobility on gel compared to the type I isoform stably expressed in human embryonic kidney 293 cells.

DISCUSSION

The H295 cell has the apparent properties of a pluripotent adrenocortical cell which, on activation of the protein kinase A pathway with agents such as forskolin or dbcAMP, induces fasciculata/reticularis-like function, that is, increased cortisol/DHEA secretion, due primarily to a marked increase in 17α-hydroxylase expression.[10,12] Alternatively, treatment with AII and subsequent activation of phospholipase C develop a glomerulosa-like functionality characterized by elevated aldosterone secretion, markedly increased aldosterone synthase expression, but low 17α-

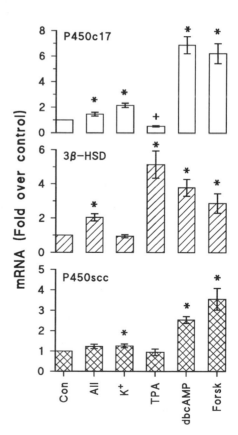

FIGURE 2. Changes in level of mRNA coding P450c17, P450scc, and 3β-HSD in response to steroidogenic agonists. Cells were maintained as described for the times shown in the presence of forskolin (10 μM), dbcAMP (1 mM), TPA (10 nM), AII (10 nM), or K⁺ (14 mM). Medium was then removed, and cellular RNA recovered and subjected to northern analysis, probing sequentially for 3β-HSD, P450c17, and P450scc mRNA. Results were quantified directly by radioimaging analysis and normalized to levels of G3PDH mRNA in the same lane. Results shown are the combined data (mean ± SE) from at least three independent experiments in each case. Data are expressed as levels relative to control at time zero.

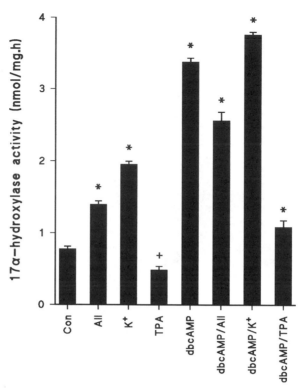

FIGURE 3. Effects of angiotensin II, K^+, phorbol ester, and dbcAMP on 17α-hydroxylase activity. Cells were treated for 48 hours in fresh media alone (control) or containing AII (10 nM), K^+ (14 mM), TPA (10 nM), or dbcAMP (1 mM). At the end of this time, media were removed and cells assayed for 17α-hydroxylase activity by metabolism of exogenous pregnenolone (2.5 μM, 4 hours) in the presence of a 3β-HSD inhibitor (4MA, 1 μM), as described. After recovery of medium for TLC analysis, cells were solubilized in protein lysis buffer and assayed for protein as described. Results are the mean ±SE of data from one of two identical experiments, each performed with quadruplicate incubations, and activity expressed as nanomoles per milligram of cellular protein per hour.

hydroxylase expression and little secretion of 17α-hydroxylated steroids.[10,14] Treatment with K^+, which acts to increase $[Ca^{2+}]_i$ through the opening of dihydropyridine-sensitive Ca^{2+} channels in H295 cells,[13] also results in increased dehydroepiandrosterone secretion in addition to increased aldosterone production.[12] The results of this study show further that this increase in DHEA secretion in response to K^+ was accompanied by an increase in P450c17 mRNA, as observed previously in response to AII.[14,15] Surprisingly, however, treatment of H295 cells with K^+ also increased expression of 17α-hydroxylase, as measured at the level of mRNA and activity, together with increased secretion of DHEA as well as cortisol. These effects of K^+ on 17α-hydroxylase expression exceed those of AII, so enhancing overall steroidogenic capacity rather than just aldosterone secretion.

Increased expression of 17α-hydroxylase is regulated by agents such as ACTH *in vivo* and forskolin or dbcAMP *in vitro*, which increase cellular cAMP and/or activate protein kinase A.[3,4,16] Agents such as AII, however, activate phosphoinositidase C in adrenocortical cells, resulting in increased $[Ca^{2+}]_i$ (through both release of intracellular stores and influx through plasma membrane Ca^{2+} channels) and activation of protein kinase C (through release of diacylglycerol).[17,18] Studies using H295 cells loaded with Fura 2 previously showed that K^+ increases $[Ca^{2+}]_i$ through the opening of nifedipine-sensitive voltage-dependent Ca^{2+} channels in the plasma membrane.[13] Thus, as seen in other mammalian adrenocortical cells,[19] treatment with K^+ activates a Ca^{2+} signaling pathway alone, whereas treatment with AII additionally stimulates protein kinase C and neither is classically regarded as signaling through direct coupling to adenylyl cyclase. However, in many cells "cross-talking" occurs between signaling pathways, and we previously hypothesized that AII may increase 17α-hydroxylase expression through indirectly increasing cAMP levels.[20] Our findings in this study suggest that such an explanation for the action of K^+ on 17α-hydroxylase expression is not valid. In addition to monitoring the effects of these and other agents on 17α-hydroxylase expression, we also studied their effects on P450scc and 3β-HSD at the level of mRNA. Both P450scc and 3β-HSD expression are increased in response to activation of protein kinase A, and 3β-HSD expression is also increased by protein kinase C activation in these cells[12] (also, Bird, Rainey, and Mason, unpublished data). While K^+ increased 17α-hydroxylase and, to a lesser extent, P450scc mRNA, it was without effect on levels of 3β-HSD mRNA. Thus, K^+ must have induced 17α-hydroxylase expression through a non-cAMP signaling mechanism which was not protein kinase C-mediated because TPA suppressed 17α-hydroxylase expression and increased 3β-HSD expression. Other evidence suggests that K^+ can regulate 17α-hydroxylase through a Ca^{2+} second messenger system (data not shown). First, BAYK8644 treatment reproduced the effects of K^+ on P450c17 mRNA, 17α-hydroxylase activity, and steroid secretion. Secondly, calcium channel blocker nifedipine blocked the action of K^+ on P450c17 mRNA. Thus, it seems likely that the intracellular signal controlling K^+-induced P450c17 expression is Ca^{2+}. (Previous studies in H295 cells using the calcium ionophore A23187 also reported a modest

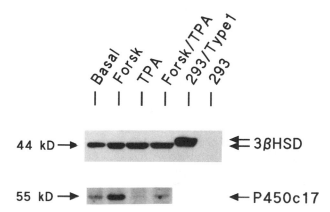

FIGURE 4. Western analysis of immunodetectable P450c17 and 3β-HSD in H295 cells in response to steroidogenic agonists. Protein (75 μg/lane) recovered from H295 cells treated as outlined with forskolin (10 μM), TPA (10 nM), or a combination was separated by polyacrylamide/SDS gel electrophoresis, transferred to a nylon membrane, and immunoblotted as described in Methods. Lysates of human embryonic kidney 293 cells stably transfected with human 3β-HSD type I and nontransfected 293 cells were also applied to separate lanes.

increase in P450c17 and P450scc mRNA in 6–12 hours, but a decline thereafter, an effect that may be attributed to long-term cellular toxicity by A23187,[21] as reported in other steroidogenic cells.[22]) Because AII also increases $[Ca^{2+}]_i$ and TPA does not reproduce this effect in H295 cells, it also seems likely that the small increase in P450c17 expression observed in response to AII treatment is also a direct consequence of increased $[Ca^{2+}]_i$.

The expression of P450c17 is principally transcriptionally regulated[23,24] and much is known about the regulatory elements that control transcription.[16,24] Two cAMP-responsive elements (CRS1 and CRS2) have been demonstrated in the bovine CYP17 gene, and studies of bovine CYP17 constructs suggest that attenuation of expression by protein kinase C is mediated through a sequence identical to or overlapping CRS1.[25] Our studies in H295 cells, as in bovine adrenocortical cells, show that combinations of dbcAMP or forskolin with AII result in attenuated expression of P450c17 and a corresponding increase in aldosterone secretion together with a marked decrease in 17α-hydroxylated steroids such as DHEA or cortisol. This action of AII is apparently mediated through the protein kinase C pathway because TPA is also a potent attenuator of dbcAMP or forskolin-induced P450c17 expression. In contrast to the action of AII and TPA, however, combined treatment of H295 cells with dbcAMP and K^+ failed to attenuate and in fact marginally increased dbcAMP-induced P450c17 expression and cortisol secretion. Although some decrease in DHEA secretion was observed, this was much less than that seen in response to dbcAMP with AII or TPA. Our data suggest that there may be an additional Ca^{2+} responsive element yet to be identified in the CYP17 gene in the human and possibly other mammalian species. Furthermore, activation of this element by increases in $[Ca^{2+}]_i$ does not appear to impair increased transcription in response to cAMP via CRS1 or CRS2 sequences. Thus, these findings suggest that the control of transcription of genes encoding key steroidogenic enzymes may occur in response to changes in $[Ca^{2+}]_i$ as well as the more well characterized protein kinase A and protein kinase C signaling pathways, and so reveals a further level of complexity in the control of zonal function in the adrenal cortex.

SUMMARY

In vitro studies of human adrenal androgen synthesis are limited because of the difficulties in obtaining adrenals. We describe the use of the human adrenocortical tumor H295 cell line as a model to evaluate mechanisms controlling C_{19}-steroid production. The cells were characterized with regard to responsiveness to a variety of agents as measured by steroid secretion and induction of 17α-hydroxylase cytochrome P450 (P450c17) expression, a key enzyme in C_{19}-steroid production. Forskolin and dibutyryl cAMP, which were more effective than ACTH, enhanced the production of DHEA and androstenedione over a 48-hour treatment period. Agents that act by increasing intracellular calcium (angiotensin II and K^+ ions) as well as protein kinase A pathway activators (ACTH, forskolin, and dibutyryl cAMP) individually increased the mRNA levels and activity of P450c17. In addition, angiotensin II but not K^+ ions attenuated the increased expression promoted by the kinase A agonists. Thus, the complexity of human adrenal P450c17 expression through multiple signaling pathways may contribute importantly to the diverse patterns of human adrenocortical steroidogenesis.

REFERENCES

1. GENAZZANI, A. R., J. H. H. THIJSSEN & P. K. SIITERI, EDS. 1980. Adrenal Androgens. Raven Press. New York.
2. PARKER, L. N. 1989. Adrenal Androgens in Clinical Medicine. Academic Press, Inc. San Diego, California.
3. HANUKOGLU, I. 1992. Steroidogenic enzymes: Structure, function, and role in regulation of steroid hormone biosynthesis. J. Steroid Biochem. Mol. Biol. **43:** 779–804.
4. SIMPSON, E. R. & M. R. WATERMAN. 1988. Regulation of the synthesis of steroidogenic enzymes in adrenal cortical cells by ACTH. Annu. Rev. Physiol. **50:** 427–440.
5. NEVILLE, A. M. & M. J. O'HARE. 1982. The Human Adrenal Cortex: Pathology and Biology—An Integrated Approach. Springer-Verlag. New York.
6. HORNSBY, P. J. & J. M. MCALLISTER. 1991. Culturing steroidogenic cells. Methods Enzymol. **206:** 371–380.
7. CHENG, C. Y., M. V. FIASCH & P. J. HORNSBY. 1992. Expression of 17 alpha-hydroxylase and 3 beta-hydroxysteroid dehydrogenase in fetal human adrenocortical cells transfected with SV40 T antigen. J. Mol. Endocrinol. **9:** 7–17.
8. MASON, J. I., B. R. CARR & W. E. RAINEY. 1986. The action of phorbol ester on steroidogenesis in cultured human fetal adrenal cells. Endocr. Res. **12:** 447–467.
9. GAZDAR, A. F., H. K. OIE, C. H. SHACKLETON, T. R. CHEN, T. J. TRICHE, C. E. MYERS, G. P. CHROUSOS, M. F. BRENNAN, C. A. STEIN & R. V. LA ROCCA. 1990. Line that expresses multiple pathways of steroid biosynthesis. Cancer Res. **50:** 5488–5496.
10. RAINEY, W. E., I. M. BIRD, C. SAWETAWAN, N. A. HANLEY, J. L. MCCARTHY, E. A. MCGEE, R. WESTER & J. I. MASON. 1993. Regulation of human adrenal carcinoma cell (NCI-H295) production of C19 steroids. J. Clin. Endocrinol. Metab. **77:** 731–737.
11. STAELS, B., D. W. HUM & W. L. MILLER. 1993. Regulation of steroidogenesis in NCI-H295 cells: A model for the human fetal adrenal. Mol. Endocrinol. **7:** 423–433.
12. RAINEY, W. E., I. M. BIRD & J. I. MASON. 1994. The NCI-H295 cell line: A pluripotent model for human adrenocortical studies. Mol. Cell Endocrinol. **100:** 45–50.
13. BIRD, I. M., R. A. WORD, C. CLYNE, J. I. MASON & W. E. RAINEY. 1995. Potassium negatively regulates angiotensin II type 1 receptor expression in human adrenocortical H295R cells. Hypertension. In press.
14. BIRD, I. M., N. A. HANLEY, A. R. WORD, J. M. MATHIS, J. L. MCCARTHY, J. I. MASON & W. E. RAINEY. 1993. Human NCI-H295 adrenocortical carcinoma cells: A model for angiotensin II-responsive aldosterone secretion. Endocrinology **133:** 1555–1561.
15. HOLLAND, O. B., J. M. MATHIS, I. M. BIRD & W. E. RAINEY. 1993. Angiotensin increases aldosterone synthase mRNA levels in human NCI-H295 cells. Mol. Cell. Endocrinol. **94:** R9–R13.
16. MOORE, C. C. & W. L. MILLER. 1991. The role of transcriptional regulation in steroid hormone biosynthesis. J. Steroid Biochem. Mol. Biol. **40:** 517–525.
17. BIRD, I. M., S. W. WALKER & B. C. WILLIAMS. 1990. Agonist-stimulated turnover of the phosphoinositides and the regulation of adrenocortical steroidogenesis. J. Mol. Endocrinol. **5:** 191–209.
18. CATT, K. J., T. BALLA, A. J. BAUKAL, W. P. HAUSDORFF & G. AGUILERA. 1988. Control of glomerulosa cell function by angiotensin II: Transduction by G-proteins and inositol polyphosphates. Clin. Exp. Pharmacol. **15:** 501–515.
19. QUINN, S. J. & G. H. WILLIAMS. 1992. Regulation of aldosterone secretion. *In* The Adrenal Gland, 2nd Ed. V. H. T. James, Ed. Ch. 8:159–189. Raven Press. New York.
20. BIRD, I. M., J. I. MASON, K. OKA & W. E. RAINEY. 1993. Angiotensin-II stimulates an increase in cAMP and expression of 17α-hydroxylase cytochrome P450 in fetal bovine adrenocortical cells. Endocrinology **132:** 932–934.
21. FARESE, R. V., M. A. SABIR & R. E. LARSON. 1981. A23187 inhibits adrenal protein synthesis and the effects of ACTH on steroidogenesis and phospholipid metabolism in rat adrenal cells *in vitro.* Endocrinology **108:** 1243–1246.
22. NAKAMURA, M. & P. F. HALL. 1978. Inhibition of steroidogenic response to corticotropin in mouse adrenal tumour cells (Y-1) by the ionophore A23187. Role of protein synthesis. Biochim. Biophys. Acta **542:** 330–339.

23. ZUBER, M. X., M. E. JOHN, T. OKAMURA, E. R. SIMPSON & M. R. WATERMAN. 1986. Bovine adrenocortical P-450$_{17\alpha}$: Regulation of gene expression by ACTH and elucidation of primary sequence. J. Biol. Chem. **261:** 2475–2482.
24. WATERMAN, M. R., N. KAGAWA, U. M. ZANGER, K. MOMOI, J. LUND & E. R. SIMPSON. 1992. Comparison of cAMP-responsive DNA sequences and their binding proteins associated with expression of the bovine CYP17 and CYP11A and human CYP21B genes. J. Steroid Biochem. Mol. Biol. **43:** 931–935.
25. BAKKE, M. & J. LUND. 1992. A novel 3',5'-cyclic adenosine monophosphate-responsive sequence in the bovine CYP17 gene is a target of negative regulation by protein kinase C. Mol. Endocrinol. **6:** 1323–1331.

Human Dehydroepiandrosterone Sulfotransferase

Purification, Molecular Cloning, and Characterization[a]

CHARLES N. FALANY,[b,c] KATHLEEN A. COMER,[b]
THOMAS P. DOOLEY,[d] AND HANSRUEDI GLATT[e]

[b]Department of Pharmacology and Toxicology
University of Alabama at Birmingham
Birmingham, Alabama 35294

[d]Southwest Foundation of Biomedical Research
San Antonio, Texas 78228

[e]Department of Toxicology
Deutsches Institute für Ernährungsforschung
Potsdam, Germany

Sulfation is an important reaction in the biotransformation of steroids in human tissues and is one of the major Phase II conjugation reactions involved in the biotransformation of drugs and xenobiotics. Sulfation involves the transfer of a sulfonate group from 3'-phosphoadenosine 5'-phosphosulfate (PAPS) to an acceptor compound to form either a sulfate ester or a sulfamate. The transfer of the sulfonate group is catalyzed by a family of enzymes termed the sulfotransferases (STs). All of the mammalian STs use PAPS as the donor of the sulfonate group. Both membrane-bound and cytosolic forms of ST are present in human tissues; however, only cytosolic STs have been reported to sulfate steroids and be involved in drug and xenobiotic metabolism. The membrane-bound STs are localized in the Golgi apparatus of the cell and are responsible for the sulfation of glycosaminoglycans, glycoproteins, and tyrosines in proteins and peptides. The majority of sulfated glycosaminoglycans, glycoproteins, and proteins are subsequently secreted by the Golgi apparatus. Golgi-associated STs are not believed to be involved in steroid and xenobiotic sulfation.

Steroid sulfation is a significant process in the synthesis and metabolism of steroids in human tissues. The addition of the charged sulfonate group to either an aliphatic or phenolic hydroxyl group on a steroid results in the formation of a sulfate moiety with a pKa of approximately 2. The presence of the charged sulfate group greatly enhances the aqueous solubility of the steroid and thereby decreases its biological activity and increases its excretion. Steroid sulfates are not capable of binding and activating steroid receptors. The most abundant steroid sulfate formed in human tissues is dehydroepiandrosterone sulfate (DHEAS). The sulfation of DHEA is shown in FIGURE 1. Circulating levels of DHEAS in the plasma are in the 2–20 μM range and result primarily from the synthesis and secretion of DHEAS

[a]This research was supported in part by National Institutes of Health grant GM38953 to C.N.F.
[c]Address for correspondence: Charles N. Falany, PhD, Department of Pharmacology and Toxicology, 1670 University Blvd., University of Alabama at Birmingham, Birmingham, AL 35294.

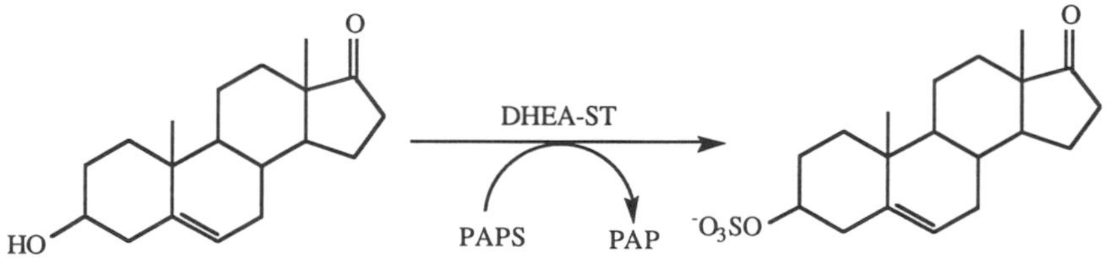

FIGURE 1. Sulfation of dehydroepiandrosterone catalyzed by DHEA-ST.

from the adrenal glands. DHEAS in the circulation may serve as a transport form for the steroid which may be converted into either androgens or estrogens in peripheral tissues.[1] The high levels of estrogen sulfates detected in plasma of pregnant women are also derived from DHEAS synthesized by the fetal adrenals. DHEAS is converted to estrogen sulfates in the fetal liver or in the placenta. Humans differ from laboratory animals such as rats, mice, and rabbits in that the large quantities of steroid sulfates present in the human circulation are not observed in these species. The physiologic role for the synthesis of large amounts of steroid sulfates in humans is not well understood.

Four forms of cytosolic ST have been identified in human tissues[2,3]: estrogen ST (hEST), two forms of phenol ST (the phenol-sulfating form, hP-PST, and the monoamine-sulfating form, hM-PST), and dehydroepiandrosterone ST (hDHEA-ST). Three of the human cytosolic STs are involved in the sulfation of steroids.[4–6] hP-PST is capable of conjugating the 3-phenolic group of estrogens but does not sulfate hydroxysteroids.[7] hEST has a high affinity for estrogen sulfation and is also capable of conjugating DHEA and pregnenolone but with a 1,500-fold lower affinity than that for estrogens.[6] hDHEA-ST sulfates both hydroxysteroids and estrogens. The small number of identified forms of cytosolic STs in human tissues differs from the situation in rats where at least six forms of PST,[8–11] six forms of hydroxysteroid ST,[8,12–14] and two forms of EST have been identified.[15]

This review briefly describes our current understanding of the biochemistry and molecular biology of human DHEA-ST and its role in steroid metabolism and carcinogen bioactivation. The activity and properties of DHEA-ST are compared with those of the other human cytosolic STs as well as those of the hydroxysteroid STs identified in rat liver. The differences in steroid sulfation and especially in DHEAS synthesis in human tissues compared to rats may help define the possibly unique role of DHEAS in human tissues.

PURIFICATION OF DHEA-ST

The involvement of DHEA-ST in the synthesis and secretion of DHEAS from the human adrenal gland has been acknowledged for many years.[16] Only recently has the characterization of DHEA-ST activity in the sulfation of steroids and bile acids in human liver been significantly investigated.[4,17,18] To increase our understanding of the sulfation of DHEA, the enzyme was purified to apparent homogeneity from both human adrenal and liver cytosols using affinity chromatography as the essential purification step. Adams and McDonald[19] purified DHEA-ST activity from adrenal cytosol using ammonium sulfate precipitation and DHEA-Sepharose 4B affinity chromatography. Falany *et al.*[4] purified DHEA-ST activity 620-fold from liver cytosol using DEAE-Sepharose Cl-6B chromatography and 3′,5′-diphosphoadenosine (PAP)-agarose affinity chromatography. Comparison of the physical, kinetic, and immunologic properties of the liver and adrenal forms of the enzyme indicate that the enzymes are probably identical.[20]

Purified DHEA-ST has a subunit molecular mass of approximately 35,000 Da as estimated by SDS-polyacrylamide gel electrophoresis.[4,19] Enzymatically active DHEA-ST has a molecular mass of approximately 68,000 Da as estimated by gel exclusion chromatography, indicating that the active form of the enzyme in tissues is most likely a dimer of two identical subunits.[4,19] Rabbit polyclonal antibodies raised to the liver form of DHEA-ST detect a single protein during immunoblot analysis of both human liver and adrenal cytosols.[20] The rabbit anti-liver DHEA-ST antibody does not react with the other three forms of human liver cytosolic ST. Additionally, human STs migrate with distinctly different masses during SDS-polyacrylamide gel electrophoresis which aids in their identification in tissue samples.[6,7,20] Immunoblot analysis of cytosols prepared from human livers did not reveal any size variants of DHEA-ST.[20]

Comparison of the levels of DHEA-ST activity in human liver cytosol with those of P-PST and M-PST does not indicate a significant correlation in their levels of expression.[5,21] Thus, expression of individual STs in human liver is apparently independently regulated. Aksoy *et al.*[21] analyzed individual variation in the levels of DHEA-ST activity in 94 adult human liver samples. DHEA-ST activity varied 4.6-fold in these liver samples, and mean activity ± SD was 317 ± 100 nmol/h/g tissue. No age-related or gender-dependent differences in the level of DHEA-ST activity were noted in these liver samples; however, a fraction of the population had significantly higher levels of activity. DHEA-ST activity assayed by bile salt sulfation was not significantly different in neonatal human liver from the activity found in adult

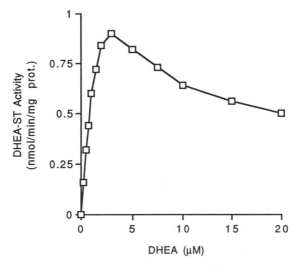

FIGURE 2. Effect of increasing DHEA concentrations on human DHEA-ST activity. The ability of partially purified human DHEA-ST expressed in *E. coli*[7] to sulfate increasing concentrations of DHEA (0.25–20 μM) was investigated. The concentration of 3′-phosphoadenosine 5′-phosphosulfate in the reactions was 25 μM. The formation of DHEA sulfate was assayed as described previously.[4]

A.

0.1 mm

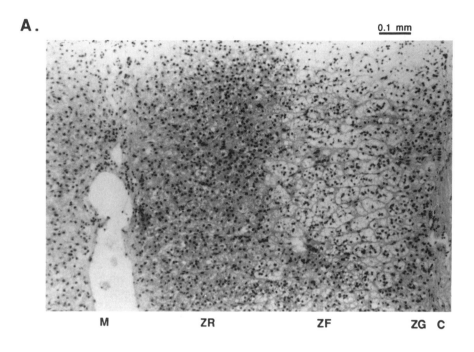

M   ZR   ZF   ZG C

B.

0.2 mm

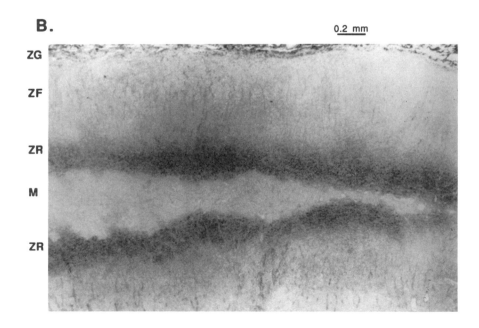

ZG

ZF

ZR

M

ZR

C.   0.1 mm

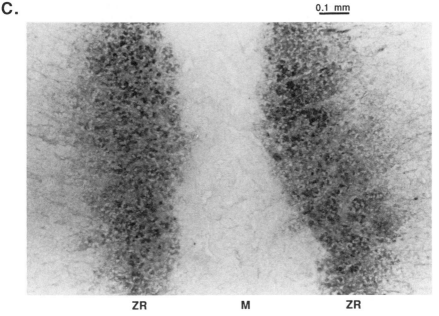

ZR   M   ZR

FIGURE 3. Immunogold localization of immunoreactive DHEA-ST in human adrenal tissue. Immunoreactive DHEA-ST was localized in human adrenal tissue (42-year-old man) using rabbit anti-human DHEA-ST IgG as the primary antibody.[20] Goat anti-rabbit IgG-gold conjugate was used as the secondary antibody and visualized by silver enhancement. The medulla (M), zona reticularis (ZR), zona fasciculata (ZF), and zona glomerulosa (ZG) are labeled. (**A**) Control (C) section of adrenal tissue stained with hematoxylin and eosin. (**B** and **C**) Bright field image of immunostained adrenal tissue.

livers. Also, bile salt sulfation activity in the liver of cholestatic infants was not significantly different from that in adult liver.[18] As with DHEA-ST, neither human PST activity displays either age- or gender-related differences in expression in human liver or platelets.[22] By comparison, hydroxysteroid ST activity in rats displays distinct gender-related differences in expression. DHEA sulfation is significantly greater in female than in male rats, and the levels of expression of the hydroxysteroid STs are regulated by growth hormone and steroid levels.[23–26]

Purified human liver DHEA-ST can sulfate the 3-hydroxyl group of all hydroxysteroids tested as well as the 17-hydroxyl of testosterone and the 3-phenolic hydroxyl of β-estradiol and estrone.[4] DHEA-ST was also reported to be responsible for the sulfation of the 3-hydroxy position of bile acids[17] and cholesterol in human liver.[27] Neither cortisol, corticosterone, betamethasone, nor dexamethasone was conjugated by liver DHEA-ST.[4,7] Sulfation of DHEA by purified liver DHEA-ST displays substrate inhibition. With increasing concentrations of DHEA in the reaction, maximal DHEA sulfation is observed at approximately 3 μM.[4] At higher DHEA concentrations, the rate of DHEA sulfation decreases but does not cease (FIG. 2). Substrate inhibition was not observed with increasing concentrations of PAPS in the reaction. Substrate inhibition is a common feature of STs and is observed with many structurally different substrates. It is believed to be the result of the formation of a nonproductive reversible enzyme–substrate–PAP complex due to the high affinity of

STs for the product of the reaction, PAP.[28] Therefore, comparison of the reactivity of STs with different substrates and analysis of the kinetic properties of the enzymes need to be carefully analyzed.

High levels of DHEA-ST activity were found in cytosol prepared from human liver and from both adult and fetal adrenal tissues.[4,19,20,29,30] In the adult human adrenal gland, tissue immunostaining of DHEA-ST occurs in the cortex. FIGURE 3 shows immunolocalization of DHEA-ST in the adult adrenal. Staining is most prominent in the reticular cell layer of the adrenal cortex and can be prevented by preabsorption of the rabbit anti-human liver DHEA-ST antibody with pure liver DHEA-ST before staining. No staining of DHEA-ST was evident in the adrenal medulla. Immunostaining of DHEA-ST in adult liver was localized to hepatocytes. Parker et al.[30] reported that DHEA-ST activity and immunoreactivity are more abundant in fetal cells than in neocortical cells in human fetal adrenal. This is consistent with the large quantities of DHEA sulfate produced by the human fetal adrenal during fetal development. DHEA-ST was also immunolocalized to epithelial cells in fetal intestinal villi, to liver hepatocytes, and to interstitial cells of the testis.

MOLECULAR CHARACTERIZATION OF HUMAN DHEA-ST

The isolation of a cDNA for human liver DHEA-ST has been reported by several research groups.[31–33] Translation of DHEA-ST cDNA results in a 285 amino acid protein with a calculated molecular mass of 33,765 Da. Northern blot analysis of RNA from both human liver and adrenal tissues with the DHEA-ST cDNA gives rise to three major bands.[33] These bands are approximately 1100, 1300, and 1800 nucleotides in length and represent messages with identical open-reading frames but variable 3'-nontranslated regions. It is not known if the different length messages for DHEA-ST are involved in regulating translation of messenger RNA. Otterness et al.[34,35] characterized the structure of the human DHEA-ST gene and localized the gene to chromosome region 19q13.3. These investigators reported the identification of only a single gene related to human DHEA-ST. The number of DNA fragments observed following Southern blot analysis of restriction enzyme-digested human genomic DNA is also consistent with a single human DHEA-ST gene.[33] The chromosomal localization of DHEA-ST is distinct from that of the PSTs which are localized to chromosome 16p12.1–p11.2.[36,37]

The cDNA for DHEA-ST has been expressed in both mammalian COS cells and in *Escherichia coli,* allowing for characterization of the expressed enzyme.[7,31–33] DHEA-ST expressed in both COS and *E. coli* cells can conjugate DHEA, and the enzyme has the same molecular mass as the native enzyme.[7,33] A comparison of the reactivity of bacterially expressed and partially purified DHEA-ST, P-PST, and EST with a number of steroids is shown in TABLE 1. The kinetic properties of DHEA-ST and P-PST expressed in bacteria are very similar to those observed with purified liver enzymes.[4,5,7,33] Of the steroids examined, DHEA-ST sulfates DHEA most efficiently with respect to the concentration generating maximal activity and to the rate of the reaction. Other 3-hydroxysteroids are rapidly conjugated irrespective of the orientation of the hydroxyl group. Human EST also conjugates DHEA; however, 10-fold higher concentrations of DHEA are necessary to observe maximal activity with EST compared to DHEA-ST.[6] In human liver, levels of EST are so low compared to those

TABLE 1. Sulfation of Steroids by Expressed Human DHEA-ST, P-PST, and EST

	Relative Activity[a,b]		
Steroids	DHEA-ST % (μM)	P-PST % (μM)	EST % (μM)
Dehydroepiandrosterone	100 (3 μM)	ND[c]	74 (30 μM)
Testosterone	26 (5 μM)	ND	ND
β-Estradiol	34 (20 μM)	45 (6 μM)	100 (20 nM)
Estrone	43 (25 μM)	100 (15 μM)	85 (20 nM)
Androsterone	65 (6 μM)	ND	53 (30 μM)
Dexamethasone	ND	ND	ND
Androstenediol	55 (12 μM)	ND	NT[d]
17α-Ethinylestradiol	14 (2 μM)	151 (1.5 μM)	355 (1 μM)

[a]ST activity is expressed relative to dehydroepiandrosterone sulfation for DHEA-ST, β-estradiol sulfation for P-PST and EST.
[b]Steroid sulfation activity was assayed with all three enzymes using steroid concentrations giving maximal activity.
[c]ND represents no detectable activity.
[d]NT indicates that the substrate was not tested with that ST.

of DHEA-ST that the conjugation of DHEA will essentially be completely catalyzed by DHEA-ST. P-PST does not sulfate hydroxysteroids or glucocorticoids[7] and M-PST does not sulfate estrogens, androgens, or glucocorticoids.[38]

FIGURE 4 compares amino acid sequences of the four human cytosolic STs that have been identified and cloned. DHEA-ST is 37% identical and 59% similar in

```
                  .          .          .          .          .          .     60
hP-PST    MELIQDTSRPPLEYVKGVPLIKYFAEALGPLQSFQARPDDLLISTYPKSGTTWVSQILDM
hM-PST                                                N
hEST      NSEL YYEKF  E H ILMY D VKYWDNVEA         V A            E VY
hDHEA-ST  SDDFLWFEGIAFPTM FRSETLRKVRDE.... VI DE VI L        N LAE  CL

                  .          .          .          .          .          .    120
hP-PST    IYQGGDLEKCHRAPIFMRVPFLEFKAPGIPSGMETLKDTPAPRLLKTHLPLALLPQTLLD
hM-PST             N    YV      VND E  L       P   I S
hEST      KE  V   KEDV  N I   CRKENLMN VKQ DEMNS  IV     PE    ASFWE
hDHEA-ST  MHSK  AKWIQSV  WE S WV SEI..... YTA SESES    FSS   IQ F KSFFS

                  .          .          .          .          .          .    180
hP-PST    QKVKVVYVARNAKDVAVSYYHFYHMAKVHPEPGTWDSFLEKFMVGEVSYGSWYQHVQEWW
hM-PST                  P           HR E A              A
hEST      KDC II LC         F Y FL VAG  N  SFPE V     Q Q P     K  KS
hDHEA-ST  S A    I LM  PR  L  G F WKNM FIKK  KS EEYF  W CQ T L     FD IHG M

                  .          .          .          .          .          .    240
hP-PST    ELSRTHPVLYLFYEDMKENPKREIQKILEFVGRSLPEETVDFMVQHTSFKEMKKNPMTNY
hM-PST                                          M
hEST      KGKSPR  F      L  DIRK VI LIH LE KPS  L  RIIH      Q     N  S
hDHEA-ST  PMREEKNF L S   EL QDTG T E   CQ L KT EP  ELNLILKNS  QS  E K S

                  .          .          .          .          .          .    296
hP-PST    TTVPQEFMDHSISPFMRKGMAGDWKTTFTVAQNERFDADYAKKMAGCSLTFRSEL*
hM-PST          L                                   E        S      *
hEST      L D I NQKL       IT      NH      L  K  KH EQQ KEST K   T I*
hDHEA-ST  SLLSVDYVVDK.AQLL     VS      NH      A D   KLFQE   DLPRELFPWE*
```

FIGURE 4. Comparison of the amino acid sequences of human cytosolic sulfotransferases. Amino acid sequences for hP-PST,[50] hM-PST,[38] hDHEA-ST,[33] and hEST[6] were aligned. Differences in the sequences when compared to the sequence of hP-PST are shown. *Asterisk* indicates a stop codon.

```
           1                                                          50
hDHEA-ST   MSDDFLWFEG IAFPTMGFRS ETLRKVRDEF VIRDEDVIIL TYPKSGTNWL
rSTa       M.P YT       P  AF IPK   QN CNK   VKE  L L
rST20      M.P YT       P HAF ISK   QN CNK   VK   L L  A
rST2-4     MS. YT       P AFW SK  I ENSCKK   VKED L
           51                                                        100
hDHEA-ST   AEILCLMHSK GDAKWIQSVP IWERSPWVES EIGYTALSES ESPRLFSSHL
rSTa       I  V  IQT    P       T   D    I T DL  DM IKK KG    IT
rST20      I  V  IQT    P       T   D    I T DV  DI IKK KG    MT
rST2-4     I  V  IQT    P       M   D    I T GS  DK TKM G     MT

           101                                                       150
hDHEA-ST   PIQLFPKSFF SSKAKVIYLM RNPRDVLVSG YFFWKNMKFI KKPKSWEEYF
rSTa         MH  S  L          I             Y   GKTTLA   D LGT V
rST20        MH  S  L          V             Y   G STLA   D LGT V
rST2-4       MH  S  L          I          A      SKIALE   D LGT V

           151                                                       200
hDHEA-ST   EWFCQGTVLY GSWFDHIHGW MPMREEKNFL LLSYEELKQD TGRTIEKICQ
rSTa         LK Y P      E  RA   LS  LD       Y   DM K   MG   K   D
rST20        LK N       E  RA   LS Q WD       Y   DM K   MG   K   D
rST2-4       LK N A      E  R    LS   WD    V Y   DM K   MGS  K   D

           201                                                       250
hDHEA-ST   FLGKTLEPEE LNLILKNSSF QSMKENKMSN YSLLSVDYVV DKAQLLRKGV
rSTa           K   D  D V  Y      V     N     N MEKELIL PGFTFM N T
rST20          K   D  D V  Y      V     D       MKKSIF TGTG M    T
rST2-4         K   D    V  Y      VV    N       MEKELIL TGFTFM    T

           251                            285
hDHEA-ST   SGDWKNHFTV AQAEDFDKLF QEKMADLPRE LFPWE*
rSTa       T            A    V        GF PG M       *
rST20      V          S  A    V        GF PG M       *
rST2-4     TN         Q  A    V        GF PG M       *
```

FIGURE 5. Comparison of the amino acid sequence of human DHEA-ST with the amino acid sequences of rat hydroxysteroid sulfotransferases. The amino acid sequence of of DHEA-ST aligned to the sequences of the rat hydroxysteroid sulfotransferases STa, ST20, and ST2–4.[25,51] Differences in the rat hydroxysteroid sulfotransferase sequences compared to the sequence of human DHEA-ST are noted. *Asterisk* indicates a stop codon.

sequence to both the human PSTs and 37% identical and 60% similar to the sequence of human EST. Differences in sequence similarity between the human STs is consistent with the inability of antibodies raised to pure human DHEA-ST to cross-react with the other human STs.[5,6,20] FIGURE 5 shows the amino acid sequence comparison of human DHEA-ST to three members of the rat hydroxysteroid ST family. The sequence of DHEA-ST is 62–64% identical and 76–78% similar to these rat hydroxysteroid ST sequences. Sequential sequence alignments of known ST sequences suggest that DHEA-ST is a member of a larger hydroxysteroid ST gene family.[39] Human PSTs and EST are members of a phenol ST gene family. Rat liver contains at least six different hydroxysteroid ST cDNAs encoded by distinct genes. Rat hydroxysteroid STs are similar to each other in amino acid sequence and kinetic properties. The functional role for the multiplicity of hydroxysteroid STs in rat liver is unknown but may be related to the regulation of steroid levels in rat liver.[40]

BIOACTIVATION REACTIONS CATALYZED BY DHEA-ST

Sulfate conjugation is involved in the bioactivation of compounds to reactive electrophilic forms that covalently bind cellular macromolecules including DNA, RNA, and protein, leading to tumorigenesis or cell death. Previous studies indicated that members of the PST gene family are primarily responsible for bioactivation of *N*-hydroxylated aromatic amines and heterocyclic amines, whereas hydroxysteroid ST activity is responsible for bioactivation of hydroxymethyl polyaromatic hydrocarbons (PAHs).[41,42] FIGURE 6 shows the mechanism for bioactivation of 9-hydroxymethylanthracene by hydroxysteroid ST activity as exemplified by DHEA-ST. The hydroxymethyl group is sulfated and undergoes subsequent spontaneous rearrangement to release the sulfate moiety and generate an electrophilic benzylic carbocation that can react with cellular nucleophiles such as DNA, RNA, and protein. The characterization of bioactivation of the hydroxymethyl PAHs by hydroxysteroid ST activity was carried out primarily with members of the rat hydroxysteroid ST family.[43–45] However, investigation of the involvement of human DHEA-ST in these reactions is intensifying.[46,47]

Glatt and coworkers[46,47] investigated the role of human DHEA-ST activity in the sulfation and bioactivation of hydroxymethyl PAHs and related compounds using a bacterial mutagenesis assay. FIGURE 7 shows the effect of increasing concentrations of hycanthone and 1-hydroxymethylpyrene on the generation of HIS⁺ revertants in *Salmonella typhimurium* TA1538 transformed with human DHEA-ST or rat STa. Rat STa and human DHEA-ST showed differences in their abilities to activate 1-hydroxymethylpyrene and hycanthone. Bioactivation of hycanthone may be clinically relevant, as hycanthone was previously used as a therapeutic anti-schistosomiasis agent; however, because of its carcinogenic and teratogenic activity in animals, the use of hycanthone in clinical practice has been discontinued.[48] TABLE 2 shows the comparison of rat STa and human DHEA-ST activity expressed in *S. typhimurium* on the bioactivation of several mutagens known to be activated by ST activity. Both STa and DHEA-ST strongly bioactivated hydroxymethyl PAHs.[47] Additionally, both hydroxysteroid STs displayed some activity in the bioactivation of compounds such as 1'-hydroxysafrole and *N*-hydroxy-2-acetylaminofluorene, which were reported as

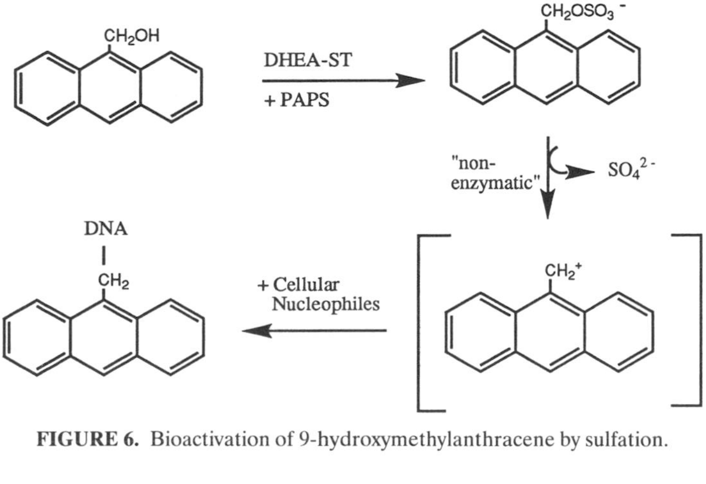

FIGURE 6. Bioactivation of 9-hydroxymethylanthracene by sulfation.

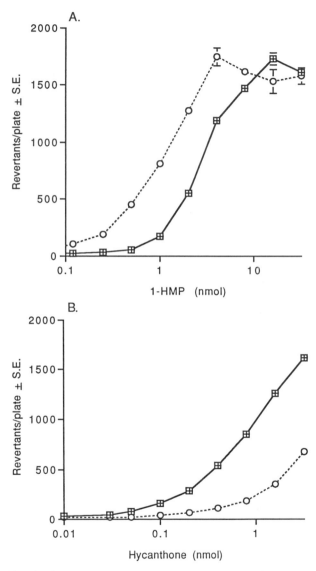

FIGURE 7. Bioactivation of 1-hydroxymethylpyrene (1-HMP) and hycanthone by human DHEA-ST and rat STa expressed in *Salmonella typhimurium.* Rat STa (*open circles*) and human DHEA-ST (*hatched squares*) cDNAs were inserted into the pKK233-2 expression vector, and these vectors were used to transform *S. typhimurium.* Various concentrations of 1-HMP and hycanthone were added to the media and the number of HIS+ revertants determined.[47] SE are within the size of the symbols, unless shown.

substrates for bioactivation by rat and human PST activities.[41,42,49] The use of cloned and expressed STs will enable investigators to more clearly elucidate and define the activity and ability of individual human STs to bioactivate structurally different procarcinogens. The role of DHEA-ST activity in the bioactivation of carcinogens or teratogens in human tissues expressing high levels of DHEA-ST activity is not well understood. The investigation of the possible role of hydroxysteroid-ST activity in the generation of reactive electrophilic compounds in the adrenal cortex must take into account the low level of hydroxysteroid-ST activity in the rat adrenal.

TABLE 2. Bioactivation of Various Compounds by Human and Rat Hydroxysteroid Sulfotransferases Heterologously Expressed in *Salmonella typhimurium* TA1538

	Induced Revertants per nmol[a]		
Compounds	TA1538	TA1538/rSTa	TA1538/hDHEA-ST
1-Hydroxymethylpyrene	<0.5[b]	750	260
6-Hydroxymethylbenzo[a]pyrene	15	NT	1,200
Hycanthone	24	250	1,400
1'-Hydroxysafrole	<0.001[b]	0.015	0.009
α-Hydroxytamoxifen	<0.05[b]	9.0	0.6
N-Hydroxy-2-acetylaminofluorene	2.7[c]	3.2[c]	7.5[c]

[a]Slopes of concentration response curves.
[b]Limit of detection.
[c]Derivatives of an acetyltransferase-deficient strain, TA1538-1,8-DNP, were used.
[d]NT means not tested.

SUMMARY

Human tissues possess at least four distinct forms of cytosolic ST, three of which are involved in the sulfation of steroids. DHEA-ST is responsible for the majority of hydroxysteroid and bile acid sulfation in human tissues and abundant levels of the enzyme are present in human liver and adrenal tissues. In the adult human adrenal, DHEA-ST has been localized immunologically to the zona reticularis of the adrenal cortex. No age- or gender-related differences in the expression of DHEA-ST activity in adult human liver cytosols have been reported. The cDNA encoding DHEA-ST has been isolated from a human liver cDNA library and expressed in both mammalian COS cells and *E. coli*. Purification and molecular characterization studies suggest a single form of DHEA-ST in human tissues. The properties of DHEA-ST expressed in either mammalian or bacterial cells are very similar to those of the native enzyme. DHEA-ST can also bioactivate a number of procarcinogens to reactive electrophilic forms. Hydroxymethyl PAHs are sulfated and bioactivated at a relatively rapid rate by DHEA-ST, whereas 1'-hydroxysafrole and N-hydroxy-2-acetylaminofluorene are bioactivated to a lesser extent.

ACKNOWLEDGMENTS

The authors thank Marion Stamp-Cole for assistance in the immunolocalization studies and Josie Falany for efforts in expressing and characterizing human liver DHEA-ST.

REFERENCES

1. MORTOLA, J. F. & S. S. C. YEN. 1990. The effects of oral dehydroepiandrosterone on endocrine-metabolic parameters in postmenopausal women. J. Clin. Endocrinol. Metab. **71:** 696–704.

2. FALANY, C. N. 1991. Molecular enzymology of human liver cytosolic sulfotransferases. Trends Pharmacol. Sci. **12:** 255–259.

3. FALANY, C. N. & J. A. ROTH. 1993. Properties of human cytosolic sulfotransferases involved in drug metabolism. *In* Human Drug Metabolism: From Molecular Biology to Man. E. H. Jeffery, Ed.: 101–115. CRC Press. Boca Raton, FL.

4. FALANY, C. N., M. E. VAZQUEZ & J. M. KALB. 1989. Purification and characterization of human liver dehydroepiandrosterone sulfotransferase. Arch. Biochem. Biophys. **260:** 641–646.

5. FALANY, C. N., M. E. VAZQUEZ, J. A. HEROUX & J. A. ROTH. 1990. Purification and characterization of human liver phenol-sulfating phenol sulfotransferase. Arch. Biochem. Biophys. **278:** 312–318.

6. FALANY, C. N., V. KRASNYKH & J. L. FALANY. 1995. Bacterial expression and characterization of a cDNA for human liver estrogen sulfotransferase. J. Steroid Biochem. Molec. Biol. **52:** 529–539.

7. FALANY, C. N., J. WHEELER, T. S. OH & J. L. FALANY. 1994. Steroid sulfation by expressed human cytosolic sulfotransferases. J. Steroid Biochem. Molec. Biol. **48:** 369–375.

8. JAKOBY, W. B., R. D. SEKURA, E. S. LYON, C. J. MARCUS & J.-L. WANG. 1980. Sulfotransferases. *In* Enzymatic Basis of Detoxication. W. B. Jakoby, Ed.: 199–227. Academic Press. New York.

9. HIRSHEY, S. J., T. P. DOOLEY, I. M. REARDON, R. L. HEINRIKSON & C. N. FALANY. 1992. Sequence analysis, *in vitro* translation and expression of the cDNA for rat liver minoxidil sulfotransferase. Mol. Pharmacol. **40:** 1027–1032.

10. OZAWA, S., K. NAGATA, D.-W. GONG, Y. YAMAZOE & R. KATO. 1990. Nucleotide sequence of a full-length cDNA (PST-1) for aryl sulfotransferase from rat liver. Nucl. Acid Res. **18:** 4001.

11. NAGATA, K., S. OZAWA, M. MIYATA, M. SHIMADA, D.-W. GONG, Y. YAMAZOE & R. KATO. 1993. Isolation and expression of a cDNA encoding a male-specific rat sulfotransferase that catalyzes activation of N-hydroxy-2-acetyl-aminofluorene. J. Biol. Chem. **268:** 24720–24725.

12. CHATTERJEE, B., D. MAJUMDAR, O. OZBILEN, C. V. RAMANA MURTY & A. K. ROY. 1987. Molecular cloning and characterization of a cDNA for androgen-repressible rat liver protein, SMP-2. J. Biol. Chem. **262:** 822–825.

13. OGURA, K., J. KAJITA, H. NARIHATA, T. WATABE, S. OZAWA, K. NAGATA, Y. YAMAZOE & R. KATO. 1989. Cloning and sequence analysis of a rat liver cDNA encoding hydroxysteroid sulfotransferase. Biochem. Biophys. Res. Comm. **165:** 168–174.

14. HOMMA, H., I. NAKAGOME, M. KAMAKURA, M. HIROTA, M. TAKAHASHI & M. MATSUI. 1994. Studies on rat hydroxysteroid sulfotransferase: Immunochemistry, development and pI varients. Chemico-Biol. Inter. **92:** 15–24.

15. FALANY, J. L., V. KRASNYKH, G. MIKHEEVA & C. N. FALANY. 1994. Isolation and expression of an isoform of rat estrogen sulfotransferase. J. Steroid Biochem. Molec. Biol. **52:** 35–44.

16. BAXTER, J. D. & J. B. TYRRELL. 1987. The adrenal cortex. *In* Endocrinology and Metabolism, P. Felig, J. D. Baxter, A. E. Broadus & L. A. Frohman, Eds.: 511–632. McGraw-Hill. New York.

17. RADOMINSKA, A., K. A. COMER, P. ZIMINAK, J. FALANY, M. ISCAN & C. N. FALANY. 1991. Human liver steroid sulfotransferase sulphates bile acids. Biochem. J. **273:** 597–604.

18. OBINATA, K., A. NEMETH, A. ELLIN & B. STRANDVIK. 1994. Bile salt sulfotransferase activity in the liver of cholestatic infants. Scand. J. Clin. Lab. Invest. **54:** 285–290.

19. ADAMS, J. B. & D. MCDONALD. 1979. Enzymatic synthesis of steroid sulphates. XII. Isolation of dehydroepiandrosterone sulphotransferase from human adrenals by affinitychromatography. Biochim. Biophys. Acta **567:** 144–153.

20. COMER, K. A. & C. N. FALANY. 1992. Immunological characterization of dehydroepiandrosterone sulfotransferase from human liver and adrenals. Mol. Pharmacol. **41:** 645–651.
21. AKSOY, I. A., V. SOCHOROVA & R. M. WEINSHILBOUM. 1993. Human liver dehydroepiandrosterone sulfotransferase: Nature and extent of individual variation. Clin. Pharmacol. & Ther. **54:** 498–506.
22. WEINSHILBOUM, R. 1990. Sulfotransferase pharmacogenetics. Pharmacol. & Ther. **45:** 93–107.
23. YAMAZOE, Y., S. MANABE, N. MURAYAMA & R. KATO. 1987. Regulation of hepatic sulfotransferase catalyzing the activation of N-hydroxyarylamide and N-hydroxyarylamine by growth hormone. Mol. Pharmacol. **32:** 536–541.
24. GONG, D.-W., S. OZAWA, Y. YAMAZOE & R. KATO. 1991. Purification of hepatic N-hydroxyarylamine sulfotransferases and their regulation by growth hormone and thyroid hormone in rats. J. Biochem. (Tokyo) **110:** 226–231.
25. LEITER, E. H., H. D. CHAPMAN & C. N. FALANY. 1991. Synergism of obesity genes with hepatic steroid sulfotransferases to mediate diabetes in mice. Diabetes **40:** 1360–1363.
26. RUNGE-MORRIS, M. & J. WILUSZ. 1991. Age and gender-related gene expression of hydroxysteroid sulfotransferase-a in rat liver. Biochem. Biophys. Res. Comm. **175:** 1051–1056.
27. AKSOY, I. A., D. M. OTTERNESS & R. M. WEINSHILBOUM. 1993. Cholesterol sulfation in human liver. Catalysis by dehydroepiandrosterone sulfotransferase. Drug Metab. Dispos. **21:** 268–276.
28. WHITTEMORE, R. M., L. B. PEARCE & J. A. ROTH. 1985. Purification and characterization of a dopamine-sulfating form of phenol sulfotransferase from human brain. Biochemistry **24:** 2477–2482.
29. ADAMS, J. B. & D. MCDONALD. 1980. Enzymatic synthesis of steroid sulphates. XIII. Isolation and properties of dehydroepiandrosterone sulphotransferase from human foetal adrenals. Biochim. Biophys. Acta **615:** 275–278.
30. PARKER, C. R., C. N. FALANY, C. R. STOCKARD, A. K. STANKOVIC & W. E. GRIZZLE. 1993. Immunohistochemical localization of dehydroepiandrosterone sulfotransferase in human fetal tissues. J. Clin. Endocrinol. Metab. **78:** 234–236.
31. OTTERNESS, D. M., E. D. WIEBEN, T. C. WOOD, R. W. G. WATSON, B. J. MADDEN, D. J. MCCORMICK & R. M. WEINSHILBOUM. 1992. Human liver dehydroepiandrosterone sulfotransferase: Molecular cloning and expression of the cDNA. Mol. Pharmacol. **41:** 865–872.
32. KONG, A.-N. T., L. YANG, M. MA, D. TAO & T. D. BJORNSSON. 1992. Molecular cloning of the alcohol/hydroxysteroid form (hSTa) of sulfotransferase from human liver. Biochem. Biophys. Res. Commun. **187:** 448–454.
33. COMER, K. A., J. L. FALANY & C. N. FALANY. 1993. Cloning and expression of human liver dehydroepiandrosterone sulfotransferase. Biochem. J. **289:** 233–240.
34. OTTERNESS, D. M., C. HER, S. AKSOY, S. KIMURA, E. D. WIEBEN & R. M. WEINSHILBOUM. 1995. Human dehydroepiandrosterone sulfotransferase gene: Molecular cloning and structural characterization. DNA Cell Biol. **14:** 331–341.
35. OTTERNESS, D., H. W. MOHRENWEISER, B. F. BRANDIFF & R. M. WEINSHILBOUM. 1995. Dehydroepiandrosterone sulfotransferase gene (STD): Localization to human chromosome 19q13.3. Cytogenet. Cell Genet. **70:** 45–52.
36. DOOLEY, T. P., H. M. MITCHISON, P. B. MUNROE, P. PROBST, M. NEAL, M. J. SICILIANO, Z. DENG, N. A. DOGGETT, D. F. CALLEN, R. M. GARDINER & S. E. MOLE. 1994. Mapping of two phenol sulphotransferase genes, *STP* and *STM,* to 16p: Candidate genes for Batten disease. Biochem. Biophys. Res. Commun. **205:** 482–489.
37. DOOLEY, T. P., P. PROBST, R. D. OBERMOELLER, M. J. SICILIANO, N. A. DOGGETT, D. F. CALLEN, H. M. MITCHISON & S. E. MOLE. 1993. Mapping of the phenol sulfotransferase gene (STP) to human chromosome 16p12.1-p11.2 and to mouse chromosome 7. Genomics **18:** 440–443.
38. GANGULY, T. C., V. KRASNYKH & C. N. FALANY. 1995. Bacterial expression and kinetic characterization of the human monoamine-sulfating form of phenol sulfotransferase. Drug Metab. Disp. **23.**

39. YAMAZOE, Y., K. NAGATA, S. OZAWA & R. KATO. 1994. Structural similarity and diversity of sulfotransferases. Chemico-Biol. Interact. **92:** 107–117.
40. LEITER, E. H. 1989. The genetics of diabetes susceptibility in mice. FASEB J. **3:** 2231–2241.
41. MILLER, E. C., J. A. MILLER, E. W. BOBERG, K. B. DELCLOS, C. C. LAI, T. R. FENNELL, R. W. WISEMAN & A. LIEM. 1985. Sulfuric acid esters as ultimate electrophilic and carcinogenic metabolites of some alkenylbenzenes and aromatic amines in mouse liver. Carcinogenesis (Lond.) **11:** 93–107.
42. MILLER, J. A., Y.-J. SURH, A. LIEM & E. C. MILLER. 1991. Electrophilic sulfuric acid ester metabolites of hydroxy-methyl aromatic hydrocarbons as precursors of hepatic benzylic DNA adducts *in vivo*. *In* Biological Reactive Intermediates. IV. C. M. Witmer *et al.,* Eds.: 555–567. Plenum Press. New York.
43. GLATT, H., K. PAULY, H. FRANK, A. SEIDEL, F. OESCH, R. G. HARVEY & G. WERLE-SCHNEIDER. 1994. Substance-dependent sex differences in the activation of benzylic alcohols to mutagens by hepatic sulfotransferases of the rat. Carcinogensis **15:** 2605–2611.
44. FALANY, C. N., J. WHEELER, L. COWARD, D. KEEHAN, J. L. FALANY & S. BARNES. 1992. Bioactivation of 7-hydroxymethyl-12-methylbenz[a]anthracene by rat liver bile acid sulfotransferase I. J. Biochem. Toxicol. **7:** 241–248.
45. SURH, Y.-J., A. LIEM, E. C. MILLER & J. A. MILLER. 1991. Age- and sex-related differences in activation of the carcinogen 7-hydroxymethyl-12-methylbenz[a]anthracene to an electrophilic sulfuric acid ester metabolite in rats: Possible involvement in hydroxysteroid sulfotransferase activity. Biochem. Pharmacol. **41:** 213–221.
46. GLATT, H., A. SEIDEL, R. G. HARVEY & M. W. COUGHTRIE. 1994. Activation of benzylic alcohols to mutagens by human hepatic sulfotransferase. Mutagenesis **9:** 553–557.
47. GLATT, H., K. PAULY, A. CZICH, J. L. FALANY & C. N. FALANY. 1995. Activation of benzylic alcohols to mutagens by rat and human sulfotransferases expressed in *E. coli.* Eur. J. Pharmacol. **293:** 173–181.
48. CIOLI, D., L. PICA-MATTOCCIA & S. ARCHER. 1993. Drug resistance in schistosomes. Parasit. Today. **9:** 162–166.
49. CHOU, H. C., N. P. LANG & F. F. KADLUBAR. 1995. Metabolic activation of *N*-hydroxy arylamines and *N*-hydroxy heterocyclic amines by human sulfotransferase(s). Cancer Res. **55:** 525–529.
50. WILBORN, T. W., K. A. COMER, T. P. DOOLEY, I. M. REARDON, R. L. HEINRIKSON & C. N. FALANY. 1993. Sequence analysis and expression of the cDNA for the phenol-sulfating form of human liver phenol sulfotransferase. Mol. Pharmacol. **43:** 70–77.
51. OGURA, K., J. KAJITA, H. NARIHATA, T. WATABE, S. OZAWA, K. NAGATA, Y. YAMAZOE & R. KATO. 1990. cDNA cloning of hydroxysteroid sulfotransferase STa sharing a strong homology in amino acid sequence with the senescence marker protein SMP-2 in rat livers. Biochem. Biophys. Res. Commun. **166:** 1494–1500.

Regulation of Human Dehydroepiandrosterone Metabolism by Insulin[a]

JOHN E. NESTLER

Division of Endocrinology and Metabolism
Medical College of Virginia / Virginia Commonwealth University
Richmond, Virginia 23298

Investigators interested in the biology of aging have increasingly focused their attention on adrenal steroids dehydroepiandrosterone (DHEA) and DHEA sulfate (DHEAS). This interest stems from the combined observations that circulating levels of DHEA and DHEAS exhibit a unique and dramatic aged-related decline and that DHEA appears to exert beneficial biologic actions. Therefore, some degenerative changes associated with aging in humans, especially atherosclerosis[1] and immune senescence,[2] are postulated to be due to a relative deficit in circulating DHEA and DHEAS.

A key question regarding DHEA metabolism is: Why do serum DHEA and DHEAS decline with aging and decline so dramatically?[3,4] This decline is selective for DHEA and is not observed with adrenal glucocorticoids or mineralocorticoids.[5] There are also two other observations that are frequently overlooked but important. Firstly, why is there such a wide range in serum DHEAS among men in any individual age group? For example, there is a 6.5-fold range in DHEAS levels among men greater than 60 years old.[3,6] One man at the age of 65 might have a serum DHEAS level of 40 µg/dl, whereas another man of identical age might have a serum DHEAS level of 260 µg/dl. Put another way, Why are DHEAS levels lower in some elderly men than in others?

Secondly, almost all studies showing an aged-related decline in serum DHEA or DHEAS have been cross-sectional. Only one study, reported by Orentreich and colleagues[7] in 1992, monitored serum levels of these steroids longitudinally. This study confirmed an overall age-related decline in serum DHEAS, but it is intriguing that serum DHEAS actually rose with aging in 15 of the 97 men studied. What could account for this unexpected and seemingly paradoxical rise in serum DHEAS?

I suggest that all three of these phenomena, that is, a component of the age-related decline in serum DHEAS, the wide variability in serum DHEAS levels among men, and the paradoxical rise in serum DHEAS in some men, may all be related to a physiologic action of insulin to reduce circulating serum DHEA and DHEAS levels in men.

INSULIN AND DHEA METABOLISM IN MEN

Several lines of evidence indicate that insulin influences human DHEA metabolism. Insulin receptors and insulin-like growth factor I receptors have both been identified on human adrenal glands,[8,9] suggesting a possible role for insulin in the

[a]Studies were supported by National Institutes of Health grants RO1AG11227, DK18903, and RR-00065 and grants from the American Diabetes Association and the Thomas F. and Kate Miller Jeffress Memorial Trust.

modulation of adrenal function. An inverse correlation apparently exists between serum insulin and DHEAS in healthy men.[10] Moreover, some epidemiologic studies report that serum DHEAS in men is reduced in pathologic states characterized by insulin resistance and hyperinsulinemia, such as obesity,[11,12] hypertension,[13,14] and untreated type II diabetes mellitus.[15]

In addition to these epidemiologic observations, my colleagues and I have shown in *men* that (1) insulin infusion acutely lowers both serum DHEA and DHEAS,[16] (2) chronic pharmacologic amelioration of insulin resistance and hyperinsulinemia is associated with a rise in serum DHEA and/or DHEAS over a broad range of ages,[17–21] (3) insulin acutely increases the metabolic clearance rate (MCR) of DHEA,[22] and (4) insulin inhibits adrenal androgen production.[23]

Moreover, studies performed in men by us[24] and others[25–27] have uniformly demonstrated a rise in serum DHEAS with weight loss or fasting. Weight loss and fasting are associated with multiple metabolic alterations, and results from such studies do not permit identification of any single cause for the rise in serum DHEAS. Nonetheless, it is well recognized that weight loss in obese individuals is accompanied by improved insulin sensitivity and reduced circulating insulin levels.[28–30] Hence, these observations are at least consistent with the possibility that insulin acts to reduce serum DHEAS concentrations in men.

I would like to highlight one study conducted in Venezuela in collaboration with Beer and Jakubowicz. To determine if a reduction in insulinemia would raise serum DHEA or DHEAS in insulin-resistant men, 29 middle-aged (30–59 years old) and 28 elderly (60–80 years old) hypertensive men were enrolled in a single-blind, placebo-controlled study in which benfluorex was administered to improve insulin sensitivity and reduce circulating insulin.[21] Benfluorex is a hypolipidemic agent that has been shown to ameliorate insulin resistance and improve glucose tolerance in both animals and humans presumably by lowering free fatty acids. Men in each age group received either benfluorex 150 mg or placebo three times daily for 6 weeks, and fasting serum steroids and hormones were determined before and after treatment. Glucose tolerance was assessed by an oral glucose tolerance test (OGTT).

Benfluorex treatment improved glucose tolerance and reduced overall insulinemia in both age groups, as evidenced by reductions in the area under the curve for both glucose and insulin during the OGTT. Concurrent with the reduction in circulating insulin, benfluorex treatment was associated with rises in both serum DHEAS (55% and 62%, respectively) and unconjugated DHEA (66% and 167%, respectively) in both middle-aged and elderly men (FIG. 1). By contrast, serum cortisol did not change with benfluorex administration in either group (FIG. 1). Serum DHEA, DHEAS, and cortisol did not change with placebo treatment in either middle-aged or elderly men (FIG. 1).

This study's findings, coupled with others performed by us,[16–23] confirm that insulin selectively lowers circulating DHEAS and DHEA levels in men. They also indicate that the age-related decline in serum DHEAS in men is not inexorable, but it can be *reversed* by improving insulin sensitivity and reducing serum insulin. Finally, the findings establish that insulin regulates DHEA and DHEAS metabolism in men under physiologic conditions and over a broad range of ages (30–80 years).

EFFECTS OF INSULIN ON THE PRODUCTION RATE AND METABOLIC CLEARANCE RATE OF DHEA

Insulin could reduce circulating DHEAS levels in men by either inhibiting the production rate (PR) or increasing the metabolic clearance rate (MCR) of these steroids. We have examined both possibilities.

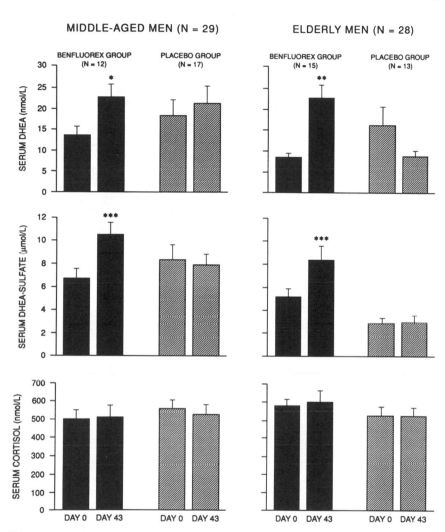

FIGURE 1. Fasting serum steroid levels in middle-aged (30–59 years old; $n = 29$) and elderly men (60–80 years old; $n = 28$) at baseline (day 0) and after receiving either benfluorex (*closed bars*) or placebo (*hatched bars*) for 6 weeks (day 43). Values are mean ± SE. *$p < 0.03$; **$p < 0.0005$; ***$p < 0.015$ (compared to day 0 value in same group). (Reproduced from Nestler *et al.*[21] with kind permission from The Endocrine Society.)

Production Rate

We speculated that insulin might inhibit adrenal 17,20-lyase activity because in our human studies insulin reduced circulating DHEAS without altering serum cortisol. Adrenal 17,20-lyase is required for the production of C_{19} steroids, such as DHEA, but it does not participate in the biosynthesis of glucocorticoids. Hence, inhibition of adrenal 17,20-lyase should yield a selective decrease in DHEA production similar to that observed with aging.

To assess the effect of hyperinsulinemia on adrenal 17,20-lyase activity, an acute ACTH stimulation test was performed in 10 healthy young men immediately following either a 5-hour insulin infusion or, 1 week later, a 5-hour saline infusion.[23] Serum molar ratios of 17α-hydroxyprogesterone to androstenedione and 17α-hydroxypregnenolone to DHEA were monitored during the ACTH test. These represent the precursor-to-product ratios for the 17,20-lyase enzyme.

Serum insulin did not change during saline infusion. Insulin infusion, however, raised serum insulin levels to ~ 88 μU/ml. Although both serum 17α-hydroxyprogesterone and androstenedione rose when ACTH was administered after the control saline infusion, there was little change in the molar ratio of these two steroids. By contrast, when the ACTH test was performed immediately after the insulin infusion, the ACTH-stimulated ratio of 17α-hydroxyprogesterone to androstenedione increased progressively. Importantly, this result was due to a relative increase in the precursor, 17α-hydroxyprogesterone, and a relative decrease in the product, androstenedione. Results for the molar ratio of 17α-hydroxypregnenolone to DHEA were similar. These findings are consistent with acute inhibition of human adrenal 17,20-lyase activity by insulin.

Metabolic Clearance Rate

Serum DHEAS fell rapidly in response to insulin infusion in our original studies,[16,31] even though the half-life of DHEAS is 9–12 hours. Therefore, we reasoned that insulin must act not only by decreasing the PR for DHEA but also by increasing the MCR for DHEA (MCR_{DHEA}). There was ample evidence in the literature to support this notion. For example, the MCR_{DHEA} is increased two- to fivefold in obesity,[32-35] an insulin-resistant and hyperinsulinemic state. The MCR_{DHEA} declines with fasting,[34,36] even when weight loss is minimal, but circulating insulin presumably decreases. Although investigators have attributed the elevated MCR_{DHEA} in obesity to increased deposition of DHEA in fat tissues, studies failed to show a clear relationship between indices of overall adiposity (such as body mass index, percent ideal body weight, or ponderal index) and serum DHEA levels.[37,38] By contrast, it was reported that a significant positive correlation exists between fasting serum insulin and the MCR_{DHEA} in women.[32,35]

To test the hypothesis that insulin increases the MCR_{DHEA}, we assessed the effect of a short-term insulin infusion (which attained a serum insulin level of ~ 150 μU/ml) or control saline infusion on the MCR_{DHEA} in 10 healthy young men.[22] Baseline MCR_{DHEA} during the insulin-glucose clamp study was similar to baseline MCR_{DHEA} during the saline control study. However, MCR_{DHEA} rose by 50% during the insulin infusion, whereas it did not change during the saline infusion. These results support the idea that insulin acutely increases the MCR_{DHEA} in men.

RELEVANCE OF INSULIN REGULATION OF HUMAN DHEA METABOLISM TO AGING

As human beings age, they become increasingly insulin-resistant and hyperinsulinemic. Basal serum insulin and glucose-stimulated insulin responses are 50–100% greater in elderly than in younger individuals.[39-41] Our observations suggest that the increasing hyperinsulinemia that accompanies aging may contribute to the selective decline in serum DHEA and DHEAS in men. In support of this idea and as discussed earlier, our data indicate that the age-related decline in DHEAS in elderly men is not inexorable, but it can be partially *reversed* by improving insulin sensitivity and reducing serum insulin.[21]

Insulin's action to lower serum DHEA and DHEAS levels in men may also provide an explanation for the wide range in serum DHEAS values among men in any individual age group. Specifically, our observations predict that serum DHEAS would function as a biologic marker for insulin resistance and hyperinsulinemia in men. Therefore, the apparent variability in serum DHEAS among men of similar age may merely reflect differences in insulin sensitivity.

Finally, our findings predict that if an individual man were to improve his insulin sensitivity (for example, through diet or exercise), serum DHEAS levels should rise and may even "mask" any decline in serum levels due to other age-related factors. This may explain the surprising finding by Orentreich and colleagues[7] that serum DHEAS actually rose in some men as they grew older!

ARE INSULIN'S EFFECTS ON HUMAN DHEA METABOLISM SEX-SPECIFIC?

As noted earlier, the majority of studies conducted by us were performed in men. More recent studies in women, conducted by ourselves and others, suggest an unexpected sex-based disparity in insulin action. To wit, there is relatively little evidence that insulin alters circulating DHEA or DHEAS levels in women under chronic conditions.

For example and in distinct contrast to men,[17-21] chronic amelioration of insulin resistance and hyperinsulinemia achieved by pharmacologic therapy either did not alter[17] or lowered[42] circulating DHEA or DHEAS levels in women. Inhibition of insulin release by diazoxide also did not alter serum DHEAS levels in either normal[43] or hyperandrogenized[44,45] women.

Moreover, and again in contradistinction to men,[24-27] four studies performed in healthy premenopausal[46] and postmenopausal[24,27] women or obese hyperandrogenized women[48] failed to show any change in serum DHEAS with amelioration of insulin resistance and hyperinsulinemia achieved through weight loss. Serum DHEAS rose in two other studies performed in women,[25,27] but it is notable that in one of these latter studies[27] a positive relationship was observed between changes in serum insulin and DHEAS ($r = 0.41$; $p < 0.05$). The positive correlation suggests that, if anything, insulin acted to augment serum DHEAS and is at least partially consistent with the conclusion that insulin does not act to reduce serum DHEAS in women.

These observations which suggest that insulin affects DHEA metabolism differently in women than in men are further bolstered by our recent finding that insulin acutely increases the MCR_{DHEA} in men but not in women.[22] We caution, however, that these studies demonstrating a sex-based disparity in insulin action are limited in number and need to be confirmed. Nonetheless, the observations are tantalizing and, if verified, may provide a clue as to the mechanism by which insulin influences human DHEA metabolism.

CLINICAL THERAPEUTIC IMPLICATIONS

How might insulin regulation of DHEA metabolism be important from a clinical or therapeutic viewpoint? DHEA may exert multiple beneficial biologic actions in humans, and oral administration of DHEA has been proposed as a preventive or therapeutic strategy in humans. However, numerous questions and obstacles to DHEA administration exist, including the appropriate form (unconjugated versus conjugated DHEA), the precise dosage and route of administration, poor availability when given orally, and the possibility of hepatotoxicity due to a bolus effect when given orally. Moreover, all oral DHEA administration studies to date have demonstrated significant *in vivo* conversion of DHEA to more potent androgens, such as testosterone and androstenedione, in both men and women. These androgens may exert undesirable and possibly deleterious biologic actions, which might negate any beneficial effects of DHEA. Therefore, it would be preferable if circulating DHEA and DHEAS levels could be raised in a more physiological manner. If further studies confirm an important physiologic role of insulin in the regulation of DHEA metabolism, the findings would suggest a therapeutic strategy of improving insulin sensitivity in men in order to raise serum DHEA and DHEAS concentrations.

Finally, our findings suggest that serum DHEAS acts as a biomarker for insulin sensitivity, at least in men, and that reduced serum DHEAS is indicative of subclinical insulin resistance. Recent studies suggest that early pharmacologic treatment of insulin-resistant but nondiabetic men may be beneficial.[18,49] Theoretically, a reduced serum DHEAS level could prove useful in identifying candidates for early intervention of this type.

ACKNOWLEDGMENTS

Studies from the author's laboratory were performed with the invaluable assistance of Drs. John Clore, William Blackard, Cornelius Barlascini, Keith Usiskin, Mark McClanahan, Ziad Kahwash, Nusen Beer, Daniela Jakubowicz, and General Clinical Research Center staff.

REFERENCES

1. NESTLER, J. E., J. N. CLORE & W. G. BLACKARD. 1992. Dehydroepiandrosterone: The "missing link" between hyperinsulinemia and atherosclerosis? FASEB J. **6:** 3073–3075.
2. DAYNES, R. A., B. A. ARANEO, W. B. ERSHLER, C. MALONEY, G. Z. LI & S. Y. RYU. 1993. Altered regulation of IL-6 production with normal aging. Possible linkage to the age-associated decline in dehydroepiandrosterone and its sulfated derivative. J. Immunol. **150:** 5219–5230.
3. ORENTREICH, N., J. L. BRIND, R. L. RIZER & J. H. VOGELMAN. 1984. Age changes and sex differences in serum dehydroepiandrosterone sulfate concentrations throughout adulthood. J. Clin. Endocrinol. Metab. **59:** 551–555.
4. MIGEON, C. J., A. R. KELLER, B. LAWRENCE & T. H. SHEPARD, II. 1957. Dehydroepiandrosterone and androsterone levels in human plasma. Effect of age and sex, day-to-day and diurnal variations. J. Clin. Endocrinol. Metab. **17:** 1051–1062.
5. PARKER, L. N. 1989. Adrenal Androgens in Clinical Medicine. Academic Press. San Diego.
6. CARLSTRÖM, K., S. BRODY, N. O. LUNELL, A. LAGRELIUS, G. MOLLERSTROM, Å. POUSETTE, G. RANNEVIK, R. STEGE & B. VON SCHOULTZ. 1988. Dehydroepiandrosterone sulfate and dehydroepiandrosterone in serum: Differences related to age and sex. Maturitas **10:** 297–306.
7. ORENTREICH, N., J. L. BRIND, J. H. VOGELMAN, R. ANDRES & H. BALDWIN. 1992. Long-term longitudinal measurements of plasma dehydroepiandrosterone sulfate in normal men. J. Clin. Endocrinol. Metab. **75:** 1002–1004.

8. KAMIO, T., K. SHIGEMATSU, K. KAWAI & H. TSUCHIYAMA. 1991. Immunoreactivity and receptor expression of insulinlike growth factor I and insulin in human adrenal tumors. An immunohistochemical study of 94 cases. Am. J. Pathol. **138:** 83–91.

9. PILLION, D. J., P. ARNOLD, M. YANG, C. R. STOCKARD & W. E. GRIZZLE. 1989. Receptors for insulin and insulin-like growth factor-I in the human adrenal gland. Biochem. Biophys. Res. Commun. **165:** 204–211.

10. HAFFNER, S. M., R. A. VALDEZ, L. MYKKÄNEN, M. P. STERN & M. S. KATZ. 1994. Decreased testosterone and dehydroepiandrosterone sulfate concentrations are associated with increased insulin and glucose concentrations in nondiabetic men. Metabolism **43:** 599–603.

11. ŠONKA, J. 1976. Dehydroepiandrosterone. Metabolic effects. In Acta Universitatis Carolinae. J. Charvát, Ed.: 1–171. Universita Karlova Praha. Prague.

12. LOPEZ-S, A. & W. A. KREHL. 1967. A possible interrelation between glucose-6-phosphate dehydrogenase and dehydroepiandrosterone in obesity. Lancet **2:** 485–487.

13. NOWACZYNSKI, W., F. FRAGACHAS, I. SILAH, B. MILLETTE & J. GENEST. 1968. Further evidence of altered adrenocortical functions in hypertension: Dehydroepiandrosterone secretion rate. Can. J. Biochem. **46:** 1031–1038.

14. NAFZIGER, A. N., D. M. HERRINGTON & T. L. BUSH. 1991. Dehydroepiandrosterone and dehydroepiandrosterone sulfate: Their relation to cardiovascular disease. Epidemiol. Rev. **13:** 267–293.

15. BARRETT-CONNOR, E. 1992. Lower endogenous androgen levels and dyslipidemia in men with non-insulin-dependent diabetes mellitus. Ann. Intern. Med. **117:** 807–811.

16. NESTLER, J. E., K. S. USISKIN, C. O. BARLASCINI, D. F. WELTY, J. N. CLORE & W. G. BLACKARD. 1989. Suppression of serum dehydroepiandrosterone sulfate levels by insulin: An evaluation of possible mechanisms. J. Clin. Endocrinol. Metab. **69:** 1040–1046.

17. BEER, N. A., D. J. JAKUBOWICZ, R. M. BEER & J. E. NESTLER. 1994. Disparate effects of insulin reduction with diltiazem on serum dehydroepiandrosterone sulfate levels in obese hypertensive men and women. J. Clin. Endocrinol. Metab. **79:** 1077–1081.

18. NESTLER, J. E., N. A. BEER, D. J. JAKUBOWICZ & R. M. BEER. 1994. Effects of a reduction in circulating insulin by metformin on serum dehydroepiandrosterone sulfate in nondiabetic men. J. Clin. Endocrinol. Metab. **78:** 549–554.

19. BEER, N. A., D. J. JAKUBOWICZ, R. M. BEER & J. E. NESTLER. 1993. The calcium channel blocker amlodipine raises serum dehydroepiandrosterone-sulfate and androstenedione, but lowers serum cortisol, in insulin-resistant obese and hypertensive men. J. Clin. Endocrinol. Metab. **76:** 1464–1469.

20. BEER, N. A., D. J. JAKUBOWICZ, R. M. BEER, I. R. AROCHA & J. E. NESTLER. 1993. Effects of nitrendipine on glucose tolerance and serum insulin and dehydroepiandrosterone sulfate levels in insulin-resistant obese and hypertensive men. J. Clin. Endocrinol. Metab. **76:** 178–183.

21. NESTLER, J. E., N. A. BEER, D. J. JAKUBOWICZ, C. COLOMBO & R. M. BEER. 1995. Effects of insulin reduction with benfluorex on serum dehydroepiandrosterone (DHEA), DHEA-sulfate, and blood pressure in hypertensive middle-aged and elderly men. J. Clin. Endocrinol. Metab. **80:** 700–706.

22. NESTLER, J. E. & Z. KAHWASH. 1994. Sex-specific action of insulin to acutely increase the metabolic clearance rate of dehydroepiandrosterone in humans. J. Clin. Invest. **94:** 1484–1489.

23. NESTLER, J. E., M. A. MCCLANAHAN, J. N. CLORE & W. G. BLACKARD. 1992. Insulin inhibits adrenal 17,20-lyase activity in man. J. Clin. Endocrinol. Metab. **74:** 362–367.

24. JAKUBOWICZ, D. J., N. A. BEER, R. M. BEER & J. E. NESTLER. 1995. Disparate effects of weight reduction by diet on serum dehydroepiandrosterone-sulfate levels in obese men and women. J. Clin. Endocrinol. Metab. In press.

25. TEGELMAN, R., P. LINDESKOG, K. CARLSTRÖM, Å. POUSETTE & R. BLOMSTRAND. 1986. Peripheral hormone levels in healthy subjects during controlled fasting. Acta Endocrinol. (Copenh) **113:** 457–462.

26. VELDHUIS, J. D., A. IRANMANESH, W. S. EVANS, G. LIZARRALDE, M. O. THORNER & M. L. VANCE. 1993. Amplitude suppression of the pulsatile mode of immunoradiometric luteinizing hormone release in fasting-induced hypoandrogenemia in normal men. J. Clin. Endocrinol. Metab. **76:** 587–593.

27. LEENEN, R., K. VAN DER KOOY, J. C. SEIDELL, P. DEURENBERG & H. P. KOPPESCHAAR. 1994. Visceral fat accumulation in relation to sex hormones in obese men and women undergoing weight loss therapy. J. Clin. Endocrinol. Metab. **78:** 1515–1520.

28. TREMBLAY, A., L. SAUVE, J. P. DESPRES, A. NADEAU, G. THERIAULT & C. BOUCHARD. 1989. Metabolic characteristics of postobese individuals. Int. J. Obes. **13:** 357–366.

29. LETIEXHE, M. R., A. J. SCHEEN, P. L. GÉRARD, C. DESAIVE & P. J. LEFÈBVRE. 1994. Insulin secretion, clearance and action before and after gastroplasty in severely obese subjects. Int. J. Obes. Relat. Metab. Disord. **18:** 295–300.

30. LETIEXHE, M. R., A. J. SCHEEN, P. L. GÉRARD, C. DESAIVE & P. J. LEFÈBVRE. 1995. Postgastroplasty recovery of ideal body weight normalizes glucose and insulin metabolism in obese women. J. Clin. Endocrinol. Metab. **80:** 364–369.

31. NESTLER, J. E., J. N. CLORE, J. F. STRAUSS, III & W. G. BLACKARD. 1987. Effects of hyperinsulinemia on serum testosterone, progesterone, dehydroepiandrosterone sulfate, and cortisol levels in normal women and in a woman with hyperandrogenism, insulin resistance and acanthosis nigricans. J. Clin. Endocrinol. Metab. **64:** 180–184.

32. KURTZ, B. R., J. R. GIVENS, S. KOMINDR, M. D. STEVENS, J. G. KARAS, J. B. BITTLE, D. JUDGE & A. E. KITABCHI. 1987. Maintenance of normal circulating levels of Δ^4-androstenedione and dehydroepiandrosterone in simple obesity despite increased metabolic clearance rates: Evidence for a servo-control mechanism. J. Clin. Endocrinol. Metab. **64:** 1261–1267.

33. FEHÉR, T. & L. HALMY. 1975. Dehydroepiandrosterone and dehydroepiandrosterone sulfate dynamics in obesity. Can. J. Biochem. **53:** 215–222.

34. KIRSCHNER, M. A., E. SAMOJLIK & D. SILBER. 1983. A comparison of androgen production and clearance in hirsute and obese women. J. Steroid Biochem. **19:** 607–614.

35. FARAH, M. J., J. R. GIVENS & A. E. KITABCHI. 1990. Bimodal correlation between the circulating insulin level and the production rate of dehydroepiandrosterone: Positive correlation in controls and negative correlation in the polycystic ovary syndrome with acanthosis nigricans. J. Clin. Endocrinol. Metab. **70:** 1075–1081.

36. HENDRIKX, A., W. HEYNS & P. DE MOOR. 1968. Influence of low-calorie diet and fasting on the metabolism of dehydroepiandrosterone sulfate in obese subjects. J. Clin. Endocrinol. Metab. **28:** 1525–1533.

37. EVANS, D. J., R. G. HOFFMANN, R. K. KALKHOFF & A. H. KISSEBAH. 1983. Relationship of androgenic activity to body fat topography, fat cell morphology, and metabolic aberrations in premenopausal women. J. Clin. Endocrinol. Metab. **57:** 304–310.

38. ELLISON, P. T. 1984. Correlations of basal oestrogens with adrenal androgens and relative weight in normal women. Ann. Human Biol. **11:** 327–336.

39. FINK, R. I., O. G. KOLTERMAN, J. GRIFFIN & J. M. OLEFSKY. 1983. Mechanisms of insulin resistance in aging. J. Clin. Invest. **71:** 1523–1535.

40. SHIMOKATA, H., D. C. MULLER, J. L. FLEG, J. SORKIN, A. W. ZIEMBA & R. ANDRES. 1991. Age as independent determinant of glucose tolerance. Diabetes **40:** 44–51.

41. MINAKER, K. L. 1987. Aging and diabetes mellitus as risk factors for vascular disease. Am. J. Med. **82 (Suppl 1B):** 47–53.

42. VELAZQUEZ, E. M., S. MENDOZA, T. HAMER, F. SOSA & C. J. GLUECK. 1994. Metformin therapy in polycystic ovary syndrome reduces hyperinsulinemia, insulin resistance, hyperandrogenemia, and systolic blood pressure, while facilitating normal menses and pregnancy. Metabolism **43:** 647–654.

43. NESTLER, J. E., R. SINGH, D. W. MATT, J. N. CLORE & W. G. BLACKARD. 1990. Suppression of serum insulin by diazoxide does not alter serum testosterone or sex hormone-binding globulin levels in healthy nonobese women. Am. J. Obstet. Gynecol. **163:** 1243–1246.

44. NESTLER, J. E., C. O. BARLASCINI, D. W. MATT, K. A. STEINGOLD, S. R. PLYMATE, J. N. CLORE & W. G. BLACKARD. 1989. Suppression of serum insulin by diazoxide reduces

serum testosterone levels in obese women with polycystic ovary syndrome. J. Clin. Endocrinol. Metab. **68:** 1027–1032.

45. NESTLER, J. E., L. P. POWERS, D. W. MATT, K. A. STEINGOLD, S. R. PLYMATE, R. S. RITTMASTER, J. N. CLORE & W. G. BLACKARD. 1991. A direct effect of hyperinsulinemia on serum sex hormone-binding globulin levels in obese women with the polycystic ovary syndrome. J. Clin. Endocrinol. Metab. **72:** 83–89.

46. KURZER, M. S. & D. H. CALLOWAY. 1986. Effects of energy deprivation on sex hormone patterns in healthy menstruating women. Am. J. Physiol. **251:** E483–E488.

47. BEITINS, I. Z., A. BARKAN, A. KLIBANSKI, N. KYUNG, S. M. REPPERT, T. M. BADGER, J. VELDHUIS & J. W. MCARTHUR. 1985. Hormonal responses to short term fasting in postmenopausal women. J. Clin. Endocrinol. Metab. **60:** 1120–1126.

48. PASQUALI, R., D. ANTENUCCI, F. CASMIRRI, S. VENTUROLI, R. PARADISI, R. FABBRI, V. BALESTRA, N. MELCHIONDA & L. BARBARA. 1989. Clinical and hormonal characteristics of obese amenorrheic hyperandrogenic women before and after weight loss. J. Clin. Endocrinol. Metab. **68:** 173–179.

49. NOLAN, J. J., B. LUDVIK, P. BEERDSEN, M. JOYCE & J. OLEFSKY. 1994. Improvement in glucose tolerance and insulin resistance in obese subjects treated with troglitazone. N. Engl. J. Med. **331:** 1188–1193.

Dehydroepiandrosterone (DHEA) Is a Neuroactive Neurosteroid

PAUL ROBEL AND ETIENNE-EMILE BAULIEU[a]

INSERM U 33
80 rue du Général Leclerc
94276 Le Kremlin-Bicêtre Cedex, France

The discovery of a steroid biosynthetic machinery in the nervous system followed the fortuitous observation of DHEA, as the unconjugated steroid and its sulfate ester (S), in the brain of adult male rats. This was an unexpected finding because the rodent steroidogenic glands, and particularly the adrenals, do not produce DHEA.[1] We review the data concerning DHEA characterization, biosynthesis, metabolism, and variations in the rat brain and extend these observations to other mammalian, or even vertebrate, species. Secondly, we provide an overview of data on the neurobiologic effects of DHEA and DHEAS.

THE RAT BRAIN

Characterization of DHEA and DHEAS in Rat Brain

Brain extracts were chromatographed on a Sephadex LH-20 column that allows complete separation of the unconjugated steroids from those conjugated to fatty acids, glucuronic acid, and sulfuric acid.[2] Fractions containing DHEAS were solvolyzed at pH 1 in ethyl acetate to quantitatively generate free DHEA, and extracts containing free DHEA or DHEA released from DHEAS were purified by chromatography on Celite 535 columns. This chromatographic step improved the specificity of DHEA radioimmunoassay. The sensitivity of the assay was such that >30 pg of DHEA or >40 pg of DHEAS could be detected in 1 ml of plasma or 1 g of tissue. Definitive identification of DHEA was obtained by gas chromatography of trimethylsilyl ethers on glass capillary columns coated with SE-30 in line with a mass spectrometer.

DHEA and DHEAS were measured in adrenals, testes, plasma, brain, and several other organs of 11-week-old Sprague-Dawley male rats (TABLE 1). Low concentrations of DHEAS were found in plasma, at the limit of sensitivity of the technique. Slightly higher concentrations were found in liver, spleen, testis, and kidney, but they were well below 1 ng/g of tissue. In sharp contrast the level of DHEAS was sometimes larger in the brain, particularly in the posterior brain (~ 5 ng/g of tissue), than in the adrenals.

Unconjugated DHEA was close to the detection limit in all organs investigated and did not permit accurate measurements. The latter were repeated in plasma, brain, and adrenals with improved methodology and confirmed initial results[3] (TABLE 2). We devised a procedure for the measurement of DHEA fatty acid esters (lipoidal derivatives,[4] L)[5] and the corresponding values are included. They are intermediate between those of DHEA and DHEAS, except in adrenals where

---

[a] To whom correspondence should be sent.

TABLE 1. DHEAS and DHEA in Plasma and Organs of Male Rats

	DHEAS (ng/g)	DHEA (ng/g)
Plasma[a]	0.3 ± 0.1 (9)	0.1 ± 0.0 (4)
Brain[b]		
Anterior	1.6 ± 0.2 (10)	0.4 ± 0.1 (4)
Posterior	4.9 ± 1.1 (11)	0.1 ± 0.0 (4)
Adrenals	2.9 ± 0.3 (4)	Nm
Liver	0.4 ± 0.1 (3)	0.04 (1)
Spleen	0.7 ± 0.1 (3)	0.06 (1)
Testes	0.4 ± 0.0 (3)	Nm
Kidneys	0.5 ± 0.0 (3)	0.05 (1)

Abbreviation: Nm = not measured.
DHEAL: [a]0.18 ± 0.05.
[b]0.41 ± 0.13. Each extract was obtained from a single animal, except for adrenals (four glands from two rats) and plasma (pools of three rats). Results represent mean ± SD. Values in parentheses are number of experiments.

DHEAL constitutes by far the major conjugate, whereas unconjugated DHEA is not detectable.

Brain DHEA Is Independent of Peripheral Steroidogenic Organs

Although DHEA production by adrenals and gonads seems minimal, it was mandatory to exclude formally their contribution to the levels of DHEA in brain. For that purpose, DHEAS was measured in plasma and brain of male rats undergoing endocrine manipulations.

Injection of long-acting zinc phosphate preparations of corticotropin ($\beta 1$–24 ACTH) or dexamethasone for 3 days, to inhibit endogenous ACTH secretion, was not accompanied by clear-cut changes in brain DHEA[2] (TABLE 3). Brain DHEAS was also unchanged 1 day after castration, whereas testosterone completely disappeared (not shown). No obvious change was observed when castrated adrenalectomized male rats were compared 15 days after operation with sham-operated controls. This finding was confirmed in a later report.[3] No significant changes in plasma DHEAS were recorded, except for a small but significant increase after corticotropin injection.

Our results might be explained by large long-standing accumulation of DHEA in the brain arising from an extraadrenal source(s). We tried to investigate this possibility by injecting radioactive DHEA in intact male rats (FIG. 1). The concentrations of radioactive DHEA were indeed several-fold larger in brain than in plasma; however, they did not approach the >20-fold difference observed between the concentrations of endogenous steroid in brain and plasma. [³H]DHEA was not

TABLE 2. DHEA, DHEAS, and DHEAL in Plasma, Brain, and Adrenals[a]

	DHEA	DHEAS	DHEAL
Plasma (ng/ml)	0.06 ± 0.06	0.20 ± 0.08	0.18 ± 0.05
Brain (ng/g)	0.24 ± 0.33	1.70 ± 0.32	0.41 ± 0.13
Adrenals (ng/g)	Nd	5.1 ± 2.6	16.1 ± 6.4

Abbreviation: Nd = not detected.
[a]Measurements were made on plasma, brain, and adrenals of single adult males ($n = 10$).

TABLE 3. DHEAS in Plasma and Brain of Male Rats Subjected to Endocrine Manipulations[a]

	Intact	Sham Operated		ORX (1 Day)	ORX + ADX		ACTH Treated	DXM Treated	EtOH Treated
		2 Days	15 Days		2 Days	15 Days			
Plasma	0.26 ± 0.13 (9)	0.59 ± 0.08[b] (6)	0.28 ± 0.09 (5)	0.21 ± 0.02 (2)	0.40 ± 0.23[b] (6)	0.36 ± 0.07 (6)	0.50 ± 0.09[b] (2)	0.14 ± 0.07 (2)	0.56 (1)
Brain									
Anterior	1.58 ± 0.14 (10)	5.77 ± 1.66[b] (6)	1.19 ± 0.27[b] (6)	1.45 ± 0.07 (2)	4.35 ± 1.33 (7)	1.63 ± 0.38[c] (7)	1.35 ± 0.36 (2)	2.10 ± 1.27 (2)	1.9 (1)
Posterior	4.89 ± 1.06 (11)	13.19 ± 2.24 (5)	2.98 ± 0.68 (5)	3.15 ± 0.78 (2)	8.99 ± 1.50 (7)	1.92 ± 0.42[c] (7)	4.00 ± 1.13 (2)	4.45 ± 1.06 (2)	4.6 (1)

Abbreviations: ORX = orchiectomized; ADX = adrenalectomized; ACTH = corticotropin; DXM = dexamethasone.

[a]Results are expressed in ng/ml or ng/g (mean ± SD). Each measurement was performed on a single animal; numbers of animals are given in parentheses. Sham-adrenalectomized and orchiectomized rats were sacrificed 2 or 15 days after operation. Orchiectomized rats were sacrificed the day after operation, and adrenalectomized and orchiectomized rats were sacrificed 2 or 15 days after operation. Corticotropin (0.5 mg/0.25 ml of solvent) was injected subcutaneously on two consecutive mornings and rats were sacrificed on the morning of the third day. Vehicle-injected controls did not differ from intact rats. Dexamethasone (1 mg/0.25 ml of absolute ethanol) was injected subcutaneously on three consecutive mornings, and rats were sacrificed 2 hours after the last injection. Ethanol (0.25 ml) was injected to control rats.

[b]Significantly different from value for intact rats at 5% level.

[c]Significantly different from sham-operated controls at 5% level.

retained in the brain any longer than in plasma and became undetectable 20 hours after injection.

On the basis of those observations, we hypothesized that DHEA(S) was synthesized in brain, and we coined it as a "neurosteroid," namely, a steroid directly synthesized in brain, whatever its precursors.[6]

DHEA Biosynthesis in Brain

As soon as solid data were obtained suggesting the possibility that DHEA was synthesized in brain, it was logical to assume that it evolved in two steps from cholesterol, as described for steroidogenic glands:

$$\text{cholesterol} \xrightarrow{\text{P450}_{scc}} \text{pregnenolone (PREG)} \xrightarrow{\text{P450}_{17\alpha}} \text{DHEA}$$

As a first step, we set up a radioimmunoassay procedure for PREG, PREGS, and PREGL in brain, and we characterized PREG by GLC-MS, as previously performed

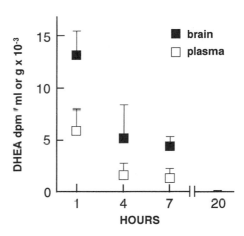

FIGURE 1. Radioactive DHEA in plasma and brain. [^{3}H]DHEA 80 × 106 dpm (0.13 μg) were injected subcutaneously in 0.2 ml of sesame oil, and rats were sacrificed 1, 4, 7, and 24 hours thereafter. Chromatographic fractions containing [^{3}H]DHEA were separated and counted.

for DHEA.[7] PREG concentrations in brain were about one order of magnitude larger than those of DHEA, as might be expected from a precursor-to-product relationship. The concentrations of PREG and PREGS were of the same order of magnitude, and they were about 10-fold larger than those in plasma. Finally, levels of PREG(S) in brain were, at least in part, independent of the presence or activity of steroidogenic glands, as previously reported for DHEA(S).

We then devoted major efforts to the elucidation of DHEA biosynthesis in the brain.[8] However, incubations of [^{3}H]PREG with brain slices, homogenates, and microsomes, with primary cultures of mixed glial cells, or with astrocytes and neurons of rat or mouse embryos, never produced a radioactive metabolite with the chromatographic behavior of [^{3}H]DHEA. Moreover, all attempts to demonstrate the P450$_{17\alpha}$ antigen immunohistochemically in the rat brain with antibodies to the enzyme purified from pig testis (kindly donated by I. Mason) and in the guinea pig brain with specific antibodies to the enzyme from guinea pig adrenal (kindly donated by S.

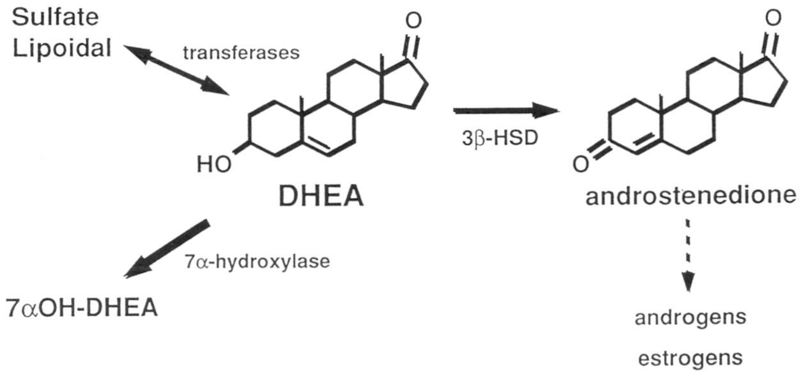

FIGURE 2. General outline of DHEA metabolism in brain.

Takemori) were unsuccessful.[9] Accordingly, Mellon and Deschepper[10] failed to detect the mRNA for $P450_{17\alpha}$ by RNase protection assays and RT-PCR. The biosynthesis of PREG also occurs in the rat retina, where it is the most abundant steroid, and which also contains tentatively identified 17α-OH PREG and DHEA.[11] Although suggested by the authors, the presence and activity of $P450_{17\alpha}$ in retina have not been conclusively demonstrated. We failed also to demonstrate the direct conversion of radioactive cholesterol or sesterpene to DHEA.[12,13] However, Prasad *et al.*[14] were able to generate PREG and DHEA from organic solvent extracts of rat brain by reaction with various reagents. They suggested the intermediate formation of cholesterol 17,20-cycloperoxide or 17-hydroperoxide in hypothetical biochemical pathway from cholesterol to DHEA. The enzyme(s) responsible for these conversions is unknown. To the best of our knowledge, DHEA biosynthesis in brain remains an open possibility.

Metabolism of DHEA in Brain

DHEA and DHEAS are involved in a series of metabolic conversions (FIG. 2) taking place peripherally that lead to the formation of biologically potent androgens and estrogens.[15]

3β-Hydroxysteroid-Dehydrogenase, Δ5 → 4 Isomerase (3β-HSD)

Preliminary observations indicated that rat brain can convert [³H]DHEA into [³H]androstenedione. The 3β-HSD activity was observed with slices or homogenates of discrete brain areas and later substantiated with [³H]PREG as substrate. Its conversion to [³H]PROG was formally established[16] and shown to occur in cultured glial cells and neurons.[17]

Four different isoforms of rat 3β-HSD have thus far been characterized.[18] It was important to determine the expression of 3β-HSD gene in the brain and to establish its degree of analogy with the isoforms already cloned. An *in situ* hybridization study, using an oligonucleotide common to the four known isoforms, demonstrated 3β-HSD mRNA in neurons of the olfactory bulb, striatum, cortex, thalamus, hypothalamus, septum, habenula, hippocampus, and cerebellum (FIG. 3). The cerebellum showed the highest level of 3β-HSD mRNA corresponding to a transcript of 1.8 kb.[19] A partial nucleotide sequence was obtained from polymerase chain reaction (PCR)-amplified cDNA fragments and indicated the expression of a 3β-HSD isoform closely resembling isoform I, the one expressed in adrenals and gonads. Moreover, antibodies to a peptide common to all 3β-HSD isoforms revealed an immunoreactive protein of ~45 kD.

Cell culture experiments indicated that 3β-HSD activity may be regulated by cell density. Purified type 1 astrocytes were obtained from fetal rat forebrain, plated at low, intermediate, or high densities, and maintained for 21 days. They were then incubated with [14C]DHEA for 24 hours and the radioactive metabolites formed were analyzed.[20] DHEA was either oxidized to androstenedione (3β-HSD activity), or converted to 7α-OH DHEA (7α-hydroxylase activity). After low density plating, the formation of androstenedione represented ~10% of incubated radioactivity, 10-fold more than 7α-OH DHEA. By contrast, after high density plating, low amounts of androstenedione were formed, whereas the conversion to 7α-OH DHEA was ≥50% (FIG. 4). When the results were expressed on a per cell basis, 3β-HSD activity was in fact almost completely inhibited at high cell density. Additional experiments suggested that 3β-HSD activity (or expression) was inhibited by cell-to-cell contacts. Thus, the nature of the metabolites formed depends on the state of cell aggregation and may take part in physiological and pathological conditions such as repair of CNS injury or astroglial tumors. DHEA and DHEAS did not decrease in the brain of male rats treated for 7 days with Trilostane, an inhibitor of 3β-HSD, thus suggesting that DHEA → androstenedione conversion is very low *in vivo*.[3]

7α-Hydroxylase

Dehydroepiandrosterone is converted by rat brain microsomes into an abundant polar metabolite, identified as its 7α-hydroxylated derivative by the "twin ion" technique of GLC-MS with deuterated substrates.[21] The reaction requires NADPH and is stimulated two- to fourfold by EDTA. Under optimal conditions (pH 7.4, 0.5 mM NADPH, 1 mM EDTA), the K_m value for DHEA is 13.8 μM, and the V_{max} is 322 pmol/min per milligram of microsomal protein. Small amounts of putative 7β-OH derivative of DHEA were detected. Formation of 7α-OH DHEA was low in prepubertal rats and increased fivefold in adults. The enzyme involved is probably identical to the 3β-diol hydroxylase described by Warner *et al.*[22]

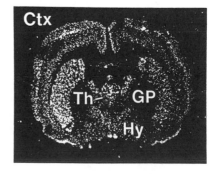

FIGURE 3. Regional distribution of 3β-HSD mRNA in rat brain. Negative print of X-ray films after hybridization of coronal brain section with 35S-labeled oligonucleotide 3β-HSD$_{I-IV}$ (3 days of exposure). Ctx = neocortex; GP = globus pallidus; Hy = hypothalamus; Th = thalamus.

The quantitatively important metabolism to 7α-OH DHEA, which strongly depends on cell density, may contribute to the control of neuroactive steroid concentrations and, consequently, activities in brain.

The gene coding for cholesterol 7α-hydroxylase was cloned in the rat and some other species including the human. The 7α-hydroxylation of side-chain oxygenated 3β-hydroxy-Δ5-C27 sterols was shown to be catalyzed by enzyme(s) other than cholesterol 7α-hydroxylase. Seven α-hydroxylation of 27-hydroxycholesterol occurs in rat brain microsomes,[23] whereas cholesterol 7α-hydroxylase mRNA present in liver was not detected on Northern blots of rat brain mRNAs. The 7α-hydroxylation of [14C]PREG was inhibited by 27-hydroxycholesterol but not by cholesterol. The

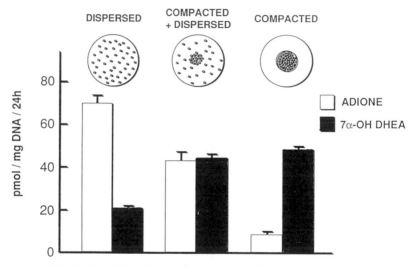

FIGURE 4. Metabolism of DHEA by primary cultures of astrocytes depends on cell density. Cells plated at different densities and grown for 21 days were incubated with 100 nM [14C]DHEA in 10 ml of SFM-NUS at 37°C for 24 hours. Radioactive steroids were extracted from media and analyzed by TLC. Metabolic conversion rates are expressed in picomoles of product formed per microgram DNA per 24 hours. Columns indicate mean ± SEM. Abbreviation: Adione = androst-4-ene-3,17-dione.

latter result is compatible with Δ5-3β-hydroxysteroids being substrates of the 7α-hydroxylase isoform(s) involved in bile acid synthesis in brain.

17β-Hydroxysteroid Oxidoreductase(s)

Several genes coding for 17β-hydroxysteroid oxidoreductase(s) (17β-HOR) enzymes have been cloned. Separate isoforms are specific for estrogenic and androgenic 17β-HSD activities.

Initially, we incubated minces of several regions of rat brain with [3H]DHEA, without added cofactor. Small amounts of [3H]androstenedione and [3H]DHEAL were obtained with hypothalamic slices, but no radioactive 5-androstene-3β,17β-diol or testosterone was found.[24] Astroglial cells from rat fetuses, kept in culture for 21 days, then incubated with [^{14}C]DHEA, yielded small amounts of DIOL (tentatively identified), which were markedly increased after bubbling the cells with CO, which inhibits cytochrome P450 activities.[20] Incubation of brain homogenates with [^{14}C]androstenedione (0.5 μM) in the presence of cofactors NADH and NADPH (1 mM) yielded [^{14}C]testosterone. The 17β-HOR activity in brain was low but significant as compared to the activity in liver homogenates.[25] Our attempts to measure DIOL in adult male rat brain extracts by radioimmunoassay were unsuccessful. Therefore, formation of the weakly estrogenic DIOL from DHEA in rat brain has probably no physiological relevance.

Acyltransferase

Dehydroepiandrosterone was characterized in rat brain not only as the unconjugated steroid or the steroid released from its sulfate ester by solvolysis, but also as the unpolar metabolite(s) converted to DHEA by saponification, supposedly fatty acid esters.[16] This led to the characterization of a Δ5-3β-hydroxysteroid acyltransferase activity in rat brain microsomes.[26] Endogenous fatty acids in the microsomal fraction served for the esterification of steroids. The enzyme system had a pH optimum of 4.5 in acetate buffer with [^{3}H]DHEA as substrate. The apparent K_m was $9.2 \pm 3.1 \times 10^{-5}$ M and V_{max} was 18.6 ± 3.4 nmol/h/mg protein (mean ± SEM). The inhibition constants of PREG and testosterone were 123 and 64 μM, respectively, and results were compatible with a competitive type of inhibition. A high level of synthetic activity was found in the brain of 1- to 3-week-old male rats, followed by a rapid decrease with aging. Contrasting with the high rates of esterification of several radioactive Δ5-3β-hydroxysteroids or 17β-hydroxysteroids, no fatty acid esters of either cholesterol, epitestosterone (with a hydroxyl group at position C-17α), or corticosterone (with hydroxyl groups at C-21 and C-11β) were formed in the same incubation conditions. The main endogenous fatty acids coupled to Δ5-3β-hydroxysteroids were palmitate, oleate, linoleate, stearate, and myristate.

The concentration of DHEAL in rat brain was of the same order of magnitude as the one of DHEAS.[3] Highest activity in 1- to 3-week-old rats may be related to the development of rat brain, particularly myelin formation, which occurs at that stage.

Steroid fatty acid esters differ from the unconjugated steroid by the production of a slow-onset sustained stimulus.[27] The sustained accumulation of DHEA observed in rat brain after combined orchiectomy and adrenalectomy may occur at the expense of DHEAL stores. In fact, DHEAL concentrations did not decrease significantly in the brain of operated rats, thus excluding it as a "reservoir molecule."

Sulfotransferases and Sulfatases

In rat brain, we have seen that concentrations of DHEAS (in mol/g) are significantly higher than those in plasma (in mol/ml) and are maintained for several weeks after adrenalectomy and/or castration. These observations, together with the blood-brain barrier's low permeability to DHEAS,[28] argue for the changes in brain DHEAS levels being independent of direct uptake from the circulation. This would mean that it is either synthesized in situ or stored in some other form, possibly analogous to the labile sulfolipid derivative(s), for which indirect evidence was obtained.[29]

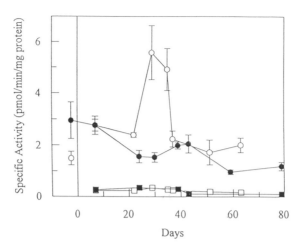

FIGURE 5. Time course of DHEA sulfotransferase activity in rat brain and blood. *Circles:* brain; *squares:* blood; *open symbols:* females; *closed symbols:* males.

Whereas estrogen sulfotransferase activity in mammalian brain is ascertained, the search for DHEA sulfotransferase was disappointing up to now.[30] However, we have detected low hydroxysteroid sulfotransferase activities in all regions of the rat brain, with the highest ones in the hypothalamus. The activity was mainly cytosolic and was not due to contamination by blood plasma.[31]

The enzyme had different properties from those of hepatic isozymes, with a pH optimum of 6.5 and a high K_m of 2.8 mM for DHEA. The enzyme was equally active with PREG as substrate. The specific activities (per milligram of cytosolic protein) in the brain were approximately 300-fold lower than those in the liver but, as in the liver, were higher in females than in males (FIG. 5). The variations in brain specific activity as a function of age did not parallel those in the liver. Relatively high activities were found in fetal brain and these declined at birth; there was a major peak in activity in pubertal female brains and a less important and later one in males.

No evidence was found to indicate that low brain enzyme activities and high K_m were due either to the presence of an inhibitor in brain cytosols or to the steroid sulfation really being a secondary activity of another brain sulfotransferase, that is, aryl or galactocerebroside sulfotransferases.

While the low brain hydroxysteroid sulfotransferase activities found here explain the lack of information in the literature, there is still the question of whether they are adequate to explain the origin of DHEAS. With a number of assumptions, we have calculated that it would take the brain over 5 days to synthesize 6 ng/g DHEAS. These data are compatible with the lack of increase of DHEAS in brain after a single subcutaneous injection of DHEA in oil solution.

DHEAS sulfatase activity in rat brain is associated with the nuclear fraction to the extent of 52%, and the latter enzyme is reported also to be present in a soluble form in the amount of 18%.[32] Moreover, rat brain homogenates hydrolyze DHEAS at an optimum pH of 6.6. Activity was maximal at 10 days of age.

It is currently difficult to evaluate the likely biologic importance of steroid sulfatases in brain. Measurements performed after combined adrenalectomy and castration do not support a significant release of DHEA or PREG from corresponding sulfate esters.

DHEAS Variations in Brain: Physiology and Pharmacology

Ontogenesis

Contrary to PREG and corticosterone, which display a perinatal burst, the concentrations of DHEA(S) were very stable between birth and postnatal day 22, in the 1.8–3.4 ng/g range, not different from the values found in adults.[33]

Circadian and Infradian Rhythms

Timing of the removal of brain, as related to the light-dark cycle, demonstrated prominent circadian rhythms of 3β-hydroxy-Δ5-steroids in rat plasma and brain. Male adult rats (11–12 weeks old) were housed in triads for 2 weeks. A combined extraction-solvolysis procedure followed by radioimmunoassay allowed measurement of the sum DHEA(S) of free and conjugated steroid.[16] Lights were on between 7 AM and 8 PM . Levels of DHEA(S) were measured at 3-hour intervals. They underwent circadian variations in the rat plasma and brain (FIG. 6). When the data were interpreted by the cosinor method, acrophases of PREG in brain and of DHEA in plasma significantly preceded the acrophase of corticosterone, suggesting partly separate coordinating mechanisms. Combined castration and adrenalectomy was followed by a disappearance of circadian variations of corticosterone in plasma and brain and of DHEA(S) in plasma. By contrast, a statistically significant rhythm of brain DHEA(S) persisted with an acrophase at the beginning of the dark span, confirming the existence of autonomous brain mechanisms coordinating the accumulation of DHEA. This did not however imply a local biosynthesis.

The same type of experiment was repeated in female Holtzman rats 3–4 months of age. The light-dark schedule was staggered in consecutive environments by 4 hours in order to approximate sampling over a 24-hour light-dark span. For 12 days, two

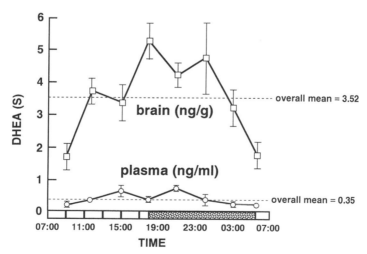

FIGURE 6. Circadian variation of dehydroepiandrosterone in rat brain. Measurements were performed every 3 hours on groups of three rats and were expressed as mean ± SEM. Span of darkness is indicated by a *shaded horizontal bar.*

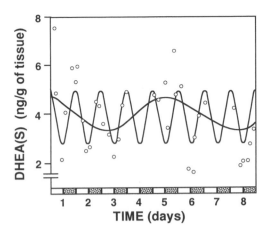

FIGURE 7. Infradian modulation of circadian rhythm of dehydroepiandrosterone in brain of female Holtzman rats. Measurements included unconjugated dehydroepiandrosterone (DHEA) and its sulfate ester (DHEAS). The experiment began at the start of a 12-hour light span indicated by *open bar.*

rats from each environment were killed at the same clock hour. The circadian and infradian variations of brain DHEA(S) were described by cosine curves with periods of 1 and 5 days with an overall probability of significance of $p < 0.001$.[34] For clarity, the cosine curves representing the circadian and infradian variations of DHEA(S) in the brain have been represented separately (FIG. 7). This result is compatible with the intervention of ovarian steroids throughout the estrous cycle in the modulation of DHEA levels in brain. Notwithstanding, no overall difference was found between DHEA(S) levels in the brain of female versus male rats.

Heterosexual Exposure

Heterosexual exposure also seems to influence DHEA(S) levels in the male rat brain. When intact male rats were exposed to the scent of estrous females (M/F), a remarkable increase in DHEA occurred in the hypothalamus, but not in olfactory bulbs, olfactory tubercles, or amygdala, by comparison to that in males exposed to the scent of other males[35] (M/M) (FIG. 8).

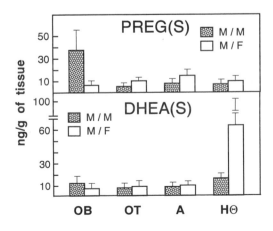

FIGURE 8. Concentrations of PREG and DHEA in the limbic system of male rats exposed to the scent of either males (M/M) or females (M/F). OB = olfactory bulb; OT = olfactory tubercle; A = amygdala; Hθ = hypothalamus. The only significant differences were the decrease of PREG in OB and the increase of DHEA in Hθ of M/F groups versus M/M ones.

The behavioral significance of this variation in hypothalamic DHEA levels is yet unknown.

Stress

The transient increase in brain DHEAS that occurs in the brain of male rats 2 days after adrenalectomy or the corresponding sham operation coincides with the heavy stress following anesthesia and surgery.[2] No increase in DHEA in cerebral cortex was observed in the brain of handling-habituated rats after CO_2 inhalation for 1 minute or 1 minute after a 5-minute foot shock.[36] This contrasting result might be due to the different intensity of stress, to the measurement of DHEA instead of

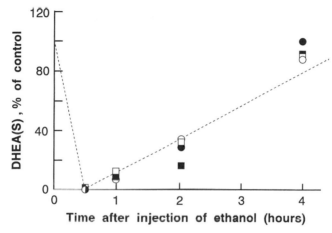

FIGURE 9. Effect of ethanol on DHEA(S) concentrations in male rat brain. Sprague-Dawley male rats (~175 g body weight) were given ethanol (16% in isotonic saline) by intraperitoneal injection to obtain a blood alcohol level of ~150 mg %. Controls were given an equal volume of saline solution. Rats were killed at 0.5, 1, 2, and 4 hours after injection; each point is the mean of 12 values measured on pools of three brains. AMY (*solid diamond*) = amygdala; HYP (*solid square*) = hypothalamus; CX (*open diamond*) = cerebral cortex; OB (*open square*) = olfactory bulbs.

DHEAS, and eventually to technical reasons, because the reported control values of DHEA are at least 10-fold larger than ours.

Acute Ethanol Intoxication

Sprague-Dawley male rats (175 g) were given ethanol (16% in saline solution) by intraperitoneal injection so as to get an alcohol level of ~150 mg % in blood. Controls were given an equal volume of saline solution. DHEA(S) was measured by the combined extraction-solvolysis procedure.[8] Ethanol injection resulted in a dramatic decrease in DHEA concentrations in brain (FIG. 9). This decrease occurred rapidly. DHEA had completely disappeared after 30 minutes, and reappeared progressively to reach control values after 4 hours. All brain areas investigated were similarly affected. PREG and PREGS did not change.

To gain some insight into the mechanisms involved in the depletion of brain DHEA, 2.5 mg of the steroid were injected intramuscularly in sesame oil, 4 hours before killing, to control or ethanol-treated rats. DHEA was cleared much more rapidly from brain under the influence of ethanol, thus suggesting that ethanol induces a rapid metabolic conversion of DHEA and DHEAS. It was previously reported that ethanol markedly increases the metabolic conversion of DHEA to DIOL.[37]

OTHER MAMMALIAN SPECIES

Mice

DHEA and DHEAS were measured in several strains of mice[38,39] (TABLE 4). The brain of male Swiss mice (13 weeks old) contains measurable levels of nonconjugated DHEA, larger than those measured in other strains and in Sprague-Dawley rats.[2] They are not modified by castration. The concentration of DHEAS in the brain of male Swiss mice is also larger than that in other strains, but similar to those in rats.

Primates

Monkey

DHEA(S) concentrations have been measured in the brain of *Macaca fascicularis* without or with suppression of adrenocortical steroid secretion by dexamethasone.[16] Two control adult spayed females and two dexamethasone (DEX)-treated females were studied. The effectiveness of adrenal suppression was indicated by the decrease in plasma cortisol to undetectable levels 20 hours after the last injection of DEX (FIG. 10). Concentrations of DHEA(S) in plasma were also much smaller after DEX treatment (91.5–93.5 ng/ml before DEX and 4.5–19.3 ng/ml after DEX, respectively). DHEA(S) concentrations in brain were about threefold smaller than those in plasma. Adrenal suppression resulted in markedly decreased brain concentrations, but the fraction of DHEA(S) remaining in brain after adrenal suppression was much larger than the corresponding fraction in plasma, suggesting that the accumulation of DHEA(S) in monkey brain is at least in part independent of peripheral endocrine glands, as previously shown in the rat.

PREG(S) concentrations were several-fold larger in brain than in plasma and did not seem influenced by adrenal suppression.

The impermeability of the blood-brain barrier to DHEAS was previously investigated in the rhesus monkey.[40] Two brains were perfused *in vivo* either with [14C]DHEA and [3H]DHEAS or with [3H]DHEA. Plasma from the jugular vein and the brain was analyzed for free and conjugated metabolites. Much more free than sulfoconju-

TABLE 4. DHEA, DHEAS, and DHEAL in the Mouse Brain[a]

Strain	Swiss	C57BL/6	B6 CBA	CSWO
DHEA	1.8 ± 0.9	0.3–0.4	1.0–1.2	0.3 ± 0.1
DHEAS	2.9 ± 1.9	1.9–2.1	0.8–1.5	1.7 ± 0.4
DHEAL	Nm	Nm	3.7 ± 1.3	1.1 ± 0.3

Abbreviation: Nm = not measured.
[a]Results are expressed as nanograms per gram of tissue, mean ± SD.

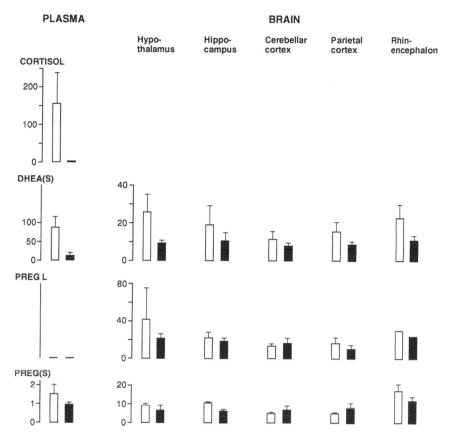

FIGURE 10. Effect of dexamethasone on plasma (ng/ml) and brain (ng/g) steroids in *Macaca fascicularis*. PREG and DHEA were measured by the combined extraction-solvolysis procedure. Four castrated adult females were used. Two were kept as controls (*open bars*), and two received 4 mg of dexamethasone daily for 3 days (*closed bars*). Plasma and brain samples were collected ~20 hours after the last injection.

gated DHEA was withdrawn from the blood. Slight conversion of [^{14}C]DHEA to [^{14}C]DHEAS and of [^{3}H]DHEAS to [^{3}H]DHEA occurred in brain. DHEA sulfatase activity has been directly demonstrated in the primate (*Macaca radiata*) brain[41]; the midbrain and hypothalamus-preoptic area showed the highest activity in females and the occipital cortex in males.

Human

Concentrations of Δ5-3β-hydroxysteroids were measured in specific regions of human brain.[42,43] Tissue samples were obtained by routine craniotomy from cadavers that had been stored at 4°C until autopsy within 24 hours.

The overall mean of PREG was 120.7 nmol/kg, or 38.2 ng/g, and the overall mean of DHEA was 19.6 nmol/kg, or 5.6 ng/g.[43] Concentrations of free steroids generally exceeded those of sulfate esters,[42] and were much higher than those of the sex steroid hormones and in the same range as those reported in the rat.

The ratios of PREG and DHEA concentrations in brain to the corresponding plasma concentrations frequently found in aged subjects were 74 and 6.5, respectively, demonstrating a remarkable tendency for the accumulation of both steroids in human brain. Hence, it is tempting to speculate that the human brain is capable of de novo biosynthesis of steroids. With the immunoperoxydase technique, we detected $P450_{scc}$, adrenodoxin, and adrenodoxin reductase in the human brain.[44] We used specific antibodies to the adrenal enzymes of cattle origin. The three enzymes were colocalized in the white matter of the cerebellum, removed at autopsy from a male cadaver 7 hours postmortem. Finally, human brain possesses DHEA sulfotransferase[40] and sulfatase activities.[32]

In conclusion, despite the prominent diversity of adrenal DHEA(S) secretion among mammalian species, from nil (rodents) to more than cortisol (primates), the picture of $\Delta5$-3β-hydroxysteroids in brain is remarkably constant, with PREG(S) predominating over DHEA(S). The biosynthesis of PREG in mammalian brain seems firmly established, whereas the one of DHEA, although likely, may not follow the classic pathway PREG $\xrightarrow{P450_{17\alpha}}$ DHEA. Because DHEAS hardly crosses the blood-brain barrier and because DHEA sulfotransferase activity has been measured, although at a low level, it appears that whatever the origin of DHEA, the formation of DHEAS is likely to occur directly in the brain, thus corresponding to the definition of "neurosteroids."

DHEA(S), A NEUROACTIVE STEROID

Neurotrophic Effects

Dissociated brains of 14-day-old mouse embryos were maintained in culture for 5 days, at which time they were found to contain closely similar numbers of cells per dish.[45] Fresh medium devoid of steroid or medium containing DHEA or DHEAS was then added, and after another 4 days the cultures were fixed and immunostained for neurofilament proteins (NF) and glial fibrillary acid protein (GFAP). In media containing one or another steroid, remarkable increases were found in the numbers of NF-positive neurons and GFAP-positive astrocytes, with extensions of the processes of both types of cells.

Results were compatible with enhanced survival and/or acceleration of the differentiation of precursors to either neurons or astrocytes. The extension of GFAP-immunoreactive astroglial cell processes was also assessed on hippocampal tissue cultures from adult male rats.[46] Although other steroids tested, including PREG and PREGS, did not affect this parameter, DHEA, DHEAS, and DHEA stearate induced the transformation of astroglial cells in hypertrophic and highly GFAP-immunoreactive cells with the morphologic characteristics of reactive astroglia.

Binding to Synaptosomal Membranes

[³H]DHEAS binding was assayed using crude synaptosomal membranes by Majewska et al.[47] They reported two categories of binding sites of, respectively, K_{d_1} = 2.9 ± 0.8 μM, B_{max_1} = 63 ± 19 pmol/mg protein; K_{d_2} = 554 ± 98 μM, B_{max_2} = 10.6 ± 2.4 mmol/mg protein.

We reinvestigated DHEAS binding with the use of purified synaptosomal membranes. Optimal conditions for the binding assay were: temperature, 23°C; pH, 5.2; protein concentration, 1.0 mg/ml; incubation time, 8–15 hours. Data were best fitted by a model of one category of specific binding sites + nonspecific binding: $K_d = 1.7 \pm 0.5 \, \mu M$, $B_{max} = 300 \pm 67$ pmol/mg protein. The K_d value is in accordance with the previous report; the B_{max} is larger due to the purification of membranes. The binding component was almost completely destroyed by proteolysis or heating at 100°C, thus indicating the proteinaceous nature of the synaptosomal binding component.

We also determined the relative competition ratios of several steroid sulfates, including in this order 3α, 5α-TH PROGS > DHEAS > PREGS (FIG. 11 and TABLE 5).

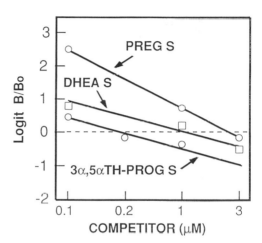

FIGURE 11. Ligand specificity of the synaptosomal binding component. Synaptosomal membranes were incubated with 25 nM [³H]DHEAS in the presence of either one of three competitors (DHEAS, PREGS, or 3α, 5α-TH PROGS) in the 100 nM–3 μM range. Nonsaturable binding was substracted. Logit-log plots were used to calculate the RCR 50s of competitors.

Dehydroepiandrosterone Sulfate Is a Naturally Occurring Excitatory Neuroactive Steroid

Dehydroepiandrosterone sulfate was reported to have proconvulsant effects when administered to laboratory animals[48] and to increase neuronal excitability (firing rate) when directly applied to septal-preoptic neurons in the guinea pig by pressure or iontophoresis.[49] The relationship of these effects to neuromodulatory functions to be described is unknown.

Neuromodulatory Functions of DHEA

GABA_A Receptors

Majewska and colleagues examined the effects of DHEAS and PREGS on the ligand binding and functional properties of $GABA_A$ receptors and reported that low micromolar concentrations of both molecules behaved as GABA antagonists[50] (see also the presentation of M.D. Majewska in this volume). However, the properties of PREGS and DHEAS were not identical. In brief, PREGS displayed mixed GABA agonistic/antagonistic features, whereas DHEAS behaved as a mere antagonist.

Indeed, DHEAS, contrary to PREGS, did not inhibit binding of the chloride channel ligands [^{35}S]TBPS and [^{3}H]TBOB and did not enhance [^{3}H]benzodiazepine binding, but rather reduced it at micromolar concentrations. Finally, DHEA mimicked the effects of DHEAS, although less potently, whereas PREG was completely inactive.

DHEAS blocked the GABA$_A$ R noncompetitively in neurons grown in primary culture from the ventral midbrains of fetal rats.[51] The apparent dissociation constant for this blockade was 4.5 μM. DHEAS did not act by occluding ion channels nor did it diminish their conductance, but it accelerated desensitization of at least one population of receptors, diminished the amplitudes of inhibitory postsynaptic currents, and shortened their decay time constants in a concentration-dependent manner.

TABLE 5. Steroid Sulfates Binding to Purified Synaptosomal Membrane ([^{3}H]DHEAS, 25 nM)

Steroid Sulfates	Relative Competition Ratio
DHEAS	100
PREGS	42
17-OH PREGS	15
Δ5-Androstene-3β, 17β-diol 3S	44
Cholesterol S	0
3α, 5α-TH PROGS	510
3β, 5α-TH PROGS	98
Testosterone S	0
Androsterone S	
3α, 5α	33
3β, 5α	155
3α, 5β	5.5
3β, 5β	45
Estradiol	
3S	30
17S	45
3, 17 di S	83
Free DHEA, 5α, 3α-TH PROG	0
GABA, muscimol, flunitrazepam, bicuculline, picrotoxin, mebubarbital up to 1 mM	0

We investigated the modulatory effects of several steroid sulfates on the muscimol-mediated influx of [^{36}Cl$^-$] into rat cerebrocortical synaptoneurosomes (FIG. 12). We confirmed that when the synaptoneurosomes were preincubated with 10 μM PREGS or DHEAS at 30°C for 15 minutes, a marked inhibition of [^{36}Cl$^-$] influx occurred.[52] We extended this observation to another Δ5-3β-hydroxysteroid-3β-sulfate, the sulfate ester of Δ5-androstene-3β, 17β-diol, which was almost as active as PREGS.

Unexpectedly, the ester sulfate of 3α-hydroxy-5α-pregnan-20-one (3α, 5α-TH PROGS) behaved as the nonconjugated steroid; it strongly and dose-dependently potentiated muscimol-mediated [^{36}Cl$^-$] uptake, whereas it was inactive by itself. This property seemed common to the 3-sulfate esters of 3α-hydroxysteroids, because it was shared by the sulfate esters of 3α, 5α-androsterone and 3α, 5β-TH PROG, whereas the ester sulfate of 3β, 5α-TH PROG was inactive. Simultaneous addition of

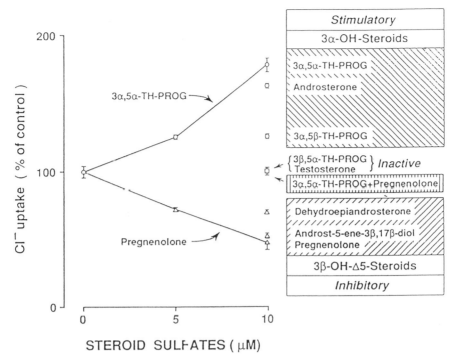

FIGURE 12. Modulation of muscimol-operated chloride ionophore by steroid sulfates. Synap toneurosomes, prepared from rat cerebral cortex, were preincubated at 30°C for 15 minutes without or with steroid sulfates, then incubated with ^{36}Cl Na (0.5 μCi) and muscimol (10 μM). Results are expressed as % change of the uptake produced by muscimol (43.8 nmol/mg protein/5 seconds). Mean ± SEM of four separate determinations.

10 μM 3α, 5α-TH PROGS and PREGS resulted in a mutual neutralization of their opposite effects. Testosterone sulfate (esterified at position 17β) was inactive.

We attempted to establish a correlation between the affinity of the steroid sulfates investigated for the synaptosomal membrane binding protein (see section on

TABLE 6. Steroid Sulfates Binding and Activity

Steroid Sulfates	Binding to Synaptosomal Membranes (affinity)	Modulation of Cl$^-$ Channel (GABA$_A$R) (agonists + antagonist−)
DHEAS	+++	−
Δ5 DIOLS	++	−−
PREGS	++	−−
TESTOS	0	0
3β, 5α-TH PROGS	+++	0
3α, 5α-TH PROGS	++++	++++
3α, 5β, TH PROGS	Nd	+
3α, 5α-androsterone S	++	+++

Abbreviation: Nd = not determined.

Binding to Synaptosomal Membranes) and their modulatory effect on [^{36}Cl$^-$] uptake (TABLE 6). For most sulfate esters tested, good correlation was observed between the relative competition ratio for the synaptosomal binding component (TABLE 5) and the activity, whether stimulatory or inhibitory. However, the activity of DHEAS was weaker than that of PREGS, whereas its affinity was larger. This discrepancy might be related to the fact that contrary to PREGS, DHEAS does not displace the ligands of the chloride channel.[50]

3β, 5α-TH PROGS was a notorious exception, because it bound to synaptosomal membranes with relatively large affinity, whereas it was completely inactive. It is not known if it counteracts the stimulatory effect of 3α, 5α-TH PROGS or the inhibitory effect of PREGS on [^{36}Cl$^-$] uptake.

Glutamate Receptors

PREGS is a positive allosteric modulator at the *N*-methyl-D-aspartate receptor; it enhances NMDA-gated currents in rat spinal cord neurons[53] (197% potentiation). However, DHEAS is weakly active; it potentiates NMDA-receptor–mediated responses by only 29%. Curiously, 3α, 5β-TH PROGS has aberrant behavior in this system, because it is a negative modulator of the NMDA-induced current.

Sigma Receptors

NMDA (200 μM) evokes the release of [^{3}H]norepinephrine ([^{3}H]NE) from preloaded rat hippocampal slices.[54] This effect is potentiated by DHEAS, whereas it is inhibited by PREGS, both at 100-nM concentrations. For the first time, opposite neuromodulatory effects of these steroid sulfates were uncovered. The σ antagonists haloperidol and 1[2-(3,4-dichlorophenyl) ethyl]-4-methyl piperazine, although inactive by themselves, completely prevent the effects of DHEAS and PREGS on NMDA-evoked [^{3}H]NE release. Progesterone (100 nM) mimicked the antagonistic effects of haloperidol and 1-[2-(3, 4-dichlorophenyl)ethyl]-4-methyl piperazine. Results indicate that the tested steroids differentially affect the NMDA response *in vitro* and suggest that DHEAS acts as a σ agonist, that PREGS acts as a σ inverse agonist, and that progesterone may act as a σ antagonist (FIG. 13). Pertussis toxin, which inactivates the Gi/o types of guanine nucleotide-binding proteins, suppresses the effects of DHEAS and reverses those of PREGS; the latter effect was interpreted as unmasking of a direct stimulatory effect of PREGS on NMDA receptors (see section on *Glutamate Receptors*). Because σ1 but not σ2 receptors are coupled to Gi/o proteins, it was suggested that DHEAS and PREGS control the NMDA response via σ1 receptors.

Calcium Channels

DHEAS (0.1–100 nM) can rapidly and reversibly depress voltage-gated calcium currents, concentration dependently, in the 0.1–100 μM range, when applied to freshly isolated adult guinea pig hippocampal CA1 pyramidal neurons.[55] This blocking action occurs in the presence of picrotoxin, thus eliminating the possible involvement of GABA$_A$ receptors. These data suggest another site at which DHEAS may exert its pharmacological actions to modulate brain excitability.

DHEA and Behavior

Memory

Roberts and his colleagues published several reports on memory enhancement in mice by DHEA and DHEAS.[45,56,57] Experiments employed an active avoidance behavioral paradigm (buzzer foot shock) in a T maze (FAAT). One week after training, T-maze training was resumed. Mice making their first avoidance in three trials or less were classed as remembering original training. Posttraining intracerebroventricular (icv) injection of DHEA in dimethyl sulfoxide prevented the amnesia for FAAT caused by the same volume of vehicle alone. DHEAS significantly enhanced retention of FAAT in weakly trained mice whether injected intracerebroventricularly or subcutaneously immediately posttraining or given in the drinking water for a 2-week period. The maximally effective doses were: icv 162 ng; sc, 700 μg; and oral 1.45 mg/mouse/day. DHEAS administered intracerebroventricularly occluded the amnestic effects of anisomycin (inhibitor of protein synthesis) and scopolamine (muscarinic cholinergic antagonist). DHEAS given intracerebroventricularly also improved retention for step-down passive avoidance. In all instances, dose-

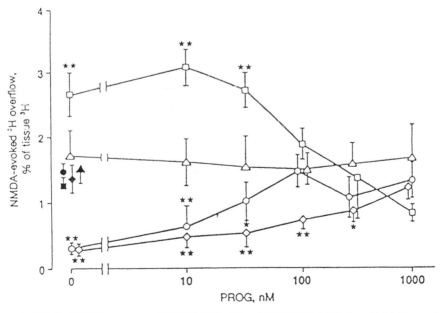

FIGURE 13. PROG counteracts PREGS (300 nM) and DTG (300 nM)-induced inhibition and DHEAS (300 nM)-induced potentiation of NMDA (200 μM) = evoked [^{3}H]norepinephrine (NE) overflow. Triangles = PROG alone; squares = DHEAS plus competitor; circles = PREGS plus competitor; diamonds = DTG plus PROG. *Solid symbols* = basal values of NMDA (200 μM)-evoked [^{3}H]NE overflow in the absence of any neurosteroid; *open symbols* = values of NMDA-evoked [^{3}H]NE overflow in the presence of various concentrations of PROG alone or in combination with DHEAS, PREGS, or DTG. Each point represents the mean ± SEM of seven to nine experiments. *$p < 0.05$ and **$p < 0.01$; Student's t test versus basal values.

dependent inverted U curves were obtained in a manner typical for memory-enhancing substances.

PREG and PREGS also improve retention for foot shock avoidance training and are more potent than DHEAS, PREGS showing significant effects at 1.1 pg/mouse. PREGS also blocks NMDA antagonist-induced deficits in a passive avoidance memory task[58] and enhances performance in a two-trial memory task when infused stereotaxically into the nucleus basalis magnocellularis (NBM) of the rat[59] (FIG. 14). The NBM is now regarded as the main source of cortical cholinergic innervation and undergoes marked cell loss and various pathological alterations in patients with Alzheimer's disease.

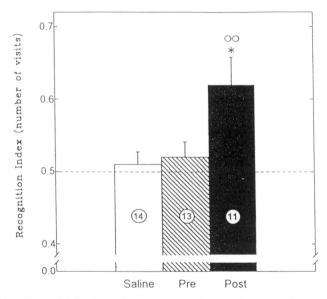

FIGURE 14. Effects of injection of 5 ng pregnenolone sulfate into the nucleus basalis magnocellularis before (Pre) or after (Post) the acquisition trial of a two-trial recognition task. The inter-trial interval (ITI) was 4 hours. Number of rats is within each bar. Difference from control group. $^*p < 0.05$; difference from chance level $^{\circ\circ}p < 0.01$.

To obtain information about the pathophysiological relevance of these observations, we evaluated the cognitive performances of aged rats. Some aged subjects are impaired, whereas others perform as well as young ones.[60] Memory performances of 29 aged rats (~ 24 months old) were measured in a water maze and in a two-trial recognition task. At the completion of the behavioral study, animals were sacrificed and brain was removed for analysis of PREGS concentrations in selected areas. A striking observations was the significant positive correlation between the concentration of PREGS in the hippocampus and memory performance, namely, animals with better performances had greater levels of PREGS ($r = -0.48, p < 0.01$).

These results support the possible neuroprotective role of PREGS (and likewise DHEAS) against neurodegenerative processes.

TABLE 7. Dehydroepiandrosterone Administration to Male Swiss Mice: DHEA(S) and Testosterone (TESTO) in Brain (ng/g)

	DHEA	DHEAS	TESTO
Intact	1.8	—	3.10
Castrated:			
Untreated	2.3	5.4	0.04
80 μg DHEA/day × 15 days	45.5	8.1	0.13

Aggression: Aggressive Behavior of Mice against Lactating Female Intruders

Group-housed triads of castrated male mice (Swiss strain) attack lactating female intruders. Previous reports indicated that testosterone (~ 1 μg/day for 15 days) and estradiol (~ 0.1 μg/day for 15 days) inhibit this aggressive behavior.[61] We observed that DHEA (80 μg/day for 15 days as the optimal dose) reproduces the effects of the sex steroids.[62] Males treated subcutaneously with an effective dose of DHEA showed more than 10-fold increased levels of DHEA in brain and a slight increase in testosterone which, although significant, remained well below its value in intact males[63] (TABLE 7). Therefore, the question arose of whether DHEA had an aggression-inhibitory action per se or through transformation to active metabolites. Indeed, DHEA is converted into testosterone (and testosterone into estradiol) after injection of large amounts to rodents. Incidentally, estrogenic androst-5-en-3β, 17β diol and DHEA sulfate, both direct metabolites of DHEA, have been discarded as the effective molecules.[63] To completely eliminate the possibility that the activity of DHEA was related to its conversion into active molecules with documented androgenic or estrogenic potency, behavioral experiments were repeated with the DHEA analog 3β-methyl-androst-5-en-17-one (M-DHEA). This molecule cannot be metabolized into sex steroids and is not demonstrably estrogenic[64] or androgenic[65] in rodents. Nevertheless, it dose-relatedly inhibited the aggressive behavior of castrated mice, at least as efficiently as did DHEA itself (TABLE 8).

Both DHEA and M-DHEA produced a marked and significant decrease in PREGS concentrations in the brain of treated mice[38] (FIG. 15). We speculated that DHEA and M-DHEA, by decreasing PREGS levels in the brain, might increase the GABAergic tone, which has repeatedly been implicated in the control of aggressiveness.[50] The time course of PREGS' decrease in brain after DHEA administration supports this conclusion. Indeed, castrated mice had to be treated for 2 weeks with DHEA before a clear-cut, significant effect on aggressive behavior was obtained.

TABLE 8. Aggressive Behavior of Castrated Swiss Male Mice towards Lactating Intruders

~ 280 nmol Steroid × 15 Days	Latency to First Bite (sec)	Number of Attacks/ 15 Minutes
DHEA	189	16
DHEAS	115	27
Δ5 DIOL	53	29
Controls	34	36
DHEA	154	21
M-DHEA[a]	309	18
Controls	59	36

[a]3β-methyl-androst-5-en-17-one.

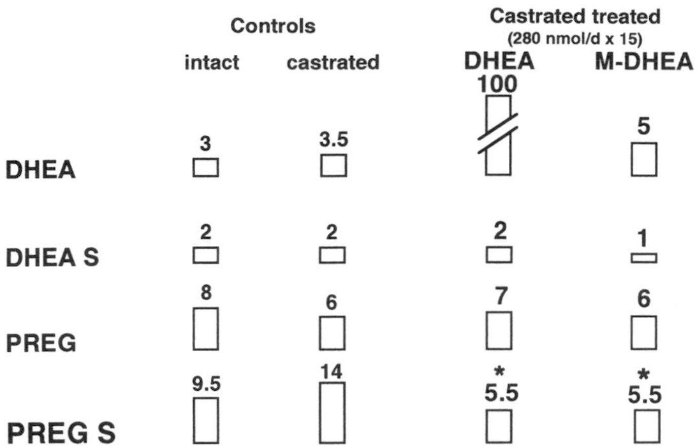

	Controls		Castrated treated (280 nmol/d x 15)	
	intact	castrated	DHEA	M-DHEA
DHEA	3 □	3.5 □	100 ⫽	5 □
DHEA S	2 □	2 □	2 □	1 ▭
PREG	8 ▯	6 ▯	7 ▯	6 ▯
PREG S	9.5 ▯	14 ▯	* 5.5 ▯	* 5.5 ▯

FIGURE 15. Neurosteroids in brain of male Swiss mice treated with DHEA or M-DHEA. *Significantly different from intact controls at 5% level (nonparametric rank order test of Kolmogorov-Smirnov).

Accordingly, the decrease of PREGS in brain was gradual and became significant only 15 days after the onset of treatment (FIG. 16).

Adult female mice also display aggressive behavior towards lactating intruders.[66] This aggressive behavior surprisingly does not depend on ovarian hormones, because it persists after ovariectomy and is not corrected by estradiol in spayed females, contrary to castrated males. As differences in hormonal control of aggressive behavior of males and females may be related to neonatal imprinting, spontaneously provoked by testosterone in males, we investigated the influence of DHEA treat-

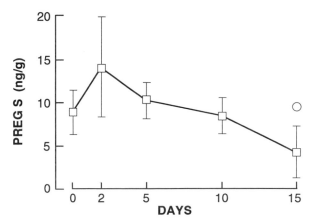

FIGURE 16. Time course of PREGS decrease in brain of castrated male mice. Forty Swiss male mice were castrated at 7 weeks. After a 4-week recovery, they received daily subcutaneous injections of DHEA 280 nmol, except the control group that received only the oil vehicle. They were killed by decapitation 2 hours after the last injection, and PREGS concentrations were measured in the whole brain. ○ Statistically different from controls at $p < 0.05$.

ment on spayed females and the modulation of this influence of DHEA by perinatal androgenization (0.5 μg testosterone injected in newborn). Indeed, females that had been androgenized at birth and then treated in adulthood with DHEA (A/D subgroup) were much less aggressive towards lactating intruders than were mice from any other experimental subgroup (FIG. 17). In accordance with this observation, the decrease in the concentration of PREGS produced by DHEA was significantly larger in the A/D subgroup than in the N/D one. The mechanisms by which DHEA or M-DHEA decreases PREGS concentrations are under current investigation. Preliminary results show that both compounds inhibit the formation of PREGS by the sulfokinase in the cytosol of the female mouse liver.

Having established a correlation between the decrease of PREGS in brain and the inhibition of aggressive behavior by DHEA and M-DHEA, we attempted to demonstrate a cause-and-effect relationship. For that purpose, it was necessary to

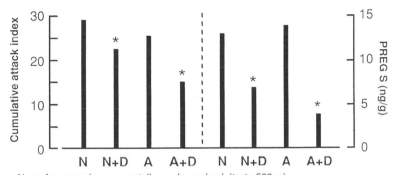

N or A : normal or neonatally androgenized (testo 500μg)
D   80 μg/d x 15 after 10 weeks of age

FIGURE 17. Effects of DHEA on aggressive behavior of female mice towards lactating intruders and on PREGS concentrations in brain. N = oil vehicle (10 μL sc); A = neonatal testosterone propionate (500 μg in oil); D = DHEA (280 nmol in oil daily for 15 days). The four experimental subgroups, made up of 30 10-week-old females each, were tested for attacks towards lactating intruders 2 hours after the last injection. PREGS was measured in whole brain 2 hours after sacrifice of similarly treated females. *Values differ significantly from oil controls.

compensate the decrease of PREGS concentrations in DHEA-treated mice. Injecting PREGS intraperitoneally was not practical because, due to the impermeability of the blood-brain barrier to steroid sulfates, enormous doses of PREGS must be used.[67] Therefore, we used trilostane (4α, 5-epoxy-17β-hydroxy-3-oxo-5α-androstane-2α-carbonitrile [TRIL]), a potent competitive inhibitor of 3β-HSD. When TRIL is given *in vivo* to rats, blockade of corticosterone biosynthesis relieves its negative feedback action on ACTH secretion, thus increasing the production of PREG, but also partly overcoming the blockade of 3β-HSD activity.

In fact, TRIL not only did not counteract the antiaggressive effect of DHEA, but also was inhibitory by itself.[68] This paradox was explained by two facts: (1) Although TRIL elicited a large increase in PREG levels in the brain of castrated mice, those of PREGS were unchanged and TRIL could not correct the decrease of PREGS induced by DHEA. (2) TRIL induced the appearance of large amounts of 3α,

21-dihydroxy-5α-pregnan-20-one (TH DOC), a brain metabolite of deoxycorticoste-rone (DOC) which had been oversecreted by the adrenals in response to endogenous ACTH. TH DOC, like TH PROG (allopregnanolone), potentiates inhibitory GABA-ergic neurotransmission. Therefore, pharmacological inhibition of the aggressive behavior of castrated male mice towards lactating intruders may result from an increase in GABAergic tone, possibly due to a decrease in PREGS (a GABA antagonist) and/or an increase in steroid metabolites such as TH PROG or TH DOC (which potentiate GABAergic neurotransmission).

CLINICAL CORRELATIONS

We have seen that the steroid biosynthetic machinery is present and seems operative in the human brain; therefore, the concept of neuroactive neurosteroids should be applicable.

This contention is supported by electroencephalographic studies. PREG (400 µg) was dissolved in oil and administrated subcutaneously to rats at the beginning of the light period. The effects on the amounts of the vigilance states and on the EEG signals within each state were investigated over 24 hours. Compared to control vehicle, PREG did not affect the duration of vigilance states. However, delta activity $(0.5–4 H_z)$ within nonrapid eye movement sleep (non-REMS) was enhanced through-out the recording period as would operate an inverse $GABA_A$-benzodiazepine agonist.[69] Similarly, the effect of a single oral dose of PREG (1 mg at 22.00 hours) upon the sleep EEG was also investigated in male volunteers. PREG increased the amount of time spent in slow wave sleep and depressed EEG sigma power.[70] On the basis of comparisons with the effects of benzodiazepines or of hypnotics such as zopiclone and zolpidem, which bind specifically to GABA-benzodiazepine receptors, the authors concluded that as in the rat, PREG exerts inverse agonistic properties at the GABA receptor, presumably after conversion to PREGS.

Single oral doses of DHEA (500 mg) were also given to normal volunteers 60 minutes before nocturnal sleep. DHEA induced a significant increase in REM sleep, whereas all other sleep variables remained unchanged. Spectral analysis of five selected EEG bands revealed marked changes during REM sleep in the first 2-hour sleep period after DHEA administration.[71] The combined effects on spectral power in the spindle frequency during REM sleep and the increase in the total amount of REM sleep pointed to a mixed $GABA_A$ agonistic/antagonistic effect of DHEA exerted through either DHEA alone or changes in steroid metabolism evoked by DHEA administration.

The observed augmentation of REM sleep, which has been implicated in memory storage, suggests potential clinical usefulness of DHEA in age-related dementia.

Indeed, serum DHEAS levels in humans reach highest values at around the age of 25 years, then decline steadily over the following decades to less than 20% of that maximum before the age of 70.[71,72] DHEAS may be seen as an individual marker because, while values decrease with age in everyone, each individual remains in his/her own class of high or low levels,[73] which is evocative of a hereditary trait.[73] As we have observed that memory performances of aged rats are positively correlated with PREGS concentrations in hippocampus, a similar relationship might be consid-ered for DHEAS in the species in which it is most abundant (primates and humans). This is being undertaken with the subjects of the Paquid program, a longitudinal survey of aging processes in an elderly community sample in France.[74]

Finally, definitive conclusions about the neuroprotective and memory-enhancing properties of DHEA in humans will rely on ongoing clinical trials, which consist of administering a relatively moderate amount of DHEA, which is massively transformed into DHEAS after oral administration, in such a way as to compensate for the decrease that occurs with aging.[75] It must be realized that the decrease of a single body component can, at most, be responsible for part of the disturbances occurring with aging and that everyone will not respond to its compensation in the same manner.

The purpose of preventing and eventually relieving the damages due to aging of the nervous system rests on the promise of physiologic and pharmacologic experiments and will necessitate several years of careful medical survey.

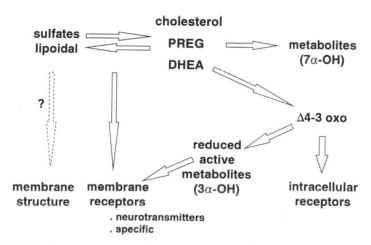

FIGURE 18. Diverse mechanisms of action of neurosteroids. Actions of neurosteroids PREG and DHEA may be direct or indirect via conversion to active metabolites and involve either intracellular receptors or several types of membrane receptors.

CONCLUDING REMARKS

Dehydroepiandrosterone may be characterized as both a neurosteroid and a neuroactive steroid.

1. A neurosteroid: *stricto sensu,* a complete description of its biosynthetic pathway(s) in brain or peripheral nervous system should be at hand to qualify DHEA as a neurosteroid. Formal demonstration is still lacking; however, strong indirect evidence has been provided, based on DHEA accumulation in brain, mostly as sulfate and fatty esters, independently of the presence or activity of peripheral steroidogenic glands. Nonclassical biosynthetic pathways have been suggested and await demonstration of the corresponding enzymatic activities.

2. A neuroactive steroid: multiple pharmacologic effects of DHEA and its sulfate ester on the nervous system have been reported. They have been described as neurotrophic, excitatory, neuromodulatory (e.g., GABA$_A$ receptor allosteric antagonist and sigma 1 receptor allosteric agonist effects), memory enhancing, and antiag-

gressive. The corresponding mechanisms of these activities are likely diverse, including direct and indirect (via metabolites) actions and effects via intracellular and several types of membrane receptors (FIG. 18).

The physiologic and pathophysiologic roles of DHEA as a neuroactive molecule, however, remain speculative. Concentrations so far measured in total brain or rather large sections of the brain, as free or conjugated steroids, are definitely too low to account for most described effects, unless there is selective accumulation of the steroid in small defined structures or areas. This is conceivable, because myelin in particular is a good candidate for accumulation of amphipathic molecules such as DHEAS; indeed, unpublished data showed a preferential accumulation of DHEAS in myelin prepared from whole brain homogenates. It should also be recalled that the DHEA biosynthetic "precursor," PREG, is an active molecule as such or after conversion to the sulfate ester and is much more abundant than DHEA in the CNS of rodents. Finally, several physiologic and/or pathologic circumstances, such as circadian variations or stress, may lead to markedly increased levels of neurosteroids.

These reservations should not preclude setting up trials aimed at compensating the profound decrease of DHEAS levels in plasma of aging human beings. The nervous system is one of the most important potential targets of the prospective trials under consideration. Experimental data on the control of mood changes and reinforcement of memory storage, combined with clinical evidence of DHEA activity on the nervous system *in vivo* in humans based on electroencephalographic data, are very encouraging.

REFERENCES

1. VINSON, G. P., B. J. WHITEHOUSE & C. GODARD. 1978. J. Steroid Biochem. **9:** 677–683.
2. CORPECHOT, C., P. ROBEL, M. AXELSON, J. SJÖVALL & E. E. BAULIEU. 1981. Proc. Natl. Acad. Sci. USA **78:** 4704–4707.
3. YOUNG, J., C. CORPECHOT, F. PERCHE, M. HAUG, E. E. BAULIEU & P. ROBEL. 1994. Endocrine **2:** 505–509.
4. MELLON-NUSSBAUM, S., L. PONTICORVO & S. LIEBERMAN. 1979. J. Biol. Chem. **254:** 12500–12505.
5. JO, D.-H., M. A. ABDALLAH, J. YOUNG, E. E. BAULIEU & P. ROBEL. 1989. Steroids **54:** 287–297.
6. BAULIEU, E. E. 1981. Steroid hormones in the brain: Several mechanisms? *In* Steroid Hormone Regulation of the Brain. K. Fuxe, J.A. Gustafsson & L. Wetterberg, Eds.: 3–14. Pergamon Press. Oxford.
7. CORPECHOT, C., M. SYNGUELAKIS, S. TALHA, M. AXELSON, J. SJÖVALL, R. VIHKO, E. E. BAULIEU & P. ROBEL. 1983. Brain Res. **270:** 119–125.
8. ROBEL, P., Y. AKWA, C. CORPECHOT, Z.-Y. HU, I., JUNG-TESTAS, K. KABBADJ, C. LE GOASCOGNE, R. MORFIN, C. VOURC'H, J. YOUNG & E. E. BAULIEU. *In* Brain Endocrinology. M. Motta, Ed.: 105–132. Raven Press, New York.
9. LE GOASCOGNE, C., N. SANANES, M. GOUEZOU, S. TAKEMORI, S. KOMINAMI, E. E. BAULIEU & P. ROBEL. 1991. J. Reprod. Fertil. **93:** 609–622.
10. MELLON, S. & C. F. DESCHEPPER. 1993. Brain Res. **629:** 283–292.
11. GUARNERI, P., R. GUARNERI, C. CASCIO, P. PAVASANT, F. PICCOLI & V. PAPADOPOULOS. 1994. J. Neurochem. **63:** 86–96.
12. JUNGMAN, R. A. 1968. Biochim. Biophys. Acta **164:** 110–123.
13. TAIT, A. D. & L. C. HODGE. 1985. J. Steroid Biochem. **22:** 237–242.
14. PRASAD, V. V. K., S. RAJU VEGESNA, M. WELCH & S. LIEBERMAN. 1994. Proc. Natl. Acad. Sci. USA **91:** 3220–3223.
15. LIEBERMAN, S. 1986. J. Endocrinol. **111:** 519–529.

16. ROBEL, P., E. BOURREAU, C. CORPECHOT, D. C. DANG, F. HALBERG, C. CLARKE, M. HAUG, M. L. SCHLEGEL, M. SYNGUELAKIS, C. VOURC'H & E. E. BAULIEU. 1987. J. Steroid Biochem. **27:** 649–655.
17. ROBEL, P., I. JUNG-TESTAS, Z.-Y. HU, Y. AKWA, N. SANANES, K. KABBADJ, B. EYCHENNE, M. J. SANCHO, K. I. KANG, D. ZUCMAN, R. MORFIN & E. E. BAULIEU. 1991. Neurosteroids: Biosynthesis and metabolism in cultured rodent glia and neurons. *In* Neurosteroids and Brain Function. E. Costa & S. M. Paul, Eds. Vol. 8: 147–154. Thieme Medical Publishers, Inc. New York.
18. PELLETIER, G., E. DUPONT, J. SIMARD, V. LUUTHE, A. BELANGER & F. LABRIE. 1992. J. Steroid Biochem. Mol. Biol. **43:** 451–467.
19. GUENNOUN, R., R. J. FIDDES, M. GOUEZOU, M. LOMBES & E. E. BAULIEU. 1995. Mol. Brain Res. **30:** 287–300.
20. AKWA, Y., N. SANANES, M. GOUEZOU, P. ROBEL, E. E. BAULIEU & C. LE GOASCOGNE. 1993. J. Cell Biol. **121:** 135–143.
21. AKWA, Y., R. F. MORFIN, P. ROBEL & E. E. BAULIEU. 1992. Biochem. J. **288:** 959–964.
22. WARNER, M., M. STRÖMSTEDT, L. MÖLLER & J. A. GUSTAFSSON. 1989. Endocrinology **124:** 2699–2706.
23. ZHANG, J., Y. AKWA, E. E. BAULIEU & J. SJÖVALL. 1995. C. R. Acad. Sci. Paris **318:** 345–349.
24. ROBEL, P., C. CORPECHOT, C. CLARKE, A. GROYER, M. SYNGUELAKIS, C. VOURC'H & E. E. BAULIEU. 1986. Neuro-steroids: 3β-hydroxy-Δ5-derivatives in the rat brain. *In* Neuroendocrine Molecular Biology. G. Fink, A. J. Harmar & K. W. McKerns, Eds.: 367–377. Plenum Press. New York.
25. MARTEL, C., E. RHEAUME, M. TAKAHASHI, C. TRUDEL, J. COUËT, V. LUU-THE, J. SIMARD & F. LABRIE. 1992. J. Steroid Biochem. Mol. Biol. **41:** 597–603.
26. VOURC'H, C., B. EYCHENNE, D.-H. JO, J. RAULIN, D. LAPOUS, E. E. BAULIEU & P. ROBEL. 1992. Steroids **57:** 210–215.
27. PAHUJA, S. L. & R. B. HOCHBERG. 1989. J. Biol. Chem. **264:** 3216–3222.
28. KISHIMOTO, Y. & M. HOSHI. 1972. J. Neurochem. **19:** 2207–2215.
29. MATHUR, C., V. V. K. PRASAD, V. S. RAJU, M. WELCH & S. LIEBERMAN. 1993. Proc. Natl. Acad. Sci. USA **90:** 85–88.
30. HOBKIRK, R. 1993. Trends Endocrinol. Metab. **4:** 69–74.
31. RAJKOWSKI, K. M., P. ROBEL & E. E. BAULIEU. Hydroxysteroid sulphotransferase activity in the rat brain and liver as a function of age and sex. Submitted.
32. HOBKIRK, R. 1985. Can. J. Biochem. Cell Biol. **63:** 1127–1144.
33. BAULIEU, E. E., P. ROBEL, O. VATIER, M. HAUG, C. LE GOASCOGNE & E. BOURREAU. 1987. Neurosteroids: Pregnenolone and dehydroepiandrosterone in the brain. *In* Receptor-Receptor Interactions. K. Fuxe & L. F. Agnati, Eds. Vol. 48: 89–104. MacMillan Press Ltd. Basingstoke.
34. JO, D. H., S. SANCHEZ DE LA PENA, F. HALBERG, F. UNGAR, E. E. BAULIEU & P. ROBEL. 1990. Circadian-infradian rhythmic variation of brain neurosteroids in the female rat. *In* Chronobiology: Its Role in Clinical Medicine, General Biology, and Agriculture, Part B. D. K. Hayes, J. E. Pauly & R. J. Reither, Eds.: 125–134. Wiley-Liss. New York.
35. CORPECHOT, C., P. LECLERC, E. E. BAULIEU & P. BRAZEAU. 1985. Steroids **45:** 229–234.
36. BARBACCIA, M. L., G. ROSCETTI, M. TRABUCCHI, T. CUCCHEDDU, A. CONCAS & G. BIGGIO. 1994. Eur. J. Pharmacol. **261:** 317–320.
37. ANDERSON, S., F. CRÖNHOLM & J. SJÖVALL. 1986. Alcohol Clin. Exp. Res. **10:** 555–615.
38. CORPECHOT, C., P. ROBEL, F. LACHAPELLE, N. BAUMANN, M. AXELSON, J. SJÖVALL & E. E. BAULIEU. 1981. C. R. Acad. Sci. Paris **292:** 231–234.
39. YOUNG, J., C. CORPECHOT, M. HAUG, S. GOBAILLE, E. E. BAULIEU & P. ROBEL. 1991. Biochem. Biophys. Res. Commun. **174:** 892–897.
40. KNAPSTEIN, P., A. DAVID, C.-H. WU, D. F. ARCHER, G. L. FLICKINGER & J. C. TOUCHSTONE. Steroids **11:** 885–896.
41. LAKSHMI, S. & A. S. BALASUBRAMANIAN. 1981. J. Neurochem. **37:** 358–362.
42. LANTHIER, A. & V. V. PATWARDHAN. 1986. J. Steroid Biochem. **25:** 445–449.
43. LACROIX, C., J. FIET, J.-P. BENAIS, B. GUEUX, R. BONETE, J.-M. VILLETTE, B. GOURMEL & C. DREUX. 1987. J. Steroid Biochem. **28:** 317–325.

44. LE GOASCOGNE, C., M. GOUEZOU, P. ROBEL, G. DEFAYE, E. CHAMBAZ, M. R. WATERMAN & E. E. BAULIEU. 1989. J. Neuroendocrinol. **1:** 153–156.
45. ROBERTS, E., L. BOLOGA, J. F. FLOOD & G. E. SMITH. 1987. Brain Res. **406:** 357–362.
46. DEL CERRO, S., J. GARCIA-ESTRADA & L. M. GARCIA-SEGURA. 1995. Glia. **14:** 65–71.
47. MAJEWSKA, M. D., S. DEMIRGÖREN, C. E. SPIVAK & E. D. LONDON. 1990. Brain Res. **526:** 143–146.
48. HEUSER, G. & E. EIDELBERG. 1961. Endocrinology **69:** 915–924.
49. CARETTE, B. & P. POULAIN. 1984. Neurosci. Lett. **45:** 205–210.
50. MAJEWSKA, M. D. 1992. Prog. Neurobiol. **38:** 379–395.
51. SPIVAK, C. E. 1994. Synapse **16:** 113–122.
52. EL-ETR, M., C. CORPECHOT, J. YOUNG, Y. AKWA, P. ROBEL & E. E. BAULIEU. 1992. Modulating effect of steroid sulfates on muscimol-stimulated ^{36}Cl uptake. Abstract of the 15th Annual Meeting of the European Neuroscience Association. Munich, September 13–17, 1992: 128. Abstract 2215.
53. WU, F.-S., T. T. GIBBS & D. H. FARB. 1990. Mol. Pharmacol. **37:** 597–602.
54. MONNET, F. P., V. MAHE, P. ROBEL & E. E. BAULIEU. Proc. Natl. Acad. Sci. USA **92:** 3774–3778.
55. FFRENCH-MULLEN, J. M. H. & K. T. SPENCE. 1991. Eur. J. Pharmacol. **202:** 269–272.
56. FLOOD, J. F., G. E. SMITH & E. ROBERTS. 1988. Brain Res. **447:** 269–278.
57. FLOOD, J. F., J. E. MORLEY & E. ROBERTS. 1992. Proc. Natl. Acad. Sci. USA **89:** 1567–1571.
58. MATHIS, C., S. M. PAUL & J. N. CRAWLEY. 1994. Psychopharmacology **116:** 201–206.
59. MAYO, W., F. DELLU, P. ROBEL, J. CHERKAOUI, M. LE MOAL, E. E. BAULIEU & H. SIMON. 1993. Brain Res. **607:** 324–328.
60. ROBEL, P., J. YOUNG, C. CORPECHOT, W. MAYO, F. PERCHE, M. HAUG, H. SIMON & E. E. BAULIEU. 1995. J. Steroid Biochem. Mol. Biol. **53:** 355–360.
61. HAUG, M. & P. F. BRAIN. 1979. Physiol. Behav. **23:** 397–400.
62. HAUG, M., J.-F. SPETZ, M.-L. SCHLEGEL & P. ROBEL. 1983. C. R. Acad. Sci. Paris **296:** 975–977.
63. SCHLEGEL, M. L., J. F. SPETZ, P. ROBEL & M. HAUG. 1985. Physiol. Behav. **34:** 867–870.
64. PASHKO, L. L., R. J. ROVITO, J. R. WILLIAMS, E. L. SOBEL & A. G. SCHWARTZ. 1984. Carcinogenesis **5:** 463–466.
65. HAUG, M., M. L. OUSS-SCHLEGEL, J. F. SPETZ, P. F. BRAIN, V. SIMON, E. E. BAULIEU & P. ROBEL. 1989. Physiol. Behav. **46:** 955–959.
66. HAUG, M., J. YOUNG, P. ROBEL & E. E. BAULIEU. 1991. C. R. Acad. Sci. Paris **312:** 511–516.
67. MAJEWSKA, M. D., M. T. BLUET-PAJOT, P. ROBEL & E. E. BAULIEU. 1989. Pharmacol. Biochem. Behav. **33:** 701–703.
68. YOUNG, J., C. CORPECHOT, F. PERCHE, B. EYCHENNE, M. HAUG, E. E. BAULIEU & P. ROBEL. 1995. Neurosteroids in the mouse brain: Behavioral and pharmacological effects of a 3β-hydroxy-steroid dehydrogenase inhibitor. Submitted.
69. LANCEL, M., T. A. M. CRÖNLEIN, P. MÜLLER-PREUB & F. HOLSBOER. 1994. Brain Res. **646:** 85–94.
70. STEIGER, A., L. TRACHSEL, J. GULDNER, U. HEMMETER, B. ROTHE, R. RUPPRECHT, H. VEDDER & F. HOLSBOER. 1993. Brain Res. **615:** 267–274.
71. FRIEB, E., L. TRACHSEL & J. GULDNER. 1994. Dehydroepiandrosterone increases REM sleep and changes EEG power spectra in men. Max Planck Institute of Psychiatry Clinical Institute. Scientific Report: 108–109.
72. MIGEON, C. J., A. R. KELLER, B. LAWRENCE & T. H. SHEPARD. 1957. J. Clin. Endocrinol. Metab. **17:** 1051–1062.
73. THOMAS, G., N. FRENOY, S. LEGRAIN, R. SEBAG-LANOE, E. E. BAULIEU & B. DEBUIRE. 1994. J. Clin. Endocrinol. Metab. **79:** 1273–1276.
74. FUHRER, R., T. C. ANTONUCCI, M. GAGON, J. F. DARTIGUES, P. BARBERGER-GATEAU & A. ALPEROVITCH. 1992. Physiol. Med. **22:** 159–172.
75. BAULIEU, E. E. 1995. C. R. Acad. Sci. Paris **318:** 7–11.

Neuronal Actions
of Dehydroepiandrosterone

Possible Roles in Brain Development, Aging, Memory, and Affect

MARIA DOROTA MAJEWSKA

Medications Development Division
National Institute on Drug Abuse
5600 Fishers Lane, Rm 11A-55
Rockville, Maryland 20857

Dehydroepiandrosterone (DHEA) and its sulfate ester (DHEAS) are major adrenal hormones in humans which, either in their native forms or as precursors of other steroids, exert remarkable diversity of biologic actions. DHEA and DHEAS are regarded as the steroids of youth, because in both women and men their levels peak in early adulthood and then monotonously decrease with age.[1,2] Several studies suggest positive correlations between plasma levels of DHEA(S) and vigor, longevity, and resistance to cancers and cardiovascular diseases,[3,4] making this steroid an intriguing object of interest for investigators studying aging.

In addition to their multifaceted peripheral actions, DHEA and DHEAS play several vital roles in the central nervous system (CNS). This chapter describes neuronal aspects of DHEA(S) activity and draws implications for their possible roles in brain development, aging, memory, and affect.

DHEA AND DHEAS AS NEUROSTEROIDS

Evidence accumulated over the last decade documented that the brain is capable of *de novo* synthesis of steroids (termed neurosteroids) independent of gonads and adrenals.[5] The mammalian brain contains large amounts of the steroid precursor cholesterol and its sulfate and lipoid derivatives,[6] and is "equipped" with several steroid-metabolizing enzymes. The presence of neurosteroids was shown in mammalian brains from rodents through primates.[5] The neurosteroids originally discovered and characterized were pregnenolone (P) and DHEA, their sulfates, PS and DHEAS, and fatty acid derivatives,[7,8] but now this class also includes many other brain-formed steroids, which are neuromodulators.

The mitochondrial enzyme cytochrome P-450$_{scc}$, responsible for cholesterol side-chain cleavage and the formation of neurosteroids with 3β-hydroxy-△5 structures, such as pregnenolone and DHEA, was found throughout the rat brain, mostly in the white matter.[9] Production of pregnenolone was found in oligodendrocytes, but not in neurons.[10] The genesis of DHEA and DHEAS in the CNS is not clear, however. In adrenal glands, gonads, and placenta, DHEA is formed by cleavage of pregnenolone by the enzyme complex 17α-hydroxylase-17-20-desmolase, which was not found in the brain,[11] thereby leading the investigators to consider an alternative path for brain biosynthesis of DHEA. In the brain, P(S) and DHEA(S) are metabolized to other neurosteroids. Pregnenolone can be converted to progesterone by 3β-hydroxy-steroid oxidoreductase, 5-ene-isomerase,[12] primarily in the glia.[10] Brain tissues also contain steroid 5α-reductase and 3α-oxidoreductase,[13-15] which can convert progesterone to 5α-pregnane-3α-ol-20-one (tetrahydroprogesterone). Likewise, DHEA can be converted in the CNS to androstenedione (4-androsten-3,17-dione) and subsequently reduced to androsterone (5α-androstane-3α-ol-17-one). Also, synthesis of 7α and 7β hydroxylated metabolites of DHEA in the brain was documented, leading to the formation of androstenediol (AED; 5-androstene-3β,17β-diol) and androstenetriol (AET; 5-androstene-3β, 7α/7β,17β-triol). Because the glia seems to be the primary site of synthesis of neurosteroids, it can be regarded as a neuroparacrine gland.

The amounts of neurosteroids, PS and DHEAS, found in rodent brain range from 2 to 16 ng per gram of fresh tissue,[7,8] but micromolar K_m values for steroid sulfatases suggest that micromolar concentrations of PS and DHEAS are present in certain CNS compartments. The neurosteroids were also found in the postmortem brain in men and women > 60 years of age.[16,17] Dehydroepiandrostereone, pregnenolone, and progesterone were present in all regions of the human brain at concentrations many times higher than those in plasma.

DEHYDROEPIANDROSTERONE SULFATE AS ANTAGONIST OF THE GABA$_A$ RECEPTORS

The ubiquitous GABA$_A$ receptor is a protein pentamer[18] whose activation by GABA opens the associated chloride channel, leading to increased chloride transport and resulting usually in hyperpolarization of neuronal membrane. In the brain, heterogeneous forms of GABA$_A$ receptors exist with different combinations of polypeptide subunits, which change during development.[19,20] Activity of the GABA$_A$ receptor is potentiated by hypnotics such as benzodiazepines and barbiturates and is reduced by convulsants such as picrotoxin.

We discovered that certain neurosteroids bimodally regulate the activity of the GABA$_A$ receptors, some behaving as agonists and others as antagonists.[21] DHEA and DHEAS at low micromolar concentrations function as allosteric antagonists of the GABA$_A$ receptors, and they noncompetitively inhibit GABA-induced currents in neurons[22,23] by accelerating desensitization of GABA$_A$ receptors.[24] The GABA$_A$-antagonistic activity of DHEAS resembles the effects of PS,[25,26] but sites of action for these two steroids at the receptor are distinct.[21] DHEAS binds at sites close to those where barbiturates act,[22,23] whereas PS interacts with sites of picrotoxin binding.[27] The neurosteroids may bind to hydrophobic pockets at the receptors.[21] The GABA$_A$-antagonistic features of DHEAS and PS contrast with the potent GABA$_A$-agonistic actions of tetrahydroprogesterone (THP), tetrahydrodeoxycorticosterone (5α-pregnane-3α,21-diol-20-one [THDOC]),[28] and androsterone (5α-androstane-3α-ol-17-one).[29]

The GABA-active steroids are modulators of synaptic events and may play a vital role in neuronal plasticity. GABA agonistic steroids prolong inhibitory postsynaptic potentials (IPSPs),[30] depress the depolarizing responses to glutamate, and block the glutamate-induced action potentials.[31] By contrast, DHEAS reduces the amplitudes of the IPSPs,[24] implying that it should enhance depolarization in neurons. Excitatory actions of DHEAS and PS on neurons were reported[32] along with their convulsant actions in animals.[33] Because different neurosteroids modulate GABA$_A$ receptor function in opposing directions, a ratio between excitatory and inhibitory steroids may ultimately shape synaptic activity.

The neuroactive effects of certain steroids were recognized in the 1920s by

Cashin and Moravek[35] who described the anesthetic action of intravenously injected cholesterol. Next, Selye[36] showed hypnotic actions of progesterone and deoxycortico-sterone, and his studies led to the development of steroidal anesthetics structurally similar to THP and THDOC.[36,37] The anesthetic effects of progesterone and of THP and THDOC[38,39] can now be explained by their potentiation of GABA$_A$ receptor function. THDOC also shows anxiolytic[40] and antiaggressive[41] effects in rodents.

The hypnotic/anxiolytic actions of THP and THDOC contrast with the behavioral effects of GABA-antagonistic neurosteroids. DHEA injected intraperitoneally in doses of 100–150 mg/kg produced tonic-clonic seizures in mice, but in lower doses it caused sedation.[33] The convulsant effects of DHEA most likely were mediated by inhibition of GABA$_A$ receptors,[22,23] whereas the sedative effects were mediated by the GABA-agonistic DHEA metabolite androsterone. Also, PS injected intracerebro-ventricularly (8 μg/10 μl) reduced barbiturate-induced sleep in rats,[42] but at lower doses it prolonged sleep.

The ubiquity of GABA$_A$ receptors in the CNS and their role in controlling neuronal excitability suggest that bimodal regulation of these receptors by neurosteroids determines many brain functions and behaviors. An increase in synaptic concentrations of DHEAS or PS should augment neuronal excitability and CNS arousal, whereas elevation in concentrations of THP or THDOC should enhance neuronal inhibition. A fine interplay may exist in the brain between the hypnotic/anxiolytic steroids and the GABA-antagonistic steroids, which not only counteract each others' actions at the GABA$_A$ receptors, but also are metabolically linked.[21] In the brain, PS and DHEAS can be desulfated[34] and then converted to THP and androsterone. This type of metabolic relationship resembles that between excitatory and inhibitory amino acids and may be part of a homeostatic mechanism of control of neural activity through precise regulation of the synthesis of counteracting neuromodulators.

DHEA(S) AND BRAIN DEVELOPMENT

Plasma levels of DHEA and DHEAS undergo dramatic developmental changes,[1,43] suggesting their involvement in CNS ontogeny. Indeed, DHEA and DHEAS enhanced neuronal and glial survival and differentiation in cultures from embryonic brains.[44] Neurodevelopmental actions of DHEA(S) may, in part, be mediated by their effects on GABA$_A$ receptors, whose subunit composition changes during fetal and neonatal development.[19,20] In early embryonic and postnatal life, GABA acting via GABA$_A$ receptors depolarizes neurons from rat cortex, cerebellum, or spinal cord,[45] and in immature neurons GABA stimulates chemokinesis,[46] thereby facilitating neuronal migration. Because "immature" GABA$_A$ receptors are modulated by neurosteroids,[47] an interaction between the expression of distinct receptor subtypes, manifesting different sensitivity to neurosteroids[48,49] and changing concentrations of steroids in fetal and neonatal brains, may sculpt neurodevelopmental processes.

DHEA(S) IN COGNITION AND BRAIN AGING

In mature neurons, stimulation of GABA$_A$ receptors produces mainly hyperpolarizing effects. Brinton[50] showed that the GABA agonist steroid THP increased chloride influx in hippocampal neuronal cultures, and it induced reversible structural regression of these neurons. This implies that GABAergic steroids play a dynamic role in shaping neuronal architecture and, as such, may have critical functions in learning, memory, and neuron survival during aging or stress. In this aspect, DHEAS, as a GABA antagonist, should facilitate neuronal structural growth. Such an effect of DHEAS was observed *in vitro* in neuronal and glial cultures, but it is not known if it was mediated by $GABA_A$ receptors.[44]

Deterioration of cognitive functions typically accompanies aging. The role of GABA in learning and memory is evidenced by the fact that GABA antagonists facilitate hippocampal long-term potentiation (LTP),[51] a synaptic process mediated through excitatory neurotransmitters and believed to be fundamental to long-term memory. Because an inhibitory input provided by the GABAergic interneurons sets a threshold for postsynaptic modification of excitatory inputs,[52] the GABAergic neurosteroids are likely to influence memory. DHEAS, DHEA, and PS, as GABA antagonists, are expected to enhance learning and memory and the GABA-agonistic steroids to impair these functions. This concept is supported by the finding that GABA agonists (barbiturates and benzodiazepines) produce amnesia,[53] whereas GABA antagonists (picrotoxin and pentylenetetrazol) reverse amnesia and improve memory.[54,55] Pentylenetetrazol was used with some success in the treatment of geriatric patients with disturbed memory.[56] Indeed, DHEAS and DHEA improved memory in aging mice[57] and prevented pharmacologically induced amnesia.[58] The potentiating effects of DHEA on automatized memory were also documented recently in humans.[59] DHEA(S), acting at the $GABA_A$ receptors, may additionally enhance memory processes by augmenting rapid eye movement sleep (REM),[60] believed to be involved in the consolidation of memory. In contrast to the memory-facilitating actions of DHEA(S), GABA-agonistic progesterone metabolites may impair automatized memory tasks.[61]

Excessive GABAergic tone may accelerate neuronal degeneration and brain aging. This concept is consistent with the marked cognitive impairments associated with some degree of cerebral atrophy[62] observed in chronic users of benzodiazepines. Marczynski[63] reported that chronic administration of the benzodiazepine antagonist flumazenil prolonged the life span and improved memory in rats, and he proposed a GABA/benzodiazepine hypothesis of brain aging. Augmentation of GABAergic tone during aging is suggested by increased activity of glutamic acid decarboxylase in the brain of aged animals[63] and by enhancement of GABA-activated currents in neurons from aged rats, resulting from the reduction in use-dependent receptor desensitization.[64] Globally, these effects would reduce neuronal excitability and might accelerate neuronal aging. In this context, because DHEAS facilitates desensitization of $GABA_A$ receptors,[24] it is expected to counteract the effect of aging in neurons, thus improving memory and promoting neuronal survival.[44,57,58] Concordantly with this notion, some studies showed lower than normal levels of DHEAS in the serum of patients diagnosed with Alzheimer's disease and multiinfarct dementia[65,66] and in men with organic brain syndrome.[67]

Although steroids can penetrate the blood-brain barrier, brain and cerebrospinal fluid (CSF) levels of DHEA and DHEAS are better forecasters of their central actions than are plasma levels. In fact, plasma DHEAS levels, while predictive of mortality, were not generally predictive of cognitive functions in the elderly.[4] Postmortem studies on individuals who died beyond 60 years of age showed higher DHEA and DHEAS levels in the cerebral cortices of women than men.[16] This intriguing observation, which needs to be replicated, may be significant despite a small sample size, because it was consistent in four cerebrocortical areas, whereas no gender differences were noted in cerebral concentrations of other steroids, and DHEA/DHEAS levels in other brain regions were not different between the two sexes.[16] In CSF of patients (50–60 years old) no gender difference was found in

DHEA levels (about 120 pg/ml), but women had significantly lower levels of DHEAS (515 pg/ml) than did men (872 pg/ml).[68] Moreover, a negative correlation was noted between CSF levels of DHEAS and aging in men but not in women. The physiologic significance of these observations is unknown, but it is intriguing to find out if the higher concentrations of DHEAS in cerebral cortices and the lack of decline of this steroid with age in women could be responsible in some way for the greater longevity of women. Conceivably, higher CSF concentrations of DHEAS in men than in women may be indicative of its greater loss from mens' brains as a result of earlier aging-related brain degeneration,[69] for elevated CSF concentrations of DHEAS were also found in patients with neuropathies.[68] Collectively, the foregoing observations, while still incomplete, suggest that declining levels of DHEA/DHEAS in the brain may accelerate brain aging and may be concordant with earlier death.

DHEA(S) AND CIRCADIAN RHYTHMS

Plasma levels of adrenal steroids typically undergo diurnal cyclical changes.[70] Likewise, circadian variations occur in the brain concentrations of neurosteroids.[71] In the brain of the rat, a nocturnal animal, DHEAS levels peak at the prenocturnal hours and remain high through the first half of the dark cycle,[71] following the plasma pattern. In humans, DHEAS manifests modest circadian rhythms, and its higher plasma levels are generally found during day hours.[71,72] The brain levels of DHEAS in humans may undergo similar diurnal changes, and DHEA and DHEAS may function as endogenous analeptics during periods of intense activity.

DHEA(S) AND PERSONALITY, AGGRESSIVITY, AND AFFECT

Neuromodulatory actions of steroids at $GABA_A$ receptors invite speculation that their profile in plasma and the CNS contributes to the manifestations of different personality traits. The steroid profile is genetically determined; it changes during development, aging, pregnancy, and stress, and it is anomalous in some pathologies. Theoretically, a higher proportion of excitatory steroids to inhibitory ones would result in an anxiety-prone, introvert type of personality characterized by a higher level of resting arousal, greater sensitivity accompanied by a tendency to augment incoming stimuli, and a low threshold for positive hedonic tone.[73] Elevated concentrations of DHEAS (and PS) may contribute to this personality trait by increasing basal CNS arousal and may be responsible for their high sedation threshold.[74] By contrast, a higher ratio of inhibitory steroids to excitatory ones could result in a personality with a tendency for blunted reaction to stimuli, extreme cases of which would be "sensation seekers" characterized by an atypically high threshold for arousal and requiring very strong stimuli to achieve positive hedonic tone. Characteristic of this personality is also a tendency for antisocial behaviors and postulated inclination towards substance abuse.

There is empiric support for this thesis, as women characterized by highly expansive personalities and men manifesting type A behavior showed markedly lower plasma levels of the excitatory steroid DHEAS than did women with low expansivity or men characterized as type B.[71,75] The type A personality was also marked by excessive secretion of cortisol. Lower levels of DHEA(S), and especially lower DHEA(S) to cortisol ratios, in type A individuals may contribute to their greater cardiovascular morbidity and generally higher mortality rates.

Aggressivity is an element of personality that remains under strong hormonal control. Androgens typically induce intermale aggression in all species, and they were shown to provoke infanticide by male rodents, whereas castration or treatment with antiandrogenic drugs results in gentling of males.[76] DHEA suppressed aggressivity of castrated males against lactating females.[77] The biologic mechanism of this effect is not known and may be complex. The antiaggressive effect of DHEA as a GABA antagonist is inconsistent with the general antiaggressive features of GABA-agonistic drugs.[78] Most benzodiazepines are antiaggressive, although sometimes they evoke paradoxic "rage reactions" and increased hostility in humans.[79] Also, the GABA-agonistic steroid THDOC reduces aggression.[41] In this context, antiaggressive effects of DHEA can be explained by its metabolism to the anxiolytic androsterone. Alternatively, DHEA may increase hypothalamic and possibly cortical levels of serotonin,[80] believed to be inversely correlated with aggressivity.[81]

In addition, DHEAS was recently shown to potentiate NMDA-induced noradrenaline release from hippocampal slices, apparently by stimulating the sigma receptors.[82] The latter mechanism, combined with DHEA proserotonergic actions, may account for the reported antidepressant effects of DHEA in humans[59] and may additionally contribute to its potentiating effect on memory, in which norepinephrine plays a pivotal role.[83,84]

DHEA(S) REPLACEMENT

Collectively, CNS actions of DHEA and DHEAS just described, along with their beneficial immune, cardiovascular, and metabolic effects, strongly suggest that supplementation of these steroids may be advantageous for aging individuals. A few controlled studies and a wealth of anecdotal evidence indicate that DHEA treatment in aging patients is both safe and beneficial.[85,86] Particularly, the recent placebo-controlled study by the Yen group[86] documented positive hormonal, physical, and psychologic effects of 3-month treatment of middle-aged women and men with 50 mg of DHEA, with an absence of side effects. This encouraging study should be a prelude to long-term controlled trials that examine the effects of DHEA(S) on a spectrum of physiologic parameters, including bone, muscle, and skin metabolism, the cardiovascular, immune, and nervous systems, and on survival. Also, more basic studies are needed to examine the molecular mechanisms of actions of DHEA(S) in different organs. Nonetheless, while we are waiting for more complete data, the existing clinical and preclinical evidence already suggests that DHEA(S) replacement may be a safe and effective means of improving health and the quality of life during aging.

REFERENCES

1. HOPPER, B. R. & S. S. C. YEN. 1975. Circulating concentrations of dehydroepiandrosterone and dehydroepiandrosterone sulfate during puberty. J. Endocrinol. Metab. **40:** 458–461.
2. ORENTREICH, N., J. L. BRIND, R. L. RITZLER & J. H. VOGELMAN. 1984. Age changes and sex differences in serum dehydroepiandrosterone sulfate concentrations throughout adulthood. J. Clin. Endocrinol. Metab. **59:** 551–555.
3. BARRETT-CONNOR, E., K. T. KHAW & S. S. C. YEN. 1986. A prospective study of dehydroepiandrosterone sulfate, mortality, and cardiovascular disease. N. Engl. J. Med. **315:** 1519–1524.

4. BARRETT-CONNOR, E. & S. EDELSTEIN. 1994. A prospective study of dehydroepiandrosterone sulfate and cognitive function in an older population: The Rancho Bernardo study. J. Am. Geriatr. Soc. **42:** 520–523.
5. BAULIEU, E.-E., P. ROBEL, O. VATIER, A. HAUG, C. LE GOASCOGNE & E. BOURREAU. 1987. Neurosteroids: Pregnenolone and dehydroepiandrosterone in the rat brain. *In* Receptor-Receptor Interaction, A New Intramembrane Integrative Mechanism. K. Fuxe & L. F. Agnati, Eds. 89–104. MacMillan. Basingstoke.
6. IWAMORI, M., H. W. MOSER & Y. KISHIMOTO. 1976. Cholesterol sulfate in rat tissues. Tissue distribution, developmental changes and brain subcellular localization. Biochem. Biophys. Acta **441:** 268–279.
7. CORPECHOT, C., P. ROBEL, M. AXELSON, J. SJOVALL & E. E. BAULIEU. 1981. Characterization and measurement of dehydroepiandrosterone sulfate in rat brain. Proc. Natl. Acad. Sci. USA **78:** 4704–4707.
8. CORPECHOT, C., M. SYNGUELAKIS, S. TALHA, M. AXELSON, J. SJOVALL, R. VIHKO, E. E. BAULIEU & P. ROBEL. 1983. Pregnenolone and its sulfate ester in the rat brain. Brain Res. **270:** 119–125.
9. LE GOASCOGNE, C., P. ROBEL, M. GOUEZOU, N. SANANES, E. E. BAULIEU & M. WATERMAN. 1987. Neurosteroids: Cytochrome P-450$_{scc}$ in rat brain. Science **237:** 1212–1214.
10. JUNG-TESTAS, I., Z. Y. HU, E. E. BAULIEU & P. ROBEL. 1989. Steroid synthesis in rat brain cell cultures. J. Steroid Biochem. **34:** 511–519.
11. ROBEL, P., Y. AKWA, C. CORPECHOT, Z. Y. HU, I. JUNG-TESTAS, K. KABBADJ, C. L. LE GOASCOGNE, R. MORFIN, C. VOURC'H, J. YOUNG & E. E. BAULIEU. 1991. Neurosteroids: Biosynthesis and function of pregnenolone and dehydroepiandrosterone in the brain. *In* Brain Endocrinology. M. Motta, Ed. Raven Press, New York.
12. WEIDENFELD, J., R. A. SIEGEL & I. CHOWERS. 1980. In vitro conversion of pregnenolone to progesterone by discrete brain areas of the male rat. J. Steroid Biochem. **13:** 961–963.
13. KARAVOLAS, H. J., P. J. BERTICS, D. HODGES & N. RUDIE. 1984. Progesterone processing by neuroendocrine structures. *In* Metabolism of Hormonal Steroids. F. Celotti *et al.,* Eds.:149–169. Raven Press, New York.
14. ROSELLI, CH. E. & CH.A. SNIPES. 1984. Progesterone 5α-reductase in mouse brain. Brain Res. **305:** 197–202.
15. KRIEGER, N. R. & R. G. SCOTT. 1989. Non-neuronal localization of steroid converting enzyme: 3α-Hydroxysteroid oxidoreductase in olfactory tubercle of rat brain. J. Neurochem. **52:** 1866–1870.
16. LANTHIER, A. & V. V. PATWARDHAN. 1986. Sex steroids and 5-en-3β-hydroxysteroids in specific regions of the human brain and cranial nerves. J. Steroid Biochem. **25:** 445–449.
17. LACROIX, C., J. FIET, J. P. BENAIS, B. GUEUX, R. BONETE, J. M. VILLETTE, B. GOURMEL & C. DREUX. 1987. Simultaneous radioimmunoassay of progesterone, androst-4-enedione, pregnenolone, dehydroepiandrosterone and 17-hydroxyprogesterone in specific regions of human brain. J. Steroid Biochem. **28:** 317–325.
18. SCHOFIELD, P. R., M. G. DARLISON, M. FUJITA, D. R. BURT, F. A. STEPHENSON, H. RODRIGUEZ, L. M. RHEE, J. RAMACHANDRAN, V. REALE, T. A. GLENCORSE, P. H. SEEBURG & E. A. BARNARD. 1987. Sequence and functional expression of the GABA$_A$ receptor shows a ligand-gated receptor super-family. Nature **328:** 8221–8227.
19. LAURIE, D. J., W. WISDEN W. & P. SEEBURG. 1992. The distribution of thirteen GABA$_A$ receptor subunit mRNAs in the rat brain. III. Embryonic and postnatal development. J. Neurosci. **12:** 4151–4172.
20. POULTER, M. O., J. L. BARKER, A. M. O'CARROLL, S. J. LOLAIT & L. C. MAHAN. 1992. Differential and transient expression of GABA$_A$ receptor alpha-subunit mRNAS in the developing rat CNS. J. Neurosci. **12:** 2888–2900.
21. MAJEWSKA, M. D. 1992. Neurosteroids: Endogenous bimodal modulators of the GABA$_A$ receptor. Mechanism of action and physiological significance. Prog. Neurobiol. **38:** 279–295.
22. MAJEWSKA, M. D., S. DEMIRGOREN, CH.E. SPIVAK & E. D. LONDON. 1990. The neurosteroid dehydroepiandrosterone sulfate is an antagonist of the GABA$_A$ receptor. Brain Res. **526:** 143–146.

23. DEMIRGOREN, S., M. D. MAJEWSKA, CH.E. SPIVAK & E. D. LONDON. 1991. Receptor binding and electrophysiological effects of dehydroepiandrosterone sulfate, an antagonist of the GABA$_A$ receptor. Neuroscience **45:** 127–135.

24. SPIVAK, CH. E. Desensitization and noncompetitive blockade of GABA$_A$ receptors in ventral midbrain neurons by a neurosteroid dehydroepiandrosterone sulfate. Synapse **16:** 113–122.

25. MAJEWSKA, M. D. & R. D. SCHWARTZ. 1987. Pregnenolone-sulfate: An endogenous antagonist of the gamma-aminobutyric acid receptor complex in brain? Brain Res. **404:** 355–360.

26. MAJEWSKA, M. D., J. M. MIENVILLE & S. VICINI. 1988. Neurosteroid pregnenolone sulfate antagonizes electrophysiological responses to GABA in neurons. Neurosci. Lett. **90:** 279–284.

27. MAJEWSKA, M. D., S. DEMIRGOREN & E. D. LONDON. 1990. Binding of pregnenolone sulfate to rat brain membranes suggests multiple sites of steroid action at the GABA$_A$ receptor. Eur. J. Pharmacol. Molec. Pharmacol. Sect. **189:** 307–315.

28. MAJEWSKA, M. D., N. L. HARRISON, R. D. SCHWARTZ & J. L. BARKER. 1986. Steroid hormone metabolites are barbiturate-like modulators of the GABA receptor. Science **232:** 1004–1007.

29. PETERS, J. A., E. F. KIRKNESS, H. CALLACHAN, J. J. LAMBERT & A. J. TURNER. 1988. Modulation of the GABA$_A$ receptor by depressant barbiturates and pregnane steroids. Br. J. Pharmacol. **94:** 1257–1269.

30. HARRISON, N. L., M. D. MAJEWSKA, J. W. HARRINGTON & J. L. BARKER. 1987. Structure-activity relationships for steroid interaction with the τ-aminobutyric acid$_A$ receptor complex. J. Pharmacol. Exp. Ther. **241:** 346–353.

31. LAMBERT, J. J., J. A. PETERS, N. C. STRUGGES & T. G. HALES. 1990. Steroid modulation of the GABA$_A$ receptor complex: Electrophysiological studies. *In* Steroids and Neuronal Activity. Ciba Foundation Symposium 153. 56–70. John Wiley & Sons. Chichester.

32. CARETTE, B. & P. POULAIN. 1984. Excitatory effect of dehydroepiandrosterone, its sulphate ester pregnenolone sulphate, applied by iontophoresis and pressure, on single neurons in the septo-optic area of the guinea pig. Neurosci. Lett. **45:** 205–210.

33. HEUSER, G. & E. EIDELBERG. 1961. Steroid induced convulsions in experimental animals. Endocrinology **69:** 915–924.

34. IWAMORI, M., H. W. MOSER & Y. KISHIMOTO. 1976. Steroid sulfatase in brain: Comparison of sulfohydrolase activities for various steroid sulfates in normal and pathological brains, including various forms of metachromatic leukodystrophy. J. Neurochem. **27:** 1389–1395.

35. CASHIN, M. F. & V. MORAVEK. 1927. The physiological actions of cholesterol. Am. J. Physiol. **82:** 294–298.

36. SELYE, H. 1942. Correlations between the chemical structure and the pharmacological actions of the steroids. Endocrinology **30:** 437–452.

37. GYERMEK, L. & L. F. SOYKA. 1975. Steroid anesthetics. Anesthesiology **42:** 331–344.

38. HOLZBAUER, M. 1976. Physiological aspects of steroids with anaesthetic properties. Med. Biol. **54:** 227–242.

39. KRAULIS, I., G. FOLDES, H. TARIKOV, B. DUBROVSKY & M. K. BIRMINGHAM. 1975. Distribution, metabolism and biological activity of deoxycorticosterone in ventral nervous system. Brain. Res. **88:** 1–14.

40. CRAWLEY, J. N., J. R. GLOWA, M. D. MAJEWSKA & S. P. PAUL. 1986. Anxiolytic activity of endogenous adrenal steroid. Brain Res. **339:** 382–386.

41. KAVALIERS, M. 1988. Inhibitory influences of adrenal steroid, 3α,5α-tetrahydrodeoxycorticosterone on aggression and defeat-induced analgesia in mice. Psychopharmacology (Berlin) **95:** 488–492.

42. MAJEWSKA, M. D., M. T. BLUET-PAJOT, P. ROBEL & E. E. BAULIEU. 1989. Pregnenolone sulfate antagonizes barbiturate-induced sleep. Pharmacol. Biochem. Behav. **33:** 701–703.

43. DE PERETTI, E. & M. G. FOREST. 1976. Unconjugated dehydroepiandrosterone plasma levels in normal subjects from birth to adolescence in human: The use of a sensitive radioimmunoassay. J. Clin. Endocrinol. Metab. **43:** 982–991.

44. ROBERTS, E., L. BOLOGA, J. F. FLOOD & G. E. SMITH. 1987. Effects of dehydroepiandrosterone and its sulfate on brain tissues in culture and on memory in mice. Brain Res. **406:** 357–362.
45. CHERUBINI, E., J. L. GAIARSA & Y. BEN-ARI. 1991. GABA: An excitatory transmitter in early postnatal life. TINS **14:** 515–519.
46. BEHAR, T. N., A. E. SCHAFFNER, C. A. COLTON, R. SAMOGYI, Z. OLAH, C. LEHEL & J. L. BARKER. 1994. GABA-induced chemokinesis and NGF-induced chemotaxis of embryonic spinal cord neurons. J. Neurosci. **14:** 29–38.
47. SMITH, S. V. & J. L. BARKER. 1991. Depolarizing responses to 3α-OH-reduced pregnane steroid metabolites and GABA occur in the majority of embryonic rat cortical cells. Soc. Neurosci. Abstr. **17:** 749.
48. SHINGAI, R., M. L. SUTHERLAND & E. A. BARNARD. 1991. Effects of subunit types of cloned GABA$_A$ receptor on the response to a neurosteroid. Eur. J. Pharmacol. Mol. Pharmacol. Sect. **206:** 77–80.
49. ZAMAN, S. H., R. SHINGAI, R. J. HARVEY, M. G. DARLISON & E. A. BARNARD. 1992. Effects of subunit types of the recombinant GABA$_A$ receptor on the response to a neurosteroid. Eur. J. Pharmacol. Mol. Pharmacol. Sect. **225:** 321–330.
50. BRINTON, R. D. 1994. The neurosteroid 3α-hydroxy-5α-pregnane-20-one induces architectural regression in cultured fetal hippocampal neurons. J. Neurosci. **14:** 2763–2774.
51. WIGSTROM, H. & B. GUSTAFFSON. 1985. Facilitation of hippocampal long-lasting potentiation by GABA-antagonists. Acta Physiol. Scand. **125:** 159–172.
52. DOUGLAS, R. M., G. V. GODDARD & M. RIVES. 1982. Inhibitory modulation of long-term potentiation: Evidence for a postsynaptic control. Brain Res. **240:** 259–272.
53. ROEHRS, T., F. J. ZORICK, J. M. SICKLESTEEL, R. M. WITTIG, K. M. HARTSE & T. ROTH. 1983. Effects of hypnotics on memory. J. Clin. Psychopharmacol. **3:** 310–313.
54. BREEN, R. A. & J. L. MCGAUGH. 1961. Facilitation of maze learning with post-trial injections of picrotoxin. J. Comp. Physiol. Psychol. **54:** 498–501.
55. IRWIN, S. & A. BENUAZIZI. 1966. Pentylenetetrazol enhances memory function. Science **152:** 100–102.
56. MORRISON, B. O. 1958. Oral metrazol in the care of the aged: A review of twenty-eight cases. J. Am. Geriatr. Soc. **8:** 895–898.
57. FLOOD, J. F. & E. ROBERTS. 1988. Dehydroepiandrosterone sulfate improves memory in aging mice. Brain Res. **448:** 178–181.
58. FLOOD, J. F., G. E. SMITH & E. ROBERTS. 1988. Dehydroepiandrosterone and its sulfate enhance memory retention in mice. Brain Res. **447:** 269–278.
59. WOLKOWITZ, O. M., V. I. REUS, E. ROBERTS, F. MANFREDI, T. CHAN, S. ORMITSON, R. JOHNSON, J. CANICK, L. BRIZENDINE & H. WEINGARTNER. 1995. Antidepressant and cognition-enhancing effects of DHEA in major depression. Dehydroepiandrosterone and Aging. Ann. N.Y. Acad. Sci. Abstr. P-19.
60. FRIESS, E., L. TRACHSEL, J. GULDNER, T. SCHIER, A. STEIGER & F. HOLSBOER. 1995. DHEA administration increases rapid eye movement sleep and EEG power in the sigma frequency range. Am. Physiol. Soc. E107–E113.
61. SANDERS, S. A. & J. M. REINISCH. 1985. Behavioral effects on humans of progesterone related compounds during development and in the adult. *In* Actions of Progesterone on the Brain. D. Ganten & D. Pfaff, Eds. 175–206. Springer, Berlin.
62. MOODLEY, P., S. GOLOMBOK, P. SHINE & M. LADER. 1993. Computerized axial brain tomograms in long-term benzodiazepine users. Psychiatry Res. **48:** 135–144.
63. MARCZYNSKI, T. J., J. ARTWOHL & B. MARCZYNSKA. 1994. Chronic administration of flumazenil increases life span and protects rats from age-related loss of cognitive functions: A benzodiazepine/GABAergic hypothesis of brain aging. Neurobiol. Aging **15:** 69–84.
64. GRIFFITH, W. H. & D. A. MURCHISON. 1995. Enhancement of GABA-activated membrane currents in aged Fisher 344 basal forebrain neurons. J. Neurosci. **15:** 2407–2416.
65. SUNDERLAND, T., C. R. MERRIL, M. G. HARRINGTON, B. A. LAWLOR, S. E. MOLCHAN, R. MARTINEZ & D. L. MURPHY. 1989. Reduced plasma dehydroepiandrosterone concentrations in Alzheimer's disease. Lancet (Sept. 2):570.

66. NASSMAN, B., T. OLSSON, T. BACKSTROM, S. ERIKSSON, K. GRAKVIST, M. VIITANEN & G. BUCHT. 1991. Serum dehydroepiandrosterone sulfate in Alzheimer's disease and multi-infarct dementia. Biol. Psychiatry **30:** 684–690.

67. RUDMAN, D., K. R. SHETTY & D. E. MATTSON. 1990. Plasma dehydroepiandrosterone sulfate in nursing home men. J. Am. Geriatr. Soc. **38:** 421–427.

68. AZUMA, T., T. MATSUBARA, Y. SHIMA, S. HAENO, T. FUJIMOTO, K. TONE, N. SHIBATA & S. SAKODA. 1993. Neurosteroids in cerebrospinal fluid in neurologic disorders. J. Neurol. Sci. **120:** 87–92.

69. COWELL, P. E., B. I. TURETSKY, R. C. GUR, R. I. GROSSMAN, D. L. SHTASI & R. E. GUR. 1994. Sex difference in aging of the human frontal and temporal lobes. J. Neurosci. **14:** 4748–4755.

70. MARTIN, C. 1985. Hormone secretion cycles. *In* Endocrine Physiology. 62–65. Oxford University Press, New York.

71. ROBEL, P., E. E. BAULIEU, M. SYNGUELAKIS & F. HALBERG. 1987. Chronobiologic dynamics of Δ_5-3β-hydroxysteroids and glucocorticoids in rat brain and plasma and human plasma. *In* Advances in Chronobiology. Part A. D. K. Hayes *et al.,* Eds.: 451–465. New York.

72. HERMIDA, R. C., F. HALBERG & F. DEL POZO. 1985. Chronobiologic pattern discrimination of plasma hormone, notably DHEAS and TSH, classifies an expansive personality. Chronobiologia **12:** 105–136.

73. EYSENEK, H. J. 1983. Psychophysiology and personality: Extraversion, neuroticism and psychoticism. *In* Physiological Correlates of Human Behaviour. 13–29. Academic Press. London.

74. LADER, M. 1983. Anxiety and depression. *In* Physiological Correlates of Human Behaviour, A. Gale & J. A. Edwards, Eds. 155–167. Academic Press. London.

75. FAVA, M., A. LITTMAN & P. HALPERIN. 1987. Neuroendocrine correlates of the type A behavior pattern: A review and hypothesis. Int. J. Psychiatry Med. **17:** 289–308.

76. CARLSON, N. R. 1991. Aggressive behavior. *In* Physiology of Behavior, 357–363. Allyn and Bacon. Boston.

77. SCHLEGEL, M. L., J. F. SPETZ, P. ROBEL & M. HAUG. 1985. Studies on the effects of dehydroepiandrosterone and its metabolites on attack by castrated mice on lactating intruders. Physiol. Behav. **34:** 867–870.

78. MOLINA, V., L. CIESIELSKI, S. GOBAILLE & P. MANDEL. 1986. Effects of potentiation of the GABAergic neurotransmission in the olfactory bulbs on mouse-killing behavior. Pharmacol. Biochem. Behav. **24:** 657–664.

79. LEVENTHAL, B. & H. K. BRODIE. 1981. The pharmacology of violence. *In* Biobehavioral Aspects of Aggression, 85–106. D. A. Hamburg & M. B. Trudeau, Eds. Liss, Inc. New York.

80. ABADIE, J., B. WRIGHT, G. CORREA, E. S. BROWNE, J. R. PORTER & F. SWEC. 1993. Effect of dehydroepiandrosterone on neurotransmitter levels and appetite regulation of the obese Zucker rat. Diabetes **42:** 662–669.

81. LINNOILA, V. M. & M. VIRKINNEN. 1992. Aggression, suicidality, and serotonin. J. Clin. Psychiatry 53 (Suppl):46–51.

82. MONNET, F. P., V. MAHE, P. ROBEL & E. E. BAULIEU. 1995. Neurosteroids, via sigma receptors, modulate the [³H]norepinephrine release evoked by N-methyl-D-aspartate in the rat hippocampus. Proc. Natl. Acad. Sci. USA **92:** 3774–3778.

83. STANTON, P. K. & J. M. SURVEY. 1985. Depletion of norepinephrine, but not serotonin, reduces long-term potentiation in dentae gyrus of rat hippocampal slices. J. Neurosci. **5:** 2169–2176.

84. SARA, S. J., A. VANKOV & A. HERVE. 1994. Locus coeruleus-evoked responses in behaving rats: A clue to the role of noradrenaline in memory. Brain. Res. Bull. **35:** 457–465.

85. MORTOLA, J. F. & S. S. C. YEN. 1990. The effects of oral dehydroepiandrosterone on endocrine-metabolic parameters in postmenopausal women. J. Clin. Endocrinol. Metab. **71:** 696–704.

86. MORALES, A., J. J. NOLAN, J. C. NELSON & S. S. C. YEN. 1994. Effects of replacement dose of dehydroepiandrosterone in men and women of advancing age. J. Clin. Endocrinol. Metab. **78:** 1360–1367.

Dehydroepiandrosterone Sulfate and Aging

A. VERMEULEN

Department of Endocrinology & Metabolism
Medical clinic-University Hospital
9000 B Ghent, Belgium

The age-associated decrease in plasma levels of dehydroepiandrosterone (DHEA) and its sulfate (DHEAS) is well established. Already in 1965,[1] using the relatively insensitive Zimmerman reaction after thin layer chromatography, we reported an age-associated decline in DHEAS levels. Since then, these data have been confirmed and extended.[2-5] It has been shown conclusively that with age levels of both DHEA and DHEAS in both sexes decrease at a relatively constant rate of 2% per year. Hence, at age 80, levels are only about 20% those at age 25 (TABLE 1). Although the overlap of values between the sexes is significant, most studies[2] report 10–30% higher DHEAS levels in men than in women. However, Zumoff *et al.*[6] report higher DHEA levels in young women, the slope of the age-associated decline being however more important than that in men. Hence, at older age (>50 years), the sex difference largely disappears. These data are based on cross-sectional studies.

Thomas *et al.*[7] in a 1-year longitudinal study calculated a relative longitudinal decline of 11% over the study year, leading to the hypothesis that higher DHEAS levels might be associated with longer survival. Therefore, there is a continuous selection of subjects with higher levels. Data from Orentreich,[8] however, do not confirm a steeper decline in DHEAS levels in longitudinal studies.

At all ages, the interindividual variability is very high and the normal range of serum DHEAS is therefore very wide. Moreover, important genetic differences appear to exist, Japanese men having significantly lower levels than American white men.[9,10] The impressive age-associated decline remains in sharp contrast to the absence of the influence of age on cortisol levels. Twelve-hour mean cortisol levels over the day (10-minute sampling) were 0.27 ± 0.07 µmol/l in a group of young men (mean age 28 ± 5 years) and 0.26 ± 0.07 µmol/l in the elderly (mean age 71 ± 3 years), whereas mean 12-hour DHEA levels declined from 17.3 ± 2.4 to 6.68 ± 0.52 nmol/l.

Dehydroepiandrosterone sulfate levels are relatively constant over the nyctohemer, a consequence of a low metabolic clearance rate ($\pm$ 15 1/24 hours). Dehydroepiandrosterone levels, on the other hand, show important nyctohemeral as well as pulsatile variations, the metabolic clearance rate being of the order of 2,000 1/24 hours. However, whereas in young adults the amplitude of the nyctohemeral rhythm was of the order of 50%, it had almost completely disappeared in the elderly.[11] For cortisol, the amplitude of the nyctohemeral variations decreases only from $\pm 75\%$ in the young to $\pm 65\%$ in the elderly. Whereas mean pulse frequency of DHEA did not change significantly with age, being 5.4 ± 1.8 in young adults against $5.4 \pm 2.0/12$ hours in the elderly, mean pulse amplitude decreased from 8.86 ± 2.32 nmol/l at age 28 ± 5 years to 2.42 ± 1.28 nmol/l at age 71 ± 3 years and total pulse amplitude from 42.0 ± 15.8 ng/dl to 10.4 ± 2.8 nmol/l in the elderly. Not only did absolute pulse amplitude decline, but also relative pulse amplitude decreased significantly from $74 \pm 12\%$ in the young to $45 \pm 22\%$ ($p < 0.05$) in elderly men.

Cortisol pulse amplitude, in comparison, decreased from 0.16 ± 0.04 μMol/l in the young to 0.13 ± 0.04 μmol/l in the elderly; the mean relative increment from 102% to 69% and the mean total amplitude from 0.67 ± 0.23 μmol/l in the young to 0.63 ± 0.35 μmol/l in the elderly (not significant). The change in secretory pattern of the adrenal cortex is clearly illustrated by the change in mean cortisol/mean DHEAS ratio, which increases from 0.042 ± 0.011 in the young to 0.21 ± 0.03 in the old.

The age-associated decline in plasma levels of DHEA(S) is reflected in the parallel decrease in tissue concentration.[12] The tissue/plasma gradient for DHEA varied between 10 and 20, but the gradient for DHEAS was always far below unity (± 0.05), indicating that tissue uptake of DHEAS is very poor or that rapid hydrolysis takes place. These gradients do not vary significantly with age.

The discordant effects of aging on cortisol and DHEA(S) levels, respectively, raise the question of the influence of age on the levels of other adrenocortical steroids. The decrease in androstenedione, a steroid of mixed adrenal and gonadal origin, is much less important than is the decrease in DHEAS levels[3,4] (TABLE 1) and in men appears to start at an older age.

In women, androstenedione levels decrease at menopause, probably reflecting the ovarian contribution, but afterwards levels remain constant. This is confirmed by

TABLE 1. Influence of Age on Plasma Androgen Levels in Men[a]

Age (Yr.)	n	DHEAS	DHEA	A	T
25–34	45	6.44 ± 2.29	15.91 ± 6.05	3.85 ± 1.25	21.38 ± 5.90
35–44	22	6.02 ± 2.18	12.65 ± 2.69	3.81 ± 2.18	23.14 ± 7.36
45–54	23	4.75 ± 2.62	11.31 ± 5.39	3.36 ± 0.90	21.02 ± 7.37
55–64	43	3.25 ± 1.48	10.20 ± 5.21	4.66 ± 1.28	19.49 ± 6.83
65–74	47	2.65 ± 1.68	7.71 ± 4.15	4.47 ± 2.17	18.15 ± 6.83
75–84	48	1.15 ± 0.52	5.36 ± 1.68	2.18 ± 1.49	16.32 ± 5.85
85–100	21	1.23 ± 0.52	3.18 ± 0.69	1.85 ± 0.91	13.05 ± 4.63

Abbreviations: A = androstenedione; DHEA = dehydroepiandrosterone; DHEAS = dehydroepiandrosterone sulfate; T = testosterone.
[a]All values in nmol/l except for DHEAS in μmol/l.

data from Loncope et al.[13] who observed that in postmenopausal women the blood production rate of androstenedione does not vary with age. Also, levels of 11-hydroxy androstenedione, a steroid of exclusive adrenal origin, are reported to be age independent,[14] which is in agreement with the data of acute ACTH stimulation tests.[15] On acute stimulation with ACTH (0.25 mg), the increase over basal levels of the Δ4-steroids, androstenedione, progesterone, and 17-hydroxyprogesterone in elderly subjects was similar or higher than that in young persons, whereas the responses of the Δ5-steroids, pregnenolone, 17-hydroxypregnenolone, and DHEA were significantly decreased in the elderly.[15,16] Similar results were reported by Carlström[17] who observed that after ACTH, the increase in DHEA levels was inversely related to age, whereas the increase in 17-hydroxyprogesterone levels was age independent or increased even with age. Hence, he observed a dramatic decrease of the Δ DHEA/Δ17 OHP ratio with age, and he considers this ratio an excellent parameter of physiological aging.

DHEA and DHEAS are interconvertible in plasma. To the best of our knowledge, no direct data on the influence of age on these interconversions are available. However, an indirect estimate can be derived from the ratio of DHEA/DHEAS in young and elderly men. We found a molar ratio of 2.50×10^{-3} at age 25–35 years and of $\pm 2.60 \times 10^{-3}$ at age 85–100 years, which indicates that no major changes in the interconversion of these steroids occur with age. It should be mentioned that the ratio is higher in women than in men, probably because of greater sulfatase activity in women.[18]

The different evolution of cortisol and DHEA levels with age suggests that other factors besides ACTH regulate DHEA(S) secretion. Although several polypeptides derived from POMC have profound effects on the adrenal cortex, such as MSH, facilitating hydrolysis of cholesterol esters and hence potentiating the steroidogenic effects of ACTH,[19] and although Parker and Odell[20] claimed to have isolated a pituitary polypeptide that apparently selectively stimulates adrenal androgen secretion, the existence of a specific adrenal androgen-stimulating hormone is still controversial. Moreover, whereas hyperprolactinemia seems to be accompanied by increased DHEAS levels,[21] prolactin evidently is not the physiological regulator of adrenal androgen secretion.

Also, the role of insulin in regulating adrenal androgen secretion is controversial. A surprising observation is that some investigators observed that insulin increases DHEA(S) secretion, whereas others claim that it decreases DHEAS secretion. Stuart and Nagamani[22] reported that in women insulin stimulates DHEA secretion, a euglycemic clamp increasing DHEA levels by 239%, although in ovariectomized women the increase was only 35%. Elkind-Hirsch et al.[23] observed in women a significant increase in DHEAS levels by acutely increased insulin levels, whereas Khaw and Barrett-Connor[24] observed that fasting plasma glucose levels correlated positively with DHEAS levels in nondiabetic postmenopausal women. In a series of publications,[25-31] Nestler's group studying the influence of insulin levels on DHEAS levels under various experimental conditions reported a decrease in these levels by insulin, although the decrease is sometimes limited to male subjects.[30] Also, Diamond et al.[32] as well as Hubert et al.[33] reported a decrease in DHEAS levels in women by an acute physiological elevation in insulin levels.

This would not be the consequence of increased hydrolysis of DHEAS, increased conversion to androstenedione, or slightly increased urinary excretion.[26] Acute elevation of insulin levels to $\pm$ 800 pmol/l in men inhibits the 17,20 lyase (but not 17-hydroxylase) activity,[31] whereas an hyperinsulinemia of 1,000–1,400 pmol/l increased the metabolic clearance rate of DHEA from 2,500 to 3,500 1/24 hours in men but not in women.[27] The authors suggest that the presence of certain sex steroids is necessary for insulin to affect the metabolic clearance rate. One wonders, however, what is the mechanism of the increased metabolic clearance rate if the metabolism (hydrolysis, interconversion) is unchanged. Also, the physiologic relevance of the inhibition of 17,20 lyase activity by insulin is questionable as, considering the large quantity of DHEAS secreted normally, one would expect plasma levels of DHEA(S) precursors to be elevated in cases of physiological hyperinsulinemia. Finally, the rapid changes in DHEAS levels are difficult to explain in view of the long half-life (9–11 hours) of DHEAS. Even total blockade of DHEAS from the blood stream would decrease plasma levels within 2 hours by only 15%.

Several investigators[1,4,34-37] reported decreased DHEAS levels in obesity in both men and women which they relate to increased insulin levels, but others reported normal DHEAS levels[38,39] without correlation with insulin levels.[39] Leenen et al.[39] report even a positive correlation ($p < 0.05$) between changes in DHEAS and insulin levels induced by a weight loss of about 13 kg in women. It should be mentioned that in obese women, whether or not a polycystic ovary syndrome is present, DHEA(S) levels are often increased, notwithstanding insulin resistance.

Although in obese men aged 25–62 years ($n = 50$) we observed moderately decreased DHEAS levels[1,34] and a significant negative correlation of DHEAS levels with BMI ($r = -0.28$, $p < 0.01$), we did not observe any significant correlation between DHEAS and insulin levels; moreover, weight loss induced a decrease in fasting insulin levels but had no effect on DHEAS levels.

As aging is accompanied by an increase in insulin levels, the latter may play a role in the age-associated decrease in DHEAS levels.[31] However, after correction for age, we observed no correlation between DHEAS and insulin levels in our normal population.

Smokers are reported to have higher DHEA(S) levels than nonsmokers,[4,40–42] and Orentreith[8] suggests that this may be a consequence of reduced pulmonary metabolism to Δ 5 androstene 3β,17βdiol.

Albumin has a high association constant for DHEAS ($\pm 2 \times 10^5$ l/mol), and it is not surprising that in the normal population aged 25–100 years, we observed a significant correlation ($p < 0.01$) between albumin and DHEAS levels. A similar correlation was reported by Tegelman et al.[43] Albumin concentration in aged patients is significantly lower than that in young adults; hence, it may contribute to the age-associated decrease in DHEAS levels.

DO DHEAS LEVELS HAVE A PROGNOSTIC VALUE AND ARE THEY RELIABLE PARAMETERS OF PHYSIOLOGICAL AGING?

Barrett-Connor et al.,[44] on the basis of data obtained by a single determination of DHEAS levels, concluded that in men but not women[45] DHEAS is independently and inversely related to the subsequent 12-year mortality from any cause as well as from cardiovascular disease. Lacroix et al.[9] reached a similar conclusion, in a study involving 138 subjects over age 85 whereas Birkenhäger et al.[46] did not find a statistically significant difference in DHEAS levels among subjects who died within 1 year ($n = 27$) and those who survived longer. In fact, men with higher DHEAS levels did not survive as long as did men with lower levels, whereas women with high DHEAS levels tended to survive longer than other women. In our study involving 110 men aged 75–80 years, we found no correlation between DHEAS levels and subsequent 3-year mortality. Hautanen et al.[47] reported that even elderly subjects with high DHEAS levels were at higher risk of developing myocardial infarction. Rudman et al.[48] reported that in men in a nursing home, DHEAS was inversely related to the presence of organic brain syndrome, but not to the 1-year mortality rate. In Alzheimer's disease, whereas Sunderland et al.[49] reported that Alzheimer's patients have lower DHEAS levels than do age-matched controls, other authors[46,50–52] could not confirm this finding.

The interpretation of studies relating DHEAS levels to physiological aging, general health condition, or life expectancy is complicated by the fact that during illness, mental depression, or other stress factors, there is a dissociation between DHEAS and cortisol levels, the former being decreased during stress situations, whereas healthy normal men have lower cortisol levels.[53]

In conclusion, more data are required before definitive statements can be made concerning the role of DHEAS in the aging process or as a predictor of life expectancy, but with Herbert[54] we can state that enough is known or suspected to warrant investigation of DHEA(S) as a worthwhile and relatively risk-free replacement therapy for advancing age.

REFERENCES

1. DE NEVE, L. & A. VERMEULEN. 1965. The determination of 17 oxosteroidsulfates in human plasma. J. Endocrinol. **32:** 295–302.

2. ORENTREICH, N., J. L. BRIND, R. L. RIZER & J. H. VOGELMAN. 1984. Age changes and sex differences in serum dehydroepiandrosterone sulfate concentration during adulthood. J. Clin. Endocrinol. Metab. **59:** 551–555.

3. BELANGER, A., B. CARRIDAS, A. DUPONT, L. CUSAN, P. DIAMOND, J. L. GOMEZ & F. LABRIE. 1994. Changes in serum concentration of conjugated and unconjugated steroids in 40 to 80 year old men. J. Clin. Endocrinol. Metab. **79:** 1086–1090.

4. FIELD, A. E., G. E. COLDITZ, W. C. WILLETT, C. LONCOPE & J. B. MCKINLAY. 1994. The relation of smoking, age, relative weight and dietary intake to serum adrenal steroids, sex hormones and sex hormone binding globulin in middle aged men. J. Clin. Endocrinol. Metab. **79:** 1310–1316.

5. VERMEULEN, A. 1980. Adrenal androgens and aging. *In* Adrenal Androgens. A. R. Genazzani, J. H. H. Thyssen & P. R. Siiteri, Eds. 201–217. Academic Press.

6. ZUMOFF, B. R., R. S. ROSENFELD, G. W. STRAIN, J. LEVIN & D. K. FUKUSHIMA. 1980. Sex differences is the twenty four hour plasma concentration of dehydroepiandrosterone (DHA) and dehydroepiandrosterone sulfate (DHAS) and the DHA/DHAS ratio in normal adults. J. Clin. Endocrinol. Metab. **51:** 330–333.

7. THOMAS, G., M. FRENOY, LEGRAIN, R. SEBAG-LANOE, E. E. BAULIEU & B. DEBUIRE. 1994. Serum dehydroepiandrosterone sulfate levels as an individual marker. J. Clin. Endocrinol. Metab. **79:** 1273–1276.

8. ORENTREICH, N., J. L. BRIND, J. H. VOGELMAN, R. ANDRES & H. BALDWIN. 1992. Long term longitudinal measurement of plasma dehydroepiandrosteronesulfate in normal men. J. Clin. Endocrinol. Metab. **75:** 1002–1004.

9. LACROIX, A. Z., K. YANO & D. M. REED. 1992. Dehydroepiandrosteronesulfate, incidence of myocardial infarction and extent of atherosclerosis in men. Circulation **786:** 1529–1535.

10. ROTTER, J. I., L. WONG, E. T. LIFRAK & L. M. PARKER. 1985. A genetic component of the variation of dehydroepiandrosterone sulfate. Metabolism **34:** 731–736.

11. DE SLYPERE, J. P. & A. VERMEULEN. 1984. Leydig cell function in normal men: Effect of age, life style, residence, diet and activity. J. Clin. Endocrinol. Metab. **59:** 955–961.

12. DE SLYPERE, J. P., L. VERDONCK & A. VERMEULEN. 1985. Fat tissue: A steroid reservoir and site of steroid metabolism. J. Clin. Endocrinol. Metab. **61:** 564–570.

13. LONGCOPE, C., W. JAFFEE & G. GRIFFING. 1981. Production rate of androgens and estrogens in postmenopausal women. Maturitas **3:** 215–223.

14. FIET, J., B. GOUMEL, J. M. VILLETTI, G. L. BRERAULT, R. JULIEN, G. CHATHELINEAU & C. DREUX. 1980. Simultaneous radioimmunoassay of androstenedione, dehydroepiandrosterone and 11 β hydroxyandro-stenedione in plasma. Hormone Res. **13:** 133–135.

15. VERMEULEN, A., J. P. DE SLIJPERE, W. SCHELFHOUT, L. VERDONCK & R. RUBENS. 1982. Adrenocortical function in old age. Response to acute ACTH stimulation. J. Clin. Endocrinol. Metab. **54:** 187–191.

16. PARKER, L., T. GRAL, V. PERRIGO & R. SKOWSKY. 1981. Decreased adrenal androgen sensitivity to ACTH during aging. Metabolism **30:** 601–604.

17. CARLSTROM, K. 1994. Andropause, fact or fiction? 1993. *In* The Modern Management of the Menopause. Proceedings of the VII international Congress on Menopause. G. Berg & H. Hammar, Eds.: 567–577. Stockholm.

18. ZUMOFF, B. & H. L. BRADLOW. 1980. Sex difference in the metabolism of dehydroisoandrosteronesulfate. J. Endocrinol. Metab. **51:** 334–336.

19. AL-DUJAILI, E. A. S., J. HOPE, F. E. ESTIVAREZ, P. J. LOWRY & R. W. EDWARDS. 1981. Circulating human pituitary pro-γ melanotropin enhances the adrenal response to ACTH. Nature **291:** 156–159.

20. PARKER, L. N. & W. D. ODELL. 1980. Control of adrenal androgen secretion. Endocr. Rev. **1:** 392–410.

21. VERMEULEN, A., E. SUY & R. RUBENS. 1977. Effect of prolactin on plasma DHEA(S) levels. J. Clin. Endocrinol. Metab. **44:** 1222–1225.

22. STUART, C. A. & M. NAGAMANI. 1990. Insulin activity augments ovarian androgen production in normal women. Fertil. Steril. **54:** 788–792.
23. ELKIND-HIRSCH, K. E., C. T. VALDES, T. G. MCCONNELL & L. R. MALINAK. 1991. Androgen response to acutely increased endogenous insulin levels in hyperandrogenic and normal cycling women. Fertil. Steril. **55:** 486–491.
24. KHAW, K. T. & E. BARRETT-CONNOR. 1991. Fasting plasma glucose levels and endogenous androgens in nondiabetic postmenopausal women. Clin. Sci. **80:** 199–203.
25. NESTLER, J. E., J. N. CLORE, I. J. F. STRAUSS & W. G. BLACKARD. 1987. The effects of hyperinsulinemia on serum testosterone, progesterone, dehydroepiandrosteronesulfate and cortisol levels in normal women and in a woman with hyperandrogenism, insulin resistance and acanthosis nigricans. J. Clin. Endocrinol. Metab. **64:** 180–184.
26. NESTLER, J. E., K. S. USISKIN, C. O. BARLASCINI, D. F. WELTY, J. N. CLORE & W. G. BLACKARD. 1989. Suppression of serum dehydroepiandrosterone-sulfate levels by insulin: An evaluation of possible mechanisms. J. Clin. Endocrinol. Metab. **69:** 1040–1046.
27. NESTLER, J. E. & Z. KAHWASH. 1994. Sex specific action of insulin to acutely increase the metabolic clearance rate of dehydroepiandrosterone in humans. J. Clin. Invest. **94:** 1484–1489.
28. NESTLER, J. E., N. A. BEER, D. J. JAKUBOWICZ & R. M. BEER. 1994. Effects of reduction in circulating insulin by metformin on serum dehydroepiandrosterone-sulfate in non-diabetic men. J. Clin. Endocrinol. Metab. **78:** 549–554.
29. NESTLER, J. E., N. E. BEER, D. J. JAKUBOWICZ, C. COLOMBO & R. M. BEER. 1995. Effects of insulin reduction by benfluorex on serum dehydroepiandrosterone (DHEA), DHEA sulfate and blood pressure in hypertensive middle aged and elderly men. J. Clin. Endocrinol. Metab. **80:** 700–706.
30. BEER, N. A., D. J. JAKUBOWICZ, R. M. BEER & J. E. NESTLER. 1994. Disparate effects of insulin reduction with Diltiazem on serum dehydroepiandrosterone-sulfate levels in obese, hypertensive men and women. J. Clin. Endocrinol. Metab. **79:** 1079–1081.
31. NESTLER, J. E., M. A. MCCANAHAN, J. M. CLORE & W. G. BLACKARD. 1992. Insulin inhibits adrenal 17,20 lyase activity in man. J. Clin. Endocrinol. Metab. **74:** 362–367.
32. DIAMOND, M. P., D. A. GRAINGER, A. J. LANDANO, K. STARICK-ZYCH & A. DE FRONZO. 1991. Effect of acute physiological elevation of insulin on circulating androgen levels in non-obese women. J. Clin. Endocrinol. Metab. **72:** 885–887.
33. HUBERT, G. D., E. D. SCHRIOCK, J. R. GIVENS & J. E. BUSTER. 1991. Suppression of circulating Δ4-androstenedione and dehydroepiandrosterone-sulfate during oral glucose tolerance test in normal females. J. Clin. Endocrinol. Metab. **73:** 781–784.
34. GIAGULLI, V. A., J. M. KAUFMAN & A. VERMEULEN. 1994. Pathogenesis of decreased androgen levels in obese men. J. Clin. Endocrinol. Metab. **79:** 997–1000.
35. LOPEZ, J. A. & W. A. KREHL. 1967. A possible relationship between 6 phosphate dehydrogenase and dehydroepiandrosterone in obesity. Lancet ii: 485–487.
36. DE PERGOLA, G., V. A. GIAGULLI, G. GARRUTI, M. R. COSPITE, F. GIORGINO, M. CIGNARELLI & R. GIORGINO. 1991. Low dehydroepiandrosterone circulating levels in premenopausal women with very high body mass index. Metabolism **40:** 181–190.
37. PASQUALI, R., F. CASIMIRRI, N. MELCHIONDA *ET AL.* 1988. Weight loss and sex steroid metabolism in massively obese men. J. Endocrinol. Invest. **11:** 205–210.
38. GRENMAN, S., T. RÖNNEMAA, K. IRJALA, H. L. KAIHOLA & M. GRÖNROOS. 1986. Sex steroids, gonadotropin, cortisol and prolactin levels in healthy, massively obese women: Correlation with abdominal fat cell size and effect of weight reduction. J. Clin. Endocrinol. Metab. **63:** 1257–1261.
39. LEENEN, R., K. VAN DER KOOY, J. C. SEIDELL, P. DEURENBERG & H. P. F. KOPPESCHAAR. 1994. Visceral fat accumulation in relation to sex hormones in obese men and women undergoing weight loss therapy. J. Clin. Endocrinol. Metab. **78:** 1515–1520.
40. BARRETT-CONNOR, E. & K. T. KHAW. 1987. Cigarette smoking and increased endogenous estrogen levels in men. Am. J. Epidemiol. **128:** 255–257.
41. DAI, W. S., J. P. GUTAI, L. H. KULLER & J. A. CAULEY. 1980. Cigarette smoking and serum sex hormones in men. Am. J. Epidemiol. **128:** 796–805.
42. SALVINI, S., M. S. STAMPFER, R. L. BARBIERI & C. H. HENNEKENS. 1992. Effects of age,

smoking and vitamins on plasma DHEAS levels: A cross sectional study. J. Clin. Endocrinol. Metab. **74:** 139–143.

43. TEGELMAN, R., P. LINDESKOG, K. CARLSTROM, A. POUSETTE & R. BLOMSTRAND. 1986. Peripheral hormone levels in healthy subjects during fasting. Acta Endocrinol. **113:** 457–462.

44. BARRETT-CONNOR, E., K. T. KHAW & S. S. C. YEN. 1986. A prospective study of dehydroepiandrosteronesulfate, mortality and cardiovascular disease. N. Engl. J. Med. **315:** 1519–1524.

45. BARRETT-CONNOR, E. & K. T. KHAW. 1987. Absence of an inverse relation of dehydroepiandrosteronesulfate with cardiovascular mortality in postmenopausal women. N. Engl. J. Med. **317:** 711–713.

46. BIRKENHAGER-GILLESSE, E. C., J. DERKSEN & A. M. LAGAAY. 1994. Dehydroepiandrosterone sulphate (DHEAS) in the oldest old, age 85 and over. Ann. N. Y. Acad. Sci. **719:** 543–552.

47. HAUTANEN, A., M. MANTTÄRI, V. MANINEN, L. TENKANEN, J. K. HUTTUNEN, M. H. FRICK & H. ADLERCREUTZ. 1994. Adrenal androgens and testosterone as coronary risk factors in the Helsinki Heart Study. Atherosclerosis **105:** 191–200.

48. RUDMAN, D., K. R. SHETTY & D. E. MATTSON. 1990. Plasma dehydroepiandrosterone sulfate in nursing home men. J. Am. Geriatr. Soc. **38:** 421–427.

49. SUNDERLAND, N., C. R. MERRILL, M. G. HARRINGTON *ET AL.* 1989. Reduced plasma dehydroepiandrosterone concentration in Alzheimer's disease. Lancet ii: 570.

50. LEBLHUBER, F., E. WINDHAGER, F. REISECKER, F. X. STEINPARZ & E. DIENSTL. 1990. Dehydroepiandrosteronesulphate in Alzheimer's disease. Lancet (Letter) **336:** 449.

51. CUCKLE, H., R. STONE, D. SMITH, N. WALD, M. BRAMMER, I. HAJIMOHAMMEDREZA, R. LEVY, T. CHARD & L. PERRY. 1990. Dehydroepiandrosteronesulphate in Alzheimer's disease. Lancet (Letter) **336:** 449–450.

52. SPÄTH-SCHWALBE, E., C. DODT, J. DITTMANN, R. SCHÜTTLER & H. L. FEHM. 1990. Dehydroepiandrosterone sulphate in Alzheimer's disease. Lancet **i:** 14112.

53. SEEMAN, T. A. & R. J. ROBBINS. 1994. Aging and hypothalamo-pituitary-adrenal response to challenge in the human. Endocrine Rev. **15:** 233–262.

54. HERBERT, J. 1995. The age of dehydroepiandrosterone (Editorial). Lancet **345:** 1193–1194.

Replacement of DHEA in Aging Men and Women

Potential Remedial Effects[a]

S. S. C. YEN, A. J. MORALES, AND O. KHORRAM

Department of Reproductive Medicine
University of California, San Diego
La Jolla, California 92093

Aging in men is associated with reduced protein synthesis, decreased lean body mass and bone mass, and increased body fat.[1] These body composition changes are accompanied by a progressive decline in adrenal secretion of dehydroepiandrosterone (DHEA) and its sulfate ester (DHEAS),[2] paralleling those of the growth hormone (GH)-insulin-like growth factor-I (GH-IGF-I) system and immune function.[1,3] Although the GH-IGF-I system is recognized to promote cellular growth and metabolism at multiple sites[1,4] and to modulate the immune system in health and disease,[3,5–7] the biologic function of DHEA and DHEAS in humans remains elusive. Extensive animal experiments have shown that DHEA may have immunoenhancing[8–11] and protective effects against viral infection,[12] glucocorticoid-induced thymic involution,[13] autoantibody formation,[14] and age-related deficits such as obesity, cardiovascular disease, and breast cancer.[15–19] Thus, DHEA may be viewed as a multifunctional steroid hormone. The relevance of these findings in human biology and diseases is perplexing, because humans and nonhuman primates are the only species with the capacity to synthesize and secrete DHEA and DHEAS in quantities surpassing all other known steroids.[20] In light of these considerations, assessments of the potential role of DHEA in human health and disease are of both biologic and clinical importance.

Until recently, limited clinical studies were conducted with mega doses of DHEA, which may induce responses beyond its physiologic action or may, through rapid biotransformation to potent androgens and estrogens, have biologic impact on target tissues, including anabolic effects. In time course studies Mortola and Yen,[21] using a 1,600-mg daily oral dose of DHEA in postmenopausal women (aged 46–61 years) for 4 weeks, demonstrated marked increments of potent androgens and estrogens within 1–2 hours. These increments reached 9-fold for testosterone (T), 20-fold for androstenedione (A) and dihydrotestosterone (DHT), and 2-fold for estrone (E_1) and estradiol (E_2) by the 3rd hour after DHEA administration, and levels were sustained during the entire duration of the study. This hyperandrogenic state imposed by a pharmacologic dose of DHEA was associated with a significant decline in sex hormone-binding globulin (SHBG), thyroid-binding globulin, total cholesterol and high density lipoprotein cholesterol, and the appearance of insulin resistance.[21]

CELLULAR MECHANISMS OF DHEA DECLINE DURING AGING

Liu *et al.*[22] reported that the progressive decline in DHEA and DHEAS during aging reflected intraadrenal changes in 17α-hydroxylase enzymatic activities, in that

[a]This work was supported by National Institutes of Health RO-1 AG-10979-03, National Institutes of Health Minority Clinical Associate Physician Award (A.M.) and General Clinical Research Center USPHA grant MO-1 Rr-00827, Ortho American College of Obstetrician and Gynecologist Award (O.K.), and in part by the Clayton Foundation for Research.

a relative deficiency in 17,20 desmolase occurs in aging women, a finding that was recently confirmed in aging men.[23] As 17α-hydroxylase and 17,20-desmolase are P450 Cα17 enzyme encoded by a single gene,[24] the selective decrease in 17,20-desmolase with unaltered 17α-hydroxylase activity observed in older individuals suggests a functional shift with aging opposite that seen during adrenarche/puberty when the selective increase in 17,20-desmolase activity leads to a preferential increase in DHEA and DHEAS levels. The mechanism(s) for this switch-on and switch-off of 17,20 desmolase activity during the anabolic state of puberty and the catabolic state of aging remains unclear. The progressive blunting of the ACTH-mediated pulsatile activity of DHEA with advancing age (FIG. 1), without affecting the pulsatile rhythm of cortisol, is highly consistent with a selective intraadrenal biosynthetic defect for DHEA.

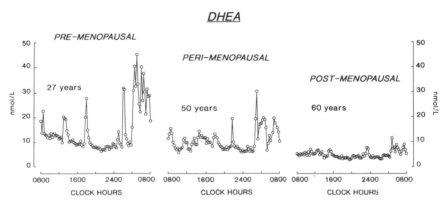

FIGURE 1. Representative 24-hour pulsatile pattern of adrenal DHEA showing a progressive decline with advancing age in pre- and postmenopausal women.

REPLACEMENT OF DHEA IN AGING MEN AND WOMEN

We tested the supposition that restoring extracellular levels of DHEA and DHEAS in individuals of advancing age to levels in young adults may have beneficial effects. Because the GH-IGF-I system and immune function decline with aging in parallel to DHEA, we hypothesized that these concomitant changes may be functionally linked. Studies of replacement doses of 50 and 100 mg of DHEA administered orally at bedtime were conducted in men and women aged 40–70 years in double-blind, placebo-controlled cross-over trials of 6- and 12-month durations. In a separate study, we determined the effects of *in vivo* administration of 50 mg DHEA on immune function in aging men.

Studies with a 50-Mg Dose of DHEA

Oral versus Sublingual Route of Administration

The time course and circulating levels of DHEA and DHEAS after oral versus sublingual routes of administration of 50 mg DHEA in gelatin capsules were

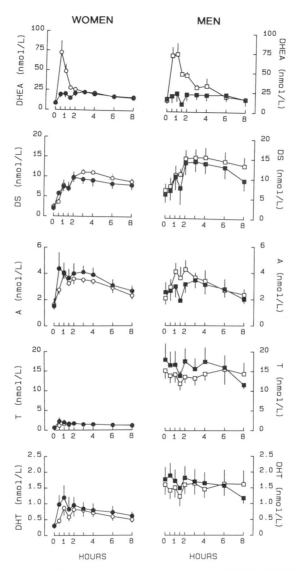

FIGURE 2. Absorption and relative increments of serum levels of DHEA, DHEAS, androstene-dione (A), testosterone (T), and dihydrotestosterone (DHT) following oral versus sublingual administration of a 50-mg dose of DHEA in aging men and women (Morales and Yen, unpublished observations).

determined in eight men and eight women. As shown in FIGURE 2, with the exception of serum DHEA levels, the increments over time of circulating DHEAS, A, T, and DHT were rapid and were similar between oral and sublingual routes of administration. DHEA levels, in contrast, showed a rapid (within 30 minutes) and marked elevation lasting for 2 hours after sublingual than after oral administration. Thereafter, all steroid levels, including those of DHEA, were similar with a slight decline towards the end of the experiment at the 8th hour. Thus, we chose the oral route of administration for subsequent studies because of its ease and reliability of administration in the aging population.

Effects of 50-Mg Oral DHEA Replacement (a 6-Month Trial)

A randomized placebo-controlled cross-over trial of nightly oral DHEA administration (50 mg) of 6-months' duration was conducted in 13 men and 17 women 40–70 years of age.[25] During each treatment period, concentrations of androgens, lipids, apolipoproteins, IGF-I, IGF-binding protein-1 (IGFBP-1), and IGFBP-3, insulin sensitivity, percentage of body fat, libido, and sense of well-being were measured. A subgroup of men ($n = 8$) and women ($n = 5$) underwent 24-hour sampling at 20-minute intervals for growth hormone determinations.

DHEA and DHEAS serum levels were restored to those found in young adults[26–28] within 2 weeks of DHEA replacement and were sustained throughout the 3 months of the study. A twofold increase in serum levels of androgens (A, T, and DHT) was observed in women, with only a small rise in A in men. These androgen increments in women remain within the range of young adults. There was no change in circulating levels of SHBG, E_1, or E_2 in either gender. High density lipoprotein levels declined slightly in women, with no other lipid changes noted for either gender. Insulin sensitivity, determined by euglycemic hyperinsulinemic clamp studies, and percentage of body fat were unaltered. Although mean 24-hour growth hormone and IGFBP-3 levels were unchanged, serum IGF-I levels increased significantly and IGFBP-1 decreased significantly, resulting in an elevated IGF-I/IGFBP-1 ratio for both genders (FIG. 3), suggesting an increased bioavailability of IGF-I to target tissues.[29] This was associated with a remarkable increase in perceived physical and psychological well-being for both men (67%) and women (84%) and no change in libido (FIG. 4). These observations and the absence of side effects constitute the first demonstration of novel effects of the replacement dose of DHEA in age-advanced men and women.[25]

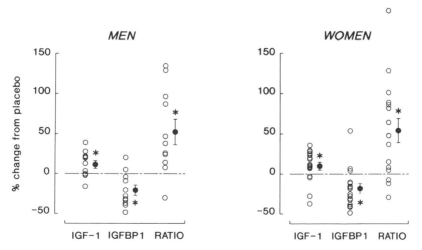

FIGURE 3. Percentage change from placebo of individual values for serum IGF-I, IGFBP-1, and IGF-I/IGFBP-1 ratio after 12 weeks of oral administration of 50 mg DHEA nightly in men and women. The mean ± SE of each measurement is also shown. *$p < 0.05$ compared with placebo (Morales and Yen[21]).

One-Year Study of a 100-Mg Dose of DHEA

A randomized double-blind placebo-controlled experiment of 1-year's duration was conducted with a 100-mg oral dose of DHEA or placebo. This study was aimed specifically to assess the effects of doubling the dose and expanding the duration of DHEA administration on *biologic end-points* in aging men (*n* = 8) and women (*n* = 8) 50–65 years of age.

Increments of Circulating Steroids

Basal concentrations of all androgenic steroids were either below or near the lower end of the normal range for young adults. Serum DHEAS levels increased several-fold in both men and women at the end of 6 months of DHEA, but not placebo, administration (FIG. 5). These values were near or beyond the upper limit of young adult levels.[26–28] Biotransformation of DHEA in men was limited to a

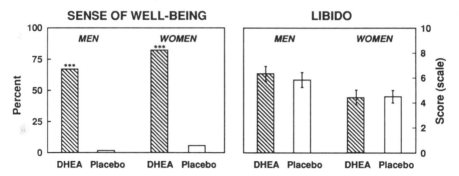

FIGURE 4. Percentage of men and women who self-reported an improved sense of well-being after 12 weeks of oral administration of 50 mg DHEA nightly and after 12 weeks of placebo administration (*left panel*). ***p < 0.005 compared with placebo values. Scored values of libido on a visual analog scale in men and women after 12 weeks of oral administration of 50 mg DHEA nightly and after 12 weeks of placebo administration are shown. **p < 0.01 compared with opposite gender values.

doubling of A levels. By contrast, there was a three- to fourfold increase in all androgenic steroids (A, T, and DHT) in women, and the levels reached were above the upper limits of normal for adult women. Although SHBG levels were unaltered in men, a 50% decline was seen in women. This gender disparity may be accounted for by the relatively greater increments of androgen levels in women, thereby exerting an inhibitory effect on hepatic production of SHBG. One woman developed facial hair that resolved by the end of the study. Gonadotropin levels in both genders were unaffected by DHEA treatment.

Biologic Markers

As seen in the 50-mg dose study, a significant (p < 0.05) increase in serum IGF-I levels occurred in both men and women after 6 months of DHEA treatment at a 100-mg daily dose (FIG. 6). The relative increment in IGF-I was greater in subjects

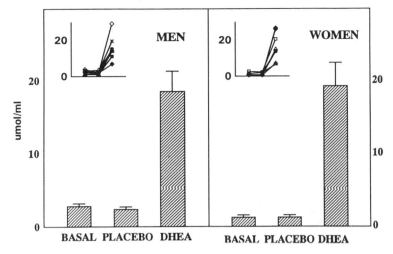

FIGURE 5. Circulating DHEAS levels (mean ± SE) at baseline and in response to placebo and DHEA (100 mg/d) administration (6 months each) in aging men ($n = 8$) and women ($n = 8$). (**Inset**) Changes in individual values.

with low DHEAS levels at baseline. Lean body mass, determined by DEXA, showed an increase in both genders, but significance ($p < 0.03$) was achieved only when both genders were analyzed together (FIG. 7). Knee extension/flexion muscle strength (MedX isometric testing) was increased in men ($p < 0.01$), but not in women, for whom a strong placebo effect was evident (FIG. 8). Lumbar muscle strength was

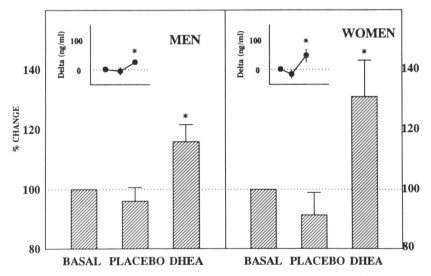

FIGURE 6. Serum IGF-I levels (mean ± SE) at baseline (100%) and the percentage change in response to placebo and DHEA (100 mg/d) administration for 6 months in aging men ($n = 8$) and women ($n = 8$). (**Inset**) Mean ± SE increments (delta). *$p < 0.05$.

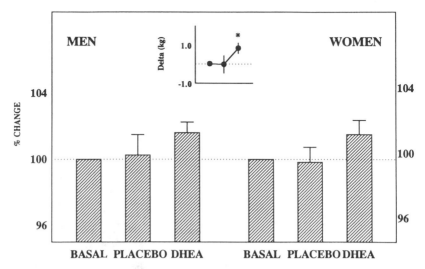

FIGURE 7. Lean body mass (LBM) measured by DEXA at baseline (100%) and the percentage change in response to placebo and DHEA (100 mg/d) administrations in aging men ($n = 8$) and women ($n = 8$). (**Inset**) Increments (delta). *$p < 0.05$.

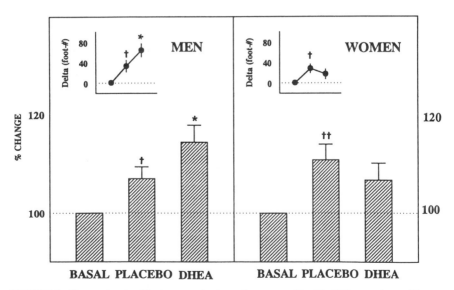

FIGURE 8. Knee extension/flexion muscle strength measured by MedX isometric machine at baseline (100%) and percentage change in response to placebo and DHEA (100 mg/d) in aging men ($n = 8$) and women ($n = 8$) expressed as number of feet. †$p < 0.05$ placebo versus baseline; *$p < 0.05$ DHEA versus placebo. (**Inset**) Incremental changes (delta).

unaltered. No time course-related changes were noted in muscle strength determinations. Fat body mass (by DEXA) was significantly decreased in men ($p < 0.05$) but not in women (FIG. 9), a finding consistent with that reported by Nestler *et al.*[30] In both genders, no change was noted in lipid profile and apolipoproteins, insulin or glucose levels, nitrogen balance, basal metabolic rate, bone mineral density, or urinary pyridiline levels.

In summary, in this extended study (1 year), we have confirmed the ability of DHEA to induce an increase in IGF-I. Furthermore, biologic end-points of increases in lean body mass and muscle strength of the knee were observed. A strong placebo effect was noted in women with regard to muscle strength measurements. A daily dose of 100 mg for 6 months appears to be excessive with respect to the increment of androgens in women and may induce undesirable androgenic effects with time. Thus, a potential gender difference in biotransformation of DHEA and biologic responses requires further study

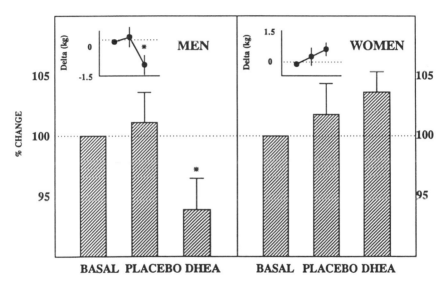

FIGURE 9. Fat body mass (FBM) measured by DEXA at baseline (100%) and the percentage change in response to placebo and DHEA (100 mg/d) for 6 months in aging men ($n = 8$) and aging women ($n = 8$). (**Inset**) Increments (delta).

DHEA Administration and Immune Function

Several lines of evidence derived primarily from animal studies have suggested a role for DHEA in modulating immune function.[8-14] In mice, DHEA administration demonstrated a protective effect against viral induced mortality,[12] and blocked the glucocorticoid-mediated thymocyte destruction *in vivo* and *in vitro*.[13] In a murine model of lupus erythematosus, oral administration of DHEA prevented the formation of antibodies to double-stranded DNA and prolonged survival.[14] *In vitro* studies with both murine[8] and human T cells[9] have shown that DHEA exerts a stimulatory effect on IL-2 secretion, inhibits NK cell differentiation,[31] and prevents the age-related increase in IL-6 production in murine lymphocytes.[10,11] A study of the therapeutic potential of DHEA (200 mg) in human systemic lupus erythematosus reported an improvement in symptoms, a reduction in corticosteroid requirements,[32] and restoration of impaired IL-2 production by T cells *in vitro.*[33]

To date, the only study examining the *in vivo* effect of a replacement dose of DHEA on human immune function is by Casson *et al.*[34] who reported that in postmenopausal women DHEA treatment with a 50-mg daily oral dose for 3 weeks increased NK cell cytotoxicity and decreased the number of CD4 (T helper) cells, but did not influence *in vitro* IL-6 production. The *in vivo* effects of DHEA treatment on the immune function of elderly men have not been reported.

DHEA Administration on Immune Function in Men

A single-blind placebo-controlled trial of 5 months' duration was conducted in nine healthy elderly men who were nonsmokers on no medications, with a mean age of 63.7 years (range 53–69) and mean body mass index of 26.7 kg/m^2 (range 22–30). Subjects took nightly placebo orally for the first 2 weeks followed by oral DHEA (50 mg) for 20 weeks. Fasting blood samples (at 8 AM) were obtained at monthly intervals

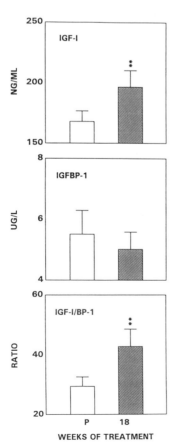

FIGURE 10. Serum levels (mean ± SE) of IGF-I, IGFBP-1, and IGF-I/IGFBP-1 ratio in response to placebo and DHEA (50 mg/d) in nine aging men during assessments of immune function. **$p < 0.01$.

TABLE 1. Effect of DHEA on Lymphocyte Subsets as Determined by Flow Cytometry[a]

Cell Marker	Weeks of Treatment						
	P	2	6	10	14	18	20
CD20 (B cells)	9.5 ± 2.1	14.5 ± 2.7*	9.5 ± 1.9	14.1 ± 3*	11.4 ± 2.8	11.4 ± 2.7	13.9 ± 4.0
CD14 (monocytes)	11.6 ± 1.9	21.2 ± 3.5**	14.0 ± 2.5	14.2 ± 2.1	14.7 ± 2.6	16.2 ± 2.9	17.9 ± 2.9**
CD3 (T cells)	68.4 ± 2.8	66.7 ± 4.3	61.7 ± 3.8	65.4 ± 3.1	69.8 ± 2.7	68.7 ± 3.7	69.1 ± 4.0
CD4 (T helper)	44.2 ± 3.4	39.4 ± 4.7	39.8 ± 2.9	40.5 ± 3.1	44.6 ± 2.4	43.9 ± 3.6	41.3 ± 4.1
CD8 (T suppressor)	32.7 ± 3.7	33.0 ± 3.0	31.2 ± 3.1	35.4 ± 3.1	33.6 ± 2.9	36.2 ± 1.9	38.3 ± 3.8
TCR α/β	59.2 ± 2.5	55.9 ± 2.9	42.6 ± 5.8	57.0 ± 3.2	51.9 ± 3.1	61.7 ± 3.9	62.0 ± 5.8
TCR γ/δ	5.7 ± 1.1	6.2 ± 0.97	6.2 ± 1.2	7.4 ± 1.1	7.7 ± 1.2	10.9 ± 1.2	10.5 ± 1.1**
CD25 (IL-2 receptor)	9.4 ± 1.2	6.7 ± 1.7	4.8 ± 0.83*	10.6 ± 2.3	11.7 ± 2.7	15.1 ± 1.5*	12.4 ± 2.4*
CD57 (NK)	24.1 ± 3.5	23.3 ± 2.9	24.0 ± 3.3	26.0 ± 2.4	22.8 ± 3.6	30.9 ± 2.9**	31.5 ± 3.2**
CD16 (NK)	15.4 ± 1.9	13.8 ± 1.4	18.1 ± 1.9	18.2 ± 2.5	15.3 ± 1.7	19.9 ± 2.2	21.0 ± 2.7*

[a]Values are expressed as % lymphocytes ± SEM.
*$p < 0.05$; **$p < 0.01$ versus placebo (P).

for assessment of immune function and determination of serum levels of IGF-I and IGFBP-1.

Our data show that DHEA treatment significantly ($p < 0.01$) elevated serum IGF-I levels with a decreasing trend for IGFBP-1 levels resulting in a significant ($p < 0.01$) elevation in the IGF-1/IGFBP-1 ratio (FIG. 10), a finding confirming our previous studies. The effect of *in vivo* DHEA treatment on lymphocyte subsets as determined by flow cytometry is shown in TABLE 1. In response to DHEA treatment a biphasic increase ($p < 0.01$) in monocytes (CD14) at 2 and 20 weeks was found. B cells (CD20) showed a fluctuating pattern with transient increases at 2 and 10 weeks ($p < 0.05$) followed by a rise (nonsignificant) at 20 weeks. Functional activation of B cells occurred as evidenced by a dose-related increase in proliferative response to the B-cell–specific mitogen pokeweed at 12 and 20 weeks (TABLE 2A and B), a response pattern parallel that seen in B-cell number. Serum IgG, IgM, and IgA were not affected (TABLE 2B). DHEA treatment did not affect basal levels of IL-6 production, but it enhanced phytohemagglutinin stimulated IL-6 production at 20 weeks (FIG. 11).

The number of total T lymphocytes (CD3) and T-cell subsets (CD4, CD8) was unaffected by DHEA treatment. However, there was a doubling in the number of T cells expressing the T-cell receptor γ/δ (TCR γ/δ) ($p < 0.01$) by 20 weeks of treatment, but not the α/β receptor (TCR α/β) (TABLE 1). T-cell function was activated as evidenced by an increased proliferative response to the T-cell–specific mitogen phytohemagglutinin (0.1 μg/ml) by 12 weeks (TABLE 2). This was accompanied by a significant ($p < 0.01$) rise in serum sIL2-R (measured by ELISA, Genzyme, Boston, Massachusetts) by 12 weeks, T cells expressing the IL-2 receptor (CD25), and the enhanced phytohemagglutinin-induced secretion of IL-2 (measured by ELISA, Bisource, Camarillo, California) by 20 weeks (FIG. 12). However, a transient decrease ($p < 0.05$) in IL-2R occurred at 6 weeks. The significance of this finding is unclear. In addition, DHEA treatment significantly ($p < 0.01$) increased NK cell number (CD16, CD57) by 18–20 weeks with a parallel rise in cytotoxicity ($p < 0.01$) as determined by a Cr-51 release assay using the K-562 cell line as the target[35] (FIG. 13).

TABLE 2A. Effect of DHEA Treatment on Lymphocytes Response to Mitogens[a]

| | | Weeks of Treatment | | | |
	Baseline	Placebo	4	12	20
Pokeweed mitogen					
0.5 μg/ml	.84 ± 0.17	1.0 ± 0.21	1.3 ± 0.18	2.1 ± 0.41*	2.1 ± 0.45*
5 μg/ml	2.2 ± 0.43	2.3 ± 0.50	2.5 ± 0.42	3.8 ± 0.64	5.3 ± 1.4**
Phytohemagglutinin					
0.1 μg/ml	1.3 ± 0.14	1.2 ± 0.13	1.7 ± 0.25	2.2 ± 0.50*	1.2 ± 0.12
2 μg/ml	6.2 ± 2.3	5.9 ± 2.3	5.9 ± 1.1	8.5 ± 2.3	5.3 ± 1.2

[a]Values are expressed as stimulation index (cpm in treatment wells/cpm in test wells) ± SEM.
*$p < 0.05$ versus placebo.

TABLE 2B. Effect of DHEA Treatment on Circulating Immunoglobulins

| | | Weeks of Treatment | | |
Immunoglobulins	Placebo	2	10	20
IgG (mg/l)	11,152 ± 757	11,015 ± 515	10,933 ± 675	11,245 ± 860
IgA (mg/l)	1,869 ± 168	1,934 ± 191	1,860 ± 192	1,914 ± 174
IgM (mg/l)	1,216 ± 208	1,187 ± 187	1,223 ± 202	1,259 ± 209

Our study demonstrates a time-related stimulatory effect of DHEA on the immune function of aging men. Peripheral lymphocytes appear to be targets of DHEA, with most effects effects occurring with a latent phase of 10–12 weeks. These results are in accord with the *in vitro* animal data showing a stimulatory effect of DHEA on IL-2 production,[11,12] but in addition we have demonstrated an increase in

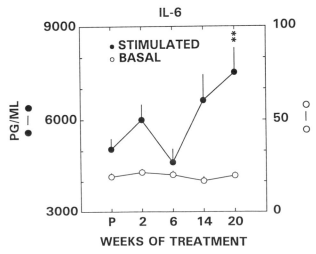

FIGURE 11. Concentrations of IL-6 (mean ± SE) in cultured lymphocytes under unstimulated (○—○) and phytohemagglutinin-stimulated (20 μg) conditions determined during placebo and during DHEA (50 mg/d) treatment. **$p < 0.01$.

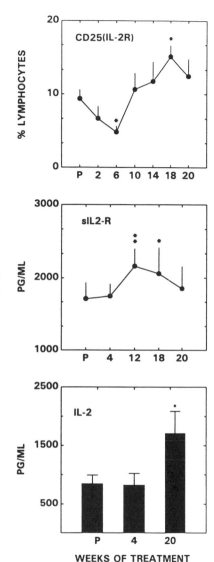

FIGURE 12. Percentage of lymphocytes expressing IL-2 receptors (*top*), concentrations of sIL-2 receptors in serum (*middle*), and IL-2 in culture (*bottom*) during placebo (p) and during DHEA (50 mg/d) treatment. *$p < 0.05$; **$p < 0.01$.

cells expressing IL-2 receptor and sIL-2 receptor in serum. In contrast with murine data showing inhibition of an age-related increase in IL-6 by DHEA,[13] we found an unaltered low level of basal secretion of IL-6, but augmented phytohemagglutinin-stimulated IL-6 production in response to DHEA treatment in men. In contrast with data obtained in postmenopausal women,[28] we did not observe a decrease in CD4+ T cells. However, a similar increase in NK cells was found with a difference in time course of activation (3 vs 18 weeks, respectively) in postmenopausal women and in our current study in men. The mechanism(s) by which DHEA exerts its lymphocyto-

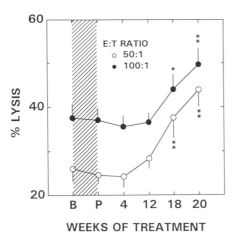

FIGURE 13. Percentage of lysis of the target cells at two effector/target (E:T) ratios at baseline (B) following placebo (P) and DHEA treatments. $*p < 0.05; **p < 0.01$.

tropic effects is unknown. The temporal synchrony of the increase in circulating IGF-I and immune activation by DHEA suggests that the immunoenhancing effects of DHEA may be mediated by IGF-I by virtue of its immune regulating properties, which have been demonstrated both *in vivo* and *in vitro*.[36,37] The question as to just how these findings translate to immunity against foreign antigens is being addressed in ongoing studies.

SUMMARY

DHEA in appropriate replacement doses appears to have remedial effects with respect to its ability to induce an anabolic growth factor, increase muscle strength and lean body mass, activate immune function, and enhance quality of life in aging men and women, with no significant adverse effects. Further studies are needed to confirm and extend our current results, particularly the gender differences.

ACKNOWLEDGMENTS

We wish to extend our appreciation for the technical assistance provided by L. Vu, S. Petze, R. Louf, J. Wong, and E. Imson and the editorial assistance by G. Laughlin.

REFERENCES

1. CORPAS, E., M. HARMAN & M. R. BLACKMAN. 1993. Human growth hormone and human aging. Endocr. Rev. **14:** 20–39.
2. ORENTREICH, N., J. L. BRIND, R. L. RIZER & J. H. VOGELMAN. 1984. Age changes and sex differences in serum dehydroepiandrosterone sulfate concentrations throughout adulthood. J. Clin. Endocrinol. Metab. **59:** 551–555.
3. MILLER, R. A. 1991. Aging and immune function. Int. Rev. Cytol. **124:** 187–215.
4. RUDMAN, D., A. G. FELLER, S. N. HOSKOTE *et al.* 1990. Effects of human growth hormone in men over 60 years old. N. Engl. J. Med. **323:** 1–54.

5. GAILLARD, R. C. 1994. Neuroendocrine-immune system interactions. Trends Endocrinol. Metab. **5:** 303–309.
6. REICHLIN, S. 1993. Neuroendocrine-immune interactions. N. Engl. J. Med. **329:** 1246–1253.
7. ADER, R., N. COHEN & D. FELTEN. 1995. Psychoneuroimmunology: Interactions between the nervous system and the immune system. Lancet **345:** 99–103.
8. DAYNES, R. A., D. J. DUDLEY & B. A. ARANEO. 1990. Regulation of murine lymphokine production in vivo. 11. Dehydroepiandrosterone is a natural enhancer of interleukin 2 synthesis by helper T cells. Eur. J. Immunol. **20:** 793.
9. SUZUKI, T., N. SUZUKI, R. A. DAYNES & E. G. ENGLEMAN. 1991. Dehydroepiandrosterone enhanced IL-2 production and cytotoxic effector function of human T cells. Clin. Immunol. Immunopathol. **61:** 202.
10. DAYNES, R. A., B. A. ARANEO, W. B. ERSHLER, C. MALONEY, G. LI & S. RYU. 1993. Altered regulation of IL-6 production with normal aging. J. Immunol. **150:** 5219.
11. DAYNES, R. A. & B. A. ARANEO. 1992. Prevention and reversal of some age-associated changes in immunologic responses by supplemental dehydroepiandrosterone sulfate therapy. Aging Immunol. Infect. Dis. **3:** 135–154.
12. LORIA, R. M., T. H. INGE, S. S. COOK, A. K. SZAKI & W. REGELSON. 1988. Protection against acute lethal viral infection with the native steroid dehydroepiandrosterone (DHEA). J. Med. Virol. **26:** 301.
13. MAY, M., E. HOLMES, W. ROGERS & M. POTH. 1990. Protection from glucocorticoid induced thymic involution by dehydroepiandrosterone. Life Sci. **46:** 1627.
14. LUCAS, J. A., A. S. ANSAR, L. CASEY & P. C. MAC DONALD. 1985. Prevention of autoantibody formation and prolonged survival in New Zealand Black/New Zealand White F1 mice fed dehydroepiandrosterone. J. Clin. Invest. **75:** 2091.
15. MCINTOSH, M. K. & C. D. BERDANIER. 1991. Antiobesity effects of DHEA are mediated by futile substrate cycling in hepatocytes of BHE/cdb rats. J. Nutr. **121:** 2037–2043.
16. GORDON, G. B., D. E. BUSH & H. F. WEISMAN. 1988. Reduction of atherosclerosis by administration of DHEA. J. Clin. Invest. **82:** 712–720.
17. EICH, D. M., J. E. NESTLER, D. E. JOHNSON, *et al.* 1993. Inhibition of accelerated coronary atherosclerosis with dehydroepiandrosterone in the heterotopic rabbit model of cardiac transplantation. Circulation **87:** 261–269.
18. MITCHELL, L. E., D. L. SPRECHER, I. B. BORECKI, T. RICE, P. M. LASKARZEWSKI & D. C. RAO. 1994. Evidence for an association between dehydroepiandrosterone sulfate and nonfatal, premature myocardial infarction in males. Circulation **89:** 89–93.
19. SCHWARTZ, A. G., J. W. WHITCOMB, J. W. NYCE, *et al.* 1988. Dehydroepiandrosterone and structural analogs: A new class of cancer chemo-preventive agents. Adv. Cancer Res. **51:** 391–424.
20. CUTLER, C. B., M. GLENN, M. BUSH, G. D. HODGEN, C. E. GRAHAM & D. L. LORIAUX. 1978. Adrenarche: A survey of rodents, domestic animals and primates. Endocrinology **103:** 2112–2118.
21. MORTOLA, J. & S. S. C. YEN. 1990. The effects of oral dehydroepiandrosterone on endocrine-metabolic parameters in postmenopausal women. J. Clin. Endocrinol. Metab. **71:** 696–704.
22. LIU, C. H., G. A. LAUGHLIN, U. G. FISCHER & S. S. C. YEN. 1990. Marked attenuation of ultradian and circadian rhythms of dehydroepiandrosterone in postmenopausal women: Evidence for a reduced 17,20-desmolase enzymatic activity. J. Clin. Endocrinol. Metab. **71:** 900–906.
23. BÉLANGER, A., B. CANDAS, A. DUPONT, L. CUSAN, P. DIAMOND, J. L. GOMEZ & F. LABRIE. 1994. Changes in serum concentrations of conjugated and unconjugated steroids in 40- to 80-year-old men. J. Clin. Endocrinol. Metab. **79:** 1086–1090.
24. MILLER, W. L. 1988. Molecular biology of steroid hormone synthesis. Endocr. Rev. **9:** 298.
25. MORALES, A. J., J. J. NOLAN, J. C. NELSON & S. S. C. YEN. 1994. Effects of replacement dose of dehydroepiandrosterone in men and women of advancing age. J. Clin. Endocrinol. Metab. **78:** 1360–1367.
26. ORENTREICH, N., J. L. BRIND, R. L. RIZER & J. H. VOGELMAN. 1984. Age changes and sex differences in serum dehydroepiandrosterone sulfate concentrations throughout adulthood. J. Clin. Endocrinol. Metab. **59:** 551–555.

27. CARLSTRÖM, K., S. BRODY, N. O. LUNELL, et al. 1988. Dehydroepiandrosterone sulfate and dehydroepiandrosterone in serum: Differences related to age and sex. Maturitas **10:** 297–306.
28. ORENTREICH, N., J. L. BRIND, J. H. VOGELMAN, R. ANDRES & H. BALDWIN. 1992. Long-term longitudinal measurements of plasma dehydroepiandrosterone sulfate in normal men. J. Clin. Endocrinol. Metab. **75:** 1002–1004.
29. JONES, J. I. & D. R. CLEMMONS. 1995. Insulin-like growth factors and their binding proteins: Biological actions. Endocrinol. Rev. **16:** 3–34.
30. NESTLER, J. E., C. O. BARLASCINI, J. N. CLORE & W. G. BLACKARD. 1988. Dehydroepiandrosterone reduces serum low-density lipoprotein levels and body fat but does not alter insulin sensitivity in normal men. J. Clin. Endocrinol. Metab. **66:** 57–61.
31. RISDON, G., T. A. MOORE, V. KUMAR & M. BENNETT. 1991. Inhibition of murine natural killer cell differentiation by dehydroepiandrosterone. Blood **78:** 2387.
32. VAN VOLLENHOVEN, R. F., E. G. ENGELMAN & J. L. MCGUIRE. 1994. An open study of dehydroepiandrosterone in systemic lupus erythematosus. Arthritis Rheum. **37:** 1305.
33. SUZUKI, T., N. SUZUKI, E. G. ENGELMAN, Y. MIZUSHIMA & T. SAKANE. 1994. Low serum levels of dehydroepiandrosterone production by lymphocytes in patients with systemic lupus erythematosus (SLE). Clin. Exp. Immunol. **99:** 251.
34. CASSON, P. R., R. N. ANDERSEN, H. G. HEROD, F. B. STENTZ, A. B. STRAUGHN, G. E. ABRAHAM & J. E. BUSTER. 1993. Oral dehydroepiandrosterone in physiologic doses modulates immune function in postmenopausal women. Am. J. Obstet. Gynecol. **169:** 1536.
35. COLIGAN, J. E., A. M. KLUISBECK, D. H. MARGULICE, E. M. SHEVACH & W. STROBER, EDS. 1992. *In* Current Protocols in Immunology. Greene Publishing Associates and Wiley Intersciences. New York.
36. TAPSON, V. F., M. BONI-SCHNETZLER, P. F. PILCH, D. M. CENTER & J. S. BERMAN. 1988. Structural and functional characterization of the human T lymphocyte receptor for insulin-like growth factor 1 in vitro. J. Clin. Invest. **82:** 950–957.
37. CLARK, R. & P. JARDIEU. 1995. Insulin-like growth factor-I: A stimulator of lymphopoiesis and immune function. 77th Annual Meeting, Endocrine Society, S11-1.

Metabolism of Dehydroepiandrosterone

CHRISTOPHER LONGCOPE

Departments of Obstetrics and Gynecology and Medicine
University of Massachusetts Medical School
Worcester, Massachusetts 01655

Dehydroepiandrosterone (DHEA) is a C-19 steroid that is secreted by the adrenals and gonads, but most circulating DHEA comes from the conversion of dehydroepiandrosterone sulfate (DHEAS) in peripheral tissues.[1]

Dehydroepiandrosterone circulates in blood in the free, that is, nonprotein-bound form and bound to albumin and sex hormone-binding globulin (SHBG).[2] Binding to SHBG is relatively small and weak and has little effect on the metabolism of DHEA. Although albumin binding plays a major role in the metabolism of its precursor DHEAS,[3,4] the binding of DHEA to albumin is relatively weak in comparison.[5]

When [³H]DHEA is administered intravenously, the disappearance of [³H]-DHEA from the blood compartment can be described as a function that is the sum of two exponentials.[4] The initial exponential represents spread into a compartment with a mean ± SEM volume of 17.0 ± 3.0 L. The mean $t_{1/2}$ for the disappearance of [³H]DHEA is 17.2 ± 6.2 minutes.[4] The second exponential represents spread into a larger compartment, and the $t_{1/2}$ for the disappearance of [³H]DHEA from this compartment is 60.2 ± 12.3 minutes. To calculate the metabolic clearance rate (MCR), the two-compartment model is necessary, and this approach gives a mean MCR for DHEA in 10 women as 1,690 ± 130 L/day.[6] In 24 women in whom the MCR for DHEA was measured using the constant infusion technique,[7–9] the mean MCR was 2,040 ± 160 L/day. These two means are not different ($p = 0.241$), and all data were pooled. The overall mean in 34 women of reproductive age is 1,935 ± 125 L/day (TABLE 1). This clearance rate is similar to those of androstenedione[10,11] and progesterone,[12] but far greater than those of estradiol and testosterone, steroids that circulate bound in part to sex hormone-binding globulin.[10,11]

The mean MCR for DHEA in 29 men is 2,050 ± 160 L/day, a value similar to that in women, $p = 0.58$ (TABLE 1). The MCR of most steroids is related to body weight,[13–15] but it is not completely clear if this relationship holds for DHEA. Feher and Halmy[16] studied two obese women and found the MCRs for DHEA were less than those in women of normal weight. In our studies in six postmenopausal women,[17] we could not find any relation between weight and the MCR for DHEA. Data from Bird *et al.*[6] do not show a relation between the MCR of DHEA and body surface area. However, Kurtz *et al.*[18] reported that the mean MCR of DHEA was increased by 81% ($p < 0.05$) in obese women whose mean weight was 99 ± 18 kg, as compared to normal women whose mean weight was 56 ± 8 kg. The design of our study[17] and that of Bird *et al.*[6] was to measure the MCR of DHEA in a normal population; therefore, although the women varied in weight and surface area, none was obese. As the study by Kurtz *et al.*[18] was designed to examine obesity and the MCR of DHEA, a different population was involved.

Nestler *et al.*[9] reported that a short-term insulin infusion resulted in a significant increase in the MCR of DHEA in men but not in women. This effect in men was suggested to be due to the vasodilatory effect of insulin that increases blood flow to DHEA-metabolizing tissues. The mechanism for the lack of effect of insulin on the

TABLE 1. Metabolic Clearance Rates of Dehydroepiandrosterone in Men and Women

Reference	n	Sex	MCR
Bird et al.[6]	15	M	$1{,}750 \pm 110^a$
Horton and Tait[7]	4	M	$1{,}865 \pm 140$
Nestler and Kahwash[9]	10	M	$2{,}440 \pm 410$
Mean	29	M	$2{,}050 \pm 160^c$
Belisle et al.[8]	4	F	$1{,}860 \pm 195$
Bird et al.[6]	16	F	$1{,}370 \pm 250$
Feher and Halmy[16]	3	F	$1{,}370 \pm 250$
Horton and Tait[7]	4	F	$1{,}535 \pm 150$
Nestler and Kahwash[9]	7	F	$2{,}525 \pm 490$
Mean	34	F	$1{,}935 \pm 125^{b,c}$

[a]Mean ± SEM.
[b]Difference between means is not significant, $p = 0.583$.
[c]Mean ± SE of all individuals.

MCR of DHEA in women was not apparent. However, the investigators commented that an infusion of insulin lowers the DHEA concentration in men but not in women.[9] However, chronic changes in insulin action or levels have not been noted to alter the MCR of DHEA.

Although the relation between DHEAS and DHEA is reversible and DHEAS is the major source of circulating DHEA, the conversion of DHEA back to circulating DHEAS is relatively small. The mean value for $[\rho]^{DHEA,DHEAS}$ (TABLE 2) is $6.25 \pm 0.54\%$ in women and $5.2 \pm 0.7\%$ in men,[6] values that are not different ($p = 0.23$). Dehydroepiandrosterone is also converted and is a source of circulating Δ^5-androstenediol, androstenedione, and testosterone.[6,11,19] The $[\rho]^{DHEA, \Delta5-A}$ is $7.1 \pm 0.3\%$ in women and $6.5 \pm 0.3\%$ in men.[6] The $[\rho]^{DHEA,A}$ values are $7.1 \pm 1.7\%$ in women and $4.7 \pm 0.3\%$ in men.[19] The $[\rho]^{DHEA,T}$ values are $0.87 \pm 0.02\%$ in women and 0.62 ± 0.06 in men. For none of these conversions is there a significant difference in the means for men as compared to those for women.

These are the major pathways for DHEA metabolism as measured in blood. These conversions are of critical importance, because conversion to T would result in binding to androgen receptors and androgenic activity. As Δ^5-androstenediol can bind to the estrogen receptor,[20,21] this could result in estrogenic activity.[21]

When radiolabeled DHEA is administered intravenously, the recovery of radioactivity in the urine is less than 100%.[22] Radiolabeled metabolites appearing in the urine include DHEAS and DHEA glucuronide and the glucuronides and sulfates of Δ^5-androstenediol, androsterone, etiocholanolone, 5α-androstane-3β-ol-17-one (isoandrosterone), and 5β-androstane-3β-ol-17-one.[22]

TABLE 2. Conversions of DHEA to DHEAS, A, T, and Δ^5-Androstenediol (Δ^5-A)

	$[\rho]^{DHEA,DHEAS}a$ (%)	$[\rho]^{DHEA,A}$ (%)	$[\rho]^{DHEA,T}$ (%)	$[\rho]^{DHEAS, \Delta5-A}$ (%)
Women	6.25 ± 0.54	7.1 ± 1.7	0.87 ± 0.02	7.1 ± 0.3
Men	5.2 ± 0.7	4.7 ± 0.3	0.62 ± 0.06	6.5 ± 0.3

[a]$[\rho]^{DHEA,DHEAS}$ is the percentage of DHEA entering the blood that is measured as DHEAS in the blood.
[b]Mean ± SE.

Dehydroepiandrosterone can also be converted to estrone (E1), although the $[\rho]^{DHEA,E1}$ value is very small, $0.16 \pm 0.04\%$.[23] This conversion contributes little to the overall production rate of E1 in young women.

In pregnancy the MCR for DHEA is markedly increased. In five pregnant women the mean MCR was 76.8 ± 18.8 L/day/kg compared to 45.7 ± 4.6 L/day/kg in five nonpregnant women.[8] This increase could be due to an increase in 16α-hydroxylation by the fetus and an increase in placental extraction.

DHEA METABOLISM AND AGING

For some but not all[24] steroids minimal changes occur with aging.[25-27] In two studies[17,28] the MCR for DHEA in 12 postmenopausal women was $1,710 \pm 90$ L/day, a value not different from that of younger women ($p = 0.56$).

Poortman et al.[28] reported a $[\rho]^{DHEA,DHEAS}$ of $30 \pm 4\%$ in 10 women and mean values of 6.8% for $[\rho]^{DHEA,A}$ and 0.5% for $[\rho]^{DHEA,T}$. Although the conversions of DHEA to androstenedione and testosterone are similar to the values in young women,[7] values for the conversion of DHEA to DHEAS are some fivefold greater than those reported in young women.[6] Whether this difference is methodologic or due to aging is uncertain.

Aging has been associated with an increase in the aromatization of androstenedione and testosterone.[29,30] We noted[17] that $[\rho]^{DHEA,E1}$ in six postmenopausal women, $0.58 \pm 0.11\%$, was significantly greater than that reported for four young women, 0.16 ± 0.04,[23] $p = 0.018$. Although the conversion of DHEA to E1 is not an important source of estrogen in young women, the decreased production rate of estrogens and the increase in aromatization of DHEA can make it a more important source of estrogen in postmenopausal women.

DEHYDROEPIANDROSTERONE SULFATE METABOLISM

Dehydroepiandrosterone sulfate is secreted by the adrenal and is the most important source of DHEA. Its pattern of metabolism is considerably different from that of DHEA.

DHEAS is strongly bound to albumin in the blood,[3,31] and undergoes renal tubular reabsorption.[32] Both these factors contribute to the very slow clearance from the blood. After the pulse administration of $[^3H]DHEAS$, the disappearance of $[^3H]DHEAS$ from the blood can be described as a function that is the sum of two exponentials.[16,33] However, because of slow clearance from the second exponential, a single compartment model can be used to determine its MCR. The $t_{1/2}$ from $[^3H]DHEAS$ from this compartment is 13.7 hours, and the mean $\pm$ SEM value for the MCR of DHEAS is 12.5 ± 1.0 L/day in women and 13.8 ± 2.7 L/day in men.[16,33-39] Thus, the MCR of DHEAS is 100-fold different from that of DHEA.

The conversion of DHEAS to DHEA is $60.5 \pm 8.2\%$[16,35-38] in normal women and $77.8 \pm 17.3\%$[36] in men. As the production rate of DHEAS is in the range of 10–15 mg/day, the high conversion of DHEAS, as noted, makes it the major source of circulating DHEA.

DHEAS is also converted to androstenedione and testosterone,[37,40] and percentage conversions are somewhat greater than the conversions of DHEA to androstenedione and testosterone. Because DHEA is an intermediate in the conversions of

DHEAS to androstenedione and testosterone, some of the conversions must occur through a pool of DHEA not in equilibrium with circulating DHEA.

Haning et al.[38,41] postulated that circulating DHEAS may be taken up by the ovarian follicle converted to androstenedione and testosterone within the follicle and secreted as such into the blood. Thus, DHEAS can serve as an important pre-hormone for circulating androgens.

DHEAS can also be aromatized to estrogens, although it does not appear to be an important source of circulating estrogens in nonpregnant women. In pregnancy, however, maternal and fetal DHEA are major precursors for the placental synthesis of estrogens. In pregnancy, the MCR of DHEAS increases fivefold due to 16α-hydroxylation in the liver and aromatization in the placenta.[42,43]

DHEAS can also be metabolized by a "direct" pathway and be excreted in the urine as Δ^5-androstenediol sulfate and other sulfated metabolites.[22]

The liver metabolizes DHEAS less than it does DHEA. Thus, following the oral administration of DHEAS, much of it will appear as such in the blood. However, after the oral administration of DHEA, the liver will metabolize most of it, and only a small fraction of DHEA will appear in the blood as DHEA, a large amount being measurable as DHEAS.

In summary, DHEA circulates in the blood bound only weakly to albumin. The MCR of DHEA is similar to that of other steroids that circulate not strongly bound to a serum protein. DHEA is metabolized to DHEA and to androstenedione and testosterone and appears in the urine as DHEAS, DHEA glucuronide, and the metabolites of androstenedione and testosterone. A small percentage of DHEA is aromatized to estrone, and this percentage increases with aging and with pregnancy. The MCR of DHEAS is smaller than that of DHEA, because DHEAS is bound much more strongly to albumin, and there is direct as well as indirect metabolism of DHEAS, so that a quantitative difference in metabolites is present.

REFERENCES

1. LONGCOPE, C. 1986. Adrenal and gonadal androgen secretion in normal females. Clin. Endocrinol. Metab. **15:** 213–228.
2. DUNN, J. F., B. C. NISULA & D. RODBARD. 1981. Transport of steroid hormones: Binding of 21 endogenous steroids to both testosterone-binding globulin and corticosteroid-binding globulin in human plasma. J. Clin. Endocrinol. Metab. **53:** 58–68.
3. PLAGER, J. E. 1965. The binding of androsterone sulfate, etiocholanolone sulfate, and dehydroisoandrosterone sulfate by human plasma protein. J. Clin. Invest. **44:** 1234–1239.
4. WANG, D. Y., R. D. BULBROOK, A. SNEDDON & T. HAMILTON. 1967. The metabolic clearance rates of dehydroepiandrosterone, testosterone, and their sulphate esters in man, rat, and rabbit. J. Endocrinol. **38:** 307–318.
5. WESTPHAL, U. 1971. Steroid interactions with serum proteins other than specific glycoproteins. In Steroid-Protein Interactions. Anonymous: 84–132. Springer-Verlag. New York.
6. BIRD, C. E., J. MURPHY, K. BOROOMAND, W. FINNIS, D. DRESSEL & A. F. CLARK. 1978. Dehydroepiandrosterone: Kinetics of metabolism in normal men and women. J. Clin. Endocrinol. Metab. **47:** 818–822.
7. HORTON, R. & J. F. TAIT. 1967. In vivo conversion of dehydroisoandrosterone to plasma androstenedione and testosterone in man. J. Clin. Endocrinol. Metab. **27:** 79–88.
8. BELISLE, S., I. SCHIFF & D. TULCHINSKY. 1980. The use of constant infusion of unlabeled dehydroepiandrosterone for the assessment of its metabolic clearance rate, its half-life, and its conversion into estrogens. J. Clin. Endocrinol. Metab. **50:** 117–121.
9. NESTLER, J. E. & Z. KAHWASH. 1994. Sex-specific action of insulin to acutely increase the metabolic clearance rate of dehydroepiandrosterone in humans. J. Clin. Invest. **94:** 1484–1489.

10. BAIRD, D., R. HORTON, C. LONGCOPE & J. F. TAIT. 1968. Steroid prehormones. Perspect. Biol. Med. **11:** 384–421.
11. BAIRD, D. T., R. HORTON, C. LONGCOPE & J. F. TAIT. 1969. Steroid dynamics under steady-state conditions. Recent Prog. Horm. Res. **25:** 611–664.
12. LIN, T. J., R. B. BILLIAR & B. LITTLE. 1972. Metabolic clearance rate of progesterone in the menstrual cycle. J. Clin. Endocrinol. Metab. **35:** 879–886.
13. KIRSCHNER, M. A., N. ERTEL & G. SCHNEIDER. 1981. Obesity, hormones and cancer. Cancer Res. **31:** 3711–3717.
14. KIRSCHNER, M. A., E. SAMOJLIK & D. SILBER. 1983. A comparison of androgen production and clearance in hirsute and obese women. J. Steroid Biochem. **19:** 607–614.
15. LONGCOPE, C., R. BAKER & C. C. JOHNSTON, JR. 1986. Androgen and estrogen metabolism in relationship to obesity. Metabolism **35:** 235–237.
16. FEHER, T. & L. HALMY. 1975. Dehydroepiandrosterone and dehydroepiandrosterone sulfate dynamics in obesity. Can. J. Biochem. **53:** 215–222.
17. LONGCOPE, C., C. BOURGET & C. FLOOD. 1982. The production and aromatization of dehydroepiandrosterone in postmenopausal women. Maturitas **4:** 325–332.
18. KURTZ, B. R., J. R. GIVENS, S. KOMINDR, M. D. STEVENS, J. G. KARAS, J. B. BITTLE, D. JUDGE & A. E. KITABCHI. 1987. Maintenance of normal circulating levels of Δ^4-androstenedione and dehydroepiandrosterone in simple obesity despite increased metabolic clearance rates: Evidence for a servo-control mechanism. J. Clin. Endocrinol. Metab. **64:** 1261–1267.
19. HORTON, R., D. ENDRES & M. GALMARINI. 1986. Ideal conditions for hydrolysis of androstane-3a,17b-diol glucuronide in plasma. J. Clin. Endocrinol. Metab. **62:** 22–27.
20. POORTMAN, J., J. A. C. PRENEN, F. SCHWARZ & J. H. H. THIJSSEN. 1975. Interaction of Δ^5-Androstene-3β,17β-diol with estradiol and dihydrotestosterone receptors in human myometrial and mammary cancer tissue. J. Clin. Endocrinol. Metab. **40:** 373–379.
21. BIRD, C. E., J. TREMBLAY, V. MASTERS & A. F. CLARK. 1982. Δ^5-Androstenediol: Kinetics of metabolism and binding to plasma proteins in normal post-menopausal women. Acta Endocrinol. **99:** 309–313.
22. BAULIEU, E. E., C. CORPECHOT & F. DRAY. 1965. An adrenal-secreted 'androgen' dehydroepiandrosterone sulfate. Its metabolism and a tentative generalization on the metabolism of other steroid conjugates in man. Recent Prog. Horm. Res. **21:** 411–500.
23. MACDONALD, P. C., C. D. EDMAN, I. J. KERBER & P. K. SIITERI. 1976. Plasma precursors of estrogen III. Conversion of plasma dehydroepiandrosterone to estrogen in young nonpregnant women. Gynecol. Invest. **7:** 165–175.
24. VERMEULEN, A., R. RUBENS & L. VERDONCK. 1972. Testosterone secretion and metabolism in male senescence. J. Clin. Endocrinol. Metab. **34:** 730–735.
25. LONGCOPE, C. 1987. The effects of age on secretion and concentration of gonadal hormones. *In:* Atherogenesis and Aging. S. R. Bates & E. C. Gangloff, Eds.: 198– 205. Springer-Verlag. New York.
26. LONGCOPE, C., W. JAFFEE & G. GRIFFING. 1980. Metabolic clearance rates of androgens and estrogens in aging women. Maturitas **2:** 283–390.
27. LONGCOPE, C. 1990. Hormone dynamics at the menopause. Ann. NY Acad. Sci. **592:** 21– 30.
28. POORTMAN, J., R. ANDRIESSE, A. AGEMA, G. H. DONKER, F. SCHWARZ & J. H. H. THIJSSEN. 1980. Adrenal androgen secretion and metabolism in postmenopausal women. *In* Adrenal Androgens. A. R. Genazzani, J. H. H. Thijssen & P. K. Siiteri, Eds.: 219– 240. Raven Press. New York.
29. HEMSELL, D. L., J. M. GRODIN, P. F. BRENNER, P. K. SIITERI & P. C. MACDONALD. 1974. Plasma precursors of estrogen. II. Correlation of the extent of conversion of plasma androstenedione to estrone with age. J. Clin. Endocrinol. Metab. **38:** 476–479.
30. LONGCOPE, C. 1987. Peripheral aromatization: Studies on controlling factors. Steroids **50:** 253–267.
31. WANG, D. Y. & R. D. BULBROOK. 1967. Binding of the sulphate esters of dehydroepiandrosterone, testosterone, 17-acetoxypregnenolone and pregnenolone in the plasma of man, rabbit, and rat. J. Endocrinol. **39:** 405–413.

32. KELLIE, A. E. & E. R. SMITH. 1957. Renal clearance of 17-oxo steroid conjugates found in human peripheral plasma. Biochem. J. **66:** 490–495.
33. OSEKO, F., T. YOSHIMI, M. FUKASE & T. KONO. 1974. Kinetics of dehydroepiandrosterone sulphate metabolism in normal controls and patients with liver cirrhosis and acute hepatitis. Acta Endocrinol. **76:** 332–342.
34. DE PERETTI, E. & M. G. FOREST. 1976. Unconjugated dehydroepiandrosterone plasma levels in normal subjects from birth to adolescence in human: The use of a sensitive radioimmunoassay. J. Clin. Endocrinol. Metab. **43:** 982–991.
35. SANDBERG, E., E. GURPRIDE & S. LIEBERMAN. 1964. Quantitative studies on the metabolism of dehydroisoandrosterone sulfate. Biochemistry **3:** 1256–1267.
36. BIRD, C. E., V. MASTERS & A. F. CLARK. 1984. Dehydroepiandrosterone sulfate: Kinetics of metabolism in normal young men and women. Clin. Invest. Med. **7:** 119–122.
37. HANING, R. V., JR., M. CHABOT, C. A. FLOOD, R. HACKETT & C. LONGCOPE. 1989. Metabolic clearance rate (MCR) of dehydroepiandrosterone sulfate (DS), its metabolism to dehydroepiandrosterone, androstenedione, testosterone, and dihydrotestosterone, and the effect of increased plasma DS concentration on DS MCR in normal women. J. Clin. Endocrinol. Metab. **69:** 1047–1052.
38. HANING, R., C. FLOOD, R. HACKETT, J. LOUGHLIN, N. MCCLURE & C. LONGCOPE. 1991. Metabolic clearance rate of dehydroepiandrosterone sulfate, its metabolism to testosterone, and its intrafollicular metabolism to dehydroepiandrosterone, androstenedione, testosterone, and dihydrotestosterone *in vivo.* J. Clin. Endocrinol. Metab. **72:** 1088–1095.
39. SCHIEBINGER, R. J., G. P. CHROUSOS, G. B. CUTLER, JR. & D. L. LORIAUX. 1986. The effect of serum prolactin on plasma adrenal androgens and the production and metabolic clearance rate of dehydroepiandrosterone sulfate in normal and hyperprolactinemic subjects. J. Clin. Endocrinol. Metab. **62:** 202–210.
40. LINDBERG, M. C., C. MCCLENAGHAN & W. L. HERRMANN. 1966. Fate of injected dehydroisoandrosterone, testosterone, and dehydroisoandrosterone sulfate in plasma in the human. Am. J. Obstet. Gynecol. **95:** 743–746.
41. HANING, R. V., R. J. HACKETT, C. A. FLOOD, J. S. LOUGHLIN, Q. Y. ZHAO & C. LONGCOPE. 1993. Plasma dehydroepiandrosterone sulfate serves as a prehormone for 48% of follicular fluid testosterone during treatment with menotropins. J. Clin. Endocrinol. Metab. **76:** 1301–1307.
42. GANT, N. F., H. T. HUTCHINSON, P. K. SIITERI & P. C. MACDONALD. 1971. Study of the metabolic clearance rate of dehydroepiandrosterone sulfate in pregnancy. Am. J. Obstet. Gynecol. **111:** 555–563.
43. BELISLE, S., R. OSATHANONDH & D. TULCHINSKY. 1977. The effect of constant infusion of unlabeled dehydroepiandrosterone sulfate on maternal plasma androgens and estrogens. J. Clin. Endocrinol. Metab. **45:** 544–550.

Pleotropic Effects of Dietary DHEA

LEON MILEWICH, FERNANDO CATALINA,
AND MICHAEL BENNETT

Departments of Obstetrics-Gynecology and Pathology
The University of Texas
Southwestern Medical Center at Dallas
Dallas, Texas 75235

The actions of dehydroepiandroserone (DHEA) have been studied at three different levels: (1) physiologic, (2) pharmacologic, and (3) dietary or suprapharmacologic.

Dehydroepiandrosterone feeding is effective in the prevention of various spontaneous and experimentally induced pathologic disorders in animals. Thus, at concentrations ranging from 0.2–1.0% in food (w/w) DHEA prevents or delays the onset of obesity,[1,2] diabetes,[3] hemolytic anemia,[4] autoimmune diseases,[5,6] immune decline,[7] nephrosis,[8] atherosclerosis,[9] neoplasias,[10] and lethal viral infections,[11] among other pathologies.

In our initial studies begun in 1986, which were directed at the identification of biochemical aspects underlying the preventive effects of dietary DHEA, we found that DHEA administration in food (0.45%, w/w) to mice and rats resulted in a decrease in body weight gain, hepatomegaly, and a change in liver color from pink to mahogany.[12] To evaluate the impact of the liver in the actions elicited by dietary DHEA, we began by studying possible changes in liver protein content by the use of polyacrylamide gel electrophoresis under denaturing conditions (SDS-PAGE) for separation[12]; in addition, we determined if morphometric changes in hepatocyte oganelles occurred with DHEA feeding.[12] Thereafter, we studied other possible effects of DHEA in rodent liver function including changes in the specific activities of protein kinases,[13,14] phosphatases,[13,14] and lipogenic enzymes.[14,15] In addition, we determined serum levels of triglycerides,[15] total cholesterol,[15] prolactin,[16] proteins,[6] DHEA, and 5-androstene-3β,17β-diol.

RESULTS AND DISCUSSION

Reduced Weight Gain, Hepatomegaly, and Liver Color Change. Dietary DHEA produces remarkable changes in the liver of rats and mice, some of which can be detected by visual inspection, such as enlarged liver and liver color change. As demonstrated by many investigators, mice and rats receiving chronic dietary DHEA (0.2–1.0% in food, by weight) experience a reduction in weight gain compared to controls, and in most cases this is accompanied by hepatomegaly or at least an increase in liver weight as a percentage of body weight. The intensity of these effects appears to be strain dependent. These effects are illustrated in our own studies as presented in TABLE 1.[17] Food intake by mice and rats receiving DHEA is also strain dependent and is not reduced on chronic DHEA administration despite a decrease in body weight gain.

The change in liver color from pink to mahogany in mice and rats produced by dietary DHEA is observable in intact liver as well as in subcellular fractions, as illustrated in FIGURE 1 for mitochondrial fractions ([200–8,000 g] obtained from the liver of control and DHEA-fed mice for 14 days [$n = 5$]). Also, blood from DHEA-

TABLE 1. Body and Liver Weights of Mice Fed Either a DHEA-Containing Diet or a Control Diet

Strain	n	Sex	Age at Time of Killing (months)	Diet	Time on Diet (months)	Mean ± SD		
						Body Weight (g)	Liver Weight (g)	Liver Weight as Percentage of Body Weight
(NZB × NZW)F₁	5	Female	6	Control		40.9 ± 4.6	2.2 ± 0.4	5.4 ± 0.5
				DHEA	5	33.6 ± 1.2*	2.7 ± 0.1**	8.0 ± 0.4**
(NZB × NZW)F₁	5	Female	7	Control		38.9 ± 3.9	2.2 ± 0.3	5.7 ± 0.8
				DHEA	6	33.7 ± 1.0*	2.5 ± 0.09**	7.5 ± 0.2*
(NZW × BXSB)F₁	5	Female	5	Control		28.5 ± 0.6	1.6 ± 0.06	5.7 ± 0.2
				DHEA	3	24.9 ± 1.1**	1.8 ± 0.1	7.3 ± 0.2**
C57BL/6	4	Female	7	Control		23.4 ± 0.7	1.0 ± 0.1	4.2 ± 0.3
				DHEA	6	20.8 ± 0.6**	1.4 ± 0.2**	6.4 ± 0.5**
C57BL/6	4	Male	7	Control		32.7 ± 0.7	1.4 ± 0.2	4.4 ± 0.7
				DHEA	6	24.4 ± 0.9**	1.4 ± 0.02	5.7 ± 0.3*

$*p \leq 0.02$; $**p < 0.001$.

treated mice is darker than that of control mice. The mahogany color is not due to hemochromogen (data not shown), and it may be due to pigments produced by peroxidation of polyunsaturated membrane lipids, such as lipofucsin. Peroxidation of polyunsaturated membrane lipids occurs by chain reactions involving reactive oxygen-

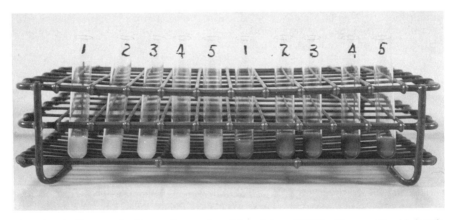

FIGURE 1. Changes in liver color produced by dietary DHEA. Two-month-old female (NZB × NZW)F₁ mice were fed either AIN-76A or the same diet containing DHEA (0.45%, by weight) for 14 days. Animals were killed by cervical dislocation under ether anesthesia, liver was removed and homogenized, and subcellular fractions were prepared. The figure presents the difference in color between mitochondrial fractions prepared from five control livers (tubes 1–5, *left side*) and that of mitochondrial fractions from livers of five mice treated with DHEA (tubes 1–5, *right side*).

free radicals, which may have their origin in normal or abnormal intracellular processes. Liver lipofucsin formation has been associated with aging. A change in liver color due to lipofucsin, associated with liver enlargement, also has been reported in mice or rats receiving hypolipidemic drugs such as clofibrate.

Separation of Liver Proteins by SDS-PAGE and Two-Dimensional Gel Electrophoresis. After separation by SDS-PAGE and staining with Coomassie blue, we observed that liver proteins of apparent $M_r \sim 72$ kD and ~ 28 kD were induced by DHEA administration, whereas a major protein of M_r app ~ 160 kD was decreased in intensity compared to that of controls (FIG. 2).[18] In addition, a protein of M_r app

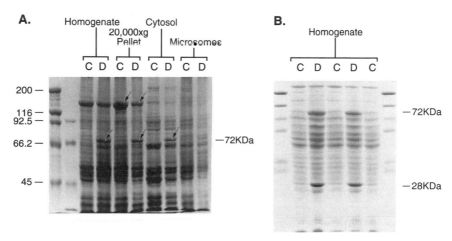

FIGURE 2. Alterations in specific liver protein levels by DHEA treatment of mice. Two month-old female (NZB × NZW)F$_1$ mice received a diet consisting of either AIN-76A or AIN-76A containing DHEA (0.45%, by weight) for 5 months. Livers were homogenized in the presence of five protease inhibitors, and subcellular fractions were prepared. (A) Proteins were separated by SDS-PAGE (10% polyacrylamide) and were visualized after staining with Coomassie blue. An induced ~ 72-kD protein was detected in liver homogenate, 200–20,000 g pellet, and cytosolic fraction of the DHEA-treated mouse, but not in microsomes. The concentration of a liver protein of $M_r \sim 160$ K was decreased with DHEA treatment; this was demonstrated with homogenate and with the 200–20,000 g pellet, but this protein was not present in cytosol or microsomes. High and low molecular weight marker proteins, respectively, are presented in the two *left lanes* of the gel. (B) A protein of $M_r \sim 28$ kD also was induced markedly by DHEA treatment, as demonstrated by the use of liver homogenate and SDS-PAGE (12% polyacrylamide). In other studies with subcellular fractions of liver homogenates, the ~ 28 kD protein was predominantly associated with the cytosolic fraction (data not shown).

~ 54 kD also was induced, but this protein was not readily observable in all gels (FIG. 3).[18] To resolve these proteins, the acrylamide content of the gels required adjustment. Thus, the ~ 160 kD protein was visualized best with 8% acrylamide gels, the $M_r \sim 72$ kD protein with 10% acrylamide gels, and the ~ 28 kD protein with 12% acrylamide gels.

When two-dimensional gel electophoreses were run with the first dimension (isoelectric focusing) under equilibrium conditions, the ~ 72 and ~ 28 kD proteins were not detected, but when the first dimension was run under nonequilibrium

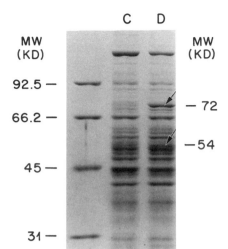

FIGURE 3. Liver protein patterns obtained by SDS-PAGE (10% polyacrylamide). Female (NZW × BXSB)F₁ mice were fed either AIN-76A (**C**) or the same diet containing DHEA (**D**, 0.45%, by weight) for 3 months, commencing at 2 months of age. Proteins were visualized after Coomassie blue staining. An induced protein of $M_r \sim 54$ K was visualized in addition to the predominant ~ 72 kD protein.

conditions, both the induced ~ 72 kD and the ~ 28 kD proteins were present, this being evidence of a basic pI for these proteins (FIG. 4).[18,19]

Identification of the Hepatic ~ 72 kD Protein Induced by DHEA. This protein was present in the 200–20,000 g pellet and in the 105,000 g supernatant fractions of liver homogenates.[18] In an attempt to determine the amino acid sequence of this protein, we found that the amino terminal was blocked and therefore sequencing could not be performed. On this account, peptide fragments of the ~ 72 kD protein were obtained by solid-phase tryptic digestion of the transblotted protein; peptides were isolated by reverse phase HPLC. Five of these peptides were reduced and alkylated and, thereafter, amino acids were sequenced using a gas phase sequencer. Comparison of these sequences with those of known proteins stored in a protein data bank enabled us to identify the induced protein as enoyl CoA hydratase/3-hydroxy-fatty acyl CoA dehydrogenase, a component of the fatty acid β-oxidation system of liver peroxisomes.[17,20]

Peroxisomes. Peroxisomes, originally termed microbodies, are cytoplasmic organelles bound by a single membrane; they have a granular matrix and in many cases a denser crystalline core. Peroxisomes were characterized from a biochemical point of view as having both oxidase activities, which participate in the oxidation of specific substrates while reducing O_2 to hydrogen peroxide, and catalase, which reduces the toxic H_2O_2 to water via peroxidatic or catalatic pathways. The oxidases, fatty acyl CoA oxidase, urate oxidase, D- and L-amino acid oxidases, L-α-hydroxy carboxylic acid oxidase, and others, together with catalase, form a primitive respiratory system in which electrons removed from the appropriate substrates are added to oxygen, ultimately producing water. By contrast to the respiratory system in mitochondria, the peroxisomal respiratory system is mediated by H_2O_2 and is not coupled to phosphorylation to store energy in the form of ATP.

In addition to oxidases and catalase, peroxisomes contain a variety of enzymes important in cellular metabolism, some of which can be induced with appropriate substrates.

DHEA Effect on Hepatic Enzyme Activities. Identification of the induced ~ 72 kD protein as enoyl CoA hydratase/3-hydroxy-fatty acyl CoA dehydrogenase, now known to contain two additional enzyme activities, namely, Δ^3/Δ^2-fatty acyl CoA isomerase and 2-cis/2-trans-fatty acyl CoA isomerase, led us to determine whether the specific activities of these and other enzymes known to be induced by hypolipidemic peroxisomal proliferators, such as clofibrate, were also induced by dietary or intraperitoneally injected DHEA. For this purpose, we used homogenates and subcellular fractions of liver prepared from mice and rats treated with either a DHEA-containing diet or a control diet to determine the specific activities of peroxisomal enoyl CoA hydratase, catalase, carnitine acetyl CoA transferase, carnitine octanoyl CoA transferase, and urate oxidase as well as mitochondrial carnitine palmitoyl CoA transferase. We found that the activities of these enzymes were increased significantly by DHEA treatment (FIG. 5).[17,20] In addition, smooth endoplasmic reticulum fatty acyl ω-hydroxylase[21-23] and cytoplasmic malic enzyme[14,15] were induced markedly by DHEA administration.

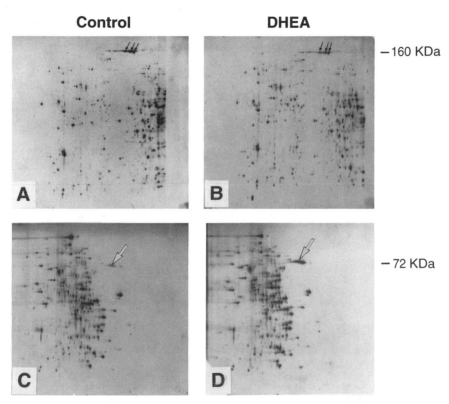

FIGURE 4. Two-dimensional gel electrophoresis of mouse liver proteins. Two-month-old female (NZB × NZW)F_1 mice were fed either AIN-76A or the same diet containing DHEA (0.45%, by weight) for 6 months. Livers were homogenized, and proteins were separated by two-dimensional electrophoresis under either equilibrium (**A, B**) or nonequilibrium conditions (**C, D**) and silver stained for visualization. Liver proteins from a control mouse (**A**) and a DHEA-treated mouse (**B**); the first dimensions were run under equilibrium conditions. Liver proteins from a control mouse (**C**) and a DHEA-treated mouse (**D**); the first dimensions were run under nonequilibrium conditions. *Black arrows* point towards the three isoforms of the protein of $M_r \sim 160$ K. *White arrows* point towards the ~72-kD protein.

Peroxisomal Proliferation. DHEA at concentrations used in the studies described in this paper behaves as a typical peroxisomal proliferator *in vivo.* Of the currently known peroxisomal proliferators, DHEA possibly is one of the very few, if not the only one, that does not have an acidic function.

Peroxisomal proliferator-activated receptors activate the transcription of genes encoding selected peroxisomal enzymes. In addition to specific peroxisomal proliferators, fatty acids also activate these receptors, whereas DHEA does not. Whether

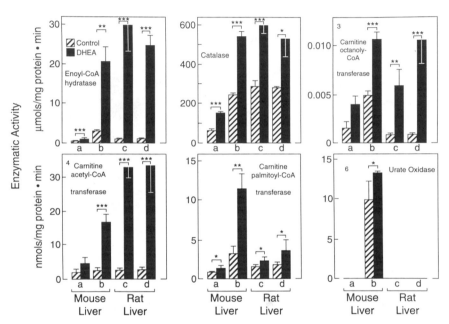

FIGURE 5. Peroxisomal and mitochondrial enzymatic activities in mouse and rat liver determined by spectrophotometric methods. Female (NZB × NZW)F$_1$ mice and male Sprague-Dawley rats were fed either AIN-76A or the AIN-76A diet containing DHEA (0.45%, by weight). Mice were started on the diets at 2 months of age and maintained on the diets for 5 months. Rats (∼100 g each) were maintained on the diets for 7 days, or alternatively they received DHEA intraperitoneally (100 mg/kg body weight, in corn oil). After killing, livers were homogenized in Tris buffer, pH 7.4, containing sucrose (0.25 M) (1:5, w/v), and a portion of each homogenate was used to prepare 105,000 g supernatant fractions. (**a**) Mouse liver 105,000 g supernatant fraction; (**b**) mouse liver homogenate; (**c**) rat liver 105,000 g supernatant (oral DHEA); (**d**) rat liver 105,000 g supernatant (intraperitoneal DHEA). *Bars* represent mean values (±SD) obtained by enzymatic determination of individual liver preparations of five animals per group. *$p <0.05$; **$p < 0.01$; ***$p < 0.005$.

DHEA sulfate (DHEAS) or DHEA fatty acyl derivatives serve this role has not currently been determined.

There is influx of fatty acids into the liver as a result of treatment with classic peroxisomal proliferators, leading to lipid excess. Activated fatty acids serve as substrates for both microsomal ω-hydroxylase and fatty acyl CoA oxidase involved in the peroxisomal β-oxidation pathway. Both enzymes are induced by administration of either peroxisomal proliferators or high fat diets. This induction is more marked with fatty acids that are poorly metabolized by mitochondria.

Lipoidal derivatives of DHEA, such as fatty acid ester derivatives of DHEA, have been identified in brain and other tissues as well as in the circulation,[24,25] and therefore it is possible that after ω-hydroxylation and further oxidation to ω-carboxylic acid derivatives followed by activation to the corresponding CoA derivative, these compounds may trigger peroxisomal enzyme induction and peroxisomal proliferation.

Recently, DHEA was demonstrated to be ineffective in the induction of peroxisomal enzymes in hepatocytes maintained in primary culture[26]; however, a previous study by other investigators showed induction capacity.[27] However, both groups of investigators demonstrated that DHEAS induces peroxisomal enzymes. Moreover, other steroids sulfated at either the C-3β, C-3α, or C-17β positions and having either C-5α or C-5β configurations also served as inducers of peroxisomal enzymes in cultured hepatocytes.[26,27] DHEAS levels increase markedly in rodents fed DHEA, and thus this conjugated steroid and/or sulfated steroid metabolites may serve as the trigger(s) for initiating the induction of peroxisomal enzymes and peroxisomal proliferation in the liver.

We observed that the common characteristics of classic peroxisomal proliferators are their hydrophobicity and the presence of either a carboxylic acid, a functional group that can be metabolized to a carboxylic acid or that otherwise has an acidic function other than a carboxylic acid. In addition, the α-carbons may have the two hydrogens substituted by alkyl or other groups, the α-carbon is substituted by another element, the β-carbon hydrogens are replaced by alkyl or other groups, or the β-carbon atoms are substituted by another element so appropriate peroxisomal oxidases cannot exert their function, with resultant substrate overload. Thus, most peroxisomal proliferators apparently may be characterized by oxidation blockade. This may lead to influx and accumulation of fatty acids in liver, as demonstrated previously in studies with classic peroxisomal proliferators, thus activating the peroxisome proliferator-dependent receptor and consequently specific gene expression.

Peroxisomal Fatty Acid Degradation. Peroxisomal enzymes degrade activated fatty acids, namely, fatty acyl CoA derivatives, via the β-oxidation pathway. In contradistinction to mitochondria, the enzyme that introduces the double bond between C-2 and C-3 in activated fatty acids is an oxidase rather than a dehydrogenase. The oxidation catalyzed by fatty acyl CoA oxidase (a flavoprotein) is the rate-limiting step in peroxisomal fatty acid degradation; the reaction consumes O_2, which is reduced to H_2O_2. The next step involves the addition of H_2O to the C-2,C-3 double bond in a reaction catalyzed by enoyl CoA hydratase to give the corresponding 3-hydroxy-fatty acyl CoA, which serves as a substrate for 3-hydroxy-fatty acyl CoA dehydrogenase, an enzyme that requires NAD^+ as the cofactor. The product, 3-oxo-fatty acyl CoA, is degraded in a reaction catalyzed by 3-oxo-fatty acyl CoA thiolase, which requires coenzyme A to produce acetyl CoA and a shortened fatty acyl CoA, which reenters the cycle of β-oxidation and degradation in peroxisomes. Peroxisomal fatty acyl CoA oxidase is not affected by cyanide, whereas the mitochondrial dehydrogenase is inhibited by it. Thus, the whole process of fatty acid degradation by peroxisomal β-oxidation enzymes can be determined spectrophotometrically by the use of palmitoyl CoA as the substrate and NAD^+ as the cofactor in the presence of potassium cyanide, to distinguish it from potassium cyanide-sensitive mitochondrial β-oxidation.

Hepatocytes: Ultrastructural Studies. The findings of peroxisomal and mitochondrial enzymes induced by DHEA led us to examine mouse hepatocytes at the ultrastructural level.

Peroxisomes were visualized after fixing liver tissue with glutaraldehyde and staining for catalase with 3,3'-diaminobenzidine in the presence of H_2O_2 (via the peroxidatic pathway). Significant morphometric differences were observed in peroxisomes and mitochondria in hepatocytes of mice treated with DHEA compared with those of control animals. The cross-sectional area, number per unit of cytoplasmic area, and volume density of peroxisomes in the liver of DHEA-treated mice were increased significantly compared to those of the controls. Proliferated peroxisomes appeared in clusters (FIG. 6 and TABLE 2).

Remarkably, the cross-sectional area of mitochondria in hepatocytes of DHEA-treated mice was decreased when compared to that of controls. The volume density of mitochondria was either decreased or increased by DHEA treatment, depending on mouse strain (FIG. 6 and TABLE 2). This is possibly one of the very few exceptions

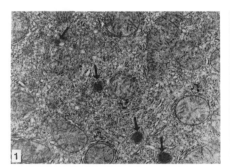
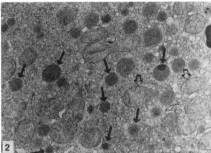

FIGURE 6. Electron micrographs of liver tissue fixed and stained for catalase (to visualize peroxisomes (×9,100). One-month-old male BALB/c mice were fed either AIN-76A or the same diet containing DHEA (0.45%, by weight) for 3 months. For ultrastructural studies, sections of liver were fixed in glutaraldehyde, incubated with 3,3'-diaminobenzidine in the presence of hydrogen peroxide (to visualize catalase in peroxisomal organelles), embedded, sectioned, and photographed using a Phyllips 301 electron microscope. (1) Liver of a control mouse; (2) liver of a DHEA-treated mouse. *Arrows* point to some of the peroxisomes present in the tissues.

to the rule that the cross-sectional area of liver mitochondria increases with physiologic changes or drug manipulation, including starvation, glucocorticoid treatment, and hypolipidemic drugs such as clofibrate.

In addition to hepatocyte peroxisomal proliferation, smooth endoplasmic reticulum also proliferated with dietary DHEA treatment, as also demonstrated with hypolipidemic peroxisomal proliferators.

Dietary DHEA and Hepatic Lipogenic Enzymes. The hypolipidemic properties of peroxisomal proliferators are well established. As demonstrated initially with clofibrate, triglyceride levels in mice, rats, and humans can be reduced significantly, particularly in obese individuals. In some instances, serum cholesterol levels also were reduced, but there is some controversy on this issue. On the basis of these reports, we determined the specific activities of hepatic lipogenic enzymes of mice that received either the control AIN-76A diet or the same diet supplemented with 0.45% DHEA (w/w). Data presented in TABLE 3 indicate that the specific activity of

TABLE 2. Morphometric Analysis of Liver Cells from Control and DHEA-Treated Mice[a]

Organelle	Mouse Strain	Treatment (weeks)	n	Cross-Sectional Area (mm^2)	p	Volume Density (%)	p
Peroxisomes	BALB/c	Control	8	0.078 ± 0.004		0.107 ± 0.15	
	(male)	DHEA (25)	8	0.107 ± 0.005	<0.001	2.77 ± 0.57	<0.05
	(C57BL/6 × DBA/2)F$_1$	Control	8	0.057 ± 0.005		0.60 ± 0.21	
	(male)	DHEA (17)	8	0.091 ± 0.003	<0.001	1.79 ± 0.20	<0.001
Mitochondria	BALB/c	Control	8	0.513 ± 0.021		21.1 ± 1.40	
	(male)	DHEA (25)	8	0.269 ± 0.096	<0.001	10.8 ± 0.88	<0.001
	(C57BL/6 × DDA/2)Γ$_1$	Control	8	0.258 ± 0.014		5.59 ± 0.30	
	(male)	DHEA (17)	8	0.092 ± 0.006	<0.001	12.0 ± 0.84	<0.001
	(NZB × NZW)F$_1$	Control	7	0.649 ± 0.090		11.3 ± 0.03	
	(female)	DHEA (1)	5	0.472 ± 0.058	0.1	9.98 ± 1.05	NS
		Control	5	0.778 ± 0.071		10.6 ± 0.36	
		DHEA (2)	9	0.396 ± 0.048	<0.01	11.4 ± 0.03	<0.05
		Control	22	0.958 ± 0.059		9.76 ± 0.23	
		DHEA (4)	13	0.572 ± 0.065	<0.001	11.6 ± 0.02	<0.001

[a]Micrographs, at an enlargement of ×9,100, were used to compute the parameters described for liver cells of BALB/c and (C57BL/6 × DBA/2)F$_1$ mice. Magnifications used in the micrographic studies for liver cells of (NZB × NZW)F$_1$ mice were in the range of ×5,700 to ×45,000. Values are given as mean ± SD. *N* represents the number of micrographs. Data were analyzed by Student's *t* test (unpaired). NS = not significant. Mice were started on the DHEA-containing diet at 2 months of age.

malic enzyme is elevated significantly by DHEA feeding in female mice and only slightly in male C57BL/6 mice.

Either a nonsignificant decrease or a significant increase in the specific activity of glucose 6-phosphate dehydrogenase was demonstrated in various strains of mice

TABLE 3. Specific Activities of Various Liver Cytosolic and Mitochondrial Enzymes of Mice Fed Either a DHEA-Containing Diet or a Control Diet

Sex	Strain	Age (months)	Diet	Time on Diet (months)	Specific Activity (munits/mg protein)[a]				
					Malic Enzyme	Glucose-6-Phosphate Dehydrogenase	Isocitrate Dehydrogenase	Citrate Cleavage Enzyme	Citrate Synthase
Female	(NZW × NZB)F$_1$	6	Control	5	17.5 ± 2.7	5.1 ± 2.2	146 ± 7	3.7 ± 0.5	15.4 ± 6.1
			DHEA		41.3 ± 4.8	3.7 ± 0.7	179 ± 12	2.0 ± 0.06	44.6 ± 10
Female	(NZW × NZB)F$_1$	7	Control	6	14.3 ± 4.7	11.1 ± 3.2	164 ± 19		103 + 736
			DHEA		43.1 ± 2.0	2.5 ± 0.8	190 ± 15		118 ± 14
Female	C57 Black/6	7	Control	6	25.3 ± 4.2	8.7 ± 1.1	154 ± 9	3.8 ± 0.4	35.3 ± 6.4
			DHEA		47.8 ± 13	11.1 ± 2.7	165 ± 36	3.9 ± 0.3	62.8 ± 10
Male	C57 Black/6	7	Control	6	40.2 ± 5.4	9.1 ± 2.0	157 ± 7	4.0 ± 0.4	75 ± 5
			DHEA		47.0 ± 3.2	11.9 ± 0.7	169 ± 28	4.0 ± 0.3	30 ± 6

[a]Specific activities shown are the mean and standard deviations obtained with five animals per group.

receiving DHEA, and therefore we expect that hepatic lipogenesis would remain almost unchanged or increased in these animals. The specific activity of $NADP^+$-linked isocitrate dehydrogenase also was increased or decreased slightly by DHEA feeding in mice of various strains, but not significantly; and no significant differences were noted between control and DHEA-treated mice in the specific activities of hepatic citrate synthase and citrate cleavage enzyme (TABLE 3).[14,15]

DHEA Effects on Serum Triglyceride and Cholesterol Levels. We determined triglyceride and cholesterol levels in mice of various strains and found that depending on the strain, triglyceride levels were either decreased slightly, but not significantly, or were increased significantly when compared to controls (TABLE 4).[15,17] Total serum cholesterol levels in DHEA-treated mice were higher than those in controls (TABLE 4).[15,17] Of interest is the finding that 7-month-old female C57BL/K_sJ *db/db* mice on DHEA for 18 weeks had a decreased triglyceride level (92 ± 10 mg/dl [$n = 5$]) compared to that of mice on the control diet (204 ± 46 mg/dl [$n = 4$]).

TABLE 4. Serum Triglyceride and Cholesterol Levels in Mice Fed Either a DHEA-Containing Diet or a Control Diet[a]

Strain	Sex	Age at Time of Killing (months)	Time on DHEA (wk)	Triglycerides (mg/dl) Controls	Triglycerides (mg/dl) DHEA-Treated	p	Cholesterol (mg/dl) Controls	Cholesterol (mg/dl) DHEA-Treated	p
(NZW × BXSB)F₁	Female	14	50	105 ± 23 (5)	93 ± 10 (6)	NS	—	—	—
(NZW × BSXB)F₁	Female	15	56	117 ± 37 (5)	108 ± 12 (5)	NS	—	—	—
(C57BL/6 × DBA/2)F₁	Male	4	8	115 ± 12 (6)	99 ± 11 (6)	NS	—	—	—
(C57BL/6 × DBA/2)F₁	Female	3	4	103 ± 25 (10)	93 ± 15 (10)	NS	59 ± 6 (10)	93 ± 15 (10)	<0.001
C3H/HeJ	Female	3.5	5	76 ± 11 (5)	112 ± 27 (8)	0.01	—	—	—
BALB/c	Female	4.5	7	93 ± 15 (8)	179 ± 24 (9)	<0.001	52 ± 8 (8)	97 ± 11 (9)	<0.001

[a]Triglycerides were determined as described by Spayd *et al.*[32] and cholesterol by the method of Allain *et al.*[33] Mean $\pm$ SD are reported; number of animals per group is indicated in parentheses. NS = not significant.

DHEA Effects on Rates of Hepatic Fatty Acid and Cholesterol Syntheses. To determine if hepatic lipogenesis was affected by DHEA, we injected tritiated water intravenously into female BALB/c mice, which had the highest increase in serum triglycerides with DHEA administration. Thereafter, we determined tritium incorporation into triglycerides and cholesterol. Unexpectedly, tritium incorporation into triglycerides was reduced ~ 70% in DHEA-treated mice, whereas the rate of hepatic cholesterol synthesis was increased ~ 40% over controls. The findings of elevated serum triglycerides and decreased hepatic lipogenesis in these mice by DHEA administration may signal a possible decrease in uptake and hydrolysis of triglycerides at sites other than the liver. The DHEA administration correlates well with the increases in serum cholesterol observed in female BALB/c mice (TABLE 4).[14,17]

DHEA, Hepatic Mitochondria, and the Urea Cycle. As mentioned previously, our electrophoretic studies with rat and mouse liver proteins allowed us to visualize a very prominent protein of M_r ~ 160 kD that was decreased in intensity in the liver of DHEA-fed animals compared with controls. We searched the literature for an abundant mouse or rat liver protein of M_r ~ 160 kD and readily identified it as mitochondrial carbamoyl phosphate synthetase-I (CPS-I). This enzyme catalyzes the first and rate-limiting step of the urea (or ornithine) cycle involved in nitrogen excretion in ureotelic organisms, a reaction that leads to the production of carbamoyl phosphate from ammonia, bicarbonate, and magnesium ATP.[28] Five enzymes are involved in the urea cycle, namely, CPS-I, which requires acetyl-L-glutamate for activation, ornithine transcarbamylase, argininosuccinate synthetase, argininosuccinase, and arginase; products at each enzymatic step in the cycle are carbamoyl phosphate, citrulline, arginine, and urea and ornithine. CPS-I and ornithine transcarbamylase are mitochondrial and the other three enzymes are cytosolic. CPS-I constitutes 15–20% of mitochondrial matrix proteins, which is in great excess of that needed for disposal of toxic ammonia.

On DHEA administration, some mitochondrial changes are apparent as determined by electron microscopy (FIG. 6). We determined CPS-I activity in liver homogenates of female (NZB × NZW)F_1 mice treated with either the DHEA-containing diet or the control diet for 5 months commencing at 2 months of age and were able to establish a profound decrease in the specific activity of CPS-I (~ 67%).[18] By the use of an anti-rat CPS-I antibody in Western blot analysis of mouse and rat hepatic proteins, polypeptides with molecular weights lower than 160 kD were detected; these appeared to be more abundant in the liver of DHEA-treated mice, possibly due to increased proteolysis (FIG. 7). Liver homogenates in these and other studies, however, were prepared in the presence of five different protease inhibitors.[18]

In addition to the foregoing, we found no significant differences in serum urea nitrogen levels between control and DHEA-treated mice[18] possibly because of the large excess of CPS-I in mitochondria. The decrease in CPS-I protein content and activity in hepatic mitochondria of DHEA-treated animals may be an adaptive characteristic of urea cycle enzymes.

Hepatic Glutathione S-Transferase and Dietary DHEA. DHEA administration in mice and rats leads to the induction of liver proteins, including a cytosolic protein of M_r ~ 28 kD (FIG. 1). After protein separation by SDS-PAGE of cytosolic mouse liver proteins, staining, and electroblotting transfer to Immobilon membrane, the portion containing the ~ 28 kD protein was excised and the protein subjected to NH_2-terminal amino acid sequence analysis. Unambiguous sequence information for the first 25 amino acid residues at the NH_2-terminal end was obtained and proved to be identical to that of the first 25 amino acids of the NH_2-terminal domain of glutathione S-transferase GT-8.7, which had been determined previously from mouse liver.[19] GT-8.7 is the major isozyme induced in mouse liver by dietary antioxidants.[29]

One of the more important functions of glutathione S-transferase is to protect cells against the toxic effects of foreign, potentially harmful electrophilic compounds by catalyzing their conjugation to glutathione to give products that are less toxic and more readily excretable. On the basis of this finding, we evaluated glutathione S-transferase activity in cytosols and microsomes prepared from liver tissue of mice fed either AIN-76A or the same diet containing 0.45% DHEA. The specific activity of this enzyme was either unchanged or slightly decreased for the first 7 days of DHEA treatment compared to controls, but it was elevated significantly after 14 days. Microsomal glutathione S-transferase activity also was elevated after 14 days of DHEA treatment; however, its activity was approximately one tenth that in cytosol.[19] Western blot analysis of cytosolic glutathione S-transferase reflected on the specific activity of the enzyme (FIG. 8). Thus, as with dietary antioxidants, dietary administration of DHEA to mice leads to the induction of hepatic glutathione S-transferase,

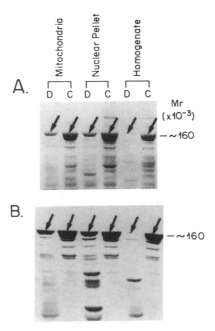

FIGURE 7. DHEA treatment and liver carbamoyl phosphate synthetase I. Two-month-old male mice of a hybrid strain (NZW × BXSB)F_1 were treated with either a DHEA-containing AIN-76A diet (**D;** 0.45%, by weight) or AIN-76A alone (**C**) for 1 month. (**A**) Liver homogenates and subcellular fractions were prepared in the presence of five different protease inhibitors; proteins were separated by SDS-PAGE (10% polyacrylamide) and detected by staining with Coomassie blue. **Arrows** point towards CPS-I ($M_r \sim 160$ K), the rate-limiting enzyme of the urea cycle. Note the relative decrease in CPS-I concentration in liver homogenate, mitochondrial fraction, and nuclear pellet in the DHEA-treated mouse compared to that of the control animal. (**B**) A duplicate gel, run in parallel with that in **A,** was used for Western immunoblot analysis. After transblotting onto nitrocellulose membrane, CPS-I was identified by treatment with rabbit anti-rat CPS-I antibody and immunostaining (**arrows**). Note the immunocross-reactive proteins of relative molecular masses lower than ~ 160 kD, particularly those in liver of the DHEA-treated animal where smaller proteolytic fragments appear. The antibody was a generous gift from Dr. Carol J. Lusty (Public Health Research Institute of the City of New York).

possibly offering a measure of protection against the action of genotoxic reactive electrophiles and thus in the prevention of various pathologies.

DHEA Effects on Hepatic Endogenous Protein Phosphorylation. Endogenous phosphorylation serves a key role in the regulation of a variety of cellular processes. Changes in protein phosphorylation appear to be intimately associated with the chemopreventive effects of agents such as retinoids.

To establish whether dietary DHEA had an effect on the phosphorylation of endogenous liver proteins as well as on various protein kinases for exogenous protein substrates, we conducted studies with homogenates prepared from liver of control and DHEA-treated mice.

The administration of DHEA in the diet of male and female (NZB × NZW)F_1 mice resulted in profound changes in the patterns of endogenous radiophosphorylated proteins obtained by fluorography after SDS-PAGE separation. Endogenous radiophosphorylation was conducted by incubation of liver homogenates prepared in either 0.25 M sucrose plus 50 mM Tris buffer or Tris buffer alone (1:5, w/v), with [γ-^{32}P]ATP (0.1 mM; 1 μCi), MgCl$_2$ (6 mM), and β-mercaptoethanol (5 mM) at 25°C for 5 minutes (FIG. 9).[13,14] The specific activities of liver protein kinases for exogenous protein substrates, namely, casein and histone H1, were not altered by DHEA and those for endogenous proteins such as cAMP-dependent protein kinase, cGMP-dependent protein kinase, and protein kinase C were not altered either, whereas that of endogenous protein phosphorylation was decreased significantly by DHEA action compared to controls (248 ± 16 vs 375 ± 2 pmol ^{32}P incorporated/mg protein · min; $p < 0.001$).[13,14] The activity observed appeared to reflect a general decrease in radiophosphorylated proteins, as also detected by SDS-PAGE (FIG. 9). Identification of the phosphorylated proteins modulated by dietary DHEA should provide an insight into their mode of action.

DHEA Effects on Liver Phosphatases. In a study designed to identify specific liver phosphatases induced by DHEA administration, we found that AMPase and GTPase were affected by the steroid. Male and female C57BL/6 mice were treated with dietary DHEA for 6 months commencing at 1 month of age. The amount of phosphate released from AMP and GTP (nmol/mg protein · min) by phosphatases in liver homogenates and subcellular fractions of mice receiving DHEA was approximately twice that produced by control liver. With other phosphorylated substrates the phosphatases remained unchanged.[13,14]

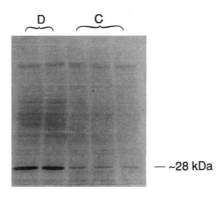

C   Control diet
D   DHEA diet

FIGURE 8. DHEA treatment and glutathione S-transferase. SDS-PAGE (10% polyacrylamide) was conducted by the use of the homogenates of liver obtained from (NZB × NZW)F$_1$ mice fed either AIN-76A or the same diet containing DHEA (0.45%, by weight) for 5 months, commencing at 2 months of age; separated proteins were transblotted onto a nitrocellulose membrane. An antibody raised against a *Saccharomyces cerevisia* protein of $M_r \sim 70$ K, which binds to the outer mitochondrial membrane through a $\sim 10,000$ mol. wt. domain (with the remainder localized in the cytoplasmic compartment), was used for Western analysis. The antibody was a generous gift from Dr. Gottfried Schatz (Biocenter, University of Basel, Switzerland). Remarkably, the antibody recognized the ~ 28-kD protein, glutathione S-transferase GT-8.7. Note the increased glutathione S-transferase concentration in the liver of DHEA-treated mice.

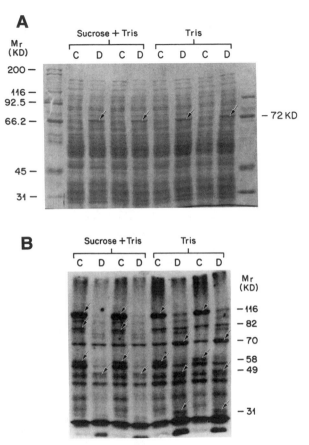

FIGURE 9. Endogenous phosphorylation of mouse liver proteins. Female (NZB × NZW)F₁ hybrid mice were fed a diet consisting of either AIN-76A or AIN-76A containing DHEA (0.45%, by weight) for 6 months commencing at 2 months of age. Mice were killed by cervical dislocation under ether anesthesia. Livers were dissected, weighed, and homogenized in either Tris buffer (50 mM, pH 7.4) or Tris buffer containing sucrose (0.25 M). Liver homogenates (10 μg protein) were incubated with $[\gamma - {}^{32}P]$ATP (0.1 M; 1 μCi), MgCl₂ (6 mM), and β-mercaptoethanol (5 mM) in a total volume of 110 μl at 25°C for 5 minutes. (**A**) Proteins were separated by SDS-PAGE (10% polyacrylamide) and stained with Coomassie blue. (**C**) Control; (**D**) DHEA-treated. Note the striking increase in the level of the ~72 kD protein in the liver of DHEA-fed animals and apparent similar concentrations of the remaining proteins when compared to those of the controls (**B**) Gel was mounted on filter paper and dried *in vacuo:* autoradiography of radiophosphorylated proteins was obtained by use of this gel. Film was exposed to the gel for 48 hours with cooling. Note the difference in endogenous protein phosphorylation obtained with Tris buffer plus sucrose for homogenization and with homogenate prepared with Tris buffer alone. Also, note the apparent decrease in endogenous protein phosphorylation in the liver of DHEA-treated mice.

GTPase is associated with intracellular membranes, and AMPase (5'-nucleotidase) was reported to be present in plasma membranes and cytosol of eukaryotic cells. The presence of these enzymatic activities in all subcellular fractions suggested cross-contamination by membrane and/or cytoplasmic-associated enzymes.[13,14] The significance of the increase in GTPase and AMPase by chronic DHEA treatment is currently unknown.

DHEA Metabolism by Rodent Liver Microsomes. In vivo, humans, rats, mice, and other species can metabolize DHEA to many metabolites, some of which are presented in FIGURE 10. A wide range of steroid-metabolizing enzymes are involved in different tissues to achieve this metabolism. Some of these steroids are metabolized back to their precursors in a reverse type of reaction. As an example, DHEAS is hydrolyzed back to DHEA in most mouse tissues.[30] Thus, it is possible that DHEA exerts some of its *in vivo* effects via conversion to androgens (testosterone, 5α-dihydrotestosterone), estrogens (estradiol-17β, 5-androstene-3β,17β-diol), sulfation (DHEAS), or 7α-hydroxy-DHEA.

Serum levels of testosterone, 5α-dihydrotestosterone, estrone, estradiol-17β, and DHEA in rodents were reported to be elevated with DHEA feeding.[31] Basal DHEA levels in brain tissue of mice also were markedly elevated compared with serum levels, and these levels were further increased in mice receiving DHEA.[32]

To identify DHEA metabolites produced by liver of control and DHEA-fed male Sprague-Dawley rats we conducted incubations of washed liver microsomes (1.25 mg [DHEA-treated rat] and 1.46 mg [control rat]) or no microsomes (blank) with [1,2-³H]DHEA (30 μM; 1.3 μCi), NADPH, NADH, NADP⁺, and NAD⁺ (5.6 mM each) in phosphate-buffered saline solution (0.1 M, pH 7.4) in a total volume of 1 ml. The radiolabeled steroids were extracted with organic solvent, and recovered substrate and products were separated by gradient elution on a celite-ethylene glycol column. The major product identified was 5-androstene-3β,17β-diol (FIG. 11).

In a similar study, we conducted incubations with 200–8,000 g and 105,000 g particulate fractions prepared from homogenates of two livers of control 5-month-old female (NZB × NZW)F₁ mice and two livers of 5-month-old female (NZB × NZW)F₁ mice treated with DHEA for 14 days with [1,2,6,7-³H]DHEA (30

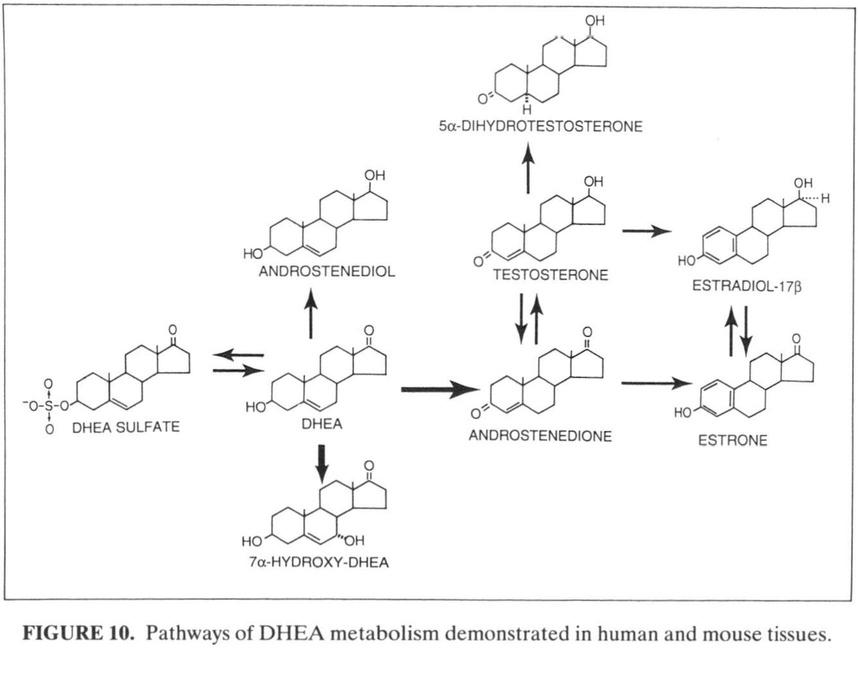

FIGURE 10. Pathways of DHEA metabolism demonstrated in human and mouse tissues.

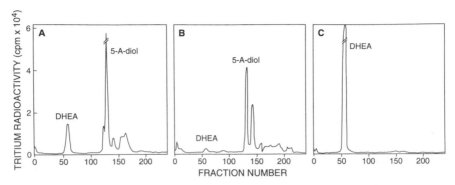

FIGURE 11. DHEA metabolism by rat liver microsomes. Male Sprague-Dawley rats weighing ~ 100 g were fed *ad libitum* either AIN-76A or AIN-76A containing DHEA (0.45%, by weight) for 7 days. Animals were killed, liver was removed and homogenized in phosphate-buffered saline (PBS) solution, and microsomes were prepared. Incubations with [1,2-^{3}H] DHEA (30 μM; 1.3 μCi), NADPH, NADH, NADP$^+$, and NAD$^+$ (5.6 mM each) in PBS solution (0.1 M; pH 7.4) were conducted in the presence or absence of microsomes for 16 minutes at 37°C. At the end of incubation, steroids (recovered substrate and metabolites) were extracted with organic solvent and separated by partition chromatography on celite-ethylene glycol columns. (**A**) DHEA treated; (**B**) control; (**C**) no microsomes. The major metabolite identified was 5-androstene-3β,17βdiol. Polar metabolites also were formed.

μM, 1.0 μCi) in the presence of an NADPH regenerating system (100 μM) in phosphate-buffered saline solution (0.1 M; pH 7.4) at 37°C for 10 minutes which resulted in the formation of 5-androstene-3β,17β-diol and polar products. Androstenedione, testosterone, and phenolic steroids were not detected (TABLE 5).

On the bases of the abundant 17β-hydroxysteroid oxidoreductase activity in rodent liver, we determined tissue and serum levels of both DHEA and 5-androstene-3β,17β-diol in male C57BL/6 mice fed either a control diet or a DHEA-containing diet (0.45%, w/w) for 14 days. After the addition of appropriate tritium-labeled steroids (6,500 dpm each) to the tissue samples, which were collected in clean 16 × 100 mm glass tubes, and trituration with nanograde methanol by means of clean glass pestles, suspensions were centrifuged at 3,000 rpm, the supernatants transferred to clean tubes, and the residues extracted once more, the solvent was evaporated, and the residues were redissolved in 5% ethyl acetate in isooctane (0.5 ml) for steroid separation by gradient elution on celite-ethylene glycol minicolumns.

Tissue steroid levels were expressed both in nanograms per gram of tissue and nanograms per organ weight in grams (FIG. 12). DHEA levels (ng/g tissue) in control

TABLE 5. DHEA Metabolism by Subcellular Fractions of Mouse Liver

| | μmol/mg protein · 10 min[a] | | | |
| | 200–8,000 g Pellet | | 105,000 g Pellet | |
Mice	5-A-3β,17β-diol	Polar Products	5-A-3β,17β-diol	Polar Products
Control	5.6	10.4	3.8	10.3
DHEA-treated	2.0	4.7	2.9	9.4

[a]Average values obtained in two incubations each.

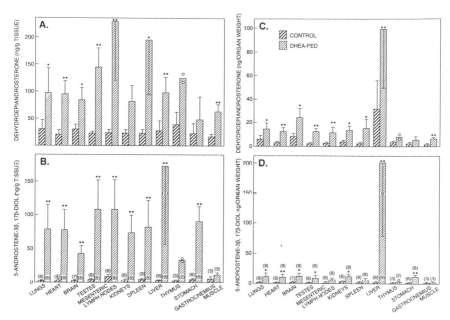

FIGURE 12. DHEA and 5-androstene-3β,17β-diol levels in male C56BL/6 mouse tissues. Four-month-old mice were fed either AIN-76A or the same diet containing DHEA (0.45%, by weight) for 14 days. Animals were killed by cervical dislocation under ethyl ether anesthesia; blood was collected for serum preparation, and tissues were dissected. Tissues were rinsed in saline solution, blotted, divided into aliquots, weighed, and frozen until analysis. After thawing, methanol (1 ml) was added and also tritium-labeled DHEA and 5-androstene-3β,17β-diol as internal recovery standards. Tissues were triturated with a glass pestle, suspensions were centrifuged at 3,000 rpm for 20 minutes, and methanolic supernatants were transferred to clean tubes. The remaining tissues were reextracted once more with methanol (1 ml); corresponding methanolic extracts were pooled, the solvent was evaporated with a stream of nitrogen, and the dried residues were treated with 5% ethyl acetate in isooctane (0.5 ml) to dissolve the steroids. These solutions were transferred to celite-ethylene glycol minicolumns. Air pressure was used after each transfer to force the solvents through the columns. Tubes were rinsed once more with isooctane (0.5 ml) and extracts transferred to the corresponding minicolumns. This step was followed by successive elutions with isooctane (3 ml), 5% ethyl acetate in isooctane (5 ml), and 20% ethyl acetate in isooctane (7.5 ml). Aliquots of column eluates were either discarded or collected to obtain peak fractions of DHEA as well as more polar fractions of the peaks containing 5-androstene-3β,17β-diol for use in radioimmunoassay. The antiserum used for radioimmunoassay of DHEA (No. D7-421) was purchased from Endocrine Sciences, California. 5-Androstene-3β,17β-diol was assayed by use of antibody R 14-02 (a generous gift from Dr. Rogerio A. Lobo, University of Southern California, Los Angeles, California). Levels are expressed as both ng steroid/g tissue (**A, B**) and ng steroid/organ weight (**C, D**). *Bars* represent mean values (± SD) obtained by the use of tissues from three or more animals, as indicated in parentheses. Steroid levels for thymus of DHEA-treated animals are presented as the average obtained from tissues of two mice.

animals were elevated (in the range of 17 ± 3 ng/g for gastrocnemius muscle to 37 ± 23 ng/g for the thymus) compared to those in serum (2.4 ± 1.2 ng/ml) (FIG. 13), as if DHEA was accumulating against a concentration gradient. DHEA tissue levels of DHEA-treated mice were in the range of 47 ± 38 ng/g for stomach and

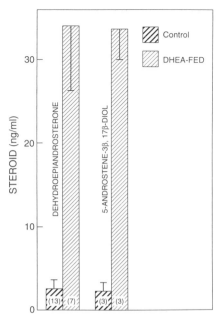

FIGURE 13. DHEA and 5-androstene-3β,17β-diol levels in the sera of male C57BL/6 mice. Tritium-labeled DHEA and 5-androstene-3β,17β-diol were added as internal recovery standards to serum samples prepared from blood of the animals described in the legend to FIGURE 12. Thereafter, sera were extracted with ethyl ether (2 × 5 ml), solvent was evaporated, and residues were dissolved in 5% ethyl acetate in isooctane (0.5 ml). Steroids were separated by chromatography as described in the legend to FIGURE 12 and used in RIA. *Bars* represent mean values (±SD). The number of serum samples analyzed are indicated in parentheses.

229 ± 108 ng/g for mesenteric lymph nodes. Serum DHEA levels in these mice were 34 ± 7.8 ng/ml. Remarkably, DHEA liver levels (ng/g) were not the highest.

When tissue DHEA concentrations in control mice were expressed in nanograms per organ weight, the highest level was found in liver (31.7 ± 24 ng per organ weight) and the lowest in gastrocnemius muscle (1.7 ± 0.8 ng per organ weight). In DHEA-treated animals, the highest level per organ weight was in the liver (98 ± 22 ng per organ weight) and this was followed by brain (24.3 ± 7.1 ng per organ weight); the lowest level was found in stomach (5 ± 3 ng per organ weight).

In regard to 5-androstene-3β,17β-diol in control animals, serum levels were 2.1 ± 1.1 ng/ml; the highest tissue level (ng/g) was found in mesenteric lymph nodes (7.6 ± 3.5 ng/g) and the lowest in thymus (1.2 ± 0.9 ng/g). In DHEA-treated mice, the highest 5-androstene-3β,17β-diol level was found in liver (170 ± 124 ng/g) and the lowest in gastrocnemius muscle (10 ± 4 ng/g) (FIG. 12).

When 5-androstene-3β,17β-dione concentrations were expressed in nanograms per organ weight, the highest level in control animals was found in kidneys (3.3 ± 1.5 ng per organ weight) and the lowest in thymus (0.3 ± 0.2 ng per organ weight); serum 5-androstene-3β,17β-diol levels were 2.1 ± 1.2 ng/ml.

In DHEA-treated mice, the 5-androstene-3β,17β-diol level was highest in liver (199 ± 145 ng per organ weight) and lowest in gastrocnemius muscle (10 ± 4 ng per organ weight); serum 5-androstene-3β,17β-diol levels were 34 ± 13 ng/ml (FIGS. 12 and 13).

Dietary DHEA Effect on Serum Prolactin Levels in Mice. The administration of DHEA in food in concentrations of 0.2–1.0% (w/w) to susceptible mice prevents or delays the onset of various autoimmune and other spontaneous or induced diseases. The administration of DHEA (0.45% in food) to mice results in ∼50% reduction in spleen, thymus, and lymph nodes cellularity, including cells of the T, B, and natural killer lineages, as well as ∼50% reduction in serum IgG levels (FIG. 14).[6] The decrease in lymphoid organ cellularity produced by DHEA administration possibly results from inhibition of lymphocyte progenitor maturation and from cell death and thus a growth block.

Neuroendocrine and immune interactions appear to be regulated by hormones that are common to both systems. Among these, prolactin (PRL) has been shown to have immunoregulatory properties as it stimulates humoral and cell-mediated immunity. In rodents, PRL levels increase with advancing age. Caloric restriction (40% or more) has reduced these levels and extended disease-free life. Hyperprolactinemic animals are characterized by premature albuminuria, elevated IgG, and

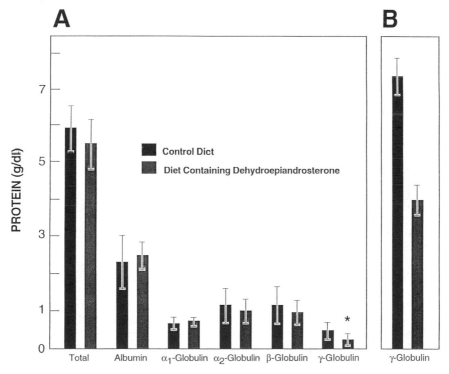

FIGURE 14. Influence of dietary DHEA on serum protein patterns. (**A**) Electrophoretic distribution of serum proteins in 13-month-old male DBA/2 mice fed either AIN-76A or the same diet containing DHEA (0.45%, by weight) for 10 months (*n* = 6). Protein levels presented are the mean values (±SD). (**B**) γGlobulin levels in 13-month-old male (NZW × BXSB)F₁ mice fed either AIN-76A or the same diet containing DHEA (0.45%, by weight) (*n* = 3) starting at 1 month of age.

accelerated mortality.[33] B and T cells contain PRL receptors, and lymphocytes also produce and secrete prolactin.

DHEA does not appear to affect lymphocytes *in vitro,* and therefore the effects of dietary DHEA on lymphopoiesis inhibition *in vivo* may be mediated, at least in part, by PRL synthesis and release from the anterior pituitary. To investigate this possibility we determined serum PRL levels in mice receiving either the control AIN-76A diet or the same diet containing DHEA (0.45, w/w) for at least 3 weeks. As positive controls, we used mice implanted with estradiol-17β pellets (15 mg) for 2 weeks (TABLE 6).[16]

The findings of this study indicate that chronic administration of DHEA in food to normal mice [C57BL/6, (B6 × DBA/2)F$_1$], mice programmed to develop an autoimmune disease [female (NZB × NZW)F$_1$], and obese-diabetic mice (C57BL/K$_s$J db$^+$/db$^+$) leads to lowered serum PRL levels, whereas, as expected, E2 administration results in a significant increase in PRL concentration. This finding applies

TABLE 6. Serum Prolactin Levels in Mice of Various Strains Fed Either AIN-76A or AIN-76A Containing DHEA (0.45%, by weight)[a]

Strain	Sex	Treatment	Age (months)	n	Time on Steroids (weeks)	Prolactin (ng/ml) (mean ± SD)
C57BL/6	♀	Control	16	5	—	185 ± 268
		DHEA	16	5	49	12 ± 9.0
C57BL/6	♀	Control	3	4	—	7.5 ± 3.0
		Estradiol-17β	3	4	2	244 ± 58
C57BL/KsJ db/db	♀	Control	13	3	—	87 ± 23
		DHEA	13	4	45	26 ± 23
(NZB × NZW)F$_1$	♀	Control	7.5	1	—	66
		DHEA	7.5	1	26	7.2
(B6 × DBA/2)F$_1$	♂	Control	3	1	—	16.4
		DHEA	3	1	3	9.4

[a]Positive controls were mice treated with silastic implants containing estradiol-17β.

particularly to aged animals with or without underlying genetic diseases. Therefore, the beneficial effects of dietary DHEA in delaying the onset of some age-associated diseases, including autoimmunity and immune decline in experimental animals, are mediated, at least in part, by reduced serum PRL levels.

SUMMARY

We present data pertaining to some of the *in vivo* effects associated with dietary DHEA administration to mice and rats. Dietary DHEA leads to: (1) decrease in body weight gain; (2) relative increases in liver weight; (3) liver color change; (4) induction of hepatic peroxisomal enzymes; (5) proliferation of hepatic peroxisomes with increased cross-sectional area; (6) decreased hepatic mitochondrial cross-sectional area; (7) elevated levels of hepatic cytosolic malic enzyme; (8) slight decreases, significant decreases, or significant increases in serum triglyceride levels, depending on mouse strain; (9) increases in total serum cholesterol levels; (10) significant decreases in the hepatic rates of fatty acid synthesis; (11) significant increases in the hepatic rates of cholesterol synthesis; (12) decreases in both protein content and specific activity of hepatic mitochondrial carbamoyl phosphate synthetase-I without concomitant changes in serum urea nitrogen; (13) induction of glutathione S-transferase activity in liver; (14) decrease in hepatic endogenous protein phosphorylation; (15) increase in hepatic AMPase and GTPase activities; (16) formation of 5-androstene-3β,17β-diol as a major metabolite of DHEA by subcellular fractions of liver, which is reflected in serum and tissue levels; and (17) reduction in serum prolactin levels.

REFERENCES

1. YEN, T. T., J. A. ALLAN, D. V. PEARSON, J. M. ACTON & M. GREENBERG. 1977. Prevention of obesity in A^{vy}/a mice by dehydroepiandrosterone. Lipids **12**: 409–413.
2. CLEARY M. P. 1991. The antiobesity effect of dehydroepiandrosterone in rats. Proc. Soc. Exp. Biol. Med. **196:** 8 15.
3. COLEMAN, D. L. 1988. Therapeutic effects of dehydroepiandrosterone (DHEA) and its metabolites in obese-hyperglycemic mutant mice. Prog. Clin. Biol. Res. **265:** 161–175.
4. TANNEN, R. H. & A. G. SCHWARTZ. 1982. Reduced weight gain and delay of Coomb's positive hemolytic anemia in NZB mice treated with dehydroepiandrosterone. Fed. Proc. **41:** 463.
5. LUCAS, J. A., S. A. AHMED, J. L. CASEY & P. C. MACDONALD. 1985. Prevention of autoantibody formation and prolonged survival in New Zealand Black/New Zealand White F$_1$ mice fed dehydroepiandrosterone. J. Clin. Invest. **75:** 2091–2093.
6. MILEWICH, L., R. S. PUTNAM, R. A. FRENKEL & M. BENNETT. 1993. Lethal autoimmunity in (NZW × BXSB)F$_1$ mice is delayed by dietary dehydroepiandrosterone and fish oil. The Endocrine Society Abstracts of Papers, 75th Annual Meeting, June 9–12, p 446.
7. WEINDRUCH, R., G. MCFEETERS & R. L. WALFORD. 1984. Food intake reduction and immunologic alterations in mice fed dehydroepiandrosterone. Exp. Gerontol. **19:** 297–304.
8. PASHKO, L. L., D. K. FAIRMAN & A. G. SCHWARTZ. 1986. Inhibition of proteinuria development in aging Sprague-Dawley rats and C57BL/6 mice by long term treatment with dehydroepiandrosterone. J. Gerontol. **41:** 433–438.
9. ARAD, Y., J. J. BADIMON, L. BADIMON, W. C. HEMBREE & H. N. GINSBERG. 1989. Dehydroepiandrosterone feeding prevents aortic fatty streak formation and cholesterol accumulation in cholesterol-fed rabbit. Arteriosclerosis **9:** 159–166.
10. SCHWARTZ, A. G., L. L. PASHKO & R. H. TANNEN. 1983. Dehydroepiandrosterone: An anti-cancer and possibly anti-aging substance. Intervention in the Aging Process, Part A: Quantitiation, Epidemiology, and Clinical Research. W. Regelson & F. M. Sinex, Eds.: 267–278. Alan R. Liss, Inc. New York.
11. LORIA, R. M., W. REGELSON & D. A. PADGETT. 1990. Immune response facilitation and resistance to virus and bacterial infections with dehydroepiandrosterone (DHEA). *In* The Biological Role of Dehydroepiandrosterone (DHEA). M. Kalimi & W. Regelson, Eds.: 107–130. Walter de Gruyter. New York.
12. MARRERO, M., J. M. SNYDER, R. A. PROUGH, P. C. MACDONALD & L. MILEWICH. 1987. Influence of orally-administered dehydroisoandrosterone (DHA) on mouse liver protein synthesis and liver mitochondria morphology: 208. The Endocrine Society Abstracts of Papers, 69th Annual Meeting, p. 208.
13. MARRERO, M., P. C. MACDONALD, R. A. PROUGH & L. MILEWICH. 1987. Effect of dehydroepiandrosterone feeding on endogenous phosphorylation-dephosphorylation in mouse liver. Am. Soc. Biol. Chem. Abstracts of Papers, 78th Annual Meeting, June 7–11, p. 2273.
14. MARRERO, M., R. A. PROUGH, R. A. FRENKEL & L. MILEWICH. 1992. Dehydroepiandrosterone feeding and protein phosphorylation, phosphatases, and lipogenic enzymes in mouse liver. Proc. Soc. Exp. Biol. Med. **193:** 110–117.
15. MILEWICH, L., M. BENNETT, R. S. PUTNAM & R. A. FRENKEL. 1988. Effects of dehydroepiandrosterone on hepatic lipogenic enzymes and plasma lipids in mice. J. Cell Biol. **107:** 645a.
16. BENNETT, M., L. KRULICH, L. MILEWICH, V. KUMAR, F. CATALINA & G. RISDON. 1992.

Dietary dehydroepiandrosterone lowers serum prolactin in mice. The Endocrine Society Abstracts of Papers, 74th Annual Meeting, June 24–27, 1992, p. 389.

17. FRENKEL, R. A., C. A. SLAUGHTER, K. ORTH, C. R. MOOMAW, S. H. HICKS, J. M. SNYDER, M. BENNETT, R. A. PROUGH, R. S. PUTNAM & L. MILEWICH 1990. Peroxisome proliferation and induction of peroxisomal enzymes in mouse and rat liver by dehydroepiandrosterone feeding. J. Steroid Biochem. 35: 333–342.

18. MARRERO, M., R. A. PROUGH, R. S. PUTNAM, M. BENNETT & L. MILEWICH. 1991. Inhibition of carbamoyl phosphate synthetase-I by dietary dehydroepiandrosterone. J. Steroid Biochem. 38: 599–609.

19. MILEWICH, L., M. MARRERO, B. U. TEZABWALA, M. BENNETT, R. A. FRENKEL & C. A. SLAUGHTER. 1993. Induction of murine glutathione S-transferase by dietary dehydroepiandrosterone. J. Steroid Biochem. 46: 321–329.

20. FRENKEL, R. A., R. A. PROUGH, S. H. HICKS & L. MILEWICH. 1988. Dehydroepiandrosterone induces peroxisomal enzymes in rodent liver. J. Cell Biol. 107: 122a.

21. WU, H.-Q., J. MASSET-BROWN, D. J. TWEEDLE, L. MILEWICH, R. A. FRENKEL, C. MARTIN WIXTROM, R. W. ESTABROOKK & R. A. PROUGH. 1989. Induction of microsomal NADPH-cytochrome P450 reductase and cytochrome P450IVA1 (P450$_{LA_\omega}$) by dehydroepiandrosterone: A possible peroxisomal proliferator. Cancer Res. 49: 2337–2343.

22. PROUGH, R. A., H.-Q. WU & L. MILEWICH. 1990. Effect of dehydroepiandrosterone on rodent liver, peroxisomal, and mitochondrial enzymes. In The Biologic Role of Dehydroepiandrosterone (DHEA). W. Regelson & M. Kalimi, Eds.: 253–279. Walter de Gruyter. New York.

23. ESTABROOK, R. W., L. MILEWICH & R. A. PROUGH. 1991. Cytochrome P450s as toxicogenic catalysts: The influence of dehydroepiandrosterone. In Xenobiotics and Cancer: Implications for Chemical Carcinogenisis and Cancer Chemotherapy. L. Earnster, H. Esumi, Y. Fujii, H. V. Gelboin, R. Kato & T. Sugimura, Eds.: 33–44. Japan Sci. Society Press, Tokyo/Taylor & Francis Ltd. London.

24. MATHUR, C., V. V. PRASAD, V. S. RAJU, M. WELCH & S. LIEBERMAN. 1993. Steroids and their conjugates in mammalian brain. Proc. Natl. Acad. Sci. USA 90: 85–88.

25. BELANGER, B., R. ROY & A. BELANGER. 1992. Administration of pregnenolone and dehydroepiandrosterone to guinea pigs and rats causes the accumulation of fatty acid esters of pregnenolone and dehydroepiandrosterone in plasma proteins. Steroids 57: 430–436.

26. RAM, P. A. & D. J. WAXMAN. 1994. Dehydroepiandrosterone 3β-sulfate is an endogenous activator of the peroxisome-proliferation pathway: Induction of cytochrome P-450 4A and acyl-CoA oxidase mRNAs in primary rat hepatocyte culture and inhibitory effects of Ca^{2+}-channel blockers. Biochem. J. 301: 753–758.

27. YAMADA, J., M. SAKUMA & T. SUGA. 1992. Induction of peroxisomal β-oxidation enzymes by dehydroepiandrosterone and its sulfate in primary cultures of rat hepatocytes. Biochim. Biophys. Acta 1137: 231–236.

28. KREBS, H., R. HEMS & P. LURD. 1973. Some regulatory mechanisms in the synthesis of urea in the mammalian liver. Adv. Enzyme Reg. 11: 361–377.

29. PEARSON, W. R., J. REINHART, S. C. SISK, K. S. ANDERSON & P. N. ADLER. 1988. Tissue specific induction of murine glutathione transferase mRNAs by butylated hydroxyanisole. J. Biol. Chem. 263: 13,324–13,332.

30. MILEWICH, L., L. R. GARCIA & L. W. GERRITY. 1984. Steroid sulfatase and 17β-hydroxysteroid oxidoreductose activities in mouse tissues. J. Steroid Biochem. 21: 529–538.

31. LEITER, E. H., W. G. BEAMER, D. L. COLEMAN & C. LONGCOPE. 1987. Androgenic and estrogenic metabolites in serum of mice fed dehydroepiandrosterone: Relationship to antihyperglycemic effects. Metabolism 36: 863–869.

32. YOUNG, J., C. CORPECHOT, M. HAUG, S. GOBAILLE, E. E. BAULIEU & P. ROBEL. 1991. Suppressive effects of dehydroepiandrosterone and 3β-methyl-androst-5-en-17-one on attack toward lactating female intruders by castrated male mice. II. Brain neurosteroids. Biochem. Biophys. Res. Commun. 174: 892–897.

33. MCMURRAY, R., D. KEISLER, K. KANUCKEL, S. IZUI & S. E. WALKER. 1991. Prolactin influences autoimmune disease activity in the female B/W mouse. J. Immunol. 147: 3780–3787.

Induction of Thermogenic Enzymes by DHEA and Its Metabolites

HENRY LARDY, NANCY KNEER, MONICA BELLEI,
AND VALENTINA BOBYLEVA

Institute for Enzyme Research
University of Wisconsin-Madison
Madison, Wisconsin 53705

Institute of General Pathology
University of Modena
Modena, Italy

MULTIPLE FUNCTIONS OF DEHYDREPIANDROSTERONE

It is not unusual for a hormone to have more than one mode of action. Some steroids may function by binding to a site on a cell membrane and influence events directly in that cell. The same steroid may also function by combining with a specific receptor to form a complex that will be recognized by a response element on specific gene promoters. However, we must be skeptical of a single steroid that can cause weight loss in obese animals, correct blood sugar concentration in diabetic animals, decrease blood cholesterol, prevent atherosclerosis, enhance the activity of the immune system, depress tumor formation, and improve the memory of aged mice.

We are willing to accept the concept that the weak androgen effect of dehydroepiandrosterone (DHEA) may rest on its conversion to testosterone and that the weak estrogen activity of androstene diol may result from its conversion to estradiol. In a logical extension, is it possible that DHEA is converted to still other metabolites which may each be responsible for one or more of the effects just mentioned above? Surely, mammals must have evolved compounds that are quantitatively much more active and qualitatively more specific than the parent DHEA. We decided to synthesize steroids that are produced from DHEA or that could be formed metabolically from DHEA by hydroxylation, hydrogenation, oxidation, carbon-carbon bond cleavage, conjugation, or other reactions and to determine their biologic activities. To carry out this program a convenient assay to guide progress was needed. What follows is a description of events that led us to use enzyme induction as a measure of steroid activity.

THERMOGENIC FUNCTIONS OF DHEA

During the metabolism in liver of lactate produced by working muscle, of consumed alcohol, and of some xenobiotics, reducing equivalents are generated in the cytosol in the reduced nicotinamide adenine denucleotide (NADH). As this electron carrier does not penetrate the mitochondria, an alternative pathway for its oxidation is required to produce pyruvate for mitochondrial function and to prevent excessive accumulation of lactate. In 1958 Estabrook and Sacktor[1] in this country and Bücher and Klingenberg[2] in Munich independently described a pathway for the oxidation of cytosolic NADH (FIG. 1). NADH can reduce dihydroxyacetone phosphate, an intermediate in glycolysis, to produce sn-glycerol 3-phosphate (G-3-P). G-3-P can be oxidized by a flavoprotein enzyme that spans the inner mitochondrial membrane. Its substrate-binding site is on the outer surface of the membrane where it can withdraw electrons from cytosolic G-3-P. The flavin-adenine dinucleotide, bound on the portion that projects into the matrix space, passes the electrons on to ubiquinone in the electron transport chain. The result is that oxidation of NADH by this pathway supports phosphorylation at only two sites on the electron transport chain, whereas oxidation of NADH in the mitochondria supports three phosphorylation sites. (The Borst pathway for transport of reducing equivalents from cytosol to mitochondrial NAD$^+$ was described years later.[3]) It was immediately apparent that the G-3-P shuttle would be thermogenic, for energy not captured as adenosine triphosphate (ATP) would perforce be released as heat.

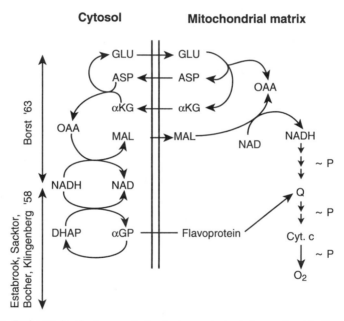

FIGURE 1. Pathways for the transport of reducing equivalents from cytosol to the mitochondrial electron transport chain. From Lardy et al.[16] with permission of Elsevier Science Publishing Co.

At that time, we were working on the thyroid hormone,[4] a classic thermogenic agent, and tested its effect on the activity of mitochondrial G-3-P dehydrogenase in various tissues of the rat.[5,6] Feeding 2% desiccated thyroid to rats for 10 days increased the concentration of this enzyme[5-7] in all tissues that exhibit enhanced oxygen consumption when animals are rendered hyperthyroid[8,9] (TABLE 1). Mitochondrial G-3-P dehydrogenase did not increase in tissues that do not show increased respiration in response to thyroid hormone.[8,9] Some time later, Tepperman and Tepperman[10] found that liver cytosolic malic enzyme also was strikingly induced by the thyroid hormone. Several other enzymes are increased in hyperthyroid animals,[11]

TABLE 1. Influence of Thyroid Hormone on Mitochondrial Glycerophosphate Dehydrogenase[a]

Tissue	Control	Thyroid-Fed (nmol/[min × mg protein])	ThX
Liver	3	66	0.6
Heart	4.2	12	1.2
Kidney	6	34	3
Adipose tissue	4.2	28	2.4
Skeletal muscle	42	48	30
Diaphragm	12	15	3.6

[a]Brain, spleen, stomach, testis, lung, and intestine did not respond. Sprague-Dawley rats (200–250 g) were maintained for 10 days on commercial rat chow. A second group received the same diet containing 2% desiccated thyroid, and the third group consisted of rats maintained for 2–5 weeks after thyroidectomy. Organs from 4–75 rats in each group were analyzed. ThX = thyroidectomized. Adapted from Lardy et al.[16]

but the magnitude of their responses to thyroid hormone is not nearly as great as are those of G-3-P dehydrogenase and malic enzyme.

In 1986 Tagliaferro et al.[12] reported that DHEA increased heat production in rats, and we were inspired to test its effect on G-3-P dehydrogenase to determine if its thermogenic effect was mediated in the same manner as was that of the thyroid hormone. Tepperman et al.[13] had found that DHEA induced a small increase in malic enzyme, but others[14,15] had found much greater responses. We confirmed the effect of DHEA on malic enzyme and found that G-3-P dehydrogenase also increased several-fold[16,17] (TABLE 2). The striking synergistic response to the combination of T_3 and DHEA indicates that the receptors for T_3 and a metabolite of DHEA may function as a heterodimer, as is the case of T_3 and some retinoic acid receptors. DHEA increases G-3-P dehydrogenase only in liver, not in other tissues that respond to thyroid hormone.

The responses of these two enzymes provide an effective assay for one type of activity of synthetic steroids related in structure to DHEA. It was important, however, to determine how these enzymes function to decrease metabolic efficiency so as to cause animals to lose weight without altering food intake.

When carbohydrate is consumed by liver, one sixth of the electrons withdrawn from the glucose molecule are used to reduce cytosolic NAD^+ to NADH; five sixths are withdrawn in the mitochondria when the generated pyruvate is oxidized in the tricarboxylic acid cycle. If the G-3-P shuttle decreases energy capture by one third and handles one sixth of the reducing equivalents, metabolic efficiency would be

TABLE 2. Responses of Rat Liver Enzymes to DHEA and Thyroid Hormone[a]

Treatment (13 days)	sn-G-3 Dehydrogenase (nmol/[min × mg protein)	Malic Enzyme
Control	5 ± 1	10 ± 1.3
DHEA 0.5%	19 ± 1	79 ± 11
ThX	1.2 ± 0.3	1.3 ± 1
ThX + DHEA	6 ± 1.1	42 ± 17
ThX + 10 μg T_3	38 ± 8.3	63 ± 34
ThX + DHEA + T_3	79 ± 2.8	338 ± 111

[a]DHEA was incorporated into the chow; 10 μg of T_3 was injected intraperitoneally daily. There were 3–5 rats per group. ThX = thyroidectomized.

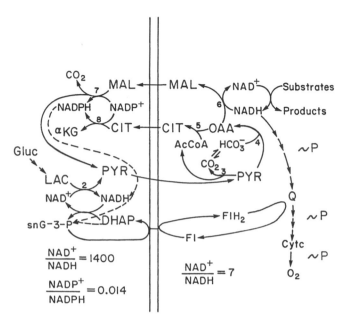

FIGURE 2. Scheme for the transport of electrons from the tricarboxylic cycle through the sn-glycerol 3-phosphate shuttle. From Lardy et al.[16]

decreased by only 5.5%. We must consider also that relatively little of the total carbohydrate consumed is metabolized in liver. Careful measurements show that the effect of either thyroid hormone[18,19] or DHEA[12] on metabolic efficiency is far greater than 5.5%.

We postulated[16] that both malic enzyme and G-3-P dehydrogenase could function as shown schematically in FIGURE 2. Pyruvate enters liver mitochondria where it is carboxylated to form oxalacetate. NADH generated by the tricarboxylic acid cycle reduces the oxalacetate to form L-malate, which moves across the mitochondrial membrane to the cytosol[20] in exchange for pyruvate moving in the opposite direction. Malic enzyme cleaves malate to produce CO_2 and pyruvate, while reducing NADP to NADPH. The pyruvate reenters the mitochondria to continue the cycle.

The unanswered question was how the reducing equivalents in NADPH could be used to convert dihydroxyacetone phosphate to sn-glycerol 3-phosphate, for the cytosolic G-3-P dehydrogenase was reported to be NAD-specific. We found that pure cytosolic enzyme can use NADPH but at a very slow rate. The rate can be increased by dropping the pH from 7.4 to 6.5. At pH 7.4 the rate can be increased by low ionic strength. The relation of these findings to the reaction in liver is unknown, but they may indicate the existence of some control mechanism that might permit NADPH to reduce dihydroxyacetone phosphate under some circumstances. NADPH must not react freely with NAD-requiring enzymes in liver because, as shown in FIGURE 2, the redox ratio of the two pyridine nucleotides differs by a factor of 100,000 despite the fact that their standard potentials are the same.[21] We found that liver cytosol from rats fed DHEA synthesizes more G-3-P during incubation with fructose 1,6-bis phosphate and NADP than does cytosol from control rats.[22] Finally, feeding rats DHEA causes the respiration of their isolated hepatocytes to be much more resistant to inhibition by rotenone than is that of control rats.[16] This indicates that in liver from DHEA-treated rats, electron transport from substrates to ubiquinone is less dependent on the intramitochondrial NADH-ubiquinone segment of the respiratory system and probably involves the G-3-P shuttle. The transport of reducing equivalents to the cytosol from the tricarboxylic acid cycle in the mitochondrial compartment ensures that mitochondrial G-3-P dehydrogenase is involved in more electron transport than that arising from glycolysis and therefore can account for the known decreased metabolic efficiency and thermogenesis. The postulated cycle[16] has been demonstrated in rat pancreatic islets.[23]

ACTIVE ANALOGS OF DHEA

Enhancement of mitochondrial G-3-P dehydrogenase and cytosolic malic enzyme was used as a semiquantitative assay for activity of nearly 150 steroid structures. The steroids were mixed into pulverized commercial rat chow and fed for 6 days. The rats were sacrificed on day 7, and the left lobe of the liver was removed, weighed, and homogenized in a solution of 70 mM sucrose, 250 mM mannitol, and 3 mM Hepes at pH 7.4. Mitochondrial and cytosolic fractions were isolated, analyzed for protein, and frozen until assayed for enzyme activity. In each experiment rats that were fed chow without steroid supplements served as controls, and a second group fed 0.05%

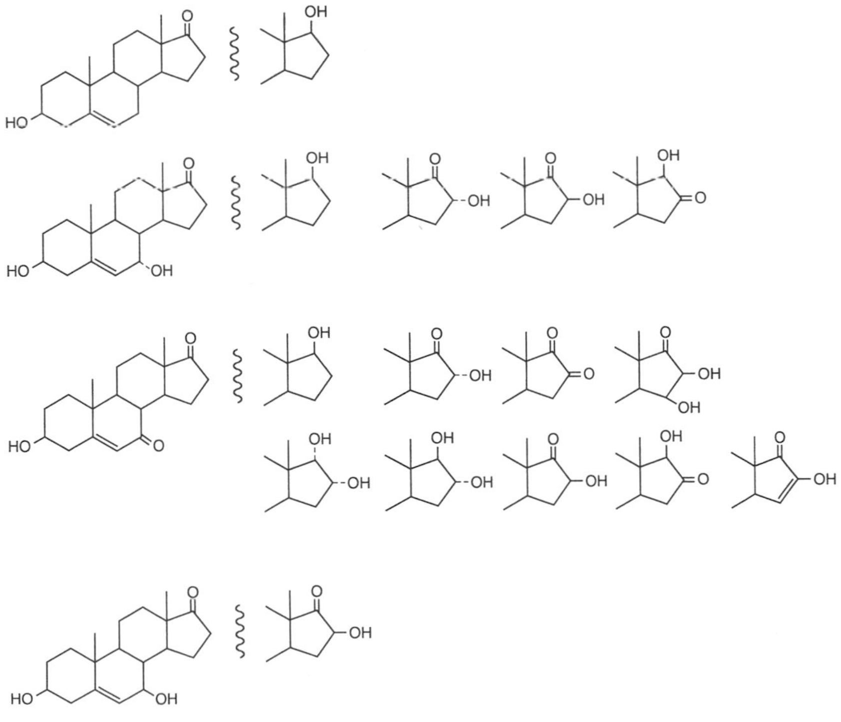

FIGURE 3. Steroids that induce the formation of both glycerophosphate (G-3-P) dehydrogenase and malic enzyme in rats' livers.

DHEA in their diet was included to assure that the animals were capable of responding. This concentration of DHEA gave about 50% of the maximum response and was chosen to enhance sensitivity of the assays. Because considerable variation existed between experiments in the enzyme activity of the control groups, compounds were considered active only if they increased activities to more than 150% of control values.

Several cytochrome P-450 enzymes hydroxylate steroids at specific positions. To test the possible activity of these metabolites, we prepared derivatives of DHEA monohydroxylated at positions 1, 2, 4, 5, 7, 15, 16, and 19. Papers describing the synthetic work will be published elsewhere in collaboration with Drs. Padma Marwah, Bruce Partridge, Ieva Reich, and Yong Wei. Of the monohydroxy derivatives only 7α- or 7β-hydroxy DHEA was active and 15β-hydroxy DHEA had some

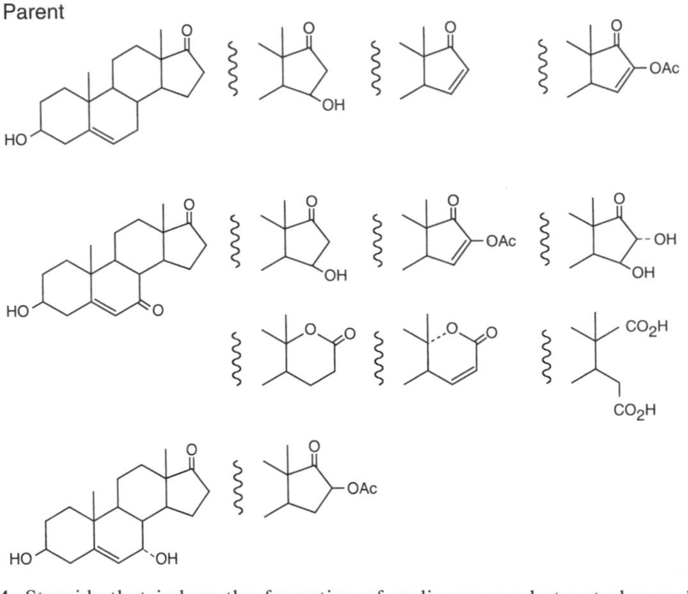

FIGURE 4. Steroids that induce the formation of malic enzyme but not glycerophosphate (G-3-P) dehydrogenase in rats' livers.

effect on the induction of malic enzyme but not on G-3-P dehydrogenase. Both of the 7-hydroxy derivatives are known to occur naturally and are converted to 7-oxo-DHEA by isolated tissue preparations.

The compounds we found capable of inducing both G-3-P dehydrogenase and malic enzyme are shown in FIGURE 3. The most active of these are the 7-oxo derivatives of DHEA and of androstene diol. Some parent compounds are completely inactive, whereas the corresponding 7-oxo derivative is active. These include the diacetyl ester of androstene diol, 16α-hydroxy DHEA, and 3β-hydroxy-androsta-5,16-diene (the 7-oxo derivative of the latter has very low activity). Isobutyryl DHEA is inactive, whereas the 7-oxo-isobutyryl ester induces both enzymes. The failure of androstenediol diacetate and of isobutyryl DHEA to induce enzyme formation must reflect their resistance to esterase activity.

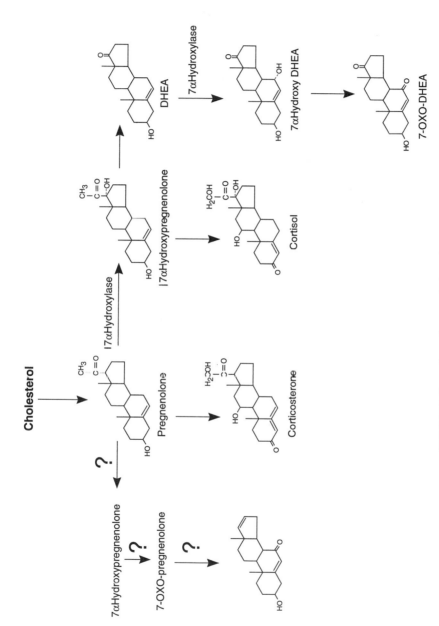

FIGURE 5. Does the rat have a substitute for DHEA?

FIGURE 4 depicts structures that induce malic enzyme but not G-3-P dehydrogenase. It will be interesting to learn if differences in the hormone response elements for the respective genes will be found to explain the selective activities.

Among the compounds shown in FIGURE 3, the 7-oxo-DHEA and 7-oxo-androstene diol are the most active.[24] Enzymatic hydroxylation of DHEA has been known for a long time and studied in many laboratories.[25-29] Lieberman and coworkers[30] isolated 7-oxo-DHEA from human urine; Schneider and Mason[31] independently found it to be produced from DHEA by rabbit liver slices, but neither group characterized it. This steroid was first prepared chemically by Billeter and Miescher[32] and its properties permitted Fukushima et al.[33] to demonstrate its presence in both normal and pathologic urines.

We must ask why the rat responds so readily to administered DHEA despite the inability of its adrenals to make enough to permit accurate detection in circulating blood. The rat's adrenals lack 17α-hydroxylase; consequently, it makes no cortisol or cortisone (FIG. 5). Hydroxylation of pregnenolone at position 11 yields corticosterone which serves the rat's need for glucocorticoid. If the two-carbon side chain of pregnenolone were removed metabolically, the product would be 3β-hydroxy-androsta-5,16-diene. We have synthesized it and found it inactive in our enzyme induction assay. We have made both 7α-hydroxy- and 7-oxo-pregnenolone, and both are inactive. Synthetic 3β-hydroxy-7-oxo-androsta-5,16-diene is active, but at 0.05% of the diet, it barely achieves the 150% activity required to gain that distinction. Rat organs other than the adrenals do form DHEA, but beyond serving as a precursor of testosterone and estrogens, little is available to the circulation. The low concentration in rat blood (0.23 ng/ml) is not influenced by ACTH but is nearly doubled by administering insulin for 8 or more days.[34]

Much remains to be learned about the metabolism and function of DHEA and its oxygenated derivatives in primates and rodents. In experiments done in collaboration with Dr. Joseph Kemnitz of the Wisconsin Primate Research Center, 7-oxo-DHEA at doses up to 140 mg/kg body weight daily for 28 days did not increase either mitochondrial G-3-P dehydrogenase or cytosolic malic enzyme. It did not alter differential blood cell counts, blood chemistry, or liver histology. The 7-oxo compounds are now being tested for possible effects on tumor formation, antiviral activity, and memory in experimental animals. Because of their natural occurrence, lack of toxicity, and the fact that they are not converted to androgens, they offer promise as therapeutic agents.

REFERENCES

1. ESTABROOK, R. & B. SACKTOR. 1958. J. Biol. Chem. **233:** 1014–1019.
2. BÜCHER, T. & M. KLINGENBERG. 1958. Angew. Chem. **70:** 552–570.
3. BORST, P. 1962. *In* Functionelle und Morphologische Organisation der Zelle. P. Karlson, Ed.: 137–162. Springer Verlag. Berlin.
4. LARDY, H., K. TOMITA, F. C. LARSON & E. ALBRIGHT. 1957. Ciba Foundation Colloquium on Endocrinology **10:** 165–164.
5. LEE, Y.-P., A. TAKEMORI & H. LARDY. 1959. J. Biol. Chem. **234:** 3051–3054.
6. LARDY, H., Y.-P. LEE & A. TAKEMORI. 1960. Ann. N.Y. Acad. Sci. **86:** 506–511.
7. LEE, Y.-P. & H. LARDY. 1965. J. Biol. Chem. **240:** 1427–1436.
8. GORDON, E. S. & A. HEMING. 1944. Endocrinology **34:** 353–360.
9. BARKER, S. B. 1951. Physiol. Rev. **31:** 205–243.
10. TEPPERMAN, H. & J. TEPPERMAN. 1964. Am. J. Physiol. **193:** 55–64.
11. PHILLIPS, A. H. & R. LANGDON. 1956. Biochim. Biophys. Acta **19:** 380–382.
12. TAGLIAFERRO, A., J. R. DAVIS, S. TRUCHON & N. VAN HAMONT. 1986. J. Nutr. **116:** 1977–1983.

13. TEPPERMAN, H., S. A. DE LA GARZA & J. TEPPERMAN. 1968. Am. J. Physiol. **214:** 1126–1132.
14. CLEARY, M. P., A. SHEPARD, J. ZISK & A. SCHWARTZ. 1983. Nutr. Behav. **1:** 127–136.
15. CASAZZA, J., W. T. SCHAFFER & R. VEECH. 1986. J. Nutr. **116:** 304–310.
16. LARDY, H., C.-Y. SU, N. KNEER & S. WIELGUS. 1989. *In* Hormones, Thermogenesis and Obesity. H. Lardy & F. Stratman, Eds.: 415–426. Elsevier. New York.
17. SU, C.-Y. & H. LARDY. 1991. J. Biochem. (Tokyo) **110:** 207–213.
18. PLUMMER, H. S. & W. M. BOOTHBY. 1923. Am. J. Physiol. **63:** 406–407.
19. BRIARD, S. P., J. T. MCCLINTOCK & C. W. BALDRIGE. 1935. Arch. Int. Med. **56:** 30–37.
20. LARDY, H., V. PAETKAU & P. WALTER. 1965. Proc. Natl. Acad. Sci. USA **53:** 1410–1415.
21. VEECH, R. L., L. V. EGGLESTON & H. KREBS. 1969. Biochem. J. **115:** 609–619.
22. BOBYLEVA, V., N. KNEER, M. BELLEI, D. BATTELLI & H. LARDY. 1993. J. Bioenergetics Biomembr. **25:** 313–321.
23. MACDONALD, M. J. 1995. J. Biol. Chem. **270:** 20051–20058.
24. LARDY, H., B. PARTRIDGE, N. KNEER & Y. WEI. 1995. Proc. Natl. Acad. Sci. USA **92:** 6617–6619.
25. STARKA, L. & J. KUTOVA. 1962. Biochim. Biophys. Acta **56:** 76–82.
26. HEINRICHS, W., R. MUSHEN & A. COLAS. 1967. Steroids **9:** 23–40.
27. FAREDIN, I., A. FAZEKAS, I. TOTH, K. KOKAI & M. JULESZ. 1969. J. Invest. Dermatol. **52:** 357–361.
28. AKWAA, Y., R. MORFIN, P. ROBEL & E.-E. BAULIEU. 1992. Biochem. J. **288:** 959–964.
29. KHALIL, M. W., B. STRUTT, D. VACHON & D. W. KILLINGER. 1994. J. Steroid Biochem. Molec. Biol. **48:** 545–552.
30. LIEBERMAN, S., K. DOBRINER, B. R. HILL, L. FIESER & C. P. RHOADS. 1948. J. Biol. Chem. **172:** 263–295.
31. SCHNEIDER, J. J. & H. L. MASON. 1948. J. Biol. Chem. **172:** 771–782.
32. BILLETER, J. R. & K. MIESCHER. 1948. Helv. Chim. Acta **31:** 629–632.
33. FUKUSHIMA, D., A. D. KEMP, R. SCHNEIDER, M. STOKEM & T. F. GALLAGHER. 1954. J. Biol. Chem. **210:** 129–137.
34. REMER, T. & K. PIETRZIK. 1993. Exp. Clin. Endocrinol. **101:** 222–229.

Mechanism of Cancer Preventive Action of DHEA

Role of Glucose-6-Phosphate Dehydrogenase[a]

ARTHUR G. SCHWARTZ AND LAURA L. PASHKO

*Fels Institute for Cancer Research and Molecular Biology and
Department of Microbiology and Immunology
Temple University School of Medicine
Philadelphia, Pennsylvania 19140*

In 1975 this laboratory demonstrated that dehydroepiandrosterone (DHEA) protected cultured rat liver epithelial-like cells and hamster embryonic fibroblasts against aflatoxin B_1- and 7,12-dimethylbenz(a)anthracene (DMBA)-induced cytotoxicity and malignant transformation.[1] Treatment with the steroid also suppressed the rate of metabolism of [^{3}H]DMBA to water-soluble products. Related steroids, such as testosterone and etiocholanolone, produced significantly less protection.

DHEA is a potent uncompetitive inhibitor (with respect to glucose-6-phosphate and NADP) of mammalian glucose-6-phosphate dehydrogenase (G6PDH) but not of algal or yeast enzyme.[2,3] G6PDH is the rate-limiting enzyme in the pentose phosphate pathway, an important source of ribose 5-phosphate and NADPH. The coenzyme NADPH is an essential reductant for the mixed function oxidases which metabolize many carcinogens into reactive electrophiles.[4] We hypothesized that DHEA protected rodent cells against aflatoxin B_1- and DMBA-induced cytotoxicity and transformation by reducing NADPH levels and thereby suppressing the rate of carcinogen activation.[1]

INHIBITION OF WEIGHT GAIN AND TUMORIGENESIS

In 1977 Yen *et al.*[5] demonstrated that oral DHEA treatment of VY-A^{vy}/a (obese) mice significantly suppressed the rate of weight gain. DHEA-treated mice consumed equivalent amounts of food as did the non-DHEA-treated mice, and thus the steroid produced its antiweight effect through an apparent metabolic alteration in the efficiency of food utilization rather than as a result of appetite suppression.

DHEA produced two biologic effects that suggested it might inhibit cancer development *in vivo:* the steroid protected cultured cells against chemical carcinogen-induced cytotoxicity and transformation, and DHEA treatment of mice inhibited weight gain. Reducing the weight of laboratory mice and rats through food restriction produces what is very likely the most marked cancer preventive effect of any known regimen.[6] The development of spontaneous,[7,8] chemically induced,[6,9] and radiation-induced tumors[10,11] is inhibited through food restriction. Underfeeding not only inhibits tumorigenesis, but also retards the rate of aging.

We did indeed find that long-term DHEA treatment inhibited the development of spontaneous breast cancer in C3H-A^{vy}//A (obese)[12] and C3H-A/A mice,[13]

[a]This work was supported by National Institutes of Health grants CA60471 and CA1227.

DMBA- and urethan-induced lung tumors in A/J mice,[14] and 1,2-dimethylhydrazine-induced colon tumors in BALB/c mice.[15] Other investigators demonstrated cancer preventive effects of DHEA in several different rat and mouse models of carcinogenesis. These include N-nitrosomorpholine-induced hemangiosarcomas in Sprague-Dawley rats,[16] diethylnitrosamine-induced liver preneoplastic foci in Wistar rats,[17] spontaneous testicular tumors in F-344 rats,[18] N-methyl-N-nitrosourea (MNU)-induced breast cancers in Sprague-Dawley rats,[19] MNU-induced prostate cancers in Sprague-Dawley rats,[20] and spontaneous lymphomas in p53 knockout transgenic mice.[21]

TWO-STAGE SKIN TUMORIGENESIS

In most of the foregoing studies demonstrating inhibition of tumor development by orally administered DHEA, DHEA treatment reduced weight gain. However, in one study, DHEA administration in the diet at 0.1 or 0.2% to MNU-treated female Sprague-Dawley rats significantly inhibited MNU-induced mammary carcinogenesis without any apparent effect on weight gain.[19] Nonetheless, we felt it important to use an experimental model of tumorigenesis in which tumor preventive activity can be dissociated from the antiweight effect. We used the two-stage skin tumorigenesis model in CD-1 mice in which DMBA, an initiating carcinogen, is applied once topically to the back, followed by twice weekly applications of the tumor promoter, 12-0-tetradecanoylphorbol-13-acetate (TPA). This treatment produces multiple skin papillomas in a few months. We applied DHEA topically to the backs of the mice 1 hour before either DMBA or TPA treatment. Topical application of DHEA had no effect on body weight, yet the steroid inhibited DMBA-initiated and TPA-promoted skin papilloma development.[22] Topical DHEA treatment also inhibited papilloma and carcinoma development induced by weekly applications of DMBA.[23] These results suggest that inhibition of skin papilloma and carcinoma development by DHEA is a result of direct action of the steroid on cells in the skin.

INHIBITION OF SKIN TUMOR PROMOTION

Topical DHEA application on mouse skin inhibits the rate of binding of [³H]DMBA to skin DNA, probably as a result of G6PDH inhibition and suppression in the rate of metabolic activation of DMBA.[22] This likely accounts for the anti-initiating action of DHEA.

Topical DHEA treatment also inhibits TPA promotion of skin papillomas. TPA, when applied to mouse skin, induces epidermal hyperplasia.[24] There is evidence that initiated epidermal cells are resistant to signals that induce terminal differentiation in normal cells, and when treated repeatedly with TPA, initiated cells undergo selective clonal expansion into papillomas.[24]

We observed in 1981 that a single intraperitoneal injection of DHEA (10 mg/kg) into ICR mice 1 hour before TPA application on the skin abolished TPA stimulation of epidermal [³H]thymidine incorporation.[25] DHEA also suppressed TPA-stimulated epidermal [³H]thymidine incorporation when administered orally[26] or applied topically[27] at dosages that inhibit TPA promotion of skin papillomas. Inhibition by DHEA of TPA-induced epidermal hyperplasia was confirmed by us using histologic examination of mouse skin as well as determining the DNA content of a 2×2 cm² section of mouse skin 48 hours after TPA application.[28,29] The synthetic steroid

16α-bromo-epiandrosterone (Epi-Br), a compound that is 30–50 times more potent than DHEA as an inhibitor of mammalian G6PDH,[3] was also much more active than DHEA in blocking TPA-stimulated epidermal [³H]thymidine incorporation; an injected dose of 0.4 mg/kg of Epi-Br was more effective than a dose of 10 mg/kg of DHEA.[25] We therefore hypothesized that the antihyperplastic effect of DHEA steroids in TPA-treated epidermis is mediated through the inhibition of G6PDH.

A major function of the pentose-phosphate pathway is the generation of NADPH as well as ribose-5-phosphate. Both NADPH and ribose 5-phosphate are used in the synthesis of purine and pyrimidine ribo- and deoxyribonucleotides. Therefore, DHEA can produce its antiproliferative effect in TPA-treated mouse skin by inhibition of deoxyribonucleotide synthesis.

Another possibility is that DHEA can produce antiproliferative effects in TPA-treated epidermis through inhibition of oxygen-free radical production. NADPH is a critical reductant for several biochemical reactions that generate oxygen-free radicals.[4,30–33] Oxygen-free radicals may serve as second messengers stimulating hyperplasia, and TPA-treated inflamed skin, with its many infiltrating white blood cells, should be an abundant source of oxygen-free radicals.[34] The importance of oxygen-free radicals in tumor promotion is underscored by marked suppression of TPA promotion of mouse skin papilloma formation by treatment with a low molecular weight copper chelate with superoxide dismutase activity.[35] DHEA, probably as a result of suppressing NADPH production, inhibits mixed-function oxidase activation of chemical carcinogens,[1,36] the NADPH-dependent generation of oxygen-free radicals from paraquat,[33] the oxidative burst generation of superoxide anion by TPA-stimulated neutrophils,[37] and nitric oxide production by lipopolysaccharide- and interferon gamma-stimulated mouse macrophages.[38]

If DHEA suppresses DNA synthesis in cells by reducing ribonucleotide and deoxyribonucleotide synthesis, then provision of these nucleosides should reverse DHEA-induced inhibition. We did indeed find that DHEA-induced growth inhibition of cultured HeLa TCRC-2 cells was overcome by adding to the culture medium a mixture of the four deoxyribonucleosides of adenine, guanine, thymine, and cytosine.[39] Gordon et al.[40] found that DHEA and Epi-Br inhibited the differentiation of cultured 3T3 fibroblasts into adipocytes, a process requiring nucleic acid synthesis, and that the addition of a mixture of the four ribonucleosides of uridine, cytosine, adenine, and guanine reversed the inhibition. Subsequently, these investigators found that intracellular levels of 6-phosphogluconate were depressed by steroid treatment, and introduction of 6-phosphogluconate into these cells via liposomes significantly reversed the block of differentiation.[41] As 6-phosphogluconate is not known to be formed by any metabolic reaction other than that mediated by G6PDH, these results strongly suggest that the suppressing action of DHEA steroids on differentiation of 3T3 fibroblasts into adipocytes results from G6PDH inhibition.

Garcea et al.[17] found that treatment with nucleosides reversed DHEA antiproliferative effects in vivo. Preneoplastic liver foci can be induced in rats by a single injection of diethylnitrosamine followed by treatment with 2-acetylaminofluorene, partial hepatectomy, and then phenobarbital for 2 weeks. If DHEA was administered during the period of phenobarbital treatment, both the size of the liver foci and the [³H]thymidine-labeling index of foci cells were reduced. Three daily intraperitoneal injections of the four ribo- or deoxyribonucleosides completely reversed DHEA-induced suppression in both focus size and labeling index of focus cells.[17]

We also found that the antihyperplastic and antitumor-promoting effects of the DHEA analog 16α-fluoro-5-androsten-17-one were completely reversed by administration of a mixture of the four deoxyribonucleosides.[29] This result strongly suggests that DHEA inhibition of TPA-stimulated epidermal hyperplasia and inhibition of

TPA tumor promotion results from inhibition of G6PDH by the steroid. The inhibition of tumor promoter-stimulated proliferation of rat hepatocytes by DHEA is also likely mediated by G6PDH inhibition, suggesting that this general mechanism may account for the inhibition of tumor promotion.

In addition to directly inhibiting ribo- and deoxyribonucleotide synthesis, DHEA inhibition of the production of oxygen-free radicals, which should be abundantly produced in tumor promoter-stimulated tissue, may also contribute to its antiproliferative action. The administration of deoxyribonucleosides would be expected to reverse DHEA-induced antiproliferative effects if DHEA suppresses deoxyribonucleotide synthesis sufficiently to inhibit DNA synthesis in target cells. Alternatively, suppression of NADPH levels could result in inhibition of the synthesis of both deoxyribonucleotides as well as various forms of oxygen-free radicals, whereas provision of exogenous deoxyribonucleosides may make more NADPH available for oxygen-free radical synthesis.

Two observations suggest that DHEA does not produce its antiproliferative effects *in vivo* by simply inhibiting deoxyribonucleotide synthesis: (1) Administration of DHEA at a dose (400 mg/kg po) that completely suppresses TPA-stimulated mouse epidermal DNA synthesis has no apparent effect on the rate of DNA synthesis in normal epidermis.[26] Oxygen-free radicals, which are likely to be produced in abundance in TPA-treated skin, may be an important mitogenic signal in TPA-treated epidermis but not in normal epidermis. (2) DHEA treatment, at doses that suppress hyperplasia in TPA-treated epidermis, does not produce any apparent mitogenic suppression in normal tissues which rapidly proliferate, such as bone marrow and intestinal epithelium (unpublished observation).

PHYSIOLOGIC ROLE OF DHEA

Food restriction of laboratory mice and rats is likely the most effective regimen known for the prevention of cancer in these animals.[6] Food restriction not only suppresses tumorigenesis, but also retards the rate of development of many age-associated pathologic changes and is believed to slow the rate of aging.[42] Caloric restriction of mice and rats impairs reproductive capacity in favor of maintenance of essential function; the slowing of aging observed in these animals may be an adaptive mechanism, enabling animals to survive periods of limited food, without breeding, until food again becomes available.[43] DHEA treatment of laboratory animals produces many of the beneficial effects of food restriction, including suppression of tumor development in many different organs,[12-21] inhibition of experimently induced atherosclerosis,[44] suppression of age-related proteinuria development,[45] and inhibition of autoimmune disease development.[46]

In 1948 Boutwell et al.[47] reported that food restriction in mice stimulates adrenocortical activity. Food restriction induced involution of the thymus gland, a decrease in the blood lymphocyte count, and an enhanced rate of deposition of liver glycogen in response to a glucose load, all of which are characteristic responses to elevated glucocorticoids.

We hypothesized that overproduction of adrenocortical steroids, such as DHEA and the glucocorticoids, contributes to the tumor-preventive and age-retarding effects of food restriction. We did indeed find that adrenalectomy of CD-1 mice before initiating food restriction completely reversed the inhibitory action of food restriction on TPA-stimulated epidermal [³H]thymidine incorporation as well as the inhibitory effect on TPA promotion of skin tumors.[48]

We recently found that adrenalectomy also completely reverses the tumor inhibitory effect of food restriction in a lung tumorigenesis model. Lung adenomas were induced in male A/J mice by a single oral dose of DMBA. A week later the mice were either adrenalectomized or sham operated and thereafter fed *ad libitum* or given 27% less food than the *ad libitum* fed group. Fourteen weeks later the mice were sacrificed and the number of alveolar adenomas was determined. Food restriction reduced the number of adenomas fourfold in the sham-operated mice, and adrenalectomy completely abolished the inhibitory effect of food restriction.[49] Results in both skin papilloma and lung adenoma tumorigenesis models suggest that secretory products from the adrenal gland play a major role in mediating the tumor inhibitory effect of food restriction in the mouse.

Two classes of adrenocortical steroids, the glucocorticoids and DHEA, both inhibit TPA-stimulated epidermal hyperplasia and TPA promotion of skin papillomas.[23,50,51] Both groups of steroids inhibit oxygen-free radical formation, the glucocorticoids as a result of their antiinflammatory action and DHEA probably through inhibition of G6PDH and suppression of NADPH production.[52] Oxygen-free radicals may contribute to the development of many age-related diseases including cancer,[53] atherosclerosis,[54] and various neurodegenerative diseases.[55] We hypothesized that food restriction in mice stimulates overproduction of glucocorticoids and DHEA, or a DHEA-like steroid, which may mediate the cancer preventive as well as the age-retarding effect of underfeeding.[52]

Our laboratory[48,49] and others[56] have found that food restriction elevates plasma corticosterone levels in several strains of mice. However, we did not find elevated levels of DHEA, as measured by radioimmunoassay, in food-restricted A/J mice.[49] These same mice had an almost threefold elevation in plasma corticosterone level in response to food restriction. Thus, either DHEA plays no direct role in mediating the tumor preventive and other age-retarding effects of food restriction or a congener of DHEA, with the biologic properties of the native steroid, exists in the mouse and does not significantly react with the antibody for DHEA in the radioimmunoassay. Recent work suggests that rat brain contains 17-ketosteroids, in addition to free DHEA, such as peroxides, hydroperoxides, and possibly even sulfolipids, which have yet to be characterized.[57] Therefore, the possible existence of biologically active steroids related to DHEA in mammals should be considered.

ACKNOWLEDGMENTS

All animal care in these experiments was in accordance with the guidelines of the Institutional Animal Care and Use Committee of Temple University.

REFERENCES

1. SCHWARTZ, A. G. & A. PERANTONI. 1975. Cancer Res. **39:** 2482–2487.
2. MARKS, P. A. & J. BANKS. 1960. Proc. Natl. Acad. Sci. USA **46:** 447–452.
3. RAINERI, R. & H. R. LEVY. 1970. Biochemistry **9:** 2233–2243.
4. SADOWSKI, I. J. & J. A. WRIGHT. 1985. Int. J. Biochem. **17:** 1023–1025.
5. YEN, T. T., J. A. ALLAN, D. V. PEARSON & J. M. ACTON. 1977. Lipids **12:** 409–413.
6. TANNENBAUM, A. & H. SILVERSTONE. 1953. Adv. Cancer Res. **1:** 451–501.
7. SHIMOKAWA, I., B. P. YU & E. J. MASORO. 1991. J. Gerontol. Biol. Sci. **46:** B228–B232.
8. HURSTING, S. D., S. N. PERKINS & J. M. PHANG. 1994. Proc. Natl. Acad. Sci. USA **91:** 7036–7040.
9. KLURFELD, D. M., M. M. WEBER & D. KRITCHEVSKY. 1987. Cancer Res. **47:** 2759–2762.
10. GROSS, L. & Y. DREYFUSS. 1984. Proc. Natl. Acad. Sci. USA **81:** 7596–7598.

11. GROSS, L. & Y. DREYFUSS. 1986. Proc. Natl. Acad. Sci. USA **83:** 7928–7931.
12. SCHWARTZ, A. G. 1979. Cancer Res. **39:** 1129–1132.
13. SCHWARTZ, A. G., G. C. HARD, L. L. PASHKO, M. ABOU-GHARBIA & D. SWERN. 1981. Nutr. Cancer **3:** 46–53.
14. SCHWARTZ, A. G. & R. H. TANNEN. 1981. Carcinogenesis **2:** 1335–1337.
15. NYCE, J. W., P. N. MAGEE, G. C. HARD & A. G. SCHWARTZ. 1984. Carcinogenesis **5:** 57–62.
16. WEBER, E., M. A. MOORE & P. BANNASCH. 1988. Carcinogenesis **9:** 1191–1195.
17. GARCEA, R., L. DAINO, S. FRASSETTO, P. COZZOLINO, M. RUGGIU, M. G. YANNINI, R. PASCALE, L. LENZERINI, M. M. SIMILE, M. PUDDU & F. FEO. 1988. Carcinogenesis **9:** 931–938.
18. RAO, M. S., V. SUBBARAO, A. V. YELDANDI & J. K. REDDY. 1992. Cancer Lett. **65:** 123–126.
19. RATKO, T. A., C. J. DETRISAC, R. G. MEHTA, G. J. KELLOFF & R. C. MOON. 1991. Cancer Res. **51:** 481–486.
20. MCCORMICK, D. L., K. V. N. RAO, M. C. BOSLAND, V. E. STEELE, R. A. LUBER & G. J. KELLOFF. 1995. Proc. Am. Assoc. Cancer Res. **36:** 126.
21. HURSTING, S. D., S. N. PERKINS & J. M. PHANG. 1995. Proc. Am. Assoc. Cancer Res. **36:** 588.
22. PASHKO, L. L., R. J. ROVITO, J. R. WILLIAMS, E. L. SOBEL & A. G. SCHWARTZ. 1984. Carcinogenesis **5:** 463–466.
23. PASHKO, L. L., G. C. HARD, R. J. ROVITO, J. R. WILLIAMS, E. L. SOBEL & A. G. SCHWARTZ. 1985. Cancer Res. **45:** 164–166.
24. HENNINGS, H. & S. H. YUSPA. 1985. J. Natl. Cancer Inst. **74:** 735–740.
25. PASHKO, L. L., A. G. SCHWARTZ, M. ABOU-GHORBIA & D. SWERN. 1981. Carcinogenesis **2:** 717–721.
26. SCHWARTZ, A. G., M. L. LEWBART & L. L. PASHKO. 1988. Cancer Res. **48:** 4817–4822.
27. SCHWARTZ, A. G. & L. L. PASHKO. 1986. Anticancer Res. **6:** 1279–1282.
28. SCHWARTZ, A. G. & L. L. PASHKO. 1993. J. Cell. Biochem. **17G:** 73–79.
29. PASHKO, L. L., M. L. LEWBART & A. G. SCHWARTZ. 1991. Carcinogenesis **12:** 2189–2192.
30. BABIOR, B. M. 1982. Can. J. Physiol. Pharmacol. **60:** 1353–1358.
31. IMLAY, J. A. & S. LINN. 1988. Science **240:** 1302–1309.
32. MARLETTA, M. A., P. S. YOON, R. IYENGAR, C. D. LEOF & J. S. WISHNOK. 1988. **27:** 8706–8711.
33. LEE, T.-C., G.-J. LAI, S.-L. KAO, I. C. HO & C.-W. WU. 1993. Biochem. Pharmacol. **45:** 1143–1147.
34. STEVENSON, M. A., S. S. POLLOCK, C. N. COLEMAN & S. K. CALDERWOOD. 1994. Cancer Res. **54:** 12–15.
35. KENSLER, T. W., D. M. BUSH & W. J. KOZUMBO. 1983. Science **221:** 75–77.
36. FEO, F., L. PIRISI, R. PASCALE, L. DAINO, S. FRASSETTO, S. ZANETTE & R. GARCEA. 1984. Toxicol. Pathol. **12:** 261–268.
37. WHITCOMB, J. M. & A. G. SCHWARTZ. 1985. Carcinogenesis **6:** 333–335.
38. MEI, J. M., S. D. HURSTING & J. M. PHANG. 1995. Proc. Am. Assoc. Cancer Res. **36:** 585.
39. DWORKIN, C. R., S. D. GORMAN, L. L. PASHKO, V. J. CRISTOFALLO & A. G. SCHWARTZ. 1986. Life Sci. **38:** 1451–1457.
40. GORDON, G. B., L. M. SHANTZ & P. TALALAY. 1987. Adv. Enzyme Regul. **26:** 355–382.
41. SHANTZ, L. M., P. TALALAY & G. B. GORDON. 1989. Proc. Natl. Acad. Sci. USA **86:** 3852–3856.
42. MASORO, E. J. 1984. Physiologist **27:** 98–101.
43. HOLLIDAY, R. 1994. *In* Genetics and Evolution of Aging. M. R. Rose & C. E. Finch, Eds.: 217–225. Kluwer Academic Publishers. Netherlands.
44. GORDON, G. B., D. E. BUSH & H. F. WEISMAN. 1988. J. Clin. Invest. **82:** 712–720.
45. PASHKO, L. L., D. K. FAIRMAN & A. G. SCHWARTZ. 1986. J. Gerontol. **41:** 433–438.
46. LUCAS, J. A., S. A. AHMED, J. L. CASEY & P. C. MACDONALD. 1985. J. Clin. Invest. **75:** 2091–2093.
47. BOUTWELL, R. K., M. K. BRUSH & H. P. RUSCH. 1948. Am. J. Physiol. **154:** 517–524.
48. PASHKO, L. L. & A. G. SCHWARTZ. 1992. Carcinogenesis **10:** 1925–1928.
49. PASHKO, L. L. & A. G. SCHWARTZ. 1995. Submitted.

50. BELMAN, S. & W. TROLL. 1972. Cancer Res. **32:** 450–454.
51. SCHWARZ, J. A., A. VIAJE, T. J. SLAGA & S. H. YUSPA. 1977. Chem.-Biol. Interact. **17:** 331–347.
52. SCHWARTZ, A. G. & L. L. PASHKO. 1994. J. Gerontol. Biol. Sci. **49:** B37–B41.
53. CERUTTI, P. 1994. Lancet **344:** 862–863.
54. WITZUM, J. L. 1994. Lancet **344:** 793–795.
55. JENNER, P. 1994. Lancet **344:** 796–798.
56. KLEBANOV, S., S. DIAIS, W. STAVINOHA, Y. SUH, T. PRIHODA & J. F. NELSON. 1995. J. Gerontol. Biol. Sci. **50A:** B78–B82.
57. MATHUR, C., V. V. K. PRASAD, V. S. RAJU, M. WELCH & S. LIEBERMAN. 1993. Proc. Natl. Acad. Sci. USA **90:** 85–88.

Regulation of Cytochromes P450
by DHEA and Its Anticarcinogenic Action

R. A. PROUGH, X.-D. LEI, G.-H. XIAO, H.-Q. WU,[a]

T. E. GEOGHEGAN, AND S. J. WEBB

Department of Biochemistry
School of Medicine
University of Louisville
Louisville, Kentucky 40292

[a] Department of Environmental Toxicology
Tongji Medical University
Wuhan, Hubei, Peoples Republic of China

Dehydroepiandrosterone (DHEA) is a C_{19} adrenal steroid that is synthesized in humans and serves as an androgen precursor for the production of the sex hormones.[1] DHEA and its reduced product, 5-*ene*-androstene-3α,17α-diol (ADIOL), circulate as 3β-sulfate conjugates *in vivo,* and after deconjugation they possess androgen activity. Bulbrook and coworkers[2] suggested that low circulating levels of DHEA in blood correlate with an increased incidence of breast cancer in older women; later studies failed to support this hypothesis.[3] However, the unique action of pharmacologic dosages of DHEA on various pathophysiologic states in rodent models, including inhibition of chemically induced cancer in colon, lung, and skin and of spontaneous breast cancer,[4-7] reduction in weight gain in animals genetically disposed toward obesity,[8,9] and the amelioration of diabetes,[10] hemolytic anemia,[11] and lupus,[1] has been extensively studied. DHEA is also an inhibitor of glucose 6-phosphate dehydrogenase activity *in vitro*[12] and appears to serve as an inhibitor of cell growth and proliferation *in vivo.*[13,14] Studies by several groups suggest that the growth inhibition action may be due to depletion of ribose phosphate pools, not cytosolic levels of NADPH in rapidly dividing cells.

The beneficial effect of DHEA on obesity may be related to its action as a peroxisome proliferator when administered at pharmacologic doses.[15,16] Peroxisome proliferation is a pathologic state characterized by increased volume and number of hepatic peroxisomes and their associated enzymes as well as induction of specific microsomal and mitochondrial enzymes.[17,18] Our past work demonstrates that administration of DHEA (either *per os* or intraperitoneally) results in induction of hepatic, microsomal cytochromes P4504A and its flavoprotein reductase as well as the peroxisomal enzymes, catalase, and fatty acyl CoA oxidase.[19] As DHEA is only effective as an inducer of *CYP*4A at pharmacologic doses, we have characterized the inductive process for microsomal and peroxisomal markers by DHEA to establish if the steroid has activity other than that as a peroxisome-proliferating agent.

INDUCTION OF MARKERS OF PEROXISOME PROLIFERATION
IN FEMALE AND MALE RATS BY DHEA

To fully characterize the role of DHEA in peroxisome proliferation in rodents, we compared its action in female and male Sprague-Dawley rats. FIGURE 1 demon-

[a] This work was supported by National Cancer Institute grant CA43839 and a postdoctoral fellowship for X.-D. Lei from the Humana Endowment for Excellence, James Graham Brown Cancer Center, University of Louisville.

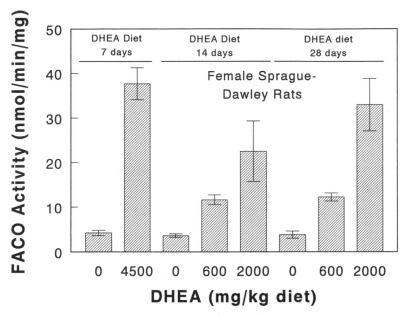

FIGURE 1. Effect of DHEA feeding on hepatic peroxisomal β-oxidation in female Sprague-Dawley rats. Female rats were fed diets containing different amounts of DHEA *per os* for 1, 2, and 4 weeks *ad libitum*. The 5,000 × *g* supernatants were prepared and FACO activity measured spectrophotometrically as described previously by Wu *et al.*[19]

strates that DHEA administration *per os* induces enzyme activity for peroxisomal fatty-CoA oxidase in the livers of female Sprague-Dawley rats. No significant differences were apparent in the induction of these activities in female and male rats (37.7 ± 3.6 vs 40.7 ± 6.1 nmol NAD^+ reduced/min/mg protein, respectively). In addition, we measured the induction of mRNA for two isoforms of cytochrome P4504A, namely, *CYP*4A1 and *CYP*4A3. Levels of hepatic mRNA for *CYP*4A1 and *CYP*4A3 were induced to similar extents by DHEA treatment in either female or male rats (FIG. 2), but hepatic levels of mRNA for *CYP*4A2 were not induced by DHEA treatment in the female rat liver (data not shown). These results are in agreement with other reports that *CYP*4A2 is not expressed or induced in the female rat liver.[20] Other than the known sexual dimorphism of *CYP*4A2, DHEA apparently induces these gene products associated with peroxisome proliferation in both female and male rats, as has been shown for other peroxisome proliferators.

MODULATION OF EXPRESSION OF OTHER HEPATIC CYTOCHROMES P450

In earlier studies we used several substrates to evaluate any changes in expression of other hepatic P450s[19] in male Sprague-Dawley rats. We demonstrated that the enzyme activities associated with P4504As were strikingly induced approximately 18-fold as expected for a peroxisome proliferator.[19] Constitutively expressed hepatic cytochromes P450 can also be characterized by their ability to metabolize various isoform specific substrates *in vitro* (FIG. 3). For several P450s (*CYP*1A, 2B, and 2E), DHEA feeding had little or no effect on the activities of the protein products of these genes. However, major changes occurred in the distribution of hydroxylated metabolites of androstenedione and testosterone formed in the presence of NADPH and oxygen by liver microsomes from DHEA-fed animals when compared to those of untreated animals. The 16α-hydroxylase activities of androstenedione and testosterone were significantly decreased (≈ 80%) in liver microsomes from DHEA-fed rats, whereas the rates of 16β-hydroxylation were increased approximately 600%. Androstenedione/testosterone 16α-hydroxylase activity has been associated with rat hepatic CYP2C11 and 2B1/2,[21] suggesting that the decrease in this enzyme activity may be due to decreased expression of these gene products in the livers of DHEA-fed animals. Androstenedione/testosterone 16β-hydroxylase activity has also been associated with CYP3A.[21] As we have shown that DHEA does not induce CYP2B1/2 activity in FIGURE 3, DHEA repression of 16α-hydroxylase activity is probably due to decreased expression of the CYP2C11 isoform. The data in FIGURE 3 clearly demonstrates that forms of cytochrome P450 induced by chemicals, such as polycyclic aromatic hydrocarbons or barbiturates, are not induced by the administration of DHEA. DHEA treatment, however, did cause the levels of hepatic mRNA for at least one constitutive cytochrome P450 (i.e., 2C11) to decrease, whereas cytochrome P4503A associated with androstene/testosterone 16β-hydroxylase activity increased (FIG. 4). We also monitored the metabolism of benzo(a)pyrene, a potent polycyclic aromatic hydrocarbon carcinogen, and found that its metabolism *in vitro* to a protein-binding intermediate was increased fivefold by DHEA feeding.[22] This result suggests that P450s other than *CYP*4A, which does not metabolize this substrate, are altered in liver microsomes of rats fed DHEA *per os* to account for changes in this activity.

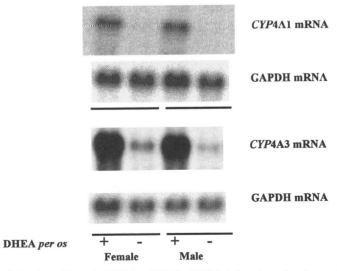

FIGURE 2. Induction of hepatic *CYP*4A mRNA by DHEA in female and male rats. Male and female rats were fed DHEA *per os* (0.45% DHEA in AIN76A diet *ad libitum*) for 7 days. mRNA was isolated, separated electrophoretically, and probed with ^{32}P-labeled oligonucleotides or cDNA specific for *CYP*4A1, 4A3, and GAPDH as described previously by Prough *et al.*[23]

ONLY DHEA AND ADIOL CAUSE PEROXISOME PROLIFERATION
AND INDUCTION OF P4504A AT PHARMACOLOGIC DOSAGES

To establish the structure-activity relationship between feeding of various intermediates of the steroid hormone biosynthetic pathway, we administered various intermediates by intraperitoneal injection at a dose of 100 mg/kg body weight, a dose that was shown to be maximal for DHEA and ADIOL.[23] As seen in FIGURE 5, only DHEA and ADIOL caused maximal induction of P4504A protein in liver microsomal fractions. These results indicate that of the intermediates of the steroid

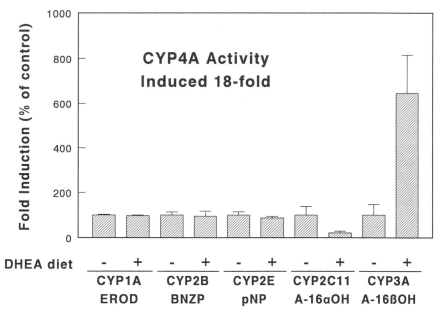

FIGURE 3. Effect of DHEA feeding on the enzyme activities of various hepatic microsomal cytochromes P450. Male rats were administered DHEA *per os* with a diet containing 0.45% DHEA in AIN76A chow for 7 days. The various enzyme assays were performed as described by Wu *et al.*[19] EROD = 7-ethoxyresorufin *O*-deethylase; BNZP = benzphetamine *N*-demethylase; pNP = *p*-nitrophenol hydroxylase; A-16αOH = androstenedione 16α-hydroxylase; and A-16βOH = androstenedione 16β-hydroxylase activities.

hormone biosynthetic pathway, only DHEA and its reduced product, ADIOL, serve as inducers of microsomal P4504A (FIG. 5) and NADPH:cytochrome P450 oxidoreductase and peroxisomal catalase and fatty acyl-CoA β-oxidation.[23] DHEA and ADIOL treatment also resulted in increased liver:body weight ratios and decreased weight gain without decreasing food intake.[19,22,23]

DHEA ENHANCES TRANSCRIPTIONAL ACTIVITY OF *CYP*4A GENES

The mechanism by which DHEA and ADIOL induce levels of *CYP*4A protein and mRNA was studied to establish whether induction occurred by a pretransla-

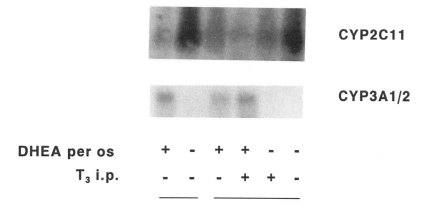

CYP2C11

CYP3A1/2

DHEA per os + - + + - -

T₃ i.p. - - - + + -

Euthyroid Thyroidectomized

FIGURE 4. Induction of hepatic cytochrome P4502C11 and 3A by DHEA in euthyroid and thyroidectomized rats. Euthyroid and thyroidectomized male rats (80–100 g) either were fed DHEA (0.45% DHEA in AIN76A diet *ad libitum*) for 1 week, were treated with 50 µg T₃/100 g body wt, or were treated with a combination of the two. Liver mRNA was prepared and analyzed as described by Prough *et al.*[23] using ³²P-labeled oligonucleotides specific for P4502C11 and 3A or cDNA for glyceraldehyde-3-phosphate dehydrogenase.

tional mechanism. Clofibrate, another peroxisome proliferator, increases peroxisomal fatty acyl-Co oxidase and microsomal P4504A mRNA and protein by increasing transcriptional activity.[24,25] We sought to determine if DHEA increased P4504A mRNA and protein by enhancing transcriptional activity. Rats were fed DHEA for 2 days and liver nuclei isolated as previously described.[23] Both DHEA and clofibrate treatment of rats resulted in the same level of transcriptional activation (11.2- vs 12.2-fold, respectively) for the nascent mRNA transcripts for *CYP*4A. These results suggest that DHEA induces *CYP*4A by a mechanism similar to that of other peroxisome proliferators, such as clofibrate and nafenopin (data not shown).

FIGURE 5. Induction of hepatic microsomal cytochrome P4504A protein content by various steroid intermediates. Male rats (80–100 g) were given the steroids in corn oil intraperitoneally at a dosage of 100 mg/kg body weight daily for 4 days and liver microsomal protein fractions prepared for Western blot analysis as described by Prough *et al.*[23] The steroid pretreatment regimens were: CONTROL = corn oil; 17OH-P = 17α-hydroxypregnenolone; DHA = dehydroepiandrosterone; ADIONE = 4-*ene*-androstene-3,17-dione; ADIOL = 5-*ene*-androsten-3β,17β-diol; T = testosterone; and EDIOL = estradiol-17β. Authentic P4504A standards purified from DHEA-treated rats were separated on the 10% gels (*far left lane*).

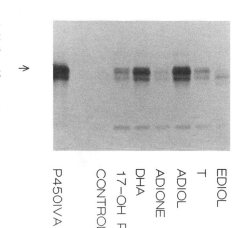

THYROID HORMONE (T₃) REGULATES INDUCTION OF *CYP*4A IN RAT LIVER *IN VIVO*

DHEA is a peroxisome-proliferating agent when administered in pharmacologic dosages, but it does not function through the peroxisome proliferator-activated receptor (PPAR) in cell-based assays.[26–28] As PPAR, like other members of the thyroid hormone/vitamin A and D nuclear receptor subfamily, heterodimerize and regulate each other's function in gene expression,[29,30] we studied DHEA and thyroid hormone interactions in regulating enzymes associated with peroxisome proliferation, namely, peroxisomal β-oxidation and microsomal cytochromes P4504A. Induction of two isozymes of *CYP*4A (4A1 and 4A3) by DHEA was suppressed over 60–80% at the hepatic mRNA level in rats administered exogenous T₃ to attain a hyperthyroid state (FIG. 6). In addition, induction of hepatic and renal *CYP*4A2 mRNA was potently inhibited (< 95%). By contrast, thyroid hormone had no effect on the induction of hepatic peroxisomal β-oxidation by either DHEA or nafenopin under any condition tested (data not shown). These results demonstrate that thyroid hormone regulation of two other marker enzymes of peroxisome proliferation, that is, fatty acyl-CoA oxidase and NADPH:cytochrome P450 oxidoreductase, is significantly different from that of *CYP*4A.

T₃ REGULATES INDUCTION OF *CYP*4A BY NAFENOPIN IN CULTURED RAT HEPATOCYTES

To establish whether this inhibitory phenomenon was a direct action of T₃ on the hepatocyte, we used cultured rat hepatocytes to measure the effect of T₃ on the expression of *CYP*4A mRNA.[31] We were unable to demonstrate reproducible

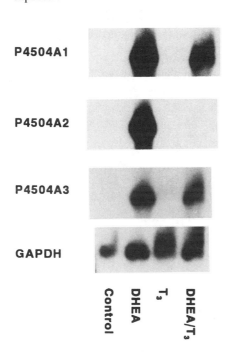

FIGURE 6. Northern analysis of hepatic poly (A)⁺ mRNA from male rats treated with DHEA and/or high doses of T₃. Male Sprague-Dawley rats were administered either DHEA *per os* (0.45% DHEA in AIN-76A *ad libitum*), T₃ intraperitoneally (50 μg daily/100 g body weight), or both daily for 7 days. Poly (A)⁺-enriched mRNA was analyzed as described by Prough *et al.*[23] using ³²P-labeled oligonucleotides specific for the individual P4504A isozymes or the cDNA for glyceraldehyde-3-phosphate dehydrogenase.

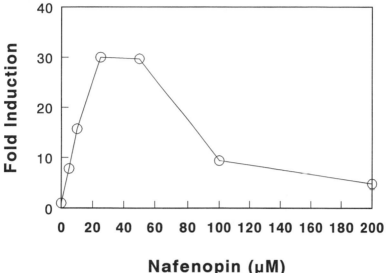

FIGURE 7. Induction of cytochrome P4504A protein by nafenopin in cultured rat hepatocytes. After plating on Matrigel-coated dishes, primary hepatocytes were cultured for 24 hours, and then nafenopin was added in graded concentrations to the media. After 72 hours, cells were collected and cell protein was isolated. Western blot analysis was performed as described in FIGURE 5.

induction of the mRNAs and protein of *CYP*4A genes by DHEA or DHEA sulfate in cultured adult rat hepatocytes[27,28] and therefore we used nafenopin, a peroxisome-proliferating agent, to increase *CYP*4A mRNA and protein expression. We noted that concentrations of up to 50 μM nafenopin caused increased levels of P4504A protein (FIG. 7) and mRNA (data not shown) for the various isozymes of *CYP*4A approximately 30-fold at 72 hours; concentrations higher than this were toxic to the cells as measured by trypan blue dye exclusion and lactic dehydrogenase leakage. We subsequently tested the effect of increasing concentrations of T_3 on nafenopin-dependent induction of *CYP*4A mRNAs in rat hepatocytes (FIG. 8). T_3 specifically suppressed the induction of mRNA specific for *CYP*4A2 by nafenopin at concentrations as low as 1×10^{-9} M, whereas concentrations as high as 1 μM T_3 had no statistically significant effect on induction of *CYP*4A1 and 4A3 mRNA. These results are nearly identical to the effect of T_3 on induction of *CYP*4A2 *in vivo,* demonstrating that T_3 apparently acts directly at the level of the hepatocyte in regulating *CYP*4A2 expression and not by altering other hormonal factors associated with the thyroid or parathyroid gland. Further studies will be required to establish whether thyroid hormone receptor functions to directly regulate these genes.[29]

DHEA BLUNTS METHYLNITROSOUREA-INDUCED BREAST CANCER AT DOSES THAT DO NOT LEAD TO PEROXISOME PROLIFERATION IN FEMALE RATS

In collaboration with National Cancer Institute study, we evaluated DHEA-dependent peroxisome proliferation in female rats treated with methylnitrosourea (MNU) to induce breast tumors. In this study, 50-day-old virgin female rats were

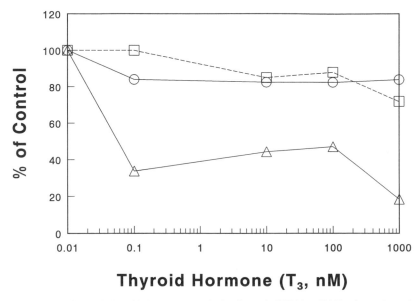

FIGURE 8. Effect of thyroid hormone on induction of *CYP*4A mRNAs by nafenopin in cultured rat hepatocytes. Primary hepatocytes were cultured as described in FIGURE 7 in the presence of 40 μM nafenopin and increasing concentrations of T_3. After 72 hours, cells were collected and the mRNA isolated.[23,31] Total mRNA was analyzed as described in FIGURE 6. Values presented are the actual optical densities of the hybridization complexes obtained from the autoradiograms normalized to glyceraldehyde-3-phosphate dehydrogenase mRNA levels. mRNA specific for *CYP*4A1, ○; *CYP*4A2, △; and *CYP*4A3, □.

administered MNU intravenously (50 mg/kg body weight), and the incidence/ multiplicity of breast tumors was observed over a 14.5-week period. Feeding up to 600 mg DHEA/kg diet *ad libitum* for 14.5 weeks to female rats significantly diminished the tumor incidence and multiplicity by more than 75% (R. A. Lubet, personal communication). Administration of smaller amounts of DHEA in the diet (i.e., 5, 24, and 120 mg DHEA/kg diet for 14.5 weeks) also displayed significant chemopreventive activity against MNU-induced breast tumors in female Sprague-Dawley rats. The liver-to-body weight ratios for female rats fed DHEA (only at levels > 2,000 mg DHEA/kg diet) were significantly increased at 4 weeks (data not shown). At 4 weeks, diets containing 2,000 and 4,500 mg DHEA/kg caused maximal induction of hepatic peroxisomal β-oxidation activity (FIG. 9) and of *CYP*4A1/4A3 mRNA levels in both female and male rats (FIG. 2). Feeding diets containing 600 mg DHEA/kg diet for 4 and 14.5 weeks resulted in only 10–15% of maximal induction of β-oxidation activity (FIG. 9) and of *CYP*4A1 mRNA levels (FIG. 10). Although effective in blunting MNU-induced mammary cancer, intake of lower amounts of DHEA by female rats resulted in little or no significant increases in markers of peroxisomal proliferation.

DISCUSSION

Initial studies on the effects of DHEA on intermediary metabolism focused on its effects on lipid metabolism.[15,32] For example, it was noted that rodents fed high levels of DHEA failed to gain weight as rapidly as did matched controls, but they consumed similar amounts of calories. Several groups observed changes in the morphology of the liver, notably, changes in the number and size of peroxisomes.[22,28] Subsequent studies demonstrated specific changes in microsomal, mitochondrial, and peroxisomal enzymes.[19,23] These studies provided information to document that DHEA was a peroxisome-proliferating agent. Specific marker enzymes of this phenomenon, peroxisomal β-oxidation and microsomal *CYP*4A, were both strikingly induced by DHEA feeding. In addition, DHEA, like other peroxisome proliferators, leads to the development of hepatocarcinoma.[16,18]

Our studies on the regulation of *CYP*4A expression by DHEA have demonstrated that two closely related *CYP*4A genes, 4A1 and 4A3, are induced in the liver and kidney of female and male Sprague-Dawley rats.[23] A third gene, *CYP*4A2, is not expressed in the liver of females,[20] but in a tissue-specific manner under a basal and DHEA-inducible state in the liver and kidneys of male rats.[23] The expression of *CYP*4A2 gene is also under developmental control, because mature rats are not as well induced as immature rats.[23] Of the various steroid intermediates of the steroid biosynthetic pathway, only DHEA and its reduced product, 5-*ene*-androstene-3β,17β-diol, served as peroxisome proliferators. However, several groups have demonstrated that DHEA itself does not directly induce *CYP*4A in hepatocytes[27,28] or activate PPAR-dependent transient transcription assays.[33] Other peroxisome proliferators, such as nafenopin, do activate PPAR-dependent transcriptional activity for the native *CYP*4A genes (FIG. 8).

Other genes associated with peroxisome proliferation are coregulated by thyroid hormone. As PPAR is part of the thyroid hormone/vitamin A/vitamin gene family

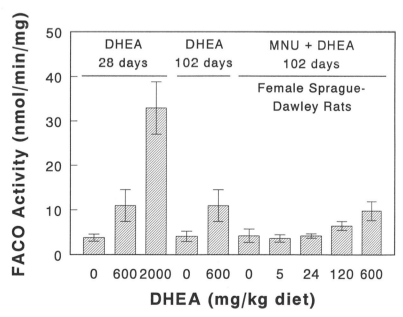

FIGURE 9. Effect of DHEA feeding for 14.5 weeks on hepatic fatty acyl CoA oxidase activity of methylnitrosourea-treated female rats. Female rats were fed diets containing different amounts of DHEA *per os* for 4 and 14.5 weeks. The FACO activities were measured on 5,000 × *g* supernatants.

which modulates each other's action by hetero- and homodimerization,[30] we sought to establish if thyroid hormone affects DHEA-induced expression of *CYP*4A genes. In hyperthyroid conditions, DHEA-induced *CYP*4A expression was strongly blunted. Induction of *CYP*4A2 mRNA and protein was most potently affected (FIG. 6), relative to *CYP*4A1 and *CYP*4A3. In addition, regulation by T_3 apparently acts directly on the hepatocyte at the level of transcription, not through some other factor expressed by the thyroid gland. Several mechanisms can be envisioned for regulation of this gene, such as direct binding of the thyroid hormone receptor to elements on the 5' flanking region of the gene.

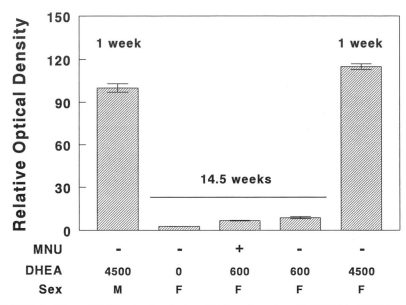

FIGURE 10. Effect of DHEA feeding for 1 and 14.5 weeks on hepatic *CYP*4A1 mRNA levels in livers of rats treated with MNU. Female and male rats were fed diets containing different amounts of DHEA *per os*. A single dose of MNU (50 mg/kg body wt.) was administered to female rats and mRNA measured at 14.5 weeks as described in FIGURE 6. Values presented are the optical densities of the hybridization complexes obtained from the autoradiograms normalized to glyceraldehyde-3-phosphate dehydrogenase mRNA levels.

The mechanism of hepatocarcinogenesis by DHEA is still unclear. To date, no data have been obtained to suggest that DHEA-induced hepatocarcinogenesis occurs by any mechanism different from that observed for other classic peroxisome proliferators. Most of the marker genes altered by peroxisome-proliferating agents are also induced to the same levels by DHEA administration, suggesting that in pharmacologic dosage, it functions like other peroxisome proliferators.

Although long-term administration of DHEA causes hepatocarcinogenesis, DHEA-induced carcinogenesis is most likely dose dependent. For example, rats eliciting hepatocarcinoma were fed diets high in DHEA, that is, 5,000 or 10,000 mg DHEA/kg diet *ad libitum*. In our study, even the highest concentration of DHEA used to blunt breast carcinogenesis, 600 mg/kg diet, was probably lower than that required for high incidences of hepatocarcinogenesis. At this lower dosage, MNU-induced breast cancer was suppressed more than 70%, yet peroxisome proliferation measured as induced fatty acyl CoA oxidase activity or levels of *CYP*4A mRNAs was only modestly increased (10–20% of maximum) compared to higher concentrations of DHEA used in studies in which maximal peroxisome proliferation was observed, that is, > 2,000 mg DHEA/kg diet. At smaller amounts of DHEA, such as 25–120 mg DHEA/kg diet, the cancer chemopreventive action of DHEA was still striking, whereas no significant increase in the markers of peroxisome proliferation was noted. Considering the effectiveness of DHEA as a cancer chemoprotective agent, the dose-dependent responses of DHEA-induced peroxisome proliferation and hepatocarcinogenesis must be considered when evaluating the potential clinical use of DHEA in humans.

ACKNOWLEDGMENTS

The authors wish to thank R. A. Lubet, C. Grubbs, and R. C. Moon for their collaboration in the studies on breast tumorigenesis in female rats. We also thank Cameron Falkner for critical review of this article.

REFERENCES

1. VANDEWIELE, R. L., P. C. MACDONALD, E. GURPIDE & S. LIEBERMAN. 1963. Studies on the secretion and interconversion of androgens. Recent Prog. Horm. Res. **19:** 275–310.
2. BULBROOK, R. D., J. L. HAYWARD & C. C. SPICER. 1971. Relationship between urinary androgen and corticoid excretion and subsequent breast cancer. Lancet **2:** 385–398.
3. BARRETT-CONNOR, E., N. J. FRIEDLANDER & K.-T. KHAW. 1990. Dehydroepiandrosterone sulfate and breast cancer risk. Cancer Res. **50:** 6571–6574.
4. SCHWARTZ, O. 1979. Inhibition of spontaneous breast cancer formation in female C3H (A$^{vy/a}$) mice by long-term treatment with dehydroepiandrosterone. Cancer Res. **39:** 1129–1132.
5. SCHWARTZ, A. G. & R. H. TANNEN. 1981. Inhibition of 7,12-dimethylbenz[a]-anthracene- and urethane-induced lung tumor formation in A/J mice by long-term treatment with dehydroepiandrosterone. Carcinogenesis **5:** 1335–1337.
6. NYCE, J. W., P. N. MAGEE, G. C. HARD & A. G. SCHWARTZ. 1984. Inhibition of 1,2-dimethylhydrazine-induced colon tumorigenesis in Balb/c mice by dehydroepiandrosterone. Carcinogenesis **5:** 57–62.
7. PASHKO, L. L., R. J. ROVITO, J. R. WILLIAMS, E. L. SOBEL & A. G. SCHWARTZ. 1984. Dehydroepiandrosterone (DHEA) and 3-β-methylandrost-5-en-17-one: Inhibitors of 7,12-dimethylbenz[a]anthracene (DMBA)-initiated and 12-O-tetradecanoyl-phorbol-13-acetate (TPA)-promoted skin papilloma formation in mice. Carcinogenesis **5:** 463–466.
8. YEN, T. T., J. A. ALLEN, D. V. PEARSON, J. M. ACTON & M. M. GREENBERG. 1977. Prevention of obesity in A$^{vy/a}$ mice by dehydroepiandrosterone. Lipids **12:** 409–413.
9. SCHWARTZ, A. G., L. L. PASHKO, E. E. HENDERSON, R. H. TANNEN, M. P. CLEARY, M. ABOU-GHARBIA & D. SWERN. 1983. Dehydroepiandrosterone: Antiobesity and anticarcinogenic agent. Comment. Res. Breast Dis. **3:** 113–130.
10. COLEMAN, D. L., E. H. LEITER & R. W. SCHWIZER. 1982. Therapeutic effects of dehydroepiandrosterone (DHEA) in diabetic mice. Diabetes **31:** 830–833.
11. TANNEN, R. H. & A. G. SCHWARTZ. 1982. Reduced weight gain and delay of Coombs positive hemolytic anemia in NZB mice treated with dehydroepiandrosterone (DHEA). Fed. Proc. **41:** 463.
12. RANIERI, R. & H. R. LEVY. 1970. On the specificity of steroid interactions with mammary glucose 6-phosphate dehydrogenase (Abstr.). Biochemistry **9:** 2233–2243.

13. SCHANTZ, L. M., P. TALALAY & G. B. GORDON. 1989. Mechanism of inhibition of growth of 3T3-L1 fibroblasts and their differentiation to adipocytes by dehydroepiandrosterone and related steroids: Role of glucose-6-phosphate dehydrogenase. Proc. Natl. Acad. Sci. USA **86:** 3852–3856.

14. GARCEA, R., L. DAINO, S. FRASSETTO, P. COZZOLINO, M. E. RIGGOI, M. G. VANNINI, R. PASCALE, L. LENZERINNI, M. M. SIMILE, M. PUDDU & F. FEO. 1988. Reversal by ribo- and deoxyribonucleosides of dehydroepiandrosterone-induced inhibition of enzyme altered foci in the liver of rats subjected to the initiation-selection process of experimental carcinogenesis. Carcinogenesis **9:** 931–938.

15. LEIGHTON, B., A. R. TAGLIAFERRO & E. A. NEWSHOLME. 1987. The effect of dehydroepiandrosterone acetate on liver peroxisomal enzyme activities on male and female rats. J. Nutr. **117:** 1287–1290.

16. HAYASHI, F., H. TAMURA, J. YAMADA, H. KASAI & T. SUGA. 1994. Characteristics of the hepatocarcinogenesis caused by dehydroepiandrosterone, a peroxisome proliferator, in male F-344 rats. Carcinogenesis **15:** 2215–2219.

17. HAWKINS, J. M., W. E. JONES, F. W. BONNER & G. G. GIBSON. 1988. The effect of peroxisome proliferators on microsomal, peroxisomal, and mitochondrial enzyme activities in the liver and kidney. Drug Metab. Rev. **18:** 441–515.

18. REDDY, J. K. & M. S. RAO. 1992. Peroxisome proliferation and hepatocarcinogenesis. IARC Sci. Publ. 225–235.

19. WU, H.-Q., J. MASSET-BROWN, D. J. TWEEDIE, L. MILEWICH, R. A. FRENKEL, C. MARTIN-WIXTROM, R. W. ESTABROOK & R. A. PROUGH. 1989. Induction of microsomal NADPH-cytochrome P-450 reductase and cytochrome P450IVA1 (P-450 laω) by dehydroepiandrosterone in rats: A possible peroxisomal proliferator. Cancer. Res. **49:** 2337–2343.

20. SUNDSETH, S. S., J. A. ALBERTA & D. J. WAXMAN. 1992. Sex-specific growth hormone-regulated transcription of the cytochrome P450 2C11 and 2C12. J. Biol. Chem. **267:** 3907–3914.

21. WAXMAN, D. J. 1991. Rat hepatic P450IIA and P450IIC subfamily expression using catalytic, immunochemical, and molecular probes. Methods Enzymol. **206:** 249–266.

22. PROUGH, R. A., WU, H.-Q. & L. MILEWICH. 1990. Effect of dehydroepiandrosterone on rodent liver microsomal, mitochondrial, and peroxisomal proteins. *In* The Biologic Role of Dehydroepiandrosterone (DHEA). M. Kalimi & W. Regelson, Eds.: 253–279. Walter de Gruyter & Co. Berlin/New York.

23. PROUGH, R. A., S. J. WEBB, H.-Q. WU, D. LAPENSON & D. J. WAXMAN. 1994. Induction of microsomal and peroxisomal enzymes by dehydroepiandrosterone and its reduced metabolite in rats. Cancer. Res. **54:** 2878–2886.

24. HARDWICK, J. P., B.-J. SONG, E. HUBERMAN & F. J. GONZALEZ. 1987. Isolation, complementary DNA sequence, and regulation of rat hepatic lauric acid ω-hydroxylase (cytochrome P450$_{LAω}$). Identification of a new cytochrome P450 gene family. J. Biol. Chem. **262:** 801–810.

25. REDDY, J. K., S. K. GOEL, M. R. NEMALI, J. J. CARRINO, T. G. LAFFLER, M. K. REDDY, S. J. SPERBECK, T. OSUMI, T. HASHIMOTO & N. D. LALWANI. 1986. Transcription regulation of peroxisomal fatty acyl-CoA oxidase and enoyl-CoA hydratase/3-hydroxyacyl-CoA dehydrogenase in rat liver by peroxisome proliferators. Proc. Natl. Acad. Sci USA **83:** 1747–1751.

26. GEARING, K. L., M. GOTTLICHER, M. TEBOUL, E. WIDMARK & J.-A. GUSTAFSSON. 1993. Interaction of the peroxisome-proliferator-activated receptor and retinoid X receptor. Proc. Natl. Acad. Sci USA **90:** 1440–1444.

27. RAM, P. A. & D. J. WAXMAN. 1994. Dehydroepiandrosterone 3-β-sulphate is an endogenous activator of the peroxisome-proliferation pathway: Induction of cytochrome P-450 4A and acyl-CoA oxidase mRNAs in primary rat hepatocyte culture and inhibitory effects of Ca^{2+}-channel blockers. Biochem. J. **301:** 753–758.

28. YAMADA, J., M. SAKUMA & T. SUGA. 1992. Induction of peroxisomal β-oxidation enzymes by dehydroepiandrosterone and its sulfate in primary cultures of rat hepatocytes. Biochim. Biophys. Acta **1160:** 231–236.

29. LEHMANN, J. M., X. K. ZHANG, G. GRAUPNER, M. O. LEE, T. HERMANN, B. HOFFMANN & M. PFAHL. 1993. Formation of retinoid X receptor homodimers leads to repression of T_3 response: Hormonal cross talk by ligand-induced squelching. Mol. Cell Biol. **13:** 7698–7707.

30. GREEN, S. & W. WAHLI. 1994. Peroxisome proliferator-activated receptors: Finding the orphan a home. Mol. Cell Endocrinol. **100:** 149–153.

31. XIAO, G.-H., J. A. PINAIRE, A. D. RODRIGUES & R. A. PROUGH. 1995. Regulation of the *Ah* gene battery via *Ah* receptor-dependent and independent processes in cultured adult rat hepatocytes. Drug Metab. Dispos. **23:** 642–650.

32. LARDY, H., C.-Y. SU, N. KNEER & S. WIELGUS. 1989. Dehydroepiandrosterone induces enzymes that permit thermogenesis and decrease metabolic efficiency. *In* Hormones, Thermogenesis, and Obesity, H. Lardy & F. Stratman, Eds.: 415–426. Elsevier Science Publ. Co. New York.

33. ISSEMANN, I. & S. GREEN. 1990. Activation of a member of the steroid hormone receptor superfamily by peroxisome proliferators. Nature **347:** 645–650.

Does DHEAS Restore Immune Competence in Aged Animals through Its Capacity to Function as a Natural Modulator of Peroxisome Activities?[a]

NINA F. L. SPENCER,[b] MATTHEW E. POYNTER,[b]
JON D. HENNEBOLD,[b] HONG-HUA MU,[b]
AND RAYMOND A. DAYNES,[b,c]

[b]Department of Pathology
University of Utah School of Medicine
Salt Lake City, Utah 84132

[c]Geriatric Research, Education and Clinical Center
Veterans Affairs Medical Center
Salt Lake City, Utah 84112

Optimum function throughout life of an individual's immune system is intimately dependent on the highly regulated production and biologic activities of a well-balanced network of protein cytokines and growth factors. Collectively, these molecules are well established to be involved in the proliferation, differentiation, and survival of the various types of lymphoid cells that constitute the mammalian immune system.[1,2] Their pleiotropic biologic activities, however, extend well beyond cell types associated with the immune system and include control over a diverse array of cellular and physiologic processes that occur in many distinct tissues and organ systems of the body.[1,2]

Age, stress, autoimmune diseases, and many infectious agents create conditions that can subvert normal host defenses through their capacity to detrimentally remodel the host's highly coordinated cytokine network by effectively altering either the production of or the cellular responses to these protein molecules. Some of these conditions can actually elicit, without exogenous stimulation, a constitutive production of certain cytokine species by hyperactive lymphoid cells. This dysregulation in gene expression results in constant exposure of all cytokine responsive cells within the vicinity of the cytokine-producing cells to the modulatory activities of the abnormally produced and secreted molecules. Dysregulations in cytokine production, therefore, can lead to an altered state of cellular reactivity to exogenous agents or antigens and may result in a lowered capacity to elicit protective types of immune and inflammatory effector responses. Overexpression of some cytokines may also lead to increased autoantibody production which may ultimately proceed to the development of autoimmune disease.

Steroids represent a class of small molecular weight bioactive molecules derived from cholesterol, many of which have long been known for their modulatory effects

[a]This work was supported by National Institutes of Health grants CA25917 and AG11475 and by DVA Medical Research Funds.
[b]Address for correspondence: R. A. Daynes, Department of Pathology, University of Utah School of Medicine, 50 N. Medical Drive, Salt Lake City, UT 84132.

on lymphocytes, macrophages, and other cell types associated with the mammalian immune system.[3] Dehydroepiandrosterone (DHEA) is a natural steroid which, in addition to being the precursor of sex steroids, has been reported by many investigators to possess immunomodulatory and immunocorrective activities.[4-13] The immunoregulatory effects of DHEA are most strikingly demonstrated in experiments employing conditions under which the host is in some way immunologically compromised.[10-12]

Before being secreted into the plasma by the adrenals, most newly synthesized DHEA in humans is efficiently sulfated to DHEA-3β-sulfate (DHEAS). DHEAS is the dominant species of steroid in the plasma of humans, yet its concentration throughout the life of an individual is known to fluctuate greatly (FIG. 1). High levels of DHEAS are present in the plasma of the late-term human fetus and in newborn infants.[14] These high circulating levels of DHEAS dramatically decline over the first 6 months of neonatal life.[14] Low plasma levels of this steroid are found in both males and females until adrenarche, which usually begins at 6–8 years of age. Plasma DHEAS levels then rise dramatically to maximum levels of between 1 and 6 μg/ml

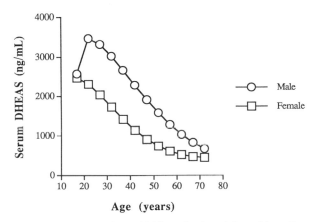

FIGURE 1. Age-associated decline in DHEAS production. Adapted from Orentreich *et al.*[15]

near the end of the second decade of life.[15] After the peak level of adrenal DHEA production is reached, adrenal DHEAS output gradually and consistently decreases. Circulating DHEAS levels ultimately decrease 80–90% by the age of 70 or later.[15-17] Interestingly, the functional competency of the immune system is less suited for optimum protective activity in very young or very old individuals, which represent times in life when endogenous DHEAS production levels are at their lowest. Analysis of plasma DHEAS levels in a large group of elderly human volunteers has established a very positive correlation between DHEAS levels and general health.[15,18] In other historical studies, the quantitation of mean circulating DHEAS levels in numerous mammalian species indicates a direct correlation between serum DHEAS levels and the average lifespan of the species under evaluation.[19]

We report an overview of the findings of our and others' laboratories describing a variety of age-associated abnormalities in both inducible and constitutive cytokine production. The possible roles of these agents in creating the senescent immune system are presented, as are the possible implications of a dysregulated cytokine network in altering the function of many organ systems distinct from the immune system. Our discussion then moves to the restorative effects of supplemental DHEAS therapy with regard to its ability to correct the dysregulated expression of cytokine genes in aged animals and the implications of this correction on the pathophysiology of the aging process. Finally, our current hypothesis of the possible mechanisms by which DHEAS exerts its diverse array of biochemical effects is discussed.

DYSREGULATION IN THE MECHANISMS THAT CONTROL THE PRODUCTION OF CERTAIN CYTOKINE SPECIES CONTRIBUTES TO THE IMMUNOSENESCENT PHENOTYPE

Dysregulation of Inducible Cytokine Production with Aging

Under normal conditions highly regulated and coordinated mechanisms exist to control the rate of cytokine production by lymphoid and nonlymphoid cells. Collectively, the cytokines serve as transiently expressed intercellular signaling molecules which are involved in providing microenvironment-specific information to the multitude of cellular elements linked directly or indirectly to the immune system.[2] Cytokines also provide biochemical information to most of the body's cell and organ systems.[2] The mechanisms that regulate cellular proliferation, the acquisition or loss of effector activities, differentiation processes, and even the resistance or susceptibility to apoptosis are directly mediated through cytokine effects.[2] These molecules, which are generally restricted in their production to the consequences of a specific cellular activation event, act principally through autocrine or paracrine pathways to influence the physiologic activities of producing as well as neighboring cells. Cytokine influences are only rarely facilitated via endocrine pathways.[2]

An abnormality or dysregulation in the inducible synthesis and secretion of certain cytokine species was observed with a number of disease states.[20–22] Numerous investigators have demonstrated that the capacity of activated lymphocytes to synthesize and secrete interleukin (IL)-2, IL-3, and granulocyte/monocyte colony-stimulating factor (GM-CSF) is significantly reduced in cells derived from aged animals and humans, whereas the capacity of these same cells to produce IL-4, IL-5, IL-6, IL-10, and gamma interferon (IFN-γ) is markedly increased.[12,23–27] It has been hypothesized that the profound qualitative and quantitative changes in activation-driven cytokine responses may explain many of the altered effector responses observed in aged individuals, including changes associated with the well-described declines in cellular and humoral immunity.[12,28,29]

Constitutive Cytokine Dysregulation with Aging

Our laboratory has observed that lymphoid cells derived from the spleen and certain lymph nodes of aged animals spontaneously secrete significant levels of IL-6, IL-10, and IFN-γ when placed into tissue culture without added stimulants.[13,30,31] IL-2 or IL-4 are not produced by these same cell populations, indicating that the presence of IL-6, IL-10, and IFN-γ is not an artifact associated with nonspecific cellular stimulation caused by the *in vitro* conditions employed.[31] The dysregulated production of IL-6 is so great that the presence of cytokine can readily be detected in the plasma of aged animals.[13,32] IL-10 and IFN-γ cannot be directly detected in serum or plasma samples from aged animals, but abnormal production is easily observed following *in vitro* culture or by using molecular techniques to quantitate cytokine messenger RNA levels.[30,31] Finally, human studies have further confirmed that IL-6 is detectable in the plasma of aged donors but absent in young individuals.[13,32]

IL-6 is a pleiotropic cytokine that plays a critical role in the generation of the acute phase and inflammatory responses.[33] In the immune system, it appears to be involved in T-cell activation, growth, and differentiation and to induce both B-cell proliferation and maturation.[33] Furthermore, analysis of the IL-6 gene knockout mouse established that this cytokine is also important to the development of the mucosal immune system.[34] The regulation of IL-6 gene expression is complex, and usually little or no IL-6 protein is produced spontaneously. With age, however, this tight regulation seems to be relaxed, and measurable levels of IL-6 appear in the plasma in the absence of an overt inflammatory stimulus. Thus, aging seems to represent a condition in which IL-6 responsive cell types in the body are relegated to undertaking their normal physiologic processes under the continual influence of this cytokine. Aberrant outcomes, such as a persistent acute phase response, continual nonspecific B-cell stimulation, or enhanced osteoclast activity resulting in greater rates of bone resorption, represent a few of the pathologic conditions that may result on the basis of the well-described bioactivities of this cytokine.[33] These as well as other cell and organ system changes that can be directly induced by IL-6 are commonly observed in aged individuals.

IL-10 is a multifunctional cytokine with strong immunomodulatory properties[35] that appears to be constitutively expressed in old age and may therefore be continuously exerting its influences on all IL-10 responsive cell types.[31] IL-10 is reportedly produced by activated T cells, B cells, and macrophages, although T-cell production of this cytokine has been studied most extensively.[35] IL-10 possesses a broad range of reported activities, including the capacity to affect numerous physiologic functions in many different cell types and organ systems.[35] For example, many age-associated changes in T-cell, macrophage, and B-cell functions that define the immunosenescent phenotype[28,36] may be closely linked to dysregulated control over endogenous IL-10 production. IL-10 can directly inhibit IL-2 gene expression by activated T cells,[37,38] reduce the expression of Class II major histocompatibility complex (MHC) molecules on monocytes/macrophages,[39] and depress B7 costimulatory molecule expression on activated macrophages.[40] Previous studies also demonstrated that IL-10 can inhibit stimulated macrophage production of numerous cytokines and alter antibody production by conventional B cells in response to either T-independent or T-dependent antigens.[41,42] Some of these conditions are similar to those that occur "naturally" as a consequence of aging.

We recently determined that the constitutive IL-10 production observed in lymphocyte populations isolated from aged animals was due to B-cell overactivity.[31] A subpopulation of B cells, termed CD5[+] B cells, are major producers of IL-10 following cellular activation.[43] Interestingly, absolute numbers of CD5[+] B cells in an individual increase with advancing age.[44–46]

It has been hypothesized that CD5[+] B cells may represent a second B-cell lineage which arises early in embryonic development from committed stem cell precursors and that renewal of bone marrow precursors for this cell type terminates shortly after birth.[45,47] B cells derived from this developmental pathway have been designated B1 cells and have now been further categorized into one of two subpopulations, B1a and B1b cells.[45,47] The only reported difference between these subpopulations of B cells is that B1a cells express the CD5 cell surface molecule whereas B1b cells do not.[45,47] No functional distinction between B1a and B1b cells has yet been identified, and both populations of lymphocytes have been implicated in the production of autoreactive antibodies.[48]

It has been well established that the presence of autoantibodies such as antithyroglobulin, antithyroid peroxidase, antigastric parietal cell, and antiadrenal cell antibodies increases in the elderly.[49,50] The age-associated elevation in autoantibody production may be attributed to the increase in B1 cells in aged individuals. Observed increases in B1 cells also occur in several clinical conditions other than aging such as rheumatoid arthritis,[51,52] systemic lupus erythematosus,[53] and cancer.[54,55] Each clinical condition in which B1 cells are increased closely correlates with increased levels of autoreactive antibodies as well as the B-cell growth factor IL-10.[51–55]

We recently ascertained that unstimulated lymphoid cells from aged mice spontaneously produce significant amounts of IFN-γ. This molecule represents a cytokine with highly pleiotropic activities that may contribute to age-associated depression in cellular and organ system function. IFN-γ can upregulate the expression of Class II MHC molecules in numerous cell types[56–59] which associate with the pathogenesis of autoimmune diseases such as rheumatoid arthritis,[60] insulin-dependent diabetes mellitus,[61,62] and multiple sclerosis.[63] IFN-γ can markedly depress the responsiveness of many cell types to a variety of growth factors including epidermal growth factor, platelet-derived growth factor, and erythropoietin.[64,65] Under conditions in which IFN-γ influences growth factor responsive cell types *in vivo,* alterations in wound healing rates, erythrocyte development, and other changes in hematopoiesis are expected. IFN-γ can also exert its modulatory effects indirectly via its synergistic activities on the stimulated production of inflammatory cytokines such as tumor necrosis factor (TNF), IL-1, and IL-6.[65,66] Normal physiologic activities promoted by these cytokines may develop into pathologic consequences under conditions in which their levels of induced production are being chronically augmented.

Our recent studies on the age-associated influences of IFN-γ *in vivo* have demonstrated that lymphocytes from aged animals lose their ability to respond to a very important cytokine, transforming growth factor (TGF)-β. TGF-β possesses a reduced capacity to inhibit inducible cytokine production by lymphoid cells from aged animals. It is appreciated that IFN-γ can antagonize many reported activities of TGF-β *in vitro,* including those believed to be essential for the stimulation of bone formation by osteoblasts.[67,68] IFN-γ can promote bone resorption and inhibit bone formation in *in vitro* and *in vivo* models, causing a net decrease in bone turnover.[69–74] The inhibitory effect of constitutively produced IFN-γ on TGF-β activities may represent a contributing factor to age-associated osteoporosis.

During our investigations into the effects of IFN-γ in aging we also observed that the inducible expression of the integrin αM290/β7, an adhesion molecule involved in the activities of T lymphocytes residing within the intraepithelial spaces of the gut, is decreased in aged animals. Others have established that the expression of αM290 by activated T cells requires the costimulatory activity of TGF-β.[75,76] Thus, a constitutive presence of IFN-γ in aged animals appears to interfere with the ability of T cells from these animals to respond normally to the regulatory activities of TGF-β, thereby decreasing αM290 expression. This hypothesis was experimentally confirmed by treating aged animals *in vivo* with anti-IFN-γ antibody and demonstrating the reacquisition of normal cellular responsiveness to TGF-β. As a sidelight to the central focus of the experiment, T lymphocytes taken from aged animals treated with the anti-IFN-γ antibody demonstrated near normal capacity to produce IL-2 and IL-4 in response to stimulation. The overexpression of IL-10 in old age, however, was not altered in animals treated with anti-IFN-γ.

As IL-6, IL-10, and IFN-γ can each exert profound modulatory activities on a wide range of target cell types, it is easy to envision how their dysregulated production *in vivo* may contribute to the aging process. Depressions in the ability of the immune system to recognize and respond to foreign antigens and a concomitant increase in the abnormal production of autoreactive antibodies are but two of many pathophysiologic changes that are predicted to occur with an abnormal expression of these cytokines. Age-associated conditions that may correlate with a dysregulated control over the expression of at least one of these cytokines include immunosenescence,[13,31,77] breast cancer,[78] B-cell lymphomas,[33,79] osteoporosis,[33,67,68,80,81] anemia,[64] autoimmunity,[22,33] and depressions in wound healing rates (FIG. 2).[82] Therapeutic

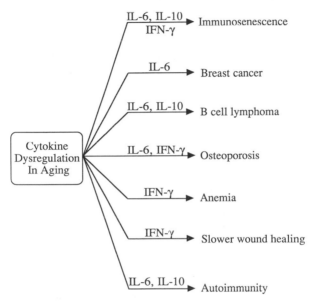

FIGURE 2. Dysregulation in the cytokine network as evidenced by constitutive expression of certain cytokines may be responsible for several age-associated diseases.

interventions designed to reestablish normal control over the inducible production of those cytokines which become dysregulated with age should significantly enhance the fidelity of many physiologic processes, especially those that are compromised by the offending cytokine species.

SUPPLEMENTAL THERAPY WITH DHEAS CORRECTS DYSREGULATED CYTOKINE GENE EXPRESSION ASSOCIATED WITH OLD AGE

A progressive decline in the amount of DHEA and DHEAS produced each day takes place as an individual ages beyond young adulthood.[15] Based on the findings that these two steroids, or their downstream metabolites, are involved in the complex mechanisms that regulate the activities of immune cells, the well-described age-associated depressions in immunocompetence could be directly linked to an individual's plasma levels of DHEA and DHEAS. We previously reported that aged animals provided with oral supplementation of DHEAS (2–4 mg/kg/day) reacquired a reasonably normal state of immunocompetence within days of treatment initiation.[12] Normal patterns of inducible cytokines were restored in treated animals, and corrective changes in the cytokine phenotype extended to cells residing in all secondary lymphoid organs tested. An example, in which IL-2 production was evaluated, is illustrated in FIGURE 3.[12] More importantly, DHEAS-supplemented aged animals regained the ability to elicit strong humoral and cellular immune responses.[12] Other investigators have now confirmed this work and have extended our findings to demonstrate the generation of antibody responses to bacterial polysaccharides[83] and distinct protein antigens in DHEAS-supplemented animals.[9,84] DHEAS supplementation appears to enhance immune responses, especially antibody production, via its capacity to promote the normal development of germinal centers in secondary lymphoid organs following vaccination.[9]

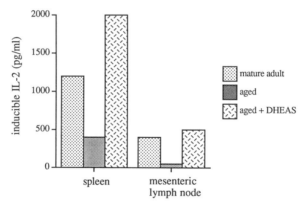

FIGURE 3. Supplemental DHEAS treatment of aged mice upregulates the capacity to produce IL-2. Splenocytes and mesenteric lymph node cells were collected from mature adult (6–12-week-old), aged (76–96-week-old), and aged (76–96-week-old) animals provided with supplemental DHEAS treatment (minimum of 3 weeks' treatment at 4 mg/kg/day). Lymphoid cells were activated with anti-CD3ε. Culture supernatants were quantitatively analyzed for the presence of IL-2 by capture ELISA.

Shortly after aged animals are placed on DHEAS supplementation or within 24 hours of systemic administration of DHEA or DHEAS at a dose of 4 mg/kg, significant changes result in restoration of near-normal control over the production of cytokines IL-6, IL-10, and IFN-γ (FIG. 4). Animals given chronic DHEAS supplementation retain normal control over cytokine expression and a normal phenotype of immunocompetence for as long as steroid treatment persists. Unfortunately, we have not yet determined if or how quickly aged animals taken off DHEAS supplementation might revert to the immunosenescent phenotype. There is little doubt, however, that DHEAS supplementation of aged rodents results in nearly complete restoration of the regulatory processes involved in normal control over the synthesis and secretion of many cytokines.

Further support for the argument that DHEAS supplementation is beneficial in aged animals comes from the finding that steroid-treated animals exhibited beneficial changes in pathologies that could be attributed to the dysregulated expression of

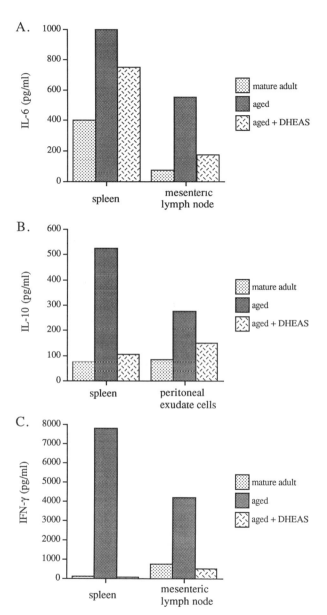

FIGURE 4. Supplemental DHEAS treatment of aged mice restores normal control over unregulated production of IL-6, IL-10, and IFN-γ. Splenocytes, mesenteric lymph node cells, and peritoneal exudate cells were collected from mature adult (6–12-week-old), aged (76–96-week-old), and aged (76–96-week-old) animals provided chronic DHEAS treatment (minimum of 3 weeks' treatment at 4 mg/kg/day). Supernatants from unstimulated cell cultures were quantitatively analyzed for IL-6, IL-10, or IFN-γ by capture ELISA.

IL-6, IFN-γ, or IL-10 *in vivo*.[13,31] Age-associated increases in the serum titers of IgM and IgG tissue-reactive autoantibodies were lowered in supplemented aged animals, as were elevated levels of antiphosphatidylcholine antibodies.[12,31] Consistent with these findings was the observation that age-associated increases in B1 cells in the peritoneal cavity, the cell type perceived to be responsible for autoantibody production, were reduced to near mature adult levels in animals following DHEAS treatment.[12,31] In addition, lymphoid cells from DHEAS-treated animals regained near normal responsiveness to the modulatory influences of TGF-β, and the activation inducible expression of the αM290/β7 integrin was also restored (Mu *et al.,* unpublished observations). These findings may help explain our recent observation that mucosal immune responses in aged animals can be induced following treatment with DHEAS, but not in untreated aged animals.[85] Collectively, the findings made in DHEAS-supplemented animals strongly suggest a linkage between age-associated depressions in the capacity to develop immune responses to foreign antigens, the dysregulated expression of certain cytokine species, the presence of autoantibodies, and age-associated depression in circulating DHEA and DHEAS levels.

DHEAS AS A NATURAL REGULATOR OF PEROXISOME ACTIVITY: A POSSIBLE MECHANISM TO EXPLAIN THE IMMUNOMODULATORY EFFECTS OF THIS STEROID *IN VIVO*

Peroxisomes are single-membrane, cytoplasmic organelles containing no DNA. These organelles are involved in numerous essential intracellular biochemical processes including antioxidant activities, cholesterol and bile acid synthesis, prostaglandin metabolism, β-oxidative metabolism of very long chain fatty acids, and the carnitinylation of fatty acids to enable their transport into the mitochondria for further breakdown.[86]

It was recently demonstrated that the chronic administration of DHEA to rodents in their feed caused significant changes in liver morphology and histopathology. These changes were caused by a massive increase in peroxisome number and volume as well as an upregulation of peroxisomal enzyme activity in this organ.[87-89] Rao *et al.*[87] reported a 200% increase in rat liver weight and a fivefold increase in the total volume of liver peroxisomes in hepatocytes following dietary administration of DHEA (0.4% w/w) for 2 weeks. Prolonged DHEA treatment protocols were responsible for significant enhancement of the peroxisomal enzyme activities associated with fatty acid β-oxidation, including acyl-CoA oxidase (the rate-limiting enzymatic component of peroxisomal fatty acid metabolism) and enoyl-CoA hydratase/3-hydroxyacyl-CoA dehydrogenase.[87-90] Dietary DHEA administration to rodents also causes an increase in some non-peroxisomal hepatic enzymes including cytochrome P450A and glutathione-S-transferase.[91,92]

A wide range of structurally dissimilar exogenous compounds and a small number of naturally occurring endogenous compounds can upregulate cellular peroxisome number, volume, and enzyme activity.[93] Control of cellular peroxisomal activity is now appreciated to be mediated by the activation of specific cytosolic receptors and their subsequent binding to appropriate hormone response elements on DNA. This unique subclass of intracellular receptors has been termed peroxisome proliferator-activated receptors (PPARs). PPARs are members of the steroid hormone family of receptors and are converted to active transcription factor subunits following activation by a diverse range of natural and xenobiotic compounds, collectively termed "peroxisome proliferators."[93,94] Several different isoforms of PPARs have now been cloned and sequenced from frogs, humans, and rodents.[95]

Each species of PPAR is differentially expressed in discrete tissues, and each species of PPAR is preferentially activated by a distinct set of "ligand" molecules.[95,96]

The basic structural requirement for peroxisome proliferators to activate PPARs was demonstrated to include an anionic group attached to a hydrophobic backbone, such as is found in DHEAS.[97,98] Yamada *et al.*[99] recently demonstrated that rat liver hepatocytes contain a high affinity (K_d 72 nM) DHEAS binding cytosolic protein.[99] These investigators evaluated many known peroxisome proliferators for their capacity to inhibit DHEAS binding to the cytosolic protein complex. Only WY-14,643 was able to effectively compete for DHEAS binding. Cultured hepatocytes exhibit markedly increased peroxisomal β-oxidation activity following direct *in vitro* exposure to DHEAS and to a much lesser extent when treated with DHEA.[98] The low level of DHEA-mediated enhancement in β-oxidation activity appears to be due to passive diffusion of the hydrophobic steroid DHEA through the hepatocyte plasma membrane, followed by endogenous sulfation of DHEA in the hepatocyte.[100-102] Intracellular DHEAS, the biologically active molecule, can then activate the appropriate PPAR.[98,99] Additionally, a number of natural and related metabolites of DHEA including 17-hydroxy- 7-hydroxy, and 7-keto derivatives of this steroid may also function as peroxisome modulators following their sulfation at the 3β-position.

Feeding normal adult animals pharmacologic doses of DHEA causes dramatic changes in the liver and probably generates large amounts of intracellular hepatocyte DHEAS.[89] We believe that the dramatic rise in hepatocyte peroxisome content and liver pathology seen in DHEA-fed animals may reflect abnormal overexpression of a normal tissue regulatory process.

Normally, most DHEA in the circulation exists in the sulfated form which is not capable of directly diffusing across the cell membranes of most cell types. The transport mechanisms used to move DHEAS into the cytoplasm of cells may represent a tightly regulated process. Appropriate biochemical mechanisms exist that allow tissue-localized desulfation of extracellular DHEAS in particular microenvironments followed by diffusion of DHEA across the plasma membrane and its intracellular resulfation in those cell types possessing the appropriate sulfotransferase activity.[102] A low density lipoprotein (LDL) receptor-mediated uptake of DHEA-fatty acid ester-LDL complexes or even direct active transport mechanisms for DHEAS directly across plasma membranes of some cell types have also been reported.[103,104]

Evidence supporting the concept that DHEAS may be playing a physiologic role in regulating peroxisomal activity has demonstrated that the liver of aged rats has reduced numbers of peroxisomes and reduced peroxisomal β-oxidation activity.[105] Plasma membrane rigidity is also appreciated to increase in most cell types with advancing age, a condition directly linked to increased fatty acid chain length and degree of fatty acid saturation.[106,107] In addition, Laganiere and Fernandes[108] recently demonstrated that membrane phospholipid content of long chain fatty acids increases with age in various lymphoid organs of Fisher rats. Similar types of age-associated increases in cellular phospholipid long chain fatty acid composition have been observed by other investigators as well.[109,110] The well described age-associated decrease in circulating DHEAS concentrations and the concomitant decrease in peroxisomal enzyme activities may be partially responsible for the increase in plasma membrane content of long chain fatty acids.

Alterations in cell membrane composition with advancing age, including increases in long chain fatty acids and the resultant decrease in membrane fluidity, may significantly contribute to the decline in a host's immune function observed in old age. Many lymphoid cell activities can be directly altered by changing cell membrane phospholipid composition. This can be accomplished experimentally by employing nutritional supplementation replete with specific fatty acids. For example, depression in lymphocyte proliferative responses was demonstrated following the dietary supplementation of animals with linoleic acid (18:2).[111,112] This may be due to an accumulation in membrane arachidonic acid (20:4) which is known to occur following elevations in phospholipid content of linoleic acid and its metabolites.[113] As a result of the enzymatic action of phospholipase A_2 upon membrane phospholipids, arachidonic acid is freely liberated from the membrane and is readily converted into bioactive lipids including the prostaglandins and leukotrienes.[114] Prostaglandins are well known modulators of lymphocyte proliferative responses and lymphokine production, whereas leukotrienes are mediators of the inflammatory response.[115]

Modifications of cellular phospholipid fatty acid composition can also result in alterations in the physical properties of cell membranes, including membrane fluidity and capacity of phospholipid and sphinyomyelin metabolites to serve as second messengers. The decrease in cell membrane fluidity with age[106,107] and the increase in cholesterol/phospholipid ratios can affect the activity of multiple receptor systems, membrane-associated enzymes, and signal transduction processes.[106,116] Lymphocytes incubated in the presence of fully saturated fatty acids acquire reduced membrane fluidity which is correlated with a depression in proliferation, reduced IL-2 production, and decreased IL-2 receptor expression following activation by a mitogen *in vitro*.[117,118] Inhibition of lymphocyte activities by fatty acids, however, does not require the generation of prostaglandins or leukotrienes, because the effect is independent of eicosanoid synthesis.[119] The consequences of decreased membrane fluidity caused by exogenous long chain fatty acid supplementation results in a phenotype similar to that observed in lymphocytes from aged mice.

Lipid second messengers are signaling molecules generated directly from the components of the cell phospholipid bilayer via the actions of cellular enzymes, such as the phospholipases, and include diacylglycerol and inositol 1,4,5,-trisphosphate which activate cellular enzymes necessary for certain proteins (i.e., cytokines) to be produced. It has been demonstrated that T lymphocytes obtained from aged rodents possess a reduced capacity to produce and respond to IL-2 following mitogenic activation because of a defect in the generation of specific second messengers.[120] It is unclear if this is a result of changes in the actual components necessary for the creation of transmembrane signals or of a reduced capacity of the enzymes to interact with the appropriate constituents of the plasma membrane. The correction of the age-associated deficiencies in immune function by DHEAS treatment may be mediated by restoration of normal peroxisomal activities in the treated recipients. This normalization would lead to changes in fatty acid content of membrane phospholipids and membrane fluidity, resulting in the restoration of optimal signal transduction processes.

The elimination of abnormally expressed cytokines in aged animals following their supplementation with DHEAS may be linked to the ability of this steroid to act as a modulator of peroxisomal activity, albeit indirectly. It is well documented that intestinal barrier function declines with advancing age,[121] a change that leads to increases in the ability of endotoxin to access the systemic circulation. Intestinal permeability increases have even been reported to allow the translocation of enteric bacteria, as evidenced by infection of the mesenteric lymph nodes.[122] It is our hypothesis that low grade, continual exposure of lymphocytes and macrophages to endotoxin serves as a stimulus for the constitutive cytokine expression observed in the aged. Abnormally produced IL-6 and IL-10 may result from direct exposure of B cells and macrophages to lipopolysaccharide,[123] while the presence of IFN-γ may represent a secondary consequence of IL-12 actions.[124]

The central issue, therefore, may actually revolve around those factors that facilitate the increased intestinal permeability of gut contents. It was recently demonstrated that platelets from aged humans and animals possess increased susceptibility to aggregation following their exposure to normal platelet agonists.[125] These effects may be due to changes in platelet membrane composition, for it is known that reduced platelet membrane fluidity is associated with greater exposure of membrane receptors to the extracellular environment which may be responsible for the increased susceptibility to activation and aggregation.[126] Platelet hyperactivity can promote the development of microthrombi followed by occlusion of blood flow within the microcapillaries of the skin, lung, and gut, resulting in the likelihood of ischemia reperfusion-mediated injury. Breakdown of the intestinal mucosa would follow, leading to endotoxin entry into the afferent lymphatic drainage and systemic circulation. Our laboratory demonstrated that the dysregulation of IL-6, IL-10, and IFN-γ production associated with aging is most pronounced in mesenteric lymph nodes and spleen (FIG. 4)[13,31] (Mu *et al.*, unpublished observations) consistent with the intestine being the source of initial cell stimulation. DHEAS, via its capacity to enhance peroxisome activity in aged tissues, would lead to normalization of fatty acid metabolism and an increase in antioxidant potential. Modifications to platelet membrane composition may eliminate platelet hyperactivity and secondarily reduce the age-associated enhancement of gut permeability. Alternatively, increased gut permeability may be due to a deficiency in peroxisomal activities in gut epithelial cells, activities required for the maintenance of a structurally intact epithelial barrier.

Support for our model of DHEAS being able to reverse immunosenescence via its influences on peroxisomal activities comes from the results of a recently completed experiment which demonstrated that the administration of low doses of WY-14,643 to aged animals partially corrected the abnormalities in inducible and constitutive cytokine expression (FIG. 5). The doses of WY-14,643 provided to the aged animals was less than 5% of the doses employed in studies designed to evaluate the ability of this drug to induce peroxisome proliferation.[127]

It was recently reported that changes in lymphocyte membrane fatty acid composition caused by chronically feeding animals a corn oil-rich diet were associated with decreased sensitivity to Fas-mediated apoptosis through a reduction of Fas gene expression.[128] This finding may account for the increased numbers and activities of B1 lymphocytes found in most elderly as well as in individuals with certain autoimmune conditions. These autoreactive B cells have been directly implicated in the production of self-reactive antibodies and appear to be significant contributors to the pathophysiology of aging and autoimmune disease-associated clinical conditions. In our hands, DHEAS administration to old mice reduced B1 cell numbers,[31] greatly depressed titers of autoreactive antibodies, and fully corrected most of the immune deficiencies associated with immunosenescence.[12,13,129]

Collectively, the published studies describing DHEAS influences on cell peroxisome activity and fatty acid metabolism provide the data for formulating an attractive hypothesis for the most afferent biochemical site by which DHEA functions to maintain normal immune homeostasis. We believe that DHEAS is facilitating these beneficial influences on the immune system through its capacity to control normal peroxisome activities which, in turn, regulate the fatty acid composition of membrane phospholipids and sphingomyelins in lymphocyte and macrophage membranes. The effects of DHEAS on peroxisome function in aging might represent the elusive linchpin needed to provide investigators with a cohesive explanation for the diverse biologic activities of this steroid.

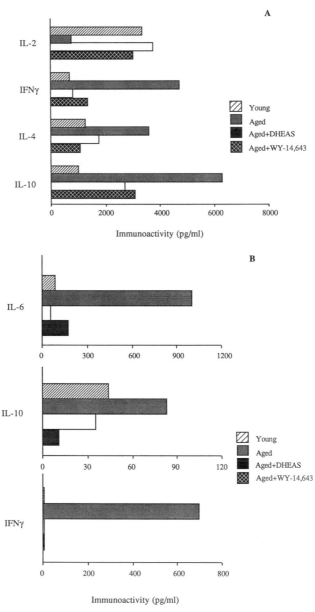

FIGURE 5. DHEAS may function to reverse immunosenescence by its capacity to modulate peroxisome activities. Splenocytes were collected from mature adult (8-week-old), aged (104-week-old), and aged (104-week-old) animals provided with DHEAS (1-week) or WY-14,643 (1-week) treatment. Both compounds were supplied at doses between 4 and 8 mg/kg/day. Cells were stimulated with anti-CD3ε (FIG. 5A) for 24 hours or left unstimulated (FIG. 5B). Culture supernatants were quantitatively analyzed for various cytokines by capture ELISA.

REFERENCES

1. PAUL, W. E. & R. A. SEDER. 1994. Cell **76:** 241–251.
2. VILCEK, J. & J. LE. 1994. Immunology of cytokines: An introduction. *In* The Cytokine Handbook. A. Thomson, Ed.: 1–19. Academic Press Inc. San Diego.
3. CUPPS, T. R. & A. S. FAUCI. 1982. Immunol. Rev. **65:** 133–155.
4. LORIA, R. M., W. REGELSON & D. A. PADGETT. 1990. Immune response facilitation and resistance to virus and bacterial infections with dehydroepiandrosterone (DHEA). *In* The Biologic Role of Dehydroepiandrosterone (DHEA). M. Kalimi & W. Regelson, Ed.: 107–130. Walter de Gruyter. New York.
5. LORIA, R. M. & D. A. PADGETT. 1992. Arch. Virol. **127:** 103–115.
6. REGELSON, W., R. LORIA & M. KALIMI. 1994. Ann. N.Y. Acad. Sci. **719:** 553–562.
7. PADGETT, D. A. & R. M. LORIA. 1994. J. Immunol. **153:** 1544–1552.
8. MORFIN, R. & G. COURCHAY. 1994. J. Steroid Biochem. Mol. Biol. **50:** 91–100.
9. CAFFREY, R. F., Z. F. KAPASI, S. T. HALEY, J. G. TEW & A. K. SZAKAL. 1994. Adv. Exp. Med. Biol. **355:** 225–229.
10. ARANEO, B. A., J. SHELBY, G.-Z. LI, W. KU & R. A. DAYNES. 1993. Arch. Surg. **128:** 318–325.
11. DAYNES, R. A., D. J. DUDLEY & B. A. ARANEO. 1990. Eur. J. Immunol. **20:** 793–802.
12. DAYNES, R. A. & B. A. ARANEO. 1992. Aging: Immunol. & Infect. Dis. **3:** 135–154.
13. DAYNES, R. A., B. A. ARANEO, W. B. ERSHLER, C. MALONEY, G.-Z. LI & S.-Y. RYU. 1993. J. Immunol. **150:** 5219–5230.
14. MEIKLE, W. A., R. A. DAYNES & B. A. ARANEO. 1991. Adrenal androgen secretion and biologic effects. *In* Endocrinology and Metabolism Clinics of North America. New Aspects of Adrenal Cortical Disease. D. H. Nelson, Ed.: 381–400. W. B. Saunders Co. Philadelphia.
15. ORENTREICH, N., J. L. BRIND, R. L. RIZER & J. H. VOGELMAN. 1984. J. Clin. Endocrinol. Metab. **59:** 551–555.
16. MELDRUM, D. R., B. J. DAVIDSON, I. V. TATARYN & H. L. JUDD. 1981. Obstet. Gynecol. **57:** 624–628.
17. MONTANINI, V. M., M. SIMONI, G. CHIOSSI, G. F. BARAGHINI, A. VERLARDO, E. BARALD & P. MARRAMA. 1988. Horm. Res. **29:** 1–6.
18. RUDMAN, D., K. R. SHETTY & D. E. MATTSON. 1990. J. Am. Geriatr. Soc. **38:** 421–427.
19. LOPEZ, A. 1984. Metabolic and endocrine factors in aging. *In* Risk Factors for Senility. H. Rothschild, Ed.: 205–219. Oxford University Press. New York.
20. HIRANO, T., T. MATSUDA, M. TURNER, N. MIYASKA, G. BUCHAN, B. TANG, K. SATO, M. SHIMUZU, R. MAINE, M. FELDMAN & T. KISHIMOTO. 1988. Eur. J. Immunol. **18:** 1797–1801.
21. HORII, Y., A. MURAGUCHI, M. IWANO, T. MATSUDA, T. HIRAYAMA, H. YAMADA, Y. FUJII, K. DOHI, I. H., Y. OHMOTO, K. YOSHIZAKI, T. HIRAMO & T. KISHIMOTO. 1989. J. Immunol. **143:** 3949–3955.
22. LLORENTE, L., Y. RICHAUD-PATIN, R. FIOR, J. ALCOCER-VARELA, J. WIJDENES, B. M. FOURRIER, P. GALANAUD & D. EMILIE. 1994. Arthritis Rheum. **37:** 1647–1655.
23. NAGEL, J. E., R. K. CHOPRA, F. J. CHREST, M. T. MCCOY, E. L. SCHNEIDER, N. J. HOLBROOK & W. H. ADLER. 1988. J. Clin. Invest. **81:** 1096–1102.
24. GILLIS, S., R. KOZAK, M. DURANTE & M. E. WEKSLER. 1981. J. Clin. Invest. **67:** 937–942.
25. ERNST, D. N., M. V. HOBBS, B. E. TORBETT, A. L. GLASEBROOK, M. A. REHSE, K. BOTTOMLY, K. HAYAKAWA, R. R. HARDY & W. O. WEIGLE. 1990. J. Immunol. **145:** 1295–12302.
26. NAGELKERKEN, L., A. HERTOGH-HUIJBREGTS, R. DOBBER & A. DRAGER. 1991. Eur. J. Immunol. **21:** 273–281.
27. WEKSLER, M. & T. H. HUTTEROTH. 1974. J. Clin. Invest. **53:** 99–104.
28. THOMAN, M. L. & W. O. WEIGLE. 1989. Adv. Immunol. **46:** 221–261.
29. SCHWAB, R., C. A. WAITERS & M. E. WEKSLER. 1989. Semin. Oncol. **16:** 20–27.
30. LI, G. Z., N. F. L. SPENCER, B. A. ARANEO & R. A. DAYNES. 1994. Cytokine abnormalities in aging: Possible linkage to losses in adrenal androgen production. *In* Experimen-

tal Biology 94. W. J. WHELAN, Ed.: 4355. Federation of American Societies for Experimental Biology. Anaheim, CA.

31. SPENCER, N. F. L., S. D. NORTON, L. L. HARRISON, G. Z. LI & R. A. DAYNES. Exp. Gerontol. In press.

32. ERSHLER, W. B., W. H. SUN, N. BINKLEY, S. GRAVENSTEIN, M. J. VOLK, G. KAMOSKE, R. G. KLOPP, E. B. ROECKER, R. A. DAYNES & R. WEINDRUCH. 1993. Lymphokine and Cytokine Res. **12:** 225–230.

33. HIRANO, T. Interleukin-6. 1994. *In* A. Thomson, Ed.: 145–168. The Cytokine Handbook. Academic Press. San Diego.

34. RAMSAY, A. J., A. J. HUSBAND, I. A. RAMSHAW, S. BAO, K. I. MATTHAEI, G. KOEHLER & M. KOPF. 1994. Science **264:** 561–563.

35. MOORE, K. W., A. O'GARRA, R. DE WAAL MALEFYT, P. VIEIRA & T. MOSMANN. 1993. Ann. Rev. Immunol. **11:** 165–190.

36. MILLER, R. A. 1991. Int. Rev. Cytol. **124:** 187–214.

37. FIORENTINO, D. F., M. W. BOND & T. R. MOSMANN. 1989. J. Exp. Med. **170:** 2081–2095.

38. TAGA, K. & G. TASOTO. 1992. J. Immunol. **148:** 1143–1148.

39. DE WAAL MALEFYT, R., J. HAANEN, H. SPITS, M. G. ROCAROLO, A. TE VELDE, C. FIGDOR, K. JOHNSON, R. KASTELEIN, H. YSSEL & J. E. DE VRIES. 1991. J. Exp. Med. **174:** 915–924.

40. DING, L., P. S. LINSLEY, L. Y. HUANG, R. GERMAIN & E. M. SHEVACH. 1993. J. Immunol. **151:** 1224–1234.

41. FIORENTINO, D. F., A. ZLOTNIK, T. R. MOSMANN, M. HOWARD & A. O'GARRA. 1991. J. Immunol. **147:** 3815–3822.

42. PECANHA, L. M., C. M. SNAPPER, A. LEES & J. J. MOND. 1992. J. Immunol. **148:** 3427–3432.

43. O'GARRA, A., R. CHANG, N. GO, R. HASTINGS, G. HAUGHTON & M. HOWARD. 1992. Eur. J. Immunol. **22:** 711–717.

44. BOOKER, J. K. & G. HAUGHTON. 1992. Ann. N. Y. Acad. Sci. **651:** 494–497.

45. BROHEE, D., M. VAN HAEUERBEEK, B. KENNES & P. NEVE. 1991. Mech. Ageing Dev. **58:** 127–138.

46. GOTTESMAN, R. S., J. EDINGTON, V. K. TSIAGBE & G. J. THORBECKE. 1993. Aging: Immunol. & Infect. Dis. **4:** 197–211.

47. HAYAKAWA, K., R. R. HARDY, L. A. HERZENBERG & L. A. HERZENBERG. 1985. J. Exp. Med. **161:** 1554–1468.

48. STALL, A. M., S. ADAMS, L. A. HERZENBERG & A. B. KANTOR. 1992. Ann. N. Y. Acad. Sci. **651:** 33–43.

49. MARIOTTI, S., P. SANSONI, G. BARBESINO, P. CATUREGLI, D. MONTI, A. COSSARIZZA, T. GIACOMELLI, G. PASSERI, U. FAGIOLO, A. PINCHERA & C. FRANCESCHI. 1992. Lancet **339:** 1506–1508.

50. FRANCESCHI, C., D. MONTI, P. SANSONI & A. COSSARIZZA. 1995. Immunol. Today **16:** 12–16.

51. PLATER-ZYBERK, C., C. M. S. BROWN, E. M. ANDREW & R. N. MAINI. 1992. Ann. N. Y. Acad. Sci. **651:** 540–550.

52. XU, H. J., P. J. ROBERTS-THOMSON, M. J. AHERN & H. AOLA. 1992. Ann. N. Y. Acad. Sci. **651:** 594–598.

53. REAP, E. A., E. S. SOBEL, P. L. COHEN & R. A. EISENBERG. 1992. Ann. N. Y. Acad. Sci. **651:** 588–590.

54. STEIN, R., I. P. WITZ, J. OVADIA, D. M. GOLDENBERG & I. YRON. 1991. Clin. Exp. Immunol. **85:** 418–423.

55. DIGHIERO, G., P. TRAVADE, S. CHEVRET, P. FENAUX, C. CHASTANG, J. L. BINET & T. F. C. G. O. CLL. 1991. Blood **78:** 1901–1914.

56. BASHAM, B. Y. & T. C. MERIGAN. 1983. J. Immunol. **130:** 1492–1494.

57. FIERZ, W., B. ENDLER, K. RESKE, H. WEKERLE & A. FONTANA. 1985. J. Immunol. **134:** 3785–3793.

58. MARKMANN, J., D. LO, A. NAJI, R. D. PALMITER, R. L. BRINSTER & E. HEBER-KATZ. 1988. Nature **336:** 476–479.

59. POBER, J. S., M. A. GIMBRONE, R. S. COTRAN, C. S. REISS, S. J. BURAKOFF, W. FIERS, R. ROTHLEIN & T. A. SPRINGER. 1983. J. Exp. Med. **157:** 1339–1353.
60. BURMESTER, G. R., B. JAHN, P. ROHWER, J. ZACHER, R. J. WINCHESTER & J. R. KALDEN. 1987. J. Clin. Invest. **80:** 595–604.
61. BOTTAZZO, G. R., R. PUJOL-BORELL & T. HANAFUSA. 1983. Lancet **2:** 1115–1119.
62. BOTTAZZO, G. F., B. M. DEAN, J. M. MCNALLY, E. H. MACKAY, P. G. F. SWIFT & D. R. GAMBLE. 1985. New Engl. J. Med. **313:** 353–360.
63. LEE, S. C., G. R. MOORE, G. GOLENWSKY & C. S. RAINE. 1990. J. Neuropathol. & Exp. Neurol. **49:** 122–136.
64. WANG, C. Q., K. B. UDUPA & D. A. LIPSCHITZ. 1995. J. Cell Physiol. **162:** 134–138.
65. FARRAR, M. A. & R. D. SCHREIBER. 1993. The molecular cell biology of interferon-γ and its receptor. *In:* W. E. Paul, C. G. Fathman & H. Metzger, Ed. Annu. Rev. Immunol. Vol 11: 571–612. Annual Reviews Inc. Palo Alto.
66. COLLART, M. A., D. BELIN, J. D. VASSALI, S. DE KOSSODO & P. VASSALI. 1986. J. Exp. Med. **164:** 2113–2118.
67. VARGA, J., A. OLSEN & S. A. JIMENEZ. 1990. Ann. N. Y. Acad. Sci. **593:** 321–322.
68. DUNHAM, D. M., S. ARKINS, C. K. R. EDWARDS, R. DANTZER & K. W. KELLEY. 1990. J. Leukocyte Biol. **48:** 473–481.
69. KLAUSHOFER, K., H. HORANDNER, O. HOFFMANN, E. CZERWENKA, U. KONIG, K. KOLLER & M. PETERLIK. 1989. J. Bone Miner. Res. **4:** 585–606.
70. FUJII, Y., K. SATO, K. KASONO, T. SATOH, T. FUJII & K. SHIZUME. 1990. Calcif. Tissues **47:** 178–182.
71. GOWEN, M. & G. R. MUNDY. 1986. J. Immunol. **136:** 2478–2482.
72. GOWEN, M., N. G. E. & G. R. MUNDY. 1986. J. Bone Miner. Res. **1:** 469–474.
73. HOFFMANN, O., K. KLAUSHOFER, H. GLEISPACH, H. J. LEIS, T. LUGER, K. KOLLER & M. PETERLIK. 1987. Biochem. Biophys. Res. Comm. **143:** 38–43.
74. MANN, G. N., T. W. JACOBS, F. J. BUCHINSKY, E. C. ARMSTRONG, M. LI, H. Z. KE, Y. F. MA, W. S. S. JEE & S. EPSTEIN. 1994. Endocrinology **135:** 1077–1083.
75. KILSHAW, P. J. & S. J. MURANT. 1990. Eur. J. Immunol. **20:** 2201–2207.
76. KILSHAW, P. J. & S. J. MURANT. 1991. Eur. J. Immunol. **21:** 2591–2597.
77. ERSHLER, W. B. 1993. J. Am. Geriatr. Soc. **41:** 176–181.
78. REED, M. J. 1995. Mol. Med. Today **1:** 98–105.
79. LEVY, Y. & J. C. BROUET. 1994. J. Clin. Invest. **93:** 424–428.
80. BELLIDO, T., R. L. JIKA, B. F. BOYCE, G. GIRASOLE, H. BROXMEYER, S. A. DALRYMPLE, R. MURRAY & S. C. MANOLAGAS. 1995. J. Clin. Invest. **95:** 2886–2895.
81. DE LA MATA, D., H. L. UY, T. A. GUISE, B. STORY, B. F. BOYCE, G. R. MUNDY & G. D. ROODMAN. 1995. J. Clin. Invest. **95:** 2846–2852.
82. VILCEK, J. 1991. Interferons. *In* Peptide Growth Factors and Their Receptors. II. M. B. Sporn & A. B. Roberts Eds.: 3–38. Springer-Verlag. New York.
83. GARG, M. & S. BONDADA. 1993. Infect. Immunol. **61:** 2238–2241.
84. SWENSON, C. D., A. R. AMIN, J. EDINGTON, S. R. S. GOTTESMAN & G. J. THORBECKE. 1994. FASEB J. **8:** A749.
85. DAYNES, R. A., B. A. ARANEO, J. D. HENNEBOLD, E. ENIOUTINA & H. H. MU. 1995. J. Invest. Dermatol. **105:** 14S–19S.
86. VAN DER BOSCH, H., R. B. H. SCHUTGENS, R. J. A. WANDERS & J. M. TAGER. 1992. Annu. Rev. Biochem. **61:** 157–197.
87. RAO, M. S., S. MUSUNURI & J. K. REDDY. 1992. Pathobiology **60:** 82–86.
88. RAO, M. S., B. REID, H. IDE, I. V. SUBBARO & J. K. REDDY. 1994. Proc. Soc. Exp. Biol. Med. **207:** 186–190.
89. FRENKEL, R. A., C. A. SLAUGHTER, K. ORTH, C. R. MOOMAW, S. H. HICKS, J. M. SNYDER, M. BENNETT, R. A. PROUGH, R. S. PUTNAM & L. MILEWICH. 1990. J. Steroid Biochem. **35:** 333–342.
90. SAKUMA, M., J. YAMADA & T. SUGA. 1992. Biochem. Pharmacol. **43:** 1269–1273.
91. PROUGH, R. A., S. J. WEBB, H.-Q. WU, D. P. LAPENSON & D. J. WAXMAN. 1994. Cancer Res. **54:** 2878–2886.
92. MILEWICH, L., M. MARRERO, B. U. TEZABWALA, M. BENNETT, R. A. FRENKEL & C. A. SLAUGHTER. 1993. J. Steroid Biochem. Mol. Biol. **46:** 321–329.

93. ISSEMANN, I. & S. GREEN. 1990. Nature **347:** 645–652.
94. ZHU, Y., K. ALVARES, Q. HUANG, M. S. RAO & J. K. REDDY. 1993. J. Biol. Chem. **268:** 26817–26820.
95. KLIEWER, S. A., B. M. FORMAN, B. BLUMBERG, E. S. ONG, U. BORGMEYER, D. J. MANGELSDORF, K. UMESONO & R. M. EVANS. 1994. Proc. Natl. Acad. Sci. USA **91:** 7355–7359.
96. KELLER, H., C. DREYER, J. MEDIN, A. MAHFOUDI, K. OZATO & W. WAHLI. 1993. Proc. Natl. Acad. Sci. USA **90:** 2160–2164.
97. EACHO, P. I., P. S. FOXWORTHY, R. P. DILLARD, C. A. WHITESITT, D. HERRON, K. & W. S. MARSHALL. 1989. Toxicol. Appl. Pharmacol. **100:** 177–184.
98. SAKUMA, M., J. YAMADA & T. SUGA. 1993. Biochim. Biophys. Acta **1169:** 66–72.
99. YAMADA, J., H. SUGIYAMA, M. SAKUMA & T. SUGA. 1994. Biochim. Biophys. Acta **1224:** 139–146.
100. YAMADA, J., M. SAKUMA, T. IKEDA, K. FUKUDA & T. SUGA. 1991. Biochim. Biophys. Acta **1092:** 233–243.
101. YAMADA, J., M. SAKUMA, T. IKEDA & T. SUGA. 1994. Arch. Biochem. Biophys. **313:** 379–381.
102. FALANY, C. N., M. E. VAZQUEZ & J. M. KALB. 1989. Biochem. J. **260:** 641–646.
103. HOLINKA, C. F. & E. GURPIDE. 1980. Endocrinology **106:** 1193–1197.
104. ROY, R. & A. BELANGER. 1989. J. Steroid Biochem. **34:** 559–561.
105. BEIER, K., A. VOLKL & H. D. FAHIMI. 1993. Virchöw's Arch. B. Cell Pathol. **63:** 139–146.
106. NADIV, O., M. SHINITZKY, H. MANU, D. HECHT, C. T. ROBERTS, JR., D. LEROITH & Y. ZICK. 1994. Biochem. J. **298:** 443–450.
107. GAREAU, R., H. GOULET, C. CHENARD, C. CARON & G. R. BRISSON. 1991. Cell. Mol. Biol. **37:** 15–19.
108. LAGANIERE, S. & G. FERNANDES. 1991. Lipids **26:** 472–478.
109. SHINITZKY, M. 1987. Gerontology **33:** 149–154.
110. HEGNER, D. 1980. Mech. Ageing Dev. **14:** 101–118.
111. HUGHES, D., E. A. CASPARY & H. M. WISNIEWSKI. 1975. Lancet **2:** 501–502.
112. THOMAS, I. K. & K. L. ERICKSON. 1985. J. Natl. Cancer Inst. **74:** 675–680.
113. JOHNSTON, P. V. 1985. Adv. Lipid Res. **21:** 103–141.
114. GOEPPELT-STRUEBE, M., C. F. KOERNER, G. HAUSMANN, D. GEMSA & K. RESCH. 1986. Prostaglandins **32:** 373–385.
115. GOODWIN, J. S., A. D. BANKHURST & R. P. MESSNER. 1977. J. Exp. Med. **146:** 1719–1734.
116. SPEIZER, L. A., M. J. WATSON & L. L. BRUNTON. 1991. Am. J. Physiol. **261:** E109–E114.
117. SØYLAND, E., M. S. NEMSETER, L. BRAATHEN & C. A. DREVON. 1993. Eur. J. Clin. Invest. **23:** 112–121.
118. CALDER, P. C., J. A. BOND, S. J. BEVAN, S. V. HUNT & E. A. NEWSHOLME. 1991. Int. J. Biochem. **23:** 579–588.
119. CALDER, P. C., S. J. BEVAN & E. A. NEWSHOLME. 1992. Immunology **75:** 108–115.
120. PROUST, J. J., C. R. FILBURN, S. A. HARRISON, M. A. BUCHHOLZ & A. A. NORDIN. 1987. J. Immunol. **139:** 1472–1478.
121. KATZ, D., D. HOLLANDER, H. M. SAID & V. DADUFALZA. 1987. Dig. Dis. Sci. **32:** 285–288.
122. DEITCH, E. A. 1990. J. Trauma **30:** S184–S189.
123. PANG, G., L. COUCH, R. BATEY, R. CLANCEY & A. CRIPPS. 1994. Clin. Exp. Immunol. **96:** 437–443.
124. WOLF, S. F., P. A. TEMPLE, M. KOBAYASHI, D. YOUNG, M. DICIG, L. LOWE, R. DZIALO, L. FITZ, C. FERENZ, R. M. HEWICK, K. KELLEHER, S. H. HERRMANN, S. C. CLARK, L. AZZONI, S. H. CHAN, G. TRINCHIERI & B. PERUSSIA. 1991. J. Immunol. **146:** 3074–3081.
125. BASTYRE, E. J. I., M. M. KADROFSKE & A. I. VINIK. 1990. Am. J. Med. **88:** 601–606.
126. WATALA, C. 1991. Med. Hypotheses **36:** 142–145.
127. CRANE, D. I., J. ZAMATTIA & C. J. MASTERS. 1990. Molec. Cell. Biochem. **96:** 153–161.
128. FERNANDES, G., B. CHANDRASEKER, J. D. MOUNTZ & W. ZHAO. 1995. FASEB J. **9:** A787.
129. ARANEO, B. A., M. L. WOODS, II & R. A. DAYNES. 1993. J. Infect. Dis. **167:** 830–840.

Adaptation to Chronic Stress in Military Trainees

Adrenal Androgens, Testosterone, Glucocorticoids, IGF-1, and Immune Function[a]

EDWARD BERNTON,[b] DAVID HOOVER,[b]
RICHARD GALLOWAY,[c] AND KATHRYN POPP[d]

[b]Department of Bacterial Diseases
Division of Communicable Diseases and Immunology

[c]Department of Clinical Physiology
Division of Medicine, and

[d]Department of Behavioral Biology
Division of Neuropsychiatry
Walter Reed Army Institute of Research
Washington, DC 20307–5100

Historically, populations stressed by natural disasters, military deployment, or wartime refugee status have demonstrated an increased incidence of infectious diseases. An example was the explosive increase in active tuberculosis and typhus in Germany towards the end of World War II. Military recruits in basic training also have incurred endemic infectious diseases such as streptococcus, meningococcus, and adenovirus. It is unclear, however, if the prevalence of infectious diseases in such situations is best attributed to defects in public health and personal hygiene or to an underlying increased suceptibility of stressed populations.

This paper summarizes some of the findings of studies investigating metabolic, cognitive, endocrinologic, and immunologic adaptation in young male soldiers enrolled at the U.S. Army Ranger School during 8 weeks of extremely stressful training. These are described in detail in three publications.[1-3] In the words of the Ranger School Manual, the Ranger Training Course "develops the leadership skills of selected male junior enlisted and officers by requiring them to perform effectively as small unit infantry leaders *in a realistic tactical environment under mental and physical stress approaching that found in combat.*"

Stressors included intentional caloric deprivation, resulting in the loss of 8–15% of body weight over 8 weeks, limitation of sleep to an average of 3.6 hours per week, long exposures to extreme environments, and continuous physical work. Psychologic stressors included constant performance evaluation and risk of academic failure and the threat of attack by simulated opposition forces. In many ways these stressors not only are militarily relevant, but also resemble stressors encountered by populations historically at risk for endemic infectious diseases. Twelve classes of approximately 300 students each attend the ranger school yearly. The uniform and predictable nature of the stressors and the homogeneity and good health of the ranger trainees provide a unique opportunity for investigating the endocrinologic and immunologic

[a]The views of the authors do not purport to reflect the position of the Department of the Army or the Department of Defense (Para. 4-3, AR360-5).

217

effects of chronic stress using a repeated measures design, with each trainee's initial status serving as his own control for later time points. The large number of subjects in each class who volunteer for these studies allows for powerful statistical analysis.

One major disadvantage is the complex mix of stressors involved in the ranger course. It is not operationally possible to eliminate or manipulate individual stressors in either all or part of the subject group due to both the training requirements and the dictates of fairness. Another disadvantage, when a repeated measures design is used, is the high attrition rate of the subjects. Approximately half the initial subject group did not finish the 8-week course. Finally, the conduct of training in three separated geographic areas and limited access to trainees during long periods of field exercises in remote terrain all add to the logistical challenges of acquiring data.

This study examined changes in serum cortisol, dehydroepiandrosterone (DHEA), DHEA sulfate (DHEAS), and testosterone in volunteers completing ranger training. During severe medical stressors such as burn or critical illness, there is selective activation of the adrenal axis, with increased cortisol and suppressed DHEA.[4–6] Strenuous exercise is reported to increase DHEA acutely, but the effect attenuates over time.[7] To our knowledge, this is the first examination of the adaptation of DHEA to chronic nonmedical stressors. We also attempted to correlate stress-induced changes in cortisol, testosterone, DHEA, and the DHEA/cortisol ratio with observed alterations in delayed-type hypersensitivity skin tests, given the published data suggesting that DHEA may antagonize certain immunosuppressive effects of glucocorticoids.[8–10]

STUDY DESIGN

During the study period, ranger training was conducted in approximately 2-week blocks at each of four locales. The first block was at Ft. Benning, Georgia, the second in the mountains at Dahlonega, Georgia, the third in the desert near Ft. Bliss, Texas, and the fourth in the swamps at Eglin AFB, Florida. Each block consisted of several days of didactic and hands-on instruction, followed by an 8- to 11-day field training exercise, or FTX. During the FTX, students are only allowed a fixed field ration daily. This ration provides fewer calories than those expended during the FTX. While daily intake of protein and micronutrients was adequate, net negative energy balance resulted in constant hunger and a progressive weight loss over the duration of the course. During the didactic portion of each block, students had access to three meals a day, at least one a hot meal with large portions, and regained some of the lost weight.

Data from two studies performed in the summers of 1991 and 1992 are presented. The ranger trainees in 1992 were allowed somewhat greater caloric intake during the non-FTX period and had about 10% less mean body weight loss.

Data were collected 2 days before the start of the course and subsequently at the immediate end of each 2-week block, when the students returned from the field-training exercise, between 6 and 9 AM. Endocrine measures, which will be discussed below, included AM cortisol, DHEAS, DHEA, insulin-like growth factor-1 (IGF-1), and testosterone, and serum interleukin-6 (IL-6). Thyroid function was also examined and will be reported elsewhere.[11]

Immune endpoints included delayed-type hypersensitivity by epicutaneous skin testing to seven antigens, using the Multitest-CM device (Connaught Labs). Skin tests were applied immediately after soldiers returned from the FTX and read 48 hours later.

Total white blood cell counts, differential, and hematocrits were measured on site with a Coulter JT analyzer. Peripheral leukocytes were incubated within 6 hours of phlebotomy with standard fluorescein or phycoerythrin-conjugated antibodies using the whole blood lysis method for determination of lymphocyte subsets (total CD-3, CD-4, CD-8, and CD-20). Analysis was performed on a Becton-Dickinson FACSCAN.

Serum IL-6 assays were performed with a competitive displacement EIA kit using enzyme-labeled rIL-6 as tracer and a solid phase anti–IL-6 polyclonal antibody (Assay Research, Inc., College Park, Maryland). Serum creatinine phosphokinase (CPK) was measured on a Beckman autoanalyzer. Serum amyloid A was determined using a sandwich EIA (Biosource International, Camarino, California).

Ex vivo studies of monokine secretion were performed by mixing heparin-anticoagulated blood with 2 volumes of Hanks'-buffered saline solution with Mg and Ca in the absence or presence of 1 μg/ml *Escherichia coli* lipopolysaccharide, sterile culture tubes. Cells were incubated in a 37-degree incubator for 3 hours, with vigorous shaking every 30 minutes. Tubes were centrifuged and culture fluids frozen for subsequent assay of IL-1 alpha, tumor necrosis factor-alpha (TNF-α), and IL-6 using EIA kits (R&D systems, Minneapolis, Minnesota).

Sleep was quantified by the use of continuously recording wrist-worn actigraphs (Precision Control Devices, Ft. Walton Beach, Florida).[12]

RESULTS

Sleep and Body Weight. Students averaged 3.6 hours/24 hours of sleep over the 8-week training period.[2] This degree of sleep debt was associated with slowing on cognitive testing and with episodes of disorientation or hallucination at times during the night. The mean percentage of body weight loss over 8 weeks in 1991 was aproximately 13.8% and in 1992 was 12.6 ± 2.8%. Body composition studies indicated a large loss of body fat and only a small loss of lean body mass.[1–3]

Endocrine Measures. In the 1991 class AM cortisol increased significantly between baseline and end-mountain phase measures. During this time DHEA and DHEAS also increased (TABLE 1), but the overall DHEA/cortisol (CS) ratio decreased significantly (from 21.1 to 16.7, $p < 0.01$ by paired t test). The DHEA/CS ratio reached a nadir at 6 weeks (14.5). Testosterone decreased significantly to clearly hypogonadal levels (TABLE 1). The change in testosterone and DHEA/CS ratio showed more variability between subjects than did the change in cortisol, which was uniform. In 1991, hormones were assessed at a recovery timepoint 3 days after the end of the last ranger school FTX, after increased sleep and ad lib access to food. After this interval, cortisol and testosterone had returned to baseline levels, but DHEAS and the DHEAS/CS ratio remained significantly suppressed. Similar changes occurred in the 1992 class, but were moderated somewhat by the increased caloric intake.

Salivary hormones were also examined at 0- and 4-week timepoints. Mean salivary cortisol increased from 300 to 707 ng/dl, while salivary DHEA increased from 22.3 to 24.5 ng/dl. The mean salivary DHEA/CS ratio, therefore, decreased from 0.076 to 0.041 ($p < 0.001$ by paired t test). As salivary hormones are thought to reflect serum concentrations of free nonprotein-bound steroids, this result suggests that changes in ratios of free or tissue cortisol and DHEA may be more marked than those of total serum cortisol and DHEAS.

Decreased testosterone did not seem mediated solely by the suppression of luteinizing hormone (LH). While LH decreased moderately (from a mean of 9.3 ng/ml to a nadir of 7.2 ng/ml), this only reached statistical significance at the end-mountain timepoint, and at the point of maximal suppression of testosterone, LH was not significantly different from baseline. Although the correlation between testosterone and weeks of ranger school had an $r = -0.73$, the overall correlation between testosterone and LH was only $r = 0.26$. Curiously, decreases in testosterone were highly correlated with decreases in both free thyroxine and serum T3 ($r = 0.55$ and 0.65, respectively). This may not reflect a causal relationship, but merely a covariance with the time-dependent decrease in thyroid function.

In a separate studies of ranger students, growth hormone and IGF-1 were measured.[1,3] Mean AM growth hormone increased aproximately fourfold, reflecting adaptation to negative energy balance. Mean serum IGF-1 decreased by 60% during ranger training, reflecting a dissociation of growth hormone from IGF-1 secretion, atributable in part to negative energy balance and high cortisol levels. Unfortunately, among the four classes of ranger trainees studied, IGF-1 and DHEA, each measured in two classes, were not measured in the same classes. Therefore, in these studies the correlation between DHEA or DHEA/CS ratios and IGF-1 cannot be directly examined.

TABLE 1. Summary of Selected Endocrine Data from 1991 and 1992 Studies[a]

Study	Baseline	End-Mountain	End-Swamp	3-Day Recovery
91 Class				
Cortisol (μg/dl)	13.1	26.5*	20.2	14.2
Free Testo (ng/ml)	3.12	1.22*	1.34*	3.36
DHEAS (μg/dl)	284	407*	276	226
DHEA (ng/ml)	297	473*	368	248
DHEAS/CS	21.1	16.7*	14.5*	17.1
92 Class				
Cortisol (μg/dl)	15.4	22.5*	17.2	
Total Testo (ng/ml)	6.5	1.9*	1.7*	
DHEAS (μg/dl)	286	330	287	
DHEAS/CS	20	18	16	

[a]Note that in 1991, data were obtained at baseline, 4 weeks, 6 weeks, and 3 days after the end of the 8-week training course. During 1992, data were obtained at baseline, 6 weeks, and 8 weeks due to the rescheduling of the desert phase from the fourth to the second block. Asterisk (*) denotes a p value of less than 0.01 using ANOVA for repeated measures, compared with the baseline value. All sera were obtained between 6 and 8 AM.

Immunologic Endpoints. Delayed type hypersensitivity responses to seven antigens were determined at baseline, at 4, 6, and 8 weeks, and after 3 days of recovery from the last ranger school FTX (TABLE 2). Significant suppression in both the mean number of positive skin tests and total millimeters of skin test induration was noted at 4, 6, and 8 weeks. Skin test responses showed significant recovery at 3 days. Lymphocyte phenotyping revealed no significant change in total lymphocyte counts, T-cell counts, or CD4/CD8 ratios which would explain the development of cutaneous anergy.

Since recruitments of monocytes and secretion of TNF-α are a crucial effector mechanism in DTH, the ability of the trainees' monocytes in whole blood to secrete TNF-α *in vitro* was examined, using *E. coli* lipopolysaccharide (LPS) as a stimulus. TNF-α secretion in response to LPS was significantly decreased during periods of maximally decreased DTH responses (FIG. 1). Production of IL-1 and IL-6 was similarly suppressed (data not shown). Of interest, when each subject's whole blood

TABLE 2. Summary of DTH Skin Test Data from 1991 and 1992 Studies[a]

Week	Mean # Positive	Mean Total (mm)	Mean (mm) d + t	% Anergic	Subjects (n)
1991					
CONT	4.15 ± 0.26	15.6 ± 1.1	10.2 ± 1.1	0	22
0	3.75 ± 0.24	13.1 ± 0.9	8.6 ± 0.7	0	31
4[b]	1.74 ± 0.15	6.2 ± 0.7	3.9 ± 0.6	9	31
6	2.33 ± 0.28	7.2 ± 1.2	4.2 ± 0.8	7	14
8 + 3 day recovery	2.94 ± 0.24	11.2 ± 1.8	6.1 ± 0.7	0	26
1992					
0	3.49 ± 0.19	17.9 ± 1.3	11.5 ± 0.9	0	40
6[b]	3.02 ± 0.25	10.5 ± 1.0	5.0 ± 0.5	2	40
8	1.82 ± 0.24	6.3 ± 1.0	4.5 ± 0.7	15	26

[a]# Positive is the number of antigens out of the seven applied to an individual resulting in 2 mm or greater induration. Mean total is the sum of the millimeters of induration of all positive tests on an individual; mm d+t is the sum of the induration to two antigens, tetanus and diphtheria. Due to prior immunizations, virtually all subjects respond to these two antigens at baseline.

[b]End-mountain phase.

TNF production (after LPS stimulation) was compared to their whole blood lymphocyte proliferation in response to the mitogen phytohemagglutinin at the 8-week point of ranger training, these two different cellular responses were highly correlated. ($r = 0.79, p < 0.001$)

Serum IL-6 was also measured using an equilibrium-type EIA capable of detecting normal levels of total IL-6. Circulating AM IL-6 levels were remarkably constant in each individual, considering the dramatic adaptive changes in most other endocrine measures. Mean levels were slightly decreased at the end of mountain phase (FIG. 2). Across all timepoints, regression analysis showed no correlation between circulating IL-6 and cortisol.

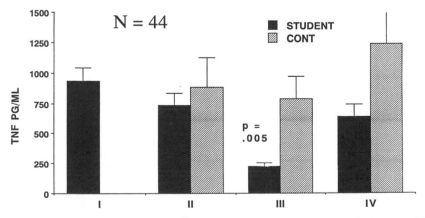

FIGURE 1. Blood leukocyte TNF secretion in ranger trainees and controls at (I) baseline, (II) 4 weeks, (III) 6 weeks, and (IV) 8 weeks of the ranger training course.

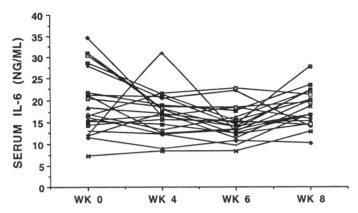

FIGURE 2. Serial determinations of serum interleukin-6 over 8 weeks in 22 ranger trainees completing the course.

Minor but statistically significant correlations were found between IL-6 and testosterone ($r = 0.27, p < 0.006$), DHEAS ($r = 0.25, p < 0.013$), and free thyroxine ($r = 0.22, p < 0.02$). No correlation existed between circulating IL-6 levels and any functional immune endpoint.

Another measure of monokine action *in vivo* is the acute phase response. This consists of altered hepatic protein synthesis, with increases in a variety of specific proteins including fibrinogen, C-reactive protein, ceruloplasmin, and serum amyloid A (SAA), a lipoprotein constituent. The SAA is an extremely sensitive and robust measure of the acute phase response; blood levels can increase 1,000-fold. IL-6, perhaps potentiated by IL-1 and TNF, is the primary stimulus for hepatocyte SAA synthesis. The SAA was measured at baseline and at 4, 6, and 8 weeks. Suprisingly, some individuals had elevated levels at baseline, and mean levels decreased significantly during ranger training.

Muscle damage is a potent stimulus for the acute phase response, and with trauma or myocardial infarction serum levels of the muscle enzyme CPK are correlated with SAA. We postulated that with heavy physical exercise in a very hot climate, some trainees had subclinical rhabdomyolysis. Indeed, some individuals had serum CPK elevations consistent with rhabdomyolysis, and at the baseline timepoint, SAA correlated with CPK. By contrast, at the end of mountain phase, no correlation existed between SAA and CPK (FIG. 3). When stimulation of SAA by muscle damage was expressed as the ratio lnSAA/lnCPK, this ratio decreased significantly between baseline and the end of mountain phase (FIG. 4). Thus, the *in vivo* association between muscle damage and cytokine-mediated hepatic SAA synthesis is present at baseline, but not at the timepoint where whole blood monokine secretion was demonstrably suppressed.

Whole blood lymphocyte mitogenic responses to the T-cell mitogen phytohemagglutinin were suppressed in ranger trainees during weeks 4 through 8 of the course.[1,2] Experiments were conducted to attempt to reconstitute suppressed T-cell mitogenic responses of ranger trainees. At the immediate end of the last FTX (8-week timepoint), heparinized blood was obtained from 44 trainees and 10 controls. Blood was incubated with 4 μg/ml of phytohemagglutinin with the addition of 4 volumes of either media alone, DHEA 10 nM, testosterone 10 nM, cimetadine 2 μg/ml, indomethacin 1 μg/ml, hIGF-1 500 ng/ml, human IL-1 20 U/ml, or human IL-2 20

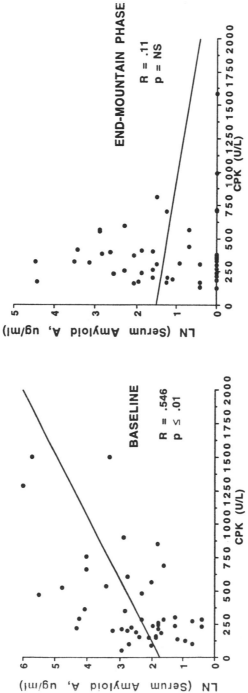

FIGURE 3. Correlation between creatinine phosphokinase (CPK) and serum amyloid A at baseline in range-- trainees is lost by the end of mountain phase 1992 (week 6).

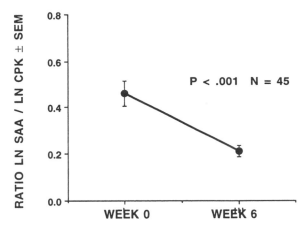

FIGURE 4. Ratio of serum amyloid A to creatinine phosphokinase decreases significantly between baseline and week 6.

U/ml. Thymidine incorporation was determined 72 hours later. Lymphocyte proliferation revealed a bimodal distribution, and subjects were divided by these responses into two groups: low, <10,000 CPM, mean CPM 4,050; and high, >10,000 CPM, mean CPM 20,254. Proliferation with each addition was calculated as a percentage of proliferation without additions, and mean changes in proliferation were determined for low and high responders for each addition. These data are shown in FIGURE 5.

At the concentrations added, DHEA, cimetadine, indomethacin, and testosterone had no effect on lymphocyte proliferation. The addition of IL-2 increased proliferation of low responders on average sixfold, in most cases normalizing T-cell

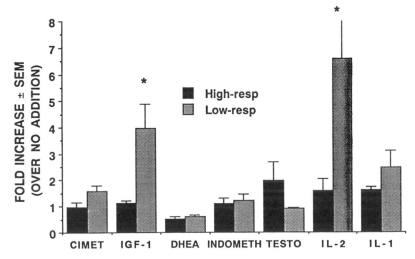

FIGURE 5. Effect of additions on phytohemagglutinin(PHA)-stimulated lymphocyte proliferation analyzed by subgroups of high- and low-responders to PHA.

responses. By contrast, IL-2 increased proliferation of high responders by less than twofold. The addition of IL-1 had a significant but lesser effect, increasing low responders by less than threefold.

The addition of recombinant human IGF-1 to lymphocytes increased low-responder responses on average over fourfold and caused no significant increase in high-responders. These data suggest that impaired T-cell proliferation is not caused by excessive prostaglandin production or histamine-like suppressor factor, as reported in some burn and surgical patients. Clearly, a defect in IL-2 production limits lymphocyte proliferation. The addition of the co-mitogen, IL-1, is less effective than IL-2 at normalizing impaired lymphocyte proliferation. Increased proliferation with the addition of IGF-1 seems to be specific for donors with suppressed T-cell proliferation, suggesting that the decreases in circulating IGF-1 may reflect decreased tissue availability, which could in turn modulate T-lymphocyte function.

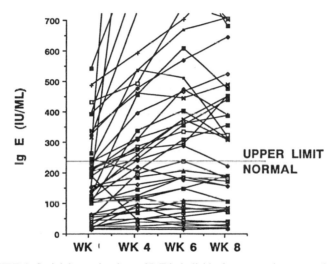

FIGURE 6. Serial determinations of IgE in individual ranger trainees over 8 weeks.

Immunoglobulins. Serum levels of IgG, IgA, IgM, and IgE were measured by USARIEM investigators. They report no significant changes in the levels of IgG, IgA, or IgM.[1] IgE levels did increase significantly during ranger training. Analysis of individual values reveals that virtually all individuals showed increases in IgE, not only those with elevated initial levels, and initial IgE was not correlated with a percentage increase over 8 weeks. Thus, the increase in mean IgE did reflect not only a large increase in atopic individuals stimulated by outdoor allergens, but also a homogeneous response by all individuals (FIG. 6).

Delayed Type Hypersensitivity Correlations with Endocrine Markers. Although over the 8-week ranger training course mean AM cortisol increased and DTH responses decreased, at any given timepoint AM cortisol was not predictive of the magnitude of the DTH response. By contrast, at 4- and 6-week timepoints, serum testosterone showed a significant positive correlation with DTH reactivity, that is, at week 4, $r = 0.47$, $p < 0.015$ (FIG. 7). The DHEA/CS ratio also showed a significant

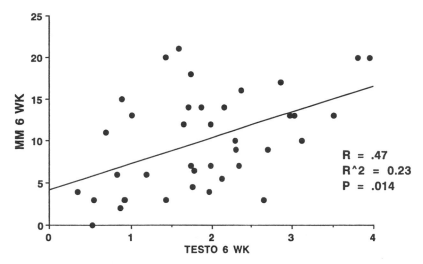

FIGURE 7. Serum testosterone levels at the end of mountain phase are significantly correlated with delayed type hypersensitivity skin test reactivity at that timepoint.

correlation with DTH (week 4, $r = 0.45$, $p < 0.02$) at these points following severe stress. DTH reactivity was also inversely correlated ($r = -0.39$, $p < 0.026$) with thyroid stimulating hormone, which increased significantly during the ranger training course. Thus, endocrine markers of adaptation to stress and to negative energy balance partially predicted the extent of impaired cellular immune responses. Of interest, when regression was performed between the percentage of body weight loss at the end of mountain phase and the total millimeters of induration on DTH testing, no correlation was found in either of the two classes analyzed (FIG. 8).

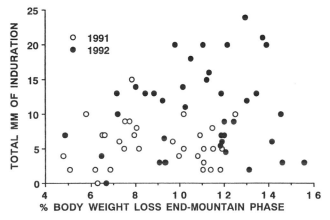

FIGURE 8. Lack of correlation between percentage of body/weight loss and delayed type hypersensitivity skin test reactivity (total millimeters' induration to seven antigens) in ranger trainees at the end of mountain phase.

DISCUSSION

These studies document endocrine adaptation in healthy young men exposed to chronic stressors and chronic energy deficit. Unlike medically ill and burn patients reported on by Parker and others, suppression of DHEA and DHEAS was not noted. Initially, both the AM cortisol, DHEA, and DHEAS levels are in the normal range and the DHEAS/CS ratio is similar to that reported in control groups by Parker *et al.*[5] and Fava *et al.*[13] At completion of the maximally stressful period of training, mountain phase, AM cortisol levels rose dramatically in all trainees, whereas the percentage increase in DHEAS and DHEA was significant, but more modest. This resulted in a significant and continuing decrease in the DHEAS/CS ratio throughout the training period, to a maximum extent of about 20% in each of two classes. However, adrenocortical adaptation to stress clearly included an increase in DHEAS production concurrent with increased cortisol secretion. Insulin secretion is judged to lower serum DHEA and DHEAS and increase DHEA clearance.[14] Blood insulin levels fell by aproximately 50% in ranger trainees during field training.[1,3] Decreased insulin along with increased ACTH would be expected to increase DHEAS, perhaps to an even greater extent than that observed.

Thus, adrenocortical adaptation to chronic stress and energy deficit does not resemble that seen with severe illness or burn injury, namely, elevated cortisol and suppressed DHEA levels with a depressed DHEA/CS ratio. By contrast, measurements of testosterone showed decreases with training stressors similar to those documented in males with both acute and chronic severe illness.[6] Both free and total testosterone levels were extremely depressed at the end of each field training period, but unlike depressed testosterone in burn patients, they demonstrated a rapid recovery 72 hours after the training period. As in medically ill patients, moderately depressed LH secretion did not correlate with or account for the suppression of testosterone.

Opstad[15] and colleagues studied Norwegian military cadets during 5 days of training involving strenuous exercise and almost total deprivation of both food and sleep. In that situation, DHEAS increased significantly, as observed in our trainees. By contrast, DHEA decreased significantly, which we did not observe at the timepoints we measured. Opstad's study suggests that DHEA and DHEAS can change in divergent directions, perhaps from inhibition of tissue desulfation of DHEAS or increased sulfatase activity. As in our study, testosterone levels fell precipitously during the stress period. At this 5-day timepoint, Opstad performed GnRH and HCG stimulation tests. The testosterone response to HCG was clearly intact, although reduced by about 25% compared to that of controls.[16] The LH response to 0.1 mg iv GnRH was greatly increased in the stressed trainees, showing the pituitary response to be intact, with increased LH release and sensitivity to GnRH compared to controls. Pituitary hypersensitivity to GnRH could reflect upregulation of receptors during a period of decreased hypothalamic GnRH release or the absence of negative feedback by testosterone following a period of low levels of androgen secretion. These data suggest that in this stress model, impaired testosterone secretion was largely hypothalamically mediated.

Opstad *et al.*[17] also noted that during this period of caloric deprivation, serum levels of insulin were decreased and those of somatostatin increased two- to fourfold. Oral or intravenous glucose temporarily normalizes somatostatin levels. *In vitro,* somatostatin has been noted to inhibit macrophage priming by gamma-interferon and the release of TNF-α.[18] The possibility that increased somatostatin secretion contributes to impaired TNF release by blood monocytes in ranger trainees cannot be excluded.

The DHEA/CS ratio itself is a difficult measure to replicate in clinical studies, being extremely dependent on circadian rhythmicity of subjects and exact timing of the AM cortisol specimen. For example, our control group of age-matched ranger school instructors had the same mean DHEAS levels as did the trainees before training, but showed significantly lower AM cortisol levels. This resulted in a twofold higher DHEAS/CS ratio than that of the trainees. These data could not be interpreted, because on average the controls were phlebotomized 90 minutes later in the day than were the trainees, and this might account for the decreased mean AM cortisol levels.

Serum IL-6 was measured across all timepoints in 28 students in one ranger class, and unlike other hormones measured, individuals maintained a remarkably consistent serum level despite chronic stress and energy deficit. Serum levels of this cytokine showed no correlation with the level of serum amyloid A, an acute phase serum protein stimulated by IL-6,[19,20] or of CPK, a marker for rhabdomyolysis, which stimulates the acute phase response presumedly via cytokines. These findings may suggest that IL-6 in the circulation serves an endocrine role, rather than reflecting immunologic responses except in cases such as sepsis where spillover of tissue cytokine is reflected in the circulation. What processes may be regulated by circulating IL-6 remain unknown, as does the mechanism by which circulating IL-6 is itself regulated. We did find significant correlations between IL-6 levels and both testosterone and free thyroxine but no correlation with cortisol levels. De Rijk et al.[19] reported that sympathetic activation increased and beta-adrenergic blockers decreased IL-6 levels in rats. This may explain why our subjects, exercising strenuously, had mean IL-6 levels, even at baseline, that were twofold higher than those of a sedentary control group of healthy volunteers (data not shown).

These studies also show a striking decrease in delayed-type hypersensitivity responses on repeated antigen skin testing. Although cutaneous anergy is common in malnutrition, ranger trainees do not develop hypoalbuminia, micronutrient deficiencies, or hypocomplementemia, hypothrombinemia, or losses of visceral lean body mass, all of which are associated with anergy in severe malnutrition. Additionally, despite great variance in percentage of body weight loss among trainees, DTH responses showed no correlation with this basic marker of energy balance. However, acute energy deficit during field training exercises certainly contributes to the marked endocrine stress responses in trainees. Other military trainee studies, such as parachute trainees, show rapid attenuation of both increased cortisol and decreased testosterone responses with repetition of stress. High insulin and growth hormone levels and low IGF-1 levels in ranger trainees suggest that elevated cortisol levels reflect, in part, the metabolic response to negative energy balance as well as a response to behavioral stressors, particularly sleep deficit.

Chronic stress with energy deficit was recently associated with decreased DTH skin test responses in Bosnian men released from Serbian detention camps.[22] Behavioral stressors without energy deficit may also be associated with suppressed DTH responses, as evidenced by DTH skin test responses before and during space flight in American astronauts.[23]

In any case, our results suggest that suppressed DTH responses can occur in the absence of medical illness or protein calorie malnutrition. The association of suppressed DTH responses and TNF-α secretion by monocytes, with an increase in circulating IgE, suggests at a tissue level a decrease in the production of the macrophage-activating factor gamma-interferon and an increase in IL-4 and IL-5 production. Behavioral stressor have been reported to increase IgE synthesis in murine models.[24] These changes suggest activation of T-helper cells expressing the TH-2–like phenotype and suppression of T cells expressing the TH-1–like phenotype. *In vitro,* cortisol also was found to increase IgE synthesis in response to IL-4 and to suppress IL-1 and TNF production by monocytes; therefore, hypercortisolinemia of ranger trainees could also cotnribute by these mechanisms to the observed changes. We hypothesize that T-helper cell responses of stressed ranger trainees shift from a TH-1 to a TH-2 pattern, a switch that is thought to be regulated in large part by the cytokine IL-12.[25] Future studies of ranger trainees or other stressed populations could use the *ex vivo* monocyte stimulation assay to directly assess IL-12 production in response to various stimuli.

The paradigm that stress can shift immune responses from a TH-1 to a TH-2 pattern provides an explanation for the clinical observations that asthma and autoimmune diseases can be exacerbated by behavioral stressors, while at the same time stressed individuals may be more susceptible to infections, particularly by intracellular pathogens and viruses. The mechanisms by which stressors can modulate T-cell function need to be clearly elucidated. It has been suggested that cortisol, vitamin D_3, dihydrotestosterone, and DHEA can all modulate T-cell function and the TH1/TH2 paradigm.[26–28] In this study, suppression of DTH responses clearly correlates with suppression of circulating testosterone, but not with increases of cortisol. Whether this implies a causal relationship or simply covariance of DTH and testosterone with another factor cannot be ascertained without any interventional study giving testosterone. Animal models of stress-induced immunosuppression such as cold-water immersion in mice[29] would easily permit such studies. This study also demonstrates a correlation between DTH skin test and thyroxine levels, which has not previously been reported. This may simply reflect the covariance seen between testosterone and free T4 at the timepoint of maximally suppressed DTH ($r = 0.55$, $p < 0.001$). This issue could also be clarified with animal studies permitting thyroid replacement.

Our data also suggest that the *in vivo* acute phase response to the simulus of subclinical rhabdomyolysis is abrogated in stressed trainees. This may reflect inhibition of IL-1, TNF, and IL-6 production noted in the *ex vivo* stimulation assay of blood monocytes with bacterial LPS. It is also possible that these results reflect tolerance to endotoxin. Increased urinary secretion of IL-1 and TNF-α along with endotoxemia and depletion of anti-LPS has been noted in long distance runners.[30,31] The combination of caloric restriction and intense exercise may alter gut permeability to LPS or reticuloendothelial clearance of LPS in the portal circulation. Subclinical endotoxemia could result in tolerance and impaired responses to LPS by monocyte/macrophages. This hypothesis could be tested by measuring anti-LPS titers and limulus lysate LPS activity in the blood of ranger trainees before and during training.

DHEA may be a counterregulatory hormone of glucocorticoids. Evidence for the antiglucocorticoid actions of DHEA have been reviewed by Regelson *et al.*[32] These include antagonism of glucocorticoid-induced suppression of T-cell proliferation in mice as well as stress- or glucocorticoid-enhanced susceptibility to viral infection. Human growth hormone and prolactin also antagonize glucocorticoid-induced immunosuppression in mice[33] DHEA was recently reported to increase IGF-1 levels in aging men and women.[34] *In vivo,* IGF-1 levels are therefore decreased by glucocorticoids and increased by lactogenic hormones and DHEA, regulated in a parallel direction as cellular immune endpoints. The reconstitution studies of T-cell proliferation responses of ranger trainees suggest that IGF-1 strikingly normalized suppressed responses.

We hypothesize that tissue ratios of DHEA to cortisol may regulate IGF-1 secretion in stressed individuals such as ranger trainees. Tissue and blood levels of

IGF-1 may then regulate T-lymphocyte function, including perhaps the TH1 to TH2 balance, possibly via IL-12 production by accessory cells. A regulatory role for IGF-1 could easily be overlooked in standard *in vitro* immunologic studies, because of the large amounts of IGF-1 in fetal calf serum, a routine cell-culture additive. In future studies of ranger trainees, salivary cortisol and DHEA as well as salivary and serum IGF-1 will be measured to aproximate tissue levels of these hormones. This will allow direct correlation of DHEA/CS ratios with IGF-1 to test the foregoing hypothesis. IGF-1 levels will also be directly correlated with changes in DTH skin test responses and T-cell proliferation assays. Finally, the effect of added IGF-1 can be examined on whole blood T-cell proliferation, IL-4, and gamma-interferon production and on the production of TNF-α and IL-12 by stimulated blood mononuclear cells.

In summary, these studies delineate the alterations in endocrine and immune function seen with exposure to multiple behavioral and metabolic stressors common to populations stressed by military deployment, refugee status, or natural disasters. Evidence of impaired cellular immune responses and of a shift from TH1 to TH2 function, which could be associated with an altered susceptibility to both infectious and autoimmune diseases. The precise mechanisms responsible for these alterations in immune function remain unclear, but a hypothesis is formulated along with an experimental method for testing that hypothesis.

REFERENCES

1. MOORE, R., K. FRIEDLE, T. KAARAMER, L. MARTINEZ-LOPEZ, R. HOYT, R. TULLEY, J. DELANY, W. ASKEW & J. VOGEL. 1992. Changes in soldier nutritional status and immune function during the ranger training course. USMRDC Tech Report T13-92.
2. Review of the results of nutritional intervention, U.S. Army Ranger Training Class 11/92. July 1993. Bernadette Marriott, Ed. National Academy Press. Washington DC.
3. SHIPPEE, R., W. ASKEW, M. MAYS, B. FAIRBROTHER, K. FRIEDLE, J. VOGEL, R. HOYT, L. MARCHITELLI, B. NINDLE, P. FRYKMAN, E. BERNTON, R. GALLOWAY, D. HOOVER, K. POPP, L. MARTINEZ-LOPEZ, T. KRAMER, R. TULLY, J. ROOD, J. DELANY, J. ARSENAULT & D. JEZIOR. 1994. Nutritional and immunologic assessment of Ranger students with increased caloric intake. USAMRDC Tech Report T95-5.
4. LEPHART, E., C. BAXTER & C. PARKER. 1987. Effect of burn trauma on adrenal and testicular steroid hormone production. J. Clin. Endocrinol. Metab. **64:** 842–849.
5. PARKER, L., E. LEVIN & E. LIFRAK. 1985. Evidence for adrenocortical adaptation to severe illness. J. Clin. Endocrinol. Metab. **60:** 947–952.
6. LUPPA, P., R. MUNKER, D. NAGEL *et al.* 1991. Serum androgens in intensive care patients: Correlations with clinical findings. Clin. Endocrinol. **34:** 305–310.
7. DUMMING, D., L. BRUNSTING, G. STRICH, *et al.* 1986. Reproductive hormone increases in response to acute exercise in men. Med. Sci. Sports **18:** 369–378.
8. BLAUER, K., L. POTH, M. ROGERS & E. BERNTON. 1991. Dehydroepiandrosterone antagonizes the suppressive effects of dexamethasone on lymphocyte proliferation. Endocrinology **129:** 3174–3180.
9. LORIA, R., T. INGE, S. COOK, A. SZAKAL & W. REGELSON. 1988. Protection against acute lethal viral infections with the native steroid DHEA. J. Med. Virol. **26:** 301–314.
10. BEN-NATHAN, D., B. LACHMI, S. LUSTIG & G. FEUERSTEIN. 1992. Protection by DHEA in mice infected with viral encephalitis.
11. GALLOWAY, R., H. FEIN, D. HOOVER, R. SMALLRIDGE & E. BERNTON. Manuscript in preparation.
12. MULLANEY, D., D. KRIPKE & S. MESSIN. 1980. Wrist-actigraphic estimation of sleep time. Sleep **3:** 83–92.
13. FAVA, M., J. ROSENBAUM, R. MACLAUGHLIN, G. TESAR, M. POLLACK, L. COHEN & M. HIRSCH. 1989. DHEA-S/cortisol ratio in panic disorder. Psychiatry Res. **28:** 345–350.
14. PARKER, L. 1995. Adrenal androgens. *In* Endocrinology, L. DeGroot, Ed.: 1836–1852. W.B. Saunders Co. Philadelphia.

15. OPSTAD, P. K. 1992. Androgenic hormones during prolonged physical stress, sleep, and energy deficiency. J. Clin. Endocrinol. Metab. **74:** 1176–1183.
16. OPSTAD, P. K. 1992. The hypothalamo-pituitary regulation of androgen secretion in young men after prolonged physical stress combined with energy and sleep deprivation. Acta Endocrinol. (Copenh.) **127:** 231–236.
17. OKTEDALEN, O., P. K. OPSTAD & J. J. HOLST. 1993. The effect of glucose on the plasma concentration of somatostatin during caloric deficiency in man. Scand. J. Gastroenterol. **28:** 652–656.
18. BERMUDEZ, L., M. WU & L. YOUNG. 1990. Effect of stress-related hormones on macrophage receptors and response to tumor necrosis factor. Lymphokine Res. **9:** 137–145.
19. DERIJK, R., A. BOELEN, F. TILDERS & F. BERKENBOSCH. 1994. Induction of plasma interleukin-6 by circulating adrenaline in the rat. Psychoneuroendocrinology **19:** 155–163.
20. FOYN BRUUN, C., M. RYGG, K. NORDSTOGA, K. SLETTEN & G. MARHAUG. 1994. Serum amyloid A protein in mink during endotoxin induced inflammation and amyloidogenesis. Scand. J. Immunol. **40:** 331–344.
21. CASL, M., B. SURINA, I. GLOJNARIC-SPASIC, E. PAPE, N. JAGARINEC & S. KRANJCEVIC. 1995. Serum amyloid A protein in patients with acute myocardial infarction. Ann. Clin. Biochem. **32:** 196–200.
22. DEKARIS, D., A. SABIONCELLO, R. MAZURAN *et al.* 1993. Multiple changes in immunologic parameters of prisoners of war. JAMA **270:** 595–599.
23. TAYLOR, G. & R. JANNEY. 1992. In vivo testing confirms a blunting of human cell-mediated immune mechanism during space flight. J. Leuk. Biol. **51:** 129–132.
24. PERSOONS, J., F. BERKENBOSCH, K. SCHORNAGEL, T. THEPEN & G. KRAAL. 1995. Increased specific IgE production in lungs after the induction of acute stress in rats. J. Allergy Clin. Immunol. **95:** 765–770.
25. GHALIB, H., J. WHITTLE, M. KUBIN, F. HASHIM, A. EL-HASSAN, K. GRABSTEIN, G. TRINCHIERI & S. REED. 1995. IL-12 enhances Th1-type responses in human Leishmania donovani infections. J. Immunol. **154:** 4623–4629.
26. DAVYNES, R., D. DUDLEY & B. ARANEO. 1990. Regulation of murine lymphokine production in vivo. II. DHEA is a natural enhancer of IL-2 synthesis by helper T cells. Eur. J. Immunol. **20:** 793–801.
27. SUZUKI, T., N. SUZUKI, R. DAYNES & E. ENGLEMAN. 1991. DHEA enhances IL-2 production and cytotoxic effector function of human T-cells. Clin. Immunol. Immunopathol. **61:** 202–211.
28. ARANEO, B., J. SHELBY, G. LI, W. KU & R. DAYNES. 1993. Administration of DHEA to burned mice preserves normal immunologic competence. Arch. Surg. **128:** 318–325.
29. JIANG, C., J. MORROW-TESCH, D. BELLER, E. LEVY & P. BLACK. 1990. Immunosupression in mice induced by cold water stress. Brain Behav. Immun. **4:** 278–291.
30. SPRENGER, H., C. JACOBS, M. NAIN, A. GRESSNER, H. PRINZ, W. WESELMANN & D. GEMSA. 1992. Enhanced release of cytokines, IL-2 receptors and neopterin after long-distance running. Clin. Immunol. Immunopathol. **63:** 188–195.
31. BROCK-UTNE, J., S. GAFFIN, M. WELLS, P. GATHIRAM, E. SOHAR, M. JAMES, D. MORRELL & R. NORMAN. 1988. Endotoxaemia in exhausted runners after a long-distance race. S. Afr. Med. J. **73:** 533–536.
32. REGELSON, W., R. LORIA & M. KALIMI. 1994. DHEA—the "Mother Steroid," I. Immunologic Action. Ann. N.Y. Acad. Sci. **719:** 553–563.
33. BERNTON, E. W., H. BRYANT, J. HOLADAY & J. DAVE. 1992. Prolactin and prolactin secretagogues reverse immunosuppression in mice treated with cysteamine, glucocorticoids, or cyclosporin-A. Brain Behav. Immun. **6:** 394–403.
34. MORALES, A., J. NOLAN, J. NELSON & S. YEN. 1994. Effects of replacement dose DHEA in men and women of advancing age. J. Clin. Endocrinol. Metab. **78:** 1360–1367.

DHEAS as an Effective Vaccine Adjuvant in Elderly Humans

Proof-of-Principle Studies

BARBARA ARANEO,[a] TAD DOWELL,[a]
MARION L. WOODS,[b] RAYMOND DAYNES,[c]
MICHAEL JUDD,[d] AND THOMAS EVANS[d]

[a]Paradigm Biosciences, Inc.
2401 Foothill Drive
Salt Lake City, Utah 84109

[b]Division of Infectious Disease
University of Utah School of Medicine
Salt Lake City, Utah 84132

[c]Department of Pathology
University of Utah School of Medicine and
Geriatric Research, Education, and Clinical Center
Office of Veteran Affairs
Salt Lake City, Utah 84132

[d]Infectious Diseases Research Lab
Veteran Affairs Medical Center
Salem, Virginia 24153

Elderly individuals often develop poor to moderate antibody production compared to younger individuals.[1] This conclusion is based on the number of vaccinees that can seroconvert in response to important vaccines such as influenza, pneumococcal polysaccharide, and hepatitis B surface antigen.[2] Attempts to vaccinate elderly persons with antigens to which the individual has never been exposed often result in significant failures in eliciting a specific immune response.[3,4] The marked reduction in the ability to stimulate primary immune responses in the elderly has become the hallmark of immunosenescense in humans.[5–7] By contrast, responses to recall antigens are induced more reliably, suggesting that immunologic memory remains intact during the aging process.[5–7]

When changes in the immune response potential become pronounced, plasma levels of the adrenal hormone dehydroepiandrosterone sulfate (DHEAS) are markedly reduced by comparison to levels achieved by humans during peak production. In preclinical studies with aged mice, immune responses improved when the hormone was administered as an adjuvant to the vaccine. Herein we present a study in aged mice which establishes a high level of functionality to the antibody response elicited using DHEAS with vaccination against tetanus toxoid. We compared the serologic response to tetanus toxoid with the resistance to local paralysis induced by a hindlimb challenge with tetanus toxin.

The main focus of this report is to present the results of two clinical studies designed to test the adjuvant activity of DHEAS in humans. Volunteers were vaccinated in a double-blind, randomized, placebo-controlled manner. In one study, DHEAS was given to test its ability to improve tetanus toxoid vaccination (a potential recall response in elderly volunteers). The other study compared DHEAS administration as an adjuvant using the 1994–1995 licensed trivalent influenza vaccine (a potential primary response in elderly volunteers). The results in humans clearly reiterate the principle of a DHEAS adjuvant effect in aged mice. The number of individuals who can generate primary responses to new antigens is markedly higher when vaccines are administered in combination with DHEAS.

MATERIALS AND METHODS

Study Subjects. Volunteers for both studies were recruited from patients in the long-term care facility at the Veterans Affairs Medical Center in Salem, Virginia, from four chronic care facilities in the area, as well as from ambulatory individuals living in the region. Inclusion criteria included age 65 years or greater, life expectancy greater than 1 month, and the ability to complete follow-up. Exclusion criteria included use of oral glucocorticoids (> 5 mg/d of prednisone), prostate cancer, or ongoing chemotherapy. For the tetanus study, exclusion criteria also included a prior adverse reaction to tetanus toxoid or a history of tetanus toxoid boosting within the past 10 years. From the influenza study, exclusion criteria included a history of allergy to chicken eggs, influenza vaccination within the previous 10 months, or a prior adverse reaction to influenza vaccination. All participants gave informed consent as approved by the Institutional Review Board.

Vaccine and DHEAS. DHEAS (lot 424721) was manufactured under GMP conditions for Paradigm Biosciences, Inc., Salt Lake City, Utah. Only material that was approved for use in two other FDA-approved trials was used in the study. Drug capsules (Eli Lilly, Indianapolis, Indiana) were filled with 50 mg of study drug or cornstarch. Licensed diphtheria-tetanus toxoid adsorbed vaccine was obtained from Wyeth Laboratories (Marietta, Pennsylvania) and was given as a 0.5 cc dose IM in the deltoid. Licensed influenza virus, trivalent, type A + B Fluogen (H1N1, H3N2, B/Panama) was obtained from Parke-Davis, (Morris Plains, New Jersey) and was given as a 0.5 cc dose in the deltoid. The two vaccine study populations did not overlap.

Tetanus Toxoid-Specific Antibody Measurement. Antibody concentration to tetanus was measured using a capture ELISA (Scimedx Co., Denville, New Jersey).[8,9] Commercial 96-well plates coated with tetanus toxoid were incubated in duplicate with 1:100 dilutions of the patient sera at 37°C for 1 hour, washed four times with phosphate-buffered saline solution-Tween 20 (pH 7.2), incubated with an IgG-peroxidase conjugate for 30 minutes, and washed again four times. O-Phenylenediamine-2HCl substrate was added along with H_2O_2 and incubated for 15 minutes at 37°C, at which time a 1m sulfuric acid stop solution was added. Optical densities were then read on a microplate reader at 492 nm. A set of standard sera (1, 2, 5, 10, 20, 50, and 100 mlU/ml) were run on each plate and used to determine antibody concentration. A protective level of antitetanus toxoid antibody is considered to be 0.1 IU/ml.

Influenza HAI Measurement. Antibody to subtype-specific influenza hemagglutinin was measured by hemagglutination inhibition according to a standard protocol.[10] Sera were treated overnight at 37°C with receptor destroying enzyme (Sigma, Cat. C8772) diluted 1:20 in calcium-saline buffer (0.9% NaCl; 0.1% $CaCl_2$ dihydrate; 0.12% boric acid anhydrous; 0.0052% sodium borate; pH 7.2), which was inactivated by incubation at 56°C for 30 minutes in 2.5% sodium citrate and diluted with phosphate-buffered saline solution to an initial concentration of 1:10 before serially diluting. Treated sera were serially diluted 1:2 in V-bottom microtiter plates (Nunc) in a volume of 25 μl before an equal volume of subtype-specific antigen containing four hemagglutinating units was added. Sera and antigen were incubated at room temperature for 30 minutes before the addition of 50 μl of 0.5% chicken red blood cells. Titers were reported as the highest dilution of sera that showed complete inhibition of agglutination.

DHEAS Measurements. DHEAS levels were measured on plasma using a commercial radioimmunoassay (Coat-a-Count DHEA-SO₄, Diagnostic Products Corporation, Los Angeles, California), following the manufacturer's recommendations. Briefly, 50 μl of the subject's serum was added to polyprophylene tubes precoated with antibodies to DHEA-SO$_4$. Then 1 ml ^{125}1 DHEA-SO$_4$ was added to each tube and incubated for 30 minutes at 37°C. Unbound sample and competitor were removed by decanting, and tubes were counted for 1 minute in a Beckman gamma-counter. The quantity of DHEA-SO$_4$ is determined by comparing the counts to a calibration curve where the amount of DHEA-SO$_4$ in the sample is inversely related to the number of counts. Sample values are expressed as μg/dL.

Statistical Analysis. Fourfold and greater than fourfold increases in antibody and protective titers were compared between groups using Fischer's exact test. Age, DHEAS levels, and prevaccination titers were compared using a two-sided Students *t* test considered significant for a $p \leq 0.05$. A Wilcoxon signed rank test was used to detect significant differences between treatment groups in the logarithmic rises in antibody levels as measured by ELISA, in the tetanus test, and HAI, in the influenza trial.

Murine Studies. Groups of six CBA/J female mice aged 6 months (mature adult) or 30 months (aged) were randomly assigned to appropriate treatment and vaccine regimens. Mature adults were injected with vaccine vehicle or 1 μg purified tetanus toxoid. Aged mice were maintained on routine water or placed on water containing 100 μg/ml DHEAS. Both aged groups of mice were immunized with 1 μg purified tetanus toxoid. Serum samples were collected from individual mice 28 days after immunization, and specific IgG antibody was detected using standard ELISA methodology. All study mice were then administered a single 2.5-ng dose of tetanus toxin intramuscularly in the left hindlimb. By 72 hours the intensity of the paralysis peaked and was irreversible. The study was terminated 7 days after challenge.

RESULTS

Concurrent DHEAS with Tetanus Toxoid Vaccination Protects against Tetanus Toxin-Induced Paralysis in Aged Mice

Immunization of adult mice with protein antigens will elicit antigen-specific primary and secondary immune responses. In stark contrast, immunization of aged mice with protein antigens is only weakly effective in stimulating primary immune responses.[11] For the generation of primary antibody responses in aged mice, previous studies in this laboratory established the adjuvant effect of DHEA or DHEAS administered concurrent with an immunogen.[11,12] The present murine study compares the *in vivo* neutralizing activity of antibodies made by tetanus toxoid immune mature adult, untreated aged, and DHEAS-treated aged mice.

Groups of six aged female mice were immunized with 1 μg of purified tetanus toxoid (a gift from M. L. Woods) as described in Materials and Methods. After 28 days, a small amount of blood was collected from each mouse to determine prechallenge tetanus toxoid-specific antibody titers by ELISA. After another 2 weeks, mice were challenged with an amount of purified tetanus toxin that would cause paralysis in the hindlimb (2.5 ng). All mice were observed daily over 7 days for the development of hindlimb paralysis, and the severity of paralysis from toxin was recorded. The response was maximal at 72 hours in all mice, and no reversal of the condition was apparent by 1 week (FIG. 1). All adult mice responded to vaccination by generating high titered serum antibody. As expected, these mice were protected

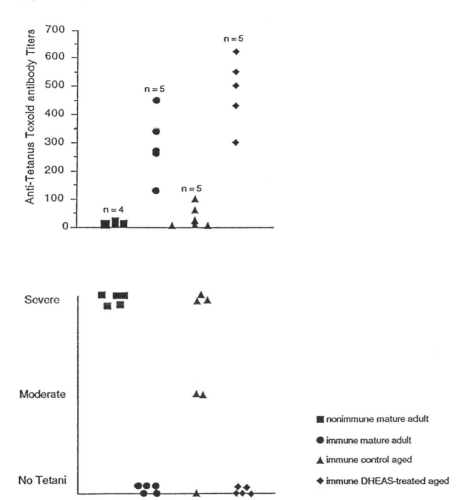

FIGURE 1. Correlation between tetanus toxoid specific serum antibody titers and protection from local tetanus toxin-induced hindlimb paralysis. (**Top**) Endpoint titers (Log 2) of antibody measured in groups of adult nonimmune, adult immune, aged immune, and DHEAS-treated aged immune mice. (**Bottom**) Development of clinical disease at 72 hours postinjection of 2.5 ng tetanus toxin.

from paralysis induced by injection tetanus toxin. Of the aged mice, a few in the untreated immunized group developed low titers of antibody and were moderately protected from paralysis. The remainder of the mice in this group had no detectable titer of tetanus toxoid-specific antibody and developed severe paralysis. Mice in the

DHEAS-treated group responded vigorously to the vaccine and were completely protected from paralysis.

The results of this experiment confirmed our earlier findings that DHEA-adjuvanted vaccines are important in assisting or boosting immune inductive processes in the elderly. They also demonstrate that the quality of the antibody, such as that required for neutralizing blood-borne toxins and pathogens, offers a level of protection equivalent to that developed by vaccinated adult mice.

Report of Trials Using DHEAS Adjuvants in Vaccination of Elderly Humans against Tetanus Toxoid or Influenza

The following studies in humans were designed to evaluate if DHEAS as a vaccine adjuvant increases the number of volunteers able to generate specific immune responses. One study employed a licensed vaccine for tetanus, which for many subjects we expected would not represent a primary exposure to tetanus toxoid. The second trial was conducted using the 1994–1995 licensed influenza vaccine. Each of the trials was run independently.

Trial 1. Vaccination of Elderly Male Volunteers with Tetanus Toxoid with or without Oral Administration of DHEAS as a Vaccine Adjuvant

Trial Design. Vaccinees for the tetanus trial were randomized in a double-blind fashion to receive oral doses of DHEAS 50 mg or placebo twice daily for 4 consecutive days beginning 2 days before vaccination. Serum samples were obtained before the first drug dose, on the day of vaccination, and on the 28th day after vaccination. All samples were frozen at $-70°C$ until tetanus toxoid-specific antibody levels were determined, as described in Materials and Methods.

Trial Results. When the study was decoded, 66 males over age 65 had been randomly assigned to a treatment group with 36 subjects randomized into the placebo group and 30 assigned to the DHEAS group. The average age of study participants was 73 with a median of 71. The relation between age and baseline DHEAS levels, presented in FIGURE 2, illustrates the expected age-related decline in endogenous levels of circulating DHEAS. A similar comparison of prevaccination tetanus titers and baseline DHEAS levels (FIG. 3) suggests that the level of prevaccination antibody titers correlates with age. Even though participants in this study had never received the childhood triple immunization regimen for tetanus, most recalled having had tetanus immunization in their adult lives. FIGURE 4 shows the distribution of prevaccination titers of tetanus toxoid specific antibody. Only 10 volunteers had baseline levels that were nonprotective (< 0.1 IU/ml), another 23 had intermediate titers (0.1–0.5 IU/ml), and the remainder exhibited titers well within the protective range. Most individuals in this study had protective titers of antitetanus serum antibody consistent with previous exposure to the immunogen. Twenty-eight days postvaccination, all but four individuals in both the placebo and the DHEAS group had a fourfold increase in response. FIGURE 5 depicts the postvaccination distribution of serum levels of anti-tetanus antibody according to the treatment regimen. We observed comparable immune responses ($>$ fourfold increase) to tetanus toxoid in both populations.

Trial Conclusions. In the absence of a notable deficiency in immunologic response in subjects treated with the placebo, it became difficult to establish a significant adjuvant effect of DHEAS. However, it had no detrimental effect on the outcome of vaccination.

Trial 2. Vaccination of Elderly Male and Female Volunteers with 1994–1995 Licensed Vaccine with or without Oral Administration of DHEAS as a Vaccine Adjuvant

Trial Design. Vaccinees were randomized in a double-blind fashion to receive DHEAS 50 mg or placebo orally for 2 consecutive days beginning the day of vaccination. Serum samples were obtained before the first drug dose and on days 28 and 90 postvaccination. All serum samples were frozen at −70°C until hemagglutination inhibition titers specific for each component (H3N2, H1N1, and B) were determined.

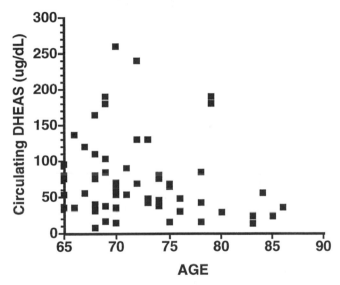

FIGURE 2. Human tetanus trial. Correlation between circulating DHEAS levels (μg/dl) and age in all subjects before vaccination.

Trial Results. Sixty-seven persons were enrolled in the influenza vaccine trial. All individuals completed the 28-day follow-up portion of the study and 62 of 67 remained in the study until its termination at 90 days. When the study was decoded, 34 had been assigned to the DHEAS treatment arm and 33 to the placebo arm. Demographically, the two groups were similar in age, in baseline serum DHEAS level, in gender, and in the percentage of entrants with < 1:40 pre-vaccination HAI titers of each component (not shown). The correlation between circulating DHEAS levels and age of all subjects before vaccination is shown in FIGURE 6. In addition, by graph we compared circulating DHEAS levels and pre-vaccination HAI titers (H3N2, H1N1, and B) in all study subjects. These data (FIGS. 7 and 8) show no striking correlation between serum DHEAS levels and pre-vaccination HAI titers.

In previous studies in aged mice, the effectiveness of DHEAS as an adjuvant was always compared to the minimal immune response by the placebo-vaccine group. To

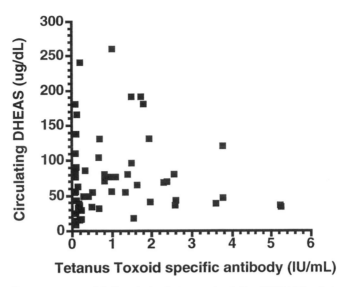

FIGURE 3. Human tetanus trial. Correlation between circulating DHEAS levels (μg/dl) and serum anti-tetanus antibody titers (IU/ml) before vaccination. Protection established at 0.1 IU/ml.

determine if DHEAS was an effective adjuvant for induction of immune responses in elderly humans, we compared the number of DHEAS-treated subjects showing a fourfold increase in antibody titers to that of the placebo group. The results of this analysis are presented graphically in FIGURES 9–11. FIGURES 9 and 10 compare the ability of subjects in the placebo versus DHEAS treatment groups to develop an immune response to H3N2. In this study 54.5% of the placebo group and 58.8% of

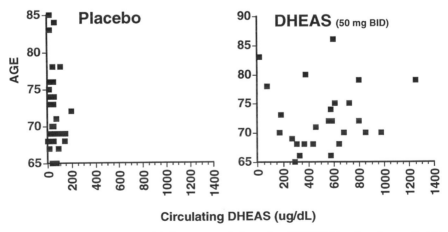

FIGURE 4. Human tetanus trial. Response to 2 days of oral DHEAS treatment according to age. Serum collected on day of vaccination.

the DHEAS-treated groups had a fourfold or greater increase in HAI titers. Only 27.3% of the placebo group and a striking 41.2% of the DHEAS-treated groups had greater than a fourfold increase in titers. FIGURES 11 and 12 illustrate the number of individuals in each treatment group that meet the minimum fourfold increase in H1N1 and influenza B HAI titers. The response to H1N1 is similar in both groups, it being 39.9% in the placebo group and 47.1% in the DHEAS-treated group. The response to influenza (Panama) B shows only three placebo-treated individuals with demonstrable increases in titer and six in the DHEAS group.

Finally, we analyzed the subset of individuals who had < 1:40 pre-vaccination HAI titers. Their responses, according to placebo or DHEAS treatment, are shown in FIGURE 13. In the placebo group, 29.6% developed a greater than fourfold increase in HAI titer. In the DHEAS group, 41.9% developed a greater than fourfold increase in HAI titer against H3N2.

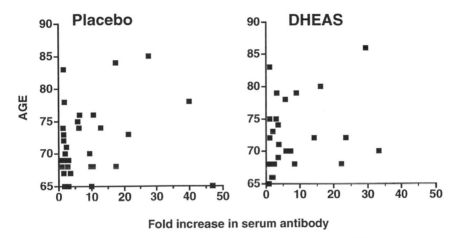

Fold increase in serum antibody

FIGURE 5. Human tetanus trial. Correlation between treatment and ability to respond to vaccination. Age versus increase in antibody levels (IU/ml).

Trial Conclusion. Although influenza may not be the perfect antigen for testing the hypothesis that DHEAS is an effective adjuvant for promoting primary response in the elderly, a strong trend towards induction of robust responses is noted in elderly individuals who receive DHEAS as an adjuvant to vaccination with this complex antigen.

DISCUSSION

The purpose of the present study was to establish proof-of-principle for DHEA/S in elderly humans as a vaccine adjuvant. On the basis of our own published murine studies,[11,12] the principal use of this adjuvant is with vaccines targeted for the elderly. Two independent studies were conducted in humans. The first assessed vaccine efficacy against tetanus toxoid and the second against the trivalent influenza vaccine in healthy volunteers aged 65 and over.

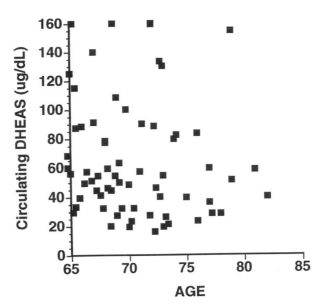

FIGURE 6. Human influenza trial. Correlation between circulating DHEAS levels and age at prevaccination screening.

The immune system of aged individuals undergoes a marked loss of efficiency with time.[4,13–15] The term immunosenescence is commonly used to refer to the age-associated decline in optimal immune function. The functional differences between adult and aged immune systems have been described in detail.[4,13,14,16] Present information, however, is largely descriptive, and progress towards understanding the physiologic basis for these changes is slow. Aberrations in immune responsiveness in the aged have been documented as depressions in cellular,[17–19] antibody-mediated,[20–23] and antitumor immunity.[24] In addition, increases in the incidence of autoimmunity and certain neoplasms in the aged have been noted.[24] Our more recent work demonstrated significant dysregulation in the production of certain cytokines, namely, interleukin-6 (IL-6), gamma-interferon (IFN-γ), and IL-10 (ref. 25 and unpublished work).

Many published studies have attempted to characterize the immunosenescent phenotype. This encumbering task requires careful assessment of the differences between specific components of the immune system in young versus old individuals. Studies have established that aging is accompanied by numerous functional and phenotypic changes in T cells, B cells, and macrophages (for review see refs. 4 and 14). The efficiency of early signal transduction events,[26–29] the ability of activated T cells to produce IL-2 or express IL-2 receptors,[28,30] the proliferative potential of activated lymphocytes,[5,31,32] differentiation of antigen-specific T cells into effector cells, and the immunologic responsiveness to new antigenic insults (for review see refs. 33 and 34) are all affected by the aging process. There is currently no consensus on the cause(s) of immunosenescence. However, this chronic condition affects most elderly individuals and plays an important role in infectious disease susceptibility, in duration and severity of disease, and in the markedly reduced efficiency of vaccination.

Our laboratory has uncovered and presented evidence that the steroid hormone dehydroepiandrosterone (DHEA) and its sulfated form (DHEAS) may play a role in immune function through their ability to influence T-cell function. DHEA has a direct effect on T-cell production of IL-2 and IFN-γ with no alteration in the production of IL-4.[11,35,36] We have demonstrated that either acute or chronic administration of DHEA/S enhances the ability of isolated T cells to produce these two cytokines.[36,37]

We recently reported that the amount of IL-2, IL-3, and GM-CSF produced *in vitro* by activated T cells from aged mice is lower than that from adult T cells.[11] Production of inducible, T-cell derived IL-4, IL-5, and IFN-γ by T cells of the aged population was markedly increased.[11] In additional experiments cytokine production appeared to be "corrected" if mice were given oral or parenteral dosing of DHEA/S.[11,12,36] This same form of therapy also conferred an enhanced ability to generate antibody responses to a test protein antigen.[11,12] The effectiveness of DHEA supplementation in reducing some of the more profound changes in immune function of the aged has led us to conclude that some of the previously described age-related alterations in immunity may be fully reversible.

Adrenal synthesis of DHEAS exhibits an age-related decline in all species that make the adrenal form of the steroid.[38,39] One avenue of research that merits further investigation is a cause-effect relationship between the decreasing DHEA/S production and the appearance of an immunosenescent phenotype. One possibility is that the declining DHEAS levels and the declining immune function in the elderly represent parallel events. Alternatively, decreasing levels of hormone may represent a risk factor for reduced immunocompetence. If individuals with low serum DHEA/S

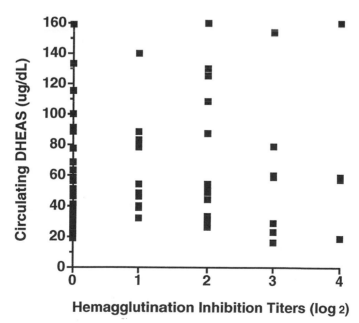

FIGURE 7. Human influenza trial. Correlation between circulating DHEAS levels and prevaccination hemagglutination inhibition titers against the H3N2 vaccine component in all study subjects.

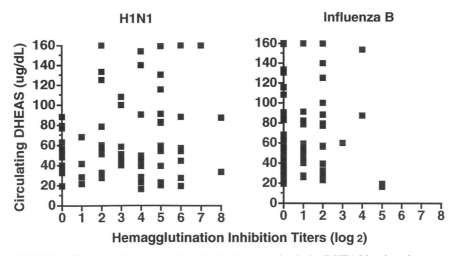

FIGURE 8. Human influenza trial. Correlation between circulating DHEAS levels and prevaccination hemagglutination inhibition titers against the H1N1 and influenza B vaccine components in all study subjects.

levels are at risk for dramatic changes in immune function, a threshold level of circulating hormone might be expected to correlate with a change in immune function. We examined the correlation between circulating DHEAS values and immune function in elderly individuals. As can be seen from FIGURE 13, there is no apparent relationship between circulating DHEAS levels and the ability of vaccinated humans to generate immune responses to the H3N2 component of the influenza vaccine. We believe that the question is not fully resolved with this test. Larger sample sizes and an analysis of immunogens that truly represent primary antigens in the elderly will be required before a definitive answer can be obtained.

On the basis of our recent murine studies in which DHEA and DHEAS augmented the capacity of aged mice to develop antibody responses to protein antigens,[11,12] we questioned if DHEAS has a similar effect on the efficacy of vaccination of elderly human volunteers. In one study, we studied the antibody response to a relatively simple protein antigen, tetanus toxoid, because it is safe, immunogenic, and currently recommended at 10-year boosting intervals in the elderly.[40,41] FIGURE 1 demonstrates the results of a study in aged mice vaccinated with tetanus toxoid using DHEAS as an adjuvant and then challenged with tetanus toxin. We saw a perfect correlation between ELISA titers of antibody and *in vivo* protection from toxin-induced paralysis. Although toxin is efficiently neutralized by circulating antibody, the results of this study indicate that the functionality of the antibody elicited in aged mice using DHEAS-adjuvanted vaccines is indistinguishable from the antibody generated by adult mice responding to antigen alone.

Tetanus is actually a rare disease in the United States. The disease continues to raise concerns because of its high mortality rate, which is preventable through immunization.[42] Despite the availability of an effective vaccine, tetanus still causes considerable morbidity.[42] Recent studies have documented that recommended protective titers of antibody are lacking in many individuals, especially those beyond their sixth decade of life.[42] In fact, surveys from various populations in the United States reveal that over half the individuals over age 60 have nonprotective levels of antitoxin.[43] Again over half of all cases of tetanus in the United States involve this age group and carry a high mortality rate.[44] The elderly are at greatest risk of tetanus either because they were never immunized or because their immunity has waned.[42,45]

Our own tetanus trial revealed interesting, yet contradictory, results. First, most volunteers in the study had been immunized more than 2 years before the present study. This may have been sufficient to explain the high percentage of individuals with protective levels of antibody before vaccination and their ability to generate a fourfold or greater increase in titers after immunization. Although it is an easy antigen to work with and validated assays can be used to ascertain reliable data, the response to this antigen apparently represented a secondary or recall immune response for the participants in the study. Earlier results in our mouse studies indicated that DHEAS was beneficial during induction of primary responses in aged, other immunocompromised mice, with little effect on recall responses. Therefore, it is not surprising that DHEAS treatment had minimal impact immune responses to tetanus in elderly humans.

Influenza, an acute, febrile respiratory illness caused by influenza A or B viruses, has an extremely high morbidity and mortality rate especially among elderly people.[41,46] During epidemics, 80–90% of influenza-associated deaths occur in individuals over age 64.[41,47] Although the exact mechanism is unknown, decreased T- and B-cell responses have been implicated.[18,23,48] Additionally, influenza-associated, bacterial superinfections have been described and may account for the serious morbidity associated with influenza.[49,50] Bacterial superinfection, in tandem with influenza infection, has a devastating effect on the elderly and may be responsible for the complications and mortality associated with influenza infections.[49,50] Adequate

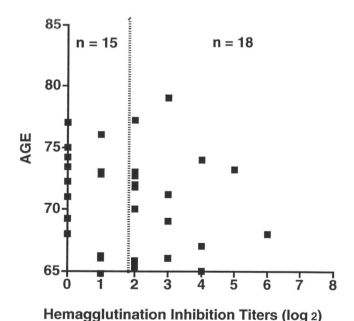

FIGURE 9. Human influenza trial. Ages and total number of subjects in the placebo group that showed a fourfold increase in HAI titers against the H3N2 component.

protection against influenza will protect against not only pulmonary disease and/or infection, but also bacterial superinfection.[49,50] A large component of the protection is mediated by IgG anti-hemagglutinating antibodies at titers of 1:40.[51] Currently, many adult subjects show protection using serologic analysis as a surrogate marker, depending on the form of vaccine. In subjects of greater than 60 years of age, both humoral and cytotoxic T-lymphocyte responses were significantly lower in the elderly than in the young.[1,46]

Results of the current influenza study demonstrated that most individuals did not have protective levels of antibody before vaccination. Furthermore, our data are consistent with published data in that roughly 55% of the participants in the placebo group could make at least a fourfold response to H3N2. Only 27% were able to

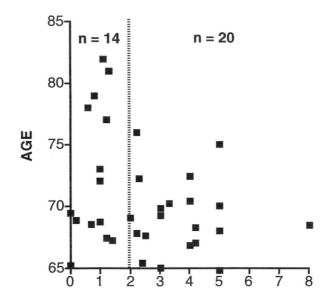

Hemagglutination Inhibition Titers (log 2)

FIGURE 10. Human influenza trial. Ages and total number of subjects in the DHEAS group that showed a fourfold increase in HAI titers against the H3N2 component.

generate responses higher than fourfold. DHEAS administered as a vaccine adjuvant enabled better response profiles, with approximately 41% showing greater than fourfold increases in HAI titers. Similar profiles were seen with responses to the other vaccine components. These data are encouraging and are based on the variance of the response; statistical significance should be attained with 500–1,000 subjects in each arm.

We currently do not completely understand the full impact of DHEA on T-cell function or the mechanism of the adjuvant activity of DHEA/S. We had set out to determine if the adjuvant effect of DHEAS in the aged mouse can be transferred to humans. The results of the influenza trial indicate that the adjuvant activity of DHEA is transferable to humans. Several studies need to be planned and carried

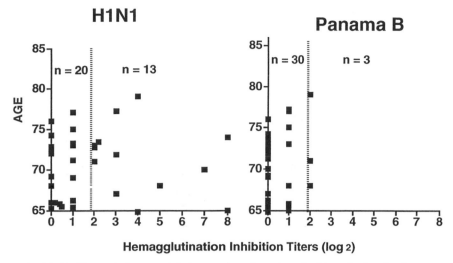

FIGURE 11. Human influenza trial. Ages and total number of subjects in the placebo group that showed a fourfold increase in HAI titers against the H1N1 and influenza B components.

out. First is a study conducted with a relevant vaccine that elicits a true primary response and GMP-quality DHEAS. Second would be a study conducted with polysaccharide antigens to expand the proof-of-principle beyond protein antigens. Finally, we would engage a number of investigators to conduct a large-scale influenza trial in community dwelling and nursing home residents, especially those in the 75–85

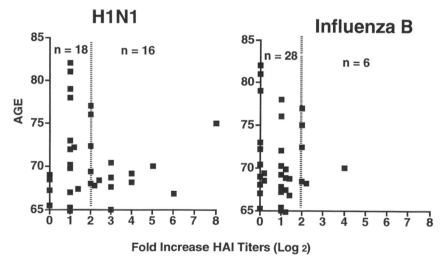

FIGURE 12. Human influenza trial. Ages and total number of subjects in the DHEAS group that showed a fourfold increase in HAI titers against the H1N1 (**left**) and influenza B (**right**) components.

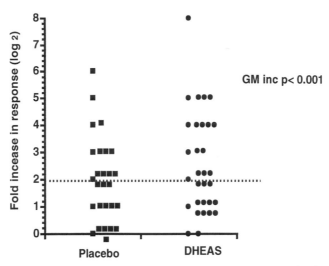

FIGURE 13. Human influenza trials. Among subjects with < 1:40 pre-vaccination HAI titers against the H3N2 component, the graph compares the number of subjects in the placebo versus those in the DHEAS treatment group that demonstrated greater than a fourfold increase in titers.

year age bracket. A large study would permit retrospective analysis to examine DHEAS risk factors and follow-up studies for infection rates in DHEAS and placebo groups.

SUMMARY

We have demonstrated that in aged mice, the titer of serum antibody induced against tetanus toxoid correlates with resistance to local paralysis caused by injection of tetanus toxin. Only mice immunized shortly after oral dosing with DHEAS demonstrated high serum antibody titers and complete protection from paralysis. These results became the basis for initiating proof-of-principle studies in human volunteers above age 65 using a licensed influenza vaccine and tetanus toxoid in two independent studies. The use of an oral delivery form of DHEAS before influenza vaccination was associated with a demonstrable increase in the number of individuals with a fourfold increase in HAI titers following vaccination. The overall mean increase in HAI titers was highest in the DHEAS-treated group. The use of DHEAS in the immunization of elderly subjects against tetanus toxoid, while unable to enhance the responses, was not a detriment to antibody response. We conclude that further studies will justify the use of DHEAS as an adjuvant for antigens that represent primary responses in the elderly.

REFERENCES

1. BEYER, W. E. P., A. M. PALACHE, M. BAKER & N. MAUREL. 1989. Vaccine **7:** 385–394.
2. STEIN, B. E. 1994. Drugs and Aging **5:** 242–253.

3. MILLER, R. A. 1989. J. Gerontol. **44:** 34–38.
4. THOMAN, M. L. & W. O. WEIGLE. 1989. Adv. Immunol. **46:** 221–261.
5. O'LEARY, J. J. & H. M. HALLGREN. 1991. Arch. Gerontol Geriatr. **12:** 199–210.
6. SANDERS, M. E., M. W. MAKGOBA & S. SHAW. 1988. Immunol. Today **9:** 195–198.
7. DE PAFOLI, P., S. BATTISTIN & G. F. SANTININ. 1988. Clin. Immunol. Immunopathol. **48:** 290–296.
8. MELVILLE-SMITH, M. E., V. A. SEAGROATT & J. T. WATKINS. 1983. J. Biol. Stand. **11:** 137–144.
9. VIRELLA, G. & B. HYMAN. 1991. J. Clin. Lab. Anal. **5:** 43–48.
10. SCHMIDT, N. S. & R. W. EMMONS. 1989. Diagnostic Procedures for Viral, Rickettsial, and Chlamydial Infections, 6th Ed. American Public Health Association. Washington, DC.
11. DAYNES, R. A. & B. A. ARANEO. 1992. Aging Immunol. Infect. Dis. **3:** 135–154.
12. ARANEO, B. A., M. L. WOODS, II & R. A. DAYNES. 1993. J. Infect. Dis. **167:** 830–840.
13. SCHWAB, R., C. A. WAITERS & M. E. WEKSLER. 1989. Host defense mechanisms and aging. Semin. Oncol. **16:** 20–27.
14. MILLER, R. A. 1991. Int. Rev. Cytol. **124:** 187–206.
15. GLATHE, H., S. BIGL & E. GROSCHE. 1993. Vaccine **11:** 702–705.
16. WALKER, C., J. F. GAUCHAT, A. L. deWECK & B. M. STADLER. 1990. Aging Immunol. Infect. Dis. **2:** 31–42.
17. WALDORF, D. S., R. F. WILKEN & J. L. DECKER. 1968. JAMA **203:** 831–837.
18. DEGELAU, J. J., J. J. O'LEARY, H. M. HALLGREN. 1994. Aging Immunol. Infect. Dis. **5:** 27–41.
19. MILLER, A. E. 1980. Neurology **30:** 582–587.
20. GOIAL, E. A., J. B. INNES & M. E. WEKSLER. 1976. J. Exp. Med. **144:** 1037–1048.
21. CZLONKOWSKA, A. & J. KORLAK. 1979. J. Gerontol. **34:** M9–M14.
22. AMMANN, A. J., G. SCHIFFMAN & R. AUSTRIAN. 1980. Exp. Soc. Exp. Biol. **164:** 312–316.
23. ERSHLER, W. B., A. L. MOORE & M. A. SOCINSKI. 1984. J. Clin. Immunol. **4:** 445–454.
24. TELLER, M. N. 1972. *In* Tolerance, Autoimmunity and Aging. M. M. Sigel & R. A. Good, Eds. Charles C. Thomas. 39–52. Springfield, IL.
25. ERSHLER, W. B., W. H. SUN, N. BINKLEY, S. GRAVENSTEIN, M. J. VOLK, G. KAMOSKE, R. G. KLOPP, E. B. ROECKER, R. A. DAYNES & R. WEINDRUCH. 1993. Lymphokine Cytokine Res. **12:** 225–230.
26. MILLER, R. A. 1991. Clin. Immunol. Immunopathol. **58:** 305–310.
27. PHILOSOPHE, B. & R. A. MILLER. 1990. J. Gerontol. **45:** 887–892.
28. ERNST, D. N., W. O. WEIGLE, D. N. McQUITTY, A. L. ROTHERMEL & M. V. HOBBS. 1989. J. Immunol. **142:** 1413.
29. BUCKLER, A. J., H. VIE, G. E. SONENSHEIN & R. A. MILLER. 1988. J. Immunol. **140:** 2442.
30. VIE, H. & R. A. MILLER. 1986. Mech. Aging Dev. **33:** 313–323.
31. NAGLE, J. E., K. K. CHOPRA, F. J. CHREST, M. T. McCOY, E. L. SCHNEIDER, N. J. HOLBROOK & W. H. ADLER. 1988. J. Clin. Invest. **81:** 1096–1106.
32. GILLIS, S., R. KOZAK, M. DURANTE & M. E. WEKSLER. 1981. J. Clin. Invest. **67:** 937–948.
33. BENDER, B. S. 1985. Rev. Biol. Res. Aging **2:** 143–155.
34. JONES, K. H. & D. L. ENNIST. 1985. Rev. Biol. Res. Aging **2:** 155–162.
35. DAYNES, R. A., D. J. DUDLEY & B. A. ARANEO. 1990. Eur. J. Immunol. **20:** 793–802.
36. ARANEO, B. A., T. DOWELL, T. TERUI, M. DEIGEL & R. A. DAYNES. 1990. Blood **78:** 688–699.
37. DAYNES, R. A., B. A. ARANEO, T. A. DOWELL, K. HUANG & D. DUDLEY. 1990. J. Exp. Med. **171:** 979–996.
38. ORENTREICH, N., J. L. BRIND, R. L. REZER & J. N. VOGELMAN. 1984. J. Clin. Endocrinol. Metab. **59:** 551–555.
39. MIGION, C. J., A. R. KELLER, B. LAWRENCE & T. H. SHEPHERD. 1957. J. Clin. Endocrinol. Metab. **17:** 1051–1062.
40. GENERAL RECOMMENDATIONS ON IMMUNIZATION. 1994. Morb. Mortal. Wkly. Rep. **43:** 1–38.
41. GUIDE FOR ADULT IMMUNIZATIONS. 1995. Am. Coll. Phys. Philadelphia, PA.: 90–97, 130–134.
42. RICHARDSON, J. P. & A. L. KNIGHT. 1993. J. Emerg. Med. **11:** 757–758.

43. GERGEN, P. J., G. M. McQULLAN, M. KIELY, T. M. EZZATI-RICE, R. W. SUTTER & G. VIVELLA. 1995. N. Engl. J. Med. **332:** 761–766.
44. SANFORD, J. P. 1995. N. Engl. J. Med. **322:** 812–813.
45. PREVOTS, R., R. W. SUTTER, P. M. STREBEL, S. L. COCHI & S. HADLER. 1992. MMWR CDC Surveill. Summ. **41:** 1–9.
46. FAGIOLO, V., A. AMADORI, E. COZZI, R. BENDO, M. LAMA, A. DOUGLAS & G. PALEE. 1993. Aging **5:** 451–458.
47. WILLIAMS, W. W., M. A. HICKSON & M. A. KANE. 1988. Ann. Int. Med. **108:** 616–625.
48. POWERS, D. C. & R. B. BELSHE. 1993. J. Infect. Dis. **167:** 584–592.
49. KILBOURNE, E. D. 1987. Influenza. Plenum. New York.
50. LOURIA, D. B., H. L. BLUMENFELD, J. T. ELLIS, E. D. KILBOURNE & D. E. ROGERS. 1959. J. Clin. Invest. **38:** 213–265.
51. GROSS, P. A., F. A. ENNIS, P. F. GOERLAN, L. J. DENSON, C. K. DENNING & D. SCHIFFMAN. 1977. J. Infect. Dis. **136:** 623–632.

Relationship between Humoral Immunoaugmenting Properties of DHEAS and IgD-Receptor Expression in Young and Aged Mice[a]

CHRISTINA D. SWENSON[b,c] SUSAN R. S. GOTTESMAN,[d]
DONALD V. BELSITO,[e] KAREN M. SAMANICH,[b]
JOANNE EDINGTON[b] AND G. JEANETTE THORBECKE[b]

[b]Department of Pathology and Kaplan Comprehensive Cancer Center
NYU Medical Center
New York, New York 10016

[d]SUNY Health Science Center
Brooklyn, New York 11203

[e]University of Kansas Medical Center
Kansas City, Kansas 66160

Injection of oligomeric IgD into young mice has immunoaugmenting properties that are mediated by IgD-receptor (IgD-R) bearing T helper cells.[1,2] Injection of oligomeric IgD in young but not in aged mice causes upregulation of IgD-R and enhances primary and secondary antibody responses, germinal center formation, and the production of all Ig isotypes except IgD itself.[1–5] IgD-R cross-linking is needed for receptor upregulation on T helper cells. Monomeric IgD injected with oligomeric IgD inhibits receptor cross-linking and subsequent IgD-R upregulation leading to the absence of immunoenhancement.[6] Augmentation induced by oligomeric IgD also fails to occur in IgD-deficient (IgD$^{-/-}$) mice that lack B-cell surface IgD.[6] These results indicate that augmentation of the humoral immune response is caused by facilitation of T-B interaction between IgD-R$^+$ T cells and surface IgD$^+$ B cells.

Injection of antigen alone also leads to upregulation of these receptors.[2] The effect of upregulation of these receptors induced by antigen alone does not occur rapidly enough to affect primary responses, but it does affect secondary responses. Monomeric IgD injected before a primary dose of antigen does not inhibit a primary response but partially inhibits IgD memory. These results suggest that the IgD-R on T cells, induced during the normal response to antigen, contributes to T-B cell interaction in priming for a secondary response.[6]

It is well known that there is an age-related decline in the immune response.[7–9] T-cell responses, including proliferative responses, delayed hypersensitivity, and antigen-specific helper T-cell functions for antibody responses,[7,8] become defective in the aged. The results just discussed suggest that induction of IgD-R on T cells might improve their helper function. We found that although IgD itself does not lead to IgD-R upregulation on cells from aged mice, exposure to various cytokines[5] and agents that activate protein kinase C and those that raise cAMP levels do so on cells

[a]This study was supported by USPHS grants AG-04980 and AG-04860.
[c]Address for correspondence: New York University, Department of Pathology, Room 523, 550 First Ave., New York, NY 10016.

from both young and aged mice.[10,11] Many of these agents are impractical or toxic for use *in vivo.* In the present study we therefore examined the effect of dehydroepiandrosterone sulfate (DHEAS), a naturally occurring prohormone that is reported to augment immune responses *in vivo,*[12-14] on the upregulation of IgD-R. We found that DHEA(S) leads to rapid upregulation of these receptors not only *in vitro,* but also in both young and aged mice *in vivo.* The results indicate, in addition, that induction of IgD-R on T cells is a major component of the humoral immunoenhancing effect of DHEAS in mice.

MATERIALS AND METHODS

Mice. Young and aged, BALB/c mice were obtained from the Charles River Breeding Lab. (Wilmington, Massachusetts). LAF_1 mice obtained from Jackson Labs. were allowed to age in the animal facility of New York University Medical Center. $CB6F_1$ mice were obtained from Biological Testing (Frederick, Maryland).

Reagents. Concanavalin A (ConA), phytohemagglutinin (PHA), lipopolysaccharide (LPS), phorbol 12-myristate 13-acetate (PMA), ionomycin, DHEA, DHEAS, and propylene glycol (p-1009) were obtained from Sigma Chemical Co. (St. Louis, Missouri). For *in vivo* use, DHEAS was dissolved in propylene glycol at a concentration of 1 mg/ml. Mice received 100 µg intraperitoneally per injection and control mice received propylene glycol. When used in drinking water, DHEAS was mixed in deionized water at a concentration of 100 µg/ml. For *in vitro* use, DHEA was dissolved in ethanol at 10 mg/ml and used at a final concentration of 20 µg/ml in medium with and without serum.

Purification of Splenic T Cells. Splenic T cells were prepared by depletion of adherent cells at 37°C for 1 hour on tissue culture grade Petri dishes (1400-1: Nunclon, Roskilde, Denmark) and of B cells by panning spleen cells on Petri dishes (Fisher 8-757-12, Fisher Scientific Co., Pittsburg, Pennsylvania) coated with affinity-purified goat anti-mouse Ig.[15] Contamination by sIg+ cells in such purified T-cell suspensions was <5%.

IgD Source and Purification. The plasmacytomas producing dimeric IgD, TEPC-1017,[16] or hybridomas producing monomeric IgD, KWD8 or KWD9,[17] were maintained in BALB/c mice. These forms of IgD were purified by affinity chromatography using a sepharose-bound lectin from *Griffonia simplicifolia*-1-(GS-1) which specifically binds murine IgD.[18]

Rosette-Forming Cell Assay. The rosette-forming cell (RFC) assay was performed as previously described.[3] In brief, purified IgD (TEPC-1017) or BSA was coupled to sheep erythrocytes (SRBC, Colorado Serum Co., Denver, Colorado) using the $CrCl_3$ coupling method.[19] IgD-SRBC or BSA-SRBC (0.2 ml of 1%) were mixed with 0.1 ml of assay T cells (2.5×10^5), incubated at 37°C for 25 minutes, centrifuged at 200 g for 3 minutes, and incubated further overnight. Lymphocytes were stained with 1% toluidine blue. T cells with ≥ 3 IgD-SRBC bound were scored as IgD-RFC, and the percentages of cells forming rosettes with BSA-SRBC were subtracted. Each sample was assayed in triplicate. The mean number ±SD of IgD-RFC among 100 lymphocytes is reported. The specificity of rosette formation for IgD was verified by inhibiting with IgD (100 µg/ml) and not with IgG (100 µg/ml).

Plaque-Forming Cell Assay. 4-Hydroxy-5-iodo-3-nitrophenyl (acetyl) (NIP)-HRBC and NIP-SRBC were prepared by coupling NIP-*O*-succinimide (Cambridge Research Biochemicals Ltd., Cheshire, England) to HRBC or SRBC.[20] Anti-NIP plaque-forming cell (PFC) assays were performed by the slide modification technique of Jerne *et al.*[21] Indirect PFC assays were performed by the addition of goat anti-μ to the agar and rabbit anti-mouse Ig to the complement as previously reported.[22]

Contact Sensitization. On day 0, all animals were sensitized on their shaved dorsal skin surface by topical application of 25 μl of 2.5% dinitrochlorobenzene (DNCB, Sigma Chemical Co., St. Louis, Missouri) in acetone:olive oil (4:1).[23] Irritant controls received solvent alone. On day 5 or 7, all animals were challenged on one ear with 25 μl of 1% DNCB. Ear swelling (as an index of sensitization) was measured 24 hours after challenge using an engineer's micrometer (Mitutoyo Mfg. Co., Tokyo, Japan) as the thickness post-challenge minus the thickness pre-challenge. Irritant controls produced negligible swelling.

Proliferation Assays. Effector cells are incubated with mitogens (Con A, 5 μg/ml; PHA, 10 μg/ml; LPS, 10 μg/ml; or PMA, 1 ng/ml plus ionomycin 1 μg/ml) or with irradiated stimulator cells in 96-well plates in Eagle's MEM with supplement: L-glutamine, penicillin-streptomycin, nonessential amino acids, heat-inactivated fetal calf serum and 2-ME. [^{3}H]Thymidine (1 μCi/well, 1.9 ci/mM) is added for the final 8 or 16 hours of incubation, and cultures are harvested with an automatic cell harvester.[8]

Interleukin-2 Assay. Interleukin-2 (IL-2) levels were measured by analyzing CTLL-1 proliferation in the presence of serial dilutions of test supernatant[24] and were calculated using probit analysis.[25] Specificity was tested by performing the assay in the presence and the absence of anti-IL-4 (11B11).[26]

Enumeration of Ia$^+$ Langerhans cells (LC) in the Skin.[27] Epidermal sheets were prepared from skin biopsies by incubation in 0.5 M NH$_4$SCN in 0.1 M phosphate buffer (pH 6.8) for 25 minutes at 37°C. To eliminate the confounding effects of regional variations in the density of LC, all experiments were performed on a 2.5 × 2.5 cm area of mid-dorsal skin. Sheets were fixed in 95% ethanol at 4°C for 20 minutes and washed in Tris buffer. Specimens were stained for the presence of cell-surface Ia antigen using monoclonal antibody M5/114 in an indirect immunoperoxidase technique.[23] The number of Ia$^+$ Langerhans cells per mm^2 in one central and four peripheral areas of each epidermal sheet was determined with a calibrated eyepiece. Areas around hair follicles were excluded. The cell density for each sheet was calculated as the arithmetic mean of the five counts. Results are expressed as the mean number of Langerhans cells per mm^2 obtained for groups of mice ± SD.

Statistical Analyses. Significance of differences between groups was determined by Student's *t* test.

RESULTS AND DISCUSSION

Effect of DHEA and DHEAS on IgD-R Expression

The effect of DHEA (20 μg/ml) on IgD-R expression on splenic T cells was examined in serum-free medium (FIG. 1). Upregulation occurred rapidly, being detectable at 15 minutes and near maximal at 30 minutes, similar to that observed previously with oligomeric IgD. We previously showed that *de novo* protein synthesis was not required for IgD-R upregulation after exposure to IgD itself.[28] IgD-R or components of the receptor must therefore be preformed and become accessible for binding IgD upon exposure to the upregulating agents, as detected in the rosette-forming assay with IgD-coated SRBC.

This rapid IgD-R upregulation induced by DHEA, similar to the effects of various pharmacologic agents examined,[10,11] indicates that DHEA triggers a signaling event leading to increased IgD-R expression.

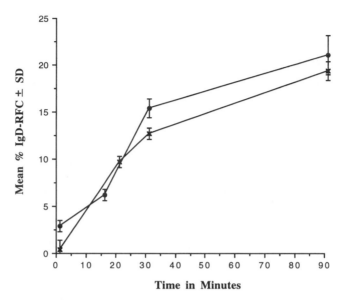

FIGURE 1. Kinetics of IgD-R upregulation on purified T cells by DHEA *in vitro* (●—●). Purified splenic T cells were exposed to DHEA at 20 μg/ml in serum-free media at 37°C for the indicated times. Cells were washed free of DHEA and assayed for IgD-RFC as described in Materials and Methods. The number of IgD-RFC obtained with T cells after exposure to medium alone for 90 minutes was 5.3 ± 0.6 and after exposure to cross-linked IgD was 19.3 ± 1.2. Similar results were obtained using medium containing 2% fetal calf serum. (*n* = 3–4). For comparison, the kinetics of IgD-RFC induction by oligomeric IgD at at 37°C are shown (x—x) (data from ref. 28).

Administration of DHEAS *in vivo* similarly induced IgD-R on spleen cells. This was observed not only after prolonged administration by adding DHEAS to the drinking water, but also within 24 hours after a single intraperitoneal injection of 100 μg. It was of particular interest that IgD-R expression was induced on cells from both aged and young mice (FIG. 2), as oligomeric IgD itself can only cause this effect on cells from young mice.

Effect of DHEAS on Antibody Production

DHEAS, administered intraperitoneally for 3–6 weeks, enhanced antibody production in both young and aged mice, as shown by an increase in the numbers of IgM and IgG antibody-forming cells per spleen (FIG. 3). The effect of DHEAS on antibody enhancement in 23-month-old mice was similar to that obtained with young mice (not shown). DHEAS was at least as effective or even more effective in enhancing antibody production in 36-month-old mice as in young mice (FIG. 3).

As just mentioned, the upregulation of IgD-R as well as the immunoaugmenting effects of IgD may be completely blocked by the simultaneous injection of monomeric IgD with oligomeric IgD. To determine if upregulated IgD-R played an important role in the enhancement of antibody production induced by DHEAS, we examined whether monomeric IgD injected at the time of antigen administration could also block the immunoaugmentation induced by DHEAS. Results in FIGURE 3 show that monomeric IgD caused a 65% reduction in DHEAS-induced enhancement in young mice and complete inhibition of DHEAS-induced enhancement of antibody production in aged mice. The results suggest that IgD-R expression is extremely important in the enhancement of antibody production by DHEAS. These results also show that IgD-R, which has already been induced by DHEAS before injection of monomeric IgD and antigen, can still be prevented from augmenting antibody production by inhibiting their interaction with $sIgD^+$ B cells. Thus, monomeric IgD blocks not only the upregulation of IgD-R, but also the interaction of IgD-R$^+$ T cells with $sIgD^+$ B cells which, as previous results indicate, is the basis of IgD-R–induced immunoaugmentation.[6]

Evaluation of Contact Sensitivity in DHEAS-Treated Mice

In view of augmented helper function for antibody production by T cells from DHEAS-treated mice, we determined if delayed type hypersensitivity was also increased in these mice. Groups of mice were sensitized by painting the skin with DNCB and were challenged 5–7 days later. No significant effect of this schedule of DHEAS administration was seen on this response in that contact sensitivity was similar in both young and aged mice with or without DHEAS treatment (TABLE 1).

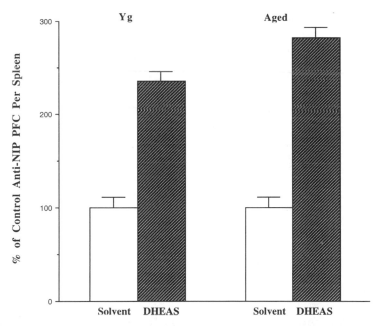

FIGURE 2. Induction of IgD-R on splenic T cells from young and aged mice by treatment with DHEAS. DHEAS as a single injection of 0.1 mg was administered intraperitoneally (ip) to CB6F$_1$ mice of 2 months (yg) and 22–25 months (aged) or by addition of 0.1 mg/ml to the drinking water for 5 weeks orally to BALB/c mice of 8 months (yg) and 23 months (aged). The percentage of IgD-RFC was determined in an IgD-RFC assay as described in Materials and Methods. $n = 2$–3 mice per group.

The variation in responsiveness in experiment 4, TABLE 1, was due to the absence of responsiveness in individual mice from each of the groups of aged mice in this experiment, regardless of their prior DHEAS treatment.

The mitogen responses of T cells from DHEAS-pretreated mice were also examined. Although no obvious effect on proliferation was observed, IL-2 contents in the supernatants harvested 24 hours after stimulation were higher with cells from DHEAS-treated than from control aged mice (see footnote c, TABLE 1).

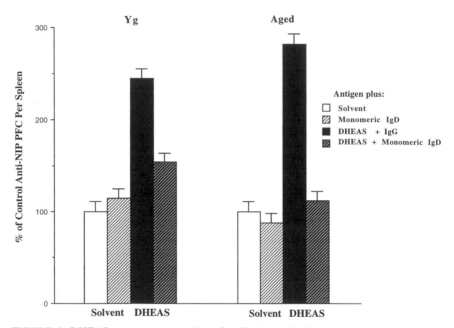

FIGURE 3. DHEAS causes augmentation of antibody production in young (9 months) and aged mice (36 months) which is prevented by monomeric IgD. Groups of LAF$_1$ mice ($n = 3$–7) received DHEAS, 0.1 mg ip, 3 times per week for 3 (yg) or 6 (aged) weeks prior to iv injection of antigen, 5×10^6 NIP-HRBC. Some mice received 0.1 mg of monomeric IgD (KWD8) or 0.1 mg IgG iv 6 hours before antigen. IgM-anti-NIP PFC per spleen were determined 4 days after antigen administration. Anti-SRBC PFC responses were subtracted from the values recorded in the figure. Results are expressed as percentages of the control response to antigen alone. The control (100%) geometric means of IgM-anti-NIP PFC/spleen were 9,400 (yg) and 9,100 (aged). Significance of differences: between primary responses obtained with spleen cells in the group of mice treated with antigen plus solvent only and the group treated with antigen plus DHEAS plus IgG, p was <0.0001 (yg) and 0.0007 (aged); between the group of mice treated with antigen and DHEAS plus IgG and the group treated with antigen and DHEAS plus monomeric IgD, p was <0.0001 (yg) and 0.006 (aged).

Effect of DHEAS on Ia Expression by (Epidermal) Langerhans Cells

Aged mice frequently exhibit lower expression of class II MHC antigen on their epidermal dendritic or Langherhans cells.[29] In view of the important role of Langerhans cells in the presentation of antigens to T cells, particularly during contact sensitization,[30] any effect on Ia antigen expression by these cells could greatly

TABLE 1. Effect of DHEAS on Contact Sensitivity

		Ear Swelling (mm $\times 10^{-2}$) $\pm$ SD $(n)^b$	
Age of Mice[a]	Exp.	In Control Mice	In DHEAS-Treated Mice[c]
Young	1	11.0 ± 2.2 (4)	15.5 ± 0.5 (4)
	2	23.8 + 2.7 (3)	21.0 ± 3.7 (4)
Mature	3	19.4 ± 2.4 (5)	21.2 ± 3.8 (5)
Aged	1	20.4 ± 3.7 (3)	25.2 ± 2.9 (3)
	4	20.7 ± 15.6 (4)	15.0 ± 13.1 (4)

[a]Young = 2–4 months; mature = 12 months; aged = 22–24 months.
[b]Sensitization was by application of 0.025 ml of 2.5% DNCB to the back of the neck on day 0. Ear swelling was measured 24 hours after challenge (application of 0.025 ml of 1% DNCB to the ear on day 5).
[c]DHEAS treatment was by subcutaneous injection of 0.1 mg in 0.1 ml propylene glycol 1 day before sensitization. Control mice received solvent only. Similarly treated mice were also used for measurements of interleukin-2 production in spleen cells. The response to stimulation by concanavalin A was measured in serum-free medium. The 24-hour supernatants contained: yg control, 1,000 ± 200 U/ml; yg DHEAS-treated, 1,100 ± 270 U/ml; aged control, 110 ± 85 U/ml; aged DHEAS-treated, 717 ± 535 U/ml of IL-2.

influence immune responses. Moreover, Langerhans cells may be considered as outposts of the dendritic cell system in the skin, where they can readily be sampled for Ia expression.[29] It was therefore of interest to determine if treatment with DHEAS would affect the expression of Ia antigen on these cells. Epidermal sheets prepared from full thickness skin were stained for Ia and the Ia$^+$ cells enumerated. No difference was observed between epidermis from control and that from DHEAS-treated young mice (TABLE 2). However, in two separate experiments with aged mice, DHEAS enhanced the number of Ia$^+$ Langerhans cells. This was even more striking because the untreated aged mice showed levels of Ia$^+$ cells that were equal to those of untreated young mice. Therefore, the augmented Ia$^+$ Langerhans cell counts observed in DHEAS-treated mice were higher than the Ia$^+$ Langerhans cell counts in epidermis from young mice. It is possible that this effect on Ia levels is

TABLE 2. Effect of DHEAS on Ia Expression on Langerhans Cells in Young and Aged Mice

		# Langerhans Cells per mm^2 $\pm$ SD $(n)^b$	
Age of Mice[a]	Exp.	In Control Mice	In DHEAS-Treated Mice[c]
Young	1	554 ± 36 (5)	628 ± 62 (5)
Aged	1	516 ± 89 (3)	1,032 ± 423 (3)
Young	2	628 ± 78 (1)	641 ± 54 (4)
Aged	2	554 ± 65 (3)[d]	925 ± 124 (3)[d]

[a]Young = 2–4 months; aged = 22–24 months.
[b]Langerhans cells were enumerated on at least five different areas of epidermal sheets stained for MHC class II antigen.
[c]DHEAS treatment was by subcutaneous injection of 0.1 mg in 0.1 ml propylene glycol 1 day before the mice were killed (Exp. 1) or by repeated ip injections (Exp. 2). Control mice received solvent only.
[d]Difference between these two groups is significant ($p = 0.01$).

mediated by cytokines activated in the epidermis when DHEAS, as reported, causes normalization of cytokine levels in aged mice.[31-33]

Possible Application of DHEAS to Humans

The effect of DHEA on IgD-R in humans has not been studied as yet. However, there is good reason to expect that it will be similar to that in mice. In the first place, the various agents that cause upregulation of IgD-R on murine T cells also have this effect on human peripheral blood cells.[34] Secondly, the ability of aged individuals to produce good antibody responses (with titers ≥ 40) to all three viral components of the 1993/1994 influenza vaccine is strongly correlated with the ability of the peripheral blood cells from these people to exhibit IgD-R on exposure to aggregated IgD *in vitro*.[35,36] In fact, aged subjects who have good responses to influenza vaccination exhibit elevated IgD-R expression on their peripheral blood T cells for at least 2 weeks after immunization, whereas aged subjects who have defective responses do not show elevated IgD-R on their T cells.[36] Thus, although reconstitution of IgD-R expression on T cells by agents such as DHEA(S) could be of help in enhancing antibody responses to vaccination in the elderly, it remains to be determined if DHEA(S) will have such effects on IgD-R expression in all aged human subjects.

SUMMARY

IgD-receptors are associated with augmented antibody production *in vivo* and are induced on CD4[+] T cells by aggregated IgD in young but not in aged mice. In the current study orally or intraperitoneally administered DHEAS was found to enhance antibody production, as measured in a plaque-forming cell assay, and also to cause an increased expression of IgD-R on T cells in both young and aged mice. IgD-R[+] T cells are enumerated by rosette cell formation with IgD-coated SRBC. Since, as shown previously, the immunoaugmenting effect of IgD-R[+] T cells is blocked by injection of monomeric IgD, the effect of monomeric IgD was also examined in DHEAS-pretreated mice. The inhibitory effect obtained with monomeric IgD in these studies indicates that upregulation of IgD-R by DHEAS plays an important role in the immunoenhancing effect of this hormone. In addition, no significant effect of DHEAS was obtained on contact hypersensitivity to DNCB or on proliferative responses of T cells from young or aged mice. Aged but not young mice showed increases in the numbers of Ia[+] epidermal Langerhans cells after DHEAS treatment.

REFERENCES

1. XUE, B., R. COICO, D. WALLACE, G. W. SISKIND, B. PERNIS & G. J. THORBECKE. 1984. Physiology of IgD. IV. Enhancement of antibody production in mice bearing IgD-secreting plasmacytomas. J. Exp. Med. **159:** 103.
2. COICO, R. F., G. W. SISKIND & G. J. THORBECKE. 1988. Role of IgD and T delta cells in the regulation of the humoral immune response. Immunol. Rev. **105:** 45.
3. SWENSON, C. D., R. F. VAN VOLLENHOVEN, B. XUE, G. W. SISKIND, G. J. THORBECKE & R. F. COICO. 1988. Physiology of IgD. IX. Effect of IgD on immunoglobulin production in young and old mice. Eur. J. Immunol. **18:** 13.
4. COICO, R. F., D. WALLACE, B. XUE, J. ROSEN, B. PERNIS, G. J. THORBECKE & G. W.

SISKIND. 1985. IgD-induced enhancement of the immune response. *In* Microenvironments in the Lymphoid System. G. G. B. Klaus, Ed.: 729. Plenum Publ. Corp. New York.

5. COICO, R. F., S. R. S. GOTTESMAN, G. W. SISKIND & G. J. THORBECKE. 1987. Physiology of IgD VIII. Age-related decline in the capacity to generate T cells with receptors for IgD and partial reversal of the defect with IL-2. J. Immunol. **138:** 2776.

6. SWENSON, C. D., E. R. RIZINASHVILI, A. R. AMIN & G. J. THORBECKE. 1995. Oligomeric IgD augments and monomeric IgD inhibits the generation of IgD memory antibody responses in normal, but not in IgD-deficient mice. J. Immunol. **154:** 653.

7. MAKINODAN, T. & M. M. B. KAY. 1980. Age influence on the immune system. Adv. Immunol. **29:** 287.

8. GOTTESMAN, S. R. S., J. A. KRISTIE & R. L. WALFORD. 1981. Proliferative and cytotoxic immune functions in aging mice. I. Sequence of decline reactivities measured under optimal and suboptimal sensitization conditions conditions. Immunology **44:** 607.

9. ERNST, D. N., W. O. WEIGLE & M. L. THOMAN. 1987. Retention of T cell reactivity to mitogens and alloantigens by Peyer's patch cell of aged mice. J. Immunol. **138:** 26.

10. AMIN, A. R., C. D. SWENSON, B. XUE, Y. ISHIDA, B. G. NAIR, T. B. PATEL, T. M. CHUSED & G. J. THORBECKE. 1993. Regulation of IgD-receptor expression on murine T cells. II. Upregulation of IgD receptors is obtained after activation of various intracellular second-messenger systems, tyrosine kinase activity is required for the effect of IgD. Cell. Immunol. **152:** 405.

11. SWENSON, C. D., A. R. AMIN, B. XUE & G. J. THORBECKE. 1993. Regulation of IgD-receptor expression on murine T cells. III. The nature of the defect in IgD-receptor expression on murine T cells from aged mice as defined by alternate IgD-receptor upregulating agents. Aging Immunol. Infect. Dis. **4:** 109.

12. DAYNES, R. A. & B. A. ARANEO. 1992. Prevention and reversal of some age-associated changes in immunologic responses by supplemental dehydroepiandrosterone sulfate therapy. Aging Immunol. Infect. Dis. **3:** 109.

13. ARANEO, B. A., M. L. WOODS, II & R. A. DAYNES. 1993. Reversal of the immunosenescent phenotype by dehydroepiandrosterone: Hormone treatment provides an adjuvant effect on the immunization of aged mice with recombinant hepatitis B surface antigen. J. Infect. Dis. **167:** 830.

14. GARG, M. & S. BONDADA. 1993. Reversal of age-associated decline in immune response to Pnu-immune vaccine by supplementation with the steroid hormone dehydroepiandrosterone. Infect. Immun. **61:** 2238.

15. WYSOCKI, L. J. & V. L. SATO. 1978. "Panning" for lymphocytes: A method for cell selection. Proc. Natl. Acad. Sci. USA **75:** 2844.

16. FINKELMAN, F. D., S. W. KESSLER, J. F. MUSHINSKI & M. POTTER. 1981. IgD secreting murine plasmacytomas: Identification and partial characterization of two IgD myeloma proteins. J. Immunol. **126:** 680.

17. OWENS, J. D., JR., F. D. FINKELMAN, J. D. MOUNTZ & J. F. MUSHINSKI. 1991. Nonhomologous recombination at sites within the mouse J_H-C-delta locus accompanies C-mu deletion and switch to immunoglobulin D secretion. Mol. Cell. Biol. **11:** 5660.

18. OPPENHEIM, J. D., A. R. AMIN & G. J. THORBECKE. 1990. A rapid one step purification procedure for murine IgD based on the specific affinity of *Bandeiraea* (*Griffonia*) *simplicifolia-1* for N-linked carbohydrates on IgD. J. Immunol. Methods **130:** 243.

19. POSTON, R. N. 1974. A buffered chromic chloride method of attaching antigens to red cells: Use in haemagglutination. J. Immunol. Methods **5:** 91.

20. SHERR, D. H., S.-T. JU, J. Z. WEINBERGER, B. BENACERRAF & M. E. DORF. 1981. Hapten-specific T cells responses to 4-hydroxy-3-nitrophenyl acetyl. VII. Idiotype-specific suppression of plaque-forming cells responses. J. Exp. Med. **153:** 640.

21. JERNE, N. K., A. A. NORDIN & C. HENRY. 1963. The agar plaque technique for recognizing the antibody-producing cells. *In* Cell-Bound Antibody. B. Amos & H. Koprowski, Eds.: 109. Wistar Institute Press. Amsterdam.

22. GOIDL, E. A., T. J. ROMANO, G. W. SISKIND & G. J. THORBECKE. 1978. Changes in affinity of 19S and 7S antibodies at the cellular level in responses to hapten conjugates of varying T dependency. Cell. Immunol. **35:** 231.

23. XUE, B., R. M. DERSARKISSIAN, R. L. BAER, G. J. THORBECKE & D. V. BELSITO. 1986. Reversal by lymphokines of the effect of cyclosporin A on contact sensitivity and antibody production in mice. J. Immunol. **136:** 4128.
24. SMITH, K. A., L. B. LARCHMAN, J. J. OPPENHEIM & M. F. FAVATA. 1980. The functional relationship of the interleukins. J. Exp. Med. **151:** 1551.
25. GILLIS, S., M. M. FERM, W. OU & K. A. SMITH. 1978. T cell growth factor: Parameters of production and a quantitative microassay for activity. J. Immunol. **120:** 2027.
26. OHARA, J. & W. E. PAUL. 1985. Production of a monoclonal antibody to and molecular characterization of B-cell stimulatory factor-1. Nature (Lond.) **315:** 333.
27. EPSTEIN, S. P., R. L. BAER, G. J. THORBECKE & D. V. BELSITO. 1991. Immunosuppressive effects of transforming growth factor β: Inhibition of induction of Ia antigen on Langerhans cells by cytokines and of the contact hypersensitivity response. J. Invest. Dermatol. **96:** 832.
28. SWENSON, C. D., A. R. AMIN, B. XUE & G. J. THORBECKE. 1993. Regulation of IgD-receptor expression on murine T cells I. Characterization and metabolic requirements of the process leading to their expression. Cell. Immunol. **152:** 405.
29. BELSITO, D. V., R. L. BAER & G. J. THORBECKE. 1986. Immunomodulation of Langerhans cell surface antigen in various immunodeficient states. *In* Primary Immunodeficiency Diseases. M. M. Eibl & F. S. Rosen, Eds.: 253–268. Elsevier Science Publ. Amsterdam.
30. SILBERBERG-SINAKIN, I., G. J. THORBECKE, R. L. BAER, S. A. ROSENTHAL & V. BEREZOWSKY. 1976. Antigen-bearing Langerhans cells in skin, dermal lymphatics and in lymph nodes. Cell. Immunol. **25:** 137.
31. DAYNES, R. A., B. A. ARANEO, W. B. ERSHLER, C. MALONEY, G. Z. LI & S. Y. RYU. 1993. Altered regulation of IL-6 production with normal aging. Possible linkage to the age-associated decline in dehydroepiandrosterone and its sulfated derivative. J. Immunol. **150:** 5219.
32. DAYNES, R. A., B. A. ARANEO, T. A. DOWELL, K. HUANG & D. DUDLEY. 1990. Regulation of murine lymphokine production *in vivo*. III. The lymphoid tissue microenvironment exerts regulatory influences over T helper cell function. J. Exp. Med. **171:** 979.
33. DAYNES, R. A., A. W. MEIKLE & B. A. ARANEO. 1991. Locally active steroid hormones may facilitate compartmentalization of immunity by regulating the types of lymphokines produced by helper T cells. Res. Immunol. **142:** 408.
34. WEI, C.-F., S. L. TAMMA, R. F. COICO, C. D. SWENSON, E. A. SECORD, A. R. AMIN & G. J. THORBECKE. 1993. The IgD-receptor positive human T lymphocytes. II. Total absence of any IgD-receptor expression in a large percentage of healthy aged individuals. Aging: Immunol. Infect. Dis. **4:** 169.
35. WEI, C.-F., A. WALI, E. P. CHERNIACK, K. SARIRIAN, M. E. WEKSLER, C. RUSSO & G. J. THORBECKE. 1992. Correlation between the ability of elderly individuals to respond to influenza vaccination and the capacity of their peripheral blood lymphocytes to express receptors for IgD. Aging Immunol. Infect. Dis. **3:** 195.
36. SWENSON, C. D., E. P. CHERNIACK, C. RUSSO & G. J. THORBECKE. 1995. Predictive value of IgD-receptor upregulation on peripheral blood T cells for the antibody response to influenza vaccination. Submitted.

The Epidemiology of DHEAS and Cardiovascular Disease

ELIZABETH BARRETT-CONNOR AND DEBORAH
GOODMAN-GRUEN

Department of Family and Preventive Medicine
University of California, San Diego
La Jolla, California 92093-0607

Dehydroepiandrosterone (DHEA) and its sulfate ester (DHEAS), the major secretory products of the human adrenal gland, are produced in larger quantity than are any other steroid hormones. Their high turnover suggests a major biologic role, but their function is uncertain. Circulating levels of these adrenal androgens show a striking linear decrease with age.[1-3] The age-related fall in DHEA or DHEAS prompted the thesis that low levels might be associated with diseases of aging such as atherosclerosis.[4] In early case-control studies, low levels in blood or urine were associated with myocardial infarction in men.[5,6] In 1986 we reported that low levels of plasma DHEAS predicted a significantly increased risk of cardiovascular death in 242 men from the Rancho Bernardo cohort who were followed up for 12 years.[7] The converse was true in a preliminary analysis of 289 Rancho Bernardo women followed for 12 years, in whom high DHEAS levels were associated with an increased risk of heart disease,[8] but these results were based on less than 30 deaths. Other studies have shown contradictory results.[9-15]

We report here an update on the distribution and covariates of DHEAS levels and the risk of fatal cardiovascular disease (CVD) and ischemic heart disease (IHD) in men and women, based on a longer (19-year) follow-up of a larger number of men (1,029) and women (942) from the same cohort. To our knowledge, this is the only prospective community-based study of DHEAS with fatal CVD outcomes in both men and women.

METHODS

Between 1972 and 1974, 82% of a geographically defined community of older adults in Rancho Bernardo, California, were recruited to study risk factors for CVD.[16] A standardized questionnaire which included questions about personal and family history of heart disease (heart attack or heart failure), smoking and exercise history, use of hormone replacement therapy, and current use of medication was completed. Blood pressure was measured with a standard mercury sphygmomanometer after the participant had been seated for at least 5 minutes. Measurement was repeated in those in whom the initial reading was greater than 160 mm Hg systolic or greater than 90 mm Hg diastolic and the lower of the two readings was recorded. Height and weight were measured with the participants in lightweight clothing and no shoes. Body mass index (BMI) was calculated as $(kg/m^2) \times 100$. Participants were seen between 7:30 and 11:00 AM after a requested 12-hour fast. Total plasma cholesterol was measured in a standardized Lipid Research Clinic laboratory using an AutoAnalyzer.[17] Fasting plasma glucose was measured in a hospital diagnostic laboratory using a hexokinase method. Plasma for DHEAS was obtained and frozen at −70°C. One third of this cohort returned within 90 days for a second evaluation, when fasting high density lipoprotein (HDL) cholesterol and low density lipoprotein (LDL) cholesterol were measured by precipitating the other lipoproteins with heparin and manganese chloride according to the standardized procedures of the Lipid Research Clinics Manual.[17] Alcohol use was determined by self-administered questionnaire (past week) and by a dietician (past 24 hours) only in this subset.

Vital status was determined annually for 99.9% of the cohort during a 19-year follow-up. Death certificates, obtained for all decedents, were coded for underlying cause of death by a certified nosologist, using the ninth revision of the International Classification of Diseases, Adapted. Cardiovascular disease included codes 400 to 438 and IHD codes 410 to 414. A panel of cardiologists reviewed medical records in a subset and confirmed a diagnosis of definite or probable CVD in 85%.

Between 1985 and 1986, specimens obtained at baseline were first thawed and DHEAS was measured by radioimmunoassay.[18] Sensitivity for the DHEAS assay was 0.02 μg per milliliter, the intraassay coefficient of variation was 5.2%, and the interassay coefficient of variation was 10.0%. Previous work had demonstrated no DHEAS deterioration in samples stored for at least 15 years.[19] Additional baseline frozen samples were assayed during the next 2 years in the same laboratory by the same technician using the same methodology. Age-specific mean DHEAS levels in the men who formed the basis of the 12-year follow-up report did not differ significantly from levels for all men reported here (FIG. 1).

Data were analyzed using Statistical Analysis Systems (SAS Inc.; Cary, North Carolina). Because DHEAS levels showed a slightly skewed distribution, analyses were performed using untransformed and transformed data. The results did not differ, so untransformed values are shown, with the p values based on analyses using the natural logarithms of DHEAS.

The 19-year CVD and IHD mortality rates were calculated for men and women according to DHEAS levels below and above the median (154 μg/dl for men and 61 μg/dl for women), adjusting for age using the Mantel-Haenszel direct-age adjustment and using a chi-square test for statistical significance. Mean age-adjusted DHEAS levels were compared by categorical risk factor status. Linear trends across quartiles were tested using linear contrasts in analysis of covariance models. The independent contribution of DHEAS to the risk of CVD and IHD mortality was assessed using Kaplan-Meier survival curves. Cox proportional hazards models were used to compare CVD or IHD deaths versus non-CVD or non-IHD deaths and to compare CVD or IHD deaths versus survivors.[20] All p values are two-tailed. Statistical significance was defined as $p < 0.05$.

RESULTS

There were 1,029 men aged 30–82 years (mean 60.4 ± 12.8 years) and 942 women aged 50–88 years (mean 65.2 ± 7.3 years) who had no heart disease at baseline. FIGURE 2 shows the mean DHEAS levels by decade of age in men, and in women with and without estrogen replacement therapy. A stepwise decline with age (based on cross-sectional data) was observed in both sexes. The slope of loss was steeper in men than women, but women had lower DHEAS levels than did men at all ages. Women taking replacement estrogen had lower levels than untreated women.

TABLE 1 shows age-adjusted DHEAS levels in men and women with or without categorically defined heart disease risk factors. Men and women who currently smoked cigarettes or had two or more drinks per day had significantly higher levels of DHEAS. Men but not women who were obese had significantly lower levels of

DHEAS than leaner men. Men and women whose plasma HDL was ≥ 45 mg/dl had significantly higher age-adjusted mean DHEAS levels compared to those whose HDL was < 45 mg/dl (men: 189.7 vs 172.2 µg/dl, $p = 0.01$; women: 86.6 vs 63.9 µg/dl, $p = 0.0001$). In men DHEAS was unrelated to total cholesterol or blood pressure, whereas mean DHEAS levels in women were significantly higher in those who had hypercholesterolemia or hypertension as well as in women who were nonusers of estrogen replacement therapy. Dehydroepiandrosterone sulfate was not related to reported physical activity, family history of coronary heart disease, or fasting plasma glucose in either sex.

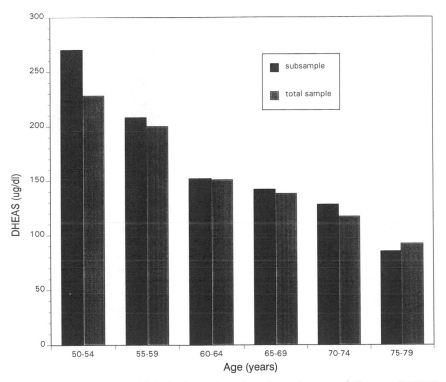

FIGURE 1. Comparison published subsample and total sample, age-specific mean DHEAS for men.

The age-adjusted mean level of DHEAS by quartile of selected heart disease risk factors is shown in TABLES 2 (men) and 3 (women). Statistically significant trends were observed for BMI in men and for cholesterol and systolic blood pressure in women, but these trends were no longer present after adjusting for alcohol intake (TABLES 2 and 3).

TABLE 4 shows the age-specific and age-adjusted mean DHEAS levels by mortality status in men. The 254 CVD deaths and the 157 IHD deaths in men were unrelated to mean DHEAS levels at baseline. Similarly in women (TABLE 5), the mean DHEAS levels did not differ by CVD (199 CVD deaths) or IHD (102 IHD

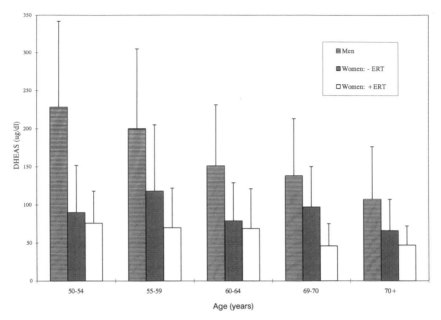

FIGURE 2. Age-specific mean DHEAS (SD) levels for men and women with and without estrogen replacement therapy.

deaths) mortality status. Comparing men with DHEAS levels above and below the median of 154 μg/dl, age-adjusted CVD and IHD mortality rates were 25.5 versus 23.3% and 15.2 versus 15.6%, respectively. In women, the age-adjusted CVD and IHD mortality rates for those with DHEAS levels above and below the median of 61 μg/dl were 42.3 versus 44.6% and 24.0 versus 24.1%, respectively.

Kaplan-Meier 19-year survival curves were used to compare CVD mortality rates by DHEAS level above and below the median in younger, middle-aged, and older men and women (FIGS. 3 and 4). At all ages, the proportion of men dying of CVD was greater among those with DHEAS levels below the median, but none of the differences was statistically significant. For the oldest women, the proportion dying of CVD was nonsignificantly greater among those with DHEAS levels above the median; the inverse, also nonsignificant, was seen in the youngest women. Similar patterns were seen for IHD and, in separate analyses, when CVD and IHD survival curves were compared by DHEAS quartile (not shown).

Using a Cox proportional hazards model, the age-adjusted relative risk (RR) of CVD death, compared to non-CVD death, for a 50 μg/dl decrease in DHEAS for men and women was 0.96 (95% CI, 0.85–1.05) and 1.05 (95% CI, 0.91–1.10) (TABLE 6). Adjustment for blood pressure, cigarette smoking, cholesterol, obesity, fasting plasma glucose, and estrogen replacement therapy did not alter these results (men: RR = 0.94, 95% CI, 0.84–1.03; women: RR = 1.11, 95% CI, 0.81–1.23). Similar analyses for IHD death showed an age-adjusted RR of 0.88 (95% CI, 0.77–1.01) for men and RR = 1.01 (95% CI, 0.99–1.02) for women. Comparable results were found after multiply adjusting the model (men: RR = 0.96, 95% CI, 0.85–1.05; women: RR = 0.92, 95% CI, 0.99–1.02).

These results were strikingly different from the apparent 12-year 70% cardioprotection in men reported in 1986. In that paper and in all of the aforementioned comparisons, CVD and IHD deaths were compared with non-CVD and IHD deaths, the latter including both deaths not attributed to CVD and survivors. Because CVD or IHD deaths may be poorly attributed as the underlying cause of death in the elderly, and because 86% of CVD deaths in men and 95% of CVD deaths in women occurred at age 70 or older, additional analyses were done comparing CVD or IHD

TABLE 1. Age-Adjusted Mean (SE) DHEAS by Risk Factor Categories for 1,029 Men and 942 Women

		Men Mean (SE) DHEAS			Women Mean (SE) DHEAS	
	n	(µg/dl)	p	n	(µg/dl)	p
Total cholesterol						
≥ 200 mg/dl	613	178.0 (3.4)	0.16	199	76.32 (2.0)	0.01
< 200 mg/dl	416	171.0 (4.2)		732	65.67 (3.8)	
Systolic blood pressure						
≥ 160 mm Hg	222	177.7 (6.4)	0.71	179	81.5 (4.1)	0.04
< 160 mm Hg	909	175.0 (3.0)		761	72.1 (2.0)	
Diastolic blood pressure						
≥ 95 mm Hg	165	171.6 (7.0)	0.54	117	82.4 (5.0)	0.07
< 95 mm Hg	966	176.2 (2.9)		825	72.9 (1.9)	
Smoking						
Current	217	200.8 (6.1)	0.0001	226	88.2 (3.6)	0.0001
Never/past	912	169.6 (2.9)		712	69.4 (2.0)	
Alcohol (2+ drinks/day)						
Yes	109	217.0 (10.2)	0.01	57	133.5 (8.3)	0.0001
No	258	187.5 (6.2)		283	85.5 (3.7)	
Physically active (>3 times/week)						
Yes	68	184.8 (13.2)	0.35	19	99.3 (14.6)	0.71
No	287	198.4 (6.1)		321	93.7 (3.9)	
ERT use						
Yes				291	56.69 (3.2)	0.001
No				651	81.7 (2.1)	
HDL-C						
≥ 45 mg/dl	226	189.7 (6.1)	0.01	382	86.6 (6.5)	0.0001
< 45 mg/dl	140	172.2 (2.9)		47	63.9 (3.2)	
LDL-C						
≥ 160 mg/dl	144	200.5 (8.1)	0.41	13	98.5 (18.1)	0.77
< 160 mg/dl	182	191.6 (7.2)		122	92.9 (5.9)	
Triglycerides						
≥ 250 mg/dl	63	161.2 (107.5)	0.17	26	75.1 (17.3)	0.71
< 250 mg/dl	966	176.5 (27.4)		616	79.3 (3.4)	
Body mass index						
≥ 27 kg/(ht)^2	354	164.4 (4.6)	0.004	159	69.9 (4.3)	0.29
< 27 kg/(ht)^2	777	180.9 (3.2)		783	74.9 (1.9)	0.29
Fasting plasma glucose						
< 140 mg/dl	1,072	175.0 (2.7)	0.34	916	74.2 (1.8)	0.71
≥ 140 mg/dl	59	186.6 (11.9)		26	70.1 (1.1)	
Family history of heart disease						
Yes	391	178.5 (4.6)	0.48	70	68.6 (5.3)	0.38
No	702	174.5 (3.4)		872	74.5 (1.9)	

death with the 19-year survivors, also shown in TABLE 6. In these multiply adjusted analyses, DHEAS levels were significantly and inversely associated with the risk of fatal CVD or IHD. These associations were not materially changed by adjusting for alcohol intake or for HDL cholesterol. In women, DHEAS levels were positively associated with CVD and particularly IHD, but none of these differences was statistically significant.

DISCUSSION

In these older men and women, cigarette smoking and alcohol intake were each positively associated with DHEAS levels. Dehydroepiandrosterone sulfate was also positively associated with HDL cholesterol in both sexes and with total cholesterol

TABLE 2. Adjusted Mean DHEAS (SE) by Quartile of Cardiovascular Disease Risk Factor: Men

| | Quartile | | | | |
	1	2	3	4	p
Body mass index					
Age-adjusted	187.1 (5.3)	176.1 (5.3)	176.7 (5.3)	162.9 (5.3)	0.003
Age-ETOH	218.6 (11.3)	200.3 (11.3)	199.1 (10.6)	193.1 (10.7)	0.11
Triglycerides					
Age-adjusted	170.7 (5.3)	178.9 (5.3)	178.8 (5.3)	173.8 (5.3)	0.70
Age-ETOH	191.5 (15.7)	195.4 (12.7)	218.7 (12.6)	200.9 (7.9)	0.34
Cholesterol					
Age-adjusted	167.7 (5.3)	175.0 (5.3)	175.0 (5.4)	183.9 (5.2)	0.04
Age-ETOH	191.5 (15.7)	195.4 (12.7)	218.7 (12.6)	200.8 (7.9)	0.34
HDL-C					
Age-adjusted	182.2 (10.6)	202.2 (10.9)	179.7 (10.7)	218.5 (10.8)	0.08
Age-ETOH	190.7 (11.1)	210.0 (11.3)	184.8 (10.8)	223.1 (10.9)	0.14
LDL-C					
Age-adjusted	195.8 (10.8)	198.9 (10.8)	184.6 (10.6)	203.2 (10.8)	0.87
Age-ETOH	202.7 (11.1)	204.6 (11.0)	192.4 (11.0)	208.7 (10.9)	0.90
Systolic blood pressure					
Age-adjusted	164.2 (5.7)	177.6 (5.4)	182.8 (5.3)	177.4 (5.7)	0.10
Age-ETOH	197.3 (12.6)	210.9 (10.9)	206.4 (11.2)	194.5 (11.3)	0.81
Diastolic blood pressure					
Age-adjusted	168.9 (5.3)	174.4 (5.0)	175.7 (6.3)	182.7 (5.0)	0.07
Age-ETOH	200.9 (12.6)	220.2 (10.3)	194.3 (13.6)	192.3 (9.3)	0.29

and blood pressure in women. It was inversely associated with obesity in men. None of these differences was statistically significant after adjusting for alcohol intake, however, suggesting that DHEAS levels have no independent effect on the heart disease risk factors measured here.

After 19 years of follow-up, high DHEAS levels were still "cardioprotective" in men but not women. In men, higher DHEAS levels were independently predictive of a significantly reduced risk of fatal CVD (RR = 0.85; 95% CI = 0.72, 0.99), but this risk reduction was much less striking than that observed at 12 years and was observed only when survivors were the comparison group rather than those not dead of cardiovascular causes, as reported at the 12-year follow-up. The survivor comparison

TABLE 3. Adjusted Mean DHEAS (SE) by Quartile of Cardiovascular Disease Risk Factor: Women

	Quartile				
	1	2	3	4	p
Body mass index					
Age-adjusted	65.3 (3.5)	79.9 (3.5)	78.0 (3.5)	72.4 (3.5)	0.21
Age-ETOH	76.7 (7.0)	100.6 (7.0)	98.9 (6.3)	95.3 (6.8)	0.08
Triglycerides					
Age-adjusted	73.3 (3.6)	72.1 (3.5)	74.2 (3.6)	76.6 (3.5)	0.44
Age-ETOH	90.9 (8.6)	91.9 (6.6)	93.8 (6.9)	95.1 (5.9)	0.65
Cholesterol					
Age-adjusted	64.2 (3.5)	71.3 (3.4)	72.4 (3.5)	87.9 (3.5)	0.0001
Age-ETOH	95.4 (9.4)	99.7 (7.7)	89.4 (7.1)	91.8 (5.1)	0.53
IIDL-C					
Age-adjusted	83.0 (6.0)	84.9 (5.9)	90.7 (6.0)	91.8 (5.9)	0.22
Age-ETOH	95.6 (7.1)	91.9 (7.2)	100.9 (7.2)	86.0 (6.9)	0.53
LDL-C					
Age-adjusted	88.0 (6.0)	87.6 (5.7)	90.4 (6.0)	84.4 (6.0)	0.77
Age-ETOH	94.3 (7.0)	86.9 (7.1)	96.6 (7.0)	95.6 (7.1)	0.67
Systolic blood pressure					
Age-adjusted	66.0 (3.6)	74.1 (3.6)	76.2 (3.4)	79.2 (3.6)	0.01
Age-ETOH	86.7 (7.0)	91.1 (6.9)	92.5 (6.3)	103.3 (7.2)	0.11
Diastolic blood pressure					
Age-adjusted	71.7 (3.5)	72.2 (3.2)	70.6 (4.2)	79.7 (3.3)	0.15
Age-ETOH	90.4 (6.9)	88.6 (6.3)	89.5 (8.4)	101.7 (6.1)	0.24

was made to minimize the effects of competing causes and the misclassification due to the expected less specific death certificate classification in old age; many of the very elderly probably die with, if not of, CVD.

We considered several possible explanations for the weakening of the DHEAS-CVD association. A low DHEAS as a marker for occult disease might be more common in the elderly; if the DHEAS level was low due to subclinical CVD, the strongest inverse association between DHEAS and CVD death would be expected to

TABLE 4. Mean Baseline DHEAS Levels (μg/dl) (SD) by Age Group and Overall Death, Death from Cardiovascular Disease (CVD), and Death from Ischemic Heart Disease (IHD) in Men

	Death from All Causes		Death from CVD		Death from IHD	
Age Group	Alive (n = 513)	Dead (n = 516)	No (n = 775)	Yes (n = 254)	No (n = 872)	Yes (n = 157)
30–44	263 ± 10	296 ± 48	264 ± 12	302 ± 97	336 ± 75	289 ± 8
45–49	218 ± 15	232 ± 31	213 ± 14	278 ± 39	278 ± 39	213 ± 14
50–54	226 ± 14	240 ± 30	225 ± 13	266 ± 43	226 ± 108	154 ± 69
55–59	196 ± 14	205 ± 18	197 ± 12	208 ± 25	196 ± 11	230 ± 31
60–64	148 ± 9	154 ± 9	148 ± 7	161 ± 12	153 ± 7	145 ± 15
65–69	136 ± 8	139 ± 6	134 ± 6	147 ± 8	135 ± 5	147 ± 10
70–74	144 ± 16	115 ± 5	121 ± 7	114 ± 8	122 ± 6	106 ± 9
75+	96 ± 20	83 ± 5	87 ± 8	82 ± 7	89 ± 6	75 ± 8
Age-adjusted mean	149	145	147	146	147	142
	p = 0.49		p = 0.99		p = 0.45	

TABLE 5. Mean Baseline DHEAS Levels (μg/dl) (SD) by Age Group and Overall Death, Death from Cardiovascular Disease (CVD), and Death from Ischemic Heart Disease (IHD) in Women

	Death from All Causes		Death from CVD		Death from IHD	
Age Group	Alive ($n = 542$)	Dead ($n = 400$)	No ($n = 743$)	Yes ($n = 199$)	No ($n = 757$)	Yes ($n = 102$)
50–54	86 ± 50	125 ± 67	89 ± 52	84 ± 54	89 ± 52	84 ± 54
55–59	87 ± 62	103 ± 109	91 ± 73	47 ± 31	90 ± 73	58 ± 34
60–64	80 ± 57	80 ± 56	79 ± 58	87 ± 47	79 ± 58	91 ± 49
65–69	70 ± 48	63 ± 47	68 ± 45	62 ± 54	67 ± 45	62 ± 66
70–74	74 ± 57	65 ± 50	70 ± 50	65 ± 57	68 ± 51	67 ± 62
75+	74 ± 47	68 ± 55	76 ± 55	66 ± 53	75 ± 54	70 ± 59
Age-adjusted mean	75	73	75	72	74	75
		$p = 0.52$		$p = 0.63$		$p = 0.87$

occur early in the follow-up period. Occult disease is an unlikely explanation, because the divergence observed in the Kaplan-Meier survival curve (FIG. 3) increased over time for at least the first 15 years in most age groups. Because DHEAS decreases with age, further decline in the aging cohort could mask a protective effect, particularly if it is the current rather than the remote level of DHEAS that determines outcome. This possibility cannot be excluded, because we have only a single DHEAS assay at one point in time, but an angiographic study[9]

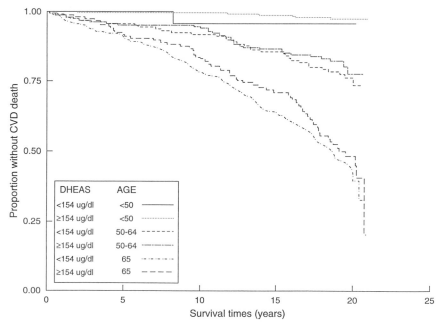

FIGURE 3. Kaplan-Meier 19-year survival curves for cardiovascular disease (CVD) mortality by age and DHEAS level for men.

showing that DHEAS was inversely associated with coronary atherosclerosis suggests a chronic process rather than an acute one.

It is possible that protection is greater at younger ages; this seems unlikely in this cohort, where less than 5% of male deaths at 12-year follow-up and 7% at the current 19-year follow-up occurred before age 65. The age-specific Kaplan-Meier curves also suggest that the protective effect is not limited to younger age groups.

The initial reports on DHEAS and CVD in Rancho Bernardo[7,8] were based on only 24% of the men and 31% of the women reported here; the remainder of the sample had their blood measured in the following years when funds became available. It seems unlikely that the longer freezing caused sample deterioration or that the weaker associations are explained by laboratory drift, because the published age-specific mean DHEAS levels in the original sample did not differ significantly from the levels in the total sample reported here (FIG. 1).

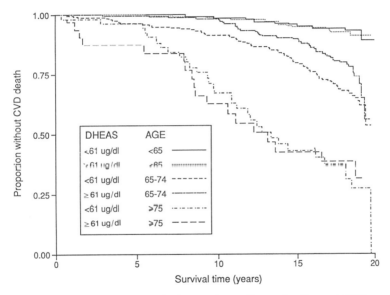

FIGURE 4. Kaplan-Meier 19-year survival curves for cardiovascular disease (CVD) mortality by age and DHEAS level for women.

Since the original sample was a true random sample of the whole cohort, it seems unlikely that the sample selection explains these differences. Furthermore, to confirm the results of the initial analysis based on a random sample of 143 men, we selected 99 additional specimens from the freezer; no differences were found in the DHEAS-CVD mortality associations, and results from both groups were pooled in the original publication. This second sample was used to test the hypothesis generated by the original sample and provides additional evidence that the 1986 report was not a chance finding. Finally, although the effect size is now smaller, the risk estimate is within the 95% confidence limits published by several other groups.[10,12,13]

This paper confirms our original observation that any cardioprotective effect of

DHEAS is limited to men. These results are similar to those of Herrington *et al.*[9] who found an inverse DHEAS-atherosclerosis association in men but no association in women. Because DHEAS is a weak androgen, we originally proposed that this sex difference reflects a benefit of androgens for men compared to estrogens for women. It is possible, however, that it is the DHEAS conversion to estrogen that explains the cardioprotective effect in men. We find this explanation less attractive, because men have higher estrogen levels than do postmenopausal women, so that the added effect of estrogen to the baseline level should be greater in women than men.

Alternatively, the sex differences in cardioprotection could be explained by alcohol consumption, which was not asked at baseline and was not considered in our original paper or in the study by Herrington.[9] Two recent studies which found a (nonsignificant) reduced risk of fatal heart disease in men with higher DHEAS levels did adjust for alcohol consumption.[12,13] We think the cardioprotective effect of alcohol is unlikely to be the whole explanation for the DHEAS-CVD association, because the statistically significant reduced risk remained after adjusting for alcohol intake. However, it is possible that self-reported alcohol intake is not sufficiently

TABLE 6. Relative Risk (95% Confidence Interval) of Overall, CVD, and IHD Death for a 50-μg/dl Decrease in DHEAS for Men and Women[a]

	Men			Women		
Risk	Overall Mortality	CVD Mortality	IHD Mortality	Overall Mortality	CVD Mortality	IHD Mortality
Age-adjusted	0.91	0.96	0.88	1.03	1.05	1.01
	(0.82, 1.01)	(0.85, 1.05)	(0.77, 1.01)	(0.91, 1.15)	(0.91, 1.10)	(0.99, 1.02)
vs survivors		0.99	0.97		1.11	1.18
		(0.92, 1.08)	(0.87, 1.08)		(0.96, 1.29)	(0.96, 1.46)
Multiply adjusted	0.93	0.94	0.96	0.94	1.11	0.92
	(0.90, 0.95)	(0.84, 1.03)	(0.85, 1.05)	(0.82, 0.97)	(0.81, 1.23)	(0.99, 1.02)
vs survivors		0.85	0.79		0.88	1.21
		(0.72, 0.99)	(0.60, 1.04)		(0.76, 1.02)	(0.81, 1.46)

[a]Adjusted for age, blood pressure, smoking, total cholesterol, body mass index, fasting plasma glucose, and replacement estrogen.

reliable to adequately control for this confounding in the analysis. More men drank alcohol (28% vs 17% of women), and the men who drank consumed significantly more alcohol than did women, which could explain some of the greater cardioprotection observed in men than women.

Cigarette smoking was associated with a raised DHEAS level and would be expected to obscure a protective effect. Cigarette smoking was an independent CVD risk factor in men in this cohort, and the inverse association of CVD or IHD with DHEAS was strengthened after adjusting for cigarette smoking. Smoking was relatively uncommon in this cohort; only 19% of men and 24% of women were current cigarette smokers at baseline, the majority of whom (61% men and 91% women) had quit smoking within the last 12 years.

The strong association of DHEAS with HDL cholesterol has been reported previously.[21,22] It is not possible to tell if this increase in HDL is caused by alcohol or DHEAS or some other factor. Perhaps HDL is the causal mechanism for the cardioprotection offered by DHEAS in men and exerts no effect in women because they already have higher HDL levels.

In conclusion, this extended analysis of the Rancho Bernardo study confirms a significant 15–25% reduction in the risk of fatal CVD in men and a nonsignificant increase in the risk of fatal CVD in women. If this cardioprotection is real, any postulates about the mechanism of action must include a thesis compatible with the unexplained sex difference.

SUMMARY

In 1986 we reported that high levels of plasma dehydroepiandrosterone sulfate (DHEAS) reduced the risk of fatal cardiovascular disease (CVD) in 242 men and increased the risk in 289 women from the Rancho Bernardo cohort who were followed up for 12 years. We report here an update on the epidemiology of DHEAS and CVD based on a 19-year follow-up of 1,029 men and 942 women aged 30–88 years from the same cohort.

In cross-sectional analyses, DHEAS levels decreased with age in both sexes and were lower in women than men. Men who were overweight were more likely to have low DHEAS levels; women who had hypercholesterolemia or hypertension or were nonusers of estrogen therapy had higher DHEAS levels. Alcohol intake and cigarette smoking were associated with higher DHEAS levels in both sexes. All differences were no longer statistically significant after adjusting for alcohol intake.

All participants were followed for vital status. After 19 years there were 254 CVD deaths in men and 199 CVD deaths in women. DHEAS was not associated with CVD or ischemic heart disease (IHD) deaths in age-adjusted analyses where the comparison group was individuals without CVD or IHD death. In contrast, when the comparison group was survivors, multiply adjusted models showed a statistically significant, modestly reduced risk of fatal CVD (RR = 0.85) in men and a nonsignificant increased risk of fatal CVD (RR = 1.11) in women.

REFERENCES

1. SMITH, M. R., B. T. RUDD, A. SHIRLEY, P. H. RAYNER, J. W. WILLIAMS, N. M. DUIGHAN & P. V. BERTRAND. 1975. A radioimmunoassay for the estimation of serum dehydroepiandrosterone sulfate in normal and pathological sera. Clin. Chem. Acta **65:** 5–13.

2. YAMAJI, T. & H. IBAYASHI. 1969. Plasma dehydroepiandrosterone sulfate in normal and pathological conditions. J. Clin. Endocrinol. Metab. **29:** 273–278.

3. ZUMOFF, B., R. ROSENFELD, G. W. STRAIN, J. LEVIN & D. K. FUKUSHIMA. 1980. Sex differences in the twenty-four-hour mean plasma concentrations of dehydroisoandrosterone (DHA) and dehydroisoandrosterone sulfate (DHAS) and the DHA to DHAS ratio in normal adults. J. Clin. Endocrinol. Metab. **51:** 330–333.

4. KASK, E. 1959. 17-Ketosteroids and arteriosclerosis. Angiology **10:** 358–368.

5. MARMORSTON, J., J. J. LEWIS, J. L. BERNSTEIN et al. 1957. Excretion of urinary steroids by men and women with myocardial infarction. Geriatrics **12:** 297–300.

6. RAO, L. G. S. 1970. Urinary steroid-excretion patterns after acute myocardial infarction. Lancet **2:** 390–391.

7. BARRETT-CONNOR, E., K. T. KHAW & S. C. C. YEN. 1986. A prospective study of dehydroepiandrosterone sulfate, mortality, and cardiovascular disease. N. Engl. J. Med. **315:** 1519–1524.

8. BARRETT-CONNOR, E. & K. T. KHAW. 1987. Absence of an inverse relation of dehydroepiandrosterone sulfate with cardiovascular mortality in postmenopausal women. N. Engl. J. Med. **317:** 711.

9. HERRINGTON, D. M., G. B. GORDON, S. C. ACHUFF, J. F. TREJO, H. F. WEISMAN, P. O. KWITEROVICH & T. A. PEARSON. 1990. Plasma dehydroepiandrosterone and dehydro-

epiandrosterone sulfate in patients undergoing diagnostic coronary angiography. J. Am. Coll. Cardiol. **16:** 862–870.

10. MITCHELL, L. E., D. L. SPRECHER, I. B. BORECKI, T. RICE, P. M. LASKARZEWSKI & D. L. RAO. 1994. Evidence for an association between dehydroepiandrosterone sulfate and nonfatal, premature myocardial infarction in males. Circulation **89:** 89–93.

11. RUDMAN, D., K. R. SHETTY & D. E. MATTSON. 1990. Plasma dehydroepiandrosterone sulfate in nursing home men. J. Am. Geriatr. Soc. **38:** 421–427.

12. LACROIX, A. Z., K. YANO & D. M. REED. 1992. Dehydroepiandrosterone sulfate incidence of myocardial infarction and extent of atherosclerosis in men. Circulation **86:** 1529–1535.

13. NEWCOMER, L. M., J. E. MANSON, R. L. BARBIERI, C. H. HENNEKENS & M. J. STAMPFER. 1994. Dehydroepiandrosterone sulfate and the risk of myocardial infarction in US male physicians: A prospective study. Am. J. Epidemiol. **140:** 870–875.

14. HAUTANEN, A., M. MANTTAR, P. KOSKINEN, V. MANNINEN, H. ALDERCRENTZ & M. H. FRICK. 1990. Dehydroepiandrosterone sulfate as a coronary risk factor in the Helsinki Heart Study. Circulation **82**(Suppl. III): III–468.

15. CORTOREGGICS, C. S., M. R. BLACKMAN, R. ANDRES, D. C. MULLER, E. G. LAKALLA, J. L. FLEG & S. M. HARMAN. 1990. Plasma levels of estradiol, testosterone, and DHEAS do not predict risk of coronary artery disease in men. J. Androl. **11:** 460–470.

16. CRIQUI, M. H., E. BARRETT-CONNOR & M. AUSTIN. 1978. Differences between respondents and non-respondents in a population-based cardiovascular disease study. Am. J. Epidemiol. **108:** 367–372.

17. LIPID RESEARCH CLINICS PROGRAM. 1974. Manual of Laboratory Operations, Vol. 1. Lipid and Lipoprotein Analysis. CHEW Publ. No (NIH) 75–628, 2nd Ed. U.S. Government Printing Office. Washington, DC.

18. HOPPER, B. R. & S. C. C. YEN. 1975. Circulating concentrations of dehydroepiandrosterone and dehydroepiandrosterone sulfate during puberty. J. Clin. Endocrinol. Metab. **40:** 458–461.

19. ORENTREICH, N., J. L. BRIND & R. L. RIZER. 1984. Age changes and sex differences in serum dehydroepiandrosterone sulfate concentrations throughout adulthood. J. Clin. Endocrinol. Metab. **59:** 551–555.

20. COX, D. R. 1972. Regression models and life-tables. J. R. Stat. Soc. **34:** 187– 220.

21. HAUTANEN, A., M. MANTTARI, U. MANNINEN & H. ALDERCREUTZ. 1994. Gemfibozil treatment is associated with elevated adrenal androgen, androstanediol glucuronide and cortisol levels in dyslipidemic men. J. Steroid Biochem. **51:** 307–313.

22. HAFFNER, S. M., L. MYKKANEN, R. A. VALDEZ & M. S. KATZ. 1993. Relationship of sex hormones to lipids and lipoproteins in nondiabetic men. J. Clin. Endocrinol. Metab. **77:** 1610–1615.

Dehydroepiandrosterone and Coronary Atherosclerosis

DAVID M. HERRINGTON[a]

Section of Cardiology
The Bowman Gray School of Medicine
Winston-Salem, North Carolina 27157

In 1959, Kask wrote, ". . . a shortage of 17-ketosteroids, especially dehydroepiandrosterone, seems to accompany, and possibly have causal significance in, cases of atherosclerotic disease. Persons with an overabundance of . . . dehydroepiandrosterone may be relatively protected."[1] Since that original speculation based on autopsy data, a modest body of evidence has accumulated suggesting that dehydroepiandrosterone (DHEA) may indeed play an important role in the pathogenesis of coronary atherosclerosis.[2]

Urinary[3] and blood[4,5] levels of DHEA or DHEA sulfate (DHEAS) fall dramatically with age, coincident with the age-associated increase in atherosclerotic disease. Cross-sectional,[6–10] case-control,[11,12] and cohort studies[10,13] have demonstrated an inverse association between plasma levels of DHEA, DHEAS, or urinary 17-ketosteroids and clinical manifestations of coronary or cerebrovascular atherosclerosis, although other observational studies have failed to detect such an association.[14,15] Orally administered DHEA has also been shown to inhibit coronary atherosclerosis,[16] aortic fatty streak formation in rabbit models of atherosclerosis,[17] and allograft vasculopathy in a rabbit heterotopic cardiac transplant model.[18] In tissue culture, DHEA inhibits fibroblast growth[19] and differentiation,[20] suggesting that DHEA may influence the cellular proliferative component of atherosclerosis.

To further characterize the relation between DHEA and DHEAS and coronary atherosclerosis, we conducted two studies. In the first study, plasma levels of DHEA and DHEAS were measured in patients undergoing elective coronary angiography.[21] In the second study, these steroid hormones were measured in a group of cardiac transplant patients at risk for accelerated cardiac allograft vasculopathy.[22]

DHEA IN PATIENTS UNDERGOING CORONARY ANGIOGRAPHY

Patients undergoing elective diagnostic coronary angiography (between April 1985 and April 1988) at the Johns Hopkins Hospital, who were enrolled in the Johns Hopkins Coronary Artery Disease Study, were included in our study. As this was designed to be a study of premature coronary artery disease, patients were eligible if they were men ≤ 50 years of age or women ≤ 60 years of age. Patients who were undergoing emergency coronary angiography or percutaneous transluminal coronary angioplasty or had had a myocardial infarction within the previous 12 weeks were

[a] Address for correspondence and requests for reprints: David M. Herrington, MD, MHS, Division of Cardiology, The Bowman Gray School of Medicine, Medical Center Blvd., Winston-Salem, NC 27157–1045.

ineligible for enrollment. On the morning of the procedure or at the time of angiographic examination, a fasting blood specimen was obtained. A portion of the plasma was stored at $-70°C$ for subsequent biochemical analysis.

Coronary angiography of the right and left coronary arteries was performed with angulated views to completely display the coronary tree. A consensus panel of three physicians experienced in coronary angiography, who did not know the DHEA and DHEAS levels, examined the film. Each of the 15 American Heart Association (AHA) designated coronary artery segments was characterized as having 0%, 1–24%, 25–49%, 50–74%, 75–99%, or 100% diameter stenosis and given a corresponding score of 0–5. Bypass grafts, native vessels proximal to bypass grafts, and poorly visualized segments were not evaluated. A global measure of the extent of coronary artery disease (coronary disease score) was calculated as the average score for all evaluated AHA segments divided by five.

Plasma DHEA and DHEAS levels were measured using commercially available radioimmunoassay kits (Wien Laboratories and Immuchem). These kits were independently validated with a chromatographic-enzymatic assay.[23] The intra- and interassay variabilities of these assays were $<10\%$ over a range of values that exceeded those observed in this study. Plasma levels of total cholesterol and triglycerides and concentrations of low and high density lipoprotein cholesterol were determined using methods of the Lipid Research Clinics Program[24] as modified by Kwiterovich et al.[25]

Age adjustment of DHEA and DHEAS levels was performed using least squares estimates of marginal mean values,[26] where age was treated as a continuous variable. Spearmans rank order correlation was used to assess the univariate association between DHEA and DHEAS levels and the coronary disease score.[27] The coronary disease score was also divided roughly into tertiles. All patients with totally normal coronary angiograms and coronary disease scores of zero were assigned to the lowest tertile. The intermediate tertile ($0 <$ coronary disease score <0.25) identified those patients with mild disease, and coronary disease scores in the highest tertile (coronary disease score >0.25) were observed in patients with extensive disease. A polycotomous logistic regression technique was used to examine the relation between DHEAS and coronary disease score tertiles after adjusting for other variables.[28] Odds ratios were calculated from logistic regression models based on a decrease of 1 standard deviation in DHEA or DHEAS plasma levels. Tests of significance for variables in the logistic regression model were based on the likelihood ratio test.

Fifty-five percent of the study subjects had at least one $\geq 50\%$ stenosis. Dehydroepiandrosterone and DHEAS levels were lower in men with at least one $\geq 50\%$ stenosis; however, the difference was only statistically significant for DHEAS (TABLE 1). Dehydroepiandrosterone and DHEAS levels were also lower in men with any coronary artery disease, regardless of the degree of stenosis, than in the group with normal appearing coronary arteries (14.0 ± 6.7 versus 16.3 ± 6.5 pmol/ml, $p = 0.13$, and 4.8 ± 2.6 versus 6.7 ± 3.6 nmol/ml, $p = 0.01$, respectively). In women, there were no differences in DHEA or DHEAS levels between those with and without any stenosis $\geq 50\%$ or those with totally normal coronary arteries compared with those with any stenosis regardless of the degree of severity.

TABLE 2 shows the relation between plasma levels of DHEA and DHEAS and the number of diseased coronary arteries. In men, there was a significant, inverse, dose-response relation between DHEAS levels and the number of diseased coronary arteries (any stenosis $\geq 50\%$) determined by angiography. For DHEA, although

TABLE 1. Dehydroepiandrosterone (DHEA) and Dehydroepiandrosterone Sulfate (DHEAS) Levels (mean ± SD) in 204 Men and Women According to Presence of Angiographically Defined Coronary Artery Disease[a] and Gender

	Men (n = 101)			Women (n = 103)		
CAD	No.	DHEA (pmol/ml)	DHEAS (nmol/ml)	No.	DHEA (pmol/ml)	DHEAS (nmol/ml)
+	61	14.2 ± 6.8	4.9 ± 2.7	51	12.1 ± 10.1[b]	2.7 ± 2.5
−	40	15.4 ± 6.5[c]	6.1 ± 3.5	52	11.7 ± 7.1	2.8 ± 1.8
p value[d]		0.40	0.05		0.83	0.80

[a]Any ≥50% stenosis; [b]based on 50 participants; [c]based on 39 participants; [d]based on two-sample t test for the presence (+) and absence (−) of coronary artery disease (CAD). Reprinted with permission from the American College of Cardiology (J. Am. Coll. Cardiol.). 1990. **16:** 862–870.

mean levels were higher in men with single vessel disease than in those with no disease, there remained an overall statistically significant trend towards lower levels with the increasing number of diseased vessels. In women, no association was noted between DHEA or DHEAS levels and the number of diseased vessels.

Both DHEA and DHEAS levels were inversely associated with the extent of coronary artery disease in men as measured by the coronary disease score (DHEA: $r = -0.26, p = 0.01$; DHEAS: $r = -0.25, p = 0.01$). FIGURE 1 shows the mean levels of DHEA sulfate in men stratified into three age groups and tertiles of the coronary disease score. Within each age group, there was a dose-response relation between the mean level of DHEAS and the extent of coronary disease. After age adjustment, mean DHEAS levels in men with extensive disease (highest coronary disease score tertile) remained significantly lower than levels in men with no disease (lowest coronary disease tertile) (4.9 ± 3.3 versus 6.5 ± 3.0 nmol/ml, $p = 0.05$). Dehydroepiandrosterone levels in men with extensive disease were only slightly lower than those in men with no disease after age adjustment (15.1 ± 7.0 versus 15.7 ± 6.4 pmol/ml, $p = 0.77$).

Logistic regression modeling demonstrated a significant association between age-adjusted levels of DHEA and DHEAS and angiographically defined coronary

TABLE 2. Correlation[a] between Dehydroepiandrosterone (DHEA) and Dehydroepiandrosterone Sulfate (DHEAS) Levels (mean ± SD) and Number of Diseased Coronary Arteries[b] in 204 Men and Women According to Gender

No. of Diseased Coronary Arteries	Men (n = 101)			Women (n = 103)		
	No.	DHEA (pmol/ml)	DHEAS (nmol/ml)	No.	DHEA (pmol/ml)	DHEAS (nmol/ml)
0	40	15.4 ± 6.5[c]	6.1 ± 3.5	52	11.7 ± 7.1[b]	2.8 ± 1.8
1	15	19.0 ± 9.7	5.5 ± 3.5	13	9.8 ± 8.9	1.5 ± 1.0
2	17	14.1 ± 5.8	5.0 ± 2.2	15	9.7 ± 8.1	2.4 ± 2.0
3	29	11.8 ± 3.9	4.4 ± 2.5	23	15.2 ± 11.5[d]	3.5 ± 3.1
r value		−0.23	−0.20		−0.04	−0.03
p value		0.02	0.05		0.05	0.78

[a]Spearman's rank order correlation coefficient; [b]≥50% stenosis; [c]based on 39 participants; [d]based on 22 participants. Reprinted with permission from the American College of Cardiology (J. Am. Coll. Cardiol.). 1990. **16:** 862–870.

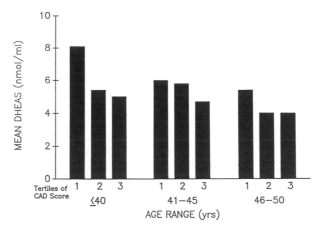

FIGURE 1. Mean plasma dehydroepiandrosterone sulfate (DHEAS) levels in 98 men according to extent of angiographically defined coronary atherosclerosis stratified by age group. The age-adjusted mean level in men with no coronary disease (coronary artery disease [CAD] score tertile = 1) was significantly higher than that in men with extensive coronary artery disease (coronary artery disease tertile = 3) (6.5 ± 3.0 versus 4.9 ± 3.3. nmol/ml, p = 0.05). Reprinted with permission from the American College of Cardiology (J. Am. Coll. Cardiol.). 1990. **16:** 862–870.

artery disease in men (relative odds: 1.15, p = 0.04, and 1.32, p = 0.03, respectively). To exclude confounding due to other coronary artery disease risk factors, the age-adjusted associations between DHEA and DHEAS levels and the extent of coronary disease were also examined after adjusting individually for smoking, diabetes mellitus, elevated LDL cholesterol (> 160 mg/dl), hypertension, positive family history of premature coronary disease, physical activity, and alcohol consumption. The age-adjusted associations between DHEA and DHEAS levels and extent of coronary disease were independent of each of the factors tested (p value range 0.05–0.01). A final model simultaneously adjusting for age, smoking, low density lipoprotein cholesterol, and diabetes continued to demonstrate a significant inverse association between DHEAS and the extent of coronary atherosclerosis (p = 0.04). No association was seen between plasma levels of DHEA and DHEAS and extent of coronary disease in women.

DHEA AND ACCELERATED ALLOGRAFT VASCULOPATHY

Adult recipients of cardiac allografts between 1984 and 1989 at the Johns Hopkins Hospital were eligible for study. Subjects with at least one annual follow-up coronary angiogram seen for routine surveillance endomyocardial biopsy between January and June 30, 1989 were included (n = 61). Morning fasting plasma specimens were obtained at the time of endomyocardial biopsy which was less than 1 year from the time of their most recent coronary angiogram. If a patient was undergoing biopsy for work-up of acute rejection, collection of plasma for DHEA and DHEAS measurements was deferred until the rejection episode had resolved. The immune suppressive regimen for these patients typically included preoperative cyclosporin, intraoperative solumedrol, and postoperative maintenance doses of prednisone, azathioprine, and cyclosporin.[29]

Each annual coronary angiogram was read by a faculty level, invasive cardiologist. Subjects were defined as having accelerated allograft vasculopathy if they had at least one major epicardial segment with >50% diameter stenosis or ≥ three segments with 1–50% narrowing on one or more of the first five annual follow-up coronary angiograms. Stenosis could include tapering or diffuse narrowing relative to a more normal appearing proximal segment or discrete focal lesions. The time from transplantation to the date of the first follow-up catheterization with evidence of accelerated allograft vasculopathy was also recorded.

Plasma levels of total DHEA and DHEAS were measured using specific and precise radioimmunoassays developed at the Bowman Gray School of Medicine.[22] Because DHEA bound to sex hormone binding globulin (SHBG) may not be available to exert any intrinsic biologic effects, levels of bioavailable or "free" DHEA (i.e., DHEA not bound to SHBG) were also measured. Free DHEA levels were calculated as the product of total plasma DHEA and the percentage of non-SHBG–bound DHEA, determined by selective ammonium sulfate precipitation of [^{3}H]DHEA labeled plasma.

Mean and age-adjusted mean plasma levels of total and free DHEA and DHEAS were compared in subjects with and without allograft vasculopathy using the two-sided, two-sample T test. The relation between these steroid hormones and allograft vasculopathy was also examined using survival analysis. Time to development of allograft vasculopathy was compared using the log rank test between subjects with high or low DHEA, free DHEA, or DHEAS based on the median values of the hormone levels in the study population.[30] Cox proportional hazards models were used to make similar comparisons after adjustment for other covariates.[31]

Mean levels of total and free DHEA and DHEAS in 61 cardiac transplant recipients with and without accelerated allograft vasculopathy are shown in TABLE 3. Total and free DHEA levels were significantly lower in subjects with than without accelerated allograft vasculopathy. FIGURE 2 shows cumulative survival free of allograft vasculopathy for up to 5 years of follow-up in subjects with low and high total and free DHEA. Patients with low total DHEA (<2.74 nm/ml) had more accelerated allograft vasculopathy and developed it earlier in the period of follow-up than did those with high free DHEA ($p = 0.062$). Similarly, patients with low free DHEA (<2.27 nm/ml) were more likely to develop premature disease ($p = 0.046$).

TABLE 3. Plasma Levels of Dehydroepiandrosterone (DHEA) and Dehydroepiandrosterone Sulfate (DHEAS) in 61 Cardiac Transplant Recipients with and without Accelerated Coronary Allograft Vasculopathy[a]

	Accelerated Allograft Vasculopathy		
	+ (n = 11)	− (n = 50)	
	Mean (SD)	Mean (SD)	p Value
DHEA (ng/ml)	2.64 (0.79)	3.86 (2.42)	0.005
Free DHEA (ng/ml)	2.19 (7.54)	3.37 (2.13)	0.003
DHEAS (ng/ml)	422.5 (267.7)	433.3 (247.4)	0.898

[a]Reprinted, with permission, from Mosby-Yearbook, Inc. J. Heart Lung Transplant. D. M. Herrington, N. Nanjee, S. C. Achuff et al. 1996. Dehydroepiandrosterone (DHEA) and Cardiac Allograft Vasculopathy. In press.

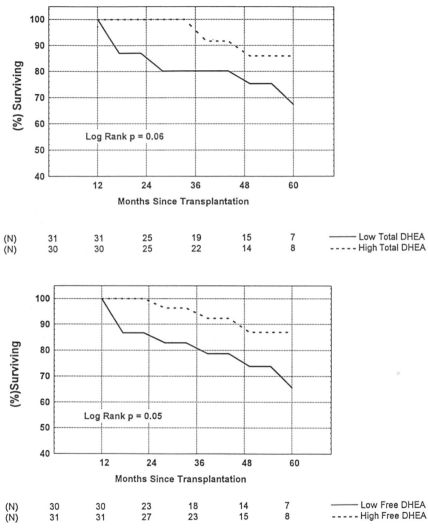

FIGURE 2. Cumulative survival free of premature allograft vasculopathy in patients with high and low total (top) and free (bottom) DHEA. Patients were divided into "high" and "low" groups based on the median values for total and free DHEA (2.74 and 2.27 nm/ml, respectively). High and low groups were compared using the log-rank test. (Reprinted, with permission, from Mosby-Yearbook, Inc. J. Heart Lung Transplant. D. M. Herrington, N. Nanjee, S. C. Achuff *et al.* 1996. Dehydroepiandrosterone (DHEA) and Cardiac Allograft Vasculopathy. In press.)

After adjusting individually for age, gender, average cholesterol, prednisone dose, systolic blood pressure, and diastolic blood pressure during follow-up, low levels of free DHEA remained independently related to risk of accelerated allograft vasculopathy with p values ranging from 0.025–0.053. The corresponding range of p values for the association between low levels of total DHEA and premature disease was 0.042–0.086. Plasma levels of DHEAS were not related to risk for allograft vasculopathy even after adjustment of potential confounders.

DISCUSSION

These two studies demonstrate a significant inverse relation between plasma levels of total or biologically available DHEA or DHEAS and angiographically defined coronary disease. These data lend further support to the clinical[6–9] and epidemiologic,[10–13] animal model,[16,18] and tissue culture[19,20] studies suggesting that DHEA may play an important role in the pathogenesis of coronary disease. Although the coronary vascular disease syndromes were distinctly different in these two studies, they have in common the histopathologic attribute of rampant cellular proliferation in the intimal medial space.[32,33] This common feature may be the avenue through which DHEA could influence the development or progression of such vascular disease syndromes because DHEA is a potent antiproliferative agent. Restenosis following mechanical revascularization procedures is another coronary disease syndrome that, like allograft vasculopathy, is dominated by cellular proliferation[34] and that may also be significantly influenced by plasma levels of DHEA. Other possible effects of DHEA that may influence the development of vascular disease include favorable effects on carbohydrate metabolism,[35] inhibition of platelet aggregation,[36] and reductions in PAI-1 levels.[37]

The major weaknesses of these two studies lie in their cross-sectional design. Such studies cannot determine if low levels of DHEA are an antecedent to, rather than a consequence of, coronary disease. Nonetheless, epidemiologic studies have shown that low levels of DHEAS precede the development of clinical manifestations of cardiovascular disease, and animal model studies have shown that oral supplementation with DHEA can prevent or attenuate the development of atherosclerosis. Cross-sectional studies are also less likely to include subjects that die quickly because of severe disease, resulting in survival bias. If DHEA is inversely related to coronary disease, survival bias would tend to weaken the apparent association, making it more difficult to detect statistically significant associations. Finally, in observational studies it is always possible that observed associations are confounded by unrecognized and unadjusted determinants of the outcome of interest.

Even taking into account the possibility of survival bias, the magnitude of the association between low DHEA and coronary artery disease in these studies is modest at best. In the first study, after adjustment for age, the risk of having extensive coronary atherosclerosis was only increased by 15% for each drop in DHEA levels of 6.8 pmol/ml (1 SD in the study population mean). Similarly, the difference in prevalence of allograft vasculopathy after 5 years among cardiac transplant patients with low versus high free DHEA was 19%. These observations are consistent with our understanding of coronary atherosclerosis as a complex multifactorial disease process[38] in which DHEA may play a small but important role. This coupled with the considerable within-subject variability of DHEA levels may also explain why some studies have detected little or no association between DHEAS and cardiovascular disease.

Whether maneuvers to alter levels of DHEA affect the development of coronary atherosclerosis remains unknown. Some studies suggest that a low calorie diet[39] or physical activity[40,41] may be associated with slightly higher levels of DHEA or DHEAS; however, other studies have failed to confirm these findings.[42,43] DHEA[44,45] or DHEAS[46] has also been successfully administered in humans for extended periods. With oral administration it appears possible to elevate plasma levels of

DHEA without significant adverse effects.[45] More data are needed on the safety of administration of DHEA for long periods, the pharmacokinetics of various orally administered forms of DHEA or similar compounds,[47] and the associated changes in plasma levels of biologically active DHEA. Armed with this additional information, it may be possible to consider clinical trials of DHEA for prevention of vascular disease syndromes that are dominated by cellular proliferation in subjects with low levels of endogenous DHEA.

SUMMARY

Tissue culture, animal model, and epidemiologic studies suggest that dehydroepiandrosterone (DHEA) may inhibit atherosclerosis through its potent antiproliferative effects. To examine the relation between DHEA and a direct measure of coronary atherosclerosis, plasma DHEA, and DHEA sulfate (DHEAS) levels were determined in 206 middle-aged patients undergoing coronary angiography. Plasma DHEAS levels were lower in subjects with at least one $\geq 50\%$ stenosis than in those with no stenosis $> 50\%$ ($p = 0.05$) and was inversely associated with the number of diseased coronary vessels and the extent of coronary atherosclerosis ($p = 0.05$ and 0.01, respectively).

Cardiac allograft vasculopathy is dominated by abnormal cellular proliferation and, therefore, may be uniquely influenced by DHEA. To study this, 61 cardiac allograft recipients with at least one annual follow-up cardiac catheterization were studied. Plasma levels of total and free DHEA were inversely related to the development of accelerated coronary allograft vasculopathy ($p = 0.005$ and 0.003, respectively). Furthermore, the time to development of accelerated allograft vasculopathy was shorter in subjects with low levels of total and free DHEA ($p = 0.062$ and 0.046, respectively).

These data suggest that low plasma levels of DHEA may facilitate, and high levels may retard, the development of coronary atherosclerosis and coronary allograft vasculopathy.

REFERENCES

1. KASK, E. 1959. 17-Ketosteroids and arteriosclerosis. Angiology **10:** 358–368.
2. NAFZIGER, A. N., D. M. HERRINGTON & T. L. BUSH. 1991. Dehydroepiandrosterone and dehydroepiandrosterone sulfate: Their relation to cardiovascular disease. Epidemiol. Rev. **13:** 267–293.
3. MARMORSTON, J., G. C. GRIFFITH, P. J. GELLER, E. I. FISHMAN, F. WLESCH & J. M. WEINER. 1975. Urinary steroids in the measurement of aging and of atherosclerosis. J. Am. Geriatr. Soc. **23:** 481–492.
4. MIGEON, C. J., A. R. KELLER, B. LAWRENCE & T. H. SHEPARD. 1957. Dehydroepiandrosterone and androsterone levels in human plasma: Effect of age, sex, day-to-day and diurnal variation. J. Clin. Endocrinol. Metab. **17:** 1051–1062.
5. ORENTREICH, N., J. L. BRIND, R. L. RIZER & J. H. VOGELMAN. 1984. Age changes and sex differences in serum dehydroepiandrosterone sulfate concentrations throughout adulthood. J. Clin. Endocrinol. Metab. **59:** 551–555.
6. MARMORSTON, J., J. J. LEWIS, J. L. BERNSTEIN et al. 1957. Excretion of urinary steroids by men and women with myocardial infarction. Geriatrics **12:** 297–300.
7. WEINER, J. M. & J. MARMORSTON. 1969. Statistical techniques of difference. Ann. N. Y. Acad. Sci. **161:** 641–669.
8. RAO, L. G. 1970. Urinary excretion patterns after acute myocardial infarction. Lancet **2:** 390–391.

9. LOPEZ-S, A. 1984. Metabolic and endocrine factors in ageing. *In* Risk Factors for Senility. H. Rothschild & C. F. Chapman, Eds.: 210–219. Oxford University Press. New York.

10. BARRETT-CONNOR, E., K. T. KHAW & S. S. YEN. 1986. A prospective study of dehydroepiandrosterone sulfate, mortality, and cardiovascular disease. N. Engl. J. Med. **315:** 1519–1524.

11. SLOWINSKA-SRZEDNICKA, J., S. ZGLICZYNSKI, M. CISWICKA-SZNAJDERMAN, P. SOSZYNSKI, M. BIERNACKA, M. WOROSZYLSKA & W. RUZYLLO. 1989. Decreased plasma dehydroepiandrosterone sulfate and dihydrotestosterone concentrations in young men after myocardial infarction. Atherosclerosis **79:** 197–203.

12. MITCHELL, L. E., D. L. SPRECHER, I. B. BORECKI, T. RICE, P. M. LASKARZEWSKI & D. C. RAO. 1994. Evidence for an association between dehydroepiandrosterone sulfate and nonfatal, premature myocardial infarction in males. Circulation **89:** 89–93.

13. LACROIX, A. Z., K. YANO & D. M. REED. 1992. Dehydroepiandrosterone sulfate, incidence of myocardial infarction, and extent of atherosclerosis in men [see comments]. Circulation **86:** 1529–1535.

14. HAUTANEN, A., M. MANTTARI, V. MANNINEN, L. TENKANEN, J. K. HUTTUNEN, M. H. FRICK & H. ADLERCREUTZ. 1994. Adrenal androgens and testosterone as coronary risk factors in the Helsinki Heart Study. Atherosclerosis **105:** 191–200.

15. NEWCOMER, L. M., J. E. MANSON, J. E. BARBIERI, C. H. HENNEKENS & M. J. STAMPFER. 1994. Dehydroepiandrosterone sulfate and the risk of myocardial infarction in US male physicians: A prospective study. Am. J. Epidemiol. **140:** 870–875.

16. GORDON, G. B., D. E. BUSH & H. F. WEISMAN. 1988. Reduction of atherosclerosis by administration of dehydroepiandrosterone. A study in the hypercholesterolemic New Zealand white rabbit with aortic intimal injury. J. Clin. Invest. **82:** 712–720.

17. ARAD, Y., J. J. BADIMON, L. BADIMON, W. C. HEMBREE & H. N. GINSBERG. 1989. Dehydroepiandrosterone feeding prevents aortic fatty streak formation and cholesterol accumulation in cholesterol-fed rabbit. Arteriosclerosis **9:** 159–166.

18. EICH, D. M., J. E. NESTLER, D. E. JOHNSON, G. H. DWORKIN, D. KO, A. S. WECHSLER & M. L. HESS. 1993. Inhibition of accelerated coronary atherosclerosis with dehydroepiandrosterone in the heterotopic rabbit model of cardiac transplantation. Circulation **87:** 261–269.

19. SAENGER, P. & M. NEW. 1977. Inhibitory action of dehydroepiandrosterone (DHEA) on fibroblast growth. Experientia **33:** 966–967.

20. GORDON, G. B., J. A. NEWITT, L. M. SHANTZ, D. E. WENG & P. TALALAY. 1986. Inhibition of the conversion of 3T3 fibroblast clones to adipocytes by dehydroepiandrosterone and related anticarcinogenic steroids. Cancer Res. **46:** 3389–3395.

21. HERRINGTON, D. M., G. B. GORDON, S. C. ACHUFF, J. F. TREJO, H. F. WEISMAN, JR. & T. A. PEARSON. 1990. Plasma dehydroepiandrosterone and dehydroepiandrosterone sulfate in patients undergoing diagnostic coronary angiography (corrected and republished with original paging, article originally printed in J. Am. Coll. Cardiol. 1990. Oct;16: 862–870). J. Am. Coll. Cardiol. **16:** 862–870.

22. HERRINGTON, D. M., N. NANJEE, S. C. ACHUFF, D. E. CAMERON, B. DOBBS & K. L. BAUGHMAN. 1996. Dehydroepiandrosterone and cardiac allograft vasculopathy. J. Heart Lung Transplant. **15:** in press.

23. HOLTZCLAW, W. D. & G. B. GORDON. 1989. Measurement of serum levels of dehydroepiandrosterone sulfate: A comparison of radioimmunoassay and enzymatic analysis. Steroids **54:** 355–371.

24. Manual of Laboratory Operations: LRC Program 1: Lipid and Lipoprotein Analysis. US Department of Health, Education and Welfare. Publication no. NIH 75-628. May 1974. (revised version issued October 1982).

25. KWITEROVICH, P. O. J., S. WHITE, T. FORTE, P. S. BACHORICK, H. SMITH & A. SNEIDERMAN. 1987. Hyperapobetalipoproteinemia in a kindred with familial combined hyperlipidemia and familial hypercholesterolemia. Atherosclerosis **7:** 211–225.

26. WILCOSKY, T. C. & L. E. CHAMBLESS. 1985. A comparison of direct adjustment and regression adjustment of epidemiologic measures. J. Chron. Dis. **38:** 849–856.

27. SNEDECOR, G. W. & W. G. COCHRAN. 1980. Statistical Methods, 7th Ed. Iowa State University Press. Ames, IA.

28. WALKER, S. H. & D. B. DUNCAN. 1967. Estimation of the probability of an event as a function of several independent variables. Biometrika **67**: 167–179.
29. BAUMGARTNER, W. A., B. A. REITZ & S. C. ACHUFF. 1990. Heart and Heart-Lung Transplantation: 149–150. W. B. Saunders Co. Philadelphia, PA.
30. COX, D. R. & D. OAKES. 1985. Analysis of Survival Data. 104. Chapman and Hall. New York.
31. COX, D. R. & D. OAKES. 1985. Analysis of Survival Data. 70. Chapman and Hall. New York.
32. SCHWARTZ, S. M. & R. ROSS. 1984. Cellular proliferation in atherosclerosis and hypertension. Prog. Cardiovasc. Dis. **26**: 355–372.
33. MILLER, L. W., R. C. SCHLANT, J. KOBASHIGAWA, S. KUBO & D. G. RENLUND. 1993. 24th Bethesda conference: Cardiac transplantation. Task Force 5: Complications. [Review]. J. Am. Coll. Cardiol. **22**: 41–54.
34. MCBRIDE, W., R. A. LANGE & L. D. HILLIS. 1988. Restenosis after successful coronary angioplasty: Pathophysiology and prevention. N. Engl. J. Med. **318**: 1734–1737.
35. NESTLER, J. E., J. N. CLORE & W. G. BLACKARD. 1990. Regulation of dehydroepiandrosterone (DHEA) metabolism by insulin and metabolic effects of dehydroepiandrosterone in man. *In* The Biologic Role of Dehydroepiandrosterone (DHEA). M. Kalimi & W. Regelson, Eds.: 189–205. Walter de Gruyter. New York.
36. JESSE, R., J. E. NESTLER, & D. M. EICH *et al.* 1991. Dehydroepiandrosterone *in vivo* and *in vitro* inhibits platelet aggregation (abstr.). J. Am. Coll. Cardiol. **17**: 376A.
37. BEER, N. A., D. J. JAKUBOWICZ, R. M. BEER & J. E. NESTLER. 1994. Effect of oral dehydroepiandrosterone administration on plasminogen activator inhibitor type 1 levels in middle-aged men (abstr.). Circulation **90**: I-179.
38. ROSS, R. 1986. The pathogenesis of atherosclerosis—An update [Review]. N. Engl. J. Med. **314**: 488–500.
39. HENDRIX, A., W. HEYNS & P. DEMOOR. 1968. Influence of low-calorie diet and fasting on the metabolism of dehydroepiandrosterone sulfate in obese subjects. J. Clin. Endocrinol. **28**: 1525–1533.
40. LOPEZ-S, A., C. WINGO & J. A. HEBERT. 1976. Total serum cholesterol and urinary dehydroepiandrosterone in humans. Atherosclerosis **24**: 471–481.
41. SONKA, J., I. GREGOROVA, Z. TOMSOVA, A. PAVLOVA, A. ZHIRKOVA, R. RATH & M. JOSIFKO. 1972. Plasma androsterone, dehydroepiandrosterone and 11-hydroxycorticoids in obesity. Effects of diet and physical activity. Steroids Lipids Res. **3**: 65–74.
42. HILL, P. B. & E. L. WYNDER. 1979. Effect of a vegetarian diet and dexamethasone on plasma prolactin, testosterone and dehydroepiandrosterone in men and women [Review]. Cancer Lett. **7**: 273–282.
43. BAKER, E. R., R. S. MATHUR, R. F. KIRK, S. C. LANDGREBE, L. O. MOODY & H. O. WILLIAMSON. 1982. Plasma gonadotropins, prolactin, and steroid hormone concentrations in female runners immediately after a long-distance run. Fertil. Steril. **38**: 38–41.
44. ADLERCREUTZ, H., J. KERSTELL, K. O. SCHAUMANN, A. SVANBORG & R. VIHKO. 1972. Plasma lipids and steroid hormones in patients with hypercholesterolaemia or hyperlipaemia during dehydroepiandrosterone sulphate administration. Eur. J. Clin. Invest. **2**: 91–95.
45. MORALES, A. J., J. J. NOLAN, J. C. NELSON & S. S. YEN. 1994. Effects of replacement dose of dehydroepiandrosterone in men and women of advancing age. J. Clin. Endocrinol. Metab. **78**: 1360–1367.
46. NESTLER, J. E., C. O. BARLASCINI, J. N. CLORE & W. G. BLACKARD. 1988. Dehydroepiandrosterone reduces serum low density lipoprotein levels and body fat but does not alter insulin sensitivity in normal men. J. Clin. Endocrinol. Metab. **66**: 57–61.
47. SCHWARTZ, A. G., L. PASHKO & J. M. WHITCOMB. 1986. Inhibition of tumor development by dehydroepiandrosterone and related steroids [Review]. Toxicol. Pathol. **14**: 357–362.

Dehydroepiandrosterone Inhibits Human Platelet Aggregation *in Vitro* and *in Vivo*[a]

ROBERT L. JESSE,[b] KATHY LOESSER, DAVID M. EICH,
YONG ZHEN QIAN, MICHAEL L. HESS,
AND JOHN E. NESTLER

Divisions of Cardiology and of Endocrinology and Metabolism
Department of Medicine
Medical College of Virginia/Virginia Commonwealth University
Richmond, Virginia 23298

Dehydroepiandrosterone (DHEA) is a major steroid hormone found in plasma in either free or conjugated form, primarily as DHEA sulfate (DHEAS). It is synthesized in the adrenal cortex and serves as a precursor to both androgens and estrogens.[1] Aside from this observation, the physiologic role of DHEA has yet to be discerned.

Recently, accumulating evidence suggests a potential role for DHEA in the prevention of atherosclerosis.[2,3] Several lines of evidence support this conclusion. Epidemiologic studies show that concentrations of DHEA and its conjugates in plasma are age-dependent, peaking during early adulthood and declining steadily thereafter.[4,5] Peak, plasma DHEAS levels of 3,000–3,500 ng/ml are present at age 20–30, decline to 1,500–2,000 ng/ml by age 50, to 1,000 ng/ml by age 60, and are typically less than 700 ng/ml by age 70.[4] By the ninth decade plasma levels are reduced by >95% of peak levels. Neither the mechanism nor the function of this reduction is known, but the rate of decline is inversely proportional to the incidence of atherosclerosis, suggesting that DHEA may protect against the development of atherosclerosis. This idea is further supported by other epidemiologic studies which show that male survivors of myocardial infarction have lower plasma DHEAS levels than do healthy age-matched controls without overt coronary disease.[6] In addition, a prospective study of a large cohort of men aged 50–79 years demonstrated an inverse association between cardiovascular mortality risk and plasma DHEAS levels over a 12-year period.[7]

A major concern in evaluating this epidemiologic data is that the association may merely be an epiphenomenon. That is, because the incidence of atherosclerosis is related to age, the decline in plasma DHEAS with aging may be coincidental and not causal. To address this issue, several animal studies were performed to prospectively test the hypothesis that DHEA protects against atherosclerosis. These studies showed that oral administration of DHEA provides substantial protection against atherosclerosis in cholesterol-fed animals using several different models of vascular injury.[8–10]

[a]This research was supported in part by National Institutes of Health grant 1RO1AG11227 (J.E.N.), a Research Award from the Virginia Affiliate of the American Diabetes Association (J.E.N.), a Grant-in-Aid from the American Heart Association, Virginia Affiliate (R.L.J.), a Research Advisory Group Award from the U.S. Veterans Administration (R.L.J.), and a National Institutes of Health training grant (Y.Z.Q., M.L.H.).

[b]Address for correspondence and reprint requests: Robert Jesse, MD, Division of Cardiology, Medical College of Virginia, MCV Station, Box 105, Richmond, VA 23298.

Platelet activation has been implicated in atherogenesis, especially in response to vascular injury.[24] Thus, we speculated that inhibition of certain platelet functions may contribute to mechanisms by which DHEA exerts antiatherogenic activity. The present study evaluates the ability of DHEA to alter platelet function in humans and describes potent antiplatelet activity by DHEA both *in vitro* and *in vivo*.

MATERIALS AND METHODS

Preparation of Platelets

All donors for these experiments were young normal individuals who had refrained from taking any medication for at least 10 days before phlebotomy. Blood from the antecubital vein was collected into 1/8 volume of acid-citrate-dextrose, centrifuged at 150 × g for 12 minutes, and the top layer comprising the platelet-rich plasma (PRP) was removed. Tubes were then centrifuged at 1,500 × g for 15 minutes, and the upper layer of platelet-poor plasma (PPP) removed. Platelet concentrations in PRP were determined electronically with a Coulter counter and adjusted to 250,000/µl by dilution with PPP. The PRP was stored in a capped syringe for the duration of the experiments which were concluded within 4 hours of phlebotomy.

Platelet Aggregation Studies

Platelet aggregation studies were performed turbidimetrically using a Sienco (Morrison, Colorado) dual channel aggregometer. Platelet-rich plasma was placed in the aggregometer cuvette and spun at 1,000 rpm, with equilibration at 37°C for 1.0 minute before the addition of agonist(s). Light transmission was recorded in arbitrary units with 100% being that set for PPP and 0% for PRP. Light transmission (LT) was recorded for at least 4 minutes or to the completion of aggregation. Each aggregation tracing was analyzed for the following parameters: extent of maximal aggregation (i.e., the highest LT), time from the addition of agonist to the nadir of the initial decrease in LT (LAG time), slope of the rise in LT (SLOPE), and time to attain half-maximal aggregation (T½MAX).

Thromboxane B_2 (TxB_2) Determination

Cuvettes were removed from the aggregometer and reactions stopped by the addition of 5.0 mM EDTA and 10.0 µM indomethacin (final concentrations), and then placed in an ice cold water bath. Contents of the cuvettes were transferred to plastic centrifuge tubes and centrifuged in the cold for 10 minutes. Supernatant was removed and assayed for TxB_2 by radioimmunoassay (Advanced Magnetics, Cambridge, Massachusetts).

Human in Vivo Studies

The study was approved by the Committee on the Conduct of Human Research at the Medical College of Virginia, and informed consent was obtained from each subject. Ten normal men between the ages of 23 and 35 were divided randomly into two groups and received either DHEA 300 mg ($n = 5$) or placebo capsule ($n = 5$) orally three times daily. Capsules were prepared by the Investigational Pharmacy Unit at the Medical College of Virginia, and randomization was directed by the Department of Biostatistics. Clinical investigators and patients were blinded to the drug regimen. Aggregation studies were performed on fasting blood samples, as already described. In addition, a plasma sample from each study was frozen at $-70°C$ for subsequent determination of DHEA and DHEAS by radioimmunoassay (Diagnostic Products Corp., Los Angeles, California). Platelet aggregation studies were performed on three occasions before drug administration (two different days in the week before starting the study, and day 0) and on three occasions while taking the drug (days 7, 10, and 14).

Reagents

Arachidonic acid was purchased from Bio-Data (Hatboro, Pennsylvania) as the sodium salt and reconstituted daily before use. DHEA and DHEAS were purchased from Sigma (St. Louis, Missouri). H_2O_2 (Sigma) was prepared as a fresh dilution from a 30% stock solution for each experiment.

RESULTS

In Vitro Studies

Platelet aggregation can be expressed quantitatively by measuring either the extent or rate of aggregation. In the following *in vitro* studies, the rate of platelet aggregation is reported as the time to reach a point that is half the maximal aggregation, recorded as the T½MAX with the units in seconds. When aggregation did occur in these experiments (i.e., when it was not completely inhibited), very little variation in the extent of maximal aggregation occurred, but any minor differences that did occur were compensated for by this method. The addition of DHEAS to PRP before the addition of agonist attenuated platelet aggregation by slowing the rates at which aggregation proceeded (i.e., by increasing T½MAX) or by completely inhibiting aggregation. Aggregation tracings from a single donor experiment, where aggregation was initiated by the addition of arachidonic acid, are illustrated in FIGURE 1. The addition of increasing concentrations of DHEAS resulted first in prolongation of the T½MAX and then eventual inhibition of aggregation. The inhibition of aggregation was a consistent observation among donors. It should be noted that inhibition occurred at a DHEAS concentration of 100 μM, which is well within the physiologic range. FIGURE 2 shows a slowing of the rate of aggregation, and at higher DHEAS concentrations, complete inhibition. By using the T½MAX as the measure of rate, results from several different donors can be pooled and expressed as a percentage of control (the rate of aggregation in the absence of DHEAS). Thus, as DHEAS concentrations increase, the rates of aggregation progressively slow relative to that of control.

A short preincubation period was required before inhibition of platelet aggregation by DHEAS became apparent (FIG. 3). No attenuation of aggregation was noted if DHEAS was added either concurrently or immediately before the addition of agonist (the 15-second time point). When DHEAS was added 1.0 minute before the

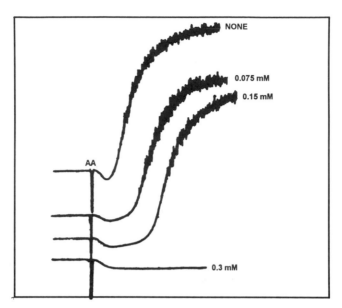

FIGURE 1. Inhibition of platelet aggregation by DHEAS. Platelet aggregation was measured turbidimetrically following the addition of arachidonic acid (AA) to citrated platelet-rich plasma. DHEAS was added at the indicated concentration 1.0 minute before the addition of AA. These tracings represent the change in light transmission (y-axis) recorded against time (x-axis). This is a representative study using platelets from a single donor for all the tracings.

agonist, a slight delay in aggregation occurred (i.e., T½MAX increased). A preincubation period of 2.5 minutes resulted in marked prolongation of T½MAX, and aggregation was completely inhibited when preincubations lasted > 3.0 minutes. Preincubation was required regardless of the amount of DHEAS added. Higher concentrations of DHEAS could cause complete inhibition with shorter preincubations, as shown in FIGURE 1 for the single donor or FIGURE 2 for pooled data; in both cases 0.3 mM DHEAS completely inhibited aggregation after just a 1.0-minute preincubation.

One potential mechanism for attenuation of platelet aggregation by DHEAS is through inhibition of TxB$_2$ synthesis by activated platelets. Very low concentrations of DHEAS, which caused only slight changes in aggregation, significantly reduced TxB$_2$ synthesis (FIG. 4). TxB$_2$ synthesis was inhibited by nearly 50% with the addition of 120 μg/ml of DHEAS (final concentration 0.3 mM).

In vivo Studies

Attenuation of platelet activation by DHEA was also observed with *in vivo* studies. In a randomized, double-blind trial, 10 normal men received either placebo capsule (*n* = 5) or DHEA 300 mg (*n* = 5) orally three times daily for 14 days. Aggregation of PRP was assessed on three occasions before starting the study and on three occasions between days 7 and 14. Rates of platelet aggregation did not change in any men in the placebo group. By contrast, platelet aggregation rates were prolonged in three of the men in the DHEA group, as measured by both the T½MAX and LAG time. Representative data from one of these individuals are shown in FIGURE 5. The effect on aggregation was manifested as an increase in the lowest dose of agonist (arachidonic acid) that could initiate aggregation, resulting in a shift of the pre-drug curves to the right (i.e., decreased sensitivity) and as slower aggregation, shifting these curves upwards. In another man in the DHEA group, platelet aggregation was inhibited completely while he was taking DHEA. Only a single subject in the DHEA group failed to manifest attenuation of platelet aggregation while taking DHEA. Thus, four of five volunteers taking DHEA had a demonstrable effect on platelet aggregation. None of the men reported any side effects while taking DHEA, and no man was able to tell if he was taking DHEA or the placebo. Compliance was determined by measuring plasma DHEA and DHEAS levels before, during, and after the dosing period.

DISCUSSION

An age-related decline in plasma DHEA and DHEAS concentrations is well described in the literature.[4,5] Although the potential relation of this decline to disease states is controversial and under investigation, multiple lines of evidence suggest that DHEA exerts antiatherogenic and cardioprotective actions. Most epidemiologic studies,[6,7,11–13] but not all,[14] demonstrated significantly lower levels of plasma DHEAS or urinary 17-ketosteroids in men with coronary disease than in matched controls. Furthermore, several animal studies demonstrated beneficial effects of DHEA on atherosclerosis.[8–10] For example, Gordon *et al.*[8] studied the effects of DHEA in cholesterol-fed rabbits after mechanical endothelial injury (balloon abrasion) to the aorta. Dietary treatment with 0.5% DHEA resulted in a 50% reduction in the development of atherosclerosis compared to controls, despite

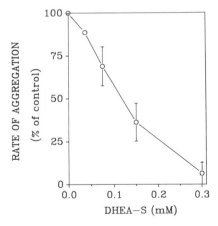

FIGURE 2. Inhibition of platelet aggregation by DHEAS. Platelet aggregation was measured turbidimetrically following the addition of arachidonic acid to citrated platelet-rich plasma. The rate of aggregation was the T½MAX derived from aggregometer tracings as defined in Methods. DHEAS was added 1.0 minute before the addition of arachidonic acid. Data are represented as a percentage of the rate determined for aggregation in the absence of DHEAS (control) and are means of studies derived from at least four donors.

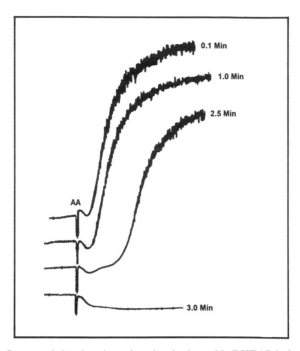

FIGURE 3. Influence of the duration of preincubation with DHEAS before initiation of aggregation. Platelet aggregation was measured turbidimetrically following the addition of 0.075 mM arachidonic acid (AA) to citrated platelet-rich plasma. DHEAS (0.075 mM) was added first, then following the indicated delay time AA was added. The control tracing (i.e., without DHEAS) was essentially superimposable on that from the 0.1-minute sample, indicating that some initial delay is required for inhibition to occur. This is a representative study using platelets from a single donor for all the tracings.

no differences in food intake, weight gain, or lipoprotein profiles. More recently, Eich et al.[10] reported reduced development of coronary atherosclerosis in heart-transplanted rabbits fed a high cholesterol diet supplemented with 0.5% DHEA compared to transplanted animals fed a high cholesterol diet alone.

The mechanism(s) underlying DHEA's protection against the development of atherosclerosis remains unclear. Hypercholesterolemia is a well recognized risk factor for the development of atherosclerosis, and oral DHEA administration reduces both serum total cholesterol and low density lipoprotein cholesterol levels in men.[15] In hypercholesterolemic rabbit models, however, no significant alteration in serum lipids was observed in animals fed DHEA compared to controls.[8–10] DHEA has also been shown to inhibit fibroblast growth[16] and differentiation[17] in culture and may inhibit the differentiation and proliferation of smooth muscle cells and fibroblasts seen in atherosclerosis.

The results of the present study suggest that DHEA-mediated inhibition of platelet activity may contribute to DHEA's putative beneficial effects on atherosclerosis and cardiovascular mortality. The inhibition we observed was relatively rapid in onset, requiring only a few minutes to reach maximal degree. It is unknown if DHEAS directly inhibited platelet aggregation or if hydrolysis occurred at the platelet surface and DHEA was the active moiety. The relatively brief time required for DHEA-mediated inhibition is consistent with a rapid and direct mechanism, mediated perhaps via binding to a cell surface receptor,[18,19] enzymic inhibition,[20,21] or membrane effects. However, it is not consonant with a mechanism more typical of steroid hormones, such as gene activation for induction of protein synthesis. This more typical steroid mechanism would not be expected to be operative in this system because platelets are anucleate.

One well described biochemical activity of DHEA in mammalian systems is inhibition of glucose-6-phosphate dehydrogenase (G6PD) activity.[20,21] G6PD is the initial enzyme in the hexose monophosphate shunt, which provides five carbon sugars for the synthesis of nucleotides and is also the major source of cellular reduction potential in the form of NADPH. Inhibition of G6PD activity could potentially explain many of the reported actions for DHEA, including antimito-genic[17] and antioxidant[22] activities. It could also explain our observed inhibition of platelet function, including attenuated aggregation and reduced thromboxane pro-duction. The cyclooxygenase enzyme PgH$_2$ synthase depends on an NADPH cofac-tor. Initial activation of the oxidase portion depends on the continuous presence of a low level of peroxide, approximately 1.0 μM, for stimulation of rapid activity.

Hence, a common underlying mechanism for the growing body of evidence supporting a role for DHEA in the amelioration of atherogenesis[2,3] may be DHEA inhibition of G6PD activity and the hexose monophosphate shunt. In this manner, DHEA could control proliferative responses by regulation of five carbon sugar synthesis, and control redox-based biochemical processes by regulation of NADPH availability.

In summary, this report adds modulation of platelet activity to the list of potential roles for DHEA. The context of this inhibition may be very important for atherogen-

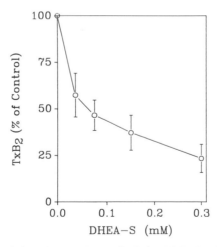

FIGURE 4. Inhibition of thromboxane B$_2$ synthesis by DHEAS. Platelet aggregation was initiated by the addition of arachidonic acid to citrated platelet-rich plasma (PRP) and allowed to continue for at least 4 minutes or to completion of the reaction (attaining a stable maximum in LT). DHEAS was added to PRP 1.0 minute before the addition of arachidonate. When complete, the reaction was stopped by the addition of EDTA and indomethacin and placed in an ice bath. Thromboxane B$_2$ was measured by radioimmunoassay as described in Methods. Data are means from four separate experiments.

esis in that DHEA not only inhibits aggregation and thromboxane synthesis by platelets, but also may temper proliferative responses to injury by vascular tissue. Moderation of platelet aggregation by DHEA is also of interest with respect to aging. Extensive evidence suggests that platelet aggregation is enhanced with age: platelets from older donors aggregate in response to lower concentrations of agonists and produce more thromboxane than do those from younger donors.[23] Enhanced platelet activity in the elderly occurs *ex vivo* in both PRP and whole blood and *in vivo* as suggested by elevated levels of urinary metabolites of TxB_2. Although speculative, our data suggest that the lower levels of plasma DHEA and DHEAS reported in the elderly may contribute to the enhanced platelet aggregation and thromboxane synthesis observed in these individuals.

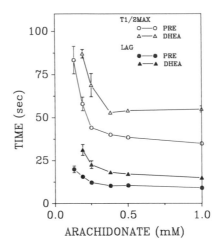

FIGURE 5. Platelet aggregation before and after administration of DHEA to men. Platelet aggregation was determined turbidimetrically following the addition of arachidonic acid (AA) to citrated platelet-rich plasma. The T½MAX and LAG times are derived from the aggregation tracing as described in Methods. Data are compiled from samples drawn on three occasions before taking DHEA and on three occasions while taking orally DHEA 300 mg three times daily. At least three aggregation curves were performed for each concentration of AA on each sample tested. The amount of AA added to initiate aggregation was titrated down until the lowest dose that would still initiate aggregation was determined. The data presented are those from a single volunteer and are the means of all determinations for a given concentration of AA before or while taking DHEA. *Error bars* represent SEMs; when not present, the error bars were too small to be charted.

SUMMARY

The hypothesis has been advanced that the adrenal steroids dehydroepiandrosterone (DHEA) and DHEA sulfate (DHEAS) exert antiatherogenic and cardioprotective actions. Platelet activation has also been implicated in atherogenesis. To determine if DHEA and DHEAS affect platelet activation, the effects of these steroids on platelet aggregation were assessed both *in vitro* and *in vivo*. When DHEAS was added to pooled platelet-rich plasma before the addition of the agonist arachidonate, either the rate of platelet aggregation was slowed or aggregation was completely inhibited. Inhibition of platelet aggregation by DHEA was both dose- and time-dependent. Inhibition of platelet aggregation by DHEA was accompanied by reduced platelet thromboxane B_2 (TxB_2) production.

Inhibition of platelet aggregation by DHEA was also demonstrated *in vivo*. In a randomized, double-blind trial, 10 normal men received either DHEA 300 mg ($n = 5$) or placebo capsule ($n = 5$) orally three times daily for 14 days. In one man in the DHEA group arachidonate-stimulated platelet aggregation was inhibited completely during DHEA administration, whereas in three other men in the DHEA group the rate of platelet aggregation was prolonged, and the sensitivity and responsiveness to agonist were reduced. None of the men in the placebo group manifested any change in platelet activity.

These findings suggest that DHEA retards platelet aggregation in humans. Inhibition of platelet activity by DHEA may contribute to the putative antiatherogenic and cardioprotective effects of DHEA.

REFERENCES

1. LEITER, E. H., W. G. BEAMER, D. L. COLEMAN, & C. LONGCOPE. 1987. Androgenic and estrogenic metabolites in serum of mice fed dehydroepiandrosterone: Relationship to antihyperglycemic effects. Metabolism **36**: 863–869.
2. NESTLER, J. E., J. N. CLORE, & W. G. BLACKARD. 1992. Dehydroepiandrosterone: The "missing link" between hyperinsulinemia and atherosclerosis? FASEB J. **6**: 3073–3075.
3. NAFZIGER, A. N., D. M. HERRINGTON & T. L. BUSH. 1991. Dehydroepiandrosterone and dehydroepiandrosterone sulfate: Their relation to cardiovascular disease. Epidemiol. Rev. **13**: 267–293.
4. ORENTREICH, N., J. L. BRIND, R. L. RIZER & J. H. VOGELMAN. 1984. Age changes and sex differences in serum dehydroepiandrosterone sulfate concentrations throughout adulthood. J. Clin. Endocrinol. Metab. **59**: 551–555.
5. MIGEON, C. J., A. R. KELLER, B. LAWRENCE & T. II. SHEPARD, II. 1957. Dehydroepiandrosterone and androsterone levels in human plasma. Effect of age and sex, day-to-day and diurnal variations. J. Clin. Endocrinol. Metab. **17**: 1051–1062.
6. SLOWINSKA-SRZEDNICKA, J., S. ZGLICZYNSKI, M. CISWICKA-SZNAJDERMAN, M. SRZEDNICKI, P. SOSZYNSKI, M. BIERNACKA, M. WOROSZYLSKA, W. RUZYLLO & Z. SADOWSKI. 1989. Decreased plasma dehydroepiandrosterone sulfate and dihydrotestosterone concentrations in young men after myocardial infarction. Atherosclerosis **79**: 197–203.
7. BARRETT-CONNOR, E., K. T. KHAW, & S. S. C. YEN. 1986. A prospective study of dehydroepiandrosterone sulfate, mortality, and cardiovascular disease. N. Engl. J. Med. **315**: 1519–1524.
8. GORDON, G. B., D. E. BUSH & H. F. WEISMAN. 1988. Reduction of atherosclerosis by administration of dehydroepiandrosterone. A study in the hypercholesterolemic New Zealand White rabbit with aortic intimal injury. J. Clin. Invest. **82**: 712–720.
9. ARAD, Y., J. O. BADIMON, L. BADIMON, W. HEMBREC & H. N. GINSBERG. 1989. Dehydroepiandrosterone feeding prevents aortic fatty streak formation and cholesterol accumulation in cholesterol-fed rabbit. Arteriosclerosis **9**: 159–166.
10. EICH, D. M., J. E. NESTLER, D. E. JOHNSON, G. H. DWORKIN, D. KO, A. S. WECHSLER & M. L. HESS. 1993. Inhibition of accelerated coronary atherosclerosis with dehydroepiandrosterone in the heterotopic rabbit model of cardiac transplantation. Circulation **87**: 261–269.
11. HERRINGTON, D. M., G. B. GORDON, S. C. ACHUFF, J. F. TREJO, H. F. WEISMAN, P. O. KWITEROVICH & T. A. PEARSON. 1990. Plasma dehydroepiandrosterone and dehydroepiandrosterone sulfate in patients undergoing diagnostic coronary angiography. J. Am. Coll. Cardiol. **16**: 862–870.
12. MARMORSTON, J., J. J. LEWIS, J. L. BERNSTEIN, H. SOBEL, O. KUZMA, R. ALEXANDER, O. MAGIDSON & F. J. MOORE. 1957. Excretion of urinary steroids by men and women with myocardial infarction. Geriatrics **12**: 297–300.

13. RAO, L. G. 1970. Urinary steroid excretion patterns after acute myocardial infarction. Lancet **2:** 390–391.
14. LACROIX, A. Z., K. YANO & D. M. REED. 1992. Dehydroepiandrosterone sulfate, incidence of myocardial infarction, and extent of atherosclerosis in men. Circulation **86:** 1529–1535.
15. NESTLER, J. E., C. O. BARLASCINI, J. N. CLORE & W. G. BLACKARD. 1988. Dehydroepiandrosterone reduces serum low-density lipoprotein levels and body fat but does not alter insulin sensitivity in normal men. J. Clin. Endocrinol. Metab. **66:** 57–61.
16. SAENGER, P. & M. NEW. 1977. Inhibitory action of dehydroepiandrosterone (DHEA) on fibroblast growth. Experientia **33:** 966–967.
17. GORDON, G. B., J. A. NEWITT, L. M. SHANTZ, D. E. WENG & P. TALALAY. 1986. Inhibition of the conversion of 3T3 fibroblast clones to adipocytes by dehydroepiandrosterone and related anticarcinogenic steroids. Cancer Res. **46:** 3389–3395.
18. KALIMI, M. & W. REGELSON. 1988. Physicochemical characterization of (^{3}H)DHEA binding in rat liver. Biochem. Biophys. Res. Commun. **156:** 22–29.
19. MEIKLE, A. W., R. W. DORCHUCK, B. A. ARANEO, J. D. STRINGHAM, T. G. EVANS, S. L. SPRUANCE & R. A. DAYNES. 1992. The presence of a dehydroepiandrosterone-specific receptor binding complex in murine T cells. J. Steroid Biochem. Mol. Biol. **42:** 293–304.
20. LOPEZ, S. A. & W. A. KREHL 1967. A possible interrelation between glucose-6-phosphate dehydrogenase and dehydroepiandrosterone in obesity. Lancet **2:** 485–487.
21. OERTEL, G. W. & P. BENES. 1972. The effects of steroids on glucose-6-phosphate dehydrogenase. J. Steroid Biochem. **3:** 493–496.
22. WHITCOMB, J. M. & A. G. SCHWARTZ. 1985. Dehydroepiandrosterone and 16α-Br-epiandrosterone inhibit 12-O-tetradecanoylphorbol-13-acetate stimulation of superoxide radical production by human polymorphonuclear leukocytes. Carcinogenesis (Lond) **6:** 333–335.
23. VILEN, L., S. JACOBSSON, H. WADENVIK & J. KUTTI. 1989. ADP-Induced platelet aggregation as a function of age in healthy humans. Thromb. Hemostasis **61:** 490–492.
24. WOOLF, N. & M. J. DAVIES. 1992. Interrelationship between atherosclerosis and thrombosis. *In* Thrombosis in Cardiovascular Disorders. V. Fuster & M. Verstraete, Eds. W. B. Saunders. Philadelphia, Pennsylvania.

Dehydroepiandrosterone Attenuates Study-Induced Declines in Insulin Sensitivity in Postmenopausal Women[a]

G. WRIGHT BATES, JR.,[b] ROBERT S. EGERMAN,[b]
EDWARD S. UMSTOT,[b] JOHN E. BUSTER,[c]
AND PETER R. CASSON[c]

[b]Department of Obstetrics and Gynecology
University of Tennessee
Memphis, Tennessee 38163

[c]Department of Obstetrics and Gynecology
Division of Reproductive Endocrinology
Baylor College of Medicine
Houston, Texas 77030

Dehydroepiandrosterone (DHEA) and its sulfated congener dehydroepiandrosterone sulfate (DHEAS) may play a role in the regulation of immune competence[1] and insulin sensitivity[2] and also may be cardioprotective.[2] Age-related declines in adrenocortical androgen secretion, independent of cortisol, may thus contribute to the increased prevalence of insulin resistance in the elderly. In rodents, DHEA decreases the severity of genetic and induced diabetes.[2] In humans, amelioration of diabetes in a DHEA-supplemented patient has been described.[3] Additionally, 17-hour DHEA infusions enhance postreceptor insulin action,[4] and 3 weeks of oral DHEA increases T-lymphocyte insulin binding and degradation.[2] We have defined a low dose preparation of DHEA that recreates the reproductive age adrenal androgen milieu in elderly subjects.[2] We hypothesize that with this system, DHEA supplementation will decrease insulin resistance in an androgen-deficient population of postmenopausal women.

MATERIALS AND METHODS

We studied 15 subjects in a 3-week prospective, randomized, double-blind, placebo-controlled trial. Fifty milligrams per day of oral micronized DHEA, or placebo, were administered at 8:00 AM. Subjects were evaluated for changes in weight, body mass index, insulin sensitivity index (SI), and insulin-independent glucose uptake (S_G). The last two parameters were derived from a tolbutamide-augmented IVGTT (Mod-IVGTT) using the minimal model program.[5] Erythrocyte insulin binding was also performed.[4]

[a]This work was supported in part by the American College of Obstetricians and Gynecologists Ortho Academic Training Fellowship, of which Dr. Casson is the 1990–1991 recipient, and by United States Public Health Service Clinical Research Center grant No. RR00211-27.

TABLE 1. Subject Characteristics ($n = 15$)

	Placebo		DHEAS	
	Mean	Range	Mean	Range
Age (yr)	57	35–68	62	48–73
Wt. (kg)	78	66–97	80	60–108
BMI (kg/m^2)	29.9	24.5–40.7	30.1	22.2–38.9
FSH (mIU/ml)	76	42.6–93.1	60.9	34.0–87.5
DHEAS (µg/dl)	69.7	36–110	63.1	12–120
Testosterone (ng/dl)	24	11–38	21	9–29
Glucose (mg/dl)	94	89–110	100	88–123

RESULTS

TABLE 1 shows the screening data on the subjects. Two subjects in the placebo group and one in the DHEA group were excluded from minimal model analysis because of uninterpretable data. FIGURE 1 demonstrates the SI data. Although in the placebo group there was a study-induced decline in SI, no such change was seen in the DHEA group. Thus, SI was significantly enhanced in the DHEA group than in the placebo group ($p = 0.04$). No difference was noted between the placebo and DHEA arms in the other parameters.

CONCLUSIONS

This study demonstrates significant amelioration of a study-induced decline in SI in DHEA-treated subjects. This decline in insulin sensitivity in the placebo group may be explained on the basis of a previously documented elevation in serum cortisol

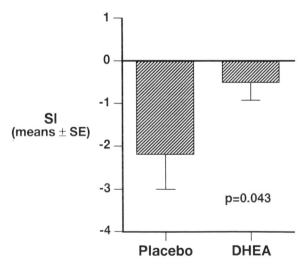

FIGURE 1. Change in the sensitivity index (SI) with DHEA or placebo ($n = 12$). DHEA ameliorated the study-induced decline in SI in the placebo group.

levels,[1] perhaps secondary to study-induced stress. Whether this effect is reproducible in larger studies remains to be determined. If DHEA supplementation in aged subjects enhances insulin sensitivity, DHEA replacement may help attenuate age-related increases in insulin resistance.

REFERENCES

1. CASSON, P. R., R. N. ANDERSON, H. G. HERROD, F. B. STENTZ, A. B. STRAUGHN, G. E. ABRAHAM & J. E. BUSTER. 1993. Oral dehydroepiandrosterone in physiologic doses modulates immune function in postmenopausal women. Am. J. Obstet. Gynecol. **169:** 1536–1539.
2. CASSON, P. R., L. C. FAQUIN, F. B. STENTZ, A. B. STRAUGHN, R. N. ANDERSON, G. E. ABRAHAM & J. E. BUSTER. 1995. Replacement of dehydroepiandrosterone (DHEA) enhances T-lymphocyte insulin binding in postmenopausal women. Fertil. Steril. **63:** 1027–1030.
3. BUFFINGTON, C. K., G. POURMOTABBED & A. E. KITABCHI. 1993. Case report: Amelioration of insulin resistance in diabetes with dehydroepiandrosterone. Am. J. Med. Sci. **306:** 320–324.
4. SCHRIOCK, E. D., C. K. BUFFINGTON, J. R. GIVENS & J. E. BUSTER. 1994. Enchanced post-receptor insulin effects in women following dehydroepiandrosterone infusion. J. Soc. Gynecol. Invest. **1:** 74–78.
5. BERGMAN, R., J. BEARD & M. CHEN. 1986. The minimal modeling method assessment of insulin sensitivity and B-cell function in vivo. *In* Methods in Diabetes Research. W. Clarke, J. Larner & S. Pohl, Eds.:15–34. John Wiley and Sons. New York.

Cloning and Expression of Hamster Adrenal Cytochrome P450C17 cDNA[a]

MARIO CLOUTIER, ALAIN FLEURY,
JEAN COURTEMANCHE, LYNE DUCHARME,
J. IAN MASON,[b] AND JEAN-GUY LEHOUX[c]

Department of Biochemistry
Faculty of Medicine
University of Sherbrooke, QC, Canada J1H 5N4

[b]*Department of Clinical Biochemistry*
The University of Edinburg
Royal Infirmary of Edinburg
Edinburg, EH3 9YW, Scotland, UK

The biosynthesis of androgens requires the action of cytochrome P450c17 (P450c17), the product of the *CYP*17 gene. Two enzymatic activities are needed to convert pregnenolone and progesterone into dehydroepiandrosterone (DHEA) and androstenedione (Δ^4), respectively, a 17α-hydroxylase to hydroxylate in position 17α, and a 17,20-desmolase to cleave the c21 lateral chain of 17α-hydroxylated steroids.

In contrast to humans and bovines, small rodents such as mice and rats do not express the *CYP*17 gene in their adrenals, and consequent formation of adrenal androgens cannot occur in these species. Like humans, however, the hamster is a cortisol producer,[1] indicating the presence of a functioning adrenal P450c17. Although these results clearly established that the hamster adrenal P450c17 possesses 17α-hydroxylase activity, whether this enzyme also possesses 17,20-desmolase activity necessary in the biosynthesis of adrenal androgens is still unknown. To verify this, P450c17 cDNA was isolated from a Uni-Zap XR cDNA library of hamster adrenals. Clones lacking the 5'-end were found and sequenced. To obtain the complete coding sequence, a Rapid Amplification of cDNA Ends (RACE) was performed by polymerase chain reaction (PCR), using Clontech's 5'-amplifinder RACE kit (Clontech, Palo Alto, California). The complete hamster P450c17 cDNA was cloned in the expression vector pSV-SPORT 1 and transfected in COS-1 cells.

RESULTS

A 511 amino acid residue coding sequence was deduced from the cDNA isolated from the hamster adrenal library (FIG. 1). FIGURE 1 also shows the amino acid sequence alignment between the hamster P450c17 and that of the guinea pig,[2] the human,[3] and the bovine.[4] A phenylalanine residue is noted at position 344 for the hamster and the guinea pig, which has been shown to be required for the preferential Δ^4-lyase pathway in the rat.[5] This phenylalanine is replaced by isoleucine in humans

[a]This work was supported by the Medical Research Council of Canada and by the Heart and Stroke Foundation of Canada.
[c]Address for correspondence: Dr. Jean-Guy LeHoux, Department of Biochemistry, University of Sherbrooke, Sherbrooke, Quebec, Canada J1H 5N4.

and bovines, which preferentially use the Δ^5-pathway to produce androgens. When COS-1 cells transiently transfected with pSV-SPORT 1 harboring the hamster P450c17 were incubated for 6 hours with [^{14}C]pregnenolone, 20% of the substrate was transformed into [^{14}C]17α-OH-pregnonolone and 1.3% into [^{14}C]DHEA (FIG.

```
HAMSTER   MWELVALLLLILLAYRFWSKSKTGGAKSPKSLPFLPLVGSLPFIPRHGHPHVNFFKLQEKY   60
G.PIG     MWELVTLLGLILLAYLFWPRQGSSGIKVPKSLPSLPVVGSLPFLPKSGHMVNFFKLQKKY    60
HUMAN     MWELVALLLLILLAYLFWPKRRCPGAKVPKSLLSLPVVGSLPFLPRHGHMHNNFFKLQKKY   60
BOVINE    MWLLLAVFILILLAYLFWPKTKHSGAKMPRSLPSLPLVGSLPFIPRRGQQHKNFFKLQEKY   60

HAMSTER   GPIYSLRLGSTTTVLIGDYQLAKEVLVKKGKEFSGRPHMVTLGLLSDQGKGIAFADSGGS   120
G.PIG     GSIYSFRLGSTTTVVIGHHQLARELLIKKGKEFSGRPLTTTVALLSDNGKGIAFADSSAT   120
HUMAN     GPIYSVRMGTTTVIVGHHQLAREVLLKKGKDFSGRPDMATLDIASNNRKGIAFADSGAH   120
BOVINE    GPIYSFRLGSKTTVMIGHHQLAREVLLKKGKRFSGRPKVATLDILSDNQKGIAFADHGAH   120

HAMSTER   WQLHRKLALSSFRLFRDGNQKLEKIIDQKASSLCDFLLTHNEESIDLSEPIFNSITNIIC   180
G.PIG     WQLHRRLVLSSFSLFRDGEQKLEKIIDQELSALCDFLRTCDGQVKDLSSSIFMTVVNIIC   180
HUMAN     WQLHRRLAMATFRLFRKDGDQKLEKIIDQEISTLCDMLRTHNGQSIDISFPVFVAVTNIIS   180
BOVINE    WQLHRQLALNAFRLFRDGNLKLEKIIHQEANVLCDFLRTQHGEAIDLSEPLSLAVTNIIS   180

HAMSTER   IICFGISVENRDPILATIKSFTEGILNSLGNDHLVDLFPVLKIFPNKTVDMIKKNVKIRD   240
G.PIG     MICFSVSVKEGDMELVTIRRFTTGFVNSLSDDNLVDIFPVLKIFPNKTLEMIRKYTELRG   240
HUMAN     LICFNTSVKNGDPELNVIQNYNEPGIIDNLSKDSLVDLVPWLKIFPNKTLEKLKSHVKIRN   240
BOVINE    FICFNFSFKNEDPALKAIDNVNDGILEVLSKEVLLDIFPVLKIFPSKAMEKMKGCVQTRN   240

HAMSTER   EVLSGILEKCKEKFHSDSISSLMDLLLQAKTNAIDNNTSEGQDSNAFSDMHLLATLADIF   300
G.PIG     AMLSKILKECKEKFRSDSVSNLIDILLQAKVNENNNNSSLDQDSNLFSDKHLLTLGDIF    300
HUMAN     DLLNKILENYKEKFRSDSITNMLDTLMQAKMNSDNGNAGPDQDSELLSDNHILTTIGDIF   300
BOVINE    ELLNEILEKCQENFHSSDSITNLLHILLQAKVNAIDNNAGPDQDSKLLSNRHMLATIGDIF   300

HAMSTER   GAGVETTASVLSWIIAFLLHNPEVKKKIQKEIDDNIGFSRTPTFNDRNHLLMLEATIREV   360
G.PIG     GAGVETSSSVVLWVIAFLLHNPQVKKKIQEFIDHNVGFSRTPTFSDRNHLLMLEATIREV   360
HUMAN     GAGVETTTSVVKWTLAFLLHNPQVKKKLYEEIDQNVGFSRTPTISDRNRLLLLEATIREV   360
BOVINE    GAGVETTTSVIKWIVAMLLHHPSLKKRIQDDIDQIIGFNRTPTISDRNRLVLLEATIREV   360

HAMSTER   LRLRPVAPMLIPHRANSDMSIGEFSIPKFTHVLINLWALHHSEKEWDQPDRFMPERFLDP   420
G.PIG     LRLRPVAPLLIPHKANTDSSIGEFAIDKDTNVLVNLWALHHNPEWDRPDQFMPERFLNP   420
HUMAN     LRLRPVAPMLIPHKANVDSSIGEFAVDKGTEVIINLWALHHNPEKEWHQPDQFMPERFLNP   420
BOVINE    LRLRPVAPTLIPHKAVIDSSIGDLTIDKGTDVVWNLWALHHSEKEWQHPDLFMPERFLDP   420

HAMSTER   TGSHLITPSLSYLPFGAGPRSCIGEVLARQELFLFMAHLLQRFDLDVPDDEQPFPLLKGNA   480
G.PIG     TGSQIIVPSSSVPFGAGPRSCVGEALARQEIFLITAWLLQKFDLEVPEGGQLPSLEGIP   480
HUMAN     AGTQLISPSVSYLPFGAGPRSCIGEILARQELFLIMAWLLQRFDLEVPDDGQLPSLEGIP   480
BOVINE    TGTQLISPSLSYLPFGAGPRSCVGEMLARQELFLFMSRLLQRFNLEIPDDGKLPSLEGHA   480

HAMSTER   NVWFLIDPFKVKILVRDAWKDAQAEVNTWRP                             511
G.PIG     KIWFLIDPFKVKILVRPAWKEAQAEGSA---                             508
HUMAN     KVWFLIDSFKVKIKVRDAWREAQAEGST---                             508
BOVINE    SLVLQIKPFKVKIEVRDAWKEAQAEGSTP--                             509
```

FIGURE 1. Sequence alignment of P450c17 from hamster, guinea pig,[2] human,[3] and bovine.[4]

2). When incubated with [^{14}C]progesterone, 11.3 and 13.4% were metabolized into [^{14}C]Δ^4 and [^{14}C]17α-OH-progesterone, respectively. Similar results were obtained when isolated adrenal cells were incubated with the aforementioned [^{14}C]substrates (results not shown).

A   B

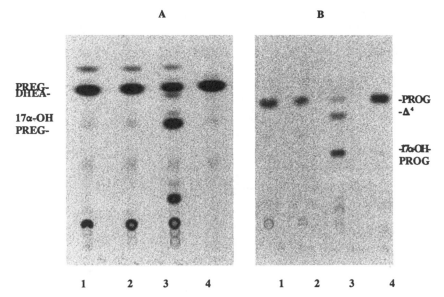

FIGURE 2. Metabolism of [^{14}C]pregnenolone (**left**) and [^{14}C]progesterone (**right**) by pSV-SPORT-1 harboring the hamster P450c17 transfected in COS-1 cells. *Lane 1:* medium; *lane 2:* pSV-SPORT-1; *lanes 3 and 4:* plasmid harboring the hamster adrenal P450c17. *Lanes 1, 2, and 3,* incubation time: 6 hours; *lane 4,* incubation time: 0 hour.

CONCLUSION

These results demonstrate the presence of P450c17 in hamster adrenals, which possesses 17α-hydroxylase and 17,20-desmolase activities. Although progesterone is a better substrate than pregnenolone for androgen formation, DHEA could also be identified from the media of transfected cells as well as from that of isolated adrenal cells. These results therefore indicate that in contrast to that of other small rodents, the hamster adrenal is capable of Δ^4 and DHEA formation much like that of the bovine and the human species.

REFERENCES

1. LEHOUX, J. G., J. I. MASON & L. DUCHARME. 1992. *In vivo* effects of adrenocorticotropin on hamster adrenal steroidogenic enzymes. Endocrinology **131:** 1874–1882.
2. TREMBLAY, Y., A. FLEURY, C. BEAUDOIN, M. VALLEE & A. BELANGER. 1994. Molecular cloning and expression of guinea pig cytochrome P450c17 cDNA (steroid 17α-hydroxylase/17,20 lyase): Tissue distribution, regulation, and substrate specificity of the expressed enzyme. DNA Cell Biol. **13:** 1199–1212.
3. CHUNG, B. C., J. PICADO-LEONARD, M. HANIU, M. BIENKOWSKI, P. F. HALL, J. E. SHEVILY & W. L. MILLER. 1987. Cytochrome P450c17 (steroid 17α-hydroxylase/17,20 lyase): Cloning of human adrenal and testis cDNA indicates the same gene is expressed in both tissues. Proc. Natl. Acad. Sci. USA **84:** 407–411.
4. ZUBER, M. X., M. J. JOHN, T. OKAMURA, E. R. SIMPSON & M. R. WATERMAN. 1986. Bovine adrenocortical cytochrome P-45017α. J. Biol. Chem. **261:** 2475–2482.
5. KOH, Y. C., E. BUCZKO & M. L. DUFAU. 1993. Requirement of phenylalanine 343 for the preferential Δ^4-lyase versus Δ^5-lyase activity of rat *CYP*17. J. Biol. Chem. **268:** 18267–18271.

Dehydroepiandrosterone Enhances Influenza Immunization in Aged Mice[a]

H. D. DANENBERG,[b,c] A. BEN-YEHUDA,[b]
Z. ZAKAY-RONES,[d] AND G. FRIEDMAN[b]

[b]Division of Medicine
Hadassah University Hospital, and
[d]Department of Virology
Hebrew University
Hadassah Medical School
Jerusalem, Israel

Influenza vaccine, while highly effective in young, healthy adults, fails to generate protective immunity in 30–50% of older persons at high risk for influenza infection.[1] A model of old mice immunized with influenza vaccine showed a decrease in both humoral response and protection against influenza virus.[2]

Dehydroepiandrosterone (DHEA) administration to mice reverses some of the typical phenomena of immunosenescence including disturbed cytokine production.[3] Recently, DHEA treatment was found to augment immunization of old mice to recombinant hepatitis B vaccine.[4] These experiments were planned to study the effects of DHEA treatment on the efficacy of immunization against influenza in old mice, as measured by the titer of antibodies and the protection against exposure with live influenza virus.

MATERIALS AND METHODS

Female C57/black mice were used. Mice of the same age and batch were immunized intraperitoneally (ip) with 1,000 hemagglutination units of live A/PR/8/34 (H1N1) influenza virus in 0.2 ml of phosphate-buffered saline solution (PBS). DHEA was dissolved in ethanol and 10 mg were administered subcutaneously. Hemagglutination inhibition assay is described elsewhere. The susceptibility of immunized mice to influenza infection was determined by an intranasal challenge with 100 μl of PBS containing 10^6 EID_{50} 5 weeks after immunization. Three days after challenge, mice were sacrificed and their lungs removed for detection of viable virus as described previously.[2]

RESULTS AND DISCUSSION

Hemagglutination inhibition antibodies against influenza were measured 4 weeks after immunization in treated and nontreated 16- and 24-month-old mice and in

[a]This work was supported in part by general scientist of the Israeli ministry of health grant S/3025 to H.D.D. and by a grant from H. J. Leir to G. F.
[c]Address for correspondence: H. D. Danenberg, Division of Medicine, Hadassah University Hospital, P.O.B. 12000, Jerusalem 91120, Israel.

young nontreated mice (FIG. 1). The humoral response significantly declined with advancing age. DHEA-treated, 16-month-old mice demonstrated complete reversal of antibody decline. The decline in humoral response was greater in 24-month-old mice. DHEA treatment significantly reversed the decline in hemagglutination inhibition activity in these mice, but not to the level recorded with young mice. To study the protective effect of immunization against influenza challenge, the resistance to pulmonary infection was compared after intranasal challenge with live A/PR/8 virus. Virus titers in the lungs 3 days after inoculation were very low in most of the young mice and negative in 16-month-old, DHEA-treated mice, whereas significant titers were recorded in the old nontreated group (FIG. 2). Absence of virus in the lungs 3 days after challenge suggests that the promotion of effective immunization increases the resistance to infection not by decreasing its magnitude but rather by preventing and blocking viral replication.

The administration of DHEA to old mice was previously shown to increase antibody formation to ovalbumin[3] and to hepatitis B surface antigen.[4] The present experiments demonstrate that administration of DHEA to old mice combined with influenza vaccine augments the humoral response against influenza. Moreover, following inoculation with live virus, effective protection against pulmonary infection is achieved. These experiments support the hypothesis of a cause-effect relationship between the age-related decline in DHEA and immunosenescence. If these findings can be repeated in humans, DHEA may be beneficial in the prevention of influenza in the aged.

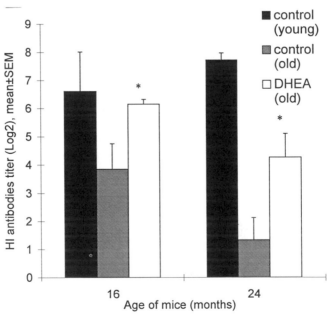

FIGURE 1. Effect of DHEA treatment on hemagglutination-inhibiting antibody formation after immunization against influenza in aged mice ($n = 6$). *$p < 0.05$ compared to nontreated mice.

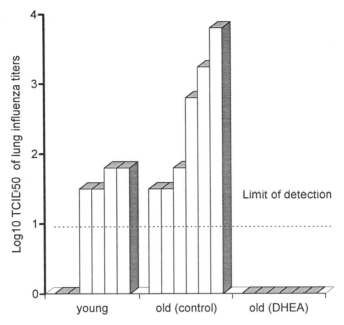

FIGURE 2. Pulmonary infection of mice 35 days after influenza immunization ± DHEA, following intranasal challenge with live A/PR/8 influenza virus. MDCK cells were plated with different dilutions of lung homogenates from infected mice 3 days after inoculation of 10^6 EID_{50}. Two days later, supernatants were assayed for hemagglutination titers, and Log_{10} tissue culture infectious dose 50% ($TCID_{50}$) from individual lungs was calculated.

SUMMARY

The effect of DHEA administration on the age-associated decline in immunity against influenza vaccine was studied. Increased humoral response was observed in 16- and 24-month-old mice immunized by live A/PR/8/34 (H1N1) influenza virus following DHEA treatment (a single injection adjacent to immunization). Furthermore, DHEA-treated mice demonstrated increased resistance to postvaccination intranasal challenge with live influenza virus. Thus, DHEA treatment overcomes the age-related defect in the immunity of old mice against influenza.

REFERENCES

1. SETIA, U., I. SERVENTI & P. LORENZ. 1985. J. Am. Geriatr. Soc. **33:** 856–858.
2. BEN-YEHUDA, A., D. EHLIETER, A. R. HU & M. E. WEXLER. 1993. J. Infect. Dis. **168:** 52–57.
3. DAYNES, R. A. & B. A. ARANEO. 1992. Aging Immunol. Infect. Dis. **3:** 135–154.
4. ARANEO, B., L. MARION, H. WOODS & R. A. DAYNES. 1993. J. Infect. Dis. **167:** 830–840.

Dehydroepiandrosterone Augments M1-Muscarinic Receptor-Stimulated Amyloid Precursor Protein Secretion in Desensitized PC12M1 Cells

H. D. DANENBERG,[a,b] R. HARING,[c] E. HELDMAN,[c]
D. GURWITZ,[c] D. BEN-NATHAN,[d] Z. PITTEL,[c]
A. ZUCKERMAN,[c] AND A. FISHER[c]

[a]Division of Medicine
Hadassah University Hospital
Jerusalem 91120, Israel

[c]Department of Organic Chemistry and
[d]Department of Virology
Israel Institute for Biological Research
P.O.B. 19
Ness-Ziona 74100, Israel

Amyloid β protein (βA4) is the major component of senile plaques, a distinct neuropathologic lesion in the brain of patients with Alzheimer's disease (AD). Deposition of aggregated βA4 amyloid deposits in plaques and the neurotoxicity that may be associated with these deposits are implicated in the etiology of AD.[1] βA4 is a proteolytic product of a larger transmembrane-associated glycoprotein, the amyloid precursor protein (APP), whose processing by "α-secretase" results in secretion of non-amyloidogenic isoforms of APP that exhibit neuroprotective properties.[2] Secretion of non-amyloidogenic APP by cultured cells was shown to be coupled to activation of m1 muscarinic acetylcholine receptors (m1AChR)[3] and is associated with decreased production of βA4. These findings suggest a possible linkage between well documented cholinergic deficiency and amyloid deposition in AD. Desensitization of muscarinic-stimulated APP release is observed after prolonged incubations with muscarinic agonists.[4] Attenuation of such desensitization mechanisms may allow increased APP secretion and thereby decreased formation of the undesirable βA4 peptide. Epidemiologic studies suggest that the age-associated decline in DHEA levels is correlated with AD.[5] To examine the effect of DHEA on m1AChR-stimulated APP secretion we used PC12 cells transfected with cDNA encoding m1AChR which release APPs in response to muscarinic stimulation.[3,4]

MATERIALS AND METHODS

PC12M1 cells were plated in complete RPMI medium and used 4–5 days after plating. Cells were either untreated or pretreated for 24 hours with carbachol and/or

[b]Address for correspondence: H. D. Danenberg, Division of Medicine, Hadassah University Hospital, P.O.B. 12000, Jerusalem 91120, Israel.

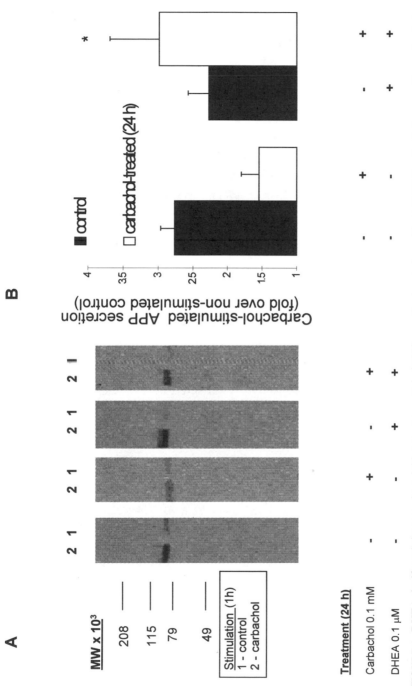

FIGURE 1. DHEA significantly increased amyloid precursor protein (APP) secretion in m1-desensitized PC12M1 cells. Cells were either untreated or treated for 24 hours with carbachol, DHEA alone, or a combination Cells were washed extensively, and APP secretion was measured following stimulation with 0.1 mM carbachol for 1 hour. (**A**) Representative immunoblot. (**B**) Video densitometry data (mean ± SEM, *n* = 3) from a representative experiment. *p < 0.05 (compared to carbachol 24 hours alone).

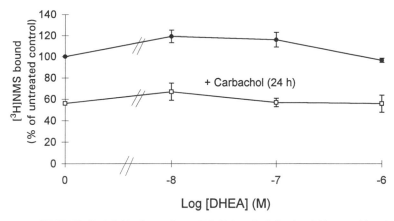

FIGURE 2. [³H]NMS (2 nM) binding to intact PC12M1 cells following 24 hours of incubation with and without DHEA and carbachol (0.1 mM).

DHEA, washed extensively with fresh medium, and APP secretion during 1 hour of incubation with carbachol (0.1 mM) was measured as described previously.[4]

RESULTS AND DISCUSSION

Stimulation of PC12M1 cells with carbachol resulted in an increased level of APP in the medium. Treatment with DHEA (0.1 μM for 24 hours before stimulation with carbachol) did not result in any significant change in carbachol-stimulated APP secretion (FIG. 1a and b). Similar observations were obtained using a wide range of DHEA concentrations (1 nM to 1 mM, data not shown). When cells were incubated for 24 hours with 0.1 mM carbachol, washed extensively, and then stimulated with carbachol, APP secretion was decreased. Cotreatment for 24 hours with DHEA and carbachol significantly increased APP secretion in such desensitized cells, almost blocking completely the decrease induced by 24 hours of incubation with carbachol alone (FIG. 1A and B).

To better understand the mechanism of DHEA action we examined whether it affected muscarinic receptors or phosphoinositide (PI) hydrolysis which constitutes its best characterized signal transduction pathway. DHEA treatment did not affect [³H]NMS binding or PI hydrolysis in basal, carbachol-stimulated, and carbachol-desensitized PC12M1 cells. (FIGURE 2 presents binding assays; data of PI hydrolysis studies are not shown.) This warrants further investigation to elucidate the mechanism by which DHEA affects m1AChR-stimulated APP secretion from these cells. These observations may constitute a clue as to the possible role of DHEA in APP processing and the pathogenesis of AD.

SUMMARY

Epidemiologic studies suggest that the age-related decline in dehydroepiandrosterone (DHEA) levels may be associated with Alzheimer's disease (AD). Cholinergic markers also decline with age, and are associated with AD pathology. Activation of m1AChR-transfected PC12 cells (PC12M1) with cholinergic agonists results in secretion of Alzheimer's β-amyloid precursor protein (APP) which in turn reduces β-amyloid production. This study examined whether DHEA affects APP processing in m1AChR-transfected PC12 cells. DHEA treatment did not significantly alter basal or m1AChR-stimulated APP secretion. However, DHEA (0.1 μM) significantly diminished the desensitization of APP secretion in cells exposed to carbachol for 24 h. The effect of DHEA on APP processing is probably not related to up-regulation of m1AChR or increased m1AChR-activated phosphoinositide hydrolysis since these parameters did not change following DHEA treatment. These findings imply a possible involvement of DHEA in APP processing. Thus, the age-associated decline in DHEA levels may contribute to decreased APP secretion and a consecutive increase in β-amyloid deposition, which in turn may play a role in the development of AD.

REFERENCES

1. SELKOE, D. J. 1993. Trends Neurosci. **16:** 403–409.
2. MATTSON, M. P., B. CHENG, A. R. CULWELL, F. S. ESCH, I. LIEBERBURG & R. E. RYDEL. 1993. Neuron **10:** 243–254.
3. BUXBAUM, J. D., M. OISHI, H. I. CHEN, R. PINKAS-KRAMARSKI, E. A. JAFFE, S. E. GANDY & P. GREENGARD. 1992. Proc. Natl. Acad. Sci. USA **89:** 10075–10078.
4. HARING, R., D. GURWITZ, J. BARG, R. PINKAS-KRAMARSKI, E. HELDMAN, Z. PITTEL, A. WENGIER, H. MESHULAM, D. MARCIANO, Y. KARTON & A. FISHER. 1994. Biochem. Biophys. Res. Commun. **203:** 652–658.
5. NASMAN, B., T. OLSSON, T. BACKSTROM, S. ERIKSSON, K. GRANKVIST, M. VIITANEN & G. BUCHT. 1991. Biol. Psychiatry **30:** 684–690.

Effects of Dehydroepiandrosterone Sulfate and Stress on Hippocampal Electrophysiological Plasticity[a]

DAVID M. DIAMOND,[b,d,f] BERRILYN J. BRANCH,[b]
MONIKA FLESHNER,[e] AND GREGORY M. ROSE[b,c,d]

[b]Department of Pharmacology
[c]Neurosciences Training Program
University of Colorado Health Sciences Center
Denver, Colorado 80262

[d]Medical Research Service
Veterans Affairs Medical Center
Denver, Colorado 80220

[e]Department of Psychology
University of Colorado
Boulder, Colorado 80309

Dehydroepiandrosterone sulfate (DHEAS) is the major secretory product of the human adrenal cortex, is described functionally as an antiglucocorticoid, and its levels decline with age.[1] Little is known, however, about the effects of DHEAS on CNS function. We studied the effects of DHEAS on hippocampal primed burst (PB) potentiation and long-term potentiation (LTP), two electrophysiological models of memory.[2-4] In both cases, relatively brief electrical stimulation of the hippocampus induces a long-lasting enhancement of synaptic transmission which has characteristics in common with memory. However, whereas LTP involves extensive high frequency electrical stimulation (25–100 pulses) which typically induces a large increase in the magnitude of an evoked response, PB potentiation involves threshold stimulation (only 5 pulses patterned to mimic endogenous electrophysiological activity) and a smaller increase in response.[4,5] In this work we evaluated the effects of the administration of DHEAS on the magnitude of hippocampal LTP and PB potentiation. Furthermore, we tested the hypothesis that stress will modulate DHEA-induced changes in PB potentiation and LTP.

Young adult 350-g male Sprague-Dawley rats were injected with DHEAS (24 mg/kg, sc) or saline solution and then 10 minutes later were anesthetized with urethane (1.25 g/kg, ip). Subjects in a second group were stressed by placing them in an unfamiliar environment for 20 minutes[6,7] and were then injected with DHEAS and urethane. A stimulating electrode was placed in the ventral hippocampal commissure, and a recording electrode was placed in the CA1 cell layer of the hippocampus, according to procedures described previously.[4,6,7] Test pulses were delivered every 30 seconds for 10 minutes before and for 30 minutes after PB and LTP stimulation. Primed burst stimulation, composed of a single pulse followed 170

[a]This work was supported by the Veterans Affairs Medical Research Service, National Institute of Aging, and Office of Naval Research.
[f]Address for correspondence: David Diamond, PhD, Department of Pharmacology, Box C236, University of Colorado Health Sciences Center, Denver, CO 80262.

ms later by 4 pulses at 200 Hz, was delivered first. Thirty minutes later the current was reduced, if necessary, to normalize the baseline to the pre-PB stimulation baseline level. Long-term potentiation stimulation, composed of 25 pulses at 200 Hz, was then delivered.

Two basic observations emerged from within the PB stimulation component of the study. First, DHEAS significantly enhanced the magnitude of PB potentiation. Second, when the rats were stressed for 20 minutes before being given DHEAS, enhancement of PB potentiation did not occur (FIG. 1). Stress, therefore, blocked the capacity of DHEAS to increase the magnitude of PB potentiation. The LTP findings contrasted with the PB potentiation findings. Long-term potentiation stimulation produced a greater increase in response in saline-injected control subjects than that with PB stimulation. However, enhancement of the response induced by LTP stimulation was not affected by either DHEAS or stress manipulations (FIG. 2). This finding is consistent with previous work demonstrating that LTP is less sensitive than PB potentiation to modulation by pharmacological or behavioral variables.[8,9]

Overall, these findings indicate that: (1) DHEAS can enhance the magnitude of hippocampal plasticity, but only when threshold (PB) stimulation is used; and (2) when subjects were stressed before being given DHEAS, PB potentiation was not enhanced. Thus, under nonstress conditions DHEAS could enhance hippocampal synaptic plasticity. However, prior exposure of a rat to an unfamiliar environment could block the DHEAS-induced enhancement of PB potentiation. Enhancement of

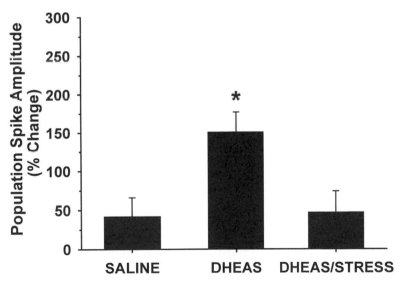

FIGURE 1. DHEAS-induced enhancement of primed burst (PB) potentiation is blocked by stress. This figure illustrates the increase in amplitude of the CA1 population spike (mean ± SEM) recorded during the 21–30-minute period after delivery of PB stimulation (5 pulses patterned to mimic theta burst activity). Subjects ($n = 8$) that were injected with saline solution exhibited a 42% (±24) increase in response, whereas subjects ($n = 6$) that were injected with DHEAS (24 mg/kg, sc) exhibited a 151% (±26) increase. Subjects ($n = 6$) that were placed in an unfamiliar environment for 20 minutes before they were injected with DHEAS exhibited an increase in response which was not significantly different from that of saline control subjects. ([F3,22] = 4.83, $p < 0.01$, *Dunnett's posthoc test.)

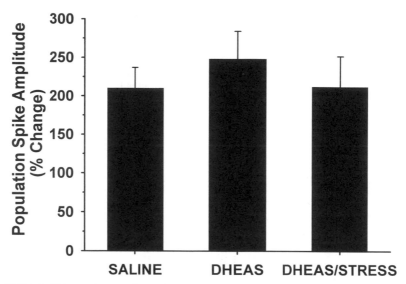

FIGURE 2. Thirty minutes after primed burst (PB) stimulation was delivered (PB data presented in FIG. 1), long-term potentiation (LTP) stimulation produced an increase in response which was unaffected by behavioral and pharmacological manipulations. There was a 210% ($\pm$27) increase in response in saline-injected control subjects, a 248% ($\pm$36) increase in DHEAS-injected subjects, and a 212% ($\pm$40) increase in subjects that were stressed before being injected with DHEAS. ($F[3,22] = 1.1, p > 0.3$.)

PB potentiation by DHEAS is consistent with previous work indicating that DHEAS can enhance memory.[10,11] The present work further demonstrates a balance between the inhibitory effects of stress on the hippocampus and the facilitatory effect of DHEAS on synaptic plasticity.

REFERENCES

1. KALIMI, M., Y. SHAFAGOJ, R. LORIA, D. PADGETT & W. REGELSON. 1994. Anti-glucocorticoid effects of dehydroepiandrosterone (DHEA). Molec. Cell. Biochem. **131:** 99–104.
2. MAREN, S. & M. BAUDRY. 1995. Properties and mechanisms of long-term synaptic plasticity in the mammalian brain: Relationships to learning and memory. Neurobiol. Learning Memory **63:** 1–18.
3. IZQUIERDO, I. 1994. Pharmacological evidence for a role of long-term potentiation in memory. FASEB J. **8:** 1139–1145.
4. DIAMOND, D. M., T. V. DUNWIDDIE & G. M. ROSE. 1988. Characteristics of hippocampal primed burst potentiation in vitro and in the awake rat. J. Neurosci. **8:** 4079–4088.
5. ROSE, G. M. & T. V. DUNWIDDIE. 1986. Induction of hippocampal long-term potentiation using physiologically patterned stimulation. Neurosci. Lett. **69:** 244–248.
6. DIAMOND, D. M., M. C. BENNETT, K. E. STEVENS, R. L. WILSON & G. M. ROSE. 1990. Exposure to a novel environment interferes with the induction of hippocampal primed burst potentiation. Psychobiology **18:** 273–281.
7. DIAMOND, D. M., M. FLESHNER & G. M. ROSE. 1994. Psychological stress repeatedly blocks hippocampal primed burst potentiation in behaving rats. Behav. Brain Res. **62:** 1–9.

8. CORRADETTI, R., L. BALLERINI, A. M. PUGLIESE & G. PEPEU. 1992. Serotonin blocks the long-term potentiation induced by primed burst stimulation in the CA1 region of rat hippocampal slices. Neuroscience **46:** 511–518.

9. MOORE, C. I., M. D. BROWNING & G. M. ROSE. 1993. Hippocampal plasticity induced by primed burst, but not long-term potentiation, stimulation is impaired in area CA1 of aged Fischer 344 rats. Hippocampus **3:** 57–66.

10. FLOOD, J. F., G. E. SMITH & E. ROBERTS. 1988. Dehydroepiandrosterone and its sulfate enhance memory retention in mice. Brain Res. **447:** 269–278.

11. ROBERTS, E., L. BOLOGA, J. F. FLOOD & G. E. SMITH. 1987. Effects of dehydroepiandrosterone and its sulfate on brain tissue in culture and on memory in mice. Brain Res. **406:** 357–362.

Sex Differences
in Dehydroepiandrosterone
Metabolism in Rodents[a]

GERHARD HOBE, RENATE SCHÖN, KATHRIN UNDISZ,
LUTZ BLEI, AND HANS-GEORG HILLESHEIM

Hans-Knöll-Institut for Natural Products Research
D-07745 Jena, Germany

Rats and mice are commonly used in studies on the pharmacologic effects of dehydroepiandrosterone (DHEA). In these studies DHEA is frequently admixed to the food. Knowledge of the plasma levels of DHEA in rodents following administration of DHEA-supplemented food and of the fate of DHEA in rodents at all is poor. Recently, 7-hydroxylated DHEA metabolites were reported to be the true active compounds in exerting DHEA effects on the immune system.[1,2]

We studied total DHEA plasma levels in male and female Sprague-Dawley rats by a specific microtiter plate enzyme immunoassay[3] after ingestion of a standard chow with 0.3% and 0.6% DHEA and also radioactivity distribution in organs and tissues, biliary elimination in animals with bile fistulas, and urinary and fecal excretion after oral administration of [3H]DHEA with a dose of 10 mg/kg body weight. DHEA metabolite patterns were obtained by TLC separation of extracts from plasma, bile, and urine of rats and NMRI mice. Using a ligand binding assay[4] with 1,2,6,7 [3H]DHEA, the existence of a DHEA receptor was examined.

RESULTS AND DISCUSSION

DHEA Plasma Levels after Food Administration

Mean DHEA and DHEA sulfate (DHEAS) plasma concentrations in female and male Sprague-Dawley rats during unrestricted feeding of 0.6% and 0.3% DHEA-supplemented chow are compiled in TABLE 1. Significant sex differences in total DHEA plasma concentrations are found in far higher concentrations in female animals than in male rats. The main part of DHEA was present as the sulfate conjugate. For control, DHEA food was withdrawn and replaced by standard chow without DHEA. Total DHEA plasma concentrations decreased to 4–23 ng/ml (mean 11.1 ± 6 ng/ml).

Radioactivity Distribution

Analysis of radioactivity distribution in organs and tissues of male and female rats 1 and 24 hours after oral administration of [3H]DHEA (10 mg/kg body weight) demonstrated at 1 hour high concentrations of DHEA and/or DHEA metabolites in

[a]This study was supported by the Ministry of Education, Science, Research and Technology of the Federal Republic of Germany (FKZ 0310591 A).

the organs for excretion, the liver and kidney. The pituitary gland and bone marrow retained remarkable concentrations even 24 hours after administration when the levels in other tissues had significantly decreased.

Biliary, Renal, and Fecal Excretion of DHEA Metabolites

In male and female rats with bile fistulas, more than 60% of intravenously administered [³H]DHEA was eliminated during the first 9 hours after administration. The male rat demonstrates rapid biliary elimination immediately after administration. In female rats urinary elimination predominates, whereas in male rats fecal excretion is higher.

TABLE 1. Mean DHEA and DHEA Sulfate (DHEAS) Plasma Concentrations (ng/ml; m ± s_D) in Female and Male Sprague-Dawley Rats during Unrestricted Feeding of 0.6% and 0.3% DHEA-Supplemented Food.

Hours of DHEA Feeding	12 (M)	48 (E)	84 (M)	120 (E)	156 (M)	192 (E)
	0.6% DHEA, ♀ Animals (n = 12)					
DHEA	0.71 ± 0.48	0.75 ± 0.38	1.07 ± 0.50	0.85 ± 0.50	1.32 ± 0.81	0.90 ± 0.35
DHEAS	16.77 ± 6.64	21.51 ± 8.52	31.93 ± 11.91	24.17 ± 10.20	29.98 ± 9.22	26.07 ± 5.44
	0.6% DHEA, ♂ Animals (n = 12)					
DHEA	0.03 ± 0.05	0.08 ± 0.05	0.03 ± 0.04	0.17 ± 0.15	0.14 ± 0.16	0.07 ± 0.06
DHEAS	0.35 ± 0.31	0.57 ± 0.38	0.74 ± 0.50	1.36 ± 1.17	0.95 ± 0.74	0.85 ± 0.50
	0.3% DHEA, ♀ Animals (n = 6)					
DHEA	0.18 ± 0.07	0.22 ± 0.08	0.21 ± 0.09	0.18 ± 0.03	0.17 ± 0.08	0.18 ± 0.06
DHEAS	8.12 ± 2.96	9.78 ± 4.65	11.08 ± 3.68	8.79 ± 2.86	10.21 ± 2.52	8.71 ± 2.86
	0.3% DHEA, ♂ Animals (n = 6)					
DHEA	0.04 ± 0.03	0.07 ± 0.03	0.08 ± 0.06	0.10 ± 0.07	0.08 ± 0.05	0.06 ± 0.04
DHEAS	0.33 ± 0.18	0.30 ± 0.10	0.41 ± 0.16	0.28 ± 0.13	0.34 ± 0.23	0.24 ± 0.17

[a]Blood was collected from the animals by retroorbital vein puncture under light ether anesthesia in 36-hour intervals in the morning (M) and evening (E), respectively.

Metabolite Pattern of DHEA

In vivo biotransformation of DHEA has been characterized by metabolite patterns obtained by chromatographic separation of extracts from plasma, urine, and bile after oral administration of [³H]DHEA. FIGURE 1 represents DHEA metabolite patterns in rat bile and urine. In the female rat DHEA is a considerable part of the extracted radioactivity as in plasma, whereas in the male rat DHEA is absent or present in minute quantities. In the urine and bile of the female rat the following DHEA metabolites were tentatively identified by TLC comparison in different solvent systems with authentic reference compounds: 5-androstene-3β, 17β-diol; 3β,7α-dihydroxy-5-androsten-17-one (7α-OH-DHEA); 3β-hydroxy-5-androsten-7,17-dione (7-Oxo-DHEA), and 3β,16α-dihydroxy-5-androsten-17-one (16α-OH-DHEA). Androsterone and etiocholanolone, which are the principal DHEA metabolites in man, occur only in small quantities in the rat.

In the urinary DHEA metabolite patterns in male and female NMRI mice after oral administration of [³H]DHEA (10 mg/kg body weight) no pronounced sex

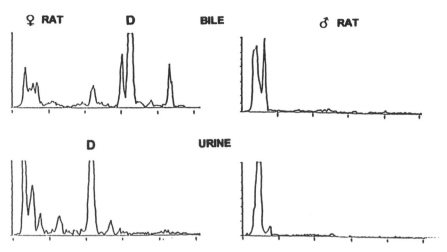

FIGURE 1. Metabolite patterns of dehydroepiandrosterone (D) in bile and urine of male and female Sprague-Dawley rats after oral administration of 10 mg [³H]DHEA/kg body weight. TLC on alumina; solvent system benzene/ether 7:3 (5×).

differences such as those found in the rat could be ascertained. Strong polar, obviously polyhydroxylated compounds dominate in the pattern of both sexes; no unchanged DHEA could be found. Noteworthy are the less polar compounds that were obtained *in vitro* by incubation of [³H]DHEA with liver homogenate of male and female NMRI mice. These compounds have been identified by high-resolving mass spectrometry and TLC comparison with authentic reference compounds to be DHEA acetate, 5-androstene-3β,17β-diol-3-acetate, and 5-androstene-3β,17-diol-3,17-diacetate.

DHEA Receptor Binding

No high affinity receptor for DHEA could be demonstrated in liver cytosol of intact and adrenalectomized male and female Sprague-Dawley rats or in bone marrow cells, using a ligand binding assay with 1,2,6,7 [³H]DHEA.

CONCLUSIONS

Sprague-Dawley rats demonstrate significant sex differences in DHEA plasma levels when the compound is admixed to food. The far higher DHEA plasma levels in the female animal have to be considered in the evaluation of pharmacologic DHEA testing in rats. As demonstrated in the metabolite pattern of bile and urine, the female rat is additionally subjected to the estrogenic effect of the DHEA metabolite 5-androstene-3β,17β-diol. In NMRI mice, the DHEA metabolite pattern is characterized by strong polar compounds, whereas *in vitro* by liver homogenate less polar DHEA metabolites are formed which were identified as DHEA-3-acetate and 5-androsten-3β,17β-diol-3-acetate and 3,17-diacetate. Evidence for a high affinity receptor for DHEA in rat liver cytosol and bone marrow was lacking.

REFERENCES

1. MORFIN, R. & G. COURCHAY. 1994. Pregnenolone and dehydroepiandrosterone as precursors of native 7-hydroxylated metabolites which increase the immune response in mice. J. Steroid Biochem. Molec. Biol. **50:** 91–100.
2. PADGETT, D. A. & R. M. LORIA. 1994. In vitro potentiation of lymphocyte activation by dehydroepiandrosterone, androstenediol, and androstentriol. J. Immunol. **153:** 1544–1552.
3. FREYMANN, E. & W. HUBL. 1990. Determination of dehydroepiandrosterone in serum by an enzyme immunoassay on microtitre plates. *In* Advances of Steroid Analysis '90. S. Görög, Ed.: 97–101. Akadémíaí Kíadó. Budapest.
4. KALIMI, M. & W. REGELSON. 1988. Physicochemical characterization of [³H]DHEA binding in rat liver. Biochem. Biophys. Res. Commun. **156:** 22–29.

Effect of Dehydroepiandrosterone on Cyclic-Guanosine Monophosphate in Men of Advancing Age

DANIELA JAKUBOWICZ, NUSEN BEER,
AND RUFINO RENGIFO

*Department of Internal Medicine
Hospital de Clinicas Caracas
Caracas, Venezuela*

Several clinical and population-based studies suggest that dehydroepiandrosterone (DHEA) and its sulfate (DHEAS) play a protective role against atherosclerosis and coronary artery disease in men,[1,2] but the mechanism of its biologic role remains elusive.

Serum DHEA demonstrates a progressive age-related decline[3] paralleling that of serum insulin-like growth factor-1 (IGF-1).[4,5] Morales *et al.*[6] reported that replacement therapy with DHEA in men of advancing age increases the bioavailability and serum levels of IGF-1. Evidence indicates that IGF-1 exerts a potent vasodilatory action presumably mediated by stimulation of nitric oxide (NO) synthesis in the endothelial cells.[7]

With that background, we hypothesized that replacement with DHEA through stimulation of IGF-1 might enhance NO activity. To test this hypothesis we conducted a double-blind and placebo-controlled study in 22 men (57 ± 1.95 years), which assessed the effects of oral DHEA 100 mg nightly ($n = 12$) or placebo ($n = 10$) for 30 days on plasma cyclic-guanosine monophosphate (c-GMP) as an indirect assay of NO activity.[7] Concurrently, IGF-1, DHEAS, glucose, and insulin serum levels were determined at baseline and after DHEA or placebo treatment.

Given that c-GMP is a second messenger of NO activity and also of the atrial natriuretic factor (ANF), to elucidate the selective contribution of NO in the DHEA-mediated increment of c-GMP, we performed an acute test in a subgroup of 14 of 22 subjects. In the test we quantified serum IGF-1 and plasma c-GMP at 0, 60, and 120 minutes after 300 mg of oral DHEA, followed by 2 hours of intravenous saline infusion (DHEA-saline group, $n = 8$). After the oral dose of DHEA instead of saline, six of them received a 2-hour intravenous infusion of L-nitro-arginine-methyl-ester (L-NAME), a specific inhibitor of NO synthase (DHEA-L-NAME group, $n = 6$).

After 30 days of treatment in the DHEA group ($n = 12$), serum DHEAS rose from 105.5 ± 5.6 to 285 ± 11 μg/ml ($p < 0.0001$). Serum IGF-1 increased from 96.7 ± 4.8 to 183 ± 8.4 ng/ml ($p < 0.001$). Serum insulin decreased from 35.3 ± 2.2 to 25.8 ± 0.8 μU/ml ($p < 0.01$) and serum glucose declined from 93.4 ± 0.5 to 88.9 ± 0.4 mg/ml ($p < 0.01$). Plasma c-GMP exhibited an increase by 54% from 2.22 ± 0.2 to 5.65 ± 0.4 pmol/ml ($p < 0.005$). Serum concentration of DHEAS, IGF-1, insulin, glucose, and plasma c-GMP did not change in the placebo group (FIG. 1).

In the acute test, after 120 minutes of the oral dose of DHEA in the DHEA-saline group ($n = 8$), serum IGF-1 increased ($p < 0.01$) by 52.9 ± 2.4 ng/ml;

concurrently, a significant rise in plasma c-GMP (from 2.64 ± 0.4 to 10.7 ± 1.6 pmol/ml, $p < 0.005$) was observed. By contrast, in the DHEA-L-NAME group ($n = 6$), although serum IGF-1 evoked a similar increase by 64.9 ± 3.2 ng/ml ($p < 0.01$), the plasma c-GMP rise in response to DHEA was completely abolished (FIG. 2).

The significant suppression by L-NAME of the DHEA-induced increase in

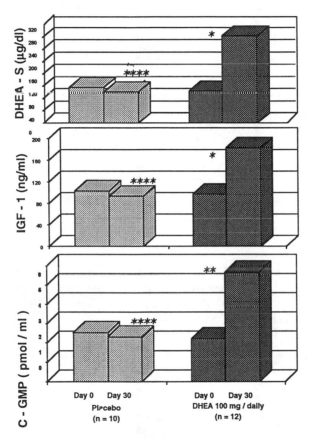

FIGURE 1. Serum DHEAS, IGF, and plasma c-GMP at baseline (day 0) and after treatment (day 30) with DHEA or placebo. *$p < 0.0001$ compared to basal value in the DHEA group; **$p < 0.005$ compared to basal value in the DHEA group; ***$p < 0.001$ compared to basal value in the DHEA group; ****p = NS compared to basal value in the placebo group.

c-GMP indicates that DHEA's effect is mediated by stimulation of NO synthesis directly or via IGF-1 stimulation.

It is noteworthy that several of the suggested mechanisms by which DHEA exerts its antiatherogenic properties, including inhibition of cellular proliferation and suppression of platelet reactivity, resemble those of NO. Hence, if DHEA promotes NO synthesis, at least some of its protective actions might be mediated through NO activation.

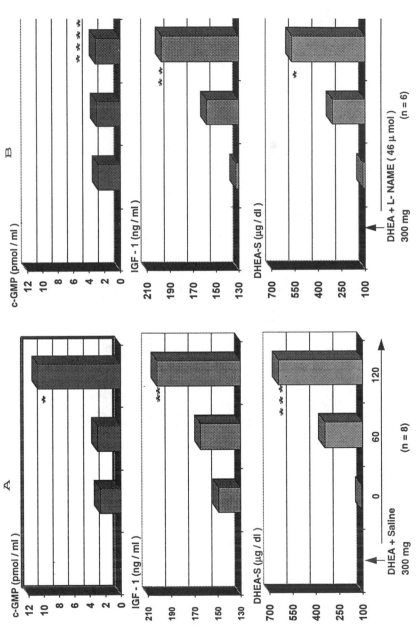

FIGURE 2. Serum DHEA, IGF-1, and plasma c-GMP at 0, 60, and 120 minutes after an oral 300-mg dose of DHEA followed by **(A)** a 2-hour saline intravenous infusion and **(B)** a 2-hour infusion of L-NAME. *p* value compared to basal in the same group. *$p < 0.005$; **$p < 0.01$; ***$p < 0.001$; ****$p =$ NS.

CONCLUSIONS

In this study, after 1 month of replacement therapy with DHEA, serum IGF-1 and plasma c-GMP increased significantly. The DHEA-induced increase in c-GMP reflected enhancement of NO activity, because it was completely suppressed by L-NAME. These findings raise the possibility that DHEA either directly or through IGF-1 stimulation promotes NO synthesis, which might be one pathway for the protective action of DHEA against coronary ischemic disease in men.

REFERENCES

1. HERRINGTON, D. M., G. B. GORDON, S. C. ACHUFF, J. F. TREJO, H. F. WEISMAN, P. O. KWITEROVICZ & T. A. PEARSON. 1990. J. Am. Coll. Cardiol. **16:** 862–887.
2. GORDON, G. B., D. E. BUCH & H. F. WEISMAN. 1988. J. Clin. Invest. **82:** 712–720.
3. ORENTREICH, N., J. BRIN, R. RIZER & J. VOGELMAN. 1984. J. Clin. Endocrinol. Metab. **59:** 551–555.
4. CORPAS, E., M. HARMAN & M. R. BLACKMAN. 1993. Endocrinol. Rev. **14:** 20–39.
5. CLEMMONS, D. 1992. J. Clin. Endocrinol. Metab. **75:** 1183–1185.
6. MORALES, A. J., J. J. NOLAN, J. C. NELSON & S. S. C. YEN. 1994. J. Clin. Endocrinol. Metab. **78:** 1360–1367.
7. TSUKAHARA, H., D. V. GORDIENKO, B. TONSHOFF, M. C. GELATO & M. S. GOLIGORSKI. 1994. Kidney Int. **45:** 598–604.

7α-Hydroxylation of the Adrenal Androgens Dehydroepiandrosterone and Androst-5-ene-3β, 17β-Diol Predominates in Differentiating Human Adipose Stromal Cells

M. W. KHALIL, B. STRUTT, AND D. W. KILLINGER

Department of Medicine and Lawson Research Institute
St. Joseph's Health Centre and
University of Western Ontario
London, Ontario, Canada N6A 4V2

Circulating levels of dehydroepiandrosterone (DHEA) and its sulfate ester dehydro-epiandrosterone sulfate (DHEAS), secreted mainly by the adrenal, peak between age 20 and 30 and decline with age. This decline may be associated with age-related illnesses such as ischemic heart disease, obesity, and noninsulin-dependent diabetes mellitus.[1]

Human adipose stromal cells obtained from adipose tissue and grown to confluence will metabolize DHEA to androstenedione and thence to estrone.[2] These cells will also differentiate into mature adipocytes when cultured in differentiation medium containing dexamethasone, thyroxine, and insulin.[3]

This study examines the effect of differentiation of human breast adipose stromal cells on their capacity to metabolize DHEA, androst-5-ene-3β, 17β-diol (Δ^5-diol), and androstenedione.

MATERIALS AND METHODS

Procedures for steroid isolation and for culturing adipose stromal cells are described elsewhere.[2,4]

RESULTS AND DISCUSSION

The major metabolite identified when differentiating breast adipose stromal cells were incubated with DHEA was 7α-OH DHEA. In cells obtained from 10 patients, 7α-OH DHEA averaged 56% of substrate (range 12–80%) (FIG. 1). A minor metabolite more polar than 7α-OH DHEA accounted for 10% of product. When Δ^5-diol was used as substrate, this metabolite was the only product (20%, 60%, two experiments).

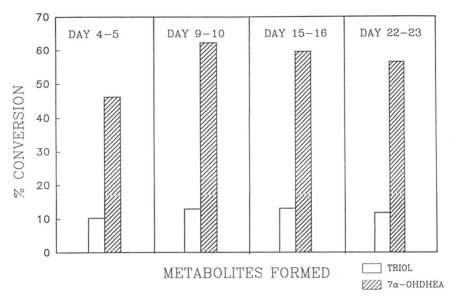

FIGURE 1. Steroid metabolism in human breast adipose stromal cells. Cells were grown in differentiation medium for 23 days to study DHEA, androst-5-ene-3β, 17β-diol or androstenedione metabolism. Medium was removed and replaced with medium containing 2μCi [³H] steroid substrate on days 4–5, 9–10, 15–16, and 22–23 and incubation proceeded for 24 hours. Metabolites were isolated as previously described.[4] The main metabolites of DHEA and androst-5-ene-3β, 17β-diol were the 7α-hydroxylated derivatives, androst 5 ene 3β, 7α-diol-17-one (7α-OH DHEA) and androst-5-ene-3β, 7α, 17β-triol, respectively. GPDH activity increased 52-fold as cells differentiated and accumulated lipids. In cells from 10 patients, 7α-OH DHEA formation from DHEA averaged 56% of total radioactivity (range 12–80%). Androst-5-ene-3β, 7α, 17β-triol was the major product formed from androst-5-ene-3β, 17β-diol.

Sufficient quantities of this metabolite were obtained by incubating adipose stromal cells from one patient with 5 μM unlabeled androst-5-ene-3β, 17β-diol; it was identified by mass spectrometry as androst-5-ene-3β, 7α, 17β-triol (FIG. 2).

Human adipose stromal cells cultured under replicating conditions can metabolize DHEA to androstenedione, estrone, and 7α-OH DHEA.[4] Under differentiating conditions, 7α-hydroxylation is the predominant pathway; the preferred substrates are Δ⁵-3β-hydroxysteroids because 7α-hydroxylated metabolites of androstenedione were not detected when cells were incubated with androstenedione.

7-Hydroxylase activity has been detected in a variety of tissues.[5] 7-Hydroxylated DHEA derivatives can increase the immune response[6] and potentiate lymphocyte activation,[7] whereas DHEA can restore interleukin-6 levels in aging mice to values found in mature animals.[8] These findings suggest that one way by which DHEA and its metabolites may play an immunomodulatory role in the aging process is through critical interactions with the immune system.

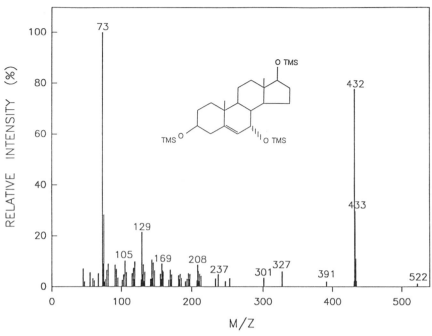

FIGURE 2. Mass spectrum of the trimethylsilyl ether derivative of androst-5-ene-3β, 7α, 17β-triol, isolated from human adipose stromal cells cultured with 5 μM androst-5-ene-3β, 17β-diol in differentiating medium. Steroid metabolites were purified and derivatized as described.[4] The GC retention time of the major component was 21.018 minutes. Then, 2 μl of sample was injected in the splitless mode on a 25 m × 0.32 mm (id) 5% phenyl methyl silicone-fused silica capillary column. Major ions are m/z 522 (molecular ion), 432 (loss of trimethylsilanol m/z 90 from the molecular ion), and other ions at 327, 129, and 73. The mass spectrum of this metabolite was identical to the spectrum obtained from a synthetic sample of androst-5-ene-3β, 7α, 17β-triol produced from Na BH₄ reduction of authentic androst-5-ene-3β, 7α-diol-17-one (7α-OH DHEA).

REFERENCES

1. HERBERT, J. 1995. Lancet **345:** 1193–1194.
2. KILLINGER, D. W., B. STRUTT, D. VACHON, R. A. RONCARI & M. W. KHALIL. 1995. J. Steroid Biochem. Molec. Biol. **52:** 195–201.
3. HAUNER, H., G. ENTENMANN, M. WABITSCH, D. GAILLARD, G. AILHAUD, R. NEGREL & E. F. PFEIFFER. 1989. J. Clin. Invest. **84:** 1663–1670.
4. KHALIL, M. W., B. STRUTT, D. VACHON & D. W. KILLINGER. 1993. J. Steroid Biochem. Molec. Biol. **46:** 585–595.
5. SULCOVA, J., A. CAPCOVA, J. E. V. JERASEK & L. STARKA. 1968. Acta Endocrinol. **59:** 1–9.
6. MORFIN, R. & G. COURCHAY. 1994. J. Steroid Biochem. Molec. Biol. **50:** 91–100.
7. PADGETT, D. A. & R. M. LORIA. 1994. J. Immunol. **153:** 1544–1552.
8. DAYNES, R. A., B. A. ARANEO, W. B. ERSHLER, C. MALONEY, G.-Z. LI & SI-Y RYU. 1993. J. Immunol. **150:** 5219–5230.

Effects of Aging and Long-Term Calorie Restriction on DHEA and DHEA Sulfate in Rhesus Monkeys

MARK A. LANE, DONALD K. INGRAM,
AND GEORGE S. ROTH

Gerontology Research Center
National Institute on Aging
Baltimore, Maryland 21224

The adrenal steroids, dehydroepiandrosterone (DHEA) and its sulfate (DHEAS), have attracted much attention for their ability to modify age-associated changes in tumorigenesis, diabetes mellitus, obesity, and immune function and because of their well documented declines with advancing age.[1] Calorie restriction (CR), which extends life span and slows physiologic aging processes, also alters the normal course of several age-associated disorders.[2] Indeed, it has been suggested that DHEA and CR might affect age-related disease through similar mechanisms.[3] The present study reports the effects of aging and calorie restriction on circulating DHEA and DHEAS in male and female rhesus monkeys.

METHOD

Thirty male and 60 female rhesus monkeys were obtained in three age groups representative of the species' life span. About half the monkeys in each age group were permitted ad libitum intake, whereas the other half were placed on CR at 70% of ad libitum levels. Calorie restriction for the males began in 1987 and for the female monkeys in 1992. There are no CR monkeys in male Group O. The diet was supplemented with extra vitamins, minerals, and trace elements to prevent malnutrition in the CR group. However, diet formulation for control and CR monkeys was not different. Circulating DHEA and DHEAS levels were determined in blood samples collected in the early morning from monkeys that had been fasted overnight.

SUMMARY/DISCUSSION

DHEA and DHEAS were negatively correlated with chronologic age of both male and female rhesus monkeys (ps < 0.05) and tended to be elevated in CR monkeys. However, statistically significant elevations were seen only for DHEAS in male rhesus monkeys, such that CR delayed the early decline to adult levels. The lack of a significant effect in female monkeys likely relates to the duration of CR (3 years) as elevations in DHEAS were not evident in male monkeys until well into the fourth year of CR. The physiologic significance of the CR effect in male monkeys is not clear, but similar CR-induced delays have been reported for both sexual[4] and skeletal development[5] in these monkeys. The slight elevations in circulating DHEA and DHEAS seen in CR monkeys might relate to a CR-induced lowering of insulin

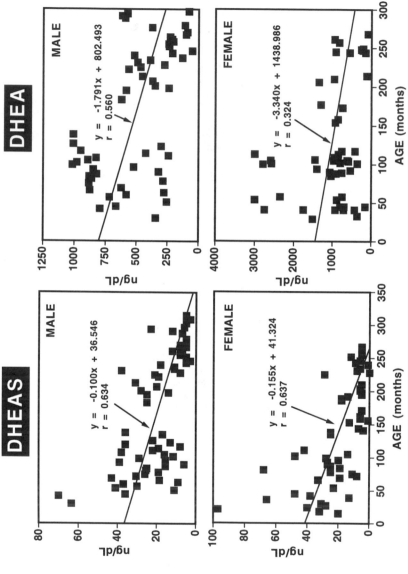

FIGURE 1. DHEA and DHEAS declined with age in male and female rhesus monkeys. Each point represents the circulating DHEA or DHEAS level for each monkey at a given age. Pearson product-moment correlations with chronologic age were significant ($p < 0.05$) for all measurements.

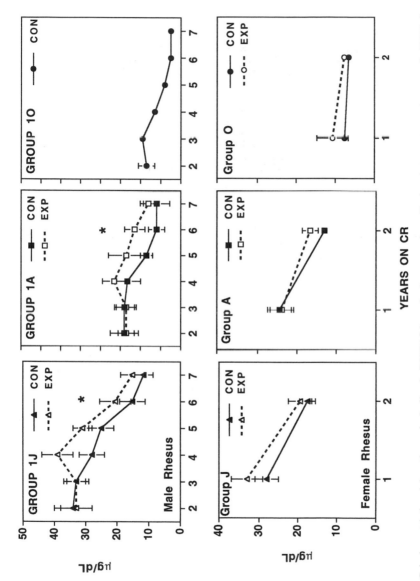

FIGURE 2. Calorie restriction delays the early decline in DHEAS in male rhesus monkeys. Each point represents the mean (±SEM) for monkeys in that group. DHEAS levels were generally elevated in all monkey groups, but the diet X time interaction was significant only for male monkeys ($p < 0.05$).

levels.[6] Nestler *et al.*[7] proposed that hyperinsulinemia could reduce DHEA and DHEAS by increasing clearance or inhibiting production of adrenal androgens (FIGS. 1 and 2).

REFERENCES

1. ORENTREICH, N., J. A. ZIMMERMAN & J. R. MATIAS. 1994. Practical Handbook of Human Biological Age Determination. 391–396. CRC Press. Boca Raton.
2. MASORO, E. J. 1993. J. Am. Geriatr. Assoc. **41:** 994–999.
3. SCHWARTZ, A. G. & L. L. PASHKO. 1986. Anti-Cancer Res. **6:** 1279–1282.
4. ROTH, G. S., M. R. BLACKMAN, D. K. INGRAM, M. A. LANE, S. S. BALL & R. G. CUTLER. 1993. Endocrine J. **1:** 227–234.
5. LANE, M. A., A. Z. REZNIK, E. M. TILMONT, A. LANIR, S. S. BALL, V. READ, D. K. INGRAM, R. G. CUTLER & G. S. ROTH. 1995. J. Nutr. **125:** 1600–1610.
6. LANE, M. A., S. S. BALL, D. K. INGRAM, R. G. CUTLER, J. ENGEL, V. READ & G. S. ROTH. 1995. Am. J. Physiol. (Endo. Metab. 31): 268.
7. NESTLER, J. E., J. N. CLORE & W. G. BLACKARD. 1992. FASEB J. **6:** 3073–3075.

Steroid Hormone Regulation
of a Polyclonal T$_H$2 Immune Response

DAVID A. PADGETT,[a] JOHN F. SHERIDAN,[a]
AND ROGER M. LORIA[b]

[a]Department of Medical Microbiology
The Ohio State University
Columbus, Ohio 43210

[b]Department of Microbiology and Immunology
VCU/MCV
Richmond, Virginia

Dehydroepiandrosterone (5-androstene-3β-ol-17-one [DHEA]) and two of its metabolites, androstenediol (5-androstene-3β-17β-diol [AED]) and androstenetriol (5-androstene-3β-7β-17β-triol [AET]), have been shown to protect mice from viral, bacterial, and parasitic infections.[1] Unlike that in intracellular viral and bacterial infections, the extracellular parasite generally invokes the production of interleukin-4 (IL-4) and subsequent isotype switch to IgE. Wu et al.[2] reported that the synthesis of IgE by IL-4–stimulated human lymphocytes was markedly increased by glucocorticoids. Therefore, because we believe that DHEA, AED, and AET counterregulate glucocorticoid function in vivo, these studies were designed to investigate the ability of each of these steroids to regulate a T$_H$2 immune response.

MATERIALS AND METHODS

Female BALB/c mice were injected intravenously with allospecific monoclonal antibodies to mouse IgD (provided by Dr. Fred Finkelman, Uniformed Services University of the Health Sciences) to generate serum IgE levels comparable to those in helminth-infected mice and approximately 100-fold greater than those in unstimulated mice.[3] One hundred micrograms of each Hδ^a/1 (a mouse IgG2a of the b allotype that binds the Fc fragment of δ chain of the a allotype) and FF1-4D5 were coinjected in 0.2 ml of 0.9% NaCl. Control mice were similarly treated with normal mouse serum, so that all mice received a total of 200 μg of protein. Before initiation of this polyclonal T$_H$2 immune response, six animals per group were subcutaneously injected with either 1.0 g/kg DHEA, 160 mg/kg AED, 40 mg/kg AET, 200 mg/kg hydrocortisone, or the control vehicle of DMSO:ethanol. Blood samples were obtained on days 0, 5, 9, and 14 to quantitate the serum concentration of total IgE and IL-4 as determined by ELISA.

RESULTS

Compared to mice receiving the control vehicle of DMSO:EtOH and monoclonal anti-IgD, mice receiving hydrocortisone 200 mg/kg had increased production of IL-4 (FIG. 1). On day 5, positive control animals peaked with an average IL-4 content of 219.4 pg/ml, whereas that of the glucocorticoid-treated mice was 274.0 pg/ml.

Although the concentration of IL-4 on days 9 and 14 from both groups had decreased, samples from glucocorticoid-treated animals on day 14 still contained 173.4 pg/ml, whereas that of the control animals was 125.6 pg/ml. Analysis of serum from DHEA-, AED-, and AET-treated animals showed that although IL-4 increased over the course of the experiment, in each group this increase was significantly lower than that in the positive control mice. Peak levels of IL-4 were obtained on day 5, with the average of the DHEA-, AED-, and AET-treated groups being 174.8, 153.1, and 170.3 pg/ml, respectively.

FIGURE 2 shows that similar to the production of IL-4 in these anti-IgD–treated mice, IgE production was likewise increased. Vehicle-treated positive control mice had serum IgE concentrations that rose from a background of 0.53 μg/ml to a peak of 14.2 μg/ml on day 9 postinjection. Glucocorticoid-treated mice had serum concentrations that also peaked on day 9 at 16.9 μg/ml, somewhat higher than that of the control mice. Similar to the effects noted with IL-4, treatment with DHEA, AED, and AET significantly reduced the peak levels of IgE stimulated by anti-IgD treatment. In each of these groups peak levels were 23–28% below control levels.

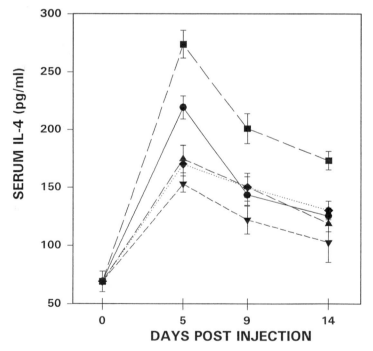

FIGURE 1. Effects of DHEA, AED, AET, and hydrocortisone on serum interleukin-4 concentrations. Female BALB/c mice, six per group, were injected iv with allotypic antibodies to IgD to induce production of IL-4 and IgE. Experimental mice were treated sc 4 hours prior with either a single dose of 1.0 g/kg DHEA (*triangles*), 160 mg/kg AED (*inverted triangles*), 40 mg/kg AET (*diamonds*), 200 mg/kg hydrocortisone (*squares*), or control vehicle of DMSO:EtOH (*circles*). On days 0, 5, 9, and 14 posttreatment, animals were bled from the tail vein, and serum IL-4 concentrations were determined by ELISA. Day 0 readings from all groups were averaged to generate baseline IL-4 levels.

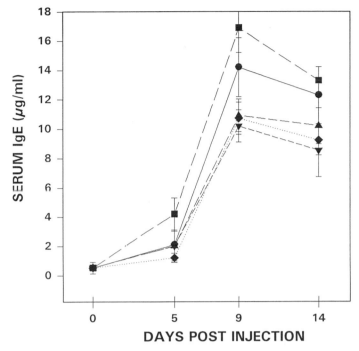

FIGURE 2. Effects of DHEA, AED, AET, and hydrocortisone on serum IgE concentrations. Female BALB/c mice, six per group, were injected iv with allotypic antibodies to IgD to induce production of IL-4 and IgE. Experimental mice were treated sc 4 hours prior with either a single dose of 1.0 g/kg DHEA (*triangles*), 160 mg/kg AED (*inverted triangles*), 40 mg/kg AET (*diamonds*), 200 mg/kg hydrocortisone (*squares*), or control vehicle of DMSO:EtOH (*circles*). On days 0, 5, 9, and 14 posttreatment, animals were bled from the tail vein, and serum IgE concentrations were determined by ELISA. Day 0 readings from all groups were averaged to generate baseline IgE levels.

CONCLUSIONS

These data show that while glucocorticoid increases the T$_H$2-related production of IL-4 and subsequent IgE synthesis, DHEA, AED, and AET function in a converse manner to downregulate the T$_H$2 response. Such observations support our assertion that *in vivo* these three steroid hormones function in a manner that is counterregulatory to glucocorticoid action.[4]

REFERENCES

1. LORIA, R. M. & D. A. PADGETT. 1992. Arch. Virol. **127:** 103–115.
2. WU, C. Y., M. SARFATI, C. HEUSSER, S. FOURNIER, M. RUBIO-TRUJILLO, R. PELEMAN & G. DELESPESSE. 1991. J. Clin. Invest. **87:** 870–877.
3. FINKELMAN, F. D., C. M. SNAPPER, J. D. MOUNTZ & I. M. KATONA. 1987. J. Immunol. **138:** 2826–2830.
4. PADGETT, D. A. & R. M. LORIA. 1994. J. Immunol. **153:** 1544–1552.

Effect of TGF-β on Dehydroepiandrosterone Sulfotransferase in Cultured Human Fetal Adrenal Cells

C. R. PARKER, JR.,[a] A. K. STANKOVIC, C. N. FALANY,
AND W. E. GRIZZLE

Departments of Obstetrics and Gynecology,
Pharmacology, and Pathology
University of Alabama at Birmingham
Birmingham, Alabama 35233-7333

TGF-β was shown previously to influence the production of steroidogenic enzymes such as cholesterol side-chain cleavage, 3β-hydroxysteroid dehydrogenase/delta 5-4 isomerase, and 17-hydroxylase/17-20-lyase in several types of adrenal cells.[1-5] We found that this cytokine also can inhibit growth and steroid production by the human fetal adrenal.[6,7] We and others found that production of dehydroepiandrosterone sulfate (DHEAS) is more sensitive to TGF-β than is the corticosteroid pathway in the human adrenal.[7,8] This study investigates the effect of TGF-β, a putative adrenal regulating cytokine, on dehydroepiandrosterone sulfotransferase (DHEA-ST) expression in cultured human adrenal cells.

To achieve this goal we used neocortex (NC) and fetal zone (FZ) from human fetal adrenals as described previously.[7] The use of these tissues was approved by the Institutional Review Board of the University of Alabama at Birmingham. Thirteen separate experiments were performed; eight on FZ cells and five on NC cells. Isolated adrenal FZ and NC cells were precultured in control medium (McCoy's 5A plus 5% fetal bovine serum) for 1–10 days before trypsinization and adherence onto glass coverslips (2×10^4 cells/250 μl of culture medium). Cells were incubated at 37°C in a humidified atmosphere (95% air, 5% CO_2) for 1–3 days in the presence or absence of 1 ng/ml porcine, platelet-derived TGF-β1 (R and D systems, Minneapolis, Minnesota) and 25 ng/ml ACTH (Cortrosyn, Organon, West Orange, New Jersey). Whenever possible, cells on duplicate coverslips were exposed to each experimental condition. At the end of the culture period the coverslips were rinsed in phosphate-buffered saline solution and fixed in 10% buffered formalin and immunostained for DHEA-ST, as described elsewhere.[9,10] After the cells were counterstained with light green or hematoxylin, we determined the relative intensity of DHEA-ST staining using a scoring scale of 0–4. This same scale was used to estimate the proportion of immunopositive adrenal cells per slide: 0 = none, 1 = 1–25%, 2 = 26–50%, 3 = 51–75%, and 4 = 76–100%.

Cells that reacted with anti-DHEA-ST antibodies were present in untreated (control) FZ and NC cells; the frequency and intensity of staining were higher in FZ cells. As we showed previously, the addition of ACTH to cultured cells increased both the relative frequency and the intensity of DHEA-ST staining in both types of

[a]Address for correspondence: C. Richard Parker, Jr., Ph.D., Department of Obstetrics & Gynecology, University of Alabama at Birmingham, Birmingham, AL 35233–7333.

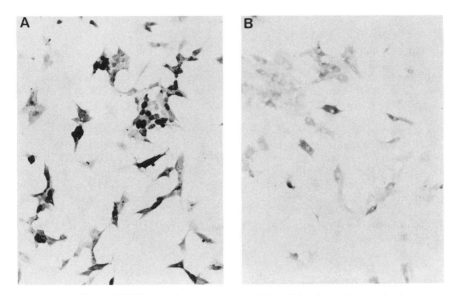

FIGURE 1. Effects of TGF-β on immunocytochemical staining for dehydroepiandrosterone sulfotransferase in cultured human fetal adrenal cells. Neocortex cells were cultured on glass coverslips for 3 days in the presence of ACTH, 25 ng/ml (**A**), or ACTH + TGF-β, 1 ng/ml (**B**) and then immunostained for dehydroepiandrosterone sulfotransferase; counterstain was light green. (Microscopic magnification 10×.)

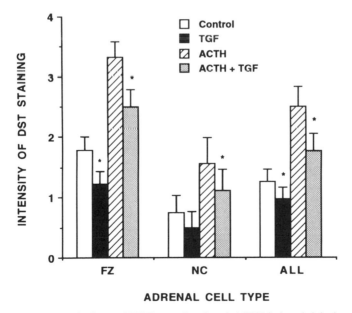

FIGURE 2. Summary of effects of TGF-β on basal and ACTH-induced dehydroepiandrosterone sulfotransferase (DHEA-ST) immunoreactivity in neocortex and fetal zone cells. The intensity scores (mean ± SE) of immunostaining for DHEA-ST after 3 days of culture are summarized. The data for fetal zone and neocortex cell cultures were analyzed separately as well as combined (ALL). *$p < 0.05$ versus cells grown in the absence of TGF-β.

adrenal cells.[10] TGF-β treatment of control and ACTH-stimulated adrenal cells decreased slightly the number of DHEA-ST–positive (data not shown) cells and significantly inhibited the relative intensity of DHEA-ST staining (FIGS. 1 and 2). This effect of TGF-β on DHEA-ST was apparent after 3 days, but not after 1 day of culture. TGF-β also inhibited the stimulatory effects of forskolin and dibutyryl cAMP on intensity of DHEA-ST staining (data not shown).

Our current results correlate well with our previous data that indicated that DHEA-ST is more abundant in FZ than in NC cells both *in vivo* and *in vitro*[9,10] and that activation of protein kinase A upregulates the expression of DHEA-ST in both cell types.[10] On the other hand, TGF-β, which was shown to inhibit DHEAS secretion by cultured fetal and adult human adrenal cells,[7,8] decreases significantly the amount of DHEA-ST present in control and ACTH-treated fetal adrenal cells. These data suggest that the effect of TGF-β on DHEAS synthesis by human fetal adrenal cells may be due, in part, to the downregulation of DHEA-ST production by this cytokine.

REFERENCES

1. FEIGE, J.-J., C. COCHET & E. M. CHAMBAZ. 1986. Biochem. Biophys. Res. Commun. **139:** 1015–1021.
2. FEIGE, J.-J., C. COCHET, W. E. RAINEY, C. MADANI & E. M. CHAMBAZ. 1987. J. Biol. Chem. **262:** 13491–13495.
3. RAINEY, W. E., D. NAVILLE, J. M. SAEZ, B. R. CARR, W. BYRD, R. R. MAGNESS & J. I. MASON. 1990. Endocrinology **127:** 1910–1915.
4. NAVILLE, D., W. E. RAINEY & J. I. MASON. 1991. Mol. Cell. Endocrinol. **75:** 257–263.
5. PERIN, A., O. PASCAL, G. DEFAYE, J.-J. FEIGE & E. M. CHAMBAZ. 1991. Endocrinology **128:** 357–362.
6. STANKOVIC, A. K., W. E. GRIZZLE, C. R. STOCKARD & C. R. PARKER, JR. 1994. Am. J. Physiol. **266:** E495–500.
7. STANKOVIC, A. K., L. D. DION & C. R. PARKER, JR. 1994. Mol. Cell. Endocrinol. **99:** 145–151.
8. LEBRETHON, M. C., C. JAILLARD, D. NAVILLE, M. BEGEOT & J. M. SAEZ. 1994. J. Clin. Endocrinol. Metab. **79:** 1033–1039.
9. PARKER, C. R., JR., C. N. FALANY, C. R. STOCKARD, A. K. STANKOVIC & W. E. GRIZZLE. 1994. J. Clin. Endocrinol. Metab. **78:** 234–236.
10. PARKER, C. R., JR., A. K. STANKOVIC, C. N. FALANY, O. FAYE-PETERSEN & W. E. GRIZZLE. 1995. J. Clin. Endocrinol. Metab. **80:** 1027–1031.

DHEA Diminishes Fat Food Intake
in Lean and Obese Zucker Rats

J. R. PORTER[a,b] AND F. SVEC[b]

Obesity Research Program
Departments of Physiology[a] and Medicine[b]
LSU Medical Center
1542 Tulane Ave.
New Orleans, Louisiana 70112

Dehydroepiandrosterone (DHEA) has been proposed as a multifunctional steriod. It affects the aging process, improves lipid markers which are related to cardiovascular disease, alters immune function, and is an antiobesity agent.

We reported that DHEA administered either as a dietary supplement, as an intraperitoneal injection, or through an intracerebroventricular cannula reduces caloric intake of the obese Zucker rat. The effect on fat consumption is most pronounced. We reported that in short-term experiments, DHEA elevates serotonin content in the lateral hypothalamus of the obese Zucker rat, a region involved in food intake regulation. Dehydroepiandrosterone alters neurotransmitters in whole hypothalamus and regional hypothalamic neurotransmitters at 1 day, 7 days, and 28 days which are commensurate with a central nervous system mechanism for the behavioral effect of DHEA on caloric intake.

In this communication we report that DHEA lowers fat intake in the "hungry rat model" in both lean and obese rats. In neurotransmitter (NT) experiments, paraventricular nucleus content of norepinephrine, dopamine, 5-hydroxytryptamine (5-HT), and 5-hydroxyindoleacetic acid (5-HIAA) were all significantly changed 2 hours postinjection of DHEA.

Lean and obese Zucker rats were obtained from our colony at the LSU Medical Center. Two studies were carried out. Rats were fed a macronutrient diet consisting of fat, carbohydrate, and protein, which was presented ad libitum in three different bowls. In the hungry rat model rats were fed this diet for 4 days for accommodation. Rats were then fasted for 24 hours and provided their bowls at the end of the 24-hour fast for 4 hours.

In the first experiment, DHEA in doses varying from 25–200 mg/kg was administered ip 2 hours before presentation of the food to lean and obese female rats. Dose response curves were constructed for lean and obese animals.

In a second experiment, obese female rats were fasted as before. DHEA was given as just described, except at the end of the 2-hour period rats were killed by decapitation. Brains were removed within 30 seconds of decapitation. Prior to microdissection, the whole brain was plunged into liquid nitrogen. The ventromedial hypothalamus, the paraventricular nucleus of the hypothalamus and the lateral hypothalamus were microdissected from slices of whole brain. Brain samples were subjected to HPLC and electrochemical detection.

In the hungry rat paradigm both lean and obese rats take in the greatest portion of their calories within the first hour after presentation of their food (unpublished observations). Biopotency curves with DHEA in the hungry rat model indicate that both lean and obese rats respond in a qualitatively similar way to varying doses of DHEA (FIG. 1). Total calories are reduced in both at the higher doses. In this

Lean

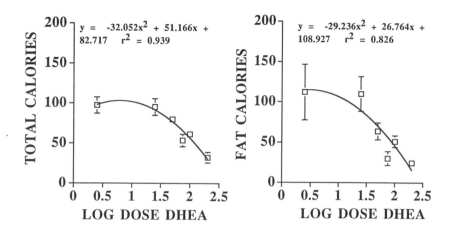

Obese

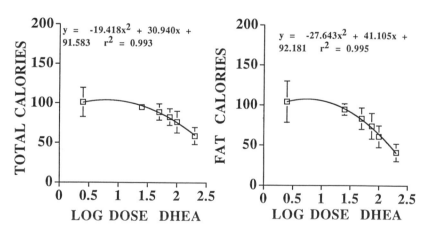

FIGURE 1. In these experiments, one group of obese and lean rats served as controls and another group was given varying doses of DHEA. To achieve uniformity, all rats were provided a control period of macronutrient feeding for 3 days. All bowls were then removed for 24 hours. Rats were injected with either vehicle (sesame oil) or the appropriate DHEA dose 2 hours before presenting the rats with their three bowls of macronutrient. Rats were allowed to eat for 4 hours and their individual macronutrient intake was calculated and analyzed. The *top two panels* are total calories and fat calories of the lean rat. The *bottom two panels* are the total calories and the fat calories of the obese rat.

TABLE 1. Regional Hypothalamic Neurotransmitter Content per Milligram of Wet Weight[a]

	NE	EPI	DPM	5-HT	5-HIAA
PVN					
Control	3.18 ± 0.30	0.05 ± 0.007	0.19 ± 0.02	0.53 ± 0.04	0.46 ± 0.04
DHEA	2.30 ± 0.17	0.03 ± 0.006	0.32 ± 0.01	0.76 ± 0.06	0.69 ± 0.07
	($p < 0.04$)	($p = 0.10$)	($p < 0.007$)	($p < 0.03$)	($p < 0.03$)
LH					
Control	3.64 ± 0.20	0.08 ± 0.02	0.32 ± 0.03	0.65 ± 0.09	0.59 ± 0.01
DHEA	2.63 ± 0.33	0.05 ± 0.01	0.38 ± 0.09	0.72 ± 0.11	0.70 ± 0.17
VMH					
Control	4.22 ± 0.51	0.09 ± 0.02	0.61 ± 0.23	0.36 ± 0.04	0.38 ± 0.10
DHEA	3.02 ± 0.12	0.06 ± 0.008	0.86 ± 0.08	0.43 ± 0.07	0.38 ± 0.05
	($p = 0.12$)				

Abbreviations: DPM = dopamine; EPI = epinephrine; LH = lateral hypothalamus; NE = norepinephrine; PVN = paraventricular nucleus; VMH = ventromedial hypothalamus.

[a]Obese female rats were fed macronutrient diet ad libitum for 3 days and then fasted for 24 hours. The control group was injected with sesame oil ip, and the experimental group was injected with DHEA (200 mg/kg). At 2 hours, all animals were decapitated and their brains frozen, regional hypothalamic areas were dissected by punch, homogenized in buffer, and centrifuged, and the supernatant was analyzed by HPLC and electrochemical detection.

paradigm, fat intake of lean rats is clearly affected by doses of 50, 75, 100, and 200 mg/kg, whereas obese rats are affected only at the 100- and 200-mg/kg dose. Protein intake was affected only at the highest dose in both phenotypes (data not shown). Carbohydrate intake was not affected by DHEA at any dose in either phenotype (data not shown). Neurotransmitter changes induced by DHEA included several changes, particularly in the PVN of the hypothalamus (TABLE 1). The PVN hypothalamic norepinephrine was decreased. Dopamine, on the other hand, was significantly increased in the same area. 5-HT and 5-HIAA were both significantly elevated in the paraventricular nucleus or PVN of the hypothalamus, corroborating our previous studies of an increase in 5-HT in the lateral hypothalamus at 1 and 7 days. The ventromedial hypothalamus norepinephrine responded to DHEA as did PVN hypothalamic norepinephrine; however, this change was not statistically significant ($p = 0.12$).

In the hungry rat paradigm both lean and obese fat caloric intake is specifically and dramatically decreased by DHEA. This appears to be a macronutrient specific affect and not a generalized phenomenon. Neurotransmitter changes in the paraventricular hypothalamus may underlie this behavioral effect of DHEA.

Synergistic Anorectic Effect of Dehydroepiandrosterone and Fenfluramine on Zucker Rat Food Intake and Selection

The Obesity Research Program

FRANK SVEC[a] AND JOHNNY R. PORTER[a,b]

Departments of Medicine[a] and Physiology[b]
LSU Medical Center
1542 Tulane Ave.
New Orleans, Louisiana 70112

We reported that dehydroepiandrosterone (DHEA) diminishes caloric intake and elevates hypothalamic serotonin content in the obese Zucker rat. Fenfluramine, an agent known to decrease serotonin uptake in the hypothalamus, also decreases food consumption. These experiments were designed to evaluate the combined effectiveness of these two agents.

TABLE 1. Neurotransmitter Content of Hypothalamic Regions of Obese Zucker Rats Treated with DHEA and Fenfluramine Individually or Together for Three Days[a]

Hypothalamic Region	NE	DA	5-HT	5-HIAA	5-HIAA/5-HT
PVN					
Control	3.30 ± 0.70	0.21 ± 0.02	0.58 ± 0.04	0.35 ± 0.03	0.62 ± 0.09
DHEA	2.98 ± 0.26	0.21 ± 0.05	0.42 ± 0.02	0.33 ± 0.04	0.77 ± 0.06
FEN	3.05 ± 0.43	0.27 ± 0.02	0.32 ± 0.04*	0.27 ± 0.01	0.88 ± 0.09*
DHEA + FEN	1.97 ± 0.13*	0.10 ± 0.03*	0.17 ± 0.02*	0.19 ± 0.03*	1.10 ± 0.06*
LH					
Control	3.14 ± 0.24	0.26 ± 0.02	0.59 ± 0.10	0.43 ± 0.05	0.79 ± 0.13
DHEA	4.17 ± 0.45	0.26 ± 0.01	0.72 ± 0.03	0.41 ± 0.05	0.58 ± 0.10
FEN	3.52 ± 0.22	0.40 ± 0.05*	0.51 ± 0.09	0.45 ± 0.03	0.93 ± 0.12
DHEA + FEN	2.38 ± 0.34	0.12 ± 0.04*	0.29 ± 0.07*	0.28 ± 0.06	1.00 ± 0.07
VMH					
Control	4.12 ± 0.27	1.31 ± 0.35	0.36 ± 0.04	0.21 ± 0.01	0.63 ± 0.12
DHEA	4.00 ± 0.30	0.46 ± 0.08*	0.32 ± 0.05	0.23 ± 0.03	0.76 ± 0.08
FEN	4.38 ± 0.65	1.01 ± 0.08	0.36 ± 0.12	0.20 ± 0.02	0.67 ± 0.12
DHEA + FEN	2.29 ± 0.16*	0.63 ± 0.06*	0.22 ± 0.05	0.14 ± 0.02	0.69 ± 0.17

Abbreviations: DA = dopamine; DHEA = dehydroepiandrosterone; FEN = fenfluramine; LH = lateral hypothalamus; NE = norepinephrine; PVN = paraventricular nucleus; VMH = ventromedial hypothalamus.

[a]Obese Zucker rats were treated ip with DHEA (100 mg/kg/day) or fenfluramine (5 mg/kg/day) either individually or in combination. Controls were injected with vehicle. After 3 days the animals were sacrificed by rapid decapitation, and three hypothalamic regions were isolated. Each was analyzed for its content of norepinephrine, dopamine, serotonin (5-HT), and 5-hydroxyindoleacetic acid (5-HIAA). Values are expressed as nanograms per milligram wet weight of tissue. Values shown are the mean ± SEM ($n = 6$). *Asterisks* indicate that statistically significant differences exist between controls and treated groups.

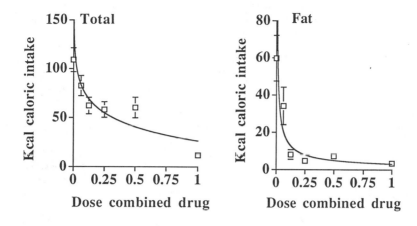

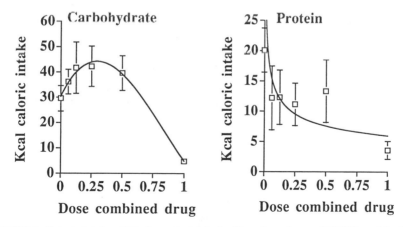

FIGURE 1. Caloric intake of Zucker rats treated with various doses of DHEA and fenfluramine. Obese male Zucker rats were divided into six groups of three animals per group. One group received DHEA 100 mg/kg/day and fenfluramine 5 mg/kg/day ip. This dose was called unity. Other groups received injections of this mixture diluted serially twofold. The fraction of the initial dose is indicated in the figure. Control animals received vehicle only. Each animal was allowed to eat the macronutrient selection diet. Intakes on the third day for each macronutrient and their total are shown. Values are the mean ± SEM of each group.

Daily caloric intake of obese and lean Zucker rats was recorded. In most experiments they were fed a diet that consisted of separate bowls of nearly pure (90%) macronutrients (carbohydrate, protein, or fat). Daily consumption of each choice was recorded as was their weight while they received DHEA and fenfluramine either individually or together.

After 3 days of treatment each agent given individually (DHEA 100 mg/kg/day and fenfluramine 5 mg/kg/day ip) affected food intake significantly, but only slightly. The combination, however, had a profound effect that was greater than would be predicted by the actions of either alone. Lean animals consumed nearly 66% fewer calories than did their controls and obese animals nearly stopped eating. The body weight of the animals treated with both agents decreased during the treatment period. When the agents were given for 28 days, fenfluramine's effect by itself waned by 14 days, but the effect of the combination continued.

Hypothalamic extracts from the four groups were analyzed for neurotransmitters. Results in the obese animals are shown in TABLE 1. The combination caused an increase in the ratio of 5-HIAA/5-HT in both the lateral hypothalamic region and the ventromedial hypothalamic region. Individually, neither agent affected this ratio.

The biopotency of the combination on food intake was evaluated in obese male Zucker rats. Doses of DHEA ranged from 6.25–100 mg/kg/day and fenfluramine 0.312–5 mg/kg/day ip. FIGURE 1 shows the total caloric intake and the consumption of each macronutrient on the third day of the experiment. Carbohydrate intake was diminished only at the highest doses. Indeed, at lower doses intake was stimulated slightly. Protein consumption was decreased variably and only significantly at the highest dose. Fat consumption, however, was decreased almost completely at every dose except the very lowest.

It is concluded that DHEA and fenfluramine form a synergistic anorectic combination that diminishes profoundly the caloric intake of the Zucker rat, both lean and obese. The effect does not show tolerance over 28 days and can cause significant weight loss in obese animals. At low doses it shows a decidedly greater effect on fat food consumption compared to that of carbohydrate and protein. This suggests that the combination is not a general anorectic, but it may exert selective suppression on the drive to consume fat foods. The mechanism of this effect is not yet known, but the combination affects the levels of hypothalamic neurotransmitters more than do the individual agents. The effect is most pronounced on the serotonin system.

Effect of Dehydroepiandrosterone on Rat Thyroxine Binding Globulin, a Protein Upregulated during Aging

ROGER VRANCKX, PATRICIA MECHIGHEL,
AND LIA SAVU

Laboratoire de Biochimie Endocrinienne
Faculté de Médecine Xavier Bichat
16, rue Henri Huchard
B.P. 416
75870 Paris Cédex 18, France

In rat serum, thyroid hormones are carried by two high affinity binding proteins, the transthyretin, which is present at all ages at virtually constant concentrations, and the thyroxine binding globulin (TBG), which is stringently developmentally regulated.[1,2] Indeed, rat TBG is actively expressed during the postnatal period, virtually undetectable during adulthood, then progressively reexpressed in aging rats from about 9 months on. Recently, among the proteins reacting to nonpathologic senescence by changes in their circulating levels, TBG was shown to be the most reliable senescence marker inasmuch as it is among the few positive (increasing) reactants and does not respond to acute inflammatory processes.[3] At least two hormonal pathways were demonstrated for the regulation of the rat TBG, one under negative control by the thyroid hormones, the other under pituitary growth hormone control, although apparently without the direct link existing in the rat between the production of thyroid hormone and growth hormone, but rather involving the action of the growth hormone on carbohydrate metabolism.[4]

On the other hand, it is well documented that DHEA behaves in many respects similar to the thyroid hormones, its thyromimetic properties including an aging-related decrease and antiobesity effects.[5–7] In light of these observations, administration of DHEA during aging has been suggested as a possible efficient rejuvenating treatment. In this study we investigated whether the senescence-upregulated, TH-downregulated rat TBG responds to the administration of the rejuvenating and thyromimetic DHEA.

Male Wistar rats aged 3 (adult) and 19 (senescent) months received a daily subcutaneous injection of either vehicle (propylene glycol, 1 ml/kg body weight) or 100 mg/kg DHEA for 20 days. Serum samples were then collected and assayed for transthyretin and TBG by the rocket immunodiffusion technique.

We found that when TBG is ontogenically extinguished (3 months), DHEA had no upregulatory effect. When it was normally reexpressed (20 months), DHEA induced a highly significant decrease (> 50%) in protein. At both ages, DHEA decreased serum transthyretin by about 50%.

Our results indicate that in the aging rat, DHEA markedly inhibits the senescence upregulation of rat TBG, a phenomenon in keeping with the hypothesis of rejuvenating action of the hormone. Our observations also represent a novel example of the thyromimetic (or thyroagonist) effect of DHEA, because its inhibitory effect on TBG mimics the negative control of the binding protein by the thyroid hormones.

Finally, they represent the first example of experimental conditions inducing a similar reaction of TBG and transthyretin.

REFERENCES

1. SAVU, L., R. VRANCKX, M. MAYA, M. ROUAZE-ROMET, E. A. NUNEZ. 1991. *In* Progress in Thyroid Research. A. Gordon, J. Gross & G. Henneman, Eds.: 789–792. Balkema. Rotterdam.
2. SAVU, L., R. VRANCKX, M. ROUAZE-ROMET, M. MAYA, E. A. NUNEZ, J. TRETON & I. L. FLINK. 1991. Biochim. Biophys. Acta **1097:** 19–22.
3. VRANCKX, R., L. SAVU, N. LAMBERT, G. VERMEIL DE CONCHARD, R. GROSSE, M. S. MOUREY & B. CORMAN. 1995. Am. J. Physiol. **268:** R536–R548.
4. VRANCKX R., M. ROUAZE-ROMET, L. SAVU, P. MECHIGHEL, M. MAYA & E. A. NUNEZ 1994. J. Endocrinol. **142:** 77–84.
5. ARANEO, B. A., M. L. WOODS & R. A. DAYNES 1993. J. Infec. Dis. **167:** 830–840.
6. BERDANIER, C. D., J. A. PARENTE & M. K. MCINTOSH. 1993. FASEB J. **7:** 414–419.
7. DAYNES, R. A., B. A. ARENO, W. B. ERSHLER, C. MALONET, G. Z. LI & S. Y. RYU. 1993 J. Immunol. **150:** 5219–5230.

Antidepressant and Cognition-Enhancing Effects of DHEA in Major Depression

O. M. WOLKOWITZ,[a] V. I. REUS,[a] E. ROBERTS,[b]
F. MANFREDI,[a] T. CHAN,[a] S. ORMISTON,[a] R. JOHNSON,[a]
J. CANICK,[a] L. BRIZENDINE,[a] AND H. WEINGARTNER[c]

[a]Department of Psychiatry
UCSF
San Francisco, California 94143-0984

[b]Department of Neurobiochemistry
City of Hope
Duarte, California 91010

[c]National Institute of Alcohol Abuse & Alcoholism
Bethesda, Maryland 20892

Several lines of evidence suggest that dehydroepiandrosterone (DHEA) and dehydroepiandrosterone sulfate (DHEAS) may be involved in behavior[1-4] and that age- or illness-related decreases in circulating levels may be pathophysiologically relevant in psychiatric illness. We recently reported that DHEA, DHEAS, and the ratios of these hormones with cortisol decrease with age in both normal subjects and patients with major depression[5] and that basal levels of these hormones were directly correlated with performance in verbal memory tasks involving "automatic," noneffortful functions, and "semantic memory" performance (i.e., knowledge rather than episode-based memory).[5]

Pilot studies of DHEA administration to medical or psychiatric patients[6] noted improvements in mood, energy, libido, and in some cases memory performance. Morales *et al.*[7] administered physiologic doses of DHEA to healthy elderly volunteers and noted improved senses of well-being. In the current open-label pilot studies, we sought to determine if DHEA administration would improve mood and cognition in middle-aged and elderly depressives. Doses of DHEA were individually adjusted to achieve circulating levels which are in the mid-normal range in younger healthy individuals.

METHODS

Six subjects (3 male, 3 female, age range 51–72 years) with DSM-III-R major depression and low basal 1600 hours serum levels of either DHEA (< 160 ng/dl) or DHEAS (< 100 μg/dl in men and 60 μg/dl in women) were orally administered DHEA 30–90 mg per day for 4 weeks. Subjects were evaluated weekly with the 21-item Hamilton Depression Rating Scale (HDRS), the Beck Depression Inventory (BDI), the Symptom Checklist 90 (SCL-90), the Bunney-Hamburg (BH) Global Depression Rating, and a test of verbal memory. The memory test assessed vigilance/attention, free recall and recognition of verbal material, frequency monitoring (an automatic memory process), and self-generation of words belonging to a given semantic category (semantic memory performance). One subject from Study 1 (a 67-year-old female) received DHEA 60 mg orally per day for 4 months followed by 90 mg orally per day for an additional 2 months. She was evaluated monthly during the

337

6-month study and for 2 months following gradual DHEA withdrawal using the measures just described.

RESULTS

Administration of DHEA resulted in significant increases in serum levels of DHEA and DHEAS and in significant improvement in HDRS, BH Global Depression, SCL-90, and BDI ratings (TABLE 1). In our test of verbal memory, DHEA administration was associated with significant improvement in automatic memory functions (i.e., frequency monitoring); $\chi_r^2 = 10.20$, $p < 0.04$; other aspects of memory performance were not significantly altered. Treatment-induced changes in serum DHEA or DHEAS levels were inversely correlated with changes in HDRS and SCL-90 ratings (all: $r_s \geq 0.70$) (i.e., greater increases in DHEA or DHEAS levels were associated with greater symptomatic improvement). The one subject who received DHEA (60–90 mg a day) for 6 months showed continued and dose-related improvement in HDRS ratings (from 23 to 12, a 48% improvement) as well as

TABLE 1. Behavioral and Biochemical Effects of DHEA Administration[a]

	n	Baseline	End of Study (Week 4)	χ_r^2	$p \leq$
DHEA (ng/dl)	6	179.2 ± 59.9	370.3* ± 144.2	14.49	0.006
DHEAS (µg/dl)	6	44.0 ± 24.6	257.2* ± 92.8	13.20	0.01
HDRS	6	24.7 ± 4.6	15.2* ± 7.8	10.62	0.03
BH Depr.	6	6.8 ± 1.7	4.2* ± 3.3	11.3	0.03
SCL-90	5	214.8 ± 58.8	159.0* ± 64.8	F = 69.4	0.001
BDI	4	25.3 ± 5.5	12.0* ± 14.1	13.13	0.01

Abbreviations: DHEA = dehydroepiandrosterone, DHEAS = dehydroepiandrosterone sulfate, HDRS = Hamilton Depression Rating Scale, BH Depr = Bunney-Hamburg Global Depression Rating, SCL 90 = Symptom Checklist 90, BDI = Beck Depression Inventory.
[a]Values are means ± SD.
*Significantly different from baseline by Fisher's PLSD test.

improvement in BH Global Depression (from 7 to 3) and BDI ratings (from 35 to 10). She also showed improved semantic memory performance (from 16 to 25 self-generated items, a 36% improvement). Each of these behavioral and cognitive measures returned to baseline following DHEA withdrawal. In this patient, serum levels of DHEA and DHEAS were significantly and inversely correlated (over the nine monthly observation points) with HDRS and BH Global Depression ratings (all: $r > 0.70$).

DISCUSSION

These preliminary results raise the possibility that age- and/or illness-associated decreases in circulating DHEA and DHEAS levels in depressed patients may be pathophysiologically relevant and are amenable to pharmacologic treatment. We noted clinically and statistically significant improvement in both objective and subjective ratings of depression in this open-label study. We also noted significant improvement in aspects of memory functions, but the selectivity of these effects requires further investigation. Consistent with a direct relationship between DHEA and the observed behavioral changes are the high correlations between DHEA and DHEAS levels and improvements in depression ratings, although our power was limited in demonstrating statistical significance. Larger scale double-blind trials to further examine these intriguing findings are currently underway.

REFERENCES

1. BOLOGA, L., J. SHARMA & E. ROBERTS. 1987. Dehydroepiandrosterone and its sulfated derivative reduce neuronal death and enhance astrocytic differentiation in brain cell cultures. J. Neurosci. Res. **17:** 225–234.
2. FLOOD, J. F. & E. ROBERTS. 1988. Dehydroepiandrosterone sulfate improves memory in aging mice. Brain Res. **448:** 178–181.
3. RUDMAN, D., K. R. SHETTY & D. E. MATTSON. 1990. Plasma dehydroepiandrosterone sulfate in nursing home men. J. Am. Geriatr. Soc. **38:** 421–427.
4. SUNDERLAND, T., C. R. MERRIL, M. G. HERRINGTON *et al.* 1989. Reduced plasma dehydroepiandrosterone in Alzheimer's disease. Lancet **ii:** 570.
5. REUS, V. I., O. W. WOLKOWITZ, E. ROBERTS, T. CHAN, N. TURETSKY, F. MANFREDI & H. WEINGARTNER. 1993. Dehydroepiandrosterone (DHEA) and memory in depressed patients. Neuropsychopharmacology **9:** 66S.
6. KALIMI, M. & W. REGELSON (Eds). 1990. The Biologic Role of Dehydroepiandrosterone. Walter de Gruyter. Berlin.
7. MORALES, A. J., J. J. NOLAN, J. C. NELSON & S. S. C. YEN. 1994. Effects of replacement dose of dehydroepiandrosterone in men and women of advancing age. J. Clin. Endocrinol. Metab. **78:** 1360–1367.

Effects of Dehydroepiandrosterone on MNU-Induced Breast Cancer in Sprague-Dawley Rats

R. A. LUBET,[a] D. M. McCORMICK, G. M. GORDON,[b]
C. GRUBBS,[d] X-D LEI,[e] R. A. PROUGH,[e] V. E. STEELE,[a]
G. J. KELLOFF,[a] C. F. THOMAS,[c] AND R. D. MOON[c]

[a]National Cancer Institute
Bethesda, Maryland 20892

[b]Oncology Center
Johns Hopkins University
Baltimore, Maryland

[c]University of Illinois at Chicago
Chicago, Illinois 60612

[d] University of Alabama at Birmingham
Birmingham, Alabama 35294

[e]University of Louisville
Louisville, Kentucky 40292

In previous studies we demonstrated that high dose dehydroepiandrosterone (DHEA) was an effective chemopreventive agent in the N-methyl-N-nitrosourea (MNU)-induced rat mammary tumor model.[1] We want to expand on these observations.

In brief, female Sprague-Dawley rats were administered a single intravenous dose of MNU at 50 days of age. Dietary DHEA was administered beginning 1 week before MNU and was administered continually throughout the duration of the experiment. These methods were previously described.[1]

Initially, DHEA was administered in the diet at 400 and 800 ppm. Although both doses profoundly inhibited tumor multiplicity (> 90%) and tumor incidence, neither dose affected body weight gain in the treated rats. This finding is of great importance because decreased body weight gain, as by caloric restriction, can by itself severely decrease tumor incidence and multiplicity. Next, the effects of a wide range of doses of DHEA were examined. The highest dose of DHEA (600 ppm) significantly decreased tumor incidence from 95% to 45%, increased tumor latency, and decreased tumor multiplicity from 4.1 to 0.5 tumors per rat. Lower doses of DHEA (120, 24, 5 ppm) decreased tumor multiplicity by 55, 40, and 28%, respectively, significantly increased tumor latency at all three doses, but minimally affected tumor incidence. The minimal effects of these various doses of DHEA on tumor incidence, as contrasted with their striking effects on tumor multiplicity, are due to the high tumor multiplicity and virtually 100% tumor incidence achieved in this model. These experiments demonstrate that DHEA has striking chemopreventive efficacy in this model at doses far below its maximally tolerated dose. Serum levels of DHEA in treated rats (120 ppm in diet; 26 pmol/ml) were similar to those in a young human female, implying chemopreventive efficacy at achievable doses.

One adverse effect of high dose DHEA treatment was the induction of liver tumors which are associated with peroxisome proliferation. Studies determining the levels of certain peroxisomal enzymes in the liver of treated rats found that although high doses of DHEA ($\geq 2,000$ ppm) highly induced these peroxisomal enzymes, lower doses (≤ 120 ppm) minimally affected these enzyme levels.[2] These latter studies imply that: (1) Peroxisomal proliferation is not necessary for the observed chemopreventive effects; and (2) Chemopreventive efficacy can be achieved at doses that do not induce peroxisomes. Furthermore, peroxisome-mediated hepatocarcinogensis, although observed in rodents, is probably not relevant in primates.

Further mechanistic studies employing 600 or 2,000 ppm DHEA in the diet were undertaken. Intermittent treatment with DHEA (3 weeks of exposure to DHEA followed by 3 weeks of exposure to control diet) is an effective preventive regimen. Treatment with DHEA only for a limited time (7 days before MNU until 42 days post-MNU exposure) inhibits MNU-induced tumor incidence 35–45% and tumor multiplicity >70%. The latter finding implies that limited exposure to DHEA has long-lasting effects on the outgrowth of mammary tumors. Our prior investigations with this tumor model had shown that exposure to DHEA for only 1 week before and 1 week after MNU treatment was ineffective as a preventive protocol in this model.[1] These results imply that although exposure just at the time of initiation is ineffective, exposure for 6 weeks causes long-term inhibition of tumor growth. Finally, DHEA was administered to rats when an animal exhibited its first palpable tumor. Although this treatment did not affect the rate of outgrowth of palpable tumors, implying minimal chemotherapeutic efficacy, DHEA did decrease the outgrowth of new primary tumors. These observations that limited exposure to DHEA or that exposure to DHEA in an adjuvant type of setting is effective are particularly intriguing.

REFERENCES

1. RATKO T. A., C. J. DETRISIAC, R. N. MEHTA, G. J. KELLOFF & R. C. MOON. 1991. Inhibition of rat mammary gland carcinogenesis by dietary DHEA or a fluorinated analogue of DHEA. Cancer Res. **51:** 481–486.
2. PROUGH R. A., X. D. LEI, G. H. XIAO, T. E. GEOGHEGAN & S. J. WEBB. 1995. Regulation of cytochromes P450 by DHEA and its anticarcinogenic action. Ann. N. Y. Acad. Sci., this volume.

Subject Index

DHEA = Dehydroepiandrosterone; DHEAS = Dehydroepiandrosterone sulfate;
DHEAS-ST = Dehydroepiandrosterone sulfotransferase

Index of Contributors